JUDITH S. KAYE
IN HER OWN WORDS

JUDITH S. KAYE
IN HER OWN WORDS

REFLECTIONS ON LIFE AND THE LAW,
WITH SELECTED JUDICIAL OPINIONS AND ARTICLES

Judith S. Kaye

EDITED BY

Henry M. Greenberg, Luisa M. Kaye,
Marilyn Marcus, and Albert M. Rosenblatt

excelsior editions

AN IMPRINT OF STATE UNIVERSITY OF NEW YORK PRESS

On the cover: Chief Judge Judith S. Kaye sits at the bench of the New York State Court of Appeals in this photo by Annie Leibovitz for the cover of a 1998 issue of *Vanity Fair* magazine. Courtesy of Annie Leibovitz. Cover design by Elise Brauckmann.

Published by State University of New York Press, Albany

Excelsior Editions is an imprint of State University of New York Press

For information, contact State University of New York Press, Albany, NY
www.sunypress.edu

Library of Congress Cataloging-in-Publication Data

Names: Kaye, Judith S., 1938–2016, author. | Greenberg, Henry M., 1961– editor. | Kaye, Luisa M., 1965– editor. | Marcus, Marilyn, editor. | Rosenblatt, Albert M., editor.
Title: Judith S. Kaye in her own words : reflections on life and the law, with selected judicial opinions and articles / edited by Henry M. Greenberg, Luisa M. Kaye, Marilyn Marcus, and Albert M. Rosenblatt.
Description: Albany : State University of New York Press, 2019. | Series: Excelsior editions | Includes bibliographical references and index.
Identifiers: LCCN 2018033290 | ISBN 9781438474793 (hardcover : alk. paper) | ISBN 9781438474816 (ebook) | ISBN 9781438474809 (pbk. : alk. paper)
Subjects: LCSH: Kaye, Judith S., 1938–2016. | Judges—New York (State)—Biography. | New York (State). Court of Appeals—History. | LCGFT: Autobiographies. | Court decisions and opinions.
Classification: LCC KF373.K394 A3 2019 | DDC 347.747/035092 [B]—dc23
LC record available at https://lccn.loc.gov/2018033290

10 9 8 7 6 5 4 3 2 1

The Historical Society of the New York Courts is grateful for the substantial financial support received for this publication from the William Nelson Cromwell Foundation, of which Judge Kaye was a trustee for many years.

We are also grateful for the approval to publish and financial support of Judith Kaye's three children: Luisa, Jonathan, and Gordon Kaye.

We wish to acknowledge Annie Leibovitz for graciously donating the use of her photo of Judge Kaye for the cover of this book.

CONTENTS

REFLECTIONS ON A LIFE IN THE JUDICIARY, THE LAW, AND THE WORLD

Part I. The Court Years (1983–2009)

Part II. Return to the Real World

Part III. Who I Am, from Day One

Photo galleries follow pages 76 and 90

OPINIONS

ARTICLES AND SPEECHES

FOREWORD

Chief Judge Janet DiFiore

I am deeply honored that Luisa Kaye has invited me to pen a foreword to the collected memoirs, opinions, and articles of Chief Judge Judith S. Kaye, an extraordinary woman, jurist, and leader who had a striking impact on the law and the administration of justice in New York State and beyond.

Judith Kaye's scholarly, eloquent, and progressive opinions—spanning a quarter century of service on the New York State Court of Appeals, one of the most influential appellate courts in the nation—will surely stand the test of time. She has influenced the course of our constitutional and common law for generations to come in momentous decisions addressing a child's right to a basic education, the death penalty, marriage and adoption rights, the scope of the rights and protections afforded by our State constitution, and on and on. Her opinions are models of judicial craftsmanship, reflecting a keen intellect; a strong command of the law; a clear, elegant writing style; and a wise understanding of human affairs.

Judith's articles reveal a prolific and sophisticated scholar with insightful and interesting perspectives on a broad range of topics. Her bold insights on judicial leadership and court reform are especially valuable, coming from a chief judge who led one of the largest and busiest court systems in the world through a period of intense social and technological change. Her vision for how the New York courts could respond more effectively to the societal problems swelling the dockets led to a "problem-solving justice revolution" that helped transform the delivery of justice at the national level.

Judith's memoirs and personal writings are a joy to read, illuminating a unique and fascinating woman: wise, cultivated, and elegant, of course, but also witty, fun-loving, and even a little mischievous. As she reflects on the different phases of her life, from her humble upbringing to her cherished court years, we are the beneficiaries of her sparkling intellect and a love of learning, language, and literature that shines through. In these writings, we are presented with a passionate, humane, and gracious woman who surmounted great challenges, won many victories, and suffered her share of disappointments. She loved her life, her profession, her court, and above all, her family.

This collection is more than a simple record of a remarkable life. It is a treasure—not only for those of us who knew and admired Judith but for all who may seek to understand and appreciate the profound impact she had on the law, the legal profession, and the administration of justice.

EDITORIAL PREFACE

Honorable Albert M. Rosenblatt

Like a symphony, Judith S. Kaye's writings consist of themes, harmonies, and resolutions, encased in creative expression, imbued with beauty and passion.

As with symphonic compositions, her writings can be divided into parts, and we have chosen three: memoir, judicial opinions, and articles. It seemed sensible to begin with the memoir, followed by the opinions and articles. That is probably how Judge Kaye would have prescribed it: "Here I am, Judith Kaye. Would you like to know something of my life? Read on."

Most everyone will. She was a felicitous writer: engaging, modest, and revealing without being indiscreet. Do not look for tell-all diatribes or attempts to settle scores. Judith was not like that, and it would be out of character for her to do so in her farewell account. Instead, she presents a remarkable life, including her childhood and her fidelity to her family, including her late husband, Steve; her children, Luisa, Jonathan, and Gordie; and her grandchildren.

She describes her battle with cancer, a foe she fought for several years, with some public concealment, so as not to be consigned (as she put it) to a "poor Judith" category. The major part of her memoir covers her years on the New York Court of Appeals, and as the state's chief judge. She observes proprieties but does not shy away from describing the background and her thoughts in important cases and about policies. She is candid.

The memoir is followed by a selection of her judicial opinions. Themes and resolutions are the bread and butter of judicial opinions, and as a writer, Judith's style and elegance gave added lift to what would otherwise be little more than superb reasoning and impeccable analysis. Those who know her might read a phrase and say, "Ah, yes, that sounds just like her; no one else could have written with such verve and clarity."

Judith's writings are vast, which required some difficult editorial choices. Covering a substantial span of those "hard-bound green books," her judicial opinion writing began in 60 NY 2d and ran up through 11 NY 3d, covering some fifty volumes over a quarter of a century, from 1983 through 2008.

In all, she wrote 522 majority opinions, 77 dissents, and 28 concurrences. The tally seems proportional, considering that she was not a "great dissenter." She preferred to lead from the front, seeking consensus when possible.

Choosing representative opinions was no easy matter. Judith's writings are so consistently good that even a random selection or the use of a dartboard might have acquainted the reader with her legacy quite well. But that would not be fair to her, as she did have her preferences, and we could identify them—or at the very least make some good guesses.

A random sampling process would also have been unfair to us as editors, because it would have denied us a frolic through a field of plenty. Presenting the opinions unadorned would have been adequate, as they stand on their own, needing no enhancement. But as an added treat for the reader, we asked Judge Kaye's former law clerks to pick an opinion or two (preferably ones they worked on) and give it a short introduction. We thank them for sharing their thoughts.

The decisions cover a wide range of topics. In the realm of family law, we have included several, most notably her dissents in *Alison D.* and *Hernandez*. In *Alison D.*, she argued for the visitation rights of a lesbian parent, and in *Hernandez* for marital rights for same-sex couples. Both dissents proved prescient. The state legislature enacted marriage equality in 2011, five years after *Hernandez*, and in 2016 the Court of Appeals came around to the viewpoint she expressed twenty-five years earlier in *Alison D.*

We have also selected others dealing with family law and intimate relations, such as sexual discrimination in student housing (*Levin*), adoption (*Piel*, *Ross*, and *Matter of Jacob*), and domestic violence (*Nicholson*).

Passionate as Judge Kaye was in these opinions, she was a commercial litigator who keenly understood the need for predictability and stability in the commercial realm. Her *Levandusky* opinion forged New York's Business Judgment Rule, and her decisions in *Deutsche Bank* and *Brandon* are models of writings in banking and insurance law. When it came to business contracts, her parol evidence discussion in *W.W.W.* is among the most cited in the field.

Although gracious, she had little tolerance for procedural laxity and drew the line sharply (as in *Kihl* and *Brill*) if court practice allowed the system to become sluggish or unresponsive. She held people to appropriate standards of accountability when it came to consumerism (*Karlin*), government (*Maybee*, *Schulz*), negligence (*532 Madison Ave.*), or medical malpractice (*Tebbutt*).

In the criminal arena, we have chosen several opinions displaying her keen sensitivity in balancing the rights of criminal defendants with those of public order (*Johnson*, *Catu*, *Wesley*, *Gonzalez*, *Hill*).

Any list of her writings would have to include *Campaign for Fiscal Equity* (*CFE*). It is one of her longest opinions, but there is hardly a wasted word, addressing the state constitutional requirement for a sound basic education for students and ruling that the state had not met its constitutional and statutory obligations for New York City schools.

Judith was a champion of the state constitution. She proclaimed it in *CFE* and elsewhere revealed her affinity for that document, never hesitating to remind us that it was ten years older than its federal counterpart. She repeatedly pointed out that while a state court could not deny anyone a constitutional right below the federal interpretative "floor," there are instances in which a state court should and will exceed the federal floor and accord greater rights and liberties than those found in the US Constitution (*Class*, *O'Neill*, *Caban*, *Immuno AG*).

Hank Greenberg, a stalwart of our editorial team, took on the duty of assembling a representative sampling of Judge Kaye's articles. As with choosing from among her opinions, it was an agreeable task, but very difficult, given the length of her publications list and breadth of her work. A search tells only a part of the story. It is easy to go online and find dozens of her articles, but that does not include her unpublished works, articles stashed away here and there, that she may have written for a synagogue or a middle-school journal. When it came to requests for essays, she was an easy touch and rarely said no. Hank surveyed the field and came up with excellent choices.

They fall into several brackets.* There are the law review–type articles, written in the classic style, with prolific notes and stellar scholarship. This includes her articles on "The Human Dimension in Appellate Judging: A Brief Reflection on a Timeless Concern" (1988); "Delivering Justice Today: A Problem-Solving Approach" (2004); and "One Judge's View of Academic Law Review Writing" (1989).

Then there are the articles advancing a cause or point of view: "Women in Law: The Law Can Change People" (1991); "Law Is Pivotal in Advancing Women's Rights" (1993); and "The Changing World of Children: The Responsibility of the Law and the Courts" (1993). Her kinship with state constitutional law comes across compellingly in her articles "Dual Constitutionalism in Practice and Principle" (1987) and "State Constitutional Common Law: The Common Law as a Full Partner in the Protection of Individual Rights" (1992), as well as in "State Courts at the Dawn of a New Century: Common-Law Courts Reading Statutes and Constitutions" (1995).

There are remembrances and tributes, of which two are especially touching: "In Memoriam: William J. Brennan, Jr." (1997) and "A Lecture about Judge Benjamin Nathan Cardozo" (1986). There is also her own account in "My Life as Chief Judge" (2006).

Beyond that, one article deserves special mention, as we all agreed that it must be included. We understand that scholarship and enduring jurisprudence were Judge Kaye's stock in trade. But those who knew her often saw a lighter side that could be hilariously funny, and we wanted to be sure that her entertaining essay "The Best Oral Argument I (N)ever Made" (2005) made the cut.

Readers will approach this volume differently; some may browse or turn to one section or another first. Judith would not decree the sequence, nor will we. No single volume or even set of volumes can fully present a life, let alone one as singular as Judge Kaye's. Her achievements are legendary and will live on long after her lifetime and ours.

---

*Needless to say, given the breadth of the various pieces collected here, and the variety of sources in which they were originally published, readers should expect to see some variation in editorial style.

BIOGRAPHICAL INTRODUCTION

Susan N. Herman

By her own account, Judith Smith Kaye was first and foremost a writer. Having started out as a journalist, she went on, as a lawyer and then judge, to write 627 judicial opinions (522 majority opinions, 28 concurrences, and 77 dissents) and over 200 articles (some of which are included here).

In writing her memoir, she did what she had done throughout her life as an author, lawyer, and judge and as a woman of impeccable integrity: defied convention to do what she thought was right. The organization of her memoir resists what her daughter, Luisa, calls a "conventional, chronologically ordered account." That was not the frame Judith wanted for telling her story. What she did want to do was to use part 1 (The Court Years) to educate readers about the life and work of the New York State Court of Appeals, from the physical courthouse, to her colleagues, to court procedures and output. It is characteristic of the Judith I knew that her story of "the" court years (as opposed to "my" court years) is about so much more than her own journey.

In part 2 (Return to the Real World), Judith talks candidly and movingly about coping with the "triple whammy" of mandatory retirement from the court; the death of her beloved husband of more than forty-two years, Stephen Rackow Kaye; and receiving a diagnosis of cancer. Her life at the time she was writing became the filter through which she reflected on her earlier years—a perspective on her story from a point near its end. Her mission here is more educational than self-centered: to offer readers her own example and her thoughts about how to cope with painfully difficult transitions.

It is only in part 3 (Who I Am, from Day One) that the memoir turns to the question most biographies start with: how did she become Judith S. Kaye, chief judge and

Susan N. Herman is Centennial Professor of Law, Brooklyn Law School; President, American Civil Liberties Union. Her collaborations and connections with Judge Kaye, including a speech at the newly renovated Court of Appeals building, and a later speech on the occasion of the hanging of Judge Kaye's portrait in the courtroom, are recounted in Susan N. Herman, *Portrait of a Judge: Judith S. Kaye, Dichotomies, and State Constitutional Law*, 75 Albany L. Rev. 1977 (2012), and Susan N. Herman, *For Judith S. Kaye*, 81 Brook. L. Rev. (2016), available at https://brooklynworks.brooklaw.edu/blr/vol81/iss4/2.

legal lion? And even here, she frequently shifts her gaze from her younger self to the reader, sharing wisdom she accumulated through the years. With her extraordinary blend of majesty and modesty, she tells the reader about what she has learned, showing her evident belief that sharing knowledge is a more important goal than talking about herself.

It is my aim to provide a "conventional, chronologically ordered" biography so that readers will have an objective frame of Judith Kaye's life to complement her memoir.

Judith Ann Smith was born in Monticello, New York, on August 8, 1943. She describes her parents, Benjamin Smith and Lena Cohen Smith, as "Jewish immigrant farmers turned small-town shopkeepers." Both had fled Eastern European poverty and persecution. Benjamin was turned away on his first attempt to enter the United States, went to Cuba and then Panama, and ultimately entered the United States illegally. Benjamin and Lena married in 1936 and settled on a farm in Maplewood, New York, near Monticello. When Benjamin's immigration status came to the attention of authorities in the 1940s, the fact that he was a responsible farmer and the parent of US citizen children (Judith and her brother, Allen, who went on to become an executive at Sony Music) helped him escape the fate of his brother, who was deported and later killed in a concentration camp in Poland.

Judith started her education at a one-room schoolhouse in Maplewood at the age of five. In a harbinger of academic successes to come, after one year of schooling she was tested and placed in the third grade. Although two years younger than most of her classmates, in her later school years she towered over them physically as well as intellectually: she was a full head taller than most.

Judith's ambitions exceeded her parents' expectations for her—that she should become a teacher or perhaps work in the ladies clothing store the family opened in Monticello, where she helped out from the age of twelve. At Monticello High School, confronted with a choice between an academic and a secretarial program, Judith took both because her parents thought secretarial skills were important for a woman, but she was not willing to consign herself to a future as a secretary. Honing skills she would need in her later life, she participated on the high school debate team, served as an editor on the school newspaper, and became an excellent typist. In juggling these multiple demands on her time, she had a role model in her mother, who worked full-time in the store and still ran a household, including cooking all the family's meals.

At the age of fifteen, Judith was admitted to Barnard ("in the wilds of New York City") where, planning to be a journalist, she majored in Latin American civilizations and was editor-in-chief of the *Barnard Bulletin*.

Judith self-deprecatingly says that she was a bit "block-headed" about the lack of opportunities for women. After graduating from Barnard, she applied for newspaper positions with little success and had to settle for a job as a social reporter—the area the male-dominated profession regarded as suitable for women—for the *Hudson Dispatch* of Union City, New Jersey. Hoping to provide herself with a platform for breaking out of the society columns, she signed up for a night program at New York University Law School in 1959. Law school agreed with her. She graduated at the top of her class; all three of the pieces she wrote while in law school were published. Law became her chosen profession.

As Judith later memorably said (in a *New York Times* quote of the day), "I take my gender with me everywhere I go." The white-shoe law firms where she applied for a position turned her away, sometimes explaining their decisions in overtly sexist terms. These rebuffs increased her determination to succeed in that world. She eventually received and accepted an offer at the highly prestigious Sullivan & Cromwell LLP, where she spent two years as the only woman in the litigation department (the firm's other two women practiced in trusts and estates). While there she met Stephen Kaye, the rare man who shared her range of passions—he had season tickets for both the New York Rangers and the Metropolitan Opera—and entered into an "almost perfect" marriage where the two were "fiercely independent and fiercely interdependent."

When Stephen left Sullivan & Cromwell to join a different firm, Judith also left for a job in the legal department of IBM, where she stayed for about a year. As was expected at the time, she gave up that job during the seventh month of her first pregnancy. From 1965 to 1969, while she had her three children, Luisa, Jonathan, and Gordon, she worked as a part-time assistant for Dean Russell Niles, first at New York University and then at the Association of the Bar of the City of New York, on research, speeches, and articles. She developed a practice of rising at 5 a.m. so she would have several hours to work before the children were up and the household's day began. Arranging for full-time help at home, she took a part-time job at Olwine, Connelly, Chase, O'Donnell & Weyhar in 1969 which turned into a fifteen-year stay, initially as the firm's first female associate and later as its first female partner.

By the 1970s, the legal profession was sufficiently defensive about its previous dismissive treatment of women that being a woman could sometimes be a benefit. Olwine offered Judith partnership after she told them that she would be leaving for a highly paid position at Exxon, which was eager to hire its first woman attorney. The firm accommodated Judith's sense of work/family life balance, which included not working all weekend, taking family vacations, and showing up for school conferences, swim meets, and concerts. She succeeded without complaining about the profession's discriminatory treatment of women, simply by doing her job well. She became a leader of the bar in the public sphere, devoting precious time to serving on the executive committee of the Association of the Bar of the City of New York, numerous committees of the New York State Bar Association, the board of the Legal Aid Society (including serving as vice president), the American Law Institute Council, and so on.

During his campaign for election in 1982, Governor Mario Cuomo (a former New York Court of Appeals law clerk) announced his intention to appoint the first woman Court of Appeals judge. He had his first opening to fill shortly after taking office with the retirement of Associate Judge Domenick L. Gabrielli in 1982. But the new governor found the list of possible nominees presented to him by the Commission on Judicial Selection consisted only of men. Not only were there no women on the Court of Appeals in that era, there were no women on the Appellate Division benches, the most obvious source of candidates. A few months later, when Associate Judge Jacob J. Fuchsberg retired, Cuomo had another opportunity. This time, the commission's list included the names of two women, one of whom was Judith Kaye.

Judith's road to the Court of Appeals was not free of bumps. The New York Women's Bar Association supported the other female nominee, an active member and past president of their association, and declared Judith Kaye to be unqualified. But other bar associations disagreed, as did Governor Cuomo, and the New York Senate unanimously approved Judith's appointment as the first woman on the New York Court of Appeals. (It was not long before the Women's Bar Association warmly embraced Judith on the basis of her performance on the court—and her former rival, Betty Weinberg Ellerin, was subsequently appointed to the Appellate Division.)

Judith Kaye was sworn in as an associate judge on September 12, 1983, a day she describes as terrifying. The job of a Court of Appeals judge was extremely intense in her first two years, as the court was required to hear many kinds of appeals and thus faced a daunting caseload. Legislation in 1985 allowing the court greater freedom to select cases reduced the sheer quantity of cases and left the judges free to spend more time on the quality of their work.

In many respects, Judith Kaye approached the court as an outsider: she had not previously been a judge, she was a woman, and she was unaccustomed to dealing with criminal cases, a substantial part of the court's work. ("I was lost in the ether of the criminal law," she says.) She was forty-five years old, in contrast with the majority of her new colleagues—Associate Judges Hugh R. Jones, Matthew J. Jasen, and Bernard S. Meyer, and Chief Judge Lawrence H. Cooke—who were all close enough to seventy that they were compelled to retire within several years of her arrival. But she quickly became part of the community of the court. She followed her lifelong practice of putting in as much time as was needed to get things right—even mastering criminal law. She worked toward consensus, as was the court's custom. But she maintained her distinct voice and perspective, calling on her "life experience as a woman, wife, daughter, mother and grandmother."

Judith Kaye's clear, confident, and empathetic voice is heard in landmark opinions in many areas, from family law to commercial litigation to criminal law, where she made some of her greatest contributions to New York jurisprudence. During her first year on the court, she cast the deciding vote and then wrote the majority opinion in *People v. Lemuel Smith*,[1] finding the state's mandatory death penalty for murder committed by an inmate already serving a term of life imprisonment to be unconstitutional. If his conviction had been affirmed, Smith would have been the first person to have been executed in New York in over twenty years. Instead, Kaye's vote took New York State a significant step down the path of questioning and ultimately abolishing capital punishment.

Among the other cases she recalls with pride is *Matter of Jacob*,[2] where her opinion (over a vigorous three-judge dissent) interpreted New York law as recognizing the rights of an unmarried partner of a child's biological mother, whether homosexual or heterosexual, to adopt the mother's child. Protecting the interests of children was a particularly important issue for Judith, who proudly served for years as chair of the New York State Permanent Judicial Commission on Justice for Children.

Jacob also sounded a theme of other cases Judith regarded as among her "best": the right of couples to structure their own relationships, regardless of whether they were

---

1. 63 NY2d 41 (1984), *cert. denied*, 469 US 1227 (1985).

2. 86 NY2d 651 (1995).

of the same sex. *Braschi v. Stahl Associates Co.*,[3] another hard-fought case, resulted in a plurality of the court defining a deceased tenant's same-sex partner as a "family" member entitled by statute to continue living in a rent-controlled apartment. These cases were especially important to Judith not just because of the legal craft involved but because they made a difference in many people's lives. It was thus a source of considerable dismay when, years later, she had to write an opinion dissenting from a plurality 2006 refusal to recognize a constitutional right to same-sex marriage in New York in *Hernandez v. Robles*.[4] (The legislature conferred that right five years later.)

Judith Kaye also had a tremendous influence in the area of state constitutional law, in New York and around the nation. Justice William Brennan's article, "State Constitutions and the Protection of Individual Rights," published in the *Harvard Law Review* in 1977,[5] inspired her to do extensive research on the New York State constitution during her early years on the court. This led to her enormously influential speech and article, "Dual Constitutionalism in Practice and Principle," first delivered at the Association of the Bar of the City of New York as the Benjamin N. Cardozo Lecture in 1987.[6] This masterful exposition of the history of the state's constitution, case law interpreting it, and a theory of dual constitutionalism encouraged lawyers to take the New York constitution seriously as an opportunity to forge law recognizing rights beyond what the US Constitution provides. I still assign this scholarly article to my law students for its comprehensive clarity and incisive analysis.

As a Court of Appeals judge, Judith Kaye took her own advice and looked to New York's constitution as a basis for rights in cases like *People v. Class*,[7] which was being argued in the Court of Appeals around the same time she was writing "Dual Constitutionalism." Judge Kaye's initial opinion in *Class* mentioned both state and federal constitutional provisions in reversing *Class*'s conviction. When the Supreme Court found that the federal Fourth Amendment had not been violated, on remand the New York Court of Appeals interpreted the New York constitution to provide greater protection against searches and seizures than the US Constitution.[8] Later cases like *People v. Scott*,[9] where Judge Kaye's concurring opinion set out a defense of her theory of state constitutional interpretation,[10] made the state's constitutional protection of privacy an essential argument for defense attorneys. The New York constitution also became the basis for the Court

---

3. 74 NY2d 201 (1989).

4. 7 NY3d 338 (2006).

5. 90 Harv. L. Rev. 489 (1977).

6. Originally published in the City Bar Association's *Record*, the article based on this speech was republished at 61 St. John's L. Rev. 399 (1987).

7. 63 NY2d 491 (1984), *rev'd*, 475 US 106 (1986) (as not violating US Constitution).

8. *People v. Class*, 67 NY2d 431 (1986) (after Supreme Court remand, finding right based on state constitution).

9. 79 NY2d 474 (1992).

10. See Susan N. Herman, *Portrait of a Judge: Judith S. Kaye, Dichotomies, and State Constitutional Law*, 75 Albany L. Rev. 1977, 1985–2002 (2012) (discussing Judith Kaye's conception of state constitutional law as a double protection for liberty and as an essential part of federal–state dialogue about rights).

of Appeals enhancing the rights of New Yorkers in areas as varied as free speech[11] and educational equity.[12]

Judge Kaye spent about ten years as an associate judge "in a place perfectly suited to me." She thrived on the challenge, the collegiality, and the practice of her craft of writing. Then the small world of the court was roiled again when Chief Judge Sol Wachtler was forced to resign in November 1992. It says something about Judith Kaye that in her account of the resignation, she chose not to revisit or even mention the circumstances surrounding Judge Wachtler.

Governor Cuomo selected Judge Kaye to be the next chief judge, the Senate unanimously confirmed the appointment, and she was sworn in as the twenty-second chief judge of the New York State Court of Appeals on March 23, 1993, the first woman ever to serve in that position.

If appointment to the Court of Appeals had enabled her to play a role in effecting changes in the substantive law, her role as chief judge of the Court of Appeals and as chief judge of the State of New York put her in a position to bring about deep and abiding changes in the state courts, in the justice system, and even in the courthouse itself.

Undertaking these challenges entailed personal sacrifice. In December 1992, while the chief judge selection process was going on, Judith was interviewed by President-elect Bill Clinton for a position as his attorney general. Even before knowing that she would be Cuomo's choice for chief judge, she withdrew from consideration because she thought the New York courts needed stability after the disruption of Judge Wachtler's departure. Janet Reno got the attorney general job; Judith Kaye got the chief judgeship. When US Supreme Court Justice Byron White announced his retirement on March 20, 1993, President Clinton had Kaye's name on a short list of those considered for that position. But having been sworn in as chief judge just a few weeks previously, she again declined to leave the New York courts, forgoing the possibility of life tenure as a Supreme Court justice. Ruth Bader Ginsburg got that job. President Clinton had been as serious as Governor Cuomo in his desire to select women for top positions.

Cuomo chose wisely. Judith's influence on the New York courts has been truly transformative. Judith credits her time on the Permanent Judicial Commission on Justice for Children (which she calls "a centerpiece of my life") with teaching her how to go about initiating reform in a stagnant system. Using what she had learned about process, she appointed commissions, consulted with experts, and enlisted allies to formulate what were sometimes audacious goals and then implement them.

One result of her efforts was the advent of specialized courts—like the Midtown Community Court, where low-level offenders received not just punishment but respectful counseling, treatment, and training. This innovative problem-solving approach was tried in other specialized courts in New York, addressing issues like drug abuse, mental health problems, and domestic violence and was emulated in other states. Judith took endless pride in the success of defendants who were empowered to turn their lives around. The

---

11. *Immuno AG v. Moor-Jankowski*, 77 NY2d 235, *cert. denied*, 500 US 954 (1991) (free speech and libel law).

12. *Campaign for Fiscal Equity, Inc. v. State of New York*, 100 NY2d 893 (2003) (educational equity).

Center for Court Innovation, a public-private collaboration inspired by Judge Kaye's vision and founded in 1996, continues to seek new approaches to the problems confronting our courts.

A similar idea led to the creation of a specialized commercial court (the Commercial Division of the Supreme Court), which enabled the New York courts to play the role Judith thought they should rightly play in one of the world's greatest commercial hubs.

One of her crowning achievements as chief judge of the State of New York was her transformation of "jury duty" into "jury service." Jury service law had become riddled with automatic exemptions for people in some twenty professions, ranging from lawyers to podiatrists to embalmers. Judith persuaded the legislature to abolish those inequitable exemptions (even the exemption for lawyers and judges), adding more than a million names to the eligibility lists. She overhauled the whole experience of jury service, finding myriad ways to respect the comfort and convenience of those called for jury service, like adding a call system so prospective jurors could be spared an unnecessary trip to the courthouse. She spoke inspirationally (including in a video welcoming prospective jurors to the court) about the key role of juries in our democracy.

Under Judith's watchful eye, the Court of Appeals courthouse itself was dramatically expanded (by 30,000 square feet), refurbished, and renovated to replace the electrical, plumbing, ventilation, heating, cooling, and telecommunications systems. On her watch, the New York courts adapted to new technologies, including electronic filing. She celebrated the rededication ceremony of the renovated courthouse in 2004 with an eclectic "law and" lecture series, sharing with the public her extraordinary range of interests. The series started with two prominent architects talking about courthouse architecture, and later included my law and literature talk about Theodore Dreiser's novel, *An American Tragedy*, and the New York case on which it had been based, *People v. Chester Gillette*.[13] Also on the program that evening was Francesca Zambello, who had just directed an opera based on *An American Tragedy*, connecting Judith's love for opera with her interest in law and literature and her pride in her court and courthouse.[14] Judith was a champion for funding improvements of deteriorating courthouses around the state.

Among other groundbreaking initiatives Judith set in motion during her tenure as chief judge—the longest serving chief judge in New York as well as the first woman—were the Committee on the Profession and the Courts, which held hearings throughout the state and issued a report leading to a number of positive reforms, including mandatory continuing legal education for all lawyers in New York, new rules regulating frivolous litigation, the adoption of standards of civility for lawyers, and the creation of what became the New York State Judicial Institute on Professionalism in the Law; the New York State Judicial Institute, the nation's first facility for judicial research and training built by the court system itself; a Special Commission on the Future of the New York State Courts, established in 2006 to evaluate the problems of the court system as a whole

---

13. See Susan N. Herman, People v. Gillette *and Theodore Dreiser's* An American Tragedy: *Law v. Literature*, http://www.nycourts.gov/history/programs-events/images2/Judicial-Notice-11.pdf#page=23.

14. See Susan N. Herman, *Portrait of a Judge: Judith S. Kaye, Dichotomies, and State Constitutional Law*, 75 Albany L. Rev. 1977, 1977–82 (2012) (describing this event).

and assess the need for further reform; review of the fiduciary appointment system, matrimonial lawyers, and judicial compensation; and the Historical Society of the New York Courts.

All in all, it is no wonder that one prisoner addressed his letter to Chief Judge Judith Kaye, "Dear Mother of Justice."

In Judith Kaye's farewell speech on November 12, 2008, she revealed how she had been able to accomplish so much as both chief judge of the Court of Appeals and chief judge of the State of New York: "Each of these jobs," she said in a line I shamelessly plagiarize, "takes 80 percent of my time."

Judith Kaye's "afterlife" at the law firm of Skadden Arps, Slate, Meagher & Flom LLP called on her judicial skills in conducting arbitrations and high-profile investigations (including an investigation of Governor David Paterson) and on her continued dedication to public service as chair of the Commission on Judicial Nominees and some dozen boards of directors. In addition to her law and policy work, she happily agreed to serve on the board of directors of Lincoln Center for the Performing Arts.

Above all, the fair treatment of children continued to occupy her attention. She chaired and served on committees on youth and citizenship, and youth and courts. When the (US) Supreme Court Historical Society invited her to give its annual lecture at the Supreme Court courtroom itself, the topic she chose was due process for children.

Among the many revelatory stories studding her memoir is her reminiscence of an American Bar Association meeting she was attending when her granddaughter, Sonja, cut her first tooth. When a reporter asked her which of those events was more important, Judith replied, "It's not even close." Fortunately, she did not have to choose between dedication to her family and dedication to being New York's "mother of justice." She met the challenges she set herself, as a woman, of having it all.

MILESTONES

August 4, 1938	Born in Monticello, New York, daughter of Benjamin Smith and Lena Cohen Smith
1954	Graduated Monticello High School at age fifteen, having skipped two grades
1958	Earned B.A., Barnard College
1958–1959	Society reporter for *Hudson Dispatch* in Union City, New Jersey
1959	Entered New York University School of Law night program
1959–1961	Copyeditor for General Features Corporation
1962	Earned LL.B., New York University School of Law
1962–1964	Associate, Sullivan & Cromwell LLP
February 11, 1964	Married Stephen Rackow Kaye
1964–1965	IBM, legal department
March 1965	Daughter Luisa born
1965–1969	Part-time assistant to Dean Russell Niles of New York University School of Law
September 1966	Son Jonathan born
September 1968	Son Gordon born
1969–1975	Associate, Olwine, Connelly, Chase, O'Donnell & Weyher
1975–1983	Partner, Olwine, Connelly, Chase, O'Donnell & Weyher
September 12, 1983	Sworn in as associate judge of the Court of Appeals of the State of New York, the first woman to hold that position
February 26, 1987	Delivered Benjamin N. Cardozo Memorial Lecture on "Dual Constitutionalism in Practice and Principle" at the New York

City Bar Association, making her one of the first to urge New Yorkers to rely on the New York State Constitution to protect individual rights not adequately protected by the US Supreme Court under the federal Constitution

1992–2016	Chair, Permanent Judicial Commission on Justice for Children, spearheading New York's efforts to promote permanency for children in foster care and comply with federal mandates on early intervention programs for infants and toddlers with developmental delays
December 1992	Met with President-elect Bill Clinton and withdrew her name from consideration to be attorney general of the United States
March 23, 1993	Sworn in as chief judge of the State of New York and chief judge of the New York State Court of Appeals, the first woman to hold those offices
October 1993	Implemented concept of problem-solving courts by establishing Midtown Community Court, where low-level crimes in and around the Times Square area of Manhattan are dealt with through a combination of punishment (often visible community service projects) and treatment, training, and counseling
1993	Established Committee on the Profession and the Courts, which made recommendations that resulted in new rules requiring continuing legal education for attorneys admitted to practice in New York, standardizing grievance committee practices, and creating a code of civility for attorneys
January 1994	Delivered first State of the Judiciary address, emphasizing the need to restore public trust and confidence in the courts by focusing on fundamental areas of concern that directly impact the public, such as how the jury system might be improved, individual courts could meet local needs, and families might be better served by the court system
1995	Expanded concept of problem-solving courts by opening the first drug court in Rochester, New York, which replaced punishment for drug abuse with treatment, monitoring, and essential services
1995	Established the Commercial Division of the New York State Supreme Court as a forum to improve the efficiency with which commercial disputes were addressed by trial courts and enhance the quality of judicial treatment of those cases
January 1996	Spearheaded comprehensive jury reform efforts, the centerpiece of which was legislation eliminating all automatic exemptions

	for jury service, thereby expanding jury pool by over a million people
1999	Received the William H. Rehnquist Award for Judicial Excellence from the National Center for State Courts at the US Supreme Court
December 2000	Established Birnbaum Commission (named after its chair, Sheila L. Birnbaum), which made recommendations for new rules for fiduciary appointments in New York
2002	Established the Historical Society of the New York Courts
2002–2003	Selected and served as the president of the Conference of Chief Justices
January 2003	Announced comprehensive three-year plan to institute statewide integrated domestic violence courts to enable the court system to address the many legal issues that domestic violence engenders
May 5, 2003	Opened New York State Judicial Institute on the campus of Pace University Law School, becoming the nation's first training and research facility for judges built by and for a state court system
May 2003	Established Adoption Now Program, which reduced the number of children awaiting adoption by 50 percent
October 2003	Created Center for Court Innovation, a public–private partnership charged with the development of new approaches to the myriad issues that confront our courts
December 31, 2008	Mandatory retirement from the New York State Court of Appeals
June 7, 2010	Delivered the Supreme Court Historical Society's thirty-fifth Annual Lecture at the US Supreme Court, with the talk "The Supreme Court and Justice for Children"
2009–2016	Of counsel, Skadden, Arps, Slate, Meagher & Flom LLP
2009–2016	Chair, New York State Commission on Judicial Nomination
January 7, 2016	Died at home in New York City

REFLECTIONS ON A
LIFE IN THE JUDICIARY,
THE LAW, AND THE WORLD

A NOTE ON THE TEXT

Luisa M. Kaye

Some notes before you begin reading our mother's telling of her story. First, a note of profound gratitude to those who made her last wish—the publication of her memoirs—come true and in such style: the Historical Society of the New York Courts, its venerable board of trustees, and its remarkable executive director, Marilyn Marcus, and her staff; our mother's esteemed colleague and inheritor of her robe, Chief Judge Janet DiFiore; her beloved colleague, friend, and confidante, Honorable Albert Rosenblatt, and her unofficial son, Hank Greenberg; the loving and wise Marge McCoy; Professor Susan Herman; James Peltz and SUNY Press; the many people who generously agreed to her requests for comments on her drafts; Susan Leon; and Annie Leibovitz for allowing us to use her incredible photograph on the cover.

Second, a note regarding editing. At the time of her death, our mother was in the process of working with editors to turn her manuscript into a more conventional, chronologically ordered autobiography. Unfortunately, fate intervened before that could be accomplished. Given how actively (to say the least) our mother controlled and influenced the editing process, we determined that it was impossible to edit the remaining raw portions authentically. At the same time, the structural difference between the edited parts and unedited parts made it too weird to use both together. Accordingly, to preserve her voice over what would have perhaps been a neater but less genuine read, we went with the original manuscript, with only the lightest technical edits. Notably, we did not edit relative time references, such as, "when I was diagnosed two years ago." Our mother wrote her manuscript over a five-year period, and thus these references are from the time she wrote them, not from when she completed her writing.

Third, a note regarding organization. Among the other aspects left untouched by editing is the organization of our mother's story. It does not start with her birth and end with her death; does not go from point A to point B; and does not necessarily conform with how most people would order and prioritize. Although—and maybe even because—our mother was an intensely organized person, we felt that even moving chapters around to create a more logical or cohesive flow would do violence to her essence. The very way she ordered her story, the points she repeated and emphasized, may reflect something about her thinking and priorities. We thought it best for the reader to extrapolate from how she let her pen flow.

Finally, we thank everyone who reads these volumes for taking an interest in our mother's story. She was a remarkable woman, jurist, lawyer, wife, mother, grandmother, sister, aunt, cousin, and friend. She will never be forgotten.

PREFACE

By nature, I am first and foremost a writer, most comfortable with pen and pad, whether the subject is the rule against perpetuities or the dynamics of dual constitutionalism. Writing, like the law itself, brings order to our experience, and I have always had a passion for words, their implications, their sequences, and their silences. This has been especially so for me since December 31, 2008, when my glorious quarter century on the Court of Appeals, New York State's highest court (fifteen of those years as chief judge) came to an end. More and more I have thought of writing a book, partly about my unlikely journey from a spare, sometimes secluded early childhood as the daughter of Jewish immigrant farmers turned small-town shopkeepers in New York's Sullivan County, to Manhattan and my discovery of the law, and then to Albany and a storied judicial experience. I was eager to explore the idea of an "afterlife" in the sense of the "after-chief-judge-life, then what?" More and more of us are blessedly finding ourselves living longer after enjoying a stimulating career, with successors on the scene understandably eager to make their own legacies. For those of us with a desire to still do things and contribute, what do our lives look like when that chapter is over? What *can* they look like?

In the course of investigating these answers, two sad facts have critically skewed the building of my afterlife. The first is the death of my beloved husband of nearly forty-three years, Stephen Kaye. I did not need for Stephen to die to know how treasured our time together was or how interwoven our lives were. What I have seen for the first time, however, is how dramatic the difference is to be without one's longtime partner or, put another way, what an enormous positive force it is to be with someone who loves and knows and supports you all the way. That is not to say that Stephen and I never disagreed; we did, often. He was even a registered Republican for many years! But disagreements with him helped me form and strengthen my own views. I miss much his presence, his companionship as we traveled the world, his optimism and zest for life. The depth of this loss is a definite disadvantage of a long, intimate relationship, but I know I was privileged to have it. It's lonely now, despite children and grandchildren who embrace and buoy me without condition.

The second sad fact that has skewed my story was the discovery in 2010 of a mass in my right lung that is indeed a cancer—due to a mutation of the EGFR gene—and more common among nonsmoking women (as I am). Triple whammy: no loving spouse, no cherished public role, now this. The diagnosis came as a bolt from the blue when I was vacationing with my family in Stone Harbor, New Jersey, unhappily sniffling away. My son Gordon suggested a visit to the nearby emergency room, where I was given a chest x-ray, and there it was, hiding in plain sight like malware. My diligent annual physical examinations did not include chest x-rays; my doctor tells me he orders a chest x-ray only when there are symptoms, and I had none.

The negative has been several tough years tacking between treatment and periods of wellness, managed within a fierce desire for public secrecy so that I can continue as long as possible living in the healthy world, not the "poor Judith" cancer world and the ugly side effects of cancer treatment. I mean to outrun this hideous disease and remain vital, defiant, and relevant as long as I can. As Emily Dickinson reminds us, "Looking at Death, is Dying."

But there's a positive here, too. A book my daughter, Luisa, gave me some time ago, Michael Morpurgo's *Alone on a Wide Wide Sea*, begins with the observation that the time to write about your life is when the end is in sight. In other words, you begin a story when you know the end. Whether or not the end is in sight for me—the statistics on stage four lung cancer are grim—I have reached a life juncture, a transformative moment that has inspired me to pick up a pen and start writing.

Maybe, just maybe, another theme will propel me through this time, one I have never felt more than I do today: fear of failure, failure to achieve something meaningful. I mean that not in a paralyzing sense but in an invigorating sense. I am equally devastated by the prospect of dying soon as I am by the notion of living many more years and achieving nothing more after my time as chief judge. That fear ignited a wonderful second act that is as much my story as my years on the court.

Always I carry with me this quote from A. A. Berle's 1969 book, *Power*:

> The post-power syndrome should be a passing phase. Sooner or later, the former power holder convinces himself that he is no longer important as a decision-maker, and that if he is to be important at all, it will be because of private or personal achievement. Then, if not crushed by the realization (and this sometimes occurs), he attacks a new life with perspectives not available to most. A surprising number of power holders have made their greatest contributions after their days in office have ended.

Having passed more than five years after being chief judge, I do not see myself making my greatest contribution in my postpower years, and I live in fear of joining that "sometimes" category of former power holders who are crushed by that realization. My post-court years have been filled, every day, with activity, satisfactions, and even joy. So I am turning to my comfort zone—writing—hoping to share that story and fulfill at least one more lifelong objective: to better inform the public about courts, particularly through the lens of the one most familiar to me during my years there, the Court of Appeals of the State of New York. The law, after all, affects virtually every aspect of our personal, professional, and communal lives. Familiarity with our system of government, its laws, and the judicial system that interprets those laws is key to better understanding our world, appreciating why certain things happen, and deciding how to change or improve circumstances we don't like.

~

Just a word about the universe I will be describing. Our great democracy rests on the three branches of federal government: the executive, the legislature, and the judiciary. The shape and reach of the judicial branch, embodied by the US Supreme Court, is a familiar one.

It comes as a surprise to many people that there is also a completely separate, parallel system of government in each state, including a constitution for each state. In New York, the governor heads the executive branch, the state Senate and Assembly make up the legislative branch, and the Court of Appeals of the State of New York (called the state Supreme Court in most other states) is at the top of the judicial branch. The New York Court of Appeals has a bench of seven judges appointed by the governor, and it sits at Court of Appeals Hall in Albany.

Though critically important to our nation and our lives, the judicial branch—for good reasons (like remoteness from the public to retain independence) and bad (obscure writing)—is less well known to the public than the other two branches. Despite their huge dockets, touching the everyday lives of our citizenry, the state courts are even more unknown than their federal counterparts. "The courts," for most people, largely start and stop with the US Supreme Court, the occasional high-profile criminal case, the often entertaining but fantastical depiction of courtroom trials in television and film, and a usually unwelcome summons for jury duty.

My story, focused principally on the Court of Appeals, will hopefully offer a bit of illumination about state courts throughout the nation that have so enriched my life.

Part I

The Court Years (1983–2009)

Chapter 1

The New York Court of Appeals

I begin with a paean to the Court of Appeals, my professional home for more than a quarter century. *Paean* means "a song of praise or thanksgiving; a shout or song of triumph, joy, or exultation," and is hardly an everyday word. But the New York Court of Appeals is hardly an ordinary place, and it deserves to be lauded and celebrated in a uniquely special way with a specific word.

I know I'm not alone in this feeling. What precipitated this segment was a call from a highly experienced New York City lawyer after his first appearance before the Court of Appeals. He's a big firm partner who has litigated for decades and even clerked for a justice of the US Supreme Court. He struggled to find words sufficient to capture the ecstasy of his experience before the Court of Appeals—the building, the courtroom, the staff, the judges, the level of their preparation and quality of argument. When I repeated this story to a law firm colleague, he continued in the same vein about his own experience two years earlier. He told me that having arrived the day before his scheduled argument—wisely intending to get a sense of the bench he would face—he was disappointed to learn that the court was not sitting that day. The court officer who conveyed that news insisted on accompanying him into the courtroom, showing him where everyone would sit and the next day's calendar, even giving him a brochure and gavel-tipped Court of Appeals pencils for his children.

Court of Appeals Hall

My paean starts with the court building itself, which is nestled between the Albany County Courthouse and City Hall, diagonally across from the Capitol, with a small park in between. Now known as Court of Appeals Hall, the white marble Greek Revival structure was originally known as State Hall and was completed in 1842 to house state officers. The Court of Appeals officially commenced in 1847—the state constitution of 1846 declares that "there shall be a Court of Appeals"—and was originally located on the third floor of the Capitol. Interestingly, an apparent contest between two leading architects of the day—H. H. Richardson and Leopold Eidlitz—as to who would design the Capitol was resolved by "dividing the baby" between them. The space occupied by the Court of Appeals in the Capitol fell to Richardson. In 1917, when the court moved from the Capitol to occupy State Hall, Richardson's courtroom—including the floor-to-ceiling hand-carved oak paneling, the furniture, and the Mexican onyx (nonworking) fireplace (what a treat it is to sit in the courtroom's fireplace!) was—except for the ceiling— dismantled and moved to what has ever since been known as Court of Appeals Hall. The ceiling was "mocked in" in plaster to match. The courtroom is not the largest, grandest, or most ornate I have ever seen, but it is the most beautiful.

I need to jump ahead a bit to 2002, when the court updated its magnificent home. That had been done only once before, in 1958, and it was high time to do so again to meet physical and technological demands. The court had earlier moved the Office of the State Reporter (responsible for publishing the court's decisions) out of Court of Appeals Hall to its own quarters, but that left insufficient space. For the first time, plans to enlarge the structure—actually add meaningfully to the size of the building, making it asymmetrical—met resistance from historic preservationists. I decided not to engage in battle with them.

As we fruitlessly searched in the city of Albany for expansion space, we miraculously received the enthusiastic endorsement of the historic preservationists and, between 2002 and 2004, went forward with enlargement of the building from roughly 60,000 to 90,000 square feet.[1] Much of what had been the former marble facade of the building became interior wall space, as we added significantly at two ends of the building and took the interior down to brick; we uncovered magnificent vaulted ceilings hidden behind acoustical tile installed in 1958. But it was scary! I am so grateful to my colleague Richard C. Wesley, who originally laid the renovation idea on the table, before beating a retreat to the US Court of Appeals for the Second Circuit. There are too many heroes of the renovation—Clerk of the Court Stuart Cohen and building manager Brian Emigh, chief among them—to mention and thank every one of them here.

Suffice it to say that given the ultimate success of the renovation, the terrors, miseries, and agonies—certainly attendant to any building overhaul—are long forgotten. In hindsight, it was a ton of fun coordinating colors (ivory, navy, deep red, and dark green throughout the building), finding matching marble for the new facade (I visited the Danby Quarry—more accurately a mine—in Vermont), selecting furnishings and materials, and allocating space. For the first time, all seven judges' chambers would now be on the same floor, instead of five on the second floor and two on the third, permitting more natural exchanges among them. Considering the extent of the renovation, my favorite

---

1. Years later, Albany's county executive, knowing that we had looked at historic Centennial Hall across the street, called me to say that we could have that then-collapsing building "for nothing" (his words), all efforts at their own private development having failed. We accepted the offer and proceeded with plans to locate the State Reporter there, as well as a modest lodging room for each nonresident judge, who otherwise stays at a mediocre local hotel, with a judicial branch museum in the lobby. That erupted into a ludicrous scandal over the so-called palatial space being planned for the judges in the midst of a state fiscal crisis, so the living quarters part was halted, and the small rooms were rented out as offices. Having spent twenty-five years largely at a hotel two weeks out of every five, it is beyond sad that the non-Albany judges can't have a small, regular room to come to, a place to leave a few personal effects and security downstairs (we had two security incidents in my years at hotels), as well as our museum in the lobby. What's more, the court saved a beautiful century-old building, which would have otherwise become a parking lot.

compliment from Court of Appeals long-timers revisiting the building is "nothing has changed," meaning the beauty and dignity of the hall are fully intact. Indeed, comprehensive though the project was, in the courtroom itself we merely spruced up the furnishings, including a return to the style of the original light fixtures—now six chandeliers instead of one, to provide more light—updating the carpeting, and recovering the chair seats. (Embarrassingly, we discovered on day one of the public reopening that they needed more stuffing—everyone had left his or her imprint on the seats at the rear of the courtroom.) Among my toughest decisions was choosing fabric texture for the new draperies—closer weave meant more sheen, looser weave meant more swag.

All of this returns me to the subject of the Richardson courtroom. To my mind, the Court of Appeals physically is vastly underappreciated, including its glorious rotunda and magnificent courtroom. One day as I wandered through our beautifully enlarged space, it occurred to me that now we had a better opportunity to bring in the public, which is something courts should strive to do. The courthouse is, after all, a public building, and sadly the public rarely visited the Court of Appeals. So we initiated a public lecture series, cosponsored with the Historical Society of the Courts of the State of New York, centered on legal subjects of wide interest and drew crowds of 200 or more Capital District residents and others. One of my favorites was "The Shape of Justice: Courthouse Architecture," delivered by two preeminent architects, Henry N. Cobb and Paul Bayard. I could not better capture the emotion our courtroom engenders than to quote the words of Henry Cobb, which I enthusiastically affirm:

> Look around you now and notice how eloquently this room gives voice to values that underlie the administration of justice in our democratic society. Notice that the room is stately yet unpretentious, highly ordered yet refreshingly nonhierarchical, beautifully crafted yet materially modest, appropriately ceremonial yet warmly human. If I were speaking to you in a lecture hall, I would be obligated to illustrate these points with projected images, but here I need only to invite you to enjoy discovering for yourself the myriad details that together constitute the eloquent voice of this room. Wherever you are seated—whether near the bench or fireplace, or in one of the ram's-head armchairs, or toward the rear with a sweeping view of the many portraits arrayed around its paneled walls, you are palpably enveloped here in the voice of architecture as spoken by a master of our art.
>
> Here, more effectively than in any other courtroom I know, the collegial character of an appeals court and the collective nature of its judgments is eloquently affirmed. When we consider the coherence and splendor of this chamber, with its magnificent fireplace and wonderful carved ornament—on its walls, on its bench, on its tables and chairs, all of which were custom-made at this site—it is easy to understand why, when the court later outgrew its quarters in the Capitol, it took the unprecedented step of dismantling the courtroom and reconstructing it virtually intact in its new quarters in the old State Hall, now appropriately renamed, of course, Court of Appeals Hall.

The Judges and Court Staff

Of course, my paean goes far beyond love for bricks and mortar. Indeed, it is truly the people of the court—the judges and staff—who create and continue this extraordinary institution. The dedication of the staff—many of whom have served for decades, and many of whom never worked anywhere else—can only be described as genetic. It's a family I joined in September 1983, knowing that I could ask anything of anyone and it would be done, and the tradition endures. We share one another's personal joys and tragedies and delight in the work of the court, whether keeping the brass interior staircase rails polished or cleaning chambers (which begins before 5 a.m., anticipating the judges' early arrivals; I often found homemade biscotti on the seat awaiting me in the morning), or ensuring that the public's needs and questions are answered promptly and courteously, or handling difficult dockets superbly. The feelings go both ways. For several years at the court we had a book club, another bridge between the judges and staff; I knitted baby sweaters when I learned that one of the court officers was expecting twins. I have no reluctance recommending that people call, write, or visit the Clerk's Office with any question, or seek information from the public information officer or the lawyer/librarian, or help from one of the court officers in the lobby. They never disappoint.

Of the 109 judges who have been privileged to sit on the Court of Appeals from 1847 to date, I have worked alongside nineteen—roughly 20 percent of the judges over the past 164 years—and have known several more of them personally. My testimony, based on decades of firsthand experience, I submit, is therefore unimpeachable: they are phenomenal. Many things I would wish to say about the judges are told in later segments and, best of all, in the massive volume *The Judges of the New York Court of Appeals: A Biographical History*, the ultimate work product of us all, under the masterful direction of Judge Albert Rosenblatt. I am reluctant to name judges individually for fear of skipping someone. My praise is universal.

The governor appoints judges from all over the state, and I think being a nonresident court helps enormously. The court—meaning all seven judges, the only way the court officially convenes—gathers in Albany for sessions of oral argument generally two weeks out of every five. The judges return between sessions to their home chambers to write and study for the intervening weeks.[2] When we were together in Albany, it was dawn to dusk (and beyond) together. In between, we exchanged tons of paper but did not often see or speak to one another. Always I looked forward to gathering with my colleagues in Albany, and after two weeks of lively debate I looked forward to leaving them. There are immense personal differences among the judges—some are genuine "buddies," some less so. But at the core I encountered human beings of quality at the peak of their careers in law, dedicated to the work of the court. Our personal rapport—even those with whom

---

2. I was fortunate that my children were old enough that I could do this relatively easily. Back in September 1983, Luisa was in her first year at Amherst; Jonathan was a senior at Dalton, headed to Cornell; and Gordie, at Fieldston, transferred to Choate (which he chose because, among the boarding school catalogs he studied, Choate's was "the only one where the kids were smiling"). A couple of years later when Gordie was at Hamilton, Stephen mastered "the circuit," visiting all of us periodically by trekking between Albany; Amherst, Massachusetts; Ithaca, New York; and Clinton, New York.

I more often disagreed on the law—I could never hope to replicate in anything I do. Lawyer heaven.

Coincidentally, in my afterlife, I discovered objective evidence of the court's distinction that even the court may not fully appreciate. In the global agreements I now routinely encounter in my arbitration practice, I find that often the parties contractually chose New York law to govern the resolution of any dispute that might arise between them, and that is because of its recognized clarity, rationality, stability, and predictability. While the Court of Appeals surely has as its objective in each case reaching a result and setting a rule that is sound for the particular parties and the law of New York, it does not necessarily consider the impact of its holdings in faraway corners of the world. Credit needs to be shared with other New York courts and the practicing bar, but nevertheless the predominance of New York jurisprudence as the choice of law speaks volumes about the deep regard our high court has earned as a sound, stable decision maker. What a joy it was to be part of and ultimately lead this institution and its people. How painful it is to be severed from them. When they say "I miss you," I honestly respond, "I miss you more."

Here are two illustrative personal anecdotes from my first months on the court, one a judge story and one a clerk story.

As one of my draft writings was being discussed at the conference table, Judge Bernard Meyer remarked that he knew of a line in an old case that would fit perfectly into the opinion. He remembered only that the line was on the left side of the page in an opinion in the *New York Reports* (each volume about 1,000 pages), about the middle of the page. This was back in 1983, pre-Internet. I reported this to my law clerk, Gary Hoppe, and after lunch went down to the courtroom to hear oral arguments. Returning to my chambers hours later, there was Gary surrounded by at least fifty volumes scattered on the floor, pulling books from the shelves and muttering, "I'll kill him. I'll kill him." But Gary found the case, and the language Meyer recalled was indeed where he remembered it to be, and indeed it fit perfectly. At conference the next morning, as my revised draft was circulated, Bernie simply whispered, "Yes, that's it," and I said "Thanks." A great communal effort.

As I reflect on my first chambers in the courthouse (the two "juniors"—Judge Richard Simons, later Judge Fritz Alexander, and I—we each started with quarters on the third floor), I am reminded of a call I received shortly after my arrival from Jack Matthews, a fearsome figure who had been with the court forty-some years, starting after law school graduation as law clerk for Chief Judge Charles Desmond and moving up to the position of conference room clerk. Jack sat in on all the court conferences, and when he spoke it was usually to call a judge's attention to a technical error in one of our drafts—"You can't do that, Judge." Everyone's blood froze around the conference table when we heard Jack clearing his throat as if to speak. One day Jack called to say he was on his way up to see me, and that was distinctly not good news. What had I done wrong? Once I composed myself, I decided that instead of remaining in my seat behind my desk, I would pull out the little shelf in the front of the desk and sit alongside him, conveying a sense of equality and collegiality. That proved unnecessary. Minutes later Jack strode into the room, went right to my seat behind the desk and proceeded to educate me about one of the innumerable technicalities of Court of Appeals procedure I had overlooked. (There are dozens of similar technicalities. The court's collection of motion and jurisdictional reports detailing them is appropriately called "The Arcanum.")

That is the tradition it was my good fortune to step into on September 12, 1983: an outstanding group of equals, all working hard together to do our individual and collective best possible job.

The Cases

One of the many stories floating around the courthouse is that once during oral argument, a lawyer was questioned about how he got to the Court of Appeals—meaning the jurisdictional basis for his case—and he answered, "By car." There are in fact several ways to get cases to the court. Here's a highly simplified version.

In the design of the New York court system there are trial courts, with case filings each year numbering in the four million range, and intermediate appellate courts, with cases numbering in the tens of thousands. Everyone basically has a right to bring a case to a trial court, and (unlike the federal court system) a right to full review of the decision once, generally by the Appellate Division, which has broad "interests of justice" jurisdiction and can address even factual disputes (differences over what words were spoken or what things were done). The Court of Appeals offers a second layer of appeal, which is more constricted and less available. The road to the court has obstacles, consistent with the goal that the opportunity for yet another layer of appeal should be more sparingly available, to resolve issues of significance going beyond factual differences between the parties—in other words, to settle and declare the law for the whole state.

To this end, there are three essentials, each with its own exceptions. First, cases reaching the court must have been finally decided below it—there is to be no piecemeal Court of Appeals review of cases. Second, the cases generally must present only questions of law, not of facts, the review of which stops at the Appellate Division. Third, the issues must have significance beyond the parties, so that in a relatively few cases the court can decide legal questions with broad impact.

This trio of requirements makes for oral arguments with little late-night TV appeal. It's usually the facts, the human tangles, the things people actually say and do to one another that draw popular interest. From the bench, we often had to remind lawyers presenting argument that ours is a law court and they should stay focused on the law. Every now and then I toyed with the idea of shaking things up by saying, "We know the law, Counsel, just stick with the facts." I consciously tried to limit humor from the bench. It's always easy for judges to get a laugh, but that sort of egotism disrupts the appropriate courtroom decorum. Though oral arguments at the Court of Appeals have been recorded for decades, we attracted no television audience. Humor and drama certainly would have made us more popular. But the Court of Appeals is not *Judge Judy*—an excellent entertainer—and we were soon dropped from local TV. Pity. I always brought home the videotaped argument in aid of opinions I was drafting. I imagine lawyers purchased copies, too, especially when they felt good about their presentation and wanted to show off to friends and family.

Before 1986, many cases came to the court "as of right"—for example, even the opinion of a single dissenting Appellate Division judge was a ticket to the Court of Appeals. In my initial years on the court we heard approximately 800 appeals annually, arriving at the courthouse Sunday afternoons for two packed weeks of argument, at least seven cases a day. That changed radically for the better in 1985 when the state constitution was amended to transform the court to a basically "cert" (or certiorari) court, meaning that the judges largely get to select the docket, pretty much like the US Supreme Court. The result has been that the Court of Appeals hears roughly 250 cases annually, and I assure you that it's still a full-time job. The nine justices of the Supreme Court hear approximately seventy appeals annually.

One further general observation: civil and criminal cases follow different pathways to the court. Since 1986 civil cases get to the court by application, or motion for leave to appeal from a decision of the intermediate appellate court. There are roughly 1,000 civil motions for leave to appeal annually. Each motion is assigned to one judge, purely in decreasing order of seniority, assisted by an attorney on the Court's Central Legal Research staff, resident in Albany (contrasted with "elbow clerks," who travel with and serve their respective judges), for preparation of a report to grant or deny leave to appeal, which is then circulated for a vote by the full court. Motions for leave to appeal are conferenced every morning the court is in session. Typically they top the daily conference agenda. It takes the vote of two judges to grant leave. As with everything else in life, there are exceptions, practically and systemically. As a practical matter, leave may be granted if even one of the seven judges very strenuously urges it. Systemically, civil cases can still occasionally reach the court as a matter of right—without a motion—as when there are two dissents at the Appellate Division or the sole issue is a substantial constitutional question.

As in the past, criminal cases come not by formal motion but by letter application to the court—in a given year the number of these applications is generally more than double the number of civil motions for leave to appeal. Each criminal leave application is assigned for review to a single judge in order of seniority, and that judge alone decides whether leave should be granted. Here I will say something that applies generally to the work of the court I am describing. My accounts of how cases are prepared by the judges individually are based strictly on my own experience—I have no idea how my colleagues, within chambers, arranges his or her own matters. For me, every criminal leave application was first fully reviewed by one of my law clerks, who prepared a written report I studied along with the underlying letter application and prior court documents. If merited, I would schedule a call or appearance with counsel. My objective always was to grant, not deny, the criminal leave application, unless convinced otherwise.

In recent years, the bar raised concerns about the low number of leave grants— perhaps some of us were a bit stingy in granting leave to appeal. With the judges' consciousness raised, the numbers have gone up a bit—but so have the relatively less significant unsigned memorandum affirmances of criminal convictions. Whether the push to grant more criminal leave applications makes any real difference to the law or to the defendants remains to be seen. An alternative suggestion from some members of the bar to put all criminal leave applications through the same formal motion process as the civil cases would add tremendously, and I believe unnecessarily, to the burdens on the court and the already insufficient pool of available counsel for indigent defendants.

While cases overwhelmingly arrive on the calendar by grant of leave, in 1985 the state constitution was further amended to open yet another significant avenue to the court: certified questions. These are requests for leave to appeal made not by the parties but by another court—a federal appellate court or high court of a sister state—and reflect the line between our parallel state-federal court systems. Although federal courts and courts of other states can opine on issues of New York law, our own state courts have the ultimate authority to speak to state law issues. For example, if the meaning of a state statute is at issue before the federal courts, they can go ahead and interpret the statute, but the state courts can later overrule their interpretation. Embarrassing and inefficient. The certification process offers these courts an opportunity to put only the state law issue to the state court for resolution while retaining the rest of the case for application of the now-explicated law to the facts.

For nearly two decades the procedure has worked remarkably well in New York. Of the court's 250 or so appeals annually, usually a half dozen or more important questions have come through the certification process, usually from the federal appellate court sitting in New York—the US Court of Appeals for the Second Circuit—eliciting quick, final resolution of the state law issue. I see at least two additional advantages. First, from the New York Court of Appeals' point of view, it's an opportunity to opine on a significant law issue "unencumbered" by the underlying facts. *Nicholson v. Scoppetta* is for me a great example where, given only a certified question of law, we were able to state a broad principle regarding removing children from domestic violence situations that continues a to be central to the disposition of many cases. It might not otherwise have been as widely impactful a decision had it arisen in the context of specific facts (in the book *Women: A Celebration of Strength*, the authors identify the writing as among "50 Key Cases for Women's Equality"). Second, I sense that the certification procedure has strengthened the relationship and promoted a sense of parity between the Second Circuit and the New York Court of Appeals. All around, a good move.

The variety of cases before the Court of Appeals, civil and criminal, is boundless. Several years ago the court's public information officer, Richard Zander, mentioned to me that the post-Christmas weeks were pretty dead news time, so in an effort to stimulate greater public awareness of what we do, I had each judge synopsize half a dozen of his or her significant decisions and we put the list out to the media during those weeks. Not surprisingly, that failed in its intended purpose, but it did become a tradition, continued today, for each Court of Appeals judge at year end to summarize five or so key decisions. The full list, arranged by category of law, is included in the *Annual Report of the Clerk of the Court*, reflecting the amazing A to Z (administrative law to zoning) range of legal issues that find their way to Albany—family law, mental hygiene, contracts, land use, municipal law, consumer protection, insurance, landlord/tenant are but a few examples. It's an interesting compilation of what each of the judges considers to be his or her "decisions of the year."

Chapter 2

My Arrival on the Court of Appeals

Morpurgo recommends that you start your life story with the first day you can be sure you really remember with complete accuracy. For me and my life at the Court of Appeals, that would be Tuesday, September 12, 1983, the day I publicly took the oath of office as the first female judge to sit on the court. I'm sure there were terrifying and momentous days in my life before that—September 1943, when my father drove me in our pickup truck from our farm down to the one-room schoolhouse in Maplewood for my first day of school; arriving at Barnard College in the wilds of New York City just days after I turned sixteen; starting night law school in 1959 against the pleas of parents dismayed at the path their daughter was taking; or starting at Sullivan & Cromwell as a Jewish woman in 1962. But as terrifying (and wonderful) as any of those days were, September 12, 1983, takes the cake.

What led up to that is somewhat clouded by the excitement, anxiety, hoopla (including an ultimately foiled plan by some to have a different person be the first woman to sit on the Court of Appeals) and euphoria of the process.

Announcement of my selection by Governor Cuomo came on August 11, 1983. Early that morning, the governor's office called to tell me to be at the World Trade Center (where Cuomo then maintained his New York City quarters) at noon, and added: "Tell ABSOLUTELY no one!" Meekly I called back minutes later to ask if it was all right to tell my husband and children. I was taking no chances. Then came the difficulty of collecting them for the nomination ceremony. No problem for my daughter, Luisa (then eighteen), summering at a downtown brokerage firm, but poor Stephen had to gather our sons, Jonathan (seventeen) and Gordon (fifteen), both working at a day camp, along with appropriate dress for the occasion.

All in all, it was nearly flawless. As the boys hurriedly changed into suits and ties on the long elevator ride up at the World Trade Center, they discovered that they had lost Gordie's tie along the way. Stephen pointed to a fellow elevator passenger and said, "I'll give you $20 for that tie." As the tie-wearer was removing his tie, he said, "This must be *Candid Camera*!" I still have that tie, which likely netted the original owner a $19 profit. There was one small glitch. When all the fanfare died down, I told Stephen in jest (I thought privately), "I'm not cooking dinner tonight." That made it into the wonderful *Times* story, along with my only *New York Times* Quotation of the Day: "I take my gender with me everywhere I go." But the cooking remark distinctly upset Sofia, our housekeeper, who (among others in the family) was delighted that I never cooked dinner.

Weeks later I was unanimously confirmed by the Senate (these days the Senate's accolades are less often unanimous) and given a joyous introduction to Court of Appeals Hall by the fabulous Clerk of the Court (later Court of Appeals judge) Joseph Bellacosa.

Shortly after my appointment was announced, my friend Arthur Liman, a renowned Paul Weiss partner, called with congratulations, adding somewhat ominously, "You had better get yourself some good law clerks. You are really going to need them." Oy! Of course he was right, and I followed his advice. I always had the very best law clerks (every one of them still dear to me), drawn from the practicing bar rather than law school, the more typical source—though it was a bit daunting at first. When I asked the lawyer with whom I had worked most closely, Gary Hoppe (then in his sixth year at the firm and headed for partnership), to come with me, his answer was, "You must be joking." I thought that meant no. Fortunately, he returned to my office the next day and accepted the offer. Together we found Darren O'Connor at the Legal Aid Society, confident that he would add just the right touch of diligence, diversion (he had been a professional actor!), and (our otherwise utterly lacking) criminal law experience. With my former law firm secretary and a block of unused space at the firm,[1] we opened a dozen or so bankers' boxes filled with briefs for the upcoming court session and set to work.

I remember taking a break from those briefs, first on August 29 for a face-to-face meeting with the judges, who were in Albany to hear *Matter of Schumer v. Holtzman* (District Attorney Elizabeth Holtzman's charges against State Assembly member Charles Schumer for alleged improper use of state employees during his congressional campaign), and second to purchase a new (taupe) suit with matching shoes (Henri Bendel, they cost a fortune) for what was one of the great days of my life. One physical change had been made in the magnificent nineteenth-century building that is the home of the Court of Appeals to accommodate its first-ever female judge: a lock was put on the bathroom door just off the robing room, in case one of the judges had to step off the bench during oral argument. They didn't need the lock for me—I never used that bathroom. (As the only woman partner at my law firm, I never used the partners' bathroom, though I insisted on having the key.)

September 12 arrived before we knew it. At the festive swearing in, I remember my Uncle Charlie's advice to me on seeing the all-male portraits of the former judges on the walls of the courtroom: get my "portrait painted right away" rather than waiting until my retirement from the court (at least) fourteen years later. After a luncheon reception at the State Bar, the court convened promptly at 2 p.m. to hear argument. The courtroom was packed until I asked my first questions in the first case (*People v. Cofresi*, a criminal

---

1. The Judiciary Law promised a Court of Appeals judge commodious chambers of "his choosing." The judges do, of course, have glorious chambers at the court in Albany—the official chambers. This was local, or home chambers I had to choose. Stephen's firm was at 300 Park Avenue, mine at 299. Usually we met downstairs and walked home to have dinner with the kids, then later returned to the office. Prakash Yerawadeker from the Office of Court Administration worked with me to find chambers space in the area, so Stephen and I could continue our walks home for dinner. How fortunate we were to find the state vacating 230 Park Avenue for the World Trade Center! At that time the rent was $17 per square foot, virtually the only affordable space for us on Park Avenue. For the next twenty-five years, that was the site of my truly beautiful New York City chambers and remains the site of my successor's chambers.

appeal presenting a search and seizure issue)—in all, about five minutes. Then the room cleared. Immediately it was as if I had been there all my life.

Given how full the court's work days are now, it's hard to imagine a tripled docket. But back in 1983, before cert or leave jurisdiction, we arrived in Albany for two-week sessions on Sunday, with arguments Monday through Friday instead of (as now) Tuesday through Thursday; a tradition of early breakfast and dinner together; longer afternoon sessions on the bench with a break for tea (or soup!); and late nights back working in chambers. My friend Peg Breen, who did a terrific TV show called *Inside Albany*, described us on her program as a "co-ed monastery."

Lunch was traditionally served by George Connair at each judge's desk as we and law clerks prepared for 2 p.m. oral arguments. Lunch for the judges was canned soup of choice (which George meticulously poured into a bowl from a silver tureen), cookies, and tea or coffee. The solemnity of the soup-pouring ceremony cracked me up. (Today the judges have much more informal and nutritional lunches, still at their desks with their law clerks, preparing for oral arguments.) Judges' breakfasts were in the Red Room (a small gem of a conference room just behind the courtroom), with blueberry muffins picked up by Bernard Meyer from Dunkin' Donuts each morning on his way to the courthouse. Hugh Jones always cut off the top of his muffin and ate it in two parts; Bernie cut his into eight parts; Matt Jasen had shredded wheat with skim milk, following his mother's good nutrition training. Mostly we read the newspapers and chatted about world events. Though the nightly dinner tradition largely continues, the collegial breakfasts went by the boards long ago.

Following lunch come oral arguments. Oral arguments are "showtime," a genuine change in the pace of the day the judges look forward to, when f they get to hear one another's questions—signifying a colleague's "take" on a case—and have lively confrontations with counsel. Do oral arguments matter?, I am often asked. Not as much as the briefs, but yes, absolutely, they do matter.

Albany sessions consisted of four to seven arguments a day for two consecutive weeks, with a three-week intersession for preparing decisions, deciding motions, and studying briefs for the next session. Thankfully, I took the advice of my friend, New Jersey Supreme Court Justice Marie Garibaldi to turn down all invitations to speak for a year or more and learn my job. At the end of each day's arguments, the judges retire to the Red Room, where a series of index cards, each bearing a case name on the underside, is spread on the table. Then, in order of seniority, each judge randomly picks a card, which becomes his or her assigned case for reporting at conference the following morning. No "vest-pocket specialists" on the Court of Appeals!

The reporting judge's Conference Room report begins with recommendation as to result and form of writing—signed opinion, unsigned per curiam or memorandum writing (opinions are at the front of the court's published reports, unsigned writings at the back). Then after a full presentation as to proposed rationale, the discussion proceeds around the table, in reverse order of seniority, beginning with the junior judge. The theory is that the junior judge should not feel unduly intimidated by "senior" opinion. Moreover, a vigorous junior judge report, if different from the reporting judge, gets the discussion off to a good start. If the reporting judge carries the court, the case remains with that judge to write; if not, the writing falls to the judge sitting immediately to the right of the reporting judge in the majority—a genuinely random writing assignment system.

Conference back then packed every morning from 9:30 or 10 until 12:30 lunch, followed by oral argument at 2 on the dot. If nothing else—and there's a lot else—the court is highly punctual. (After twenty-five years, I have become neurotically punctual in my personal life as well.) In my last years on the court, the morning Conference Room discussions became shorter and less robust. Individual personalities matter. Some people like to explore or argue more than others, on the bench and off. Some are virtually impossible to persuade, and more extended discussion at the conference table is utterly useless.

It's a terrific system that I found in place and burnished just a bit over the years. It's a good system largely because of the judges and court personnel—their acute preparation, self-discipline, and dedication to the business of the court and the collegiality that defines the institution. With little exception, cases heard by the Court of Appeals one session are resolved in writings carefully reviewed by the colleagues and made public the next session, a genuine service to the law and litigants. I know no other court that does this. When a case has been held over more than one session, that's a sign of divisions within the court and the desire for further discussion. A prime example—one of my proudest decisions—is the four-three decision upholding same-sex adoption under the New York Domestic Relations Law, *Matter of Jacob*, argued June 5 and not decided until November 5, 1995. For the Court of Appeals, a five-month delay between argument and release of a decision to this day is most unusual, signaling not only disagreement (evidenced by the dissent) but also that someone in that four-three mix—thankfully, in retrospect—was keeping the door ajar, unwilling to finalize the vote.

Obviously that rigorous schedule requires the judges' intense preparation of the cases before oral argument, readiness to cast a fully informed vote the day following argument, and commitment to circulating a draft writing from home chambers before the court convenes next in Albany. Quite a feat—but it works! When I arrived back home from my very first session with a half-dozen or so decisions to write and upcoming cases to prepare, Stephen attempted to relieve my anxiety with "Don't worry, what you don't get done this month, you'll do next month." Well . . . no. The Court of Appeals doesn't work that way. Cases argued one session are, with rare exception, resolved by the court the very next session. Period. Remarkably, no one deviates.

Chapter 3

Getting to Work

Despite the public's general lack of awareness of the work of the judicial branch, the state court dockets—over 90 percent of our nation's litigation, on every subject imaginable—most closely reflect the everyday lives of our citizenry. As I write this, I have, for example, been following news reports of the controversy surrounding the Picasso wall hanging at the Four Seasons restaurant in Manhattan. The Court of Appeals upheld the landmarking of the *interior* of that restaurant. If only the painting that fills an entire wall had been included in the landmarking! (*Matter of Teachers Ins. & Annuity Assn. of Am. v. City of New York*). In my neighborhood, I regularly pass and often visit Symphony Space, a delightful entertainment venue that would not exist today but for a Court of Appeals decision under an ancient doctrine—the Rule Against Perpetuities—that confounds law students but protects against limitless conveyances that would long ago have gobbled up Symphony Space (*Symphony Space v. Pergola Properties*). I return home with a now clearly permissible large soda bottle (*Matter of New York Statewide Coalition v. NYC Dep't of Health and Mental Hygiene*) to a board meeting of my apartment co-op, where the applicable standard of care for directors has been defined by the Court of Appeals (*Matter of Levandusky v. One Fifth Ave.*). That is, of course, only a tiny taste. State court decisions are everywhere!

The cases may be divided into three categories. First, unique to the state (as opposed to federal) courts, are common law cases, where the courts draw the lines defining lawful and unlawful conduct, based on a combination of prior court decisions (precedents) and contemporary wisdom. "Common law" describes a tool of judging and a body of judge-made law. It is static at its core, yet case by case it proceeds and grows incrementally, in restrained yet principled fashion to fit an inherently stable yet constantly changing society.

Second, the courts interpret statutes enacted by the legislature—the criminal law, for example, is essentially statutory. There are volumes of statutes on civil practice, domestic relations, eminent domain, real property, trusts and estates, town and village law—everything. In statutory interpretation cases, the courts attempt to implement the legislature's will as expressed in provisions often written long before any dispute arises. Over the decades, statutes have proliferated, as have the state court decisions necessarily updating, narrowing, or broadening statutory language, which the legislature may thereafter amend if, in its view, the court got it wrong.

Third are constitutional law cases, requiring courts to give modern-day significance to the protections framed centuries ago by our founders. All three categories of cases present a singular challenge: the law at its core must remain rational and stable, yet it must reflect—and sometimes incentivize—the progress and protection of our fundamental values. In each category there are inevitably gaps to be filled. Inevitably the courts make law as well as policy decisions.

The array of cases presenting these issues is dazzling, and the crammed September 1983 session (fifty or more cases) was no exception: murder and other criminal law matters, Medicaid reimbursement, attorney discipline, workers' compensation, municipal liability, personal injury, family law, commercial law, administrative law. You name it, we heard it—each case purportedly raising a novel issue of significance meriting the second layer of appellate review the state court system provides. My law clerk Gary Hoppe tells me that, as I sat across the desk from him after the first day's arguments, I said, "I have absolutely no idea what I am supposed to do here, do you?"

Quickly we learned. Indeed, during that first two-week session in Albany, I miraculously produced a few unsigned writings (called memorandum opinions) that actually made it into the published court reports. My first random pick—a case argued on September 12, my very first day on the bench—was *Humphrey v. State of New York* (still possibly cited more than my other writings), standing for the thoroughly unremarkable proposition that the Court of Appeals is without power to review trial-level findings of fact that are affirmed by the intermediate appellate court and supported by the record. In those initial weeks following that first Albany session, I produced three signed opinions publicly released the following month: *Consolidated Edison v. Red Hook* (the law on power plant siting and my first signed opinion!), *Braten v. Bankers Trust* (contracts), and *Campbell v. Pesce* (criminal). Having gone to the highest appellate court without the customary years of prior judicial service—somewhat of an outsider—I still found a zone of comfort stemming from my years of experience as a litigator. Indeed, a high court is strengthened by diversity, including the litigators' experience. Even today it astounds me to think that every single volume of the *New York Reports* from 60 New York Second to 11 New York Third—fifty-one books in all—contains at least a dozen of my writings. I am not aware that anything I authored has yet been overruled, though that always remains a possibility.

Scanning those first weeks of the court's writings is still breathtaking—the array of subject matter, certainly, but even more the articulation and importance of the holdings, enduring to this day and unquestionably into the future, the bedrock law, despite a rapidly evolving society. From those September session days we produced, for example, *DeLong v. County of Erie*, Sol Wachtler's writing for a unanimous court upholding the county's liability for failure to respond to the plaintiff's call for emergency assistance despite the municipality's assurance that help was on the way; *Matter of Alessi*, on remand from the US Supreme Court, Bernie Meyer's writing on professional standards required of attorneys concerning letters soliciting legal business; and *Sega v. State of New York*, Larry Cooke's writing settling the parameters for state landowners' liability when the public is gratuitously allowed on state property.

How well I remember *Matter of Suffolk Outdoor Advertising v. Town of Southampton*, a case involving billboard advertising that had been marked for "reargument." I had no idea what that signaled. Though I had carefully prepared my extensive junior judge report for conference the morning following reargument, when the case was called the chief asked only for my vote. I said, "Affirm." That did it! The three-three split (the court had been reduced to six by the departure of Jack Fuchsberg, whose seat I filled) was resolved and the court issued a single unanimous opinion. No one needed to hear my exquisitely reasoned take on the case.

Those days we generally tried to be unanimous. The early training I received at the conference table was that the court splits—and we surely did—only when we really have to. I remember several "dissents" circulated by Judge Jones, not with the intention that they be published but to better inform the majority opinion writer in crafting what ultimately became a unanimous opinion. Back in my day, just about every one of us on the Court of Appeals had the experience of writing, and withdrawing, separate concurring or dissenting opinions that were solely intended to spawn modifications in what then became a unanimous writing. Today the tradition is visibly different, with many more four-three benches and separate writings, delightful fodder for the commentators.

What I learned over my quarter-century on the court is that unanimity or consensus can be achieved only if every judge at the conference table believes it is a desirable objective. No chief judge, however brilliant or beloved, can impose it. It was my good fortune, during most of my years on the court, that working hard to achieve consensus, when possible without compromising principle, was a shared value. When it was not possible, no one hesitated to write separately and vigorously.

A personal word about the colleagues (or "collies" as we jokingly referred to them in chambers): when I arrived on the court I had just turned forty-five. Four of the six were approaching seventy, mandatory retirement age. So imagine what life was like for the court's first female judge, ensconced among Chief Judge Lawrence Cooke (learning to call him "Larry" was among the hardest things I had to do) and associate judges Matthew J. Jasen, Hugh R. Jones, and Bernard Meyer. I had a special attachment to each of those great gentlemen. The "juniors," Sol Wachtler and Richard Simons, were pretty terrific, too. If there is any advantage I failed to take—by reason of unique age, gender, or commercial litigation experience—that is my sole regret.

The judges' long-standing tradition was to assemble for dinner at the University Club[1] every night the court was sitting—a wonderful tradition that continues, but to a more limited extent, and now at restaurants around the city. Back then no one missed. Once, when I had thoughtlessly arranged for dinner with a friend visiting Albany, we met early so that I could join the court for dinner (again) afterward. Our meals were in fact a good break from diligent morning preparation for conference, then conference followed by lunchtime preparation for oral argument, and several hours of back-and-forth with the lawyers. Having discovered that one of our favorite restaurants, Jack's, offered a free birthday cake with singing waiters, Judge Vito Titone secretly informed the staff that it was my birthday several times a year—they very politely went along with it.

---

1. In the distant past, the judges had dined regularly at Albany's Fort Orange Club, but then moved to the University Club because the Fort Orange Club did not allow women members at the time. That changed, and I even became a member for a while. I have heard that earlier the Fort Orange Club also did not accept Jews, causing Chief Judge Lehman to dine elsewhere, but I have not verified that story.

Dinnertime conversation among the Colleagues was usually about our personal lives, sometimes about lawyers appearing before us, but never about the cases, which were discussed only in conference. Though it was at the time regarded as "sinful" for the judges to talk among themselves about the cases outside the conference room—it was looked on as lobbying—Judge Simons and I developed the habit of walking up three flights to our chambers after argument, when we talked about you-know-what, merely searching for a clue as to the vote we would cast the next morning. (At the conference table, Judge Simons and I often disagreed—more like "battled," as he said—the most on the law. Our staircase exchanges merely helped us better prepare for the battle.)

The seven of us got to know one another well, and I think those dinners really promoted the extraordinary collegiality we enjoyed. Afterward we returned to chambers to work, except for Chief Judge Cooke, who preferred burning the candle at the other end, going "home" after dinner to the DeWitt Clinton Hotel, where he maintained an apartment, and arriving at the court for the day at 3:30 to 4 a.m.

Back to September 12, 1983: at our very first dinner together, as we chatted around the table, I watched with horror as a salad dressing–drenched lettuce leaf drifted from my fork onto the tip of that brand-new taupe shoe that matched my brand-new suit. The colleagues watched, too. Without missing a beat, Judge Jones announced that if, after dinner, I brought the shoe to his chambers, he would remove the stain. And that is how the first official day ended for the first female judge in the history of the Court of Appeals of the State of New York. At around 10 p.m., I brought the shoe to Judge Jones's chambers, he sprayed the tip with a heavy coat of Goddard's (he could not possibly have imagined the cost of that shoe), let it dry, then gently wiped it off. And it worked! Though as the first woman on the court I neither sought nor received any deference, I can think of no courtesy my colleagues failed to extend to assure me that I was welcome and valued.

From 1993 (when I became chief) to the end of my years on the court, each year I celebrated September 12—that magical first day—with a small gift to every member of the court staff, usually a book or a T-shirt, along with a personal note. That anniversary tradition actually began on September 12, 1984, when Public Information Officer Walter Mordaunt (and later his widow) presented me with a sprig from a floribunda rosebush in his front yard, a tradition he continued—adding one rose each year—even after his retirement. September 12, 1983 was a very special day for me.

Chapter 4

The Courts' Dockets and Enduring Personal Lessons

Having identified three general categories of cases—common law, statutory interpretation, and constitutional—I illustrate each, enriched with enduring personal lessons from my court years.

Common Law Cases

The common law is judge-made law, most familiar in the area of tort and contract cases, where the judges draw the lines defining the duty or obligation owed to others and when it is breached. We have, for example, defined the duty of care owed to baseball spectators, baseball players, jockeys, firefighters, swimmers, divers, and fetuses; we have defined duties of property owners, lessees, trespassers, donation recipients, heirs, and countless others. In the commercial area, as a matter of common law we have set a standard for enforcing contractual agreements that is often specified by parties as the law of choice to govern major worldwide disputes.

Today, the statutory cases probably predominate in the courts—so much of our law has now been codified by the legislature. But courts like ours still are principally described as common law courts because case-by-case lawmaking is our traditional role. Ours is, after all, the court of the great Benjamin Nathan Cardozo, who served as a judge there from 1914 to 1927 (having come virtually directly to the court from private commercial practice), and then as its chief judge from 1927 to 1932, when he was appointed to the US Supreme Court (distinctly less happy years for him). What a joy it was, every now and again in an opinion, to hook a sentence of mine to one of his, leading with: "As we have held."

Cardozo's writings—judicial and scholarly—are a bible of the common law. Time and again I return to his book, *The Nature of the Judicial Process*. I know no better statement of what our task is: we are there not merely to paste existing precedents—law rulings in prior cases—to new facts, with a view to the stability of the law, but to ensure that the lines defining lawful and unlawful conduct remain fair and just for the litigants and for a constantly evolving society. I could not imagine on September 12, 1983, that I would so soon have a firsthand lesson in the nature of the judicial process.

I refer to *Bovsun v. Sanperi*, a memorable chapter in my early education. *Bovsun* dealt with two separate personal injury cases consolidated for presentation to the court because of a common core issue. What follows is a description of one of the cases.

A father and mother were riding with their young daughters in a van, the mother in the front seat holding her one-year-old daughter in her lap when the car was struck, resulting in the child's death. The mother was not physically harmed. The legal issue was whether she could recover damages for the emotional distress suffered by witnessing her child's death. Our court had previously steadfastly declined to allow emotional distress damages in such cases, fearful that emotional distress damages suffered by a bystander, untethered to any personal physical injury, could precipitate limitless litigation, the proverbial floodgates. There were lots of precedents saying exactly that.

I vividly recall the court's conference the morning following oral argument—December 14, 1983. Especially as the junior judge (and to the very last day of my tenure on the court, whenever I was the reporting judge on a case) I meticulously prepared for my oral presentation at conference. In effect the reporting judge is arguing to the full court, without a clue as to how the others will vote, so with a good report there is still an opportunity to capture an undecided vote. Hugh Jones was the reporting judge in *Bovsun*. That's the card he had picked in the Red Room following oral argument the previous afternoon. I was stunned when Hugh reported to reverse and allow the mother's cause of action, applying what he called a "zone of danger" rule that would allow close family members (but not bystanders generally) to recover emotional distress damages even in the absence of any physical harm to them.

That was simply not the law of the State of New York! Speaking next (as the junior judge), I very confidently reported to affirm the dismissal of the mother's claim, reciting each of the court's precedents denying emotional distress damages to bystanders who had themselves suffered no physical injury. Judge Jones responded "with due respect" (a tipoff) that he knew the law. Of course he did. The question before the court, however, was whether the time had come to tweak our rule just a bit, and he underscored the careful lines he proposed to draw in sustaining the new cause of action. Oh my! In my own diligent analysis of the cases, I had not sufficiently factored in that perhaps the Court of Appeals should modify or update its own prior precedents, just as Cardozo had done in so many instances that trip off a law student's tongue. It's why we're there!

After my exchange with Hugh, the case proceeded around the table for other votes. Imagine my surprise when the four senior judges stood together, allowing the mother's claim to proceed, leaving the three juniors mired in the dust of the past. I wrote a vigorous dissent predicting runaway phony claims for all sorts of bystander emotional injury, the end of the world of money damages, ultimately paid for by the public.

Hugh's cogent writing for the court beautifully reflects the development of the common law nationwide, as well as the care courts take in drawing the lines of liability, reflecting on prior precedents over the decades and envisioning where any change might take the law in the future. The court has to draw careful lines because it knows that inevitably the winning side of an issue immediately will attempt to move the law even further. That's how the law develops in a changing society.

Judge Jones began his writing with a summary of the law to date: the reluctance of courts to recognize liability for mental distress resulting from merely observing harm to a third person, fearing massive liability; California's deviation from that principle to permit recovery by a close relative when that injury was reasonably foreseeable; a division around the country—several courts following California, others (including New York's) not; the position on the issue of the *Restatement of Torts* (a respected, scholarly, forward-looking compilation of the law); and the factual nuances of the *Bovsun* cases that boded in favor of change (a narrower change than California's rule) in our rule. I especially love his observation, taken from an earlier decision, underscoring that expediency alone cannot commend itself to a court of justice, thereby resulting in the denial of a logical legal right and remedy in all cases because a fictitious injury might later be urged as a real one—particularly given the sophistication of modern medicine and fact finders' ability to weed out false claims.

And they did it, they did it! Four-three. Since *Bovsun*, New York allows recovery for emotional damage that was serious and verifiable, the allowable compensation must be tied to observation of the serious injury or death of an immediate family member, and the injury or death must have been caused by the conduct of the defendant. Though "zone of danger" cases have regularly followed, requiring the court to draw lines defining liability in all sorts of negligence cases, the end of the world of massive damages that I predicted in my dissent never came. (By wonderful coincidence, on August 27, 2014, a *New York Law Journal* article summed up three decades of "bystander" liability cases, concluding that—though the claims have moved well beyond automobile accidents to such events as fires, assaults, and elevator accidents—the foundational pillars erected by Judge Jones remain firmly and sensibly in place.)

All in all, I had a powerful firsthand lesson in the conscientious, careful development of the common law, echoing Oliver Wendell Holmes's observation that "the life of the law has not been logic; it has been experience." When that moment of realization actually dawned, I cannot define with precision—Court of Appeals cases are by definition close and difficult or they would not have reached a second layer of appeal. I surely would not have dissented had I for a moment doubted the correctness of my position, and I had very good company in Judges Wachtler and Simons. But *Bovsun* was a critical first step into the deep waters of judging on a common law court.

Common law cases cover the entire range of human imagination, and of particular interest to me, of course, were the commercial cases, which had been the centerpiece of my prior years at the bar. Again, given New York's preeminence as a world commercial center, the court is responsible for articulating a rational, stable body of commercial law—a favorable coincidence for me, as I learned from day one. No, it was actually day three—September 14, 1983—when *Braten v. Bankers Trust Co.* was argued. *Braten* was a consolidation of four cases challenging termination by the defendant bank of an oral promise of forbearance on a loan so that the plaintiffs—two of whom had given personal guarantees—might continue their apparel business.

I remember the debate accelerating around the conference table the morning following argument in *Braten* and one of the colleagues pausing to ask, "Well, what does Judith think about that point?" I was a new arrival from the commercial law world, and it was the first of many times over the next quarter century that I got to underscore in our discussions and writings the critical importance of the parties' written contract. Predictability and stability of the law is particularly important in commercial dealings—what the law is is fundamental to how the parties' prospective conduct, how they negotiate and structure their transactions. The unconditional guaranty negotiated and signed by all the parties in *Braten*, which made no reference to the bank's purported earlier oral promise, to my mind could not overcome their meticulous signed writing. "Evidence of what may have been orally agreed between the parties prior to the execution of an integrated written instrument cannot be received to vary the terms of the writing." That theme resounded for me all the way to the end of my term, and continues now in my afterlife back at the bar.

Though not every jurisdiction and every commentator might agree, a hallmark line of Court of Appeals cases underscores the heavy presumption that a clear negotiated, executed written instrument manifests the true intention of the parties. I resist identifying any one opinion as particularly memorable in this regard, but I have to give a small nod to *W.W.W. Assoc. v. Giancontieri*, as much for my hours of serious study as for the anguish that preceded its resolution. Do we, like some other jurisdictions—most notably California—allow "parol evidence" (evidence outside the agreement) to show ambiguity in the language of the contract, or do we stay with the facially unambiguous agreement of the parties? I am dazzled by the number of times that key principle has figured prominently in subsequent cases (cases much more felicitously named—like *Greenfield v. Philles Records* and *Vermont Teddy Bear Co. v. 538 Madison Realty Co.*).

The long-established New York common law principle, well known to contract lawyers, is that when parties set down their agreement in a clear, complete document, that writing should be enforced according to its terms. Evidence outside the four corners of the document as to what might have been intended is generally inadmissible to vary the writing or create an ambiguity where there otherwise is none. Whether the writing is clear and complete is a question of law to be resolved by the courts, again within the four corners of the document, rather than through outside evidence. Universal, clear, simple, and incontestable as those principles might seem, they are challenged to this day—and have stood the test of time.

Much to my delight, when I returned to the real world of commercial dispute resolution (including arbitration), I saw New York recognized throughout the world for adhering to the four-corners rule, which underscores the care parties should take in preparing their contracts and the desirability of specifying New York law as the governing law in contractual dispute resolution clauses. The message is clear and simple: take care to say what you mean and mean what you say in written contracts, because these words will be taken seriously should a dispute reach the courts later. Maybe best of all, I have just written the foreword for a book on contract law, *New York Contract Law for Non-New York Lawyers*, where the author (Glen Banks) describes 200 years of New York law on the subject as "a thing of beauty."

Finally, a brief note about a related area of the court's commercial docket to which I will later return: arbitration. The subject belongs here because cases relating to arbitration fall into the area of common law but, as a product of our modern globalized world, also transcend that category today. There are governing statutes and sometimes even constitutional issues in cases dealing with arbitration.

My very first exposure came months after I joined the court, in *Silverman v. Benmor Coats*, one of the many arbitration cases that come to the court simply for confirmation of an award, so that it can become and enforceable judgment. Through *Silverman*, I learned an essential lesson when it comes to court review of arbitration awards: deference. Courts are extremely deferential to arbitration awards, virtually always confirming them. After all, parties choose arbitration to avoid the complexities and delays of litigation. Back then, however, I had the temerity to dissent from that understanding of the courts' role, ultimately persuading two of my colleagues to sort of join in. I concluded my dissent with a warning that arbitration becomes tantamount to "assumption of the risk," when there is no later hope of any real judicial supervision. I doubt I would write those words today.

As a last word, for now, on common law and a transition to the rest of the court's docket, I reemphasize that in truth and in practice, common law is not just a body of judge-made law. It is also a case-by-case process of judicial analysis and decision making that pertains across the court's docket, as the following sections illustrate.

Statutory Interpretation Cases

Although statutory interpretation cases are, at their essence, different—courts are applying laws written by the legislature, not self-made principles—in many respects these cases also present the agony of case-by-case drawing of the lines defining lawful and unlawful conduct. The statute in question may have been enacted years or decades before the parties' dispute raising question as to its meaning. A signal difference here is that the legislature can simply amend the statute if the courts have misread its words.

Once again, I soon had a superb lesson in the artistry of justice in the area of statutory interpretation. I refer to *People v. Bruce Register* (argued September 20, 1983, my eighth day as a judge), a criminal law case that more than thirty years later continues to torment the state and federal courts. The issue was one of statutory interpretation involving the meaning of the statutory crime of "depraved indifference murder." Plainly, writing statutes in the abstract is one thing. Applying the words of a statute to real-life situations, tested in the crucible of litigation, can be quite another.

The phrase "depraved indifference murder" pretty well captures the intended viciousness of the crime. It tops the categories of nonintentional, or reckless, crime; nonintentional crime is presumably less harshly punished than intentional crime. The court in 1983 had not considered the depraved indifference statute for a long time. *Register* was a significant juncture and a particular misery for me, having arrived on the bench after twenty-one years as a commercial litigator. I was lost in the ether of the criminal law.

The defendant, Bruce Register, at about 12:30 a.m. had wandered into a bar in downtown Rochester, already pretty drunk. He got into a fight, shot two people, and wound up killing a person trying to flee the bar. The jury acquitted Register of intentional murder. But was this "depraved indifference murder" as envisioned by the legislature? It sure seemed to be as depraved and indifferent a murder as I could imagine. The discussion at the conference table, however, quickly morphed into something far more sophisticated than my commonsense reading of the statutes had led me to, as phrases like *actus reus* and *mens rea* were bandied about by my colleagues. Even worse, the court was decidedly split three-three, with Judge Simons to affirm (upholding defendant's conviction for depraved indifference murder) and Judge Jasen to reverse (overturning the conviction). They awaited only my vote, and I was not at all sure what it should be.

Even worse than all of that was Judge Simons's growing impatience with my indecision. The case had to be put over, unresolved and unassigned, from September to the October session. Despite daily conferencing, my indecision worsened. I remember Judge Simons's angry words as the October session drew to a close: "I don't care whether I am writing the majority or the dissent, Judith. I just want to know which it is before we leave Albany." Trouble from day one. Ultimately, I voted to affirm the conviction, creating the four-three majority, because getting drunk, repeatedly shooting into a crowded bar, and killing someone seemed to me the epitome of depraved indifference murder. Whatever the subject, good sense was my last touch point in reaching a result.

After our decision upholding the conviction, depraved indifference murder prosecutions blossomed throughout the state, as district attorneys built on the majority's interpretation of the statute, essentially allowing an objective assessment of the degree of recklessness based on the act itself (*actus reus*) rather than proof of a defendant's culpable mental state—utter indifference to the value of human life (*mens rea*). Again, it's my "smell of blood" theory—the side that prevails on an issue then carries the proposition out further and further, until it goes way over the top. I saw that happen several times during my years on the court.

The depraved indifference statute did not become confrontational for the court until the arrival sixteen years later of Judge Albert Rosenblatt, himself a former district attorney, who saw abuse of the statute as the court's majority had interpreted it and prosecutors had increasingly expanded it. After an evolution of more than twenty years, in another split opinion, the court actually overruled *Register* in *People v. Feingold*, a rare event for a court that values stability (though not rigidity) in the law. The crime of depraved indifference murder, identical in severity of sanction to intentional murder, apparently had been misused as the basis for twin-count indictments—an example of pushing the court-defined line of legality to the limit—allowing juries reluctant to impose an intentional murder conviction to take refuge in depraved indifference murder as what they believed was a lesser crime, when in truth it was not.

Feingold is hardly the end of this story. Despite the passage of decades, and legislative refinements, depraved indifference murder continues to torment our state and federal courts, including such issues as retroactivity and *habeas corpus*. On November 21, 2013, for example, the Court of Appeals issued its (again divided) opinion in *People v. Heidgen*, three consolidated cases upholding depraved indifference murder convictions for taking lives in the course of drunk driving. For me, the most potent words are those of dissenting Judge Susan Philips Read: "Essentially, the majority has resurrected the *Register* standard for cases in which intoxicated drivers kill innocent people, or at least has done so here in order to salvage these three convictions." Wouldn't you know, on July 1, 2014, the Court of Appeals divided yet again—this time reducing the conviction (wild death-producing driving) from depraved indifference murder (*People v. Maldonado*), with Judge Pigott in dissent taking the majority to task for "treating this crime with unfathomable and unjustified leniency."

With *Register* a classic example of a significant statutory challenge time and again eluding absolutely last-word final determination, I offer two additional criminal case examples of the phenomenon referred to earlier: that whichever side prevails on an issue quickly takes the decision to its extreme, inevitably posing the judicial, policy-making conundrum the court faces in each case: if we conclude X in this case, what will tomorrow bring? Hopefully not the sleepless nights of the two following examples.

In *People v. Rosario* and *People v. Consolazio*—long before my time—the court had concluded that it was absolute, irremediable error for the prosecutor to fail to turn over to the defendant material relevant to the testimony of a prosecution witness. Perfectly sensible, and several cases throughout the years reversing convictions reaffirmed this as "the right sense of justice." There would be no inquiry whatever as to whether the district attorney's failure was "harmless," trivial, or inadvertent. All went well until the light went on over the head of the defense bar: why not apply the same principle to *all* posttrial motions allowed under another section of the Criminal Procedure Law, even long after all of a defendant's direct appeals had been completed? Indeed, in a case that reached the court in 1991, *People v. Jackson*, the crime had been committed thirteen years earlier, and the defendant had exhausted all direct appeals more than six years before. Again, the delay between oral argument date (May 31, 1991) and decision (December 19, 1991), if not the bitter division evidenced in the writings of Chief Judge Wachtler (writing for four, ultimately including me) and Judge Titone (writing for three) offer a clue as to the difficult juncture we had reached in how to read that particular Criminal Procedure Law section.

The arguments on both sides made perfectly good sense. Which was the better policy choice? I remember the remark of one of my law clerks (in jest) that if the Titone view prevailed, once back in private practice she intended to ensure that every prisoner knew that every single conviction was up for grabs—they had only to find some scrap of unproduced paper, however insignificant. Ultimately, I decided to join Judge Wachtler's triumvirate, persuaded that as a matter of policy it had the better reading of the particular section at issue, requiring a trial court in posttrial motions under Criminal Procedure Law § 440.10 to determine whether there was a reasonable possibility—some minimal showing—that the failure to turn over a document in any way contributed to defendant's conviction. We abated the storm.

Even more vivid is the frenzy that followed the court's decision in *People v. Antommarchi*, an appeal centered on a challenge to the trial court's charge on reasonable doubt. Though the court concluded that the charge could have been better framed, it found it unnecessary to decide whether that alone was reversible error because of a subsidiary point pressed by defense counsel and largely unaddressed by the prosecution: that the court had neglected to include the defendant in chats it held with prospective jurors (sidebar conferences) regarding their ability to serve. I remember Judge Simons's deft writing for a unanimous court that since the sidebar issue required reversal anyway under Criminal Procedure Law § 260.20 (providing the defendant's right to be present during any material stage of the trial), this omission required reversal of the defendant's conviction and a new trial, when the judge could address the imperfection in his reasonable doubt charge.

Then lightning struck. Sidebar conferences are common during trials—lawyers frequently confer with the court on matters ranging from bathroom breaks to missing witnesses. Much to our shock, chagrin, and horror, thousands of convictions immediately were thrown into doubt. Fortunately, we were "saved" some months later by an opportunity to narrow the holding, making clear that *Antommarchi*, decided as a matter of state statutory law, should be applied only prospectively (*People v. Mitchell*). The front-page *New York Times* article that followed on December 18 noted that the court had avoided a potential legal calamity. Whew!

Though I could easily multiply statutory law examples many times over in the civil law arena, I limit this discussion to one significant segment of the civil statutory law: adoption law. If depraved indifference statutes exemplify the state's attempt to protect its citizens by laws prohibiting dangerous criminal conduct, in the civil arena New York's adoption laws illustrate how this state has sought to protect its most vulnerable citizens: children.

Matter of Jacob rises to the top of my list—two consolidated cases in which the court was asked to decide whether the unmarried partner of a child's biological mother (whether homosexual or heterosexual) could become the child's second parent by way of adoption. Ultimately, after a long and significant struggle among the seven judges (noted earlier), the court in a majority of four answered with a vigorous yes, notwithstanding an equally vigorous dissent of three.

New York's adoption statute was first enacted in 1873—more than a century earlier— had been amended innumerable times, and was last consolidated into a single body of law in 1938. Not uncommonly, at the time of these appeals, the statute contained language from the 1870s alongside language from the 1990s—plainly a challenge for the court to stitch together, let alone to take into account that the legislature likely never envisioned families that included two adult life partners whose relationship was characterized solely by emotional and financial interdependence, with no marriage license.

Because adoption is purely a creature of statute, the majority opinion began with the familiar principle that the words of the statute must be read against the backdrop of the humanitarian principle that adoption is a means of securing the best possible home for a child. In other words, the court's focus in stitching together the various statutory sections drawn from our history must be on the statute's purpose—the child's best interest, a purpose surely advanced by allowing two adults who function as the child's parents to become the child's legal parents. Apart from the plain economic benefits would be the emotional security of knowing that in the event of the biological parent's death or disability, the other parent would have presumptive custody and the child's relationship with his or her parents, siblings, and other relatives would continue. Viewed from this perspective, the court also saw the words of the statute as a shield to protect new adoptive families, never intended as a sword to prohibit otherwise beneficial intrafamily adoption by second parents. To say that the dissenters disagreed is a mammoth understatement: they found no discernible authorization for what was permitted by the court's holdings. "Nowhere do statutes, or any case law previously, recognize de facto, functional or second parent adoptions in joint circumstances as presented here."

Possibly this statutory interpretation decision has been my greatest source of satisfaction, as I see so many families—including the family of my godson, Cooper Mandell—lovingly cared for by their two forever parents. Significantly, the legislature never saw fit to amend the statute after the court's ruling—as it might have—to say that we had gotten it "wrong."

Uniformly heart wrenching, our adoption cases regrettably were rarely as personally satisfying as *Jacob*. Two sides battling for a child's life, one loses—this is not fertile ground for a decisively happy result. But the following examples each offers a lesson that goes beyond the actual court decision.

The first—*Matter of Male Infant L.*—was more than anything an enduring lesson in what the parties, not the court, can achieve between themselves. This was a petition by a poor, unwed immigrant from El Salvador then living in California (she later moved to New York) to regain custody of her son whom, before his birth, she had voluntarily arranged to place with a New York couple for foster care and eventual adoption. The issue on appeal was whether the foster parents could retain custody of the boy they had raised from birth—it took a full four years for the case to reach the court—where the birth mother had never surrendered, abandoned, or neglected the child and was never found to be unfit but simply had no current, settled plans for the child's (or her own) future.

Fortunately I had to step off the case, because my friend Eric Seiff worked with the adoptive family's lawyer and had mentioned the case to me over the years. This was good fortune, because the court unanimously concluded that the adoption statute absolutely required that the child be returned to his birth mother. Hard to imagine the impact on a four-year-old child or the wonderful family of which he had become a part of returning him to his birth mother, who planned to take him, alone, to El Salvador. Happily, as I later learned from Eric and from a wonderful book written by the adoptive mother under a pseudonym, the family had retained a counselor who advised them to encourage visits and include the birth mother in family events, eventually leading to her decision to leave the child with them. There I learned that not every case ends at the solid, fully reasoned law decision of the Court of Appeals. We know from subsequent cases how our decisions affect the law. Often I think it would be nice to know how they actually affected the lives of the parties, as in *Male Infant L.* and my next example.

Matter of Joyce T. came to the court a year later, again a heart-wrenching scenario seeking termination of the parental rights of a mentally disabled couple. Years earlier, when the couple's parental rights had been challenged, the trial court had concluded that with appropriate support they could manage the care of Joyce and her older brother, Christopher. This time, the evidence showed convincingly that they were wholly incapable of providing proper and adequate child care for the foreseeable future, and their parental rights were terminated. Once again, a humane resolution trumped Social Services Law § 384-b(4)(c): as reflected in a footnote in the opinion, even after her adoption, Joyce was able to continue to visit her birth parents and with Christopher, also freed for adoption. A tough result to be sure, but one where everyone involved was at least assured of a pathway to retaining a familial relationship. Hopefully they followed it.

Finally comes *Matter of Sarah K.*, just months after *Joyce T.*, yet another resolution going somewhat beyond the pure issues of law. I ran through another box of tissues in my chambers as I studied the record and contemplated the consequences for the parties involved, whatever the court decided. Here the birth mother, cruelly advised in the hospital recovery room that her child had Down syndrome and could immediately be placed with adoptive parents, signed a consent form, and the child was taken from the hospital to be raised by a loving family. The statutory section, last amended in 1972, plainly directed the court's conclusion: a parent's consent to the release of a child for adoption cannot simply be undone at will. That was a clear legislative directive, yet the facts of this case hardly made for an easy decision. We could not ignore the law; we ourselves could not rewrite the statutory directive. But the court in its opinion noted the statute's history—a response to controversy and uncertainty that at the time overhung adoption, impelling the legislature to give absolutely preclusive effect to a signed consent. However, as the court wrote, "Because certain dissatisfactions with the statute in its actual application have now several times been identified in the case law and literature, we believe it would be highly desirable for the Legislature to examine [the statute] in the light of 13 years' experience, for it appears that the well-founded concerns that engendered the law are not yet dispelled." Thankfully—taking into account the court's admonition—the legislature indeed wrote into the Domestic Relations Law a provision requiring a minimum of sixty days before a parent's consent to adoption might be recognized. Many times over the years we found similar examples of a constructive two-way conversation among branches of government benefiting the law and society.

Lawyer heaven? Absolutely. A privilege beyond description to serve as a judge of the Court of Appeals of the State of New York? For sure. Easy? Most definitely not. The quest for a just solution, for the parties, for the issue, and for the law, is never easy, even when the legislature has carefully spelled out the governing provisions courts are obliged to recognize. For the courts it's never a mechanical cut-and-paste process. Inevitably there are human concerns that have to be addressed when real-life disputes reach the courts.

Constitutional Cases (Starting with Federal)

Reflecting on my initial days on the Court of Appeals and my education in the art of judging in the area of constitutional law leads me naturally to *People v. Lemuel Smith*, argued April 23, 1984, a mere seven months after my arrival directly from the world of commercial law practice. This was a death penalty case—as it turned out, the last of the death penalty cases for New York until George Pataki wrested the governorship from Mario Cuomo in 1994 and succeeded in restoring it. Cuomo opposed the death penalty, Pataki supported it, and that difference ranked high among the campaign issues.

I feel especially proud that although we had a death penalty statute throughout my tenure on the court, in each case that reached us at least four of the seven judges (of mixed political affiliation) concluded that the conviction was unlawful. I believe that today, surely in New York, there is less desire for a death penalty. Maybe that's just what Stephen used to call my "east of the Mississippi thinking." In any event, I'm glad that as judges and citizens, we didn't have to put a human to death.

Lemuel Smith was tough. The facts were gruesome, including bite marks on the victim's breasts, and her body stuffed into a barrel. Smith had previously murdered five people and was serving a prison sentence of twenty-five years to life at Green Haven, a maximum security correctional facility, when he murdered Donna Payant, a prison guard. On his appeal to the court we even had the barrel in which her body had been found in the prison garbage dump, which had been marked as a trial exhibit.

The law was tough, too, as the US Supreme Court wavered on the constitutionality of the death penalty. Was it "cruel and unusual punishment" precluded by the Eighth and Fourteenth Amendments to the Constitution? Though the death penalty had been struck down by the Supreme Court in 1972 and reinstated in 1976, as of 1984, questions lingered among the states about the constitutionality of a mandatory death sentence—meaning that if the defendant was found guilty of intentional murder the court had to impose a sentence of death, whatever the circumstances. That is what New York's statute provided. In case after case, the Supreme Court struck down a mandatory death sentence with the reservation that maybe it would be constitutional in the case of a life-term inmate who committed murder. Lemuel Smith was such an inmate. Death penalty cases were especially tough as well because they were a rare exception to the court's jurisdictional power, as the judges had the responsibility to review not only the law but also the facts—and the facts in this case were truly gruesome.

Again, as discussion proceeded around the conference table the day following oral argument, the court (excluding my vote) was split three-three, Judge Simons reporting to affirm on the facts—the evidence of guilt was convincing beyond a reasonable doubt—and uphold the constitutionality of the mandatory death sentence. I had no hesitancy in concluding that the mandatory sentence was cruel and unusual punishment and therefore violated the US Constitution, and I was in good company to strike down the remaining shred of the state death penalty—Hugh Jones, Bernard Meyer, and Sol Wachtler. But the combination of Chief Judge Cooke's vote to affirm, the half-dozen "maybes" in the Supreme Court opinions, and the tradition of a writing automatically falling from the reporting judge who failed to carry the court to a junior judge in the majority (me) was worrisome. Having only months earlier been found "unqualified" for the Court of Appeals by the Women's Bar Association (remember the hoopla I referred to leading up to my appointment? That was one of the working parts of the plan to obstruct it), the prospect of overturning the death penalty on these disgusting facts, and then being reversed by the Supreme Court, would not have done much for my reputation as a sound jurist.

My opinion for the court striking down the death penalty was released on July 2, 1984—meaning that the case had gone over the May session and was finalized during our June "decision days." (Two days at the end of December, and two days at the end of June, are marked as decision days, when no new arguments are heard and the court simply resolves cases left on its docket.) There was, of course, tremendous public clamor when the decision was released. I remember condemnation of the decision by New York City Mayor Ed Koch, merciless attacks by the press, and vile mail (one letter including feces, several wishing me the same fate as Donna Payant). Most of all I remember my dear Aunt Libby—my father's sister-in-law, then age-shrunken to barely five feet tall with a heavy Jewish accent, sidling up to me during a private moment at a family gathering, and in her harshest tone saying, "Juditl ("little Judith" in Yiddish), how could *you* do such a thing." I responded instinctively, "I'm sorry, I'm sorry," because something I had done—more accurately, the negative press—had upset my Aunt Libby. But of course I wasn't sorry at all. I was only apprehensive that the Supreme court would take certiorari, that our court would be reversed, and that the public would see that indeed I was an unqualified, criminal-loving liberal.

Actually, I think we did a pretty fine job—Gary, Darren, and I—as I now reread our thirty printed pages (in fact only twenty-nine pages, the thirtieth is a drawing Gary assembled of the Green Haven Correctional Facility; we were amazed to discover the roaming privileges Green Haven had allowed Lemuel Smith, a multiple murderer). I refer not only to the size and significance of the opinion but also to the fact that we had additional writing responsibilities for the session. Gary dived into the transcript—fourteen hefty volumes I kept in chambers until the day I left the bench—Darren into the law, and I lived in both worlds. I number among my happiest ever the day the Supreme Court—despite all its "maybes"—denied certiorari, declining the district attorney's invitation to hear the appeal.

But my greatest benefit from *People v. Lemuel Smith* is that it led to an enduring friendship with the trial judge, Al Rosenblatt. Al had been unfairly berated by Smith's attorney, William Kunstler, personally for failing to recuse himself from the case and legally for imposing the death penalty, which Al had concluded was required by law. How nice that our bond was never discovered when, years later, Al was vetted by the Pataki people for the Court of Appeals appointment. I can't believe that our association would have helped him reach the Court of Appeals, where he clearly deserved to be.

So much for the death penalty in the state of New York for over a decade, until Pataki's 1995 fulfillment of his campaign promise to restore it. Reinstating the death penalty was the very first legislation he introduced.

Over the ensuing years, until 2007 (my penultimate year on the court), the Court of Appeals heard five death penalty appeals under the new statute—a required step in the capital process.[1] "Death is different," Supreme Court Justice Potter Stewart wrote in *Gregg v. Georgia*, and indeed that was my experience as a judge hearing these cases. Everyone geared up—prosecutors, defense lawyers, amici, and the court. Court submissions were mountainous. We each hired an additional law clerk, adopted special capital procedural rules, and assigned an Albany staffer to keep an eye on the calendar status of death cases—extra demands every step of the way. The court heard each death penalty argument on its own special, full day, distinctive in its somber ambience, the courtroom overflowing, press interest off the charts. Why a death penalty?, I still ask myself.

First, of course, the facts are always repulsive, and the public hungers for every ugly detail. I remember being in the back seat of a taxicab as the driver listened on the radio to the minute description of a pre-execution last meal in another state, down to chocolate chip cookies. Then, too, there's the societal desire for revenge, which might be better satisfied by the well-attended public hangings of an earlier day. It's hard for me to line all of this up with deterrence, a major justification for having a death penalty in the first place. Rather, it's the defendant's fifteen minutes (more likely fifteen years—because of procedural safeguards, these cases drag on) of fame, being noticed, even with its own groupies. Sadly, it's more attention than most of these defendants have had in all their lives.

All that aside, what interests me most in retrospect is my firsthand experience as a judge in what is on one hand perhaps the ultimate political legislative-executive

---

1. *People v. Harris*; *People v. Cahill*; *People v. Mateo*; *People v. LaValle*; *People v. Shulman* (decapitalized after *LaValle*); *People v. Taylor*.

choice and, on the other hand, perhaps the ultimate nonpolitical judicial choice. Those separate spheres of responsibility/authority in the abstract are easy to define. In actual application, less so. By now, given all the new technology, we know that innocent people have been condemned to death and we have established the arbitrariness of imposing the death penalty.

Where do the values of a hopefully "progressing society" fit: the political legislative-executive sphere or nonpolitical judicial sphere? Clearly both. Again I think how fortunate we were—I was. In every capital case that came to us, there were at least four votes against upholding the conviction or sentence. The last came from (of all people) Judge Robert Smith, a Pataki appointee, a dissenter in prior cases, who cast the definitive vote to strike down the statute in *People v. Taylor* because the court's holding in *LaValle* required that result as a matter of stare decisis.

After *Taylor*, and the millions New York spent on the death penalty apparatus, I believe the legislature, the governor, and the people had enough of the death penalty. They could easily have fixed the flaw the court identified in *Taylor*, but chose not to. Though I recognize that some states are regularly killing people—the Texans gave Rick Perry a huge round of applause when he mentioned the hundreds that state had put to death, cash-strapped California is spending a fortune to house and feed its cadre of death-convicted inmates, and Troy Davis was executed by Georgia despite new evidence of his innocence—I see that the political branches of government in states such as New Jersey, Illinois, Ohio, New Mexico, Connecticut, and most recently Washington have also lost their taste for a death penalty. From time to time I am pleased to encounter reports of increasing nationwide recognition of major systemic problems with capital punishment, further confirming its slow demise.

Capital punishment remains a good illustration of the interaction among the three branches on a hot political issue. Surely judicial review by federal and state courts—to say nothing of DNA results, botched executions, and budgetary considerations—has contributed to shifting public attitudes toward the death penalty.

I like the words of former Supreme Court Justice David Souter in his Harvard commencement address of May 27, 2010. He explained what judges properly and appropriately do when they decide cases involving the many indefinite constitutional guarantees like religious freedom, due process, equal protection, unreasonable searches and seizures, and proscriptions against cruel and unreasonable punishment. He used the best of all examples—*Brown v. Board of Education*, in which the Supreme Court overturned its own 1896 decision, finding an unconstitutional meaning in laws segregating races that its predecessors did not see. I remember the unrest that followed *Brown* back in 1954 (the year of my high school graduation), and I see the decision celebrated as a proud moment in US history. Today it is clear that the court was right and indeed heroic in its unanimous vote.

In Justice Souter's words: "If we cannot share every intellectual assumption that formed the minds of those who framed the charter, we can still address the constitutional uncertainties the way they must have envisioned, by relying on reason, by respecting all the words the Framers wrote, by facing facts, and by seeking to understand their meaning for living people."

By "living people," Justice Souter meant people living in the twenty-first century, not the eighteenth. Plainly, our brilliant framers used phrases like "equal protection of the law," "due process," and "cruel and unusual punishment" because they meant the principles those concepts embody to govern through the ages, to serve an evolving society over time, and to vest those with authority across all three branches of government to give their words meaning for people living in the contemporary world. Where precisely is the line to be drawn between the popularly elected branches and the independent courts in attaining this goal? Most often, we only know for sure in retrospect, sometimes not even then. In the meantime, we each simply do the best we can, with appropriate integrity, independence, respect, and deference, in decisively discharging our distinctly separate responsibilities. Seems to have worked pretty well for more than two centuries.

State Constitutions: Raising the Ceiling

Constitutions, we might well expect, define how we are "constituted"—organized, built, structured. Indeed, our federal Constitution (adopted in 1789) begins with a definition of the separate powers of the three branches of government and ends with the amendments that two years later became the Bill of Rights. By contrast, New York's state constitution begins with our Bill of Rights (Article 1), then proceeds in Articles 3, 4, and 6 to define the separate powers of the legislature, executive and judiciary. In this section on state constitutions, I follow New York's model, beginning with my discovery of our parallel Bill of Rights and concluding with the role of the Court of Appeals in the separation and distribution of this state's governmental powers.

Instinctively, like most people, I had assumed that "constitutional" issues refer to the US Constitution, the law of the land, a nifty little document that easily slips into one's pocket. We learn in school about the US Constitution and its essential role in safeguarding our nation's fundamental values. Freedom of speech? The First Amendment, of course. Refusal to testify on the ground of possible self-incrimination? You just take "the Fifth." Today, for example, debate rages over "the right to bear arms"—what exactly did our framers have in mind about guns back in 1791, when the Second Amendment was added? What should the Second Amendment mean today?

Early in 1984, only months after my arrival on the Court of Appeals, Chief Judge Cooke extended a terrific opportunity to me: to attend a conference on state constitutions sponsored by the National Center for State Courts, in Williamsburg, Virginia. *State* constitutions? Surely I was aware of the existence of New York's constitution. The oath of office I took on September 12, 1983 (if not my attorney oath decades earlier), included a pledge to support the constitution of the state of New York as well as the Constitution of the United States. The oath of every public officer in New York includes that pledge. I surely knew that every other state had its own constitution as well. Frankly, that was about the limit of my knowledge—I never encountered state constitutional law issues in law school or in my law practice. I never thought about the potential interrelationships, or conflicts, or opportunities that might arise from the "dual blessing" of having two separate constitutions, with many singular and many common provisions.

Dual blessings, dual challenges: where do we draw the line on unique state constitutional provisions, recognizing that court decisions resting on interpretation of *a* constitution will be hardest to change? The court can tinker with its common law precedent, the legislature can modify its statutes. A constitutional precedent is, however, a constitutional precedent—by definition, harder to change. Where do we draw the line on state constitutional provisions that are identical in both charters? In other words, how do state judges "support" their state constitutions when the rights or protections afforded virtually or actually mimic the federal charter?

What spurred the 1984 Williamsburg conference was a 1977 *Harvard Law Review* article authored by Supreme Court Justice William J. Brennan, "State Constitutions and the Protection of Individual Rights." Often dissatisfied with Supreme Court holdings narrowly reading rights under the federal constitution, Justice Brennan began urging that for the full realization of our fundamental liberties, state courts should look to their own constitutions instead of limiting their decisions to analysis under the federal charter. This is among the blessings of federalism—our remarkable system of parallel sovereignties, federal and state. But we are also the *United* States, no longer a confederation. How does this work in actual practice? A good question.

Over the years, we have learned to accommodate the blessing of a dual constitutional system by having the Supreme Court set the floor of constitutional rights uniformly applicable across the nation, recognizing that state high courts under their parallel constitutional provisions could also fix a higher ceiling—establish greater rights—within their borders when the terms of their constitutions, or their particular histories or local traditions, supported greater rights. There is even a potential virtue in state courts serving as "laboratories" under their constitutions for what might later become constitutional standards adopted nationwide by the Supreme Court. We have some terrific examples, like the historic 1963 decision in *Gideon v. Wainwright*, where the Supreme Court overruled its earlier decision and adopted a widely recognized state constitutional right to counsel for defendants charged with serious crime. More recently the Supreme Court, again looking to persuasive state court decisions under their own constitutions, reversed course and adopted the state constitutional approach of striking down the discriminatory use of peremptory challenges to remove potential jurors. Notably, Justice Anthony Kennedy—writing for the Supreme Court in two separate classes of cases (death penalty and consensual sodomy)—looked to the various state law conclusions in deciding those cases as a matter of federal law.

Justice Brennan's article touched off an avalanche of judicial and academic interest in the subject of state constitutions, which was gathering force by early 1984. For me, the Williamsburg conference was eye-opening and life-altering. I began serious study of the New York state constitution—a bulky document that most definitely does not slip easily into one's pocket—and the rapidly growing commentary.

In fact, the New York state constitution was among the first in the nation, adopted April 20, 1777, drafted principally by John Jay, Gouverneur Morris, and Robert Livingston. In many ways it served as a model for our federal constitution. Amazingly, it established our three discrete, separate branches of government and spelled out their authority—including a bicameral legislature, popularly elected governor to head the executive branch, and an independent judiciary. Our state constitution included not only the structural framework of what is today our federal and state government but also such enduring values as the guarantee of religious freedom, trial by jury, the right to counsel, and the right to vote. Many of the core provisions of that 1777 constitution survive to this day in our state and federal charters. No surprise, given that they had some of the same drafters.

The New York state constitution has been amended many times—in 2008, for example, to make it gender-neutral. But the "it" I refer to is not the 1777 version. Rather, it's our amended constitution, adopted in 1938.

The New York state constitution had been entirely rewritten several times between 1777 and 1938. Indeed, by contrast to the US Constitution, amended a mere twenty-six times in its entire 226-year lifetime, New York's constitution (today forty-six tightly printed pages, containing everything under the sun) is on its face very amendment-friendly. Article 19 provides that every twenty years the people are to be asked: "Shall there be a convention to revise the constitution and amend the same?" Our state constitution's drafters saw the desirability of having the people—in addition to the courts—take a look at our charter periodically in a changing world, though amendments require the vote of two successive legislatures and a public referendum. It is, after all, a constitution we are amending! Our last constitutional convention was in 1967, and the proposed wholesale revision was overwhelmingly defeated at the polls. Shall we have another? Seems unlikely. Too little public interest, too much at stake.

Although we New Yorkers have resisted the wholesale rewriting of our charter, we have hardly shirked from piecemeal amendments to the 1938 constitution—in 2013, for example, legitimizing state-run casino gambling. At the same time, a proposal to extend mandatory judicial retirement from age seventy to age eighty, also having secured the approval of two successive legislatures, failed at the polls.

Back to 1984: I returned from Williamsburg with new friends, new reading, and new zeal for state constitutional law. I cannot recall which came first, my speech on the subject at the City Bar Association or *People v. Benigno Class*. I mention the City Bar speech only because lawyers, once their consciousness was raised to our state constitution, got pretty excited, too. After my remarks, a lawyer came up to me overflowing with delight in first discovering that New York even had a constitution. I will never forget his words: "I feel like I'm swimming in a whole new sea of culture." He was far from alone in his discovery and his feeling.

Class was argued October 12, 1984—just after my first anniversary as a judge— and decided November 12, 1984. At the time it hardly seemed momentous. After a lawful stop, police had reached into defendant's car to look at the vehicle identification number, which was obscured by clutter on the dashboard. They simply reached into the car and moved all the clutter—how would you feel about that?—and they found a gun in plain view. A five-judge majority, in an opinion I wrote for the court, reversed the defendant's conviction for criminal possession of a weapon and declared the police action unreasonable, citing both the Fourth Amendment to the US Constitution and the New York Constitution Article 1, § 12. In virtually identical language, both constitutions secure the people against "unreasonable searches and seizures." It was important to framers of these documents that people not be subject to unwarranted police stops and invasions of our property and privacy.

Fresh from Williamsburg, in the very first sentence of the opinion, I cited both constitutions but said nothing more (neither had the lawyers on the case before us) as to why the result should be different under either constitution. Judge Jones (joined by Judge Jasen) dissented. He strongly disagreed with the conclusion that reaching into the dashboard to view an obscured VIN was an unreasonable search, but he made no reference to the constitutional basis for his dissent.

Much to my disappointment, the Supreme Court (in an opinion authored by Justice Sandra Day O'Connor) reversed our decision and sent the case back to the court "for further proceedings not inconsistent with this opinion" (*New York v. Class*). Having your carefully crafted majority opinion overturned by the Supreme Court is not a happy experience. A prisoner months earlier had written to me as "Dear Mother of Justice." Now my law clerks teased that the Mother of Justice had just been overruled by the Grandmother of Justice. Fortunately the Supreme Court docket is largely federal. Our cases rarely go there—and once I even had the pleasure of a Supreme Court reversal of our court where my dissent prevailed. In *People v. Eulogio Cruz*, I had argued unsuccessfully with my colleagues that defendant Cruz should have been tried for murder separately from his brother because his brother's long, videotaped confession explicitly detailed their roles in the homicide, while the defendant's own confession did not. Justice Antonin Scalia, writing for the majority of a sharply divided Supreme Court, agreed!

But back to Benigno Class. Though he clearly was the greatest beneficiary of all this federal and state constitutional analysis—his conviction was reversed—*People v. Class* greatly supplemented my education in state constitutional law that began in earnest in Williamsburg.

While I have referred to our state-federal constitutional system as a dual blessing—and indeed it is—*Class* is an example of where our nation's system of dual sovereignties creates a challenge for the courts. What should judges do to "support" their state constitutions, as we have sworn to do? When should a state court raise its constitutional ceiling above the federal constitutional floor? Those questions are a bit more easily answered where the constitutional language is different—though still difficult line drawing—and there are many examples of unique constitutional provisions. Most notable for me is our constitutional directive that the legislature must "provide for the maintenance and support of a system of free common schools, wherein all the children of the state may be educated" (N.Y. Const. Art. 11, § 1). Indeed, in June 2014, a California judge struck down that state's teacher tenure system under the state's constitutional commitment to provide a "basically equal opportunity to achieve a quality education." In addition to "free common schools," provision for workers compensation is in our Bill of Rights, alongside free speech and freedom of worship, to name a few.

Where the language of the two charters is virtually identical—as in the case of "unreasonable searches and seizures" (though, significantly, New York does have an additional state constitutional protection "against interception of telephone and telegraph communications")—what should the state courts do?

When *Class* returned to us from the Supreme Court, this time the Court of Appeals unanimously reversed the conviction—even Judges Jones and Jasen signed on—pointing out in an unsigned writing that the majority opinion had relied not only on the federal constitution but also on the New York state constitution in concluding that the search was unconstitutionally unreasonable. Previously, Justice O'Connor in *Michigan v. Long*, had written that where the decision rests on an adequate and independent state ground, the court should so indicate in a "plain statement." What could have been plainer than the first paragraph of my writing in *People v. Class*? I learned.

While striking the right balance between state and federal jurisdiction is still bedeviling, we have advanced well beyond *Class* in articulating and satisfying the Supreme Court's plain statement requirement. Indeed, I am forever grateful that I was not the author of a virtually contemporaneous opinion, *Massachusetts v. Upton*, another Fourth Amendment case. As in *Class*, the Supreme Court reversed the Massachusetts high court's federal constitutional analysis and returned the case to the state court for further proceedings. This time, however, Justice Stevens, separately concurring in the judgment, chewed out the Supreme Judicial Court of Massachusetts for not first deciding the issue solely as a matter of state law, which might well have resolved it and avoided the trip to Washington, as state courts have the last word on their own constitutions. He wrote:

> The maintenance of [the proper balance between state and federal courts] is . . . a two-way street. It is also important that state judges do not unneces-sarily invite this Court to undertake review of state-court judgments. I believe the Supreme Judicial Court of Massachusetts unwisely and unnecessarily invited just such review in this case. Its judgment in this regard reflects a misconception of our constitutional heritage and the respective jurisdictions of state and federal courts.

Ouch!

Despite mountainous law review writing on how and where to draw the line between reliance on state or federal charters where the provisions are similar if not identical, the answer remains somewhat elusive. But one thing is clear today: from the outset of the litigation, the issue must be raised by counsel for New York state courts to address the state constitution separately from the federal constitution, "raised" meaning more than a parallel citation in the first sentence of counsel's brief. Once the issue is deemed to be "raised," the Court of Appeals looks to the particular language of the different charters and, even where the language is identical, to their history and meaning within the state before deciding whether to start down a separate road of interpretation. (Our methodology was set out in *People v. P.J. Video*, after that case similarly was returned to us by the Supreme Court.) Regrettably, this sort of analysis is not often undertaken by lawyers in New York, reflecting perhaps the bent of national law schools in exposing law students only to the federal charter. Today, I am sad to say, I suspect that many lawyers are "swimming in a whole new sea of culture" when it comes to state constitutional law.

During my tenure as a judge of the Court of Appeals, we had several watershed state constitutional law cases. Most often they were criminal cases, sometimes civil ones.

Almost invariably what was common to these cases was how sharply they divided the court and still do. State courts generally (with several notable exceptions) just have not been all that comfortable going their separate ways from the Supremes, especially as to common constitutional provisions. It's the *United* that tends to prevail.

What follows, however, are two good illustrations, one from my day, the second from after I left the court. Mine is decidedly the easier example—a free speech case, where our constitutional language and our long-standing tradition have historically been far more protective than those of the federal courts.

Mere mention of state constitutional law for me always brings to mind *Immuno AG v. Moor-Jankowski*, a 1989 decision I was especially proud to write. The case arose out of a letter to the editor published in the *Journal of Medical Primatology*, where the author criticized Immuno AG, a manufacturer of biologic products derived from blood plasma, of harming chimpanzees in the course of its research efforts in Sierra Leone. The company claimed damages for defamation against the publisher and seven defendants, all of whom settled for substantial sums, except Jan Moor-Jankowski, co-founder and editor of the journal, who continued to pursue the case with vigor. The trial court refused to dismiss the case on the law, concluding that a trial was required; the intermediate appellate court reversed; our court unanimously agreed that the case should simply be dismissed. There was no actionable defamation. As I wrote for the court, the public forum function of letters to the editor is closely related to the treasured privilege of fair comment and the constitutional immunity accorded the expression of opinion. A publication that provides a forum for comments on controversial matters is not acting at odds with the premises of democratic government but is fostering our core values protected by the state and federal constitutions.

I suspect that on the first round in our court, distinguished counsel raised no particular state constitutional law claim; my writing healthily mixed state and federal authorities regarding protected speech. I do, however, remember with crystal clarity the phone call I received while vacationing in Switzerland from my law clerk, Hank Greenberg, telling me that the Supreme Court had "GVR'd" our *Immuno*. That was not a familiar term to me, but I soon learned it meant that the Supreme Court had granted certiorari, vacated our order of affirmance, and remanded the decision to us. The reason was that during the pendency of the appellate process in *Immuno*, the Supreme Court had decided another case—*Milkovich v. Lorain Journal*—on a similar issue. Instead of itself reviewing our decision, the Supreme Court was in effect giving the Court of Appeals the first opportunity to reconsider its own decision in light of the newly minted and narrower *Milkovich* defamation standard. The second time around, one year later, esteemed counsel before us strenuously underscored Article 1, § 12 of the New York state constitution as an independent ground for decision (as well as mentioning the First Amendment to the US Constitution). We bought the state constitutional argument, deciding to dismiss the defamation claim solely on state constitutional grounds, persuaded by New York's long tradition of independent speech protection and by the public value of ourselves settling the issue once and for all.

I think *Immuno II* is one of the court's most interesting opinions, not simply because it rests on our state constitution and thus put a decisive end to the litigation, and not simply because Anthony Lewis in his book *Make No Law: The Sullivan Case and the First Amendment*, calls it a "memorable opinion." What distinguishes our second *Immuno* decision is that while the court voted unanimously in favor of the wouldn't-give-up defendant Moor-Jankowski, there are four separate opinions for that result. I cannot recall another case that yielded four separate opinions all in favor of a single result. Chief Judge Wachtler and Judges Alexander and Bellacosa wisely joined in my writing to make the magic four votes and end the agony. Judge Simons thought that we should have decided only as a matter of federal constitutional law, allowing the Supreme Court itself to define the borders of *Milkovich*. Judge Hancock, separately concurring, agreed with Judge Simons that the appeal was properly resolved on federal constitutional grounds, but felt we had misread *Milkovich*. Finally, Judge Titone would have dismissed the claim solely based on New York common law, never reaching either constitution (and, by the way, citing one of my own articles in support of that view!).

Though I see less fuss over state constitutional law today—the subject peaked in the 1990s, in the aftermath of Justice Brennan's 1977 article—the balance between the two charters remains a delicate, sometimes controversial issue, particularly where the language of the provisions in issue is virtually the same. At least lawyers today know that they have to "raise the roof" for the Court of Appeals to raise the ceiling. That's what happened in *People v. Weaver*, decided by the Court of Appeals on May 12, 2009, this time generating three separate writings. In effect, my successor, Chief Judge Jonathan Lippman, did precisely what Supreme Court Justice O'Connor had spelled out in *Michigan v. Long* and Supreme Court Justice Stevens had urged in *Massachusetts v. Upton*: the Court of Appeals decided the search and seizure issue plainly under the state constitution, said why, and thus put the matter to rest in New York.

Weaver concerned a new police tracking system, a global positioning system (GPS) tracking device that had stealthily been installed by the police inside the bumper of defendant's street-parked van. Not a particularly welcome stealth companion! For sixty-five days, without a warrant, the police monitored the position of the van, culminating in the defendant's arrest and conviction relating to two burglaries. Defendant claimed that evidence obtained from the GPS device should not have been admitted and that the use of the device violated his right against unreasonable searches and seizures under the Fourth Amendment and the parallel if not identical Article 1, § 12 of the New York state constitution.

While recognizing that the issue remains unsettled as a matter of federal constitutional law, Chief Judge Lippman (writing as well for Judges Ciparick, Pigott, and Jones) concluded that on these facts installation of the device was an invasion of defendant's right to privacy and therefore an unreasonable search in violation of the state constitution. He pointed to the many occasions when the Court of Appeals has interpreted the state constitution to provide broader protection (including *Class*) and to decisions of other state high courts that had reached the same conclusion regarding the GPS. This reasoning elicited a strong dissent from Judge Smith, and a separate dissent from Judge Read, in which Judge Graffeo joined. What most troubled Judge Smith was the surreptitious attachment of the device, which may have violated common law property (but not constitutionally protected privacy) rights. Judges Read and Graffeo were especially concerned that the majority had improperly brushed aside state jurisprudence on methodology and precluded the legislature—better able to set limits applicable to this new surveillance technology—from acting by constitutionalizing the subject.

Like *Immuno II*, the Court of Appeals decision in *Weaver* under the state constitution is definitive in New York. Unlike *Immuno II*, however, the issue of whether GPS tracking violates the Fourth Amendment also captured the attention of state and federal courts throughout the nation. Weeks after *Weaver*, the Supreme Court granted review in a case coming out of the federal appeals court for the DC Circuit, *United States v. Jones*, among the most important Fourth Amendment cases in decades. Did police need a warrant to monitor the movements of a car with a tracking device? Could the police legally install such a device without the target's consent?

On January 23, 2012, the Supreme Court unanimously answered that the surreptitious attachment of a GPS global tracking device constitutes a "search" in violation of the Fourth Amendment as a physical intrusion on property for the purpose of obtaining information, but the Court split five-four on the privacy issue. Justice Sonia Sotomayor was the swing vote, concurring separately in Justice Scalia's curious eighteenth-century analysis (an "uber-historical approach," as one commentator described it) to note her preference to defer more precise determination of the privacy issue. In her view, it's a highly complicated question in this digital age and was unnecessary to reach in the instant case. She did, however, quote a great sentence from Chief Judge Lippman's opinion, which beautifully captures the essence of the Court of Appeals determination (and likely ultimate Supreme Court determination):

> Disclosed in (GPS) data . . . will be trips the indisputably private nature of which takes little imagination to conjure: trips to the psychiatrist, the plastic surgeon, the abortion clinic, the AIDS treatment center, the strip club, the criminal defense attorney, the by-the-hour motel, the union meeting, the mosque, synagogue or church, the gay bar and on and on.

I found Justice Samuel Alito's concurrence on privacy grounds most persuasive—and surprising in its sweep and tone. Plainly the Supreme Court has left the door ajar for serious confrontation with the Fourth Amendment privacy protections in a day when few things are truly private. For New York, the line has been definitively drawn in favor of broader protection under our state constitution.

So where are we today on matters of state constitutional law that relate to the federal constitution as well? Divided, if at all interested, on the political issue of whether to hold a convention to revise our 1938 charter to bring the words of the document into the modern world. Though a few state constitutional law textbooks have emerged, I see little interest in the law reviews, and perhaps most significant of all, little interest in the top-ranked law schools—that would be the surest sign of scholarly movement. Since Justice Brennan's call to action in 1977, and since my own introduction to the subject in 1983, although much remains to be done, surely consciousness has been raised as to our state charters. Given the many ways that New York's charter, history, and values are unique, I am confident that the bar and the bench will continue to "raise the roof" to ensure that those differences are recognized. *Weaver* is my Exhibit A that in New York, the Court of Appeals (likely in split opinions) will continue to give life to the entirety of our charter, and that its decisions, as those of our sister states under their charters, will continue to influence the development of federal constitutional law.

All of this brings me to my concluding segment on our state constitution. Our constitution of course sets forth the rights and obligations of its citizens and—most importantly—defines the respective powers of the three branches of government. Article 3 of our state constitution delineates the scope of legislative power and describes the general contours of legislative jurisdiction and power. The authority and duties of the governor and lieutenant governor, the executive power, are enumerated in Article 4. Executive branch agencies and civil departments are addressed in Article 5. Finally, Article 6 is the repository of judicial branch power and responsibility—determining the scope and limits of legislative and executive action.

Most significantly, unlike issues concerning the constitutional rights and obligations of New York citizens and officials arising under the federal constitution, the Supreme Court has no authority to review or otherwise intervene in matters involving separation of powers arising under our state constitution. These are purely issues of New York state sovereignty. The Court of Appeals is the final arbiter of what our state constitution means and requires.

Throughout my tenure on the court, "separation of powers" cases consistently found their way onto our docket. The cases ended up in the court, of course, because our constitutional system vests the judiciary with the ultimate power of judicial review—and unquestionably the cases will continue to arrive, presenting new and vexing issues of separation of powers.

Two such unforgettable cases, *Pataki v. New York State Assembly* and *Silver v. Pataki*, consolidated into a single appeal, involved traded accusations between the governor and legislature of unconstitutional budget making. As with other matters of state constitutional import, these cases divided the Court of Appeals three ways: a three-judge plurality adopting the position of the governor, a more limited concurrence by two judges (thereby making a majority), and a two-judge dissent.

The plurality of three judges determined that in both cases, the legislature had altered the governor's appropriation bills in ways not permitted by the state constitution and that the governor had not exceeded constitutional limits on what his appropriation bills could contain. The two concurring judges basically agreed but thought the plurality should have gone further to draw a line between executive and legislative power. The plurality stated it doubted a line could be drawn, but the concurrence noted that "we are, however, in the business of drawing lines; that is what we do in our decisional law." Two judges (including myself) in dissent concluded that the governor had overstepped the line separating his budget-making authority from the legislature's law-making responsibility, and that the state constitution's executive budgeting scheme was simply not the system the court now sanctioned. Later, I was more than interested to find the court's decision closely scrutinized and criticized by former Lieutenant Governor Richard Ravitch, a nationally recognized expert in governmental fiscal planning and co-chair (with Paul Volcker) of the State Budget Crisis Task Force, who advocated reversing the court's decision. Under Ravitch's proposal to redistribute New York's budget-making powers, the executive and legislative branches would each give up some of its constitutional authority, thereby creating a new balance of power regarding the public fisc. Plainly, there was more to come.

Into this "separation of powers" bucket I cannot resist adding a few words about the long, ongoing battle over public school funding encapsulated in *Campaign for Fiscal Equity v. State of New York*.

As noted earlier, our constitution uniquely emphasizes the particular importance of education to our society, with an entire article directing the legislature to "provide for the maintenance and support of free common schools, wherein all the children of the state may be educated." Central to this mandate, as the Court of Appeals concluded decades ago, is a requirement that the state offer all children the opportunity for a "sound basic education" (*Levittown Union Free District v. Nyquist*). But whose role is it to define that term, against which the adequacy of funding will then be measured—the legislative and executive branches, in which event they limit the constitutional guaranty simply to whatever they say it is, or the courts, the ultimate arbiters of the constitution? This is another question the courts are mightily trying to put to rest—our court having clearly and decisively answered on the law, its partners in government still ignoring, fighting back on the mandated remedy. So, sadly, the struggle goes on.

What did I learn from the separation of powers cases that came to the court during my tenure? I learned first that whatever their personal views and experiences, and no matter how they came to their position, courts must be sensitive to and protective of separation of powers principles in all their ramifications and complexities, yet unflinching in their responsibility to safeguard our constitutional values. Having no power over the sword or the purse, the strength of the judiciary lies in its independence and integrity. I learned that no matter how big the headlines or heated the societal debate, issues concerning the distribution of power among branches of government must be approached on all sides with dignity, respect, cool heads, and profound admiration for the constitutional scheme at the foundation of our democracy.

Lawyer heaven? Absolutely. A privilege beyond description to serve as a judge of the Court of Appeals of the state of New York? For sure. But easy? Let's just call it a labor of love.

The Spectrum of "Family" Issues

Ironically, it was Mario Cuomo's son, Andrew (Governor Cuomo II), who built a bridge for me that connects the preceding sections—common law, statutory interpretation, and state and federal constitutional law. His words were quoted by Maureen Dowd in her June 28, 2011 column in the *New York Times*:

> My father was against the death penalty, and that was hard in the Son of Sam summer when fear was driving the desire for the death penalty. You see a line of continuity from the death penalty to choice to marriage equality. You could argue there's a 30-year span of the pressing social, moral and legal issues of the day.

Only rarely does a pressing social, moral, or legal issue of the day present itself across the entire expanse of our docket. Marriage equality, same-sex—indeed, changing family—issues were perhaps the most potent example of a monumental new societal issue confronting our court during my tenure. In fact, to go beyond matters of statutory interpretation and constitutional law (state and federal), in *Bovsun*—my quintessential common law example recognizing the right of immediate family members to recover emotional distress damages—Judge Jones explicitly deferred defining "the immediate family," noting simply that the plaintiffs before the court were "married or related in the first degree of consanguinity to the deceased child."

I wonder whether Judge Jones had in mind that in a future case the woman holding the child might be the same-sex partner of the biological mother. Would he have concluded, as a matter of common law, that she was a member of the child's "immediate family" entitled to recover emotional distress damages? This was, after all, the same Judge Jones who only three years earlier, in *People v. Onofre*, cogently and presciently set aside as an unconstitutional violation of the rights to privacy and equal protection of the law two same-sex couples' criminal convictions for consensual sodomy! It took the Supreme Court an additional twenty-three years to reach that same conclusion in *Lawrence v. Texas*.

Slowly, over the past several decades, all across the spectrum, courts have been grappling with the meaning of "family" as society itself has actively redefined the term.

My own first fiery confrontation—and for sure, these cases resulted in bitterly divided courts—was *Braschi v. Stahl Associates*, where the court had to decide whether a deceased tenant's homosexual partner was a "family" member (the term used in the New York City Rent Control Law), and thus entitled to succeed to a rent-regulated apartment on the death of his partner, the named lessor. In answering "yes," a bare plurality of the court reasoned that the overwhelming policy expressed in the statute (passed originally in 1946) was to protect a class of occupants from sudden loss of their homes. That was hardly an easy lift, as is clear from the separate concurring opinion, underscoring the narrowness of the decision, and the vigorous dissent opting for "the ordinary and popular meaning of family in the traditional sense."

Just a few years later, in *Matter of Alison D.*, I was the one in vigorous dissent—my six colleagues confidently dismissing the petition of a same-sex partner for visitation rights to the couple's child, on the ground that she was not a "parent" within the meaning of the Domestic Relations Law. Period. Or perhaps more accurately, "comma." Not far around the bend was another "family" case—*Matter of Jacob*, in which a bare but robust majority of the court concluded that New York state's adoption statute permitted same-sex adoption.

I see a line of continuity, evolution, progress over the decades, and surely the courts have had a significant part in maintaining and advancing that line. Courts do not themselves instigate or create cases to impose their views. Through cases, parties bring issues, including hot-button issues, to the courts for resolution under laws they are obliged to interpret and apply. How much do shifting modern values figure in court determinations? For me, most notable—awesome, jaw-dropping—is the sudden sweep of attitudinal and legal change toward marriage equality that every day captures headlines across the nation. This brings me to *Hernandez v. Robles*.

Back in 2006, the novel question before our court in *Hernandez* was whether the state constitution compelled the recognition of marriages between members of the same sex. That is virtually a direct quote from Judge Robert Smith's first sentence for the majority, illustrating the principle that ideally the opinion's first paragraph should succinctly posit the issue and the answer. It's the second sentence of the opening paragraph that I found far less than ideal: the answer was no. "Whether such marriages should be recognized is a question to be addressed by the Legislature." Really? Fortunately, Governor Cuomo II succeeded in achieving with the legislature overnight what at the time seemed a miracle; year after year, bills authorizing same-sex marriage or domestic partnerships had been routinely dismissed, never even making it out of committee to be considered by the full legislature.

Looking back, an amazing personal coincidence for me is that as I prepared for the *Hernandez* oral argument and then engaged in the heartbreaking process of crafting a dissent (joined by Judge Ciparick), I was also preparing to perform the wedding ceremony of my law clerk Megan Bennett to her very long-term live-in boyfriend, David Ratzen. Performing a wedding ceremony for me means significant time talking to the couple, to ensure that my words sufficiently capture the sense of this unique occasion in their lives. Despite their long and beautiful relationship, Megan and David were especially emotional with me about what it meant for them openly and officially to declare their lifetime commitment to one another before family and friends. That experience powerfully underscored the words of the briefs of the many couples before us in *Hernandez*—including a doctor, a police officer, a public school teacher, a nurse, an artist, and a state legislator, many in long relationships, raising children—a cross-section of New Yorkers, who wanted only to live full lives, raise their children, better their communities, and be good neighbors. Just like Megan and David.

Also powerful were the words of our state and federal constitutions declaring fundamental rights to equal protection and due process. As the Supreme Court recognized nearly half a century ago in *Loving v. Virginia* (vacating a couple's criminal sentences for violating a ban on interracial marriages), "The freedom to marry has long been recognized as one of the vital personal rights essential to the orderly pursuit of happiness by free men. Marriage is one of the 'basic civil rights of man,' fundamental to our very existence and survival." Fundamental rights are fundamental rights; they are not defined in terms of who is entitled to exercise them. In Judge Ciparick's and my view, there was no legitimate basis for excluding same-sex couples, not in the constitutions and not in the statutes, and it was emphatically for the courts to say so. That's what judges are there to do: protect fundamental rights and values, as viewed in the light of contemporary society.

It did not occur to me until years later that there is yet another basic inconsistency in the majority's conclusion in *Hernandez*. Judge Smith, in his opinion advocating for sole legislative authority to declare a right to marry, underscores the importance of marriage to procreation—that the legislature could find an important function of marriage to create greater stability and permanence for children. This wholly overlooks the fact that a full decade earlier, the Court of Appeals had read New York's adoption statute to permit same-sex adoption—a conclusion never altered by the legislature. Indeed, many such families flourished around us. Those children also deserved the stability and security of two parents permanently dedicated to them.

Although confident that I would have written a persuasive opinion in *Hernandez* at any time during my tenure, I cannot help but think back to *Bovsun v. Sanperi* and my first days on the court. I have no question that my *Hernandez* dissent in 2006 benefited from the many lessons I learned over my years on the court; the breadth and depth of my tenure as chief judge; my work with families and children; and of course my own life experience, as a woman, wife, daughter, mother, and grandmother—each a facet of the human dimension of judging. *Hernandez* for me epitomizes the challenge and role of the court—whether statutory or constitutional interpretation, or common law judging—ensuring wisdom, fairness, stability, rationality, and modern-day relevance and significance. In a word: justice.

Chapter 5

My Transition to Chief Judge

For close to a decade I was in a place perfectly suited to me. The demands of the court were clear and enormous. I could have briefs with me and study and write around the clock, and I was surrounded by extraordinary staff of my choosing. Though the mandatory age seventy retirement provision of the state constitution radically changed the composition of the court—within two years I found myself number three in seniority, seated on the bench just to the left of Chief Judge Sol Wachtler, with Richard Simons (senior associate judge) to his right—the extraordinary personal rapport among us continued.

At that time, we were all Cuomo appointees, but we were politically diverse. Sol joked that many had feared appointments from the political clubhouse but didn't anticipate Mario's appointments from the Republican clubhouse. My court life was supplemented by Sol's success in persuading me to head his Permanent Judicial Commission on Justice for Children and by public speaking and law review writing (my speeches typically morphed into articles, of which I have published more than 200).

On the personal front, I was an avid exerciser (daily workouts at the Reebok Club and frequent runs in Central Park) and enjoyed good health. I had Stephen to keep a loving eye on me and, with our children, provide fun and balance in my life. Beginning in July 1984 (and continuing for twenty-one Julys thereafter), Stephen and I traveled to Villars-sur-Ollon, Switzerland, for essentially the month, where we rented a house and created a paradise combination of reading (we took with us the decisions from the entire Supreme Court term just ended, which makes great reading in the Alps, as well as a ton of books), running and hiking, dieting, and travel to nearby European cities for opera and sightseeing.

Crisis at the Court

With everything so perfect, obviously change was on the horizon. In life, nothing that good goes on forever.

The first rumble in the foundation was November 5, 1992. As the end of the court's Albany session grew near, I learned that Sol would be speaking the next Friday night at the Fort Orange Club, necessitating a stayover in the area, and I asked if he would come the next morning to see me receive the Ruth Schapiro Award at the State Bar headquarters. Stephen was driving up for the occasion, and I had invited my law clerk Hank Greenberg and his fiancée (now wife of more than twenty years), Hope Engel. Sol politely declined, telling me he was due on Long Island Saturday morning, and nothing more was said of it.

The four of us did indeed have a lovely day Saturday, capped off by a late lunch at Jack's restaurant in Albany, and Stephen and I stopped at a movie on the way down to New York City. We arrived home close to midnight, the phone ringing furiously. It was Uncle Leonard, urging us to turn on the TV immediately because the chief judge had just been arrested. I remember whispering to Stephen that it was perhaps time to look into some sort of care for Uncle Leonard (then in his seventies). What he was saying was utterly preposterous.

But as we know, it was not preposterous, only heartbreakingly tragic. Sol was indeed arrested on his way back to Long Island. I recall hearing that he was stopped and surrounded by dozens of officers, and then he was prosecuted and ultimately imprisoned.[1] I could not begin to tell his story (which he has done), only ours. Having described the personal feeling that pervaded Court of Appeals Hall, you can imagine the sense of loss and devastation that greeted us in Albany when the judges gathered there days later to determine what to do. Did I (we) see this coming? Absolutely not. Sol performed brilliantly in every respect we witnessed.

Thankfully, it fell to Judge Simons, as acting chief judge, to address the court staff some days later. Everyone dissolved in tears; we were in mourning. Along with Judge Simons, the six of us decided to allow Sol to retire from the court, instead of seeking his resignation, which evoked some nasty commentary in the press. I recall a photo of me the day we convened in Albany for our decision about Sol, printed the next day in the *Times*. It was the most devastated picture of me that I can recall.

Another Surprise

As my application for the position of chief judge was in process, another shocker hit. On December 9, 1992, I was shocked to find my photo on the front page of the *New York Times*, along with those of Brooksley Born, Amalya Kearse, and Patricia Wald as "finalists" for President-elect Bill Clinton's appointment as attorney general of the United States, the promised first woman AG. This was the first I had heard of my candidacy. Indeed, the article mentioned me "as a potential nominee to the Supreme Court," though there was no vacancy at the time.

Some days later, very early on a cold and snowy morning, I picked up the phone to hear Warren Christopher, soon to be sworn in as Clinton's secretary of State, on the other end of the line: "Judge Kaye, the president-elect would like to see you in Little Rock tomorrow. Just call back and give us your arrival time. We'll have someone at the airport to meet you." Click.

---

1. Ed. note: Wachtler was arrested on a number of charges that included extortion, blackmail, and racketeering.

As my staff began filtering in to my chambers that December morning, I shared the news of the call, as well as my reluctance to go to Little Rock. I had never thought of myself as an attorney general, and besides, our hard-working court was in an uncharacteristic state of turmoil. New York's Court of Appeals needed a new chief judge, and I was one of the candidates under consideration. No, I decided, most definitely I would not go to Little Rock, despite my staff's importuning. My law clerk Joe Matalon even insisted that it was "unpatriotic" for me not to go. My former law clerk Hank Greenberg, then working for the US Attorney in Albany, came rushing over to the courthouse to beg me to go to Little Rock. Hank is hard to resist.

By the conclusion of the court's morning conference (where the judges discuss and decide cases argued the previous afternoon), word was out about the call, and by the end of the day three notable things had happened. First, I called back Warren with my flight information. Second, I spoke with the Fordham Law School librarian (I frequently studied in the stacks there and came to know her well), who located a doctoral thesis on the position of attorney general, which she would let me borrow overnight. I wanted to know more about what the job entailed. Finally, when I hugged Judge Joseph Bellacosa farewell, he observed that we might never again see one another as court colleagues. The office of attorney general would obviously take me from Court of Appeals Hall to a whole new world. I took the train back to the city, picked up the volume at Fordham, read late into the night, and the next morning flew off to Arkansas.

Every detail of that day in Little Rock is forever etched in my mind—the preliminary exchange with Warren Christopher at transition headquarters, during which I told him I wasn't sure I wanted to be the attorney general; the pre-Christmas bustle at the Governor's Mansion, with holiday gifts being logged in; the wait for the president-elect in the library, the sun pouring in over a round table with a legal pad positioned exactly for handwriting by a(nother) left-handed person (probably his Inaugural Address). Within minutes a strikingly tall, handsome gentleman entered the room, held out his right hand and said, "Hi, I'm Bill."

We chatted at that round table for surely an hour—with Bill Clinton that's not hard to do—mostly talking about the Supreme Court, which was a great mutual interest of ours. Somewhere in our exchange I complimented him on his commitment to appointing a female attorney general, but added definitively, "I'm not your man." On my return to New York City late that night, Stephen told me those words would ensure my choice even though it's not at all what I had intended.

I knew we were going on too long because I could see someone anxiously pacing back and forth outside the door, concerned about getting me to the airport in time for my flight. Clinton, however, had one more stop in mind: the kitchen, spread with fabric samples, where Hillary, with whom a friendship had flowered around the American Bar Association Commission on Women in the Profession, was making choices for the upcoming inauguration. Frankly, I didn't need an airplane to get me back to New York City—I was flying on my own.

Nonetheless, first thing the next morning I called Warren Christopher to withdraw my name from consideration. On one hand I could not imagine a more challenging or fulfilling job than the one I had—let alone the chief judgeship position I had applied for.

New York's Judicial Branch needed stability in the Court of Appeals, not another vacancy. Furthermore, I could not see myself as attorney general. I think the president made a great choice in Janet Reno. I've never had a moment's regret about my own decision.

My Selection as Chief

Meanwhile, the chief judge selection process was going forward, with my name in the hat. This time the list of seven was otherwise all male (Will Hellerstein, Lewis Kaplan, Howard Levine, Leo Milonas, Dick Simons, and Joe Sullivan). Dick and I were plainly the frontrunners. Hard as I tried to be level-headed, I could not imagine Mario picking Dick (a Republican, eleven years my senior, four years short of mandatory retirement) over me. Just to heighten the anxiety, however, in the evening on February 21, Governor Cuomo's office called us both to inform us that he would announce his choice the following morning. Despite a snowstorm, Stephen and I went out to see *Chinatown*—not much of a movie, but a good distraction. At 7:20 the following morning, I received Mario's call to tell me I had been selected, and we were off to Albany. It did not escape notice that the *Times* story announcing my selection included the line "after Wachtler's resignation, a steady hand is sought." That was my hope and my firm intention.

Following my confirmation by the New York State Senate, on March 23, 1993 (coincidentally, Dick Simons's birthday, as well as my daughter's), Dick swore me in as the 22nd chief judge of the Court of Appeals and chief judge of the state of New York.

Yet Another Surprise

Seemingly minutes before my swearing in as chief judge, Byron White had announced his resignation from the Supreme Court, and my potential candidacy for another job was again in the press.

One week especially stands out in my mind—starting April 6, 1993 (my second week as chief judge), when my photo was again in the paper, mentioning me along with Governor Cuomo and Judge Wald as Supreme Court candidates identified by Clinton administration officials, with the president openly preferring a woman for the position. Within two days, the papers announced that Mario had withdrawn his name from consideration. Immensely concerned about the impact of all of the fuss on my treasured court, and on my own role as its chief, that morning I phoned Stephen at the office and asked him to meet to talk this through with me, which we did over coffee at what was then Barclays Hotel (now the Intercontinental). Stephen's words crystallized it all for me: "Do you really want this? Whether you do is a question of strategy. If yes, then the rest is tactics."

Strategy? Tactics? For a new position for the brand new chief judge? Only days earlier, in Court of Appeals Hall, I had taken an oath to perform the duties of my extraordinary office to the best of my ability so help me God and now, at the very moment when the upheaval in our court might be settling down—and indeed, I planned to be a force in helping it settle down—I was devising strategy and tactics for personal advancement? No. I walked back to chambers, phoned Bernie Nussbaum, a longtime friend and President Clinton's counsel, and withdrew my name. Bernie fussed a bit: "What is it with you New York City people? First Mario and now you. It must be something in the water." "The stars will never again be aligned for you as they are today" were his last words.

I knew that once I withdrew my name it was unlikely that the opportunity would ever present itself again. But I felt a great weight had been lifted from my shoulders as I contemplated the magnificent opportunity that lay before me as chief judge. Over the course of my decade as a judge of the Court of Appeals, my views on the role of the state judiciary as a mechanism for positive social change and the cases ruled on had evolved in important and unexpected ways. When I spoke with Bernie Nussbaum, along with my treasured judicial role, I continued to serve as chair of the Permanent Judicial Commission on Justice for Children; I had seen Sol introduce several effective reforms; and I saw how, as New York's chief judge, I could spearhead initiatives that would improve the efficacy of the state courts and the experience of New Yorkers. Community Courts, Drug Treatment Courts, jury reform, a Commercial Division—all of these were on the horizon.

I found myself excited and energized by this enormous potential for change, and as I reflected on my conversation with Bernie, I had to agree that the stars were indeed perfectly aligned for me at that moment. It's just that they pointed me in a direction other than the one others might have taken. I was ready to follow that direction and get to work.[2]

Those Unforgettable Early Days as CEO

In New York, the chief judge has two roles and thus two boxes of stationery: chief judge of the State of New York (a chief executive officer or CEO position) and chief judge of the Court of Appeals of the State of New York (the first among seven equals, hearing and deciding cases). Each is a full-time position occupying about 80 percent of the day. I used to describe my job as 5 to 9 (5 a.m. to 9 p.m., and sometimes beyond). The New York court system—more than 1,200 judges, 15,000 employees, 4 million annual filings, and a budget exceeding $2 billion—is among the largest, most complex court systems in the nation. Looking back and still today, I think my plan was to fill the daily calendar to the brim, and then add a few engagements, just to be sure that I would awaken many times during the night filled with anxiety.

Demanding though it may be, the dual chief judge roles are, in my experience, properly lodged in a single person, aided by a strong chief administrator or (even better) chief administrative judge (the chief operating officer, or COO). I was fortunate, during my entire tenure as chief judge, to have three great COOs: Leo Milonas, Jonathan Lippman (for twelve of my fifteen years), and Ann Pfau.

---

2. Jeff Greenfield wrote a delightful piece offering himself as a candidate for the Supreme Court because one who openly declines is praised to the skies. The accolades were nice, but unavailing!

As contrasted with New York State's trial courts (Civil, Criminal, Surrogate, Housing, Family, Supreme, etc.)—splintered into a dozen different courts, greatly in need of consolidation—our administrative system since 1977 has sensibly been organized around the chief judge and the Administrative Board (composed of the chief judge and the four presiding justices [PJs] of the Appellate Division). Unlike the PJs, the Court of Appeals judges are not heavily involved in day-to-day court administration. Court of Appeals Judges review and approve the budget annually. Individually they oversee various important committee matters from time to time assigned to them by the chief judge, and the chief judge keeps them informed of key issues percolating in the various courts. Despite a solid decade observing two chief judges in their role, I had a lot to learn about actually being CEO of the New York court system.

I have spoken of my good fortune at the Court of Appeals and declined to credit any particular people for fear of inadvertently skipping others. Double that for my role as chief judge. Though much of my tenure was clouded by the judicial compensation issue (which I'll get to), it is fair to say that I enjoyed and returned enormous respect and friendship throughout the court system. Nothing good could or would have happened without the skill, integrity, and dedication of the judges and court personnel.

In two particular respects I lucked out right at the beginning. First, then-Chief Administrator Matt Crosson conducted a series of private tutorials that were an utterly invaluable introduction to the technical intricacies of our court system. He did so even knowing that I did not intend to have him continue in that role. Second, in 1992 I had been a member of Sol Wachtler's Committee to Examine Lawyer Conduct in Matrimonial Actions, charged with studying and recommending vitally needed reform in the area of matrimonial practice. To this day, matrimonials are a far-too-painful court process, even after the appointment of specialized judges and a superb statewide administrative judge for matrimonial matters. The committee was chaired by Appellate Division Justice E. Leo Milonas, who was an enormously effective leader and quickly became (and remains) a close friend, along with his Barnard alum spouse, Helen. One evening over drinks at the Century Association shortly after my appointment was announced, Leo told me that he would be willing to become my chief administrative judge. Wow! What a gift!

An only slightly less wonderful coincidence is that service on that matrimonial committee, along with leadership of the Permanent Judicial Commission on Justice for Children, provided extraordinary insight into how to accomplish reform in a system where the overriding sentiment too often is "Everything stinks, don't change a thing." Here's the formula: start with a great idea (not necessarily a new idea) and a commitment to change; enlist the highest placed, very best people across the spectrum (proponents and opponents)—everyone accepts the chief judge's invitation—pick a phenomenal leader, preferably out of a large, well-resourced law firm; staff the projects well; and assiduously follow through on the group's recommendations. While the idea of reform through chief judge commissions surely existed long before me, we took them to a new level. Lippman has even super-towered the dozens we built together, with widely heralded groups tackling access to justice, wrongful convictions, sentencing reform, law school, pro bono, and innumerable other essential matters.

The fact is, chief judges are great conveners, and engaging large law firms in these projects adds enormously to the meager resources available to the court system. At Skadden, to use one example, I see that several of our first-rate (high billable hour) people are assiduously at work on Chief Judge Lippman's sentencing reform project, to say nothing of providing the services supporting all of the group's functions. Ditto for our Commercial Division Task Force, which in addition to the thirty-some first-class members and super facilities, had half a dozen or more (again high billable hour) private firm lawyers assisting in every possible way. Honestly, are there any truly new ideas in the world? Someone always is there to lay claim to the idea, and in the end what really counts is not the idea but the far more important ability and vision to actually implement it. That and unflagging optimism. "Chief judge of the state of New York" is no job for a pessimist. Or, to use the words of the late New Jersey Chief Justice (and former NYU Law School dean) Arthur Vanderbilt, "Judicial reform is no sport for the short-winded."

Also overlooked by the bar and others is the authority the chief judge has, through administrative rule making, to spearhead reform of the justice system. I am left breathless by the sweep of Lippman's current reforms—breathless but not one bit surprised, given his lifelong service in and intimate knowledge of our court system, and his extensive dealings with our partners in government as chief administrative judge. It's sort of like Lyndon Johnson's success with Congress—I think, for example, of the Civil Rights Act and healthcare reform—though I liken neither Lippman nor myself to Johnson or Obama.

There are in fact dozens of chief judges and administrative rules in every area of court practice. The requirement of continuing legal education, ensuring that the profession stays fresh, is one example; admission of foreign lawyers to limited practice in New York is another; Lippman's imposition of a required attorney affidavit supporting the filing of a foreclosure action is yet a third; his proposal to require pro bono service for bar admission is a fourth; the sweeping reforms bringing the Commercial Division into today's world is a fifth. The list grows longer every day.

It's a mistake to think that every reform has to be legislative. Chief judges' committees, commissions, and task forces are an effective (and relatively inexpensive) route to significant administrative—sometimes ultimately legislative—reform. The committee reports alone are a storehouse of fabulous research and great ideas. Excellent examples (and there are many more) during my tenure are the task force on the future of the courts chaired by Carey Dunne, the commission on judicial selection chaired by John Feerick, the commission on probation chaired by John Dunne, commissions on drug courts chaired by Bob Fiske, and indigent defense chaired by Burt Roberts and Will Hellerstein—all of incalculable value for chief judges and others to build on.

The matrimonial rules were my first announced reforms, which included the requirement of a statement of client rights and responsibilities, the prohibition against nonrefundable retainers, and (at the client's election) the provision for fee arbitration. The announcement naturally sparked controversy. Indeed, from day one as Chief judge, the word "pushback" topped my lexicon. Someone always objects. Years later I learned from a matrimonial lawyer in Buffalo that when the new chief judge's reforms were announced and complaints began surfacing, then Presiding Justice Dolores Denman got into her car with some lawyers she conscripted and traveled the Fourth Department to ensure the success of the new program. Change does not just happen in our tradition- and precedent-bound court system. It takes enormous effort "in house" before even venturing into the outside world of critics.

An understandable part of the pushback from matrimonial lawyers was, "Why just us? Why not also the rest of the bar?" Good point. I succeeded in convincing my lawyer friend Lou Craco to head a committee on the profession and the courts, which he did to perfection. So many of that committee's recommendations remain the standard today, including the requirement of continuing legal education for all New York lawyers, with which I now dutifully comply. I am pleased to see, more than a decade later, that the Institute on Professionalism that Lou's committee spawned remains alive and well, convening serious summits on the legal profession around the state. Indeed, in May 2014, the institute held a hugely significant full-day conference—the summit of summits—focused on the many profound changes in the profession. I was proud of the sponsor and the location (the Judicial Institute), though a great deal remains to be done in this era of profound change in law school education and law practice.

Just another note before getting into the "weeds" of chief judging: in August 1993, barely five months after I had stepped into office, the American Bar Association had its summer meeting in New York City—13,000 lawyers from around the nation gathered in my home city, and I was front and center, hosting in every sense. There were at the time possibly one or two other women chief judges in state courts and of course two on the Supreme Court (Justice Ruth Bader Ginsburg was in attendance). The following week, David Margolick's article appeared in the Living section of the *New York Times*: "In the Matter of Prestigious Jobs, Red Shoes and Grandchildren." It's a cherished piece. (I was saddened when David's column "At the Bar" was dropped from the *Times*. Though not always complimentary, he gave the public an otherwise wholly lacking insight into the operation of courts other than the Supreme Court, the only court the press regularly covers. The public needs more of that.)

David's article reported on my ten speeches to the Bar Association covering issues from raising breast cancer awareness (together with Judges Sondra Miller, Willie Thompson, and Karla Moskowitz, we launched the amazing Judges and Lawyers Breast Cancer Alert), to jury duty, to my affinity for red shoes (I've often said that we need more people wearing red shoes—meaning women—on the bench). The article is something I pull out every now and then when I need a lift. It's delightful, concluding with the fact that as I was hobnobbing around the Bar Association, my granddaughter Sonja (now a college graduate) sprouted her first tooth. David concluded our interview by asking me which event mattered more. I responded, "It's not even close." It never was.

Chapter 6

The Best . . .

First Initiatives

After my decades as a commercial litigator, two issues topped my list of things to be addressed during my tenure as chief judge. The first was the difficulty of conducting complex, paper-heavy commercial litigation in the state courts, which were (and are) utterly swamped with every imaginable type of dispute. In my early law firm days, we always tried to remove cases to the federal court if possible. A corporate executive decades ago told me that an element of a case settlement he had just concluded was that the parties would never again have to litigate in the state courts of New York. Painful for the chief judge to hear.

The second issue of interest was our jury system, about which there was widespread disdain, especially regrettable because, through actual jury service instead of popular fiction or the popular press, we have an opportunity to show the public a justice system that works well. The size of our caseloads required availability of a substantial number of jurors, but over the years groups had caught on to the idea of lobbying the legislature to adopt statutes providing them with automatic exemptions from jury service. By 1993, the state had about two dozen automatic statutory exemptions—doctors, lawyers, police and firefighters, Christian Science nurses, people who wore prosthetic devices and people who made prosthetic devices, and so on. Just check a box and you had an automatic exemption from jury service. The exemptions so depleted the number of available jurors that the court system had to keep Permanent Qualified Lists—you didn't want to be on that list—from which every two years the same jurors were summoned for a minimum of two weeks, longer if a case went longer. Not good for those poor souls on the Permanent Qualified List. Not good for the public perception of jury service or the experience. Not good for the court system.

Both ideas were ripe for commissions.

The Commercial Division

The first commission actually built on four specialized commercial parts Sol Wachtler had instituted in Manhattan during his tenure. Today there are Commercial Divisions of the New York State Supreme Court located all through the state. I loved the lament of US District Court Chief Judge Tom Griesa that the state court Commercial Division was taking all the really good commercial cases away from the federal courts. Music to my ears.

Pushback? Of course there was pushback. I remember receiving a petition signed by all the sitting Supreme Court justices in one judicial district objecting to a specialized commercial court, which in their view was unnecessary, and they simply would not be a part of it. The next day I appeared before them, and we calmed things down. The concern was that with this added attention and resources, we were favoring people who needed no favors at the expense of those who did. But here, too, the statewide Bench-Bar Task Force, working assiduously with Chief Administrative Judge Milonas, managed to overcome the resistance and give us a first-rate commercial court equal to the needs and demands of our world financial capital. It thrills me to see Robert Haig's authoritative treatise, *Commercial Litigation in New York State Courts*, eight hefty volumes on New York commercial law.

The Jury Project

The Jury Project, surely a highlight of my years on the bench. I made a very careful choice of chair—Colleen MacMahon, then a Paul Weiss partner, today an outstanding judge of the US District Court for the Southern District of New York. I have known Colleen for decades—a family friend introduced us while she was still in school. Colleen exceeded all of my wildly unreasonable expectations and within six months, with the fantastic Roberta Kaplan (later my law clerk, now a Paul Weiss partner, counsel for Edie Windsor in *United States v. Windsor*) as her counsel, delivered a start-to-finish blueprint for reform that was astounding. And we did it all.

The greatest change, the greatest accomplishment, was surely attitudinal, the public's and ours. Through lots of hard work the concept of jury "duty" moved closer to jury "service"—measures such as public awareness training for court staff; up-to-date work space and comfortable jury rooms for the inevitable waiting time; an objective of one day or one trial for length of service; and four or more years between jury summonses.

As a practical matter, the system took a giant step forward when all the automatic exemptions were swept off the statute books, more than a million names were added to potential juror list, and the Permanent Qualified List bit the dust. Though Jonathan Lippman by then had become my chief administrator (soon to be chief administrative judge), a role he thankfully held for a dozen years, and he deserves great praise for the jury revolution, I also have to credit Senator (later judge) James Lack, head of the Senate Judiciary Committee. Statutory exemptions from jury service could be erased only by statute, not by court rule. Jim scheduled hearings on the issue, as had been done in the past. This time, however, no one showed up to defend the exemptions, expecting (as always in the past) that they would remain untouched. Hearing no objection, the legislature abolished them—all of them, including even the statutory exemption for lawyers and judges. Cries of distress and outrage rang from every quarter.

Most memorable of all was the issue initiated by New York County Clerk Norman Goodman when he encountered Cardinal John O'Connor at some official luncheon and teased, "Soon I will have you on one of my juries." Not long after, we faced protest from the Catholic Church and other religious orders, which demanded return of the automatic exemption for clergy. If one exemption returned, obviously all would soon follow. Judge Lippman and I began a series of meetings with Cardinal O'Connor's representatives to see whether a satisfactory alternative could be found. The promise was that if we could work out something, we would be invited for breakfast with the cardinal. We did, and we were! Our compromise was that any member of a recognized religious order who felt that he or she could not sit on a jury would present an authorized certificate so stating and receive a two-year deferral. What a wonderful breakfast it was! But as a matter of fact, my own former rabbi, Marc Angel, served on a jury to verdict and wrote a piece describing it as one of the great experiences of his life. Many regular "resisters" were won over by the improved experience of jury service, genuinely a public service for them, for us an opportunity to show the public a court system that works well, as it does to this day (confirmed by my own recent jury service—though regrettably I was rejected once again).

Another benefit: one day while in Albany I received a call from my daughter, then on jury service in Manhattan. "Mom, this is a great place to meet guys!" A public service in every respect.

Most moving moment? While visiting the courts the week after September 11, 2001, I was told that a number of jurors had shown up for service and I might have the privilege of discharging them. Imagine that: although the courthouse area was filled with the smell and horror of the attack on the nearby World Trade Center, dozens responded to their summonses, seeing that as a display of their dedication to American values. Though we struggled to keep the court system operational, there was too much uncertainty for jury trials at that moment. The heroic individuals who showed up were openly disappointed to be discharged.

Another milestone was getting the US Postal Service to issue a stamp honoring jury service—a beautiful 41-cent stamp regrettably quickly superseded by rising postal rates. That took years of effort, including a barrage of letters to the postmaster general from chief justices around the nation. Why did it have to be so hard? Even the Muppets had gotten a stamp! As the postmaster general acknowledged in *Scott Stamp Catalogue* 2007, what ultimately did it for the postal service was the Freedom of Information Act request made by Greg Joseph. It was the last straw for the Postal Service, and it cost Greg several hundred dollars. Though surely the "culture shift" from jury duty to jury service was the product of lots of effort by many people, and much remains to be done, I cherish the thanks of individuals—sometimes even lawyers and judges—who every now and then stop to tell me that they have served as jurors and appreciated the experience. "Hardest thing I ever had to do," one appellate judge told me after serving to verdict in a criminal case.

The Jury Project was a magical moment in the life of the new chief judge. Once the mountain moves, even a millimeter, it's very intoxicating, invigorating, and inspiring.

. . . And More

The beginnings of what came to be called our problem-solving courts came soon thereafter, as well as the Permanent Judicial Commission on Justice for Children.

Problem-solving courts include Community Courts, Drug Courts, Mental Health Courts, and the like. As the name suggests, their objective is constructive: reducing recidivism and unnecessary rearrests and incarceration, while holding violators accountable for unlawful conduct and hopefully putting them on a positive life path. Here's how it began in New York state.

As with the commercial courts, in March 1993 I inherited the idea of a "community court" in midtown Manhattan. Literally the interest and pressure to do this came from the community—local residents, businesses, and theater owners—disgusted with the area's degradation by repeated, corrosive, nonviolent criminal conduct, such as drug abuse, prostitution, shoplifting, illegal vending, fare jumping, graffiti, and so on. Ironically, on 54th Street between Eighth and Ninth Avenues stands a building with the words "Municipal. Dist. Court" carved on its facade, one of the many courthouses scattered throughout the city before the courthouses were moved to downtown Foley Square. Back in 1993 a theater company occupied the entire six-story building on 54th Street. Today, the theater retains one floor. The building otherwise houses the Midtown Community Court.

Between March and October 1993—when Mayor David Dinkins officially handed me the keys to the courthouse—everyone worked hard to burnish the idea and the facility. Again, there are many people to thank for carefully nurturing the seeds of what became the Midtown Community Court, the Red Hook Community Justice Center, the Center for Court Innovation (a seeming oxymoron), and other problem-solving courts. With the Center for Court Innovation, the state court system has its own publicly/privately funded research and development arm.

Courts operating at their best take in or docket cases and they move them through procedural steps to fair and efficient disposition; there are time limits and rules every step of the way. Above all, numbers of dispositions count. The Midtown Community Court emerged by turning the prism a bit. People arrested for the sort of repeated nonviolent conduct that was degrading the Midtown area would be right back at it again—indeed, on the same street corner—in no time, only to be rearrested, with the process starting anew. Typically the punishment would be "time served"—the time it took to get through all the procedural steps to disposition. In effect, the process became the punishment, with ever lengthening criminal records, worsening behavior, and swelling dockets.

The idea of the Community Court was to offer a meaningful off-ramp, a constructive intervention, for people deemed to be worth the risk, to hold them accountable for their admitted misconduct but to do so under judicial supervision through measures such as community service combined with drug treatment. Everything about the court communicated a positive belief that offenders given this opportunity could and would succeed in rerouting their lives—from the spiffed-up physical structure of the court to the glass (instead of iron-barred) holding cells, to the attention paid to the person by the judge and staff, to the auxiliary services made available in the building—drug testing and counseling, job training and interview skills, connections to employment, and classes in the English language. Somebody cared. I loved the January 31, 2012, statement of Assistant US Attorney General Laurie Robinson that community courts make offenders feel like they have been treated with respect and thus more likely to accept court decisions, even unfavorable ones.

Today, even the most skeptical among us (well, almost all of them; we never did win over District Attorney Robert Morgenthau) applaud the idea, as it has spread throughout New York and the nation and even to distant places like England and Africa. Always there were visitors, from other courts and other countries, from schools and governments. I remember one extraordinary visit from US Barry McCaffrey, then director of the Office of National Drug Control Policy. We had gathered a group of Midtown Community Court graduates to meet with him, and around a large table they told their stories of how before their Community Court experience, they were never able to retain a job or have a credit card, an apartment. It wasn't long before all of us, including McCaffrey, were in tears.

The best thing about good ideas is that invariably they are pregnant with more good ideas. Early in the life of the Community Court, I met a visiting judge from Rochester, who greeted me with my four favorite words: "I have an idea." His name was John Schwartz, and that was the first I heard of drug courts, apparently then flourishing in Dade County, Florida, today common throughout New York, the nation, the world. Nearly two decades later, in May 2011, I visited Judge Schwartz in Rochester, still presiding over the Monroe County Drug Court (as well as its Mental Health Court), with the same vigor and highly contagious commitment he had back in 1993. He saw himself as saving lives, and so did I.

In many ways, the Drug Courts and Mental Health Courts (actually specialized parts of our Criminal, City, or Family Courts) have at their core the same idea that drives the success of the Community Courts: a single dedicated (in every sense) judge with knowledgeable support services focused on rehabilitation and accountability of the individual—a sharp contrast to the largely anonymous, packed courtrooms they would otherwise face.

At a Rochester Drug Court graduation ceremony (signaling the offender's successful completion of the program, a highly emotional moment), I heard these words from a college graduate who had fallen into a homeless, penniless, malnourished, friendless abyss of addiction, with no support system and no incentive to stop: "Drug Court fosters human motivation and the will to change and provides a framework within which that change can take place." Another graduate at a Family Drug Treatment Court ceremony spoke of a daily call she received from her Aunt Dorothy simply saying, "I love you," that got her through and enabled the court to return her children from foster care. At a Suffolk Drug Court graduation, a young boy stood up as his mother stepped forward to receive her completion certificate and shouted out: "Mom, I'm proud of you!" At a ceremony in Queens I heard a woman say to Judge Leslie Leach: "My head was bowed low when I was brought before you in handcuffs. But slowly I lifted my head higher and higher. Today my head is high. Today, Judge, I am looking you right in the eye." It's the consequence of at least one person, often several people, showing an offender they care about whether he or she lives or dies, and best of all connecting them with family and friends. So many people before the courts, especially the overburdened criminal and family courts, don't ever have that. No sense of self-worth is what drives them to the abyss.

Just a note about another category of special courts particularly meaningful to me— our specialized Domestic Violence Courts. They had their origin in a public clamor over a murder-suicide in Westchester County. That was my first encounter, back in 1993, with the highly vocal domestic violence community, who have truly moved the mountain in terms of public awareness of the scourge—thousands upon thousands of intimate-partner violence cases in our courts every year. "The courts absolutely must do something about this," they insisted. Murder and then suicide, I came to understand, are typical scenarios. No longer in New York.

Here the problem to be addressed stemmed from the splintered court system and from a lack of understanding about domestic violence; we've learned so much more about it in recent decades. Now we know that a judge adjudicating a domestic violence case needs comprehensive information about the people and the general situation, an objective not served by separate proceedings in, say, Criminal Court, Family Court, and Supreme Court. There is a need for life resources—can the victim continue to live safely in the home? Are there weapons? Prior violence? If safety was at issue, housing and food were necessary. What of any children? How are they surviving in what must be a tumultuous household? All of this brilliantly came together under the aegis of Deputy Administrative Judge Judy Harris Kluger (now heading Sanctuary for Families), working with the domestic violence groups. Again, a creative new approach for the courts to offer a constructive off-ramp from a devastating life experience.

Of course there was pushback—that's a constant. Fortunately, these were relatively good years for the economy and the courts, and for a few years we were able to secure federal and private financial support, so funding was less a problem than attitude. Change is rarely welcomed—people prefer to continue doing what they're doing and simply complain about it. In the court system, the pushback to problem-solving courts is best illustrated by arms folded across one's chest with a caption reading "Not my job." These are the people simply committed to plodding through standards and goals to case dispositions—though we surely need those people, too—rather than trying to address the human part of the legal issues. Clearly those were not the right people for the new initiative. Fortunately, there were many judges all across the court spectrum eager to be part of it, indeed, today they are still in these specialized parts with the same enthusiasm and dedication they had at the start. We have the statistics and the real-life stories to showcase their courage, hard work, and humanity.

In July 2012, the Urban Institute released a new evaluation showing that participants in our Mental Health Courts are significantly less likely to reoffend than are similar offenders in the traditional court system. What a pleasure it was to observe these courts in operation, particularly at "graduations," as often I did. Above all, we were fortunate to have had no mass murderers among our graduates, which would have stopped the initiative dead in its tracks. It was always a worry.

THE CHILDREN'S COMMISSION

Though technically a commission, this initiative is different from a regular commission. For starters, it's organized around the broad subject of children, not a particular issue, and it's permanent. Having now been around for twenty-five years (and still going strong), the Permanent Judicial Commission on Justice for Children is worthy of a whole book.

In fact, a book was written by its former executive director, Sheryl Dicker: *Reversing the Odds, Improving Outcomes for Babies in the Child Welfare System.*

This was one of Sol Wachtler's best ideas. Kids (especially poor, unloved, troubled kids) and their courts (especially family courts) definitely get the short end of the stick. Sol told me that his announcement of the formation of this commission in 1988 elicited the greatest response he had ever had on a new initiative—everyone wanted to be on it. Sadly, it foundered at the start, and Sol began pestering me to take over as chair. Having had no exposure to the field, I adamantly refused. Thankfully he persisted, and we struck a deal: I would do it if he provided a co-chair who had some experience in the area of justice for children. He certainly made good on his commitment: Ellen Schall, formerly New York City commissioner of Juvenile Justice, then dean of the NYU Wagner School of Social Policy, a genuine treasure. To this day I chair the commission, and it is a centerpiece of my life.

"Justice for children"—quite a challenge! What on earth does that mean? Ellen, Sheryl, and I fixed on a good way to answer that question—the modified Delphi method. We assembled a list of knowledgeable people in the field of children and courts, and we wrote to each of them outlining our new responsibility, seeking their suggestions, and telling them we would phone them for their advice about formulating a realistic agenda. By the time we had completed our calls, we had a good list of projects, centering on the zero-to-three population.

Two early initiatives especially stand out in my mind. The first stemmed from the complaint that too many young children were being brought into courtrooms because their caregivers had nowhere else to leave them. This was potentially disruptive to the proceedings and dangerous to the children, exposing them to things they should not hear. That plus a shooting in the Brooklyn Family Court precipitated our statewide children's centers, where children can be constructively occupied while their caregivers tend to their court business. In one year, the children's centers saw more than 55,000 children, taking the additional opportunity to connect their families to vital information about Head Start and food programs, if needed. In better days, every child left the center with a new book.

The commission's second project focused on securing early intervention health services, which at the time required a court order, unnecessarily adding thousands of petitions to our Family Court dockets and depriving those without a lawyer of access to these publicly funded services. The commission pressed for legislation routing these applicants directly to county Health Departments, where they belonged, instead of Family Court. In the process of conducting hearings alongside State Senator Mary Goodhue and pressing the legislature for statutory reform, I learned a great lesson, which remained with me all my chief judge years: never be negative. It's (more or less) the words of General Jan Smuts, "Never give up hope. You don't know what morning reinforcements are on the horizon." We fought to the end, despite initial legislative disinterest, and ultimately we prevailed.

Fast-forward to September 2011: I was the closing speaker at a nationwide convocation of Judicial Commissions on the Protection of Children in Salt Lake City, Utah. Ours was the first such commission. Today, twenty-one states—from Delaware to Hawaii, from California to Vermont—have them! The air sizzled with enthusiasm, ideas, success stories—not your everyday atmosphere when it comes to discussions of securing justice for children. I closed my remarks with these words of Margaret Mead that I always kept posted in my chambers: "A small group of thoughtful people could change the world. Indeed, it is the only thing that ever has." I believe it to the depths of my soul.

There was also pushback here, but of a different sort. More than pushback, it's really more public neglect and disinterest in children's issues. Kids don't vote. Overwhelmingly, children's issues have long been seen as women's province, though increasingly, superb men have stepped into the field. It continues to surprise and disappoint me that particularly in the big-firm lawyer community most familiar to me, there has long been comparatively less interest in children and families, though again I have lately seen encouraging signs of change, as both brain research and adolescent incarceration have awakened public interest. Sadly, Family Court has rarely been one's choice for lifetime judicial or even sporadic pro bono service. Apart from the humanity of it, as a practical matter we simply need to give more attention to the benefits of early intervention and education generally. Kids are, after all, our future. Troubled, neglected, expelled, and suspended kids are the core of our next generation of violent criminals. We have proof beyond all doubt of that fact.

I place the Children's Commission among my top moments for yet another reason: it opened my eyes to the need for attention to the hundreds of thousands of kids involved in our courts and to our overburdened, under-resourced Family Courts—which became a passion in my chief judge life and now my afterlife. I recognize and appreciate Chief Judge Lippman's continued commitment to the commission, despite huge budget hits.

Happily, as I already touched on, the subjects of this section—commercial courts, jury reform, problem-solving courts, and the children's commission—has not only netted significant benefit for the New York state justice system but also has been widely replicated by others. In preparing to co-chair Lippman's Task Force on Commercial Litigation in the 21st Century, I stumbled across this footnote in a 128-page article in *The Business Lawyer* by Mitchell Bach and Lee Applebaum, "A History of the Creation and Jurisdiction of Business Courts in the Last Decade": "[Robert Haig identified] Chief Judge Kaye as the only truly indispensable person in creating the Commercial Division. . . . In light of New York's influence on creating business courts nationally, her efforts and decisions lay behind more than the creation of New York's Commercial Division." Twenty-one states replicating our children's commission? Truly indispensable in creating the highly effective and widely replicated Commercial Division? Nice.

Chapter 7

The Worst . . .

September 11, 2001

Who among us will ever forget where we were on that Tuesday morning when one plane and then another flew into the World Trade Center towers and cast our city and nation into turmoil? I was at my desk at Court of Appeals Hall, preparing a speech for that evening's nationwide Access to Justice Conference, when my law clerk (now judge) Jennifer Schecter rushed in to turn on the TV set in my chambers. Perhaps thematic of the next hours, days, weeks, and months, we all reached out to locate loved ones; we gathered and hugged at every opportunity. The conference even convened that evening—people wanted to be together, to console one another; there were no formal speeches—simply words from the heart. We determined that the courts (even those located in lower Manhattan, right in the shadow of the twin towers) would be up and running. The courts perform an essential service but even more, terrorists needed to see that they cannot defeat us and what we stand for.

Of course, people were the first concern. As the hours passed, we learned that three of the many valiant court officers who had rushed to the site were missing and were never found. Dozens of our court family members were unable to locate spouses, children, siblings, cousins, nieces, nephews. An estimated 14,000 lawyers were lost or displaced— more than 1,300 attorneys registered the World Trade Center as their business address. Holding cells had to be evacuated, emergency applications heard, air filters changed, and structural damage assessed to determine whether it was even possible to safely occupy the downtown courthouses. Through the weekend, Chief Administrative Judge Lippman and I, after visiting the Ground Zero site of one of our courthouses, met with court personnel—grim-faced, red-eyed but there, on duty—to plan for Monday morning.

I've talked about heroic judges, court personnel, and jurors, but the New York Bar was also simply amazing. Quickly we learned of the enormous need for legal services—for, example, to implement a streamlined system for obtaining death certificates where no bodies and no remains could be found, so that insurance could be accessed. A call had gone out for volunteers to be trained at the City Bar Association on a day I was meeting there with bar representatives from neighboring states who offered to help. I was asked to step out of the meeting to "say a few words" to the crowd that had gathered—the stairway and lobby were filled, the line stretching out onto the street. I was speechless, moved beyond words. Though I girded myself before court visits after 9/11, there were times I just lost it completely, like the time spent with a Queens County clerk who had lost two firefighter sons and had a third searching for his brothers' remains. Her faith strengthened her—and me—beyond belief. I remember her saying, "I'm okay, I'm okay," as I wept in her arms. I remember visits to the special facility set up at the pier, staffed constantly by lawyers and others to offer counseling, services, and support of every sort. Lots of tears. Lots of heroes.

That such goodness and kindness were expressed and evidenced; that we came together to grieve with, comfort, and assist our court family and the public; that we overcame so many daily challenges in the courts—lost family members, missed court appearances, accumulating backlogs, irretrievable files—in my mind still does not lessen the incomparable, unforgettable pain for us all of September 11, 2001.

Judicial Compensation

In their brilliant design of our federal government, the framers provided for the independence of the judiciary and, while putting the power of the purse in the legislature, of judicial compensation said only that it shall not be diminished during the judge's term of office. Thus, through the combination of long terms of office and a prohibition against diminution of compensation, the Framers seemingly provided some measure of protection for the independence of the Judiciary. They could never have imagined how their assumption of fair judicial compensation could have been perverted, as it was in New York.

One more stage-setting fact. We are not talking about huge salaries. No one becomes a judge to get rich. Becoming a judge is a privilege, public service of the highest order, a genuine career culmination for lawyers, who on average have spent a dozen or more years at the bar before seeking judicial office. Lawyers know there are many avenues of practice, most notably private firms, if significant earnings matter. Nonetheless, there are life concerns common to everyone—even judges—like food, shelter, and the care and education of one's children. There is another element worthy of consideration here, too. Call it dignity, respect, value. We all want and need to draw from and retain the very best and brightest for the bench. The point is that indifference to some element of fairness in setting judicial compensation inevitably takes a toll on the quality of our judiciary. The persistent need to seek and be denied pay raises doesn't do a lot for public esteem either.

Sadly, our system for determining judicial compensation in New York rested on linkage: after a period of static salary, every few years the legislature would add catch-up cost-of-living increases for the judges. That happened only when the legislators saw an opportunity to increase their own compensation. (In New York, legislators, unlike judges, are only part-time, many of them with substantial additional employment.) Judicial raises thus functioned as cover for legislative raises. That perverted system reached a zenith, or nadir, during the twelve-year tenure of Governor George Pataki, who openly advocated raises for judges—which always got a round of applause from the judges—but not for legislators unless. . . . . (fill in the desired legislative reform the governor was seeking).

The consequence of that posturing was obvious. No raises for legislators, which required approval of the governor. So no raises for judges, which required approval of the legislature. More than a dozen years passed with utterly frozen judicial compensation as political issues flared between our "partners" in government and the cost of living soared.

The nub of the problem was likely best captured on the front page of the July 20, 2007, issue of the *New York Times*: "Deal in Albany Tightens Limits on Election Cash." The article announced that Governor Eliot Spitzer and legislative leaders had agreed to the broadest overhaul of New York's notoriously lax campaign finance laws since the end of Watergate, ending a stalemate that halted action in Albany for nearly a month The article proceeded to describe in detail the deal they had hammered out, which was a triumph for Spitzer. Several paragraphs down, still on the front page, the governor was quoted as saying that now he would support pay increases for the legislature. Not in the article, but the clear subtext is that with legislative pay increases, the judges could have them, too. Indeed, a day earlier I had received separate exultant calls from Governor Spitzer and Assembly Speaker Sheldon Silver, each informing me that as promised, he had cleared the way for judicial pay increases. I remember Silver's words: "See, I told you I would not let (the governor) leave the room until we shook hands on pay increases for judges." I need not point out that the legislature was not in session in Albany at the time—there couldn't have been a deal actually concluded then. It was just the usual three men in a room. In fact, the heralded reform never materialized. No campaign finance reform for Governor Spitzer, no raises for the legislators. If there couldn't be raises for the legislators, there would be none for the judges. Is that a good system? Does that ensure we will attract and retain the very best lawyers to the bench? Does that appropriately value our valued independent third branch of government? Plainly not.

And that, in a nutshell, has been our system for determining judicial compensation for as far back as I can remember. Fortunately, in December 2010, in Governor David Paterson's final days in office, he and Chief Judge Lippman succeeded in putting our long-urged Judicial Compensation Commission bill to the legislature—and this time it passed! Now every four years a tripartite commission will independently determine judicial compensation, which can be overturned only by a super-majority of the legislature. I thought of it as a miracle of the holiday season and most fervently hope that will prove to be so.

I am pleased by the prospect of a genuinely good system now in place to ultimately secure both independence and fairness in determining judicial compensation. I am comforted, looking back, in knowing that there is not a single thing my extraordinary Chief Administrative Judge Lippman and I could have done, might have done, should have done that we did not do to secure this objective, including very hard-fought litigation magnificently led by Bernie Nussbaum and the firm of Wachtell Lipton, resulting in a favorable decision by the Court of Appeals (legislature). Above all else, I am devastated that it took so long and has cost so much in terms of impact on our judges, in dollars, discontent and dismay. Definitely among the very worst times of my life.

Chapter 8

... And Everything in Between

During my chief judge years, I sometimes kept a journal, and it has been fun flipping back through it, though the overwhelming theme quickly grew tiresome: *yikes*! So much going on! So many pushes and pulls! Confrontation every day from every quarter! The treasures from my journals could fill many volumes of "everything in between," but here are just a few.

The Public Nature of the Chief Judge Role

Fortunately, when I was a new mother, I had developed the habit of rising by 5 a.m. to work in the silence of the dining room for an hour or two before the household awakened. (Often I've quipped that motherhood was excellent training in dispute resolution generally.) That became the ideal time for studying cases during my Court of Appeals years, supplemented by trips to work out and early morning runs with Judge Wesley in Albany. That second box of stationery—Chief Judge of the State of New York, head of the state's third branch of government—adds amazingly to what is already a very full-time job. Unlike the highly ordered judicial role, as CEO of the court system, you often can't tell what's coming next or where it will be coming from.

My diaries (all made during Lippman's COO years) are filled with unmitigated praise for my "left-hand man" (we are both left-handed). We usually began each day with a very early morning phone call, often as I was walking to chambers. Except for the day after his father's death, he invariably began the conversation with "Everything is great." That attitude helped enormously. Having spent his entire legal career in the state court system, knowing every crevice of it, every penny of every expenditure, and being a trusted, skilled, admired human being, he managed to make his daily opening statement largely true.

What tops the "Everything in Between" list is the public nature of the role—my first ever as a CEO—and the unequaled opportunity/challenge that presented. Nothing in my past had involved working with mayors, governors, legislators, and all sorts of public officials, with whom we met regularly, usually pleasant exchanges to update them on our new initiatives. Administering the oath of office to many of them at least got us off to a good start. (I've done a lot of swearings in and, even more fun, well over one hundred weddings, most recently several same-sex weddings.)

My other favorite time with public officials was ribbon cutting, because that often signaled a new court facility, a topic that could itself fill this chapter. During my tenure as chief, the state at long last took over responsibility for maintaining court facilities, regrettably still too often far short of the clean, dignified space the public deserves, and we were fortunate to secure several new court buildings, including the Judicial Institute (dedicated to education and training), a million square feet of beautiful new space in Brooklyn and a new Queens Family Court. Unforgettable is the agony of many of those new facilities—starting with the Bronx Housing Court, where the general contractor walked off the project midway, and the Bronx Criminal Court, where every imaginable thing went wrong.

Given that the budget, court facilities, and judicial raises most often topped our inter-branch agenda, and that the Court of Appeals had before it sensitive political cases bound to upset someone in the executive or legislative branch (sometimes both) and that our role is not generally understood by the public, I think that overall we did pretty well with our partners in government. Despite our own healthy legislative agenda, we never did join the "three men in a room" for the really critical decision making. By that I mean specifically in Albany and more generally throughout the nation, that despite its critical role in the preservation of our great democracy, the judiciary has never truly stood shoulder to shoulder with the other branches in its ability to run itself. I think, with the wisdom of more than two centuries' hindsight, the framers might have done a better job on funding the courts if they meant for us to be truly independent.

Another way that my life changed dramatically was dealing with the public through constant interviews and speeches—an annual State of the Judiciary, endless bar functions, judicial events of all sorts, Law Day and other official ceremonies, conferences, commencements (dozens of commencement speeches!), TV appearances, and all sorts of public events. Even if not the featured speaker, I would invariably be called on to "say a few words." Flipping through my journal, I notice that in May, June, and early July 1993 I made thirty-one speeches, including two commencement speeches, a memorial, drug court openings, and a host of judge and bar association events.

Even today I remain uncomfortable as a public speaker. I write out and endlessly revise my message, often continuing to refine the remarks even after the event and ultimately publish them. I say that this is a sign of respect for my audience, but in truth I am terrified of speaking without a text. What a joy it was to encounter in my journal a copy of an article by syndicated columnist Kyle Hughes (*Mount Vernon Daily Argus*, May 8, 1997) after our Law Day ceremony, titled "Pataki Again Upstaged, This Time by Chief Judge Kaye." "It was the second year in a row Kaye has upstaged Pataki. In 1996, the governor sat steaming while Kaye gently but firmly rebuked him for a series of attacks on court decisions and judges." Hughes concluded by suggesting that groups that have been paying Pataki $15,000 for a speech might well look into hiring me instead: "she puts some real thought beforehand into what she wants to say." Tediously writing out and revising speeches, as I do to this day, does indeed force me to put some real thought into what my message will be.

The Press

Despite my sense of identification with journalists, dealing with the press was another new challenge. As a Court of Appeals judge, public comment on decisions was a no-no: the opinion "speaks for itself." For the head of the third branch of government, it's an entirely different story. Regularly we (usually the chief administrative judge, the court system's press officer, and I) met with editorial boards, we scheduled press conferences on new initiatives and newsmaking events, granted interviews, made public appearances, and answered press questions as appropriate. I learned from former Chief Judge Charles Breitel during my stormy ascent to the Court of Appeals back in 1983 never to leave a press call unanswered, even if the answer is "No comment." He forced me to sit down in his presence and return every press call I had received, which I did. It at least surprises them to receive a callback.

Again, I think we pretty well held our own with the media during my tenure, though it was a great personal disappointment that we could never interest the press in regular coverage of the state courts in aid of greater public understanding of our role and function. By definition, news usually needs a touch of poison. During Paul Browne's years as Court of Appeals public information officer, we embarked on what in retrospect was a risky (maybe foolish is a better word) venture by inviting Joe Lelyveld and Joyce Purnick of the *Times* to my chambers to urge more sustained court coverage. Though I still believe in the message we sought to convey, I don't think they appreciated our effort to tell them how to do their job. (In 2007, shortly after Stephen's death, I declined Joyce Purnick's invitation to participate in an interview for my obituary. Now I know that many of those extensive obituaries are coauthored by the deceased! At least I won't know whether my turning down her invitation also was a mistake.) Pity that in general we can't all do better on civic education, a cause Sandra Day O'Connor and now Second Circuit Chief Judge Robert Katzmann have taken on with great zeal, to ensure that the public has a better understanding of the essential role of the courts in maintaining our nation's fundamental values and ideals.

The Conference of Chief Justices

I've spoken of several challenges of my new role within New York state. As chief judge, I also became a member of the Conference of Chief Justices, a nationwide organization of chiefs—fifty-six jurisdictions in all (the states plus US territories and commonwealths). The organization grew out of an initiative sponsored by Supreme Court Chief Justice Warren Burger—the National Center for State Courts—and offered excellent opportunities for synergies among our state courts, the repositories of the largest portion of our nation's litigation. The conference centered on two annual meetings, one in the summer at a location sponsored by a member state, the second in the fall, often in Washington, DC, or Williamsburg, Virginia (where the National Center is headquartered).

My introduction to the organization, back in 1993, was rocky, to say the least. One of very few women chiefs at the time, I found the holiday flavor of the summer meeting irritating and told them so. Stephen and I took our vacation in July, and each of us returned ready to work. The overwhelmingly male chiefs, by contrast, gathered in August for a week with their spouses (I went alone), so we were not exactly on the same wavelength at these meetings. When I complained, for example, about the day off in the middle of the week, I was pretty soundly chewed out by the organization's president at the time, who in effect told me that I had to learn to have some fun. I could read his mind: pushy New York woman. Fast forward fifteen years, during which time I even served as president of the organization. There were a lot of changes, including the fact that by 2005 approximately one-third of the Conference of Chief Justices was female, and the business docket at summer meetings was crammed to the brim with interesting policy innovations. Coincidental, or chromosomal? Clearly some of both.

I cherish many wonderful memories of my years with the Conference of Chief Justices and the National Center for State Courts. We accomplished a lot together, and we had a lot of fun, too. But right at the top of my list of treasured memories are these words appearing in their August 7, 2008, newsletter:

> Past CCJ President Judith Kaye will also retire in December. During one of our plenary sessions, Randy Shepard [then Chief Justice of Indiana] paid a spontaneous tribute to Judith. As Randy noted, no one has contributed more to improving state courts in this country than Judith. Judith redefined the role of Chief Justice in New York and because of her charismatic leadership, redefined it nationally. Almost every innovation of the past decade and more, every new focus of attention, be it children in our courts or jury service, bears Judith's stamp. Randy's remarks drew a standing ovation, an outward recognition of our deep respect for all that Judith has done.

This brings me to the subject of my retirement from the court. Back in New York state, it seemed that every day between August and December 2008 overflowed with tributes and accolades. Possibly the most memorable for me was my last day on the bench at Court of Appeals Hall. Our long tradition is that on the last day of oral argument for a retiring judge, the courtroom gradually fills with former colleagues, staff, family, and Albany friends. When the last argument concludes, everyone assembled in the courtroom rises and bursts into applause. Over the years, I have watched as some of my departing colleagues at that moment have filled with tears, and I was determined not to allow that to happen to me. So on that day of days—November 20, 2008—as I watched the courtroom fill (noting particularly the arrival into the audience of former Judges Bellacosa, Simons, Smith, and Wachtler), I grew more determined to avoid a waterfall, and there was only one way to do it. As the applause began, I held out my right hand and requested just a moment's quiet to say that I had broken tradition a quarter of a century earlier as the first woman to arrive on that bench and wished to break tradition on my departure. I wanted to be the one to express overwhelming gratitude to all those alongside me and before me for the unimaginably, indescribably sensational experience of being part of this extraordinary family, this phenomenal institution—and it worked. No tears until I left the room!

Through the balance of November and December the tributes continued, including a private ceremony in the court's conference room on December 11, in which the court family exchanged our ultimate farewells. Here were my words:

> A lot is written about the common law process, but the books and commentaries do not begin to capture the real-life experience, the anguish and joy of actually developing the law so as to retain stability, recognize growth, and render justice for the parties. For a day, a month, a year, let alone a quarter-century, it is a privilege beyond description—beyond imagination—to be part of the common law process, and part of the people who implement, honor, and preserve the process, at the greatest court on Earth, the Court of Appeals of the State of New York.

> Then the curtain came down. Thud.

1. Judge Kaye's first year on the bench of the New York State Court of Appeals, 1983. Pictured left to right: Richard D. Simons, Sol Wachtler, Matthew J. Jasen, Chief Judge Lawrence H. Cooke, Hugh R. Jones, Bernard S. Meyer, Judith S. Kaye.

2. New York State Court of Appeals bench, 1987. Pictured left to right: Joseph W. Bellacosa, Vito J. Titone, Judith S. Kaye, Chief Judge Sol Wachtler, Richard D. Simons, Fritz W. Alexander II, Stewart F. Hancock Jr.

3. Judge Kaye's first bench portrait as chief judge, 1993. Pictured left to right: George Bundy Smith, Stewart F. Hancock Jr., Richard D. Simons, Chief Judge Judith S. Kaye, Vito J. Titone, Joseph W. Bellacosa. Judge Kaye's elevation to chief judge created a vacancy for an associate judge.

4. New York State Court of Appeals bench, 1993. Pictured left to right: George Bundy Smith, Stewart F. Hancock Jr., Richard D. Simons, Chief Judge Judith S. Kaye, Vito J. Titone, Joseph W. Bellacosa, Howard A. Levine. Judge Levine filled the vacancy in September 1993.

5. New York State Court of Appeals bench, 1994. Pictured left to right: Howard A. Levine, Joseph W. Bellacosa, Richard D. Simons, Chief Judge Judith S. Kaye, Vito J. Titone, George Bundy Smith, Carmen Beauchamp Ciparick.

6. New York State Court of Appeals bench, 1997. Pictured left to right: Richard C. Wesley, Howard A. Levine, Joseph W. Bellacosa, Chief Judge Judith S. Kaye, George Bundy Smith, Carmen Beauchamp Ciparick, Albert M. Rosenblatt.

7. Judge Kaye's last bench portrait as chief judge, 2008. Pictured left to right: Eugene F. Pigott Jr., Susan Phillips Read, Carmen Beauchamp Ciparick, Chief Judge Judith S. Kaye, Victoria A. Graffeo, Robert S. Smith, Theodore T. Jones Jr.

Cuomo Selects First Woman For High Court

By DAVID MARGOLICK

The New York Times/Neal Boenzi
Judith S. Kaye after her nomination to the Court of Appeals.

Judith S. Kaye, a partner in a Manhattan law firm and vice president of the Legal Aid Society, was nominated by Governor Cuomo yesterday to be the first woman to serve as a judge on the state's highest court.

The appointment of Mrs. Kaye to the Court of Appeals is subject to confirmation by the State Senate.

At a news conference in his office at the World Trade Center, Mr. Cuomo praised Mrs. Kaye's "extraordinary qualifications" and called her a "lawyer of unusual ability, integrity and determination."

Referring to the absence of a woman on the court, he said, "In addition to adding excellence to the court, the appointment of Judith Kaye erases a stigma it has borne for too long a time."

No Experience as a Judge

Mrs. Kaye, a partner at the firm of Olwine, Connelly, Chase, O'Donnell & Weyher, has never been a judge. Mr. Cuomo said this would not be a handicap and noted that several Court of Appeals judges had not previously served on the bench, including Adrian P. Burke, for whom he once was clerk.

"Like other great Court of Appeals judges who came to the bench directly from the practice of law," he said, "her day-to-day life as an advocate has demonstrated the character, temperament, capacity for collegial activity and ability to articulate that are essential."

Mrs. Kaye said she felt both "inexpli-

Continued on Page B6, Column 1

8. *New York Times*, August 12, 1983. Copyright the New York Times.

9. Judith S. Kaye upon her appointment to the New York State Court of Appeals, 1983.

10. Judge Kaye was a keynote speaker at an event in Washington, DC.

David Jennings for The New York Times

Gov. Mario M. Cuomo introducing Judge Judith S. Kaye, his choice for Chief Judge of the Court of Appeals.

Cuomo Nominates Judith Kaye For Top New York Judicial Post

By SARAH LYALL
Special to The New York Times

ALBANY, Feb. 22 — Gov. Mario M. Cuomo today nominated Judge Judith S. Kaye, a centrist on the New York State Court of Appeals who has worked to expand individual rights under the State Constitution, to become the first woman to be Chief Judge of the court.

If confirmed by the State Senate, she would succeed Sol Wachtler, who resigned in November after being arrested on charges that he extorted money from a former lover.

While Mr. Wachtler was considered a charming but combative jurist, Judge Kaye is known as a consensus-builder. In nominating her, Mr. Cuomo not only was naming a woman to the state's top judicial position but he also was selecting a well-liked, well-known judge after the upheaval of Mr. Wachtler's departure.

In addition, the Governor, who has selected all the judges now on the Court of Appeals, guarantees himself another nomination in choosing Judge Kaye's replacement.

Legal scholars said Judge Kaye's appointment was a victory for the principle she has espoused in a number of recent rulings — that provisions of the State Constitution can be applied when they afford more protection of individual rights than those afforded by the United States Constitution. [Woman in the News, page B2.]

As Chief Judge, Judge Kaye, who is 54, would preside over the court for a 14-year term and be charged not only with leading its deliberations but also with running the state's court system, the largest in the country with 1,149 judges, 12,000 other employees and a yearly budget approaching $1 billion.

A 'Bright New Leader'

At a news conference this morning, Mr. Cuomo praised the judge, the only woman who has ever served on the Court of Appeals, as a "bright new leader whose credentials as a lawyer, legal scholar and judge are superior and whose collegiality and leadership capacities have been proved."

Judge Kaye said that "I feel wonderful from the tip of my head to the tip of my toes."

"I became a lawyer 30 years ago, and 30 years ago, this day would have

Continued on Page B2, Column 6

11. *New York Times*, February 23, 1993. Copyright the New York Times.

12. Chief Judge Kaye posing with her Unified Court System security officers (from left to right), Jack and Mark Vobis and their brothers, Matt and Jim Vobis.

13. With children in a Court Children's Center, a project initiated by Chief Judge Kaye to provide a safe space for children while their parents and guardians were in court.

14. Chief Judge Kaye, pictured with WABC-TV anchor Sade Baderinwa, at the launch of the Jury Duty Social Awareness postage stamp in 2007. Judge Kaye worked with the federal government and the US Postal Service to create the commemorative stamp, which was designed to call attention to the importance of jury service.

15. The official New York State Court of Appeals portrait of Chief Judge Judith S. Kaye, 2001.

16. Chief Judge Kaye in a New York State Court of Appeals publicity photograph, which she often used to publicize upcoming speeches and events.

17. Chief Judge Kaye, pictured with Elijah Fagan-Solis in the Richardson Courtroom at Court of Appeals Hall, Albany. Elijah was the winner of the first annual David A. Garfinkel Essay Competition (2008).

18. Chief Judge Kaye pictured with fellow women judges on the New York State Court of Appeals (counterclockwise), Carmen Beauchamp Ciparick, Victoria A. Graffeo, and Susan Phillips Read.

19. Judge Kaye giving a speech at A Summit on Children.

20. Judge Kaye addressing the public in the courtroom of the New York State Court of Appeals.

Part II

Return to the Real World

Chapter 9

The Afterlife

Stephen's Death

Although my term as chief judge continued until December 31, 2008, I mark October 30, 2006, the day Stephen died, as the start of my afterlife. Life changed profoundly. As my daughter reminds me when I begin sobbing, we did have nearly forty-three years of a remarkable marriage, but I have never stopped missing him with a terrible, always-present ache.

Back in September 1962, when I joined Sullivan & Cromwell, Stephen Rackow Kaye, then a senior associate there, was immediately and immensely attractive to me. He had a season pass to the New York Rangers and the Metropolitan Opera, and faithfully attended performances of both. He wore distinctive bowties, suspenders, and hats. He was a prized litigation associate at the firm—openly dating him would not have added to my credit as a serious lawyer back in 1962. And he was Jewish, although it concerned my parents that he was more than seven years my senior. Our romance was clandestine. We only once ran into a firm partner—on a date with a person not his wife—so our secret was safe. We were generally able to attend public events secure in the knowledge that our colleagues were at the office late into the night.

While I cannot swear that our marriage was absolute perfection, free of tension and argument, from February 11, 1964, to October 30, 2006, it came pretty close, especially in its last decades. We were fiercely independent and fiercely interdependent.

I attribute much of Stephen's strength to what doctors then called the sudden—what his doctors even called an "electric"—death of his father, when Stephen was only five years old. His seemingly hale and hearty father went out to play tennis one fiery hot August morning and dropped dead for no discernible reason. Forever after, Stephen was the go-to person for his mother and two sisters, and then for me and the kids. Like his father, who was a lawyer, Stephen loved the law—studying it (he always carried a copy of the US Constitution with him; you didn't lightly challenge him on that subject); writing about it; and practicing it days, nights, and weekends (always with family dinnertime at home). He loved being Jewish, observing traditions of our faith, studying Jewish texts, once in his early teens even having considered becoming a rabbi (an idea he surrendered when his own rabbi became the subject of a scandal).

Stephen was a faithful Cornell University alumnus (undergraduate and law school, again, like his father). He combined his senior undergraduate year with his first law school year—at that time known as "the professional option." At the end of that combined year, when he received his bachelor's degree, under his robe he wore his army uniform and was immediately shipped off to Korea. Devotion to his country was also one of the many high principles Stephen held.

Perhaps the most challenging, and at the same time most strengthening, times for me were the nearly two years that Stephen spent in Connecticut, living in Hartford, with daily calls and occasional visits home, leaving me to cope with three young children and my law practice. I did it! Equally strengthening was Stephen's boundless optimism. Who else would have traveled to Bayreuth, Germany, for the Wagner Festival without opera tickets or a hotel reservation? Who else would have flown to Vancouver, Canada, to see the New York Rangers in the Stanley Cup playoffs (a rare event) without a ticket for the game? We did it; he did it! Stephen's love, strength, and optimism were highly contagious. With him, through him, I learned to project enormous self-confidence in my personal and professional life, while grinding my fingers to the bone under the table.

Though we had treasured friends, given our three children, the family, and our opera, hockey, baseball, and other passions, we tended not to be "dinner party" people. Mostly we were a couple, with our kids, at work, at endless swim meets, games, and other events. Stephen had our kids on the ice (the boys in hockey gear, Luisa in figure skates), in the pool, in card games, and at the racetrack by the time they were four. Above all else, he was an extraordinary father and grandfather, as our children and six of our seven grandchildren (Stella Rose Kaye—another SRK, and named for him—was born after his death) can attest. All holidays were family time: Thanksgivings at the Hotel Hershey in Pennsylvania, and often throughout the year at Mohonk Mountain House outside of New Paltz. Summer vacations with the children for many years were at Hilton Head Island, South Carolina, and when they were grown, Stephen and I enjoyed twenty-two July paradises in Switzerland, hiking, reading, and traveling through Europe.

By summer 2006, Stephen had been diagnosed with bladder cancer, and we decided it would be foolish to go abroad. So we rented a house in Dutchess County, intending to replicate our Swiss paradise there. Exactly one week after moving in, Stephen awoke one morning with no hearing. That was the beginning of the end, four months later.

Devastated by the loss of Stephen, I was comforted by my family—biological and professional—and by the familiar though rigorous schedule of the Court of Appeals. On December 31, 2008, that joy of my life also came to an end.

My Route Off the Court

Unlike federal judges, who have life tenure, New York State judges have terms of office fixed by the state constitution. For Court of Appeals judges (and State Supreme Court judges), it's a curious fourteen years, a compromise reached back in the nineteenth century between those who advocated life tenure for judges (to secure independence) and those who feared that life tenure ceded too much power to the officeholder. Back in 1846, fourteen years was the average number of years actually served by those judges blessed with life tenure. What would that number be today? Plainly much higher. The New York state constitution further provides that a judge "shall retire on the last day of December in the year in which he or she reaches the age of seventy." For me that was December 31, 2008.

On September 12, 1983, when I joined the court, fourteen years in the future may have just as well been a century. Even on March 23, 1993, when I became chief judge, December 31, 2008, seemed a far distant future. When newly elected Governor Eliot Spitzer suggested that I reapply in 2006, with the end of my fourteen-year term (to say nothing of my seventieth birthday) looming on the horizon, it was a no-brainer. I would have stayed forever, even though Stephen (before the onset of his disease) urged that it was time for me to move on to something else.

As the dreaded end date drew near, I knew only two things for sure. First, I would spend no appreciable time job-hunting, I would be chief judge to the very end, enjoying every second of the unique opportunity that remained and the spectacular send-off that was lavished on me. Second, with Stephen gone, I wanted to be on the job, some job, immediately after my judgeship ended. This was not a coherent plan. As I look back on it, I realize it was probably driven more by fear that froze me in place than by a genuine choice not to consider a wide range of alternatives. After all, this would be the first time in decades that I would be without the care and counsel of Stephen (or anyone else in that role, which I consciously decided not to try to fill) and without the rigor and nurture of my Court of Appeals life. The challenge was to earn or invent a new identity. Had Stephen been around, we would have traveled the world for a while, spent blocks of time with our children and grandchildren, and carefully plotted our next steps.

To put another face on the issue, in September 2011, I was in Indianapolis to deliver a lecture on legal education when, in a question and answer period at the Indiana Supreme Court, I was asked (in essence), "What on Earth, after a long and distinguished record of public service—including being chief judge of the state of New York—are you doing at the law firm of Skadden, Arps" (or indeed any money-oriented entity)? Immediately I felt the barb in that question and bumbled about with an answer, which I now give in greater detail.

Glorious as it is to be chief judge of the state of New York, unlike service on the Supreme Court of the United States, there is no "retired" stationery, staff, space, service, or stardom. Quite the reverse. When you're out, you're out. Even my healthy roster of bar association and pro bono attachments had been wiped clean. What's more, there is a new chief judge in place, brimful of projects, with the clock ticking on his own initiatives. Having observed my predecessors and former state chiefs around the nation, I know of none who has blazed a trail I would wish follow.

I did take two directional steps before my retirement. One was toward the Barack Obama administration, which seemed a good place for me. My thought was to be somewhere in his agenda for children. Was there any? I reached out to Marian Wright Edelman and others, who gave me several leads to Obama that I followed up on, but to no avail. No response. Looking back, I suspect his attention at that moment was not on "kids," as it is today. Alternatively, I thought about the foundation world. Ellen Schall put me in touch with a foundation headhunter, a seemingly knowledgeable woman in her early seventies, who after a pleasant back-and-forth said in no uncertain terms, "Forget it. You're too old." None of the innumerable foundations, agencies, or public service organizations reached out to me. Even more significantly, I didn't reach out to them either, to "network aggressively," as my friend Ellen Futter advised me to do. Good advice. Would my path have been different? No point dwelling on a path not taken.

Although I received dozens of calls from law firms—"don't make a move until you talk to us" was part of virtually every conversation—I chose to speak to only three: Sullivan & Cromwell (too many memories; too far downtown), Proskauer (Stephen's firm; I cry just getting on their elevator), and Skadden. Skadden said magic words, in effect: "Come here and do what you want." Even more, they had special appeal as a genuine force in the pro bono world. The Skadden fellows alone are a monumental example of dedication to the public interest. Through January and early February, as my successor's selection proceeded, I attacked twenty-five years of stuff at 230 Park Avenue and sent a lot of it up to Albany. As for the major part of my papers—years of case reports, each in a separate folder, and dozens of file cabinets full of memos and correspondence—I ultimately made a critical decision. Except for my first year or so, everything went into shredding bins. The alternative was to keep the paper, requiring me first to go through it all. Unthinkable.

Fast-forwarding to today, I ask myself, should I have been more aggressive in plotting my own next move as my chief judge days waned? Did I fantasize my afterlife at a large law firm? Frankly, no. I thought of something essentially public service–oriented. But my predominating thought as December 2008 drew to an end, without Stephen, was to leave no space between the close of chambers and the opening of the next chapter. Though I made a few attempts to reach the Obama administration, public service–oriented opportunities did not knock on my door; law firms did. While I think that things have worked out well for me, junctures like this, even for "accomplished" people, need effort, direction, consultation, questioning, if only because the value of one's prior visibility fades rather quickly. ("Let me tell you who I was.") If your intent is to contribute meaningfully, if your ambition is to achieve, you cannot just stumble into it. You have to thoughtfully, diligently, persistently seek it out—or you may miss the boat, and the tide very quickly moves on.

By February 12, 2009, enough was enough, and I brought the daily drudgery of writing notes and filling shredding bins to a close. I ended my last morning in Suite 826 at 230 Park Avenue with a final tour through my spacious, beautiful, much-loved home chambers, and decided to leave behind the beautiful light oak desk and credenza I had purchased when I became an Olwine partner in 1979. I sealed the chambers key in an envelope, laid it on the shelf at the front door, and let the door lock behind me. After a small fit of tears in the arms of the guards in the building lobby, I proceeded to a long-fixed lunch date with former police commissioner Ray Kelly at the Harvard Club. A memorable lunch for Commissioner Kelly, I am sure, as I tried unsuccessfully to control my emotion. He was great! I managed to fritter away the next few days, and on February 17, 2009, showed up for work at Skadden. My first call was to chambers, to get my desk back. Too much gone in my life. I left the credenza, and still see it behind Chief Judge Lippman in some of his videos. It's my connection to him!

The credenza and the connection lead me to consider writing a section, or at least a footnote (I'm not overly fond of footnotes, but they are sometimes necessary), on the art of being a good predecessor/successor. How does the successor best use, value, maintain the connection; how does the predecessor support yet steer clear of the new legacy being built? I don't think either Chief Judge Lippman or I have perfectly mastered the art, if anyone ever does. But ultimately I gave up the idea. No good can come of it. Suffice it to say that I am grateful for the continued life of the Children's Commission, and when Lippman called in late October 2011 to invite me to co-chair (with Marty Lipton) an initiative on commercial litigation, I was thrilled. Months later, we delivered a first-rate blueprint to him, now being masterfully implemented through an advisory council overseen by Bob Haig.

My Life at Skadden

After Stephen's death, I became transfixed on Steve Jobs. I've read everything about him, and seen the recording of his 2005 Stanford University commencement address, filled with thoughts along the following lines: You can connect the dots looking backward, not forward; learn from failure; don't lose faith, find what you love, have the courage and creativity to become a beginner again; follow your heart; don't waste your time. If today were the last day of your life, would you want to do what you are about to do today? If not, for too many days in a row, you need to change something.

A different Steve, but he's definitely talking to me, his words made less relevant or more relevant (I don't know which, and it doesn't matter) by my personal circumstances.

Against that backdrop, how do I evaluate my life at Skadden? Every single day, I spend time at the peak of happiness and in the depths of despair—it's known as life. Then again, connecting the dots looking backward over my years at the firm—not bad. Every now and then I call Office Services to ask how much I owe Skadden, having in mind the charges that accumulate for personal postage, car service, and the like. I think the right answer is that the amount I owe Skadden is huge, utterly incalculable, a conclusion multiplied several times over by my disease. The extraordinary kindness of Eric Friedman, Skadden's executive partner, and other trusted colleagues has enabled me to live in the active, productive world instead of being mentally, if not physically, consumed by the ubiquitous symptoms and signposts of cancer.

That is an insight that came to me only recently. Until then, I struggled. Indeed, I have rewritten this chapter many times, as I have rewritten my life at Skadden many times over the past few years.

Most distressing still is the personal quality of life at a large law firm today—or lack thereof, a disappointment I did not sufficiently anticipate. The opportunity for some personal interaction is what most drew me to a firm. I knew it would be impossible to replicate the personal quality that defined my court life, or even what I recalled of my law firm days—wandering into a neighbor's office to toss around interesting legal issues, even a bit of social interchange. It's just not the "culture" today, which I suppose is driven by what the business of law has become. With a couple of notable exceptions, doors are closed, people are out or unavailable, pitching business, on conference calls, attending meetings in places like London, Brazil, and Taiwan, working offsite—maybe even from home—or simply disengaged. The other day I watched a young lawyer on a long elevator ride up to the office participate in what was plainly a multiparty, likely international, telephone conference on her smartphone.

When I lamented the lack of personal interaction to a group of young associates, one of them challenged me. He said, "You are dead wrong. We have more communication than you ever did. We're always talking to each other—just in a different form." I'll accept that for what it's worth, though it seems tragically sad to me that someone would believe that. I cannot believe that Tweeting, texting, and instant messaging are truly a substitute for the eyeball-to-eyeball kind of conversations I had in mind, and I grieve the loss of them.

In addition, looking back, I think that both the firm and I might have done a better job on orientation and expectations. To say that Skadden gave me a royal welcome—and it still does—would be a vast understatement. But just where and how do I fit? After twenty-five years in lawyer heaven I really needed (and was too embarrassed to admit it) a bit of reintroduction to the real world, someone to point me in directions I might pursue, introduce me to people, or suggest programs I could offer within the firm or even to clients of the firm. Surprisingly, nothing came to me naturally simply by virtue of my having been a long-serving, well-regarded chief judge.

Frankly, I don't know what the firm had in mind, if anything more than an affiliation, when they invited me to join them. They surely did not see me as (say) a Simon Rifkind or Harold Tyler, for whom law firms were renamed when they left the bench and joined them. Does anyone care, or (as I now see) is it simply another version of the need for me to have seized the lead, spoken up, plowed my own turf, and been aggressive? I was given a very nice office on the forty-first floor, just a few doors down from the legendary Joe Flom, still honeymooning around the world. My next-door neighbor (with whom I shared a secretary) told me on day one that he billed fourteen or so hours a day, six days a week, then he promptly left for another firm, taking our secretary with him. The prevailing noise was silence.

Another perfect trifecta: Skadden was making certain that I knew they were thrilled to have me; they were not imposing on me or "using" me at all; and I was just being glum, saying nothing about it. I've often thought of those words to my law clerk Gary Hoppe at Court of Appeals Hall back on September 12, 1983: "I have absolutely no idea what I am supposed to do here, do you?" That was equally true on February 17, 2009, except that there was no one seated across the desk for me to say this to, and no one at home to toss it around with. What was my strategy? Meaningfully (over)fill the work day and stay off A. A. Berle's "sometimes" list of former power-holders crushed by the realization of their subsequent lack of private or personal achievement. The tactics? A hard question to answer.

That has indeed changed, but it took time. The first break came when I moved my office up to the forty-seventh floor, right next to my longtime friend Barry Garfinkel, whom I could drop in on every now and again for discussion of esoteric legal issues (that always interests Barry) or just chat. At an interview session with a prospective partner, for the first time I heard a lateral partner who had arrived at Skadden from government explain how she had built her own very busy practice at the firm: partners had taken her around to various Skadden offices, where she had made vital connections. Oh, so that's how it's done! So I signed on for travel with a partner to other offices to build personal connections, to help where I could (for example, by speaking with women in the firm), to help define my own place in this new universe, which is what I wanted to do. Then fate intervened. Before the start of my first "tour"—scheduled for the Boston office—came the cancer diagnosis, loss of my voice, and several months of vile chemotherapy and surgery. Back to square one.

So with all of life a trade-off, here's how mine has evolved: I'm doing lots and seeking more. Fortunately, shortly after my arrival I was called on to lead several investigations (some public and some private), a few of which received a fair amount of attention. One was for the State University of New York at Binghamton involving college basketball (Pete Thamel in the February 29, 2012, *Times* said the report read like "a Grisham novel"), and a second for then–Attorney General Andrew Cuomo involving claims against Governor David Paterson and an aide. Those created an impression that I have found to be a good niche; indeed, I am enormously busy and productive. Home (alone) is my least favorite place to be. My goal is never to be there. Also, I need a purpose or I am broken (to paraphrase Brian Selznick's Hugo Cabret).

Five solid years after arriving at Skadden, I can honestly say that my life has shaped itself around several discrete categories—passions, purposes, projects—that could happily make up the last day of my life.

The first category encompasses the vestiges of my public life, including the investigations I have described. At this moment I am busily chairing the Commission on Judicial Nomination, which this year will offer the governor up to seven candidates for each of two Court of Appeals seats (one vacated by reason of age retirement, one by expiration of a fourteen-year term) and over the upcoming years will have additional slots to fill. It's a time-consuming process for our twelve-member commission (four appointed by the governor, four by the legislature, four by the chief judge), starting with raising awareness among potential applicants to maximize the pool, then carefully vetting the candidates and coming to consensus on a list for the governor. Having myself gone through the process three times as a candidate (1983, 1992, and 2006), and now twice as commission chair, I believe that (despite my own initial experience) we have an excellent process in place, as evidenced by the two most recent appointees, Judges Jenny Rivera and Sheila Abdus-Salaam.

Into this first category I also place my board responsibilities, starting with the dream of dreams, my service as a Lincoln Center board member. As a longtime Lincoln Center devotee, I am so proud to contribute to this extraordinary institution that in so many ways enriches our lives—including special efforts I am involved in to reach young people. Each of the boards I have been a part of represents not only a significant public interest but also something especially meaningful to me—for example, Volunteers of Legal Services; the Museum of Jewish Heritage; the American Arbitration Association and Institute for Conflict Prevention and Resolution; the Robert H. Jackson Foundation; the Fund for Modern Courts; the State Bar Committee on Law, Youth and Citizenship; the Youth Courts Committee I chair; the Historical Society of the Courts of the State of New York; and the Skadden Fellows Foundation. Quite a list!

In the "giving glass and getting glass" seasons—when organizations hold their principal fund-raising events—I have also been the giver or receiver of an award, again enabling me to lend support to public-oriented causes and organizations that I believe in. Every now and then I get to officiate a wedding (my favorite) or give a speech (my least favorite). In September 2014, I performed my approximately 150th wedding ceremony, joining two women who had been life partners for thirty-three years. Their seventeen-year-old daughter had inspired the idea of a formal, legal union of her parents.

Blending from this first category into the second category is my interest in children. Without question, a plum of my afterlife the first year or more was the invitation of the Supreme Court Historical Society to deliver its annual lecture in the Chamber of the US Supreme Court, which I did on June 10, 2010.

The subject was mine to choose, as long as it concerned the history of the Supreme Court. Though I knew immediately that my topic would be in the area of children (hardly an everyday subject for the Supreme Court), it took me some time and a cherished collaboration with former deputy clerk of the Court of Appeals Marge McCoy (another former Dick Simons law clerk), to hit on the subject of *In re Gault*, an extraordinary 1967 decision, the Court back then in its heyday of due process. In *Gault*, the Court set aside a six-year sentence imposed by an Arizona juvenile court (Justice Fortas called it a "kangaroo court") on a fifteen-year-old boy for (possibly) one (possibly) obscene phone call to a neighbor. The Supreme Court concluded that, in the guise of benevolence, young Gerald Gault had been denied several essential constitutional protections. Similar conduct by an adult would have resulted in a $50 fine.

I loved every gut-grinding minute of that experience: the plodding research, hundreds of manuscript revisions, and ultimate presentation of the lecture, attended by many family members and others very dear to me (including Supreme Court Justice Sonia Sotomayor; Justice Ruth Bader Ginsburg's husband was hospitalized at the time and she was not in attendance). Nothing in my litigation career compared to standing in the "well" of the Supreme Court and for nearly an hour speaking on a subject enormously meaningful to me (though regrettably not to a lot of big-firm litigators). Most exciting, as I buried myself in the literature, was the rise of public interest in the subject of adolescent misbehavior. Suddenly the subject of troubled adolescents was everywhere I looked, including new brain development science, a positive sign. Why fund all this research if no one in the judicial system is going to put it to use in addressing adolescent misbehavior?

Best of all, Justice Anthony Kennedy's opinion in *Graham v. Florida*, setting aside a juvenile sentence of life without parole, appeared in the magical months I was preparing my lecture, and the opinion relied on brain science in concluding that the sentence was unconstitutionally harsh given juveniles' impulsiveness, difficulty thinking in terms of long-term benefits, and reluctance to trust adults. What next? I ended my lecture with reference to the "sequelae" that tortured me as a Court of Appeals judge—meaning that once you start down a pathway, you will get carried further along, case by case. I was not at all surprised to see, on June 25, 2012, two more juvenile mandatory life-without-parole cases were reversed by the Supreme Court. *Graham* was a nonhomicide case; the two later cases, captioned *Miller v. Alabama*, involved homicides by fourteen-year-olds. (I joined in Skadden's amicus brief to the Supreme Court on the juveniles' behalf.) Where will all that scientific research about the adolescent brain take the courts in addressing future cases involving youth misconduct—or more hopefully and optimistically, in helping prevent juvenile crime?

Somewhat relatedly, my last Chief Justices Conference, in Anchorage in summer 2008, opened my eyes to the idea of youth courts. In his welcome to us all, then-Anchorage mayor (now senator) Mark Begich[1] lauded those courts for their effective intervention in the lives of troubled youths, and off we went (Chief Administrative Judge Ann Pfau and I) to watch them in operation. Really impressive. After signing a confidentiality pledge, we were permitted to sit in on a disposition by three teenagers in a courtroom of a case involving joyriding by a teen (we had missed the factual presentation). It was dazzling. Most impressive, the offender was compellingly told by his peers about the consequences of the proceeding (he had previously acknowledged his guilt) and the judgment that would be imposed, because wrongdoing had to be redressed. If he accepted and fully satisfied his sentence, he could participate in future Youth Court sessions in any capacity but one—defendant. This was his one chance to avoid the lifetime stigma of a criminal conviction for illegal conduct that would otherwise plague him throughout his life in every job, academic, and employment application.

Suffice it to say that Ann and I were lifted off our seats, filled with enthusiasm, and eager to bring a really important idea (confirmed by then Chief Justice Dana Fabe) back to New York. When I related this to Staten Island District Attorney Dan Donovan (then president of the New York District Attorneys' Association), his words were, "Great, let's do it here." We are doing it in Staten Island and dozens of other places throughout the state. Best of all, I continue to be involved! While hardly essential to the initiative, through the State Bar Association we attempted to secure legislation embracing the idea of youth courts, leaving flexibility in their actual organization. The legislation was a no-brainer—already there are 80 to 100 youth courts operating in New York state. The statute simply might have encouraged even wider use as an alternative to unnecessary arrest and prosecutions of kids for truly criminally insignificant misbehavior. But guess what? The statute failed. Our legislature never ceases to amaze me. Fortunately, the youth court initiative thrives anyway,

A centerpiece of this second category of children's issues is the Permanent Judicial Commission on Justice for Children mentioned earlier—the fortunate consequence of Sol Wachtler's insistence decades earlier that I step into the role of chair. "Permanent" has indeed meant permanent: I still chair this wonderful commission. The commission and my interest in and passion for kids has given birth to yet another more recent initiative, a Task Force on Keeping Kids in School and Out of Courts. When Atlantic Philanthropies approached Mayor Michael Bloomberg with the idea that they would fund a city initiative with me as an affiliate, the mayor declined the offer. So Atlantic came directly to me, with funding to enable me to grow the idea, and indeed it has grown.

The idea addresses our nation's decades-long affinity for zero-tolerance school discipline, resulting in a great many out-of-school detentions, drop-outs, and arrests of children—mostly young black men—for minor misbehavior, step one in their education

---

1. Ed. note: Begich served as senator through January 2015.

as lifetime violent criminals. As we bemoan our nation's outstanding leadership in mass incarceration—costly in so many ways—it can hardly escape notice that a large portion of our prison population consists of school dropouts. Time for change. In the words of Frederick Douglass, "It is easier to build strong children than to repair broken men [and women]."

With the support of Skadden, Atlantic, and the Permanent Judicial Commission on Justice for Children (magnificently steered by Executive Director Kathleen DeCataldo, and Deputy Director Toni Lang), we have dedicated ourselves to this idea, ultimately producing a definitive report carried all through this state, with the prospect of a convening in Washington, DC, by the federal government in October 2014. What a joy it has been to watch the rise in public attention and recognition, to move into the headlines of public consciousness. For me, it is ultimate proof of a lesson learned during my chief judge years: that judges have enormous convening power. They may not know the right course to take in matters outside their bailiwick, but they surely can bring together and incentivize the people who do.

A third discrete category or purpose in my afterlife has been a return to the field of dispute resolution, though until recently I have deliberately chosen to stay out of the courts—not put my name on court papers—and headed more toward arbitration, a form of private dispute resolution and private judging. Many retired judges become arbitrators. While I was certainly familiar with alternative dispute resolution—and had powerful lessons in judicial deference to arbitral awards—as with much of life, the field has changed dramatically from the time I left for the bench in 1983. Most significantly, in this modern world, firms like Skadden are heavily at the center of worldwide arbitration, as global clients find new ways to resolve their far-flung differences. As with the world of justice for children, after leaving the bench, I connected with many friends in the commercial litigation world and headed in the direction of international arbitration, which has included a hearing in London and travel to conferences in Singapore, Mauritius, and Brazil.

Today, in addition to serving as an arbitrator, I chair the New York International Arbitration Center, a collaboration of thirty-seven law firms and two state bar association sections. Amazing that it has taken New York—a world commercial capital—so long to get this off the ground. "It's forty years overdue," one prominent arbitrator commented. Though the center will need to rent space to help support its operations, the major objective—the mission—is to promote New York as a site for international arbitration. It's good for our economy, for our citizens, for our law, but a challenge in that many others throughout the United States and the world (such as Florida, Atlanta, Toronto, and Singapore) now see what London saw decades ago, when law firms there collaborated to open the International Dispute Resolution Center. We were fortunate to find a great executive director, Alexandra Dosman, and are busily designing programs to advance our mission, bringing together prominent spokespersons to raise awareness to the differences in and opportunities for dispute resolution in this vastly growing cross-cultural field.

Ironically, it's in the world of arbitration that several parts of my life have come together. I'm not referring to the fact that to this day it's still harder for women to get choice appointments in international commercial matters. "Pale, stale, male" is the phrase I have encountered and see in this world as well—reminiscent of the early 1960s, with women, especially younger women, pushing open the door. I'm doing OK in this respect, and most definitely enjoy both serving as an arbitrator and helping the center grow.

By parts of my life "coming together," I had in mind the connection between international arbitration and my beloved Court of Appeals, as far-flung disputes that have been resolved elsewhere often land in New York for judicial enforcement. Most global entities, after all, have some sort of assets here. Decades ago, the state legislature, perceiving the potential commercial value in hosting huge arbitrations, enacted a statute allowing for major matters to be sited here, even if the parties had no other connection to the state. At Skadden, I have had the opportunity to witness and participate in such matters, now seeing them from the other side of the bench.

Indeed, as I write, a major issue circles its way to the Court of Appeals and—given the focus of my story—seems an appropriate way to complete this segment: right back at Court of Appeals Hall. The issue I refer to is the "separate entity" rule, a long-standing common-law principle that precludes a judgment creditor from using postjudgment enforcement procedures to compel a bank with a New York branch to turn over client money held in non–New York accounts. It hardly needs stating that many banks maintain branches and affiliates in New York, a global financial capital which—but for the protective boundary the separate entity rule provides them—would be subject to attachment for judgments of foreign courts.

I missed by a few months the case that sparked the current controversy—*Koehler v. The Bank of Bermuda, Ltd.*—argued April 28, 2009, likely already in the pipeline when I left the court. In *Koehler*, the Second Circuit certified to our Court of Appeals the question whether a New York court may order a bank over which it has personal jurisdiction to deliver assets of a judgment debtor to a judgment creditor when those assets were located outside New York (in this case, Bermuda). The court, in a four-three decision, answered yes, touching off a flurry of cases and commentary—even some legislative activity, fearing adverse impact on our state's commercial preeminence.

Even the US Supreme Court coincidentally weighed in, in 2014, decisively limiting the permissible reach of a court's exercise of personal jurisdiction over foreign corporations unless those corporations themselves have significant presence here (*Daimler AG v. Bauman*). Wouldn't you know, the Second Circuit has followed with another certified question to the Court of Appeals—this time specifically serving up the applicability of the separate entity rule to foreign bank branches, in an appeal to be heard in September 2014 (*Motorola Credit Corp. v. Standard Chartered Bank*). Although I have not formally participated in the several cases serving up this critical issue for final resolution, I am pleased to have lent assistance within the firm on these, as well as several other significant matters.

This being neither bar exam preparation nor an effort to inject my own two cents into the pending controversy, I note only that so many themes identified earlier echo in this scenario: a common-law principle (the separate entity rule) adopted into New York statutes, with constitutional law ramifications, now to be construed ultimately and finally by a common-law court; the majority's effort in *Koehler* to highlight the particular facts, the dissent's astute observation that the result reached by the majority seems a "recipe for trouble"; the new world, with amici from far and wide, including Ireland, the United Kingdom, and Jordan, claiming adverse impact on themselves and New York State.

However heavy the burden on counsel, the hundreds upon hundreds of hours that have gone into the substantial stack of papers that now faces the Court of Appeals in *Motorola*, still the most nightmarish, haunting challenge of all falls on the Court of Appeals—to get the result right for the parties and the case before the court and fix a rule that takes into account the sequelae of what the consequences will be, as each stakeholder carries the articulated principle to its ends. Surely the court has seen "recipes for trouble" many times. Getting it just right is hugely challenging, yet satisfying beyond words.

Having identified these three passions, projects, and purposes that now make up my chief judge afterlife, whether looking backward or forward, it's hard to connect the dots. As a great fan of the artist Dale Chihuly, I think of his ingenuity, talent, and creativity of actually weaving glass into tapestries—stunning surfaces, patterns and forms—and I search for an analogy to the tapestry of my professional life. While I would not say that I consider these my "greatest contributions" (to use the words of A. A. Berle), my days are challenging, busy—and sometimes even beautiful.

21. Benjamin Smith, age unknown, selling ties on the street in Cuba.

22. The future chief judge's father, Ben Smith, in the family's Monticello store.

23. Judith Smith with her mother, Lena, and brother, Allen, in front of Smith's Apparel.

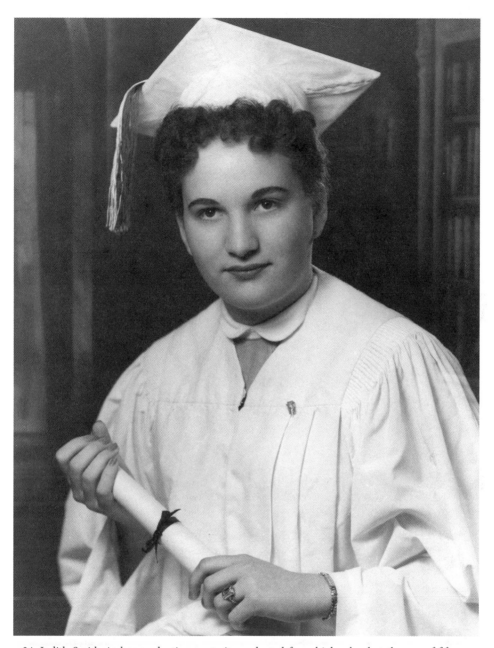

24. Judith Smith, in her graduation portrait, graduated from high school at the age of fifteen.

25. Judith S. Kaye pictured with her husband, Stephen R. Kaye, at their daughter Luisa's wedding, 1991.

26. Kaye family reunion at Mohonk, May 2006 (Stella Kaye, born June 30, 2007, inset).

27. Judith with her brother, Allen Smith, and first cousin Martin Smith (son of Ben's brother, Velvel "Willy" Smith) at commemoration of historical marker, Maplewood, New York, summer 2007.

TIMES UNION

timesunion.com

OUTLYING AREAS

ALBANY, NEW YORK ■ FRIDAY, NOVEMBER 21, 2008

End of an era

SKIP DICKSTEIN/TIMES UNION

Chief Judge Judith S. Kaye responds to praise Thursday after her final case in Albany. The first woman to serve on the state Court of Appeals, she later became the first to lead the state's highest court. She is joined by three top women jurists, Associate Judge Susan Phillips Read, left, Senior Associate Judge Carmen Beauchamp Ciparick, Kaye, and Associate Judge Victoria A. Graffeo. **Story/A3**

28. *Times Union*, November 21, 2008. Copyright Times Union.

29. Chief Judge Judith S. Kaye pictured with then–Chief Administrative Judge of the Courts Jonathan Lippman and Chief Justice of the United States John G. Roberts Jr.

30. Judge Kaye with panelists at the 2011 Historical Society of the New York Courts public lecture "Lincoln, the Civil War, and Freedom of the Press: New York Divided."

31. Judge Kaye with then–Chief Administrative Judge of the Courts Jonathan Lippman and former Associate Judge of the New York State Court of Appeals Albert M. Rosenblatt.

Part III

Who I Am, from Day One

Chapter 10

From Day One through Law School

Although I set out to write about courts and the justice system, there can be no question that the person of the judge always is a relevant subject, however scholarly or arcane the legal issue might be. So here's a little take on who I am.

My parents—Lena and Ben Smith—were kind, loving people, immigrants from Eastern Europe, neither having completed school. Sadly, in those pre-*Roots* days, we spent no time talking about their (our) roots, though I learned to speak Yiddish, mostly because that's how they spoke to each other when we were not supposed to understand what they were saying. For me, that made learning Yiddish essential. Back then, for my family, it was demeaning to be a "greenhorn," honorable only to be an American.

I do know that my mother arrived (with her family) on July 18, 1914, as a child of ten from Stavisk, Poland (I have a copy of the ship's manifest), lived on the Lower East Side where her father was a tailor (he soon passed away), and worked to help support the family from the first moment she could. My father came to the United States in his early twenties from Drahichyn (now Belarus) through Cuba, was deported, and did not return for several years. I have a photo of him selling ties on a street in Havana. When I was preparing a speech on immigration years ago and obtained a copy of their naturalization papers from the Sullivan County clerk, I learned that my father's country of last residence was not Cuba but Panama. I understand that when his illegal status was discovered in the 1940s, there was trouble, but the fact that my parents were farmers with American-born children enabled them to secure citizenship. Where would we have been today, I wonder. Our family album has a photo of one of my father's brothers who was caught, deported back to Drahichyn, and exterminated.

Both my parents passed away before I reached the Court of Appeals and before my brother reached executive status at Sony Music Corporation. My mother died in August 1964 (age sixty); my father in September 1968 (age sixty-one or so, I never knew for sure). They would have been very proud that what was for them a totally skewed, upsetting scenario—their bookish daughter a lawyer, their beatnik-hippie son a musician—had such a grand finale. Even more, it would have pleased them to no end that their children, traveling down radically different life paths, never enemies but never friends, are so close today. (I also acquired an adored sister-in-law.)

When I was born (August 4, 1938), my parents were farmers in rural Maplewood, with cows and chickens. I remember my Aunt Fagel skimming the foam from the top of the milk buckets my father carried in from the barn and applying it to her face. I remember my mother's handmade farmer cheese. I remember the day Bossie, a calf, was shackled and driven off the farm in a truck, separated from her mother and sold, and I cried for days. Upon turning five, I began my education in a one-room schoolhouse, unquestionably the best year of my entire academic life. After a year there, I was tested and placed into the third grade.

When I was six, the family moved into the village of Monticello, where my parents were shopkeepers—first they had a general dry goods store (where you could buy apparel for the whole family, yard goods, and household items) and then a ladies' clothing store (Smith's Apparel). Ralph Lauren's parents also were from Drahichyn and spent summers up with us at a bungalow colony of "landsmen." Ralph has reminded me that he bought his first pair of jeans in my parents' store, and today he owns a half-billion-dollar clothing company. He still remembers the smell of all the denim in the store, and so do I. That's America—or at least it used to be—for hard-working, ambitious immigrants.

We lived in an apartment over the dry goods store, and then rented the ground floor of a two-family house that was just behind Smith's Apparel. Amazingly, my father, a man of the soil with a pronounced Jewish accent, did the shopping for the ladies' clothing store in New York City. He even bought my senior prom dress on a shopping trip into New York City showrooms! My mother effortlessly managed the store and our home, including three meals a day. We had only one family vacation, a weekend in (of all places) Atlantic City.

Throughout, my parents were committed to the American dream for their children. For their daughter, that meant excelling in school and working in the store (no one wraps a gift package better than I do), becoming a teacher, then marrying and raising children. My dream was different.

At Monticello High School, we had the choice of a secretarial or academic program. My mother insisted that I take the secretarial option (for safety), so I took both. Still I am an extraordinary typist. Learning Gregg shorthand was like learning a foreign language, and I like learning foreign languages. Blessedly (though a personal misery) I was a head taller than most of my classmates, even though I was two years younger. My poor parents actually took me to a doctor because they feared that I was on my way to becoming a freak. But only the seventh-grade math teacher, Miss Galligan, openly mocked me, calling me "The Baby." Maybe that's why I have no math skills. But I made it into the Senior Honor Society anyway.

My parent's plan was not my plan—anything but—as evidenced by my choice of Barnard College (a first so far as I know for a Monticello High School graduate; I had never met anyone who attended Barnard), a major in Latin American civilizations, and the ambition to be a journalist with a focus on Latin America. Coming to Barnard instead of the usual choices for my Monticello classmates who went to college—state teachers college, or for the better students Syracuse or Cornell—was plainly a transformative decision in my life. I cannot imagine that I ever would have been editor-in-chief of their student papers, as I was of the *Barnard Bulletin*. It was struggle enough getting started at the small, caring, all-female Barnard College, where fate intervened as I faced first semester exams. I came down with the mumps and had the privilege of "make-ups" when I was far better acclimated. Had I gone to Cornell or Syracuse, just having turned sixteen, I likely would have been overwhelmed and returned to life in Monticello, running Smith's Apparel (which would have been all right in my parents' view). Indeed, I was engaged to a nice Monticello boy after my freshman year, but I broke it off on my return to college. In my senior year I applied for a Fulbright to Peru, which I believe I must have received a response and my parents destroyed it. Wouldn't I have heard back by now?

Maybe it was just perverseness—to do the unexpected and to do it in my own quiet yet fiercely determined way—that became my life theme. That and an incredible gift of two years added to my life by Miss Kitz at that Maplewood one-room schoolhouse, where she taught a five-year-old the equivalent of kindergarten, first, and second grades. Would I otherwise have experimented with night law school back in 1959 simply as a means of burnishing my résumé as a serious journalist? I had no intention of becoming a lawyer.

In June 1958, Barnard degree in hand, I embarked on a fruitless search for a job at a newspaper. I remember little of the year that passed before I applied to the Evening Division of New York University School of Law, which I entered in September 1959. At the time I was employed as a social reporter for the *Hudson Dispatch* of Union City, New Jersey, the only sort of newspaper job reasonably attainable by a woman. Two things I do recall. First, the bus I took over from Port Authority each work day stopped at the Burlesque Theater in Union City, and I like thinking that fellow passengers concluded I was on my way to work at the theater. Second, word for word I remember the Club Collect that began every women's club meeting: "Please, God, keep us from pettiness. Let us be large in word, in thought and in deed." An unanswered prayer.

Alongside several other women under the supervision of a woman, I mostly wrote about weddings, engagements, and social events, until I could stand it no more. I was definitely going nowhere and not enjoying it one bit.

I believe the example of Tony Lewis—who after a year of law school was reporting on courts for the *Times*—led me to law school, at night, simply to garner some serious attention in the world of journalism. I had to go at night, because this zany idea did not have the support of my parents in any sense. So for one and a half years I remained in the Evening Division (long since gone, as NYU's reputation soared), working full-time as a copyeditor for General Features Corporation, just across the street from the chambers I later occupied as judge and chief judge.

When I graduated with the class of 1962 (having transferred into the Day Division in the spring semester of my second year, with a full scholarship, and having attended summers as well) we were about 10 women in a class of 300 people. I remember only two women in my night school class, who soon dropped out; surely there were a few more. The men in the Evening Division were largely police officers, accountants, and engineers. An impressive bunch.

To this day I cannot believe I was so block-headed about how different things were for women—I just barreled ahead, having the very first day or so of law school encountered two especially good friends (Steve Fisher and Mike Weinberg) to make a sort of study group. I was mostly at sea in the various courses, especially contracts, where classroom exchanges were totally dominated by the men; there were no female professors. Women were not allowed to live in the dormitory (I rented a tiny bedroom atop 43 Fifth Avenue, undoubtedly former maid's quarters) or become Root-Tilden Scholars (the elite program that paid for everything).

Thankfully the only course that first year that had a midterm exam was civil procedure, where to my horror the exam question was framed in the context of a contracts law case. The person who sat alongside me in civil procedure was an older, brilliant engineer, always advancing intriguing comments, but when the exam grades came back, mine was at the top, his was at the bottom. I was convinced that our papers had been switched, an improbability since they were identified only by number. After an anxious day for us both—he went to inspect his paper—I realized what had happened: he had written about contracts while I, understanding little of the subject, had instead written about civil procedure. That was, after all, the subject of the class. A good life lesson: however brilliant you might be, always be sure to address the subject of the inquiry.

That got me off to a good start in law school—the stellar grade in civil procedure and the paper I produced for our introductory writing course. I wrote on journalists' testimonial privilege, a subject dear to my heart, which captivated the professor, who gave it some sort of prize and got it published as an article in the *Intramural Law Review*. Indeed, all three of my serious writings during law school were published, the latter two in the *NYU Law Review*, which, based on my grades, I was invited to join. By August 1962, when I graduated from law school near the top of my class, I had long ditched the dream of being a serious journalist. I was bound for a career in the law.

I can't leave "the Catskills" years without reference to a genuine mountaintop in my life: May 12, 2007, when the Town of Thompson, Sullivan County, dedicated a historical marker at Smith Brothers Farm in Maplewood, where the house, barn, and chicken coop built by my father and his brothers still stand. The welcome was breathtaking—state and local officials, a Boy Scout troop, the high school chorus, a bagpiper, my classmates holding a sign "Welcome Home Judith Kaye and Allen Smith," judges and friends from Albany, Maplewood, and Monticello, ending with a reception at the local firehouse where I was presented with the bell from the one-room schoolhouse. Even today stands the following roadside historical marker, capturing my parents' dream, my dream, the essence of America:

> Benjamin Smith and his brothers Willie (Velvel) and Nathan established Smith Brothers Farm on the site in the 1930's after fleeing poverty and discrimination in what is now Drohiczyn, Poland. Benjamin and his wife, Lena (born in Stavisk, Poland), made this their home until 1944, when they moved into Monticello with their children, Judith and Allen. Judith (a lawyer) in 1983 became a judge of the Court of Appeals (New York's highest court) and in 1993 became Chief Judge of the State of New York. Allen (a musician) became vice president of Sony Music Corporation. For Ben and Lena, their children's achievements were "the American Dream Come True."

Chapter 11

My Years as a Lawyer

An Albany reporter in a telephone interview some years ago referred to my career as spanning the "entire epoch of women in the law." A bit of an overstatement, given "Gentleman Margaret Brent" back in the 1600s, and Kate Stoneman, the first woman admitted to the New York Bar, in 1868. But I see the point: perhaps the early 1960s were a sort of starting point for the modern era of women in the law. Surely they were for me, with few if any role models.

I've heard former Supreme Court Justice Sandra Day O'Connor, just a couple of years ahead of me in graduating from law school, describe her job searches on the West Coast, ultimately resulting only in a secretarial offer from a major firm. The NYU Law School Placement Office told me that it would be "interesting" to see how I did. Like today, government agencies were a good prospect. Early on I pocketed an offer from the Federal Trade Commission in Washington, DC, having enjoyed intellectual property–related courses. But the more I was turned away by the white-shoe law firms (as the large, prestigious Wall Street firms are known) the more determined I became to penetrate that world. "Turned away," by the way, was overwhelmingly by a curt letter of rejection. I received dozens of them—I wish I had saved some. No one back then minded saying, even writing, "Our quota of women is filled." It never crossed my mind, or theirs, that this was blatant gender discrimination. Among the accepted reasons for turning away women lawyers were that clients wouldn't want them; travel, hotel stays, and overnights working at the office or at the printers were unthinkable; and women were interested only in finding husbands and leaving the law.

I was thrilled to be invited back for a second interview—once. It was the firm of Casey, Lane & Mittendorf (no longer in existence), which even had a woman preparing herself for bar admission through law practice, Christine Beshar, who ultimately made her career at Cravath, Swaine & Moore. This was a good sign. The partner who greeted me on that second visit, later US District Judge Robert Sweet, however, had a dismaying message: "My partners insist that I make you this offer, though I find it offensive and hope you will reject it. We are offering your male classmates $7200 [the going rate] and you $6800." Ironically, wonderfully, Judge Sweet decades later employed my daughter as his law clerk.

As I began contemplating where I would live in DC when I worked for the Federal Trade Commission, lightning struck. I had (among other things) sent my résumé to every member of a City Bar Association IP-related committee, which netted me an interview with Sullivan & Cromwell—among the most prestigious of prestigious firms—and ultimately, one glorious day, a job offer at the going rate. Hard for me to believe my response to the hiring partner: "I'll get back to you." What was I thinking? Thank you, Sullivan & Cromwell, for the offer, for tolerating that insipid response, and for nearly two glorious years as the only woman in the Litigation Department (there were two in Trusts and Estates, a traditional place back then for a woman lawyer or two).

I never did take trips with firm clients, but I thoroughly enjoyed my time working with the lawyers in the Litigation Department. I will never forget at the table where S&C lawyers gathered for evening dinners before returning to the office, one night hearing one of the associates, after reviewing the wine list, remark to the waiter, "I see you've brought your '57 reds up to market." I could not imagine a long career there. My job-hunting classmates would ask firms their "attrition rate," meaning what were their chances of becoming a partner. Partnership never crossed my mind—just to have crossed the threshold was monumental.

Several superb gentlemen stand out: Bob MacCrate, with whom I worked on a complex litigation (he encouraged me always to speak up at meetings when I had some-thing to say); Bill Piel, who opened Litigation Department meetings (at a downtown club I had to access through the Ladies' Entrance) with "Gentlemen and Judy"; Michael Cooper, John Cannon, and Paul Grand, three enduring friends; and Stephen Rackow Kaye, whom I married. Oh, and an American Motors salesman, my witness as I defended the company against negligence charges in Queens County Civil Court (one of my two small trials while at S&C; the other was for General Tire, involving the theft of four expensive tires from a turquoise Cadillac parked on a city street—the owner sued the tire company of all things). One evening as we were concluding a court appearance, the American Motors salesman invited me to watch "submarine races" on a ride home with him, which I accepted. I wound up walking a good part of the way back to Manhattan.

Stephen decided to leave Sullivan & Cromwell for Proskauer and, as we contem-plated marriage, it just seemed a better idea, though for me bitterly painful one—in the interest of family harmony—also to go elsewhere. As I said my goodbyes with no further plan in mind—the news of our upcoming marriage was jaw-dropping enough—an S&C lawyer told me that someone had just left the firm for IBM, and I might reach out to him regarding future employment, which I did. That resulted in an interview with one of the most delightful gentlemen I have ever known—Bartow Farr, son of the Willkie, Farr founder; father of preeminent Supreme Court advocate Bartow Farr III; holder of an Actors' Equity card, who had appeared on *Divorce Court*; a genuine character in every sense (emphasis on genuine). Bartow oversaw the IBM in-house counsel staff, and when he extended an offer to join them, I accepted immediately. Again, I cannot imagine what my thought process was—a client's legal department was where firms "farmed out" their exited associates, with the expectation of future business in return. It was not considered "a first-choice" job by any means. My how things have changed.

What fun it was to work with Bartow and others there. As it turns out, I remained with IBM for one year of an incredible array of fascinating legal matters—among them simultaneous translation copyright issues and contracts relating to IBM's entry into the photocopy business—and left late in my first pregnancy. Company policy required departure by the seventh month. Again, how things have changed.

It amazes me, looking back over my half-century as a lawyer, that I happened into such a fortunate succession of positions, none more fortuitous than my post-IBM years (roughly February 1965 to February 1969), during which I had three children (Luisa on March 23, 1965; Jonathan on September 4, 1966; and Gordon on September 17, 1968, three of the happiest days of my life). Simply staying in was the objective. Above all else I feared losing my foothold (more accurately, toehold) in the profession, that if I left for any time I would never be able to return. Having been (generously) turned out by IBM, I showed up on the doorstep of NYU Law School, about eight months pregnant, and learned that Dean Russell Niles was looking for someone to update his real property casebook (ugh), which I enthusiastically agreed to do. It seemed perfect in the circumstances. Luisa was born weeks later, and thankfully, before I got through chapter 1, Niles was installed as president of the Association of the Bar of the City of New York (today the City Bar Association).

I went with him to the association as his assistant, with a beautiful office right across from his and an amazing array of speeches and articles to work on (none on real property law). Every significant issue in the law, in one form or another, hits the City Bar Association. During our two years together, I asked Niles for a modest increase in my modest wages, and he responded, "Just work less." Happily, Stephen and I had a third child. When Niles's City Bar presidency came to an end, he arranged for me to work with Dean Miguel DeCapriles, again on some unusually absorbing research and writing, this time in the area of corporate finance for a conference in Uppsala, Sweden, that he (not I) would be attending. By February 1969, with a six-month-old, two-year old, and three-year-old, I hungered to return to the world of law firms and big-time commercial litigation. We had fortunately found great live-in help—the key to all my subsequent working years—and my Aunt Libby was around to pitch in any time more was needed. Even Stephen agreed it was a good idea.

Thus began my nearly fifteen-year attachment to the firm of Olwine, Connelly, Chase, O'Donnell & Weyher, all male, predominantly Irish and Catholic, one of the offshoots of Cravath, Swaine & Moore. Stephen had called Jack O'Donnell (head of Olwine's Litigation Department), whom he had met on a case, to ask whether the firm might be interested in a part-time litigator at half-salary. I think it was the half-salary that attracted them. What began with three days a week morphed into four, then five and, and, and. In 1969, I was the firm's first female associate; in 1975, I became the firm's first female partner. When I left Olwine for the Court of Appeals in September 1983, Jack called Stephen to ask if he could recommend another part-time litigator. They were losing theirs. (I usually tear up when I say that.)

Olwine was my first face-to-face encounter with daunting women's issues. Until then, I simply accepted that I was privileged to be there—law school, S&C, IBM, NYU—an oddity, with no expectation of advancement to a leadership role. Just as I credit Miss Kitz for adding two years to my education, for my solid toehold in the law—from law school to Olwine—I credit my experience as a journalist or at least the confidence that I was good at ferreting out what's important and writing articulately. Research and writing are, after all, a large part of what lawyers do, especially young lawyers. Until I reached Olwine, and maybe throughout my early years there, my analytical and writing skills earned me the kudos I needed to gain my employers' appreciation, and I was busy with the kids. It wasn't long before I wanted more.

I've spoken about the obstacles and difficulties for women lawyers back in the 1960s and 1970s. Incredible as I look back on them! Long into the 1970s, at the Sky Club where the Olwine partners often lunched, if I was with them we had to sit in the separate Ladies Dining Room across the hall from the main dining facility, which is where you would rather be seen. I was politely disinvited to the firm outing at Piping Rock Country Club because remarks might sometimes get a bit "raunchy" and I would presumably suffer embarrassment if I were there. In later years, when the embarrassment of my exclusion became known, I was—less happily—obliged to go to the firm outing.

I might say, nonworking women friends did not necessarily make it easier. I remember one "friend" telling me that she had seen my daughter at school that day and "she looked so unhappy." What a comfort! An article I did at the time on the value of part-time opportunities for working moms was roundly criticized ("the mommy track") and later, as the new chief judge of the Court of Appeals, when I addressed an annual American Law Institute dinner in Washington, DC, on family law, the *Law Journal* reported the disappointment of women attendees in my choice of subject. We can be very hard on one another.

I'd like to spend just a moment on the other side of the coin—yes, as with most everything in life, there as another side: the positive shock value of being "outstanding," meaning one of a very few. Somewhere along the decades it became desirable to have a woman attorney or two around, and I think I was well regarded as a sound, productive associate. I even survived a few trials second-chairing Jack O'Donnell and Jim Tolan (one against Roy Cohn). I distinctly remember a young female attorney coming into my office one day, closing the door behind her, and saying to me: "You're so prissy. You make me sick." I took that as a compliment—I was throughout it all my genuine self ("hellegant"), while she felt the need to parade as a bitch. She did not last long.

At the firm, Jack O'Donnell headed the litigation practice and the tradition of lunching out as a group on Saturdays. I never went to the lunches. I never showed up at the office on Saturdays. Another of Jack's traditions was never taking a vacation. Busy as we were, Stephen and I always took generous holiday and summer vacations with our children. Once, returning from a long vacation, I poked my head into a filled conference room to greet Jack and let him know I was back. He said, "I have only two words to say to you, young lady: 'Drop dead.'" We took our vacations, and I had my dinners, weekends, and lots of time with the kids. When I found myself in pretrial proceedings in a case removed from Delaware (easily commutable) to Florida, and had to be away from the family Monday to Friday, after a couple of months I simply declared it intolerable, and someone else had to step in. In many ways they just had to live with it, something that likely would not happen today.

Happily, one of my contemporaries was my lifelong friend Charlie McCaghey. Charlie never minced words, within the firm, with clients, or whatever. Fortunately for me, I never had to press for respect or compensation. What he got, I got. Then Charlie became a partner.

Valued as I was as an associate, partnership at Olwine was an entirely different matter. The list of partners was small, the list of waiting associates large, and I had no business of my own. So I read the handwriting on the wall and reached out to a headhunter who put me in touch with Exxon General Counsel, then headquartered in midtown Manhattan. Exxon was eager to have its first woman lawyer and made me a great offer, which I accepted immediately. When I returned to the firm and reported that I was leaving, they went wild and offered me an immediate partnership, leapfrogging over about eight others. Again I am unsure that would be replicated today. Before I accepted, I insisted that the partners confirm that they really, really wanted me as their partner, which they did. In so many ways that was extraordinary good fortune, not the least that Exxon soon moved its corporate headquarters to Houston, Texas.

You never do forget the slights that were so common back then—"Lady, get a lawyer," a court officer once told me; or the judge who took all the lawyers and my client into his chambers for a conference, excluding me because he "did not have a comfortable chair to offer a woman"; or the clients at group meetings who would ask me (the only woman at the table) to make copies of documents or find a phone number for them, until they were made aware of my hourly billing rate for those services. When I tried checking into a Florida hotel for an unanticipated overnight on a case, the steely eyed receptionist asked, "Do you have any luggage?" He thought I had come to work the hotel as an escort, as it was the site of an American Legion convention.

Did I respond meaningfully to the insults within and outside the firm? Did I ask someone to give me legal business? No, I never would have done that. Today the law and the culture expect and demand both. But I sensed that my presence and performance were noted in positive ways, too, especially by other women I encountered in litigation, few though we were. Marcia Goldstein, a prominent bankruptcy lawyer at Weil Gotshal, introduced me at a conference and noted that I was the first woman she observed conducting serious proceedings in a bankruptcy courtroom; so did Betsy Siedman. To learn that my courtroom presence and performance were important to them pleases me greatly.

I happen to remember well those cases. The bankruptcy matter was for the Lionel Corporation, a firm client, and more—several of the Olwine partners had been Lionel investors, but the other parties chose to waive any conflict and allow the firm to remain as counsel in the litigation. Bankruptcy at the time was not the jewel it is today. It was more of a bazaar—what an experience! Leonard Connolly (who did the corporate work) and I (the litigator) often commiserated: "How did two nice people like us get involved in a mess like this?" We managed to get the corporation through Chapter 11—once. It pleased me later to learn that the adversaries referred to me as "D.L."—Dragon Lady. Yes, you can be prissy and a dragon lady at the same time!

I first encountered Betsy Siedman when our firm represented the New York Produce Exchange (predecessor to the Commodities Exchange) in the last case flowing out of "the great salad oil swindle," about which books have been written. We had a six-week jury trial before Judge Robert Carter, where I worked with my later Court of Appeals colleague (then a Paul Weiss associate) Robert Smith. Amazingly, co-counsel (from several large law firms) chose me to argue for the entire team in the Second Circuit. If we hadn't prevailed, I wouldn't be telling this story. Charlotte Fishman and I were co-counsel, battling a tender offer that exploded into a half-dozen or more litigations in state and federal courts in several jurisdictions. I litigated a case with Hughes Hubbard, Amalya Kearse's firm, the start of a long friendship. Every one of the few women I encountered in court I remember with clarity, as they remember me.

Largely Olwine was in federal court, escaping pre–Commercial Division state court at every opportunity. The most comprehensive lessons I received in being a trial lawyer were at the hands of US District Court Judges Milton Pollack, Charles Brieant, and Edward Weinfeld. They were tough judges and good teachers. The first matter was a feisty litigation that settled just before trial, and the latter two bitterly contested jury trials fought to the end. Judge Brieant's was a tax case concerning (of all things) the depreciation rate for ornamental stone used in asphalt shingles. I think the firm handed me that case because of its apparent hopelessness. When the client complained that one of the jurors kept nodding off, I told him how amazing it was that the others remained awake. It definitely pepped him up when we prevailed at trial and were affirmed by the Second Circuit.

I don't know which was the greatest joy in the Judge Weinfeld matter—that Weinfeld (a legendary jurist) at the end complimented my adversary and me for having done a superb job (immediately I secured the page of the transcript, which to this day proudly hangs on my office wall), or that my adversary's client subsequently sued his firm for malpractice; or that it was my own client (Bartow Farr's post-IBM employer, the Singer Company) for whom I netted the victory. I'll be honest—definitely the third. Nothing quite as sweet as trouncing the adversary for your own client.

In yet another respect (the first being the lack of face-to-face personal sociability), I find that law firm culture has changed radically from my last round. I recognize that it was a huge plus to bring in business, to be a "rainmaker." It's something that was especially important to Stephen, to his very last days. He felt it gave him independence and freedom, which it undeniably does. Yet back then, in addition to the finders, there were the valued "minders" and "grinders," and I clearly fell into the latter categories. Now the day-and-night drive is having, finding, pitching for clients. It's not just independence and freedom anymore, it's life and death. The other night at an event, a seasoned female litigator from another firm and I greeted the general counsel of a major client of each of our firms. In a flash, she told him, with a bright smile, how pleased she was to be handling his matter and added, "We'd love more." Impressive. Never miss an opportunity. Still hard for me.

I've been back and forth on whether I am happier or unhappier with not having kept any record of how I managed that critical decade or so, from my Olwine awakening to arrival on the Court of Appeals, and here I have in mind the gut-grinding family issues. I cannot imagine life without my fabulous children and grandchildren. These continue to be among the toughest issues of all for women lawyers. Plainly both Stephen and I worked hard back then, Stephen most weekends as well as long days. In addition to a healthy caseload, I became active at the City Bar Association (ultimately winding up on the executive committee), the State Bar Association (many committees), the Legal Aid Society (a board member, ultimately vice president), the American Law Institute Council, and goodness knows what more. I even took one pro bono criminal assignment in the Eastern District, just to get a bit of criminal law experience. (I could use my central argument only once though: "If this was a really serious criminal case, Your Honor, they never would have assigned it to me.")

During this period, Stephen and I made several conscious decisions to remain living in the middle of Manhattan. With the birth of our second child, Jonathan, we moved from the East Side (where Stephen had grown up) to the Upper West Side, where we have remained ever since. From time to time we reevaluated these choices as friends with young children moved to the suburbs, but we steadfastly remained on the Upper West Side, giving us maximum family time around which to arrange professional commitments. Although all three children began at the Ethical Culture School right down the street from our apartment, Luisa and Jonathan transferred to the Dalton School, and Gordie transferred to Choate when my Albany absences would have left him basically alone at home. Luisa went on to Amherst and NYU Law School, Jonathan to Cornell and a Ph.D. from the University of Pennsylvania, and Gordie to Hamilton, a master's in sports administration from Indiana University, and an MBA from Columbia. Later, there were three glorious weddings—Luisa and Jan (now divorced), Jonathan and Nielufar, Gordie and Anna; and then seven spectacular grandchildren (Sonja, Andrea, Bennett— "the Prince," the only boy; Shirin and Shayna; Amelia and Stella).

Yet I remember—and hope and believe that my wonderful children would confirm—that throughout we had an active, strong family life, in addition to significant vacation time, being home together weekends and for dinner most evenings, even if it meant returning to the office afterward (as Stephen inevitably, and I sometimes, did). But no cell phone or email accessibility! I remember Gordie, age seven or so, calling one day when I was in a large conference—the instruction always was to interrupt if it was one of my children on the phone—to ask if I knew where his other sneaker was. And I did! Just a small sample of how involved we were in our kids' lives despite considerable professional pressures. I tried never to miss the conferences, concerts, swim meets, school, and other events important to them. I loved being "Mommy." And I loved being a law firm partner and active bar leader.

Chapter 12

One Continuous Role

As a Woman

Given my *Times* quotation of the day ("I take my gender with me wherever I go"), this seems a fair subject on which to conclude the section titled "Who I Am." Plainly we all take our gender, our upbringing, our ethnicity, and our occupational and personal experiences with us wherever we go. Thankfully, in recent years, we have come to recognize the desirability of a diverse legal profession and diverse judiciary, for judges in particular enriching rather than prejudicing their determinations.

Memorable as my early years as a woman lawyer were in a negative sense, I unquestionably reaped a benefit once people began to remember that there are indeed two genders. Regrettably, being a woman in the law world is still a less than entirely happy subject. Among women today, lawyers unquestionably have the very best of it. I note a number of recent women's events.

My personal zenith was a ceremony at the Court of Appeals on October 14, 2011. It all began with Susan Dautel, a Court of Appeals assistant deputy clerk, inviting me on behalf of the Capital District Women's Bar Association to be the subject of a continuing legal education program (CLE) in the courtroom centering on my portrait (the first of a woman; the first portrait to include a judge's spouse, children, and grandchildren, instead of just books). My portrait had gone up several months earlier, unheralded, as portrait installations at the Court of Appeals always are. They are simply installed within the frames that are part of the magnificent walls. I especially wanted my portrait to be hung immediately and unceremoniously, because viewers would not be able to tell that it was exceptionally flattering likeness of me.

Susan proposed that the program be called "Portrait of a Judge." My response was outright rejection of the idea but thankfully she (with the assistance of Dana Salazar, one of Court of Appeals Judge Susan Read's former law clerks) persisted, and persisted as well with the court—the courtroom is rarely if ever given over to outside events. The result was official installation of the portrait by the court (thank you especially to Chief Judge Lippman and Clerk of the Court Andrew Klein), with the present and former judges in attendance—that was great!—followed by the CLE program.

I did not fully appreciate how magnificently the Women's Bar program was conceived and executed until it was over—first an introduction to the Court's portrait collection by Judge Read; then virtually an hour each by Brooklyn Law School Professor/NYCLU President Susan Herman on my jurisprudence and Judge/Judicial Institute Dean Juanita Newton on my Access to Justice reforms; concluding with a panel of women "of a certain age," who had succeeded as law firm partners and judges despite gender obstacles, engagingly presided over by Albany Law School Professor Patrick Connors (a former Dick Simons law clerk). It would be everyone's dream to have your life work portrayed as they did mine—Herman's breathtaking tribute was even published in the *Albany Law Review*! At the end of the program, someone looked out the window and noticed that there was a rainbow over the courthouse, and it was immediately evident that the proverbial pot of gold was right there.

The unanimous view of the panel was that much has changed for women in the law, though much remains the same—the gender bias is just more subtle, more nuanced today. But for me the air sparkled with the panelists' optimism: we've been all over the profession, all over the state, these past decades and yes, it's really tough; we've had bad days, we get through them; learn how to respond meaningfully to the slurs and slights, but never miss a chance to do so; take every opportunity for guidance and mentoring—we're there for you; find your own style and stick with it; live with your choices and don't torture yourself about them; hang in there, persevere. My life experience, personal and professional, has shown me that credit and opportunity go to people who claim them, demand them, absolutely insist on their right to have them, and never give up. If you want something, you can't be passive. You have to ask for it. Rarely do advantage, credit, and opportunity simply flow naturally from talent or good deeds. It's something women especially need to know and do in balanced, positive ways, in the legal profession and beyond.

That these messages were delivered against the backdrop of the dedication of the portrait of a woman—any woman—who has reached a significant position gave them unique context and credibility. Yes, you can be a chief judge. You can travel from rural Maplewood (or wherever) to the center seat of the state's highest court. You can have the life evidenced by the canvas portrait (including children and grandchildren) and the verbal portrait. The opportunities for a satisfying personal and professional life are there for you. If you are unduly negative, if you unnecessarily close doors, you may miss that pot of gold at the end of a rainbow.

Coincidentally, at around the same time as the Albany program, the *New York Times* turned again and again to the subject of gender. On Sunday, October 9, 2011, an editorial celebrated the thirtieth anniversary of the arrival of Sandra Day O'Connor on the US Supreme Court—our nation's first female justice on the Court. The editorial, however, was hardly celebratory. Instead, it recited the grim statistics on the "cracking" but not yet "shattering" of the law world's glass ceiling, concluding that unless legal employers retain a higher share of women, the profession will continue to lose talented lawyers and lose the opportunity for gender equality that O'Connor's appointment had signaled. It is indeed remarkable (the editorial points out) that as women have been about half of law school graduates for close to thirty years, still today they are only 15 percent of equity partners in law firms (6 percent in our nation's largest firms) and less than a quarter in our judiciary, and women with children have the hardest time even remaining in the profession. The editorial argued for flexible schedules, for men as well as women, as well as transparent systems for evaluating, assigning, and paying lawyers. The battle goes on.

Weeks later, on October 28, 2011, the *Times*'s "Business Day" section featured IBM's new chief executive, Ginni Rometty, under the headline "For Incoming IBM Chief, Self-Confidence Rewarded." The article (written by a woman, Claire Cain Miller) (brava!) began with the fact that when Rometty was offered a big job early in her career, she told the recruiter that she needed more time to think about it because she felt that she lacked sufficient experience. Her husband asked, "Do you think a man would have ever answered the question that way?" That led her to the perception that you have to be outwardly self-confident, whatever your gut may be telling you about what you don't know. Though featuring Rometty, the article really was all about self-confidence, risk, and reward for women in the business world, an important subject today, particularly at a time when corporations—and derivatively their lawyers—have begun to truly recognize the value of diversity.

Wouldn't you know it, the *Times* followed up a week or so later (November 5, 2011), with a large photo of Rometty and a very different, equally fascinating theme. In an article by James B. Stewart, Rometty gives full credit to her top aide, her husband, for pursuing a career that gave him time and flexibility to support her ascension to the pinnacle of the global business world, not unlike the vast majority of CEO spouses. The Romettys are, by the way, childless. The article notes that for women in this CEO category, divorce is relatively rare. It references books and studies on the engrossing subject of family life balance, as do the prior article and the editorial. All three pieces could have cited an intriguing book, *Courageous Counsel* (I wrote the foreword, at the invitation of the coauthors), that emerged in these same weeks—the biographies of a new phenomenon, women general counsels of Fortune 500 companies. The October issue of *Fortune* magazine featured "The 50 Most Powerful Women" in the United States, including fifteen CEOs of Fortune 500 companies (up from two when the list debuted in 1998), lamenting that the percentages are still very low.

I could go on and on with this avalanche of "women" stuff—my own raised consciousness, or truly a new day?—but I will stop with the *60 Minutes* interview of Christine Lagarde, managing director of the International Monetary Fund. She's a knockout on all fronts, including sartorial. Her observations regarding Lehman Brothers (she would have saved it) and the need for better regulation earlier reminded me of Brooksley Born's lone call years ago for greater market regulation. Would (more) women in powerful Wall Street positions have made a difference? To this day, they are still too few and far between. In a small way, in my own world, Christine Lagarde and Brooksley Born reminded me of a dissent I wrote years ago questioning the electronic bundling of mortgages, which I thought posed a danger for borrowers that the legislature should look into, but no one listened (*Merscorp v. Romaine* [8 NY3d (2006)]). Today I see massive damages being paid by banks as a consequence of state and federal prosecutions challenging their bundling and sale of residential mortgage-backed securities. Pity no one bothered to take a look back then.

Would the world not be in such shambles today with more women leaders? As Harvard University psychologist Steven Pinker has noted in his book *The Better Angels of Our Nature* (Penguin, 2011), the parts of the world that lag in the decline of violence are also the parts that lag in the empowerment of women. We are different, by birth, by experience, or both. Having just encountered a Harvard study by Jack Zenger and Joseph Folkman documenting that women are viewed as better leaders overall, I would have to say unequivocally that the world would indeed be a better place with more women in leadership positions or with equal opportunity to reach them.

I regret not having better answers to questions I am often asked by young women about the daunting family and work balance issue. Most often I answer, jokingly, that the only advice I give to women lawyers is never buy a wrap skirt. I don't mean to be flippant. It's just that I have no good answer—these are immensely personal dilemmas to be resolved within families. I genuinely believe that it's harder on the moms than it is on the kids. Despite wild tantrums before I left the house, once the door closed behind me, I was satisfied that the kids were fine. I have even fewer answers for the working mothers, often single, without reliable care for their children, for whom the choices are heartbreaking and the struggle monumental.

In the back of a taxicab one day, I caught a bit of serious radio commentary on the general history of women moving into the labor force, starting in the 1970s, for a full life. The point the speaker was making was that it was the women who had traditionally held the families together, their mates not playing an equal role at home. He had no good answer to the current dilemma, observing that that balance has not changed appreciably. Though you do see different models, with the woman as principal wage-earner (with or without children), decades later it's still predominantly (in male-female-parented families) the dad in charge of putting the bread on the table, the mom of serving it. In a way, it's even harder in the legal field today, with Grandma a law firm partner, or chief judge or general counsel, unable to pitch in as grandmothers did in days past. Surely we need better balance, and I do not know the key to comprehensive change, if indeed there is one.

So how do we have something roughly equivalent to our male counterparts—in other words, equal opportunity for what satisfies us as a full life? How do we bring our special talents, our perspective, life experience, innate nature to leadership positions in the profession, to benefit society, to make this a better world? How do we get a fair shake?

Bringing my chief judgely optimism to the question, I would start with the numbers. Numbers matter. The fact that half or more of law school classes are female, the fact that increasing numbers are making those headline breakthroughs to chief judge, partnership, dean, general counsel, CEO just has to make a difference. There is first and foremost the fact that there are more of us, as groups and as individuals, to stand as models to show it can be done, to share our experiences, to commiserate, to mentor, to help other women through that glass ceiling. (Isn't glass a symbol of fragility? It's in fact a ceiling packed with men.) As a Court of Appeals judge, I remember the sheer joy of Carmen Ciparick's arrival—then Judges Victoria Graffeo and Susan Phillips Read—joining the court. To this day, frequent calls from and dinners with Carmen, visits and even a singing Valentine from Vicki, ballet invitations from Susan are uniquely cheering, afterlife-sustaining.

In numbers, there is not only the pleasure of shared experiences but also shared pride and strength, emboldening us to act and take risks we might otherwise have declined. During my fifteen chief judge years, as I watched the composition of the nationwide Chief Justices Conference genderize, I saw shifts in approaches such as restorative justice, problem-solving courts, and children's commissions. In my mind I cannot disconnect initiatives such as these from the rising numbers of women chiefs. Even on the Lincoln Center Board, the female chair has brought a new level of personal connection and inter-action to meetings that supplement the relentless drive for funds. Whether or not we are innately different, whether or not we are indeed the "better angels," women's experience surely has made us different. We deserve an equal spot, we have something—a lot—to contribute, and having risen through the ranks we are there to be an integral part as leaders and colleagues, not simply paid assistants.

Hopefully, with more of us in leadership positions at institutions, we also can be more attentive to the special challenges of family and work balance, as well as the opportunities offered by technology today. As one of my former law clerks, a partner in a large law firm, told me, she needs to know only her associates' family limitations—given modern technology, they can work within them. A good message. As with the pressure for diversity generally within the profession, the women in power simply have to be on the front line on this issue for there to be meaningful change. It matters that there are sensitized women on policy committees, on pitches, seen and heard with respect to critical decision making. While "reentry" after significant time at home still has proved generally unworkable for women, its time has come, to add yet another choice for those who feel the need to leave the front lines for a while without career-killing effect.

One thing is for sure: as important as it is for women, organized and individual women, to change the grim picture, it matters equally that there are powerful, sensitized men, preferably with wives, mothers, and daughters seeking a full life, in all of the above. I have twice recently seen the changed tone of such sessions when supportive men are also at the table. The first time was a meeting with law firm women partners in another city, meaningfully joined by the male head of the local office. All-women women's committees at law firms are not the right message or messenger. The problem crosses gender lines. The second time was my extraordinary visit to Mexico City, when I looked across the table of women law firm associates to the genuinely caring male associate and realized how significant his presence was. His wife has an advanced degree in finance, and although they do not yet have a family, the family-work balance subject clearly is on his mind as well. It will, after all, affect his life, personally and professionally. We need more of that.

We need the strength and self-esteem offered by increasing numbers of success-ful women in the profession and by associations of all sorts, women's associations and others—whatever works for us individually. We need to engage men to help change those statistics, for their good as well as ours. But the fact that we are still knee-deep in this dialogue, the fact that the numbers are still so daunting, to me signals the need to underscore the most important message of all: that each of us needs to maintain a positive attitude and stay in the game, however tenuous the toehold. If you are not there, you have absolutely no chance for a miracle to befall you or for lightning to strike. You have no shot at that pot of gold at the end of the rainbow—whatever that means for you. That is the simplest, profoundest, inarguable truth.

In one respect I end this writing as my life will: widowed and often overcome with profound aloneness despite continuing professional engagement and the love and attention of my incredible grandchildren, children, family, and friends. If nothing else,

I recognize that my medical condition probably seals my fate in this respect, but I want to put that aside for the moment and speak more generally to another sort of gender disparity at this stage of life.

Despite treasured visits with my family and women friends, more and more as the weeks, months, and years pass, I yearn for my partner, for *a* partner, a man with whom I might share an evening, someone to dress up for, banter or make plans with. It's just different. Yesterday after brunch I enviously watched the back-and-forth of two contemporaries—each widowed, now a couple, though living separately—about how they would pass the next hours of a glorious Sunday afternoon together. I went to the office, always a good refuge, knowing how fortunate I am to have that option.

I recognize that at the time of Stephen's death, I was chief judge—a bit intimidating, even off-putting—and one or two men did make oblique suggestions that might perhaps have been offers of a date. I wasn't sure and decided not to seek clarification. One of them has just written me of his exotic marriage plans, including a transatlantic luxury liner voyage. I'm glad I didn't seek clarification. Perhaps there were more, but I don't think so. I remember Stephen once asking me—since as a lawyer I traveled often for business—whether anyone ever had made a pass at me. I thought that was a sweet question, after decades of marriage. I responded honestly: "If anyone did, I didn't notice." Someone must have made a pass, I think today. I'm just not good at projecting or even noticing that sort of interest.

Anyway, once again I think it's a lot harder for widows. On the surface we seem effortlessly to step into the role of taking care of ourselves; men are just so much more obviously lost and needy. But there's a lot more to losing a soulmate than the grocery shopping and dry cleaning.

This "true confessions" segment is the social afterlife of a long-married, recently widowed woman of seventy-six years, apparently healthy (I have my voice, hair, and energy back), plainly secure financially, intellectually, and professionally. As I have seen, my male equivalent gets swamped, eaten alive by women virtually the second he comes back "on the market." At the shiva for a friend, I watched someone try to pass a phone number to the grieving husband. (He has since remarried, though not to that particularly opportunistic lady.) I've seen male friends—after decades of blissful marriage—move again into blissful relationships after the deaths of their wives, traveling to distant places I yearn to go (but not alone), organizing dinner dates with other couple friends, or just holding hands on the street or at public events. From the new David Dorsen book on Henry Friendly (Belknap Press, 2012), I learned that after the death of the judge's long-time beloved spouse, it was in his words "widows, widows, widows" flinging themselves and being flung at him. For me, none.

Though they may founder for a time, if a widower of seventy-five or older has any stature (and I don't mean height—that's irrelevant), he's a huge target, even for much younger women. With hair and money, he's a rock star. Were the situation reversed, I have no doubt that Stephen would have been besieged. The least narcissistic, most modest, bereaved man would have to be blown away by the attention and opportunities, even though the hourly rate for services rendered, particularly across generations, may be high. A couple of eightyish men I know have babies.

Then I had an epiphany. At a museum event where I serve as a trustee, I was approached by a gentleman I did not immediately recognize, but shortly did, as a childhood friend. He teared up when he told me of the recent death of his wife. Instantly one of the women with whom I was chatting pulled out her card and said, "I'm single, too. Give me a call." And then it hit me, as I was reminded of the lawyer not missing a beat in thanking the general counsel for business and adding, "We'd like more." It's the pitch! The pitch, risk-taking, and relentless perseverance—a modern-day necessity for women, whether their objective is personal or professional.

Wonder of wonders, I reached this point in my story when I encountered a slew of significant writings on the subject of women—Debora Spar's book (*Wonder Women: Sex, Power and the Quest for Perfection*; Picador, 2013) and Sheryl Sandberg's *Lean In* (Knopf, 2013) highly informative and impactful. They brought back Anne-Marie Slaughter's attention-grabbing article, "Why Women Still Can't Have It All," leading *Atlantic*'s July–August 2012 "Ideas Issue." The title upset me. What is the meaning of "all," anyway? How many of us in the world have it—male or female? Though her stated objective is to offer sympathy to women feeling they have to drop out (it's not their fault), in fact it's a distressing message for young women contemplating the vexing family-work balance issues, especially at a time when our progress to leadership positions, though still disappointing, is becoming more visible.

As the Slaughter describes herself, she is a tenured professor at Princeton University (former dean of Princeton's Woodrow Wilson School of Public and International Affairs), teaching a full course load, writing regular print and online columns on foreign policy, giving forty to fifty speeches a year, appearing regularly on TV and radio, and working on a book. She enjoyed a two-year leave from Princeton (the university policy for tenured professors) to be the first woman director of policy planning at the State Department ("a foreign-policy dream job"). She has a great marriage to another Princeton professor (noting the flexibility academics have in setting their own schedules), "who has always done everything possible to support [her] career," including caring for their children She looks great.

This is not "all" at this stage of her life? Reminds me of the debate over what the meaning of "is" is. Among the examples she uses to prove her negative conclusion is Ruth Bader Ginsburg, "who began her career as a judge only when her younger child was almost grown," ignoring the significant child-rearing years during which Ginsburg had to distinguish herself elsewhere in the profession. Several times the author rips into Sheryl Sandberg's 2011 Barnard commencement message, in effect that we can have it all. This is not what young people most need to hear at a critical time in their lives.

When I returned to the article some days later, and carefully read through to the end, I saw that the author and I are in substantial agreement about the picture, meaning what needs to be done—by men and women—to continue the trajectory of progress toward gender parity. I would have selected a different frame for the picture. No need to be so negative, and a definite need to be more positive, to encourage more risk-taking. That there are now choices women can successfully make—we have the evidence—is progress. It's good news, not bad.

But guess what: I am now at peace with her choice of the frame. You don't get the buzz Slaughter has garnered with a positive message. You need spice, controversy, to earn a cover story. I bought several copies of the magazine for friends. I like the hard copy (you're welcome, *Atlantic*), especially the image projected by the color photo of the author with her sons in a comfortable, lovely home. I've followed the buzz—largely female, largely outraged. We do need attention—it's a key to reform.

The fact is that both extremes—you can or can't have it "all," whatever "all" might be at any stage or circumstance of a person's life—are equally fatuous (a word used in her article). The decisions are so individual, and at least in the legal profession we have terrific role models for a full range of difficult personal life choices, including single, cohabiting, married (same-sex or otherwise), divorced, and widowed women with(out) children; tech-savvy (or not) full-time and part-time working women; stay-at-home moms, with(out) crammed pro bono schedules; primary wage-earner women with stay-at-home partners; and women with career- and child-supportive working partners. We even have great examples of wise Latinas, African American, and other women across a racial and ethnic spectrum.

What's important today is the discussion, the consciousness raising, the ideas and the inspiration, whether individual or organizational, for leadership, mentorship, sponsorship, and above all change that will enable us to have the confidence in ourselves and opportunity we need to achieve a secure, satisfying, personally meaningful life. That's "all."

POSTSCRIPT

As I turn back to the opening pages, this indeed was the time to write about my life. It has been personally satisfying, even strengthening, to look back on decisions made and not made, paths taken and not taken. Cancer treatment, concerns about my children, loneliness—in life no one gets away with nothing. But whether connecting dots, aligning stars, or weaving tapestries, I can only celebrate the bold choices that brought me at age sixteen from rural Monticello to Barnard College and kept me in New York City despite several diversions; from the *Hudson Dispatch* of Union City, New Jersey, to night law school and the practice of law; to the attention of a remarkable, courageous governor who not once but twice handed me the keys to lawyer heaven; and beyond all else to an extraordinary husband, children, and grandchildren.

If this were the last day of my life, I'd be OK doing what I am about to do today.

CITATIONS TO CASES
AND OTHER MATERIALS

Cases

Board of Education, Levittown Union Free School District et al. v. Nyquist, 57 NY2d 27 (1982)

Bovsun v. Sanperi, 61 NY2d 219 (1984)

Braschi v. Stahl Associates, 74 NY2d 201 (1989)

Braten v. Bankers Trust, 60 NY2d 155 (1983), reargument denied 61 NY2d 670 (1984)

Brown v. Board of Education, 347 US 483 (1954)

Campaign for Fiscal Equity, Inc. v. State of New York, 86 NY2d 307 (1995) (CFE I); 100 NY2d 893 (2003) (CFE II); 8 NY3d 14 (2006) (CFE III)

Campbell v. Pesce, 60 NY2d 165 (1983)

Consolidated Edison Co. of N.Y. v. Town of Red Hook, 60 NY2d 99 (1983)

Daimler AG v. Bauman, 134 S. Ct. 746 (2014)

DeLong v. County of Erie, 60 NY2d 296 (1983)

Gideon v. Wainwright, 372 US 335 (1963)

Graham v. Florida, 130 S. Ct. 2011 (2010)

Greenfield v. Philles Records, 98 NY2d 562 (2002)

Gregg v. Georgia, 428 US 153 (1976)

Hernandez v. Robles, 7 NY3d 338 (2006)

Humphrey v. State of New York, 60 NY2d 742 (1983)

Immuno AG v. Moor-Jankowski, 74 NY2d 548 (1989); 497 US 1021 (1990); 77 NY2d 235 (1991)

Koehler v. Bank of Bermuda, 12 NY3d 533 (2009)

Lawrence v. Texas, 539 US 558 (2003)

Loving v. Virginia, 388 US 1 (1967)

Massachusetts v. Upton, 466 US 727 (1984)

Matter of Alessi, 60 NY2d 229 (1983)

Matter of Alison D., 77 NY2d 651 (1991)

Matter of Jacob, 86 NY2d 651 (1995)

Matter of Joyce T., 65 NY2d 39 (1985)

Matter of Levandusky v. One Fifth Ave. Apt. Corp., 75 NY2d 530 (1990)

Matter of Male Infant L., 61 NY2d 420 (1984)

Matter of New York Statewide Coalition of Hispanic Chambers of Commerce, et al. v. New York City Dept. of Health & Mental Hygiene, 23 NY3d 681 (2014)

Matter of Sarah K., 66 NY2d 223 (1985)

Matter of Schumer v. Holtzman, 60 NY2d 46 (1983)

Matter of Silverman (Benmor Coats), 61 NY2d 299 (1984)

Matter of Suffolk Outdoor Advertising v. Town of Southampton, 60 NY2d 70 (1983)

Matter of Teachers Ins. & Annuity Assn. of Am. v. City of New York, 82 NY2d 35 (1993)

Merscorp, Inc. v. Romaine, 8 NY3d 90 (2006)

Michigan v. Long, 463 US 1032 (1983)

Milkovich v. Lorain Journal Co., 497 US 1 (1990)

Miller v. Alabama, 132 S. Ct. 2455 (2012)

Motorola Credit Corp. v. Standard Chartered Bank, 771 F.3d 160 (2014)

Nicholson v. Scoppetta, 3 NY3d 357 (2004)

Pataki v. New York State Assembly, 4 NY3d 75 (2004)

People v. Antommarchi, 80 NY2d 247 (1992)

People v. Cahill, 2 NY3d 14 (2003)

People v. Class, 63 NY2d 491 (1984), reversed and remanded sub nom. *New York v. Class*, 475 US 106 (1986), on remand 67 NY2d 431 (1986)

People v. Cofresi, 60 NY2d 728 (1983)

People v. Consolazio, 40 NY2d 446 (1976)

People v. Cruz, 66 NY2d 61 (1985), reversed sub nom. *Cruz v. New York*, 481 US 186 (1987)

People v. Feingold, 7 NY3d 288 (2006)

People v. Harris, 98 NY2d 452 (2002)

People v. Heidgen, 22 NY3d 259 (2013)

People v. Jackson, 78 NY2d 638 (1991)

People v. LaValle, 3 NY3d 88 (2004)

People v. Maldonado, 24 NY3d 48 (2014)

People v. Mateo, 2 NY3d 383 (2004)

People v. Mitchell, 80 NY2d 519 (1992)

People v. Onofre, 51 NY2d 476 (1980)

People v. P.J. Video, 68 NY2d 296 (1986)

People v. Register, 60 NY2d 270 (1983)

People v. Rosario, 9 NY2d 286 (1961)

People v. Shulman, 6 NY3d 1 (2005)

People v. Smith, 63 NY2d 41 (1984), cert. denied, 469 US 1227 (1985)

People v. Taylor, 9 NY3d 129 (2007)

People v. Weaver, 12 NY3d 433 (2009)

Sega v. State of New York, 60 NY2d 183 (1983)

Suffolk Outdoor Advertising v. Hulse, 43 NY2d 483 (1977)

Symphony Space v. Pergola Properties, 88 NY2d 466 (1996)

United States v. Jones, 565 US 400 (2012)

United States v. Windsor, 133 S. Ct. 2675 (2013)

Vermont Teddy Bear Co. v. 538 Madison Realty Co., 1 NY3d 470 (2004)

W.W.W. Assoc. v. Giancontieri, 77 NY2d 157 (1990)

Other Materials

Brennan, William J., Jr. "State Constitutions and the Protection of Individual Rights." *Harvard Law Review* 90, no. 489 (1977).

Cardozo, Benjamin N. *The Nature of the Judicial Process*. New Haven: Yale University Press, 1921.

Dewitt, Karen. "Lt. Gov. Ravitch Working on State Borrowing Bailout Plan." *WXXI News*, March 10, 2010. http://wxxinews.org/post/ravitch-presents-bail-out-plan (accessed August 26, 2014).

Dicker, Sheryl. *Reversing the Odds: Improving Outcomes for Babies in the Child Welfare System*. Baltimore: Paul H. Brookes Publishing Company, 2009.

Gikow, Louise A., Kathy Rodgers, and Lynn Hecht Schafran. *Women: A Celebration of Strength*. New York: Legal Momentum, 2007.

Haig, Robert L. *Commercial Litigation in New York State Courts*. New York: West Publishing Company, 1995.

Herman, Susan. "Portrait of a Judge: Judith S. Kaye, Dichotomies, and State Constitutional Law." *Albany Law Review* 75, no. 1977 (2012).

Kaye, Judith S. "The Supreme Court and Juvenile Justice." *Journal of Supreme Court History* 36, no. 62 (March 2011).

Lewis, Anthony. *Make No Law: The Sullivan Case and the First Amendment*. New York: Random House, 1991.

Pinker, Steven. *The Better Angels of Our Nature*. New York: Penguin, 2011.

Rosenblatt, Albert M., and Judith S. Kaye. *The Judges of the New York Court of Appeals: A Biographical History*. New York: Fordham University Press, 2007.

Spar, Debora L. *Wonder Women: Sex, Power, and the Quest for Perfection*. New York: Sarah Crichton Books, 2013.

OPINIONS

INTRODUCTION

Honorable Albert M. Rosenblatt

The decisions of Chief Judge Judith S. Kaye graced the New York reports from her first writing, published in October 1983, until her last, on December 17, 2008, spanning fifty-two volumes, from 60 NY 2d to 11 NY 3d. It is a vast array of wisdom and scholarship covering an even quarter of a century. In all, she authored some 627 writings with an interesting breakdown: of her total judicial output, she wrote for the court's majority 522 times (some 83 percent of the time), dissenting 77 times and concurring 28 times. Her colleagues would say that this speaks to her collegiality and credibility. Every writing reflects her masterful choice of words, her unerring logic, and her consummate sense of fairness. Although all her writings are important, we have selected a sampling of the most revealing or eminent to include here.

As many know, the relationship between judges and their law clerks is close and abiding; occasionally they are called "confidential law clerks," signifying the importance of discretion and fidelity. Often, and surely in Judge Kaye's chambers, the law clerks were part of a family that adored their "boss." She was, after all, in charge of the operation and the product, but the relationships were marked by enduring friendship, personal regard, and deep affection in both directions.

We thought it apt, in selecting these cases, that the introductions should be made by Judge Kaye's law clerks, and in many cases by the clerk who worked on the case. In keeping with their pledges and sense of propriety, they tell no tales out of school but are well situated to make general comments about the nature of each decision. We have included their names accordingly, with our appreciation.

If readers note the exquisite editing and formatting of the selected cases, it is with our hearty thanks to William J. Hooks, former state reporter, Law Reporting Bureau, New York State Court of Appeals, and his talented staff.

People v. Class,
63 NY2d 491 (1984), rev'd 475 US 106 (1986)

Very early in her tenure on the Court of Appeals, Judge Kaye received a lesson in the importance of carefully stating the reasons for a higher state constitutional ceiling from an unexpected source, the US Supreme Court. In *People v. Class*, a divided court reversed a criminal conviction based on both the Fourth Amendment to the US Constitution and the identically worded article 1, § 12 of the New York State Constitution. Justice Sandra Day O'Connor wrote the opinion reversing and remanding *Class*, holding in pertinent part that the decision of the New York Court of Appeals did not rest on an adequate and independent state ground. Writing about *Class* in an essay for *The Green Bag*, Judge Kaye wrote that "back in Chambers, I was teased that the 'Grandmother of Justice' had just reversed the 'Mother of Justice.'" (Judith S. Kaye, *The Brennan Lecture—A Bit of History*, 17 Green Bag 2d 133, 134 [Winter 2014].) On remand in *Class*, the Court of Appeals unanimously upheld its earlier determination, this time solely on state grounds.

—Introduction by Jennifer L. Smith, worked with Judge Kaye
at Skadden, Arps, Slate, Meagher & Flom LLP 2012–2016

A police officer's nonconsensual entry into an individual's automobile to determine the vehicle identification number violates the Federal and State Constitutions where it is based solely on a stop for a traffic infraction (US Const, 4th Amend; NY Const, art I, § 12).

On May 11, 1981, in the late afternoon, Police Officers Lawrence Meyer and William McNamee observed defendant driving 5 to 10 miles per hour above the speed limit, in a car with the windshield cracked on the passenger side. The officers drove alongside defendant's car and instructed him to pull over. Defendant followed this directive, emerged from his car and approached Officer Meyer, the driver of the police car. He provided Meyer with his registration and proof of insurance but stated that he did not have a driver's license in his possession. Meanwhile, Officer McNamee had gone directly to defendant's car, opened the door and checked the left door jamb for the vehicle identification number (VIN). Since the VIN was not located on the door jamb, McNamee reached in and moved papers on the dashboard to enable him to view the VIN. In doing so, he saw a handle of a gun protruding from underneath the seat, seized it, and defendant was promptly arrested.

The hearing court denied defendant's motion to suppress the gun. Although the court concluded that the officers had "no reason to believe the vehicle . . . was stolen" when defendant was stopped, it found their action reasonable in light of defendant's "immediately exiting the car and walking over to the police car, instead of waiting in his automobile, coupled with the fact that the defendant did not have a driver's license in his possession." Defendant then pleaded guilty to criminal possession of a weapon in the third degree and was sentenced to five years' probation. On appeal to the Appellate Division, the four-Justice majority affirmed, without opinion. The dissenting Justice found the search impermissible because "there was absolutely no predicate for believing the car was stolen." (97 AD2d at 742.)

VIN inspections typically involve opening a car door to locate the VIN on the doorpost, opening the hood to locate the VIN on the engine, or looking for the hidden VIN in obscure parts of an automobile. While this court has not previously considered the legality of such inspections conducted without consent, lower courts in this State, as well as courts in other jurisdictions, have approached the question from divergent perspectives. Initially, courts are divided on the threshold issue of whether a VIN inspection constitutes a search.[1] On the facts presented by this appeal, we conclude that a search was conducted.

The Fourth Amendment "protects people from unreasonable government intrusions into their legitimate expectations of privacy" (*United States v Chadwick*, 433 US 1, 7 [1977]; *see also Katz v United States*, 389 US 347 [1967]; *People v Perel*, 34 NY2d 462, 466 [1974]). One has no legitimate expectation of privacy in locations in a car which are observable by passersby. Accordingly, an officer's simply peering inside an automobile does not constitute a search and the Fourth Amendment consequently does not limit this activity (*Texas v Brown*, 460 US 730 [1983]; *People v Cruz*, 34 NY2d 362, 370 [1974]). But there are many places inside a car—including the area underneath the seats—which cannot be viewed from the outside and which an individual legitimately expects will remain private. The government intrusion here, Officer McNamee's opening the door and reaching inside, was undertaken to obtain information and it exposed these hidden areas. It therefore constituted a search (*cf. United States v Place*, 462 US 696 [1983]; *People v Miller*, 43 NY2d 789 [1977], *affg* 52 AD2d 425, 428 [1976]; *People v Sullivan*, 29 NY2d 69 [1971]).[2]

The absence of any legitimate expectation of privacy in the VIN itself is not determinative of the issue presented. The fact that certain information must be kept,

---

1. Compare, for example, *United States v Polk* (433 F2d 644 [1970]); *United States v Johnson* (413 F2d 1396 [1969], *affd en banc* 431 F2d 441 [1970]); *Cotton v United States* (371 F2d 385 [1967]); *People v Valoppi* (61 Mich App 470 [1975]); and *People v Hart* (75 Misc 2d 908 [1973]), with *United States v Powers* (439 F2d 373 [1971], *cert den* 402 US 1011 [1971]); *Simpson v United States* (346 F2d 291 [1965]); *State v Moore* (— Haw —, 659 P2d 70 [1983]); *People v Piper* (101 Ill App 3d 296 [1981]); and *State v Simpson* (95 Wash 2d 170 [1980]). Though not treating a VIN inspection as a search, some courts have limited the officers' right to check the VIN "to those cases in which there is a legitimate reason to do so" (*see e.g. Cotton v United States*, 371 F2d 385, 393 [1969], *supra*). The basis for imposing this limitation is not clear.

2. Although the gun was "protruding" from underneath the seat, Officer McNamee first observed it while conducting the search. The only question, then, is whether the officer had a right to be in the position from which he made his observation.

or that it may be of a public nature, does not automatically sanction police intrusion into private space in order to obtain it. In particular, the existence of a VIN on every automobile cannot enable police, without any basis, to make "wholesale entries of cars on nothing more than a hope that one of them might turn out to be stolen" (1 LaFave, Search and Seizure, § 2.5, p 360).[3]

A VIN inspection normally involves a lesser invasion of privacy than a full-blown search because of the fixed, known and readily accessible location of the VIN on the automobile. Additionally, there is a compelling police interest, in situations such as automobile thefts and accidents, in the positive identification of vehicles. Consequently, it may well be that some lesser justification than probable cause would be appropriate. However, it is unnecessary in this case to determine whether probable cause or a lesser justification should have been required to support the search, because here there was no semblance of either. The trial court based its apparent finding of reasonable suspicion to believe the car was stolen on two factors: defendant's exiting the vehicle and approaching the officers, and his failure to produce a driver's license. But a driver's emergence from a car upon being stopped by police is not indicative of criminal activity. Nor was reliance properly placed by the court on defendant's failure to produce a license because McNamee, having proceeded directly to defendant's car, was not even aware of that fact when he entered the automobile. Since competing inferences cannot reasonably be drawn from the undisputed facts presented, the hearing court erred as a matter of law in finding reasonable suspicion to believe the car was stolen (*see People v Harrison*, 57 NY2d 470, 477 [1982]). The facts reveal no reason for the officer to suspect other criminal activity or to act to protect his own safety (*compare People v David L.*, 56 NY2d 698 [1982], *cert den* 459 US 866 [1982]). The sole predicate for the officer's action here was defendant's commission of an ordinary traffic infraction, an offense which, standing alone, did not justify the search (*cf. People v Marsh*, 20 NY2d 98 [1967]).

Some lower court cases in New York have interpreted subdivision 4 of section 401 of the Vehicle and Traffic Law as authorizing VIN inspections (*see e.g. People v Gohn*, 49 AD2d 585 [1975]; *People v Frank*, 61 Misc 2d 450 [1969]; *People v Goldstein*, 60 Misc 2d 745 [1969]). That section provides, in pertinent part: "Carrying certificate of registration. Every person operating a motor vehicle or a motor vehicle and a trailer, registered or transferred in accordance with any of the provisions of this chapter, shall upon demand of any magistrate, motor vehicle inspector, peace officer, acting pursuant to his special duties, or police officer produce for inspection the certificate of registration or the registration renewal stub for such vehicle and shall furnish to such magistrate, inspector, officer or police officer any information necessary for the identification of such vehicle and its owner, and all information required concerning his license to operate, if he is required by law to have such a license, and shall, if required, sign his name in the presence of such magistrate, inspector, peace officer or police officer as a further means of identification."

---

3. We are not confronted with a governmental intrusion so circumscribed as to expose only information or articles in which there is no legitimate expectation of privacy (*compare United States v Place*, 462 US 696 [1983]; *Smith v Maryland*, 442 US 735 [1979]). Nor are we concerned here with an inventory of an impounded car.

In section 401, however, the Legislature has seen fit only to authorize an officer to *demand* information necessary to identify the car, as he may *demand* the certificate of registration for the vehicle.[4] No basis has been shown for ignoring this legislative direction. Here, had the officer complied with the statute and demanded exhibition of the VIN, defendant could have avoided the intrusion on his privacy interests by simply moving the papers on the dashboard, thereby facilitating the officer's observation of the VIN through the windshield. Section 401, therefore, provided no justification for the officer's entry of defendant's car.

Accordingly, the order should be reversed, the motion to suppress granted, the conviction vacated and the indictment dismissed.

---

4. No suggestion has been made that the police without basis could search the person of the driver or the interior of the vehicle to obtain a registration certificate, yet the statutory provision is no different for the VIN and the certificate of registration; in both instances the information must be provided on demand of a police officer.

Tebbutt v. Virostek,
65 NY2d 931, 940 (1985)

Judge Kaye's dissent in this case is a model of brevity, astuteness, and efficiency. It proved prescient; the court, recognizing that *Tebbutt* could no longer stand the test of time, reversed it in *Broadnax v. Gonzalez* (2 NY3d 148, 153 [2004]), stating: "*Tebbutt* reflected our longstanding reluctance to recognize causes of action for negligent infliction of emotional distress, especially in cases where the plaintiff suffered no independent physical or economic injury. Its holding was in keeping with our view that tort liability is not a panacea capable of redressing every substantial wrong. Although these concerns weigh heavily on us today, we are no longer able to defend *Tebbutt*'s logic or reasoning." Her words, nineteen years earlier, follow.

—Introduction by Hon. Albert M. Rosenblatt

(Dissenting) Dismissal of plaintiff's complaint in this instance leaves no one who can recover for alleged wrongdoing, and frees defendant from responsibility. Defendant performed the complained-of acts on a person in his care. Were the child born alive, a remedy would lie against defendant (*see Woods v Lancet*, 303 NY 349 [1951]). An arguably more grievous injury while the child is in utero, resulting in a stillbirth, should not go unredressed. Where the law declares that the stillborn child is not a person who can bring suit, then it must follow in the eyes of the law that any injury here was done to the mother. I would therefore reverse the order below, and reinstate the complaint.

O'Neill v. Oakgrove Constr., 71 NY2d 521 (1988)

In this landmark intellectual property decision authored by Judge Stewart Hancock Jr., the court recognized a qualified reporter's privilege under the state or federal constitutions extending to confidential and nonconfidential materials prepared or collected in the course of newsgathering. Judge Kaye concurred—solely for the purpose of chastising the court for deciding the issue under the federal constitution at all, when New York's State Constitution alone provided more than adequate authority. Judge Kaye's concurrence in *O'Neill* foreshadows the excitement she found and dedicated toward reinvigorating the state constitution, a mantle she gladly assumed from Justice William J. Brennan Jr. Decisions to follow such as *Immuno AG v Moor-Jankowski* are indicative of her years of advocacy for the important role of common-law courts in construing state constitutions.

—Introduction by Anne C. Reddy, law clerk 2006–2008

(Concurring) I concur in the result reached today and in the court's opinion, except insofar as the court decides the case under the Federal Constitution. In my view the case is correctly resolved under the State Constitution alone.

Issues involving free expression have long been viewed as matters peculiarly implicating local concerns and local standards (*see e.g. People v P. J. Video*, 68 NY2d 296, 308 [1986]; *People ex rel. Arcara v Cloud Books*, 68 NY2d 553, 557 [1986]). As the opinion acknowledges, the language of article I, § 8 of our State Constitution is materially different—more expansive—than the First Amendment; article I, § 8 has a longer, independent history; and we have maintained a consistent tradition in this State of providing the broadest possible protection to "the sensitive role of gathering and disseminating news of public events" (*Matter of Beach v Shanley*, 62 NY2d 241, 256 [1984, Wachtler, J., concurring]). I therefore cannot understand—or join—the decision to premise the qualified privilege we now adopt on the Federal Constitution in addition to the State Constitution. The fact that Federal law remains unsettled (*see* majority op at 528) leads me particularly to question why we would deliberately choose to surround our new privilege with any of the uncertainty that presently accompanies the Federal law, when we could very respectably resolve the issue with clarity and finality for the citizens of this State under the State Constitution.

The court offers two answers: that we decide the issue under both Constitutions because we have used that methodology before, and because it accords with our proper role in the Federal system (majority op at 524–525). But neither answer is satisfactory here. *First*, in resolving issues raised under parallel provisions of the State and Federal Constitutions, this court has not been wedded to any particular methodology. Depending on the matter at issue, we have decided parallel constitutional questions under the State Constitution alone (*see e.g. Rivers v Katz*, 67 NY2d 485, 498 [1986]) and under both (*see e.g. People v Stith*, 69 NY2d 313, 316, n [1987]). The issue before us is strikingly appropriate for disposition under the State Constitution without the additional overlay of the First Amendment: this court balances the interests of the press against the State statutory rights of New York litigants seeking particular materials in discovery, and adopts a solution that best accommodates the interests of both. *Second*, in resolving the question solely as a matter of State law, we still might look to Federal precedents as well as those of other States, and by our decision help to expound Federal law and furnish guidance for sister States. We thereby do fulfill our proper role in the Federal system, which is first and foremost to settle issues as definitively as possible for the people of this State.

Matter of Levandusky v. One Fifth Ave. Apt. Corp., 75 NY2d 530 (1990)

Here, under Judge Kaye's pen, the New York Court of Appeals adopted the "business judgment rule" as its test for postdeclaration action by common interest communities (CICs). This relatively deferential rule requires that a decision made by an agent be "rational." Adopting the business judgment rule means that judges should not inquire into actions taken in good faith "in the lawful and legitimate furtherance of corporate purposes." California agreed with New York's *Levandusky* opinion and adopted the business judgment rule approach. Thus, in at least the two of the most populous states, CIC governance decisions are unconstrained by substantive judicial oversight (*see* A. J. Boyack, *Common Interest Community Covenants and the Freedom of Contract Myth*, 22 J L & Pol'y 767 [2014]).

—Introduction by Hon. Albert M. Rosenblatt

This appeal by a residential cooperative corporation concerning apartment renovations by one of its proprietary lessees, factually centers on a two-inch steam riser and three air conditioners, but fundamentally presents the legal question of what standard of review should apply when a board of directors of a cooperative corporation seeks to enforce a matter of building policy against a tenant-shareholder. We conclude that the business judgment rule furnishes the correct standard of review.

In the main, the parties agree that the operative events transpired as follows. In 1987, respondent (Ronald Levandusky) decided to enlarge the kitchen area of his apartment at One Fifth Avenue in New York City. According to Levandusky, some time after reaching that decision, and while he was president of the cooperative's board of directors, he told Elliot Glass, the architect retained by the corporation, that he intended to realign or "jog" a steam riser in the kitchen area, and Glass orally approved the alteration. According to Glass, however, the conversation was a general one; Levandusky never specifically told him that he intended to move any particular pipe, and Glass never gave him approval to do so. In any event, Levandusky's proprietary lease provided that no "alteration of or addition to the water, gas or steam risers or pipes" could be made without appellant's prior written consent.

Levandusky had his architect prepare plans for the renovation, which were approved by Glass and submitted for approval to the board of directors. Although the plans show details of a number of other proposed structural modifications, including changes in plumbing risers, no change in the steam riser is shown or discussed anywhere in the plans.

The board approved Levandusky's plans at a meeting held March 14, 1988, and the next day he executed an "Alteration Agreement" with appellant, which incorporated "Renovation Guidelines" that had originally been drafted, in large part, by Levandusky himself. These guidelines, like the proprietary lease, specified that advance written approval was required for any renovation affecting the building's heating system. Board consideration of the plans—appropriately detailed to indicate all structural changes—was to follow their submission to the corporation's architect, and the board reserved the power to disapprove any plans, even those that had received the architect's approval.

In late spring 1988, the building's managing agent learned from Levandusky that he intended to move the steam riser in his apartment, and so informed the board. Both Levandusky and the board contacted John Flynn, an engineer who had served as consulting agent for the board. In a letter and in a subsequent presentation at a June 13 board meeting, Flynn opined that relocating steam risers was technically feasible and, if carefully done, would not necessarily cause any problem. However, he also advised that any change in an established old piping system risked causing difficulties ("gremlins"). In Flynn's view, such alterations were to be avoided whenever possible.

At the June 13 meeting, which Levandusky attended, the board enacted a resolution to "reaffirm the policy—no relocation of risers." At a June 23 meeting, the board voted to deny Levandusky a variance to move his riser, and to modify its previous approval of his renovation plans, conditioning approval upon an acceptable redesign of the kitchen area.

Levandusky nonetheless hired a contractor, who severed and jogged the kitchen steam riser. In August 1988, when the board learned of this, it issued a "stop work" order, pursuant to the "Renovation Guidelines." Levandusky then commenced this article 78 proceeding, seeking to have the stop work order set aside. The corporation cross-petitioned for an order compelling Levandusky to return the riser to its original position. The board also sought an order compelling him to remove certain air-conditioning units he had installed, which allegedly were not in conformity with the requirements of the Landmarks Preservation Commission.

Supreme Court initially granted Levandusky's petition, and annulled the stop work order, on the ground that there was no evidence that the jogged pipe had caused any damage, but on the contrary, the building engineer had inspected it and believed it would likely not have any adverse effect. Therefore, balancing the hardship to Levandusky in redoing the already completed renovations against the harm to the building, the court determined that the board's decision to stop the renovations was arbitrary and capricious, and should be annulled. Both counterclaims were dismissed, the court ruling that the corporation had no standing to complain of violations of the Landmarks Preservation Law, particularly as the building had not been cited for any violation.

On reargument, however, Supreme Court withdrew its decision, dismissed Levandusky's petition, and ordered him to restore the riser to its original position and submit redrawn plans to the board, on the ground that the court was precluded by the business judgment rule from reviewing the board's determination. The court adhered to its original ruling with respect to the branch of the cross motion concerning the air conditioners, notwithstanding that the Landmarks Preservation Commission had in the interim cited them as violations.

On Levandusky's appeal, the Appellate Division modified the judgment. The court was unanimous in affirming the Supreme Court's disposition of the air conditioner claim, but divided concerning the stop work order. A majority of the court agreed with Supreme Court's original decision, while two Justices dissented on the ground that the board's action was within the scope of its business judgment and hence not subject to judicial review. Concluding that the business judgment rule applies to the decisions of cooperative governing associations enforcing building policy, and that the action taken by the board in this case falls within the purview of the rule, we now modify the order of the Appellate Division.

At the outset, we agree with the Appellate Division that the corporation's cross claim concerning Levandusky's three air-conditioning units was properly dismissed, as the appropriate forum for resolution of the complaint at this stage is an administrative review proceeding. That brings us to the issue that divided the Appellate Division: the standard to be applied in judicial review of this challenge to a decision of the board of directors of a residential cooperative corporation.

As cooperative and condominium home ownership has grown increasingly popular, courts confronting disputes between tenant-owners and governing boards have fashioned a variety of rules for adjudicating such claims (*see generally* Goldberg, *Community Association Use Restrictions: Applying the Business Judgment Doctrine*, 64 Chi-Kent L Rev 653 [1988] [hereinafter Goldberg, *Community Association Use Restrictions*]; Note, *Judicial Review of Condominium Rulemaking*, 94 Harv L Rev 647 [1981]). In the process, several salient characteristics of the governing board homeowner relationship have been identified as relevant to the judicial inquiry.

As courts and commentators have noted, the cooperative or condominium association is a quasi-government—"a little democratic sub society of necessity" (*Hidden Harbour Estates v Norman*, 309 So 2d 180, 182 [Fla Dist Ct App 1975]). The proprietary lessees or condominium owners consent to be governed, in certain respects, by the decisions of a board. Like a municipal government, such governing boards are responsible for running the day-to-day affairs of the cooperative and to that end, often have broad powers in areas that range from financial decisionmaking to promulgating regulations regarding pets and parking spaces (*see generally* Note, *Promulgation and Enforcement of House Rules*, 48 St John's L Rev 1132 [1974]). Authority to approve or disapprove structural alterations, as in this case, is commonly given to the governing board (*see* Siegler, *Apartment Alterations*, NYLJ, May 4, 1988 at 1, col 1).

Through the exercise of this authority, to which would-be apartment owners must generally acquiesce, a governing board may significantly restrict the bundle of rights a property owner normally enjoys. Moreover, as with any authority to govern, the broad powers of a cooperative board hold potential for abuse through arbitrary and malicious decisionmaking, favoritism, discrimination and the like.

On the other hand, agreement to submit to the decisionmaking authority of a cooperative board is voluntary in a sense that submission to government authority is not; there is always the freedom not to purchase the apartment. The stability offered by community control, through a board, has its own economic and social benefits, and purchase of a cooperative apartment represents a voluntary choice to cede certain of the privileges of single ownership to a governing body, often made up of fellow tenants who volunteer their time, without compensation. The board, in return, takes on the burden of managing the property for the benefit of the proprietary lessees. As one court observed: "Every man may justly consider his home his castle and himself as the king thereof; nonetheless his sovereign fiat to use his property as he pleases must yield, at least in degree, where ownership is in common or cooperation with others. The benefits of condominium living and ownership demand no less" (*Sterling Vil. Condominium v Breitenbach*, 251 So 2d 685, 688, n 6 [Fla Dist Ct App 1971]).

It is apparent, then, that a standard for judicial review of the actions of a cooperative or condominium governing board must be sensitive to a variety of concerns—sometimes competing concerns. Even when the governing board acts within the scope of its authority, some check on its potential powers to regulate residents' conduct, life-style and property rights is necessary to protect individual residents from abusive exercise, notwithstanding that the residents have, to an extent, consented to be regulated and even selected their representatives (*see* Note, *The Rule of Law in Residential Associations*, 99 Harv L Rev 472 [1985]). At the same time, the chosen standard of review should not undermine the purposes for which the residential community and its governing structure were formed: protection of the interest of the entire community of residents in an environment managed by the board for the common benefit.

We conclude that these goals are best served by a standard of review that is analogous to the business judgment rule applied by courts to determine challenges to decisions made by corporate directors (*see Auerbach v Bennett*, 47 NY2d 619, 629 [1979]). A number of courts in this and other states have applied such a standard in reviewing the decisions of cooperative and condominium boards [citing cases]. We agree with those courts that such a test best balances the individual and collective interests at stake.

Developed in the context of commercial enterprises, the business judgment rule prohibits judicial inquiry into actions of corporate directors "taken in good faith and in the exercise of honest judgment in the lawful and legitimate furtherance of corporate purposes" (*Auerbach v Bennett*, 47 NY2d 619, 629 [1979], *supra*). So long as the corporation's directors have not breached their fiduciary obligation to the corporation, "the exercise of [their powers] for the common and general interests of the corporation may not be questioned, although the results show that what they did was unwise or inexpedient" (*Pollitz v Wabash R. R. Co.*, 207 NY 113, 124 [1912]).

Application of a similar doctrine is appropriate because a cooperative corporation is—in fact and function—a corporation, acting through the management of its board of directors, and subject to the Business Corporation Law. There is no cause to create a special new category in law for corporate actions by coop boards.

We emphasize that reference to the business judgment rule is for the purpose of analogy only. Clearly, in light of the doctrine's origins in the quite different world of commerce, the fiduciary principles identified in the existing case law—primarily emphasizing avoidance of self-dealing and financial self-aggrandizement—will of necessity be adapted over time in order to apply to directors of not-for-profit homeowners' cooperative corporations (*see* Goldberg, *Community Association Use Restrictions, op. cit.* at 677–683). For present purposes, we need not, nor should we determine the entire range of the fiduciary obligations of a cooperative board, other than to note that the board owes its duty of loyalty to the cooperative—that is, it must act for the benefit of the residents collectively. So long as the board acts for the purposes of the cooperative, within the scope of its authority and in good faith, courts will not substitute their judgment for the board's. Stated somewhat differently, unless a resident challenging the board's action is able to demonstrate a breach of this duty, judicial review is not available.

In reaching this conclusion, we reject the test seemingly applied by the Appellate Division majority and explicitly applied by Supreme Court in its initial decision. That inquiry was directed at the *reasonableness* of the board's decision; having itself found that relocation of the riser posed no "dangerous aspect" to the building, the Appellate Division concluded that the renovation should remain. Like the business judgment rule, this reasonableness standard—originating in the quite different world of governmental agency decisionmaking—has found favor with courts reviewing board decisions [citing cases].

As applied in condominium and cooperative cases, review of a board's decision under a reasonableness standard has much in common with the rule we adopt today. A primary focus of the inquiry is whether board action is in furtherance of a legitimate purpose of the cooperative or condominium, in which case it will generally be upheld. The difference between the reasonableness test and the rule we adopt is twofold. First— unlike the business judgment rule, which places on the owner seeking review the burden to demonstrate a breach of the board's fiduciary duty—reasonableness review requires the board to demonstrate that its decision was reasonable. Second, although in practice a certain amount of deference appears to be accorded to board decisions, reasonableness review permits—indeed, in theory requires—the court itself to evaluate the merits or wisdom of the board's decision just as the Appellate Division did in the present case [citation omitted].

The more limited judicial review embodied in the business judgment rule is preferable. In the context of the decisions of a for-profit corporation, "courts are ill equipped and infrequently called on to evaluate what are and must be essentially business judgments . . . by definition the responsibility for business judgments must rest with the corporate directors; their individual capabilities and experience peculiarly qualify them for the discharge of that responsibility" (*Auerbach v Bennett*, 47 NY2d at 630–631). Even if decisions of a cooperative board do not generally involve expertise beyond the usual ken of the judiciary, at the least board members will possess experience of the peculiar needs of their building and its residents not shared by the court.

Several related concerns persuade us that such a rule should apply here. As this case exemplifies, board decisions concerning what residents may or may not do with their living space may be highly charged and emotional. A cooperative or condominium is by nature a myriad of often competing views regarding personal living space, and decisions taken to benefit the collective interest may be unpalatable to one resident or another, creating the prospect that board decisions will be subjected to undue court involvement and judicial second-guessing. Allowing an owner who is simply dissatisfied with particular board action a second opportunity to reopen the matter completely before a court, which—generally without knowing the property—may or may not agree with the reasonableness of the board's determination, threatens the stability of the common living arrangement.

Moreover, the prospect that each board decision may be subjected to full judicial review hampers the effectiveness of the board's managing authority. The business judgment rule protects the board's business decisions and managerial authority from indiscriminate attack. At the same time, it permits review of improper decisions, as when the challenger demonstrates that the board's action has no legitimate relationship to the welfare of the cooperative, deliberately singles out individuals for harmful treatment, is taken without notice or consideration of the relevant facts, or is beyond the scope of the board's authority.

Levandusky failed to meet this burden, and Supreme Court properly dismissed his petition. His argument that having once granted its approval, the board was powerless to rescind its decision after he had spent considerable sums on the renovations is without merit. There is no dispute that Levandusky failed to comply with the provisions of the "Alteration Agreement" or "Renovation Guidelines" designed to give the board explicit written notice before it approved a change in the building's heating system. Once made aware of Levandusky's intent, the board promptly consulted its engineer, and notified Levandusky that it would not depart from a policy of refusing to permit the movement of pipes. That he then went ahead and moved the pipe hardly allows him to claim reliance on the board's initial approval of his plans. Indeed, recognition of such an argument would frustrate any systematic effort to enforce uniform policies.

Levandusky's additional allegations that the board's decision was motivated by the personal animosity of another board member toward him, and that the board had in fact permitted other residents to jog their steam risers, are wholly conclusory. The board submitted evidence—unrefuted by Levandusky—that it was acting pursuant to the advice of its engineer, and that it had not previously approved such jogging. Finally, the fact that allowing Levandusky an exception to the policy might not have resulted in harm to the building does not require that the exception be allowed. Under the rule we articulate today, we decline to review the merits of the board's determination that it was preferable to adhere to a uniform policy regarding the building's piping system.

Turning to the concurrence, it is apparent that in many respects we are in agreement concerning the appropriate standard of judicial review of cooperative board decisions; it is more a matter of label that divides us. For these additional reasons, we believe our choice is the better one.

For the guidance of the courts and all other interested parties, obviously a single standard for judicial review of the propriety of board action is desirable, irrespective of the happenstance of the form of the lawsuit challenging that action.[1] Unlike challenges

---

1. We of course do not disregard the form of action. In determining whether appellant's decision was "arbitrary and capricious or an abuse of discretion" (CPLR 7803 [3]), we would use "business judgment," the concurrence some form of "rationality" or "reasonableness." By analogy, we hold today in *Akpan v Koch* (75 NY2d 561, 574 ([decided today])) that because a governmental agency took the required "hard look" under the State's environmental protection laws, its action cannot be characterized as arbitrary and capricious or an abuse of discretion under CPLR 7803 (3). So too here, board action that comes within the business judgment rule cannot be characterized as arbitrary and capricious, or an abuse of discretion.

to administrative agency decisions, which take the form of article 78 proceedings, challenges to the propriety of corporate board action have been lodged as derivative suits, injunction actions, and all manner of civil suits, including article 78 proceedings. While the nomenclature will vary with the form of suit, we see no purpose in allowing the form of the action to dictate the substance of the standard by which the legitimacy of corporate action is to be measured.

By the same token, unnecessary confusion is generated by prescribing different standards for different categories of issues that come before cooperative boards—for example, a standard of business judgment for choices between competing economic options, but rationality for the administration of corporate bylaws and rules governing shareholder-tenant rights. . . . There is no need for two rules when one will do, particularly since corporate action often partakes of each category of issues. Indeed, even the decision here might be portrayed as the administration of corporate bylaws and rules governing shareholder-tenant rights, or more broadly as a policy choice based on the economic consequences of tampering with the building's piping system.

Finally, we reiterate that "business judgment" appears to strike the best balance. It establishes that board action undertaken in furtherance of a legitimate corporate purpose will generally not be pronounced "arbitrary and capricious or an abuse of discretion" (CPLR 7803 [3]) in article 78 proceedings, or otherwise unlawful in other types of litigation. It is preferable to a standard that requires Judges, rather than directors, to decide what action is "reasonable" for the cooperative. It avoids drawing sometimes elusive semantical distinctions between what is "reasonable" and what is "rational" (the concurrence rejects the former but embraces the latter as the appropriate test). And it better protects tenant-shareholders against bad faith and self-dealing than a test that insulates board decisions "if there is a rational basis to explain them" or if "an articulable and rational basis for the board's decision exists" (concurring op at 548). The mere presence of an engineer's report, for example—"certainly a rational explanation for the board's decision" (concurring op at 548)—should not end all inquiry, foreclosing review of nonconclusory assertions of malevolent conduct; under the business judgment test, it would not.

W.W.W. Assoc. v. Giancontieri,
77 NY2d 157 (1990)

W.W.W. Assoc. v. Giancontieri is one of Judge Kaye's most-cited civil opinions and is a guide for contractual interpretation. It establishes that "clear, complete writings should generally be enforced according to their terms," and that "evidence outside of the four corners of the document as to what was really intended but unstated or misstated is generally inadmissible to add to or vary the writing." Judge Kaye, writing for the unanimous court, explained that use of extrinsic evidence to create ambiguity in an otherwise clear contract would allow a party to rewrite "the bargain that was struck" and would undermine the stability of commercial transactions (163). Judge Kaye emphasized that an "analysis that begins with consideration of extrinsic evidence of what the parties meant, instead of looking first to what they said and reaching extrinsic evidence only when required to do so because of identified ambiguity, unnecessarily denigrates the contract and unsettles the law."

—Introduction by Hon. Jennifer G. Schecter, law clerk 1998–2001

In this action for specific performance of a contract to sell real property, the issue is whether an unambiguous reciprocal cancellation provision should be read in light of extrinsic evidence, as a contingency clause for the sole benefit of plaintiff purchaser, subject to its unilateral waiver. Applying the principle that clear, complete writings should generally be enforced according to their terms, we reject plaintiff's reading of the contract and dismiss its complaint.

Defendants, owners of a two-acre parcel in Suffolk County, on October 16, 1986 contracted for the sale of the property to plaintiff, a real estate investor and developer. The purchase price was fixed at $750,000—$25,000 payable on contract execution, $225,000 to be paid in cash on closing (to take place "on or about December 1, 1986"), and the $500,000 balance secured by a purchase-money mortgage payable two years later.

The parties signed a printed form Contract of Sale, supplemented by several of their own paragraphs. Two provisions of the contract have particular relevance to the present dispute—a reciprocal cancellation provision (para 31) and a merger clause (para 19). Paragraph 31, one of the provisions the parties added to the contract form, reads: "The parties acknowledge that Sellers have been served with process instituting an action concerned with the real property which is the subject of this agreement. In the event the

137

closing of title is delayed by reason of such litigation it is agreed that closing of title will in a like manner be adjourned until after the conclusion of such litigation provided, *in the event such litigation is not concluded, by or before 6-1-87 either party shall have the right to cancel this contract whereupon the down payment shall be returned and there shall be no further rights hereunder*" (emphasis supplied). Paragraph 19 is the form merger provision, reading: "All prior understandings and agreements between seller and purchaser are merged in this contract [and it] completely expresses their full agreement. It has been entered into after full investigation, neither party relying upon any statements made by anyone else that are not set forth in this contract."

The Contract of Sale, in other paragraphs the parties added to the printed form, provided that the purchaser alone had the unconditional right to cancel the contract within 10 days of signing (para 32), and that the purchaser alone had the option to cancel if, at closing, the seller was unable to deliver building permits for 50 senior citizen housing units (para 29).

The contract in fact did not close on December 1, 1986, as originally contemplated. As June 1, 1987 neared, with the litigation still unresolved, plaintiff on May 13 wrote defendants that it was prepared to close and would appear for closing on May 28; plaintiff also instituted the present action for specific performance. On June 2, 1987, defendants canceled the contract and returned the down payment, which plaintiff refused. Defendants thereafter sought summary judgment dismissing the specific performance action, on the ground that the contract gave them the absolute right to cancel.

Plaintiff's claim to specific performance rests upon its recitation of how paragraph 31 originated. Those facts are set forth in the affidavit of plaintiff's vice-president, submitted in opposition to defendants' summary judgment motion.

As plaintiff explains, during contract negotiations it learned that, as a result of unrelated litigation against defendants, a lis pendens had been filed against the property. Although assured by defendants that the suit was meritless, plaintiff anticipated difficulty obtaining a construction loan (including title insurance for the loan) needed to implement its plans to build senior citizen housing units. According to the affidavit, it was therefore agreed that paragraph 31 would be added for plaintiff's sole benefit, as contract vendee. As it developed, plaintiff's fears proved groundless—the lis pendens did not impede its ability to secure construction financing. However, around March 1987, plaintiff claims it learned from the broker on the transaction that one of the defendants had told him they were doing nothing to defend the litigation, awaiting June 2, 1987 to cancel the contract and suggesting the broker might get a higher price.

Defendants made no response to these factual assertions. Rather, its summary judgment motion rested entirely on the language of the Contract of Sale, which it argued was, under the law, determinative of its right to cancel.

The trial court granted defendants' motion and dismissed the complaint, holding that the agreement unambiguously conferred the right to cancel on defendants as well as plaintiff. The Appellate Division, however, reversed and, after searching the record and adopting the facts alleged by plaintiff in its affidavit, granted summary judgment to plaintiff directing specific performance of the contract. We now reverse and dismiss the complaint.

Critical to the success of plaintiff's position is consideration of the extrinsic evidence that paragraph 31 was added to the contract solely for its benefit. . . .

We conclude . . . that the extrinsic evidence tendered by plaintiff is not material. In its reliance on extrinsic evidence to bring itself within the "party benefitted" cases, plaintiff ignores a vital first step in the analysis: before looking to evidence of what was in the parties' minds, a court must give due weight to what was in their contract.

A familiar and eminently sensible proposition of law is that, when parties set down their agreement in a clear, complete document, their writing should as a rule be enforced according to its terms. Evidence outside the four corners of the document as to what was really intended but unstated or misstated is generally inadmissible to add to or vary the writing. That rule imparts "stability to commercial transactions by safeguarding against fraudulent claims, perjury, death of witnesses . . . infirmity of memory . . . [and] the fear that the jury will improperly evaluate the extrinsic evidence." Such considerations are all the more compelling in the context of real property transactions, where commercial certainty is a paramount concern.

Whether or not a writing is ambiguous is a question of law to be resolved by the courts. In the present case, the contract, read as a whole to determine its purpose and intent plainly manifests the intention that defendants, as well as plaintiff, should have the right to cancel after June 1, 1987 if the litigation had not concluded by that date; and it further plainly manifests the intention that all prior understandings be merged into the contract, which expresses the parties' full agreement. Moreover, the face of the contract reveals a "logical reason" for the explicit provision that the cancellation right contained in paragraph 31 should run to the seller as well as the purchaser. A seller taking back a purchase-money mortgage for two thirds of the purchase price might well wish to reserve its option to sell the property for cash on an "as is" basis if third-party litigation affecting the property remained unresolved past a certain date.

Thus, we conclude there is no ambiguity as to the cancellation clause in issue, read in the context of the entire agreement, and that it confers a reciprocal right on both parties to the contract.

The question next raised is whether extrinsic evidence should be considered in order to *create* an ambiguity in the agreement. That question must be answered in the negative. It is well settled that "extrinsic and parol evidence is not admissible to create an ambiguity in a written agreement which is complete and clear and unambiguous upon its face."

Plaintiff's rejoinder—that defendants indeed had the specified absolute right to cancel the contract, but it was subject to plaintiff's absolute prior right of waiver—suffers from a logical inconsistency that is evident in a mere statement of the argument. But there is an even greater problem. Here, sophisticated businessmen reduced their negotiations to a clear, complete writing. In the paragraphs immediately surrounding paragraph 31, they expressly bestowed certain options on the purchaser alone, but in paragraph 31 they chose otherwise, explicitly allowing both buyer and seller to cancel in the event the litigation was unresolved by June 1, 1987. By ignoring the plain language of the contract, plaintiff effectively rewrites the bargain that was struck. An analysis that begins with consideration of extrinsic evidence of what the parties meant, instead of looking first to what they said and reaching extrinsic evidence only when required to do so because of some identified ambiguity, unnecessarily denigrates the contract and unsettles the law. . . .

Even viewing the burden of a summary judgment opponent more generously than that of the summary judgment proponent, plaintiff fails to raise a triable issue of fact.

Accordingly, the Appellate Division order should be reversed, with costs, defendants' motion for summary judgment granted, and the complaint dismissed.

Alison D. v. Virginia M.,
77 NY2d 651 (1991)

Judge Kaye frequently looked back on her time on the bench as "lawyer heaven." It was the relationships with her fellow judges—the collegiality, mutual respect, and camaraderie they enjoyed—that she found truly sacred. She was particularly proud that the court made it a priority to speak with one voice and, by doing so, handed down New York law in an efficient, stable, and predictable manner. When she chose to dissent, as she did in *Alison D. v. Virginia M.*, she did not do so lightly. The majority held that a lesbian co-parent of a child could not seek visitation rights against the wishes of the biological parent, but Judge Kaye presciently and poignantly recognized the error of "fixing biology as the key to visitation rights." Unsurprisingly, history has proven her correct.

—Introduction by Jennifer L. Smith, worked with
Judge Kaye at Skadden, Arps, Slate, Meagher & Flom 2012–2016

(Dissenting) The Court's decision, fixing biology[1] as the key to visitation rights, has impact far beyond this particular controversy, one that may affect a wide spectrum of relationships—including those of longtime heterosexual stepparents, "common-law" and nonheterosexual partners such as involved here, and even participants in scientific reproduction procedures. Estimates that more than 15.5 million children do not live with two biological parents, and that as many as 8 to 10 million children are born into families with a gay or lesbian parent, suggest just how widespread the impact may be (*see* Polikoff, *This Child Does Have Two Mothers: Redefining Parenthood to Meet the Needs of Children in Lesbian–Mother and Other Nontraditional Families*, 78 Geo L J 459, 461 n 2 [1990]; Bartlett, *Rethinking Parenthood as an Exclusive Status: The Need for Legal Alternatives When the Premise of the Nuclear Family Has Failed*, 70 Va L Rev 879, 880–881 [1984]; *see generally Developments in the Law—Sexual Orientation and the Law*, 102 Harv L Rev 1508, 1629 [1989]).

But the impact of today's decision falls hardest on the children of those relationships, limiting their opportunity to maintain bonds that may be crucial to their development. The majority's retreat from the courts' proper role—its tightening of rules that should

---

1. While the opinion speaks of biological *and legal* parenthood, this Court has not yet passed on the legality of adoption by a second mother.

in visitation petitions, above all, retain the capacity to take the children's interests into account—compels this dissent.

In focusing the difference, it is perhaps helpful to begin with what is *not* at issue. This is not a custody case, but solely a visitation petition. The issue on this appeal is not whether petitioner should actually have visitation rights. Nor is the issue the relationship between Alison D. and Virginia M. Rather, the sole issue is the relationship between Alison D. and A.D.M., in particular whether Alison D.'s petition for visitation should even be considered on its merits. I would conclude that the trial court had jurisdiction to hear the merits of this petition.

The relevant facts are amply described in the Court's opinion. Most significantly, Virginia M. agrees that, after long cohabitation with Alison D. and before A.D.M.'s conception, it was "explicitly planned that the child would be theirs to raise together." It is also uncontested that the two shared "financial and emotional preparations" for the birth, and that for several years Alison D. actually filled the role of coparent to A.D.M., both tangibly and intangibly. In all, a parent-child relationship—encouraged or at least condoned by Virginia M.—apparently existed between A.D.M. and Alison D. during the first six years of the child's life.

While acknowledging that relationship, the Court nonetheless proclaims powerlessness to consider the child's interest at all, because the word "parent" in the statute imposes an absolute barrier to Alison D.'s petition for visitation. That same conclusion would follow, as the Appellate Division dissenter noted, were the coparenting relationship one of 10 or more years, and irrespective of how close or deep the emotional ties might be between petitioner and child, or how devastating isolation might be to the child. I cannot agree that such a result is mandated by section 70, or any other law.

Domestic Relations Law § 70 provides a mechanism for "either parent" to bring a habeas corpus proceeding to determine a child's custody. Other State Legislatures, in comparable statutes, have defined "parent" specifically (*see e.g.* Cal Civ Code § 7001 [defining parent-child relationship as between "a child and his natural or adoptive parents"]), and that definition has of course bound the courts (*see Nancy S. v Michele G.*, 228 Cal App 3d 831, 279 Cal Rptr 212 [1991] [applying the statutory definition]). Significantly, the Domestic Relations Law contains no such limitation. Indeed, it does not define the term "parent" at all. That remains for the courts to do, as often happens when statutory terms are undefined.

The majority insists, however, that the word "parent" in this case can only be read to mean biological parent; the response "one fit parent" now forecloses all inquiry into the child's best interest, even in visitation proceedings. We have not previously taken such a hard line in these matters, but in the absence of express legislative direction have attempted to read otherwise undefined words of the statute so as to effectuate the legislative purposes. The Legislature has made plain an objective in section 70 to promote "the best interest of the child" and the child's "welfare and happiness" (Domestic Relations Law § 70). Those words should not be ignored by us in defining standing for visitation purposes—they have not been in prior case law.

Domestic Relations Law § 70 was amended in 1964 to broaden the category of persons entitled to seek habeas corpus relief (L 1964, ch 564, § 1). Previously, only a husband or wife living within the State, and legally separated from the spouse, had standing to bring such a proceeding. The courts, however, refused to apply the statute so literally. In amending the statute to make domicile of the child the touchstone, and eliminate the separation requirement, the Legislature acted to bring section 70 into conformity with what the courts were already doing (*see* Mem of Joint Legis Comm on Matrimonial and Family Laws, 1964 McKinney's Session Laws of NY at 1880 [amendment deleted "needless limitations which are not, in fact, observed by the Courts"]).

This amendment to bring the statute into line with the practice reflects Supreme Court's equitable powers that complement the special habeas statute (*see Langerman v Langerman*, 303 NY 465, 471; *see generally* NY Const, art VI, § 7 [a]). In *Finlay v Finlay* (240 NY 429, 433), this Court established that where the section 70 writ is denied to the petitioner seeking custody "there would remain his remedy by petition to the chancellor or to the court that has succeeded to the chancellor's prerogative [and] [n]othing in the habeas corpus act affects that jurisdiction." In such an action, the Chancellor "may act at the intervention or on the motion of a kinsman . . . but equally he may act at the instance of any one else" (240 NY at 434). Jurisdiction rests on the parens patriae power—concern for the welfare of the child (*id.*; *see also Matter of Bachman v Mejias*, 1 NY2d 575, 581).

As the Court wrote in *Matter of Bennett v Jeffreys* (40 NY2d 543, 546)—even in recognizing the superior right of a biological parent to the custody of her child—"when there is a conflict, the best interest of the child has always been regarded as superior to the right of parental custody. Indeed, analysis of the cases reveals a shifting of emphasis rather than a remaking of substance. This shifting reflects more the modern principle that a child is a person, and not a sub-person over whom the parent has an absolute possessory interest."

Apart from imposing upon itself an unnecessarily restrictive definition of "parent," and apart from turning its back on a tradition of reading of section 70 so as to promote the welfare of the children, in accord with the parens patriae power, the Court also overlooks the significant distinction between visitation and custody proceedings.

While both are of special concern to the State, custody and visitation are significantly different (*see Weiss v Weiss*, 52 NY2d 170, 175; *Matter of Ronald FF. v Cindy GG.*, 70 NY2d 141, 144).[2] Custody disputes implicate a parent's right to rear a child—with the child's corresponding right to be raised by a parent (*see Matter of Bennett v Jeffreys*, 40 NY2d at 546). Infringement of that right must be based on the fitness—more precisely the lack of fitness—of the custodial parent.

Visitation rights also implicate a right of the custodial parent, but it is the right to choose with whom the child associates (*see Matter of Ronald FF. v Cindy GG.*, 70 NY2d at 144). Any burden on the exercise of that right must be based on the child's overriding need to maintain a particular relationship (*see Weiss v Weiss*, 52 NY2d at 174–175). Logically,

2. The majority's opinion rests on a fundamental inconsistency. It cannot be that visitation is the same as custody—"a limited form of custody" (majority op at 656)—and yet at the same time different from custody in that the "extraordinary circumstances" doctrine is inapplicable (*Matter of Ronald FF. v Cindy GG.*, 70 NY2d 141; see also *Matter of Mark V. v Gale P.*, 143 Misc 2d 487, 489).

the fitness concern present in custody disputes is irrelevant in visitation petitions, where continuing contact with the child rather than severing of a parental tie is in issue. For that reason, we refused to extend the *Bennett* "extraordinary circumstances" doctrine—which relates to the fitness of the custodial parent—to visitation petitions (*Matter of Ronald FF. v Cindy GG.*, 70 NY2d 141, *supra*).

The Court now takes the law a step beyond *Ronald FF.* by establishing the *Bennett* "extraordinary circumstances" test as the only way to reach the child's best interest in a section 70 proceeding. In that *Ronald FF.* determined that extraordinary circumstances are irrelevant in the visitation context, our holding today thus firmly closes the door on all consideration of the child's best interest in visitation proceedings such as the one before us, unless petitioner is a biological parent.

Of course there must be some limitation on who can petition for visitation. Domestic Relations Law § 70 specifies that the person must be the child's "parent," and the law additionally recognizes certain rights of biological and legal parents. Arguments that every dedicated caretaker could sue for visitation if the term "parent" were broadened, or that such action would necessarily effect sweeping change throughout the law, overlook and misportray the Court's role in defining otherwise undefined statutory terms to effect particular statutory purposes, and to do so narrowly, for those purposes only.

Countless examples of that process may be found in our case law, the Court looking to modern-day realities in giving definition to statutory concepts (*see e.g. People v Eulo*, 63 NY2d 341, 354 [defining "death" for purposes of homicide prosecutions]). Only recently, we defined the term "family" in the eviction provisions of the rent stabilization laws so as to advance the legislative objective, making abundantly clear that the definition was limited to the statute in issue and did not effect a wholesale change in the law (*see Braschi v Stahl Assocs. Co.*, 74 NY2d 201, 211–213).

In discharging this responsibility, recent decisions from other jurisdictions, for the most part concerning visitation rights of stepparents, are instructive (*see e.g. Gribble v Gribble*, 583 P2d 64 [Utah]; *Spells v Spells*, 250 Pa Super 168, 378 A2d 879). For example in *Spells* (250 Pa Super at 172–173, 378 A2d at 881–882), the court fashioned a test for "parental status" or "in loco parentis" requiring that the petitioner demonstrate actual assumption of the parental role and discharge of parental responsibilities. It should be required that the relationship with the child came into being with the consent of the biological or legal parent, and that the petitioner at least have had joint custody of the child for a significant period of time (*see Rethinking Parenthood as an Exclusive Status, op. cit.*, 70 Va L Rev at 945–946). Other factors likely should be added to constitute a test that protects all relevant interests—much as we did in *Braschi*. Indeed, the criteria described by the Court in *Braschi* to be applied on a case-by-case basis later became the nucleus of formal standards (*see* 9 NYCRR 2520.6).

It is not my intention to spell out a definition but only to point out that it is surely within our competence to do so. It is indeed regrettable that we decline to exercise that authority in this visitation matter, given the explicit statutory objectives, the courts' power, and the fact that all consideration of the child's interest is, for the future, otherwise absolutely foreclosed.

I would remand the case to Supreme Court for an exercise of its discretion in determining whether Alison D. stands in loco parentis to A.D.M. and, if so, whether it is in the child's best interest to allow her the visitation rights she claims.

~

In August 2016, in *Brooke S.B. v Elizabeth A.C.C.* (28 NY3d 1), the Court of Appeals overruled *Alison D.*, holding that if prior to conception, partners plan to both be parents of a child, the nonbiological partner has standing to seek custody and visitation in the event of a split.

This surely is a triumph for Judge Kaye's position, which she voiced in *Alison*, a quarter of a century earlier.

Immuno AG v. Moor-Jankowski,
77 NY2d 235 (1991)

Judge Kaye was a champion of the state constitution, continually reminding us that in appropriate cases it accords New Yorkers greater rights than does the federal constitution. *Immuno* deals with free speech.

In its 1990 decision in *Milkovich v. Lorain Journal Co.* (497 US 1), the Supreme Court held that couching a statement in the form of an opinion does not cloak it with constitutional immunity from libel rules. A year after *Milkovich*, the issue reached the New York Court of Appeals in *Immuno AG*. Disagreeing with the Supreme Court's analysis of the opinion issue, Judge Kaye, speaking for the court, interpreted that provision to provide broader protection for free speech than did the First Amendment—sufficient to create a free speech privilege for expressions of opinion. The decision employs a "totality of circumstances" test as its constitutional standard for distinguishing fact from opinion. After examining the context of the article and the editor's disclaimer, the court concluded that even if the language was serious and restrained, the average reader of the journal would view the statements as an expression of opinion, protecting it under New York's constitution.

—Introduction by Hon. Albert M. Rosenblatt

One year ago, applying what appeared to be settled law, we affirmed the dismissal of plaintiff's libel action against the editor of a scientific journal, essentially for his publication of a signed letter to the editor on a subject of public controversy. We concluded that there was no triable issue of fact as to the falsity of the threshold factual assertions of the letter, that—beyond those threshold factual assertions—the letter writer's statements of opinion were entitled to the absolute protection of the State and Federal constitutional free speech guarantees, and that charges of defendant's deliberate incitement to have a defamatory letter published lacked factual foundation (*Immuno AG v Moor-Jankowski*, 74 NY2d 548).

On plaintiff's petition, the United States Supreme Court granted certiorari, vacated our judgment, and remanded the case for further consideration in light of *Milkovich v Lorain Journal Co.* (497 US 1 [1990]). For the reasons stated below, we adhere to our determination that defendant's summary judgment motion was properly granted and the complaint dismissed, premising our decision on independent State constitutional grounds as well as the Federal review directed by the Supreme Court.

I.

This libel action arises out of a letter to the editor published in the *Journal of Medical Primatology* in December 1983. The letter was written by Dr. Shirley McGreal as Chairwoman of the International Primate Protection League (IPPL), an organization known for its vigorous advocacy on behalf of primates, particularly those used for biomedical research. Defendant Dr. J. Moor-Jankowski, a professor of medical research at New York University School of Medicine and director of the Laboratory for Experimental Medicine and Surgery in Primates of the New York University Medical Center, is cofounder and editor of the Journal.

The subject of McGreal's letter was a plan by plaintiff, Immuno AG—a multinational corporation based in Austria that manufactures biologic products derived from blood plasma—to establish a facility in Sierra Leone, West Africa, for hepatitis research using chimpanzees. Voicing the concerns of IPPL, McGreal's letter was critical of Immuno's proposal on a number of grounds: (1) that the motivation for the plan was presumably to avoid international policies or legal restrictions on the importation of chimpanzees, an endangered species; (2) that it could decimate the wild chimpanzee population, as capture of chimpanzees generally involved killing their mothers, and it was questionable whether experimental animals could be returned to the wild, as plaintiff proposed; and (3) that returning the animals to the wild could well spread hepatitis to the rest of the chimpanzee population. McGreal stated that the current population of captive chimpanzees should be adequate to supply any legitimate requirements.

The letter was prefaced by an Editorial Note written by defendant that set out its background. Identifying McGreal as Chairwoman of IPPL, the Note stated that the Journal had received the initial version of the letter in January 1983 and had submitted it to plaintiff for comment or reply. Plaintiff had acknowledged receipt of defendant's letter in February, offering no comment but that it was referring the matter to its New York lawyers. Thereafter, plaintiff's lawyers wrote that the statements were inaccurate, unfair and reckless, and requested the documents upon which the accusations were based, threatening legal action if the letter were printed before plaintiff had a meaningful opportunity to reply. The Editorial Note went on to state that the editors had advised plaintiff's attorneys that they should obtain the documentation directly from McGreal, and extended the period for plaintiff's reply by two months. The letter was published nearly a year after its receipt. In the meantime, articles had appeared in the Austrian press apparently confirming much of what McGreal had written, and defendant received no further word from plaintiff or its lawyers.

In addition to the letter that is the focus of contention, plaintiff complains that it was defamed by comments made by defendant quoted in an article entitled "Loophole May Allow Trade in African Chimps" that appeared in the *New Scientist* magazine shortly before McGreal's letter was published. Defendant is quoted as saying that the supply of captive chimpanzees was sufficient for research, describing plaintiff's attempts to circumvent controls on endangered species as "scientific imperialism," and warning that they will "backfire on people like me involved in the bona fide use of chimpanzees and other primate animals" for research.

In December 1984, plaintiff commenced this lawsuit against Moor-Jankowski and seven other defendants, including McGreal and the publishers and distributors of the *New Scientist* and the *Journal of Medical Primatology*, and it has since been vigorously litigated. By now, all the defendants except Moor-Jankowski have settled with plaintiff for what the motion court described as "substantial sums," and the complaint has been dismissed as to them. After extensive discovery—his own deposition conducted over 14 days—defendant moved for summary judgment. Supreme Court granted the motion to the extent of dismissing a claim for prima facie tort. It denied the motion as to the defamation claims, ruling that the statements at issue were statements of fact and, regardless of whether plaintiff was a public figure, there were triable issues of fact concerning whether defendant acted with actual malice in making or publishing the statements.

II.

Our analysis first focuses on *Milkovich*, in compliance with the Supreme Court's direction on remand.

As the Supreme Court wrote, *Milkovich* leaves in place all previously existing Federal constitutional protections, including the " 'breathing space' " which " 'freedoms of expression require in order to survive' " and specifically including immunity for statements of opinion relating to matters of public concern that do not contain a provably false factual connotation *Milkovich*, however, puts an end to the perception—as it turns out, misperception—traceable to dictum in *Gertz v Robert Welch, Inc.* (418 US 323, 339–340) that, in addition to all other Federal constitutional protections, there is a "wholesale defamation exemption for anything that might be labeled 'opinion.' "

Thus, statements of opinion relating to matters of public concern are today no less subject to constitutional protection, but speech earns no greater protection simply because it is labeled "opinion."

The key inquiry is whether challenged expression, however labeled by defendant, would reasonably appear to state or imply assertions of objective fact. In making this inquiry, courts cannot stop at literalism. The literal words of challenged statements do not entitle a media defendant to "opinion" immunity or a libel plaintiff to go forward with its action. In determining whether speech is actionable, courts must additionally consider the impression created by the words used as well as the general tenor of the expression, from the point of view of the reasonable person. . . .

The United States Supreme Court, looking at basically the same first two *Ollman* factors (*Ollman v Evans*, 750 F2d 970 [DC Cir 1984]), determined that a reasonable fact finder could conclude that the challenged statements in *Milkovich* implied an assertion that petitioner had perjured himself in a judicial proceeding, and the connotation that petitioner had committed a felony was sufficiently factual to be susceptible of being proved true or false. Those were the same conclusions that had been reached by the Ohio court.

The critical difference lay in the Supreme Court's treatment of the second two *Ollman* factors—the immediate and broader context of the article—reduced essentially to one: type of speech. Moreover, the Court made clear that by protected type of speech it had in mind the rhetorical hyperbole, vigorous epithets, and lusty and imaginative expression found in *Hustler Mag. v Falwell* (485 US 46 [ad parody]); *Letter Carriers v Austin* (418 US 264 [labor dispute]), and *Greenbelt Publ. Assn. v Bresler* (398 US 6 [heated real estate negotiation])—all instances where the Court had determined that the imprecise language and unusual setting would signal the reasonable observer that no actual facts were being conveyed about an individual.

In *Milkovich*, the Supreme Court resolved "type of speech" considerations in two sentences: "This is not the sort of loose, figurative or hyperbolic language which would negate the impression that the writer was seriously maintaining petitioner committed the crime of perjury. Nor does the general tenor of the article negate this impression" (*Milkovich v Lorain Journal Co.*, 497 US at 21).

In this analysis, the Supreme Court said nothing of either the conjectural language of the disputed article, or the format of the piece—a signed editorial column appearing on the sports page. Both those considerations occupied the Ohio court and the dissent at length (*see* Brennan, J., dissenting), ultimately persuading those Judges that no reasonable reader would have regarded the challenged assertions, *in their context*, as factual. The Supreme Court's failure to mention either point becomes particularly telling when its writing is laid against the State court opinion and Justice Brennan's dissent.

Thus, if not alone from the Supreme Court's statement of the governing rules, then from its application of those rules to the facts of *Milkovich*, it appears that the following balance has been struck between First Amendment protection for media defendants and protection for individual reputation: except for special situations of loose, figurative, hyperbolic language, statements that contain or imply assertions of provably false fact will likely be actionable.

We next apply *Milkovich* to the facts before us.

In general, as previously observed, it is hard to conceive that any published statement could be without some factual grounding. In particular, we recognized that the McGreal letter was provoked by a certain state of affairs, that it set out limited points of factual reference, and that to the extent that letter contained defamatory factual statements about plaintiff, they would be actionable if false (74 NY2d at 559).

Unlike the Supreme Court's characterization of the analysis done in *Scott v News-Herald*, we did not, and do not, hold that the assertions of verifiable fact in the McGreal letter were overridden or "trumped" by their immediate or broader context and therefore automatically and categorically protected as opinion. We did not, and do not, hold that all letters to the editor are absolutely immune from defamation actions, or that there is a wholesale exemption for anything that might be labeled "opinion."

But a libel plaintiff has the burden of showing the falsity of factual assertions, and we concluded that plaintiff did not meet that burden. Given the thorough Appellate Division review of the factual assertions in issue, there hardly seemed a need for repetition of the charges and the relevant evidence. . . .

According to plaintiff, the core premise of the letter is as follows: "Release of chimpanzee 'veterans' of hepatitis non-A, non-B research would be hazardous to wild populations, as there is no way to determine that an animal is definitely not a carrier of the disease."

Applying *Milkovich*, we discern two assertions of fact, one express and one implied. First, the statement asserts that there is no scientific method for determining if a chimpanzee exposed to the non-A, non-B virus is not a carrier of the disease. Second, the statement implies that plaintiff will release possible carrier-chimpanzees who may endanger the wild population. Both assertions—the existence of a scientific test to determine carrier status, and plaintiff's plans—are verifiable. Finally, the "type of speech," unlike *Falwell*, *Letter Carriers* or *Greenbelt*, is restrained, the statements are seriously maintained, and they have an apparent basis in fact.

Though this core premise could be actionable, plaintiff's complaint was nonetheless properly dismissed because, on the record presented, it was apparent that plaintiff did not satisfy its burden of proving those statements false. . . .

As for the express assertion of the absence of a test, plaintiff has pointed us to no proof establishing a scientific test in the relevant period that could conclusively determine the carrier state in chimpanzees or, more specifically, could definitely rule out that a veteran chimpanzee was not a carrier of the virus. When considered against the extensive record, plaintiff's effort to establish that there was a fail-proof test, by weaving together isolated fragments of the testimony of various experts (including defendant), simply does not satisfy its legal burden.

To the contrary, what is apparent from the record is that in the relevant period there was an ongoing process of discovery and debate centering on the very existence of a carrier state of the virus, all of which was made even more inconclusive by ambiguity as to precisely when relevant technology was acquired. When asked if it was possible that certain tests for detecting the carrier state would yield negative results even though the chimpanzee carried the virus, plaintiff's Dr. Johann Eibl replied "there is no proof on that." Finally, even if the express assertion of the "core premise" had been shown to be false, that assertion would not itself libel plaintiff, because it does not " 'stat[e] actual facts' about [that] individual" (*Milkovich v Lorain Journal Co.*, 497 US at 20; *see also King Prods. v Douglas*, 742 F Supp 778, 784 [SD NY]).

Similarly, as the Appellate Division concluded, there was no proof of falsity of the implied assertion of fact—that plaintiff in the relevant period planned to release chimpanzees with no means of definitely determining that they were not carriers of the disease, thus endangering the wild populations. It is clear from the record that plaintiff, in 1983, was considering the option of rehabilitating chimpanzees used at the projected Sierra Leone facility, for return to a natural state (*see* 145 AD2d at 136). With no proof of the falsity of the express assertion that there was a conclusive test of carrier status available in 1983, it follows that there was also no proof of the falsity of the implied assertion that plaintiff planned to return its veteran test animals with no means of definitely determining that they were not hepatitis carriers.

As an additional matter, the Appellate Division considered infectiousness as well as carrier status (the "core premise" refers only to carriers [*see* 145 AD2d at 139]). Although there was testimony that infectiousness might be tested by inoculating a healthy chimpanzee with the blood of a potentially infected animal to see whether the healthy animal developed hepatitis symptoms, plaintiff produced no proof that it would in fact be implementing that procedure at its facility. That procedure was described by Dr. Alfred Prince, a leading expert, as "expensive," "laborious" and "wasteful," in that it involved the deliberate infection of healthy chimpanzees to test the infectiousness of animals that had been exposed to the virus. As the Appellate Division noted, "McGreal can hardly be faulted for not assuming that Immuno would necessarily perform the inoculation procedure on every one of the many chimps it intended to return to the wild" (145 AD2d at 140).

In sum, our "further consideration in light of *Milkovich*" using the core premise as illustrative, confirms our conclusion that, on this factual record, summary judgment was properly granted to defendant. . . .

III.

We next proceed to a State law analysis, and also conclude on this separate and independent ground that the complaint was correctly dismissed.

A.

It has long been recognized that matters of free expression in books, movies and the arts generally, are particularly suited to resolution as a matter of State common law and State constitutional law, the Supreme Court under the Federal Constitution fixing only the minimum standards applicable throughout the Nation, and the State courts supplementing those standards to meet local needs and expectations (*see e.g. People ex rel. Arcara v Cloud Books*, 68 NY2d 553, 557–558). Indeed, striking an appropriate balance "between the need for vigorous public discourse and the need to redress injury to citizens wrought by invidious or irresponsible speech" (*Milkovich v Lorain Journal Co.*, 497 US at 14), is consistent with the traditional role of State courts in applying privileges, including the opinion privilege, which have their roots in the common law. . . .

This State, a cultural center for the Nation, has long provided a hospitable climate for the free exchange of ideas . . . That tradition is embodied in the free speech guarantee of the New York State Constitution, beginning with the ringing declaration that "every citizen may freely speak, write and publish . . . sentiments on all subjects" (NY Const, art I, § 8). Those words, unchanged since the adoption of the constitutional provision in 1821, reflect the deliberate choice of the New York State Constitutional Convention not to follow the language of the First Amendment, ratified 30 years earlier, but instead to set forth our basic democratic ideal of liberty of the press in strong affirmative terms (*see* Forkosch, *Freedom of the Press: Croswell's Case*, 33 Fordham L Rev 415 [1965]).

"The expansive language of our State constitutional guarantee (*compare* NY Const, art I, § 8, *with* US Const 1st Amend), its formulation and adoption prior to the Supreme

Court's application of the First Amendment to the States . . . the recognition in very early New York history of a constitutionally guaranteed liberty of the press . . . and the consistent tradition in this State of providing the broadest possible protection to 'the sensitive role of gathering and disseminating news of public events' . . . all call for particular vigilance by the courts of this State in safeguarding the free press against undue interference" (*O'Neill v Oakgrove Constr.*, 71 NY2d 521, 528–529).

Thus, whether by the application of "interpretive" (*e.g.* text, history) or "noninterpretive" (*e.g.* tradition, policy) factors, the "protection afforded by the guarantees of free press and speech in the New York Constitution is often broader than the minimum required by" the Federal Constitution (*O'Neill v Oakgrove Constr.*, 71 NY2d at 529 n 3).

Had defendant initially presented the issue as one of independent State constitutional law, instead of as an undenominated argument premised on the assumed identity of State and Federal law, it might have been resolved on that basis a year ago. The intervening occurrence of *Milkovich*, however, does not cause us to change our explicit conclusion that the case was correctly analyzed and decided in accordance with the core values protected by the State Constitution. . . . Several considerations impel us to restate those conclusions separately now, underscoring that we decide this case on the basis of State law independently, and that in our State law analysis reference to Federal cases is for the purpose of guidance only, not because it compels the result we reach (*see Michigan v Long*, 463 US 1032, 1038 n 4, 1041–1042).

First and foremost, we look to our State law because of the nature of the issue in controversy—liberty of the press—where this State has its own exceptional history and rich tradition (*see* discussion at 249, *supra*). While we look to the unique New York State constitutional text and history, our analysis also is informed by the common law of this State. It has long been our standard in defamation actions to read published articles in context to test their effect on the average reader, not to isolate particular phrases but to consider the publication as a whole. . . .

Second, we are mindful not only of our role in the Federal system but also of our responsibility to settle the law of this State. As has been observed, *Milkovich* may leave an area of uncertainty for future litigation, with courts and authors in the interim lacking clear guidance regarding the opinion privilege; while all of the Supreme Court Justices agreed on the rule, they differed sharply as to how the rule should be applied. If we again assume the identity of State and Federal law, and assume that *Milkovich* has effected no change in the law, we perpetuate the uncertainty in our State law. Moreover, we are concerned that—if indeed "type of speech" is to be construed narrowly—insufficient protection may be accorded to central values protected by the law of this State. We would begin the analysis—just as we did previously in this case, and just as we did in *Steinhilber* (68 NY2d at 293) with the content of the whole communication, its tone and apparent purpose. That is a clear and familiar standard that in our view properly balances the interests involved. It has been consistently applied throughout the State for several years, following State common law and following *Steinhilber*.

Finally, the case comes to us in the posture of a summary judgment motion, which searches the record and presents only issues of law. The State law issues have now been fully briefed, and there are no factual questions to be resolved. . . .

Any independent State law activity in one sense can frustrate the pronouncement of Federal law. In another sense, however, State constitutional law review—which is a responsibility of State courts and a strength of our Federal system—advances the process of pronouncing Federal law; a State can act as a "laboratory" in more ways than one, as indeed Justice Brandeis recognized in *New State Ice Co. v Liebmann* in his reference to State statutes (285 US 262, 311 [dissenting]; *see also Batson v Kentucky*, 476 US 79, *especially* at 82 n 1). By the same token, Federal cases, including Supreme Court cases— even *Milkovich* itself—can act as a source of guidance for State courts in formulating State law, even though interpretation of those cases in State law decisions reached on adequate and independent State grounds will be unreviewable by the Supreme Court (*see Michigan v Long*, 463 US at 1041).

In analyzing cases under the State Constitution, this Court has not wedded itself to any single methodology, recognizing that the proper approach may vary with the circumstances. . . . The Supreme Court has specifically directed us to consider the case in light of *Milkovich*, and we comply with that direction, as courts throughout the Nation have done in similar circumstances (*see e.g. People v Duncan*, 124 Ill 2d 400, 530 NE2d 423 [1988]). But that does not compel us to ignore our prior decision or the arguments fully presented on remand that provide an alternative basis for resolving the case. . . . Turning our back on the now developed, controlling State law issues would be no service to the Supreme Court, or the litigants, or the law of this State.

We therefore proceed to resolve this case independently as a matter of State law, concluding that—as we previously held in *Immuno*—the standard articulated and applied in *Steinhilber* furnishes the operative standard in this State for separating actionable fact from protected opinion.

B.

Letters to the editor, unlike ordinary reporting, are not published on the authority of the newspaper or journal. In this case, for instance, defendant's prefatory Editorial Note signaled that the letter was to be given only the weight its readers chose to accord McGreal's views; such reservations may be generally understood even when letters are not accompanied by any editorial note. Thus, any damage to reputation done by a letter to the editor generally depends on its inherent persuasiveness and the credibility of the writer, not on the belief that it is true because it appears in a particular publication.

Significantly, for many members of the public, a letter to the editor may be the only available opportunity to air concerns about issues affecting them. A citizen troubled by things going wrong "should be free to 'write to the newspaper': and the newspaper should be free to publish [the] letter. It is often the only way to get things put right." . . . The availability of such a forum is important not only because it allows persons or groups with views on a subject of public interest to reach and persuade the broader community but also because it allows the readership to learn about grievances, both from the original writers and from those who respond, that perhaps had previously circulated only as rumor; such a forum can advance an issue beyond invective. Finally, at the least, the public may learn something, for better or worse, about the person or group that wrote such a letter. . . .

Passing from the broader social setting to the immediate context of the letter, we note that the common expectation regarding letters to the editor has particular pertinence here.

As the Appellate Division observed, the *Journal of Medical Primatology* is directed to a highly specialized group of readers—medical doctors, researchers and the medical and science libraries of academic institutions. . . .

The letter itself related to a public controversy regarding use of live animals belonging to endangered species, including chimpanzees, in animal experimentation and research. McGreal (a known animal rights activist) and IPPL (whose very name broadcasts its point of view) were fully identified to readers of the letter. The letter made clear that its purpose was to voice the conservationist concerns of this partisan group in order "to draw this situation to the attention of interested parties." . . . Thus, like the broader social setting of McGreal's letter, the immediate context of the letter, together with the prefatory Note, would induce the average reader of this Journal to look upon the communication as an expression of opinion rather than a statement of fact, even though the language was serious and restrained.

Given the purpose of court review—to determine whether the reasonable reader would have believed that the challenged statements were conveying facts about the libel plaintiff—we believe that an analysis that begins by looking at the content of the whole communication, its tone and apparent purpose (*Steinhilber v Alphonse*, 68 NY2d at 293) better balances the values at stake than an analysis that first examines the challenged statements for express and implied factual assertions, and finds them actionable unless couched in loose, figurative or hyperbolic language in charged circumstances. . . .

The difference is more than theoretical. In the present case, for example, we conclude that what plaintiff now characterizes as the "core premise" of the IPPL letter both expressed and implied statements of fact that, if shown to be false (which they were not), would be actionable. That is true as well of other factual reference points considered by the Appellate Division and held to be lacking in demonstrated falsity. Our State law analysis of the remainder of the letter, however, would not involve the fine parsing of its length and breadth that might now be required under Federal law for speech that is not loose, figurative or hyperbolic. . . . Isolating challenged speech and first extracting its express and implied factual statements, without knowing the full context in which they were uttered, indeed may result in identifying many more implied factual assertions than would a reasonable person encountering that expression in context.

We conclude that the body of the letter in issue communicated the accusations of a group committed to the protection of primates, and that the writer's presumptions and predictions as to what "appeared to be" or "might well be" or "could well happen" or "should be" would not have been viewed by the average reader of the Journal as conveying actual facts about plaintiff. . . .

The public forum function of letters to the editor is closely related in spirit to the "marketplace of ideas" and oversight and informational values that compelled recognition of the privileges of fair comment, fair report and the immunity accorded expression of opinion. These values are best effectuated by according defendant some latitude to publish a letter to the editor on a matter of legitimate public concern—the letter's author, affiliation, bias and premises fully disclosed, rebuttal openly invited—free of defamation litigation.

A publication that provides a forum for such statements on controversial matters is not acting in a fashion "at odds with the premises of democratic government and with the orderly manner in which economic, social, or political change is to be effected" . . . but to the contrary is fostering those very values.

Finally, we reaffirm our regard for the particular value of summary judgment, where appropriate, in libel cases. . . . Indeed, this is an additional ground for preferring the independent State law approach to one that might make summary disposition less likely. . . . The chilling effect of protracted litigation can be especially severe for scholarly journals, such as defendant's, whose editors will likely have more than a passing familiarity with the subject matter of the specialized materials they publish. . . .

Hope v. Perales,
83 NY2d 563 (1994)

The court rejected state constitutional challenges to the Prenatal Care Assistance Program (PCAP), holding that the failure to include medically necessary abortions in a prenatal care public funding scheme for women with incomes up to 85 percent over the federal poverty level did not deprive such women of due process or equal protection. In so holding, the court concluded that the statutory failure to include abortions among PCAP's entitlements while nevertheless subsidizing certain prenatal services did not create an impermissible inducement for women to carry their pregnancies to term and relinquish their fundamental right of reproductive choice.

—Introduction by Hon. Robert M. Mandelbaum, law clerk 2003–2006

At issue is the validity, under the State Constitution, of New York's Prenatal Care Assistance Program (PCAP) (Public Health Law § 2520 *et seq.*). Plaintiffs claim that the statute is facially unconstitutional by reason of underinclusiveness, for its failure to include medically necessary abortions in a prenatal care public funding scheme for women with incomes up to 85% over the Federal poverty level (meaning annual income for a single pregnant woman of between $9,840 and $18,204).[1] We now reverse the Appellate Division order and declare the statute constitutional.

The Statute in Issue

New York's PCAP statute is best understood against the backdrop of related programs.

Medicaid was created by Congress in 1965 to provide Federal reimbursement to participating States for a portion of the cost of all medically necessary services for qualified individuals. Medicaid eligibility is determined by financial need, ultimately assessed by reference to the Federal poverty level—currently annual income below $9,840 for a single pregnant woman. Federal Medicaid reimbursement is available for abortion only in cases of rape or incest, or to save the life of the mother (*see* Pub L 103-112, § 509). States may, however, at their own option and expense, offer services additional to

---

1. Used throughout are the 1994 Federal poverty figures (59 Fed Reg 6277). Monthly income for PCAP-eligible single women would thus range from $820 to $1,517.

those reimbursed under Medicaid, and New York has consistently included all medically necessary abortions in its State Medicaid program (Social Services Law § 365-a [2], [5] [b]; 18 NYCRR 505.2 [e]).

In 1987, Congress created PCAP to afford Federal reimbursement to States providing prenatal care and related services for needy pregnant women with household incomes exceeding the Medicaid eligibility standard (*see* Omnibus Budget Reconciliation Act of 1987, Pub L 100-203, § 4101). Every State *must* offer PCAP to women with incomes at or below 133% of the poverty level, and *may* extend eligibility up to 185% of the poverty level, without regard to other resources these women may have (*see* 42 USC § 1396a *[l]* [2] [A]).

Effective January 1, 1990, New York amended its Public Health and Social Services Laws to participate in PCAP,[2] offering the maximum coverage for which Federal reimbursement is authorized (L 1989, ch 584).[3] Thus, in New York, a single pregnant woman with annual income between $9,840 and $18,204 is eligible for PCAP, which covers enumerated pregnancy-related services: prenatal risk assessment, prenatal care visits, laboratory services, parental health education, referrals for pediatric care and nutrition services, mental health and related social services, transportation to and from appointments, labor and delivery, post-pregnancy services such as family planning, inpatient care, dental services, emergency room services, home care and pharmaceuticals (Public Health Law § 2522 [1] [a]–[o]).

PCAP does not provide funding for an abortion, or transportation to or from an abortion.[4] An eligible woman who elects to have an abortion, however, may receive all other covered pregnancy and post-pregnancy services. PCAP coverage continues, without regard to a change in income, for 60 days after the month in which the pregnancy terminates, even if by abortion (*see* Public Health Law § 2521 [3]).

While Medicaid eligibility generally depends upon verification of the application (*see* Social Services Law § 366-a [2]), a pregnant woman applying for PCAP is immediately presumed eligible upon a preliminary showing to a qualified provider that her household income falls below 185% of the poverty level (*see* Public Health Law § 2529 [2]). Similarly, Medicaid applicants are required to exhaust certain household resources for eligibility (*see* Social Services Law § 366 [2]), while PCAP applicants need only satisfy the income requirement (*see* Public Health Law § 2521 [3]; Social Services Law § 366 [4] [o] [2]). These differences are rooted in the exigencies attendant upon the need for prenatal care.

As was made explicit at the time of New York's adoption of PCAP, the available benefits are tailored to the statutory objective of combatting the State's "unacceptably high rate of low birthweight and infant mortality"—reportedly higher than the national average—and

---

2. PCAP replaced New York's pilot Prenatal Care Assistance Program, created in 1987, which authorized the Commissioner of Health to provide grants of State funds to prenatal care service providers (*see* L 1987, ch 822). PCAP is funded and administered through the Medicaid program (*see* Social Services Law § 366 [4] [n], [o]; § 368-a [1] *[l]*).

3. In conjunction with PCAP, New York expanded its Medicaid program to provide Medicaid coverage for pregnant women with incomes at or below the Federal poverty level (*see* Social Services Law § 366 [4] [m]).

4. New York City, at its own expense, provides abortions free of charge to PCAP-eligible women.

increasing healthy births by ensuring adequate prenatal care to pregnant women who, although not indigent, are deemed less likely to spend their available resources to obtain good prenatal care (*see* Mem of State Exec Dept, 1989 McKinney's Session Laws of NY at 2218). Studies have documented the correlation between infant mortality and neurological abnormalities on the one hand, and low birthweight and premature birth on the other— conditions ameliorated by proper care throughout pregnancy, which can be costly (*see e.g.* House Report No. 99-727 to Pub L 99-509 at 99, *reprinted in* 1986 US Code Cong & Admin News 3689). PCAP unquestionably is highly effective in meeting its objective.

Proceedings Below

In September 1990, plaintiffs, led by PCAP-eligible women Jane Hope and Jane Moe,[5] commenced this action against the Commissioners of Social Services and Health seeking a preliminary injunction against implementation of the PCAP program to the extent it excludes funding for medically necessary abortions, and a declaration that PCAP-eligible women are entitled to such funding.

Citing evidence that abortions in New York cost between $200 and $3,500 (depending on the facility and the stage of pregnancy), plaintiffs alleged that PCAP-eligible women are otherwise unable to afford abortions. Jane Hope, age 19, was then a PCAP-eligible pregnant woman advised by her doctor that an abortion was medically necessary, and unable to afford the procedure on her earnings of $230 per week. Jane Moe was income eligible under PCAP and, although not pregnant at that time, is a carrier of a fatal genetic defect that would compel her to have an abortion if she were to become pregnant.

Defendants cross-moved for summary judgment declaring the constitutionality of chapter 584. Supreme Court granted the injunction, holding that PCAP violates the Due Process (NY Const, art I, § 6), Equal Protection (NY Const, art I, § 11), Aid to the Needy (NY Const, art XVII, § 1) and Public Health (NY Const, art XVII, § 3) Clauses of the State Constitution by affirmatively and impermissibly pressuring women to choose childbirth over abortion. The court considered and rejected plaintiffs' additional argument that PCAP impinges upon the free exercise of religion under the State Constitution (NY Const, art I, § 3), a holding not challenged on appeal. Instead of invalidating PCAP as underinclusive, Supreme Court enlarged the beneficial statute to include medically necessary abortions, staying its order pending appellate review. The Appellate Division affirmed (the Presiding Justice dissenting), agreeing with the trial court that the statute was unconstitutional because it coerced, steered or pressured low-income women into choosing childbirth, thus abridging their fundamental right to choose.

Because a substantial constitutional question is directly involved, defendants appeal as of right (*see* CPLR 5601 [b] [1]). We granted leave to intervenor-respondent Alma Poindexter, a PCAP recipient.

---

5. The other plaintiffs are four obstetricians/gynecologists, a nurse-midwife, seven health care clinics serving low-income women, four reproductive rights advocacy organizations and two members of the clergy. Supreme Court determined that Moe and the clergy members lacked standing to bring this action, a conclusion not challenged on appeal.

Analysis

Analysis begins by articulating the common ground. Plainly, PCAP satisfies Federal constitutional standards (*see Harris v McRae*, 448 US 297, 316–318, and n 19; *Maher v Roe*, 432 US 464, 474–475). Only the State Constitution is in issue. Moreover, no one disputes that, as every enactment of a coequal branch of government, PCAP is entitled to a strong presumption of constitutionality, and that plaintiffs bear the heavy burden of establishing the contrary beyond a reasonable doubt (*see Matter of Klein [Hartnett]*, 78 NY2d 662, 666, *cert denied* 504 US 912). It is not the role of the courts to pass upon the wisdom of the Legislature's policy choice, even though there may be differences of views about the decision to exclude a medically necessary service from an otherwise comprehensive prenatal care program.

Similarly, it is undisputed by defendants that the fundamental right of reproductive choice, inherent in the due process liberty right guaranteed by our State Constitution, is at least as extensive as the Federal constitutional right (*see Roe v Wade*, 410 US 113, 153–154; *Rivers v Katz*, 67 NY2d 485, 493; *see also Planned Parenthood of Southeastern Pa. v Casey*, 505 US 833, 868–872). Nor do defendants challenge New York's long-standing commitment to fund abortions for poor women under the Medicaid program (*see* Social Services Law § 365-a [2], [5] [b]; *see also Matter of City of New York v Wyman*, 30 NY2d 537, *revg on dissent below* 37 AD2d 700).

Finally, plaintiffs do not contend that the statute imposes any direct burden, that it makes abortions any less accessible or less affordable for PCAP-eligible women (*see Golden v Clark*, 76 NY2d 618, 626; *Matter of Schulman v New York City Health & Hosps. Corp.*, 38 NY2d 234, 240). PCAP-eligible women (who have income above the poverty level and need not exhaust other resources to establish eligibility) are presumptively able to afford abortion, a legislative premise not rebutted on the record before us. As defendants point out, PCAP may even make abortion more affordable for these women as—irrespective of pregnancy outcome—the statute offers free testing for fetal abnormalities that may early in pregnancy indicate the need for (and thereby reduce the cost of) an abortion, mental health and social services, family planning and 60-day postpartum care.

Instead, the heart of plaintiffs' challenge is that by funding certain childbirth services for these women, but not abortion, the Legislature has violated an obligation under the Due Process Clause not to influence the exercise of a fundamental right.[6] Plaintiffs recognize that the fundamental right of reproductive choice does not carry with it an entitlement to sufficient public funds to exercise that right, and that the State is not required to remove burdens, such as indigence, not of its creation. They urge, however, that by failing to include abortions among PCAP entitlements, the statute creates an impermissible inducement for women to carry their pregnancies to term and relinquish their fundamental right of choice.

Plaintiffs have failed to establish their contention that PCAP even indirectly infringes the right of reproductive choice. There is no evidence that eligible women are coerced, pressured, steered or induced by PCAP to carry pregnancies to term. Thus, even if we

---

6. While plaintiffs also assert a denial of equal protection, equal protection is at the core of their due process argument, and both challenges fail for much the same reasons.

were to recognize a governmental obligation to stand neutral—an issue we need not and do not reach in this case—no violation of such a requirement has been demonstrated here.

Plaintiffs' contention that a selective allocation of public funds in favor of childbirth over abortion can be an indirect burden on the fundamental abortion right arises from the dissenting opinions of the United States Supreme Court concerning Medicaid funding (*see Harris*, 448 US at 330 [Brennan, J., dissenting] [the "denial of funds for medically necessary abortions plainly intrudes upon this constitutionally protected (abortion) decision, for both by design and in effect it serves to coerce indigent pregnant women to bear children that they would otherwise elect not to have"]; *see also Maher*, 432 US at 484 [Brennan, J., dissenting]). Put succinctly, "[i]t matters not that . . . the Government has used the carrot rather than the stick" (*see Harris*, 448 US at 334 [Brennan, J., dissenting]).[7]

This principle has been embraced by several States as a matter of State constitutional law, invalidating Medicaid funding schemes that exclude medically necessary abortions from comprehensive medical care for the indigent (*see Moe v Secretary of Admin. & Fin.*, 382 Mass 629, 654–655, 417 NE2d 387, 402 [1981]; *Committee to Defend Reproductive Rights v Myers*, 29 Cal 3d 252, 270, 284–285, 172 Cal Rptr 866, 876, 885–886, 625 P2d 779, 789, 798–799 [1981]; *Right to Choose v Byrne*, 91 NJ 287, 307 n 5, 450 A2d 925, 935 n 5 [1982]; *Women's Health Ctr. v Panepinto*, 446 SE2d 658, 661 [W Va]).

The case before us is significantly different. Unlike an indigent woman, whose option to choose an abortion is arguably foreclosed by her lack of resources, the PCAP-eligible woman—not ordinarily a recipient of State assistance—presumptively has the financial means to exercise her fundamental right of choice. That the Legislature in these circumstances elects to subsidize certain prenatal services cannot, in and of itself, be deemed coercive, and no showing has been made that such a woman would be influenced by PCAP to carry a child to term.

Nor does the statute impermissibly penalize women for exercising their right to choose. In *Regan v Taxation with Representation of Wash.* (461 US 540, 545), for example, the Supreme Court upheld Congress' refusal to extend a tax deduction to charitable contributions made for lobbying activities, concluding that a mere failure to subsidize the exercise of plaintiffs' right of free speech, even though the deduction was available to those who did not lobby, was constitutionally permissible. Like the regulation in *Regan*, PCAP simply fails to subsidize abortion. Eligibility for the program does not terminate if a participant aborts her pregnancy, nor does the statute require reimbursement for any services received before abortion. PCAP does not penalize the exercise of the right of choice, as it does not deny eligibility for any benefit to which participants choosing to abort would otherwise be entitled.

We thus conclude that PCAP does not in any sense burden a fundamental right, and accordingly the statute is valid if it bears a rational relationship to the State's interest

---

7. This principle may be traced to *Sherbert v Verner* (374 US 398, 404), in which the Supreme Court invalidated a State provision denying unemployment benefits based on the refusal of a Seventh-day Adventist to accept Saturday work, holding that "the liberties of religion and expression may be infringed by the denial of or placing of conditions upon a benefit or privilege." The Supreme Court itself has limited the neutrality obligation recognized in *Sherbert* to regulations that infringe on rights arising under the Establishment and Freedom of Religion Clauses of the First Amendment (*see Maher v Roe*, 432 US at 475 n 8).

in providing much-needed prenatal care to low-income women (*see Golden v Clark*, 76 NY2d at 624). Because plaintiffs concede the laudable goals and effectiveness of PCAP in ameliorating infant mortality and morbidity, we conclude that it does satisfy the rational relationship test.

We briefly address plaintiffs' remaining constitutional claims, which arise from the Aid to the Needy (NY Const, art XVII, § 1) and Public Health (NY Const, art XVII, § 3) Clauses of the State Constitution. Plaintiffs urge that PCAP violates those provisions by excluding coverage for medically necessary abortions without regard to the financial or medical need of the participants. This contention fails because, as discussed previously, we are bound to accept the legislative determination that PCAP-eligible women are not indigent or in need of public assistance to meet their medical needs. We cannot infer the contrary from the mere fact that PCAP—aimed neither at the protection of public health nor at the support of the needy—was enacted (*see Tucker v Toia*, 43 NY2d 1, 8 [art XVII, § 1 imposes affirmative obligation on the Legislature to aid "those whom it has classified as needy"]).

Moreover, both clauses expressly accord to the Legislature discretion to promote the State's interest in aiding the needy and promoting public health "in such manner, and by such means as the legislature may from time to time determine" (NY Const, art XVII, §§ 1, 3). We cannot say beyond a reasonable doubt that, by not including abortion funding in PCAP the Legislature has transgressed its powers.

Accordingly, the order of the Appellate Division should be reversed, with costs, and judgment granted declaring valid chapter 584 of the Laws of 1989.

People v. Wesley,
83 NY2d 417 (1994)

This case presented the court with two important questions: admissibility of DNA profiling evidence in a criminal proceeding, and whether admissibility of novel scientific evidence met the long-held New York standard derived from *Frye v. United States* (293 F 1013 [D.C. Cir 1923]). Under *Frye*, admissibility turns on whether the scientific evidence in question is "generally accepted" in the scientific community. The majority in *Wesley* construed the lack of expert controversy about the technique as evidence of its reliability, but Chief Judge Kaye pointed out that this dearth of reporting reflected the novel and unreliable nature of the technique. She also emphasized that it was not enough to show that a technique was accepted as reliable; it must also be shown that the technique was performed in conformity with those standards in the case at trial. Her concurrence was cited with enduring frequency in numerous jurisdictions as DNA evidence became more common in the courtroom. Notably, the very concerns she raised in this opinion were still alive more than twenty years later, as described in an article in *The Atlantic*, "The False Promise of DNA Testing" (June 2016). Despite the great attention the *Wesley* case garnered at the time, it was an odd vehicle for exploring the utility of DNA evidence in criminal cases because the evidence at trial did not purport to establish the identity of the perpetrator of the crime; rather, the bloodstain that was typed belonged to the victim and was found on the defendant's shirt. The defendant had never denied being present in the room with the victim. The forensic evidence was therefore ultimately inconclusive.

—Introduction by Mary Rothwell Davis, law clerk 1993–1995

(Concurring) We conclude that it was error to admit the DNA bloodstain analysis evidence in this case. We nevertheless agree that defendant's conviction should be affirmed, because that evidence comprised only a minor part of the People's case. Although the result is unaffected, we write separately out of concern, for future cases, that the principles governing admission of novel scientific evidence be correctly articulated and applied.

Lest we add to rather than ameliorate confusion, we begin by stating points on which the Court is unanimous.

The Court agrees unanimously that where the scientific evidence sought to be presented is novel, the test is that articulated in *Frye v United States* (293 F 1013, 1014 [1923]), in essence whether there is general acceptance in the relevant scientific community that a technique or procedure is capable of being performed reliably (*People v Middleton*, 54 NY2d 42, 49 [1981]).[1] In the present case, such an inquiry required assessment of whether the technique employed in forensic DNA analysis had gained scientific acceptance—that is, whether the six steps of the Restriction Fragment Length Polymorphic (RFLP) procedure, the procedure for declaring that two samples of DNA were identical (step seven), and assessment of the significance of a "match" (step eight) were generally accepted as reliable by experts in the field.

The Court is unanimous, moreover, in concluding that three inquiries are involved in the consideration of novel scientific evidence. The first—the *Frye* hearing—asks whether, theoretically, the accepted techniques, when performed as they should be, generate results generally accepted as reliable within the scientific community. Once a scientific procedure has been proved reliable, a *Frye* inquiry need not be conducted each time such evidence is offered. Courts thereafter may take judicial notice of reliability of the general procedure.

Next, a foundational inquiry must be satisfied before such evidence is placed before the jury: in each case the court must determine that the laboratory actually employed the accepted techniques. This foundational inquiry also goes to admissibility of the evidence, not simply its weight (*People v Middleton*, 54 NY2d at 45, 50, *supra*).[2] Finally, infirmities in collection and analysis of the evidence not affecting its trustworthiness go to weight, to be assessed by the jury.[3]

Where we part company with our colleagues is in the application of these principles. We do not agree that the eight steps of forensic analysis, then in its infancy, were shown to have been accepted as reliable within the scientific community. Rather, the standard for general acceptance of the new techniques was seen as commensurate with the standards adopted by Lifecodes, the commercial laboratory hired to conduct the actual tests and which virtually occupied the field of forensic DNA analysis. Additionally, the hearing court made very clear to the parties in its *Frye* decision that it considered only the theory of forensic DNA analysis as going to admissibility, and relegated the remaining questions for weighing by the jury, including such foundational inquiries as whether Lifecodes' methodology and procedures were adequate to assure the reliability and accuracy of the

---

1. Even the new federal test articulated in *Daubert v Merrell Dow Pharms.* (509 US 579 [1993]) would require proof of reliability of novel scientific evidence.

2. We disagree with the conclusion of the court in *People v Castro* (144 Misc 2d 956, 959 [1989]) that the foundational inquiry is part of a special "DNA Frye test." Our cases have always required a foundational inquiry before scientific evidence can be admitted (*see e.g. People v Middleton*, 54 NY2d at 45), even after a particular technique has passed out of the "twilight zone" of "novel" evidence that is the subject of *Frye* and is judicially noticed as reliable (*see People v Knight*, 72 NY2d 481, 487 [1988] [radar speed detection]; *People v Campbell*, 73 NY2d 481, 485 [1989] [blood alcohol content test]; *People v Mertz*, 68 NY2d 136, 148 [1986] [same]; *People v Freeland*, 68 NY2d 699, 701 [1986] [same]; *Pereira v Pereira*, 35 NY2d 301, 307 [1974] [polygraph test used for investigative purposes]). While the *Frye* hearing and foundational inquiry may proceed simultaneously, in the present case the *Frye* inquiry was conducted before any samples were taken, so that a foundational inquiry was not possible at that time.

3. Brief gaps in the chain of custody, for example, may not affect trustworthiness of the test results, while challenges to the forensic laboratory analysis may go to the heart of reliability of results and require preclusion (Imwinkelreid, *The Debate in the DNA Cases Over the Foundation for the Admission of Scientific Evidence: The Importance of Human Error as a Cause of Forensic Misanalysis*, 69 Wash U LQ 19, 27).

results (140 Misc 2d 306, 317 [1988]; *see also* 183 AD2d 75, 78 [1992]). In our view admission of this evidence was error.

The *Frye* Hearing in This Case

The *Frye* hearing in this case was virtually the first in the nation to consider whether forensic application of DNA analysis had been generally accepted as reliable. While the mere fact that a court is the first to evaluate novel scientific evidence does not mean the evidence is unreliable, it increases the task of the hearing court. If no court opinions, texts, laboratory standards or scholarly articles have been issued on the technique—the types of materials relevant to a determination of general acceptability (*Matter of Lahey v Kelly*, 71 NY2d 135, 144 [1987]; *People v Middleton*, 54 NY2d 42, 50, *supra*; *People v Leone*, 25 NY2d 511, 516–517 [1969]; *People v Magri*, 3 NY2d 562 [1958])—the court may, as it did here, take the testimony of expert witnesses.[4]

The People offered detailed testimony concerning the RFLP procedure—an accepted procedure for separating strands of DNA and locating their unique fragments—which had been in use for research and diagnostic purposes long before its forensic application was proposed. Dr. Kenneth Kidd and Dr. Richard Roberts, experts in molecular biology and population genetics, and Dr. Sandra Nierzwicki-Bauer, a molecular biologist specializing in the study of blue-green algae, vouched on behalf of the People for the reliability of RFLP procedure. None of these witnesses, however, was expert in forensic DNA analysis.

In defining the relevant scientific field, the court must seek to comply with the *Frye* objective of containing a consensus of the scientific community. If the field is too narrowly defined, the judgment of the scientific community will devolve into the opinion of a few experts. The field must still include scientists who would be expected to be familiar with the particular use of the evidence at issue, however, whether through actual or theoretical research (Giannelli, *The Admissibility of Novel Scientific Evidence: Frye v United States, a Half-Century Later*, 80 Colum L Rev 1197, 1209–1210).

Focusing on DNA profiling in the forensic setting is crucial because "DNA fingerprinting is far more technically demanding than DNA diagnostics," particularly in the art of declaring a "match" between samples (Lander, *DNA Fingerprinting on Trial*, 339 Nature 501). Traditional RFLP procedure was developed to enable scientists to identify the DNA structure contained within a particular sample, and had been in use for more

---

4. It is not for a court to take pioneering risks on promising new scientific techniques, because premature admission both prejudices litigants and short-circuits debate necessary to determination of the accuracy of a technique. Premature acceptance of "revolutionary" forensic techniques has led to wrongful conviction (*see* Giannelli, *The Admissibility of Novel Scientific Evidence: Frye v United States, a Half-Century Later*, 80 Colum L Rev 1197, 1224–1225 [discussing belated discovery of inaccuracy of paraffin test]; Neufeld and Colman, *When Science Takes the Witness Stand*, 262 [No. 5] Scientific Am 46 [discussing belated discovery of inaccuracy of gunpowder detection test]). In *People v Leone* (25 NY2d 511, 517–518, *supra*) we also warned against introduction of scientific evidence before its general reliability have been resolved in the scientific community, because " 'the value of the test . . . could easily become the question in the trial rather than that person's guilt or credibility' " (quoting *People v Davis*, 343 Mich 348, 372, 72 NW2d 269, 282 [1955]). Surely this case is an example of such diversion of focus.

than a decade at the time of this hearing. Its forensic application—comparison of DNA between two or more samples, one from an unknown source—is far more susceptible to error (*id.*). Techniques must be adapted to the special requirements of crime scene samples, which are subject to contamination that can confuse results. Moreover, steps seven and eight—the steps unique to forensic analysis of DNA—were truly novel.

The theoretical use of DNA profiling as a method for identifying perpetrators of crimes was first posited in 1985 in a series of articles by British researchers (Jeffreys, Wilson and Thein, *Hypervariable Minisatellite Regions in Human DNA*, 314 Nature 67–69; Jeffreys, Wilson and Thein, *Individual-Specific "Fingerprints" of Human DNA*, 316 Nature 76; Gill, Jeffreys and Werrett, *Forensic Application of DNA "Fingerprints,"* 318 Nature 577). By 1988, the only practitioners of the technique in this country were the commercial laboratories Cellmark (founded by Dr. Jeffreys), Cetus and Lifecodes, which began forensic analysis just one year before the hearing in this case. Little peer review of their techniques had taken place by 1988 because these enterprises endeavored to keep their methods secret to protect their proprietary interests. According to the defense witness Dr. Neville Colman, the procedures were still so new that there had not yet been efforts in the field to "validate by replication" the methods employed at Lifecodes; there had been neither refutation nor support of the technique in the professional literature.[5]

The point of noting controversy about the reliability of the forensic technique is not for our Court to determine whether the method was or was not reliable in 1988, but whether there was consensus in the scientific community as to its reliability. The *Frye* test emphasizes "counting scientists' votes, rather than on verifying the soundness of a scientific conclusion" (*Jones v United States*, 548 A2d 35, 42 [DC Ct App 1988]; *accord State v Montalbo*, 73 Haw 130, 828 P2d 1274, 1279 [1992]). Where controversy rages, a court may conclude that no consensus has been reached. Here, however, the problem was more subtle: absence of controversy reflected not the endorsement perceived by our colleagues, but the prematurity of admitting this evidence. Insufficient time had passed for competing points of view to emerge.[6]

The inquiry into forensic analysis of DNA in this case also demonstrates the "pitfalls of self-validation by a small group" (Hoeffel, *The Dark Side of DNA Profiling: Unreliable Scientific Evidence Meets the Criminal Defendant*, 42 Stan L Rev 465, 502, citing Black, *A Unified Theory of Scientific Evidence*, 56 Fordham L Rev 595, 625). Before bringing novel evidence to court, proponents of new techniques must subject their methods to the

---

5. The earliest law review study of forensic DNA profiling, however, completed about the same time as the decision on the suppression motion in this case, warned that "[u]nforeseen exceptions to the test's reliability are already beginning to surface" and that it was not yet ready for *Frye* scrutiny, citing concerns raised by Dr. Alec Jeffreys himself (Burk, *DNA Fingerprinting: Possibilities and Pitfalls of a New Technique*, 28 Jurimetrics 455, 468, 470 n 68 [summer 1988]).

6. In the six years between the *Frye* hearing in this case and our review of it, debate within the scientific community has exploded about forensic application of DNA analysis. In New York, the Governor's Panel on Forensic DNA Analysis issued an interim report in September 1989 (Poklemba Report) with recommendations for a model program. No final recommendations have been issued. In April 1992, the National Research Council (NRC) issued its report, *DNA Technology in Forensic Science*, initiated in January 1990. In fall 1993, the NRC announced its intention to issue an amended report with modified recommendations.

scrutiny of fellow scientists, unimpeded by commercial concerns (Thompson, *Evaluating the Admissibility of New Genetic Identification Tests: Lessons From the "DNA War,"* 84 Crim L & Criminology 22, 95).

A *Frye* court should be particularly cautious when—as here—"the supporting research is conducted by someone with a professional or commercial interest in the technique" (Giannelli, *The Admissibility of Novel Scientific Evidence: Frye v United States, a Half-Century Later,* 80 Colum L Rev 1197, 1213). DNA forensic analysis was developed in commercial laboratories under conditions of secrecy, preventing emergence of independent views. No independent academic or governmental laboratories were publishing studies concerning forensic use of DNA profiling. The Federal Bureau of Investigation did not consider use of the technique until 1989. Because no other facilities were apparently conducting research in the field, the commercial laboratory's unchallenged endorsement of the reliability of its own techniques was accepted by the hearing court as sufficient to represent acceptance of the technique by scientists generally. The sole forensic witness at the hearing in this case was Dr. Michael Baird, Director of Forensics at Lifecodes laboratory, where the samples were to be analyzed. While he assured the court of the reliability of the forensic application of DNA, virtually the sole publications on forensic use of DNA were his own or those of Dr. Jeffreys, the founder of Cellmark, one of Lifecodes' competitors. Nor had the forensic procedure been subjected to thorough peer review.

The absence of agreed-upon standards and laboratory protocol for the conduct of a technique can also serve to establish that the technique has not yet gained general acceptance (*People v Leone,* 25 NY2d 511, *supra*). Here, no laboratory conducting DNA analysis had been accredited for that purpose. As early as 1984, the legislature set standards, in the Family Court Act, for admissibility of blood genetic marker tests. Analysis of DNA samples considered on the question of paternity—where laboratories must also declare that two samples "match"—must be shown to have been performed in accordance with proper procedures by a laboratory authorized by the Commissioner of Health to conduct such tests (Family Ct Act §§ 418, 532). As of July 1992, however, no laboratory, including Lifecodes, had yet been authorized by the Commissioner of Health to conduct DNA testing (*Matter of S.L.B. v K.A.,* 155 Misc 2d 458, 459 [1992]). The defense introduced testimony from Dr. Anne Willey of the Department of Health establishing that no licensing or certification standards governing DNA profiling evidence had yet been developed in New York State, although discussions were ongoing. Lifecodes was licensed only to conduct genetic tests of amniotic fluid. As defendant pointed out to the hearing court, the evidence proffered against him to prove murder would not have been admissible in this state on the question of paternity.

The opinions of two scientists, both with commercial interests in the work under consideration and both the primary developers and proponents of the technique, were insufficient to establish "general acceptance" in the scientific field (*People v Leone,* 25 NY2d 511, 514, *supra*). The People's effort to gain a consensus by having their own witnesses "peer review" the relevant studies in time to return to court with supporting testimony was hardly an appropriate substitute for the thoughtful exchange of ideas in an unbiased scientific community envisioned by *Frye*. Our colleagues' characterization of a dearth of publications on this novel technique as the equivalent of unanimous endorsement of its reliability ignores the plain reality that this technique was not yet being discussed and tested in the scientific community.[7]

The hearing court also erred in failing to scrutinize the seventh and eighth steps of forensic DNA analysis pursuant to *Frye* standards. Our colleagues obscure this shortcoming by focusing on the wealth of evidence establishing the reliability of the first six steps of forensic analysis (the RFLP procedure)—a question that was not even disputed at the hearing. It is the absence of evidence concerning accepted standards for steps seven and eight that compels me to conclude admission of this evidence was error.

It is the declaration of a match between two samples of DNA, depicted on two separate autorads, that distinguishes forensic use of DNA from traditional, research-based application of RFLP procedure. The only evidence offered on this point was, again, the testimony of Dr. Michael Baird, who testified as to how a Lifecodes technician would visually compare the bands on two autorads to determine if they were the same. During the testimony of Dr. Borowsky, the court had the following exchange with the District Attorney:

> Let me ask you this. Let's just keep on this field. Is there some person who looks at the autorad, gentlemen, and says "All right, this is included, this one is not included?" or is the autorad read by computer or some kind of machine?
>
> DISTRICT ATTORNEY: It's read by a person.
>
> THE COURT: It's read by a person?
>
> DISTRICT ATTORNEY: Yes.
>
> THE COURT: All right. And a person with what expertise?
>
> DISTRICT ATTORNEY: Well, Dr. Balasz from Lifecodes, who's a Ph.D., he has read the auto[rads].

The People presented no evidence as to whether this was the procedure generally accepted as reliable in determining whether two DNA samples match beyond Dr. Baird's broad assertion that it was. Given the testimony from Dr. Borowsky indicating that autorad readings could lead to highly subjective results, it cannot be said that the People

---

7. While DNA evidence had been admitted in some criminal cases by mid-1988, the defense in this case was the very first to "mount . . . a serious challenge to DNA typing" (Thompson and Ford, *DNA Typing: Acceptance and Weight of the New Genetic Identification Tests*, 75 Va L Rev 45, 46 n 4). Contrary to the observations of our colleagues, therefore (majority op at 426), the fact that Lifecodes DNA evidence had been admitted without objection prior to the time of the hearing in this case was of little significance. This is particularly so since Dr. Michael Baird was also the witness vouching for the reliability of the unopposed Lifecodes evidence in those cases as well (Thompson and Ford, *op. cit.*, 75 Va L Rev 45, 49 n 20). The mere fact that the same assertions he made here had been repeated elsewhere—without challenge—did not render those statements more reliable.

met their burden of clearly establishing that there were generally accepted procedures for "reading" autorads in the scientific community.

Moreover, we can take note that the "visual" matching technique was rejected as unreliable once it came to the attention of neutral peers in the scientific community (National Research Council, *DNA Technology in Forensic Science* ["NRC Report"] § 2.3.5).[8] We now know that "visual matches" must be confirmed by a computerized measurement of the apparently matching bands. Only if these bands fall within certain defined parameters, called a "match window," will a match be declared (Attorney-General's amicus brief at 20). Moreover, band appearance and position may be altered by testing conditions, environmental factors or sample contamination, compelling scientists to employ a wide "latitude of acceptance" to account for discrepancies between prints and to permit declaration of a match even where bands are not identical. This creates a danger that DNA prints of different individuals will be mistakenly declared to match, and no formal standards existed for declaring a match in 1988 (Thompson and Ford, *DNA Typing: Acceptance and Weight of the New Genetic Identification Techniques*, 75 Va L Rev 45, 87–89 [1989]).

The People's failure to adduce evidence on the matching standards was pointed out by the defense at the hearing. In the course of examining Lifecodes' methods for assessing the statistical significance of a match, the defense witness Dr. Richard Borowsky, a population geneticist, repeatedly questioned the criteria employed by Lifecodes for determining that two autorads "matched." Defense counsel emphasized that "the way they read" autorads raises issues relevant to the reliability of the testing and that a negative result "may be just a matter of interpretation." Dr. Borowsky specifically cautioned that "the probability of error" in evaluating the frequency with which a particular gene will appear on an autorad band "has not been evaluated by the scientific community," and declared that "interpretation is as much as part of the print test as the molecular biology."

Our colleagues' conclusion that the reliability of the procedures employed in the instant case had been satisfactorily established overlooks that the samples had not been tested at the time of the *Frye* hearing, and the autoradiographs never examined prior to their admission at trial. Establishing a proper foundation requires at a minimum a determination that the autoradiographs were of a quality susceptible to interpretation (*People v Castro*, 144 Misc 2d 956, 967, 973–979 [1989]), an inquiry that was here foreclosed by the court's erroneous determination in its *Frye* decision that all questions as to how a sample was tested go to weight, not admissibility.

---

8. Because the question of admissibility of novel evidence is one of law, our determination on appeal should acknowledge when subsequent developments have cast doubt upon the result of the *Frye* hearing (*see e.g. People v Hughes*, 59 NY2d 523, 543 [1983]; *People v Taylor*, 75 NY2d 277 [1990]; *People v Williams*, 6 NY2d 18, 26 [1959]; *People v Magri*, 3 NY2d 562, 566 [1958]). Defendant unsuccessfully brought a motion pursuant to CPL 440.10 (1) (g) to vacate the conviction on April 18, 1990, alleging that the technique for declaring a "match" employed in 1988 had been proven unreliable. Indeed, the slip opinion—relying on 1990 and 1993 texts describes step seven as including both visual studies and computer imaging analysis. No such evidence was before the hearing court when it passed on the techniques at issue; it dispensed with this crucial phase of determining that an autoradiograph is suitable for analysis, and that two samples match, in just one sentence: "When comparing two DNA fragment patterns . . . one simply looks to see where the probe 'landed'" (140 Misc 2d 306, 317 [1988]).

Defendant also challenged the reliability of step eight, application of statistical methods to determine the significance of a "match." In its written decision, the court summarized what it saw as part of "[t]he defense attack": "that Lifecodes' population studies are inadequate to establish a claimed power of identity for its results under the laws of population genetics" (140 Misc 2d at 317). Dr. Borowsky sought to evaluate independently the autorads which comprised the population genetics database, warning that the absence of standards in the field led to subjective results.

Step eight is an integral part of DNA forensic analysis. Indeed, evidence of a "match" is virtually meaningless without resort to the statistical interpretation; population genetics is arguably the most crucial step of the analysis. It is the area of greatest controversy among the experts.[9] Whether the statistical technique employed by the laboratory meets the standards in the field and is capable of producing reliable results goes directly to admissibility. The hearing court erroneously characterized these concerns as affecting only the weight of the population genetics evidence.

We therefore conclude that the court erred in holding that DNA forensic analysis was generally accepted as reliable in 1988.

Harmless Error

Because of the overwhelming evidence of defendant's guilt, we join in affirming defendant's conviction in this instance where it can fairly be said that use of DNA evidence was harmless beyond a reasonable doubt (*People v Crimmins*, 36 NY2d 230, 237 [1975]). At the time the People raised the possibility of introducing DNA evidence, they apparently hoped tests would establish that semen found on the body of the deceased originated from defendant, establishing his guilt of her sexual assault. It is unclear why the court instigated a *Frye* hearing before these tests had even been conducted, for it turned out that the DNA tests on the semen sample were inconclusive. While evidence concerning the source of the semen would have been probative, it never materialized and was not introduced at trial.

Instead, the People presented evidence that DNA contained in blood found on defendant's shirt matched that of the deceased and was not defendant's. This evidence added nothing to the People's case, however, since defendant admitted that he had been at the deceased's apartment at the time of her death and touched her body, albeit in an attempt to revive her (majority op at 421). Moreover, independent forensic analysis of fibers found at the crime scene also established that defendant had been present at the

---

9. Some jurisdictions have barred DNA evidence altogether because of the uncertainty of the statistical significance of a match (*Commonwealth v Curnin*, 409 Mass 218, 565 NE2d 440, 443 [1991]; *Ex parte Perry*, 586 So 2d 242, 254 [Ala 1991]; *People v Barney*, 8 Cal App 4th 798, 10 Cal Rptr 2d 731, 742 [1992]). Others have simply barred any statistical evidence of a match, while allowing testimony that the DNA test did not exclude the defendant as a suspect (*Prater v State*, 307 Ark 180, 820 SW2d 429 [1991]; *State v Bible*, 175 Ariz 549, 858 P2d 1152 [1993]; *State v Pennell*, 584 A2d 513 [Del 1989]; *State v Schwartz*, 447 NW2d 422 [Minn 1989]; *State v Houser*, 241 Neb 525, 490 NW2d 168 [1992]; *State v Vandebogart*, 136 NH 365, 616 A2d 483 [1992]; *State v Anderson*, 115 NM 433, 853 P2d 135 [1993]; *Rivera v State*, 840 P2d 933 [Wyo 1993]; *United States v Porter*, 618 A2d 629 [DC Ct App 1992]).

apartment. The DNA evidence, therefore, was simply cumulative on this point, as both parties acknowledged on summation:

> [DEFENDANT'S LAWYER]: What does [the DNA evidence] establish? That Helen Kendrick's blood was on George Wesley's T-shirt. That's all it establishes. It establishes nothing else. What it establishes is exactly what George Wesley admitted, that he was there . . .

> [DISTRICT ATTORNEY]: In this case, as it turns out, [the DNA evidence's] significance is perhaps less than we anticipated, because it's unquestioned that the victim's blood is on the defendant's clothing.

Future Use of Forensic DNA Analysis

We join our colleagues in concluding that RFLP-based forensic analysis is today generally accepted as reliable. We know that, in principle, DNA polymorphisms provide a reliable method of comparing samples, that other than identical twins, each person has unique DNA, and that the current laboratory procedures for detecting DNA sequence variations are fundamentally sound. While the general acceptability of these techniques is no longer an open question, and trial courts may take judicial notice of their reliability, the adequacy of the methods used to acquire and analyze samples must be resolved case by case. As new forensic procedures are developed, *Frye* hearings will have to be conducted to assess the reliability of those methods.

The NRC panel called for formal quality-control programs in all laboratories, called on Congress to require external accreditation and proficiency testing of laboratories by a governmental body, and recommended the establishment of a National Committee on Forensic DNA Typing to provide scientific and technical advice on new methods of DNA typing and related issues as they arise (Annas, *Setting Standards for the Use of DNA-Typing Results in the Courtroom—The State of the Art*, 326 N Eng J of Med 1641, 1642). Such a call is a useful reminder, even in 1994. As the NRC recommended:

> [f]orensic DNA analysis should be governed by the highest standards of scientific rigor in analysis and interpretation. Such high standards are appropriate for two reasons: the probative power of DNA typing can be so great that it can outweigh all other evidence in a trial; and the procedures for DNA typing are complex, and judges and juries cannot properly weigh and evaluate conclusions based on differing standards of rigor. (NRC § 2.1.)

Accordingly, we would affirm defendant's conviction, but only because, in the unusual circumstances of this case, the erroneous admission of the DNA evidence was harmless beyond a reasonable doubt.

Schulz v. State of New York, 84 NY2d 231 (1994)

Robert L. Schulz initiated this voter standing action to challenge a New York public works financing practice, the "moral obligation bond." This mechanism was created to avoid running afoul of a state constitutional prohibition against accruing debt without voter approval. The law authorizing these bonds declared that the obligations incurred thereby were "not debt." Schulz took the position that simply declaring an obligation "not debt" did not actually make it not debt. While the court ultimately ruled that Schulz lacked standing to bring the action, in private Chief Judge Kaye noted more than once that she appreciated Schulz's determination to ensure the state's compliance with its own constitution. In its detailed recounting of the state's history with debt, the opinion also reflects Kaye's enjoyment of legal history and her belief that following a principle back to its original genesis often revealed the principles that should guide the Court in the present. She was particularly pleased to have occasion to invoke the memory of Assemblyman Arphaxed Loomis of Herkimer County, who tackled the debt issue in 1841.

—Introduction by Mary Rothwell Davis, law clerk 1993–1995

This challenge to a 1993 statute authorizing a multibillion dollar bond issue for state and local transportation improvements continues a debate on financing public works projects that has engaged our state throughout its history. The instant litigation attacks the statute both as imprudent fiscal policy and as violative of debt-limiting provisions of the State Constitution. The wisdom of legislation, of course, is not a matter for the courts. As to legality, we conclude—as did both the trial court and Appellate Division—that the statute before us does not violate the State Constitution.

I

On April 15, 1993 Governor Mario Cuomo signed into law, as chapter 56 of the Laws of 1993 (the Act), a four-year, $20 billion financing plan for the State's transportation system.

The plan provides $10.47 billion for the Dedicated Highway and Bridge Trust Fund (Highway Fund) operated by the State Thruway Authority, and $9.56 billion for the Dedicated Mass Transportation Trust Fund (Mass Transportation Fund), operated by the Metropolitan Transportation Authority (MTA).[1] Both funds, created in 1991, would under the 1993 statute receive revenues—subject to annual appropriation by the legislature—from taxes and fees derived from use of the Authorities' facilities: vehicle registration fees, the motor fuel tax, the petroleum and aviation fuel business tax, and miscellaneous highway use taxes (State Finance Law §§ 89-b [3]; 89-c; Tax Law §§ 289-e, 515; Vehicle and Traffic Law § 401; L 1993, ch 56, §§ 16, 31, 33).

The Thruway Authority

The Act authorizes the Thruway Authority to issue up to $4 billion in 30-year bonds for highway and bridge construction.[2] Part of the Highway Fund, therefore, is a special reserve to be used by the Authority for debt service and administrative expenses on its bonds. The bond proceeds, in turn, finance improvements for highways, bridges, railways and aviation facilities. Some of the bonds are to be secured by service contracts and sale-and-leaseback agreements between the Authority and the State (L 1993, ch 56, §§ 16, 33).

The Act sets forth several provisos relating to Thruway Authority bonds. Any bonds issued pursuant to authorizations contained in the Act do not constitute a debt of the State. In the words of the Act:

> The notes, bonds or other obligations of the authority authorized by this section shall not be a debt of the state and the state shall not be liable thereon, nor shall they be payable out of any funds other than those of the authority pledged therefor; and such bonds and notes shall contain on the face thereof a statement to such effect. (L 1993, ch 56, § 34, adding Public Authorities Law § 385 [1] [d]; *see also* L 1993, ch 56, §§ 16, 33; Public Authorities Law §§ 386 [4]; 1269 [8]; Highway Law § 10-e [5]).

Moreover, the statute in the same section declares that the State has "no continuing legal or moral obligation to appropriate money for payments due" under any agreements entered into to effect the implementation of the goals of the Act.

---

1. The Thruway Authority was created in 1950 by the New York State Thruway Authority Act (Public Authorities Law § 352). It operates and maintains the 641-mile New York State Thruway, as well as New York's 524-mile canal system. In addition, it finances and performs economic development and transportation projects, and since 1972 has through bonds financed state and local highway capital projects. The MTA was created in 1967 by Public Authorities Law § 1263 (*City of Rye v Metropolitan Transp. Auth.*, 24 NY2d 627 [1969]). Through its affiliates and subsidiaries—the New York City Transit Authority, Manhattan and Bronx Surface Transit Operating Authority, the Long Island Rail Road Company, Metro-North Commuter Railroad Company, and the Triborough Bridge and Tunnel Authority—MTA is charged with implementing and operating a unified mass transportation system in New York City and the nearby suburban counties.

2. Sections 13 and 14 of the Act authorize the Thruway Authority to issue bonds to finance $1.01 billion over the next four years for local highways and bridges through three programs: (a) the Consolidated Local Highway Assistance Program for local highway and bridge projects; (b) the Municipal Streets and Highways Program; and (c) the Suburban Highway Improvement Program for improvements on local and state highways and bridges in the Hudson Valley and on Long Island.

Restrictions on state liability must be included in any cooperative agreements flowing from the Act:

> Each dedicated highway and bridge trust fund cooperative agreement or agreements pursuant to this section shall contain a clause that such agreement or agreements of the state thereunder are not a debt of the state and that such agreement or agreements shall be deemed executory only to the extent of the monies available to the state and no liability on account thereof shall be incurred by the state beyond the monies available for the purpose thereof. (L 1993, ch 56, § 33, adding Highway Law § 10-e [5]; *see also* L 1993, ch 56, §§ 16, 19, 34; Public Authorities Law §§ 385 [1] [d]; 386 [2]; L 1991, ch 329, § 11 [d]).

Further, Thruway Authority bonds issued pursuant to the Act are payable only by legislative appropriations from the Highway Fund and no other source:

> Such obligations . . . shall be special obligations of the authority secured by and payable solely out of amounts appropriated by the legislature as authorized pursuant to section eight-nine-b of the state finance law without recourse against any other assets, revenues or funds of or other payments due to the authority. (Public Authorities Law § 385 [1] [c], added by L 1993, ch 56, § 34; *see also* Public Authorities Law § 385 [1] [d])

Finally, the Act specifies that the State may assume the obligations of the Authority or substitute state security for the obligations of the Authority only upon constitutional amendment (L 1993, ch 56, § 34, adding Public Authorities Law § 385 [10]).

The MTA

With regard to the MTA, the Act sets up a $9.56 billion capital funding program for the five-year period ending December 31, 1996. The existing—but not previously funded—Mass Transportation Trust Fund and the Metropolitan Mass Transportation Operating Assistance Fund would receive appropriations from user-derived taxes and fees and, in turn, would pay into a newly created MTA Dedicated Tax Fund (L 1993, ch 56, § 7, adding Public Authorities Law § 1270-c). Appropriated under the Aid to Localities law as financial assistance for the operations and programs of the MTA, those expenditures are not subject to any restrictions.

The Act does not require the MTA to issue bonds, but if it chooses to do so, it may use the Tax Fund for security and debt service. Any bonds issued by the MTA are subject to the same statutory provisos on state liability as the Thruway Authority bonds. Tax Fund money not used in connection with issuance of bonds can be applied to operating and capital costs of MTA subsidiaries (L 1993, ch 56, §§ 6, 7, 10; Public Authorities Law §§ 1269 [12]; 1270-c; State Finance Law § 89-c).

Asserting voter standing, plaintiffs commenced this action on May 24, 1993, alleging that the Act misuses public authorities to circumvent constitutional limitations on contracting debt, including the prohibitions against contracting state debt without a public referendum (NY Const, art VII, § 11), the lending of credit to public corporations (NY Const, art VII, § 8), and assumption of liability of debt obligation of public corporations (NY Const, art X, § 5).

On cross motions for summary judgment, Supreme Court concluded that under *Matter of Schulz v State of New York* (81 NY2d 336 [1993]), plaintiffs lacked standing to challenge the legislation as violative of any constitutional provision other than article VII, § 11 and, on the strength of *Wein v City of New York* (36 NY2d 610 [1975] [*Wein I*]), upheld the statute as constitutional. The Appellate Division affirmed those conclusions, as do we.

II

Because plaintiffs assert voter standing, Supreme Court correctly held that the only cognizable challenge to the Act is under article VII, § 11, the constitutional mandate that state contracts for debt be submitted for public referendum. Plaintiffs contend first that debt contracted by the public authorities is indistinguishable from debt contracted by the State and thus within the referendum requirement. Alternatively, they argue that the Act—by pledging appropriation of public revenues—compromises the legal independence of the public authorities involved, subjecting them to the debt-limiting provisions imposed on the State. They urge moreover, that as a practical matter the Legislature always will appropriate money for the Funds rather than risk damaging the State's credit rating. The effect of long-term appropriation-risk bonds, they say, is to "contract debt" within the meaning of article VII, § 11, and the failure to submit the proposed law to a public referendum renders the enactment unconstitutional.

Before proceeding to an examination of each claim, we note that plaintiffs' burden is a heavy one. It is true that when the main purpose of a statute is to effect " 'indirectly that which cannot be done directly, the act is to that extent void, because it violates the spirit of the fundamental law' " (*Wein v State of New York*, 39 NY2d 136, 145 [1976] [*Wein II*], quoting *People ex rel. Burby v Howland*, 155 NY 270, 280 [1898]). It is also true, however, that enactments of the legislature—a coequal branch of government—enjoy a strong presumption of constitutionality. In particular, we give deference to public funding programs essential to addressing the problems of modern life, unless such programs are "patently illegal" (*see Hotel Dorset Co. v Trust for Cultural Resources*, 46 NY2d 358, 369–370 [1978], quoting *Comereski v City of Elmira*, 308 NY 248, 254 [1955]).

Plaintiffs have not satisfied their burden of proving unconstitutionality beyond a reasonable doubt.

III

In considering plaintiffs' first contention—that the debt of the Authorities is debt of the State—we begin analysis with a history of the referendum requirement and the origin of public authorities.

The State Constitution of 1777, our first, provided that the legislative power of this state is to be vested in the Senate and Assembly (art II). The unlimited grant of legislative authority—when exercised in the arena of borrowing and spending—led to abuses and prompted a movement for reform of state borrowing practices (*see Matter of Schulz v State of New York*, 81 NY2d 336, 346 [1993]; *People v Westchester County Natl. Bank*, 231 NY 465, 471–473 [1921]). Of particular concern, and the impetus for change, was the lending of public credit to private, "irresponsible" corporations. Following the onset of economic depression in 1837, private railroad corporations defaulted on obligations that had been assumed on the strength of liberally granted state credit. The State assumed the liabilities, with no hope of reimbursement, and by 1845 more than three fifths of the entire state debt was the result of such loans. Public works were suspended in response to the debt crisis (*see Wein II*, 39 NY2d at 142–143, *supra*; 2 Lincoln, *Constitutional History of New York* at 87, 100 [1906]).

The precursor to the referendum requirement of article VII, § 11, proposed in 1841 by Assembly Member Arphaxed Loomis of Herkimer County, was adopted under the Constitution of 1846 (former art VII, § 12) as part of a sweeping reform of public borrowing practices, in an effort to protect the State from the uncertain and possibly disastrous consequences of incurring future liabilities—"liabilities easy for a current generation to project but a burden on future generations" (*Wein II*, 39 NY2d at 144). Known as "the people's resolution," the amendment reserved to voters the power to determine, by referendum, whether a proposed law creating debt would take effect (2 Lincoln, *op. cit.* at 73–83). In its present form, the Constitution provides:

> Except the debts specified in sections 9 and 10 of this article, no debt shall be hereafter contracted by or in behalf of the state, unless such debt shall be authorized by law, for some single work or purpose, to be distinctly specified therein. No such law shall take effect until it shall, at a general election, have been submitted to the people, and have received a majority of all the votes cast for it and against it at such election nor shall it be submitted to be voted on within three months after its passage nor at any general election when any other law or any bill shall be submitted to be voted for or against.
>
> The legislature may, at any time after the approval of such law by the people, if no debt shall have been contracted in pursuance thereof, repeal the same; and may at any time, by law, forbid the contracting of any further debt or liability under such law. (art VII, § 11)

Long-term state obligations are the concern of article VII, § 11 (*Wein v Levitt*, 42 NY2d 300, 304 [1977] [*Wein III*]). By article VII, § 9, the State may validly contract short-term debt in authentic anticipation of the receipt of taxes and revenues, for the purposes and within the amounts of appropriations previously made, if repaid within one year (NY Const, art VII, § 9; *Wein II*, 39 NY2d at 146). State debt that extends beyond one year, therefore, is subject to the referendum requirement of article VII, § 11. Simultaneously, a provision was adopted forbidding gifts or loans of state credit to "any individual, association, or corporation" (NY Const of 1846, art VII, § 9).[3]

The referendum requirement is not simply a limit on discretion. In *People ex rel. Hopkins v Board of Supervisors* (52 NY 556 [1873]), we observed that it was legally impossible for the legislature to contract debt in the absence of approval by the people through referendum: such approval is a condition precedent to the creation of debt. Any purported long-term debt created in the absence of a public referendum is simply not legally binding on the State.

Following adoption of the referendum requirement, the legislature sought ways to provide long-term funding for public works projects that would not require public referendum. In 1851, without public referendum, the legislature authorized issuance of canal certificates, to be paid from canal revenues, which by their terms were not to be deemed to create a debt against the State. While we struck down the statute because it failed to comply with a constitutional mandate as to application of canal revenues (*see Newell v People*, 7 NY 9, 92 [1852]), we noted in passing that even though purchasers of the canal certificates may have no legal remedy against the State if canal revenues proved insufficient to pay the certificates, the State would no doubt make good on them by reason of moral obligation. Moreover, canal revenues paid out to certificate holders represented money that would be diverted from public coffers. The declaration that the certificates were not to be deemed debt was therefore "an evasion, if not a direct violation, of the constitution" (*Newell*, 7 NY at 93).

The legislature then passed a series of town bonding acts that authorized—and later compelled—cities to borrow money to invest in railroad company stock. The question whether the State could authorize one of its instrumentalities to undertake commitments the Constitution prohibited the State itself from undertaking reached this Court in *Bank of Rome v Village of Rome* (18 NY 38 [1858]). We upheld the scheme, leading to ratification of constitutional restrictions on municipal debt in 1874, 1884 and 1894.

Shortly after the turn of the century, the legislature devised a new vehicle for funding public works projects that appeared to insulate the State from the burden of long-term debt: legislative creation of legally separate public benefit corporations, known as public authorities, to discharge particular functions. The first such entity was the Port of New York Authority, created in 1921 (*see Collins v Manhattan & Bronx Surface Tr. Operating Auth.*, 62 NY2d 361, 367 [1984]). In theory, a public authority would be self-supporting, able to meet debt obligations through revenues obtained from its own valuable assets, such as fares and user fees. Such public benefit corporations would separate their administrative and fiscal functions from those of the State (1929 Ops Atty Gen 223, 224), to " 'protect the State from liability and enable public projects to be carried on free from restrictions otherwise applicable' " (*Matter of Plumbing, Heating, Piping & Air Conditioning Contrs. Assn. v New York State Thruway Auth.*, 5 NY2d 420, 423 [1959], citing 1951 Ops Atty Gen 130, 132).

We rejected an early challenge to the effectiveness of language disclaiming the State's liability for public authority debts, where bonds were secured solely by the revenues of

---

3. This prohibition was made binding on cities and other local governments by article VIII, § 11 of the 1874 amendments.

the issuing authority (*see Robertson v Zimmermann*, 268 NY 52, 62). Although public authority debt was not legally binding on the State, we nevertheless recognized in *Williamsburgh Sav Bank v State of New York* (243 NY 231) that the State might choose to honor a liability as a moral obligation. We stated, however, that whether to recognize a moral obligation is within the discretion of the State:

> [I]t rests solely with the State through its Legislature to determine whether it will recognize a claim even though founded upon equity and justice and allow it to be developed into a legal demand and . . . the exercise of this choice cannot be delegated to anyone else[.] . . . Practically the sole power of the courts in this respect is to determine whether all of the facts established in a given case and presumably within the knowledge of the Legislature do establish such a foundation of equity and justice that the Legislature within the rules established by the courts was authorized, *if it saw fit so to do*, to recognize the justice of the claim. (243 NY at 244–245 [emphasis added])

In *Williamsburgh*, the State had indicated its intent to allow enforcement of a moral obligation, permitting judicial determination of a claim (*id.*; *see also Board of Supervisors v State of New York*, 153 NY 279, 293 [1897] [unenforceable moral obligation paid by the State]).

To prevent the State from assuming public authority debt as a moral obligation—and to overrule constitutionally the effect of *Williamsburgh*—the 1938 Constitution (our present Constitution) explicitly empowered public authorities to issue bonds and incur debt but prevented the State from assuming that liability:

> Neither the state nor any political subdivision thereof shall at any time be liable for the payment of any obligations issued by such a public corporation heretofore or hereafter created, nor may the legislature accept, authorize acceptance of or impose such liability upon the state or any political subdivision thereof; but the state or a political subdivision thereof may, if authorized by the legislature, acquire the properties of any such corporation and pay the indebtedness thereof. (NY Const, art X, § 5; *see* 3 Revised Record of 1938 Constitutional Convention of State of NY at 2259–2283; Galie, *New York State Constitution* at 226–228)

To limit proliferation of public authorities, the new Constitution specified that only the legislature, through special act, could create them (*see City of Rye v Metropolitan Transp. Auth.*, 24 NY2d 627 [1969]).

Those who spoke in opposition to allowing public authorities expansive discretion in performing formerly state functions were in the minority. Debate at the Constitutional Convention included discussion of whether the State would be liable in the event an authority were unable to meet its obligations, and the language of the amendment was tailored to make clear that it would not. The Chair of the Committee on the Legislature and its Powers, George Fearon, supported the new provision, stating, " 'I believe that when people buy [authority] bonds they should know definitely and certainly that the credit of the State of New York and that the credit of the municipality is not behind those bonds. There should not be any question about it'" (Quirk and Wein, *A Short Constitutional History of Entities Commonly Known as Authorities*, 56 Cornell L Rev 521, 573 [1971], quoting 3 Revised Record of 1938 Constitutional Convention, *op. cit.* at 2276).

By article VII, § 8 and article VIII, § 1 of the 1938 Constitution, the prohibition against gifts or loans of state credit was made applicable to public corporations (*see Wein II*, 39 NY2d at 144). While the provision bars the State from lending its "credit" to a public corporation, the State is nonetheless free to give money to a public authority and to commit itself to giving future gifts (*see Comereski v City of Elmira*, 308 NY 248 [1955]). The distinction is rooted in the fact that the granting of state money—while depleting current state coffers and making those funds unavailable for other purposes—nevertheless does not bind future generations or create the same dangers of collapse, insolvency and crisis associated with the abuse of credit. Such a distinction presumes, of course, that the State has adequate funds to support a gift (*Wein II*, 39 NY2d at 154 [Jasen, J., dissenting]).

The Constitution was adopted by the people on November 8, 1938 at a general election, giving full recognition to the existence of public benefit corporations, their independent capacity to contract debt, and the continued power of the State to make gifts of money to those authorities.[4] Thus, contrary to plaintiffs' contention, there can be no question that—for the purpose of contracting their own legally binding obligations—the Thruway Authority and the MTA are public benefit corporations existing independently of the State (NY Const, art X, § 5; *Matter of Plumbing, Heating, Piping & Air Conditioning Contrs. Assn. v New York State Thruway Auth.*, 5 NY2d 420, 424–425, *supra*; *Metropolitan Transp. Auth. v County of Nassau*, 28 NY2d 385, 390 [1971]).[5] Moreover, contracting of debt by public authorities was unquestionably not the aim of the referendum requirement, adopted in 1846, since those entities did not exist at the time.

That the 1938 Constitution expressly empowered public authorities to contract debt independently of the State lends further support to the conclusion that the Act, by authorizing the Thruway Authority and the MTA to issue bonds, does not contract legally binding debt upon the State. The power of the State and these Authorities to engage in this practice has been secured by vote of the people, through article X, § 5 of the Constitution, and any change must come by constitutional amendment. The courts have not made the Constitution and they cannot unmake it (*see Sgaglione v Levitt*, 37 NY2d 507, 514 [1975]).

---

4. We have consistently recognized public authorities as legal entities separate from the State, enjoying an existence separate and apart from the State, its agencies and political subdivisions (*see e.g. Matter of New York Pub. Interest Research Group v New York State Thruway Auth.*, 77 NY2d 86, 92–93 [1990]; *Methodist Hosp. v State Ins. Fund*, 64 NY2d 365 [1985]; *Collins*, 62 NY2d 361, 367, *supra*; *Grace & Co. v State Univ Constr. Fund*, 44 NY2d 84, 88 [1978]; *Patterson v Carey*, 41 NY2d 714 [1977]; *Matter of Dormitory Auth. [Span Elec. Corp.]*, 18 NY2d 114 [1966]; *Matter of Plumbing, Heating, Piping & Air Conditioning Contrs. Assn. v New York State Thruway Auth.*, 5 NY2d 420, 423–424 [1959]).

5. *McCabe v Gross* (274 NY 39 [1937]), holding unlawful the City of Troy's effort to issue bonds through a school district "authority" is not to the contrary. There, we construed the effect of a constitutional provision limiting city debt as extending to debt of city school districts, which are subdivisions of the city. By contrast, the Constitution, through article X, § 5, separates debt of public benefit corporations and that of the State. Public authority bonds are—by constitutional mandate—not legal liabilities of the State.

Though the debt of the Thruway Authority and MTA are not a legal obligation of the State, plaintiffs also contend that the Act contracts debt of the State by imposing a moral obligation on the legislature to continue appropriating revenue to the special Funds. A moral obligation, however, is not in and of itself "debt" (*see Firestone Tire & Rubber Co. v Agnew*, 194 NY 165, 170 [1909])—although it may constitute sufficient consideration to support a promise to pay (*see Meyer v Price*, 250 NY 370, 376 [1929]).[6] Debt, within the contemplation of the state constitutional debt-limiting provisions, has a settled meaning (*see Wein I*, 36 NY2d 610, *supra*), and we are not persuaded that plaintiffs' argument for an expanded definition has merit.

To bring themselves within article VII, § 11, plaintiffs characterize the Act as creating "moral obligation" debt—a term apparently coined in the 1960s to describe appropriation-risk bonds that could not legally bind the legislature beyond a session but would create a "moral obligation" to appropriate money should a public authority be unable to redeem its bonds (*see* Quirk and Wein, *Rockefeller's Constitutional Sleight of Hand*, Empire State Report at 430 [Nov 1975]; *see also* Tyler, *The Steady Growth of Backdoor Financing*, Empire State Report at 213, 222 [June 1975]). The existence of such a moral obligation would provide some assurance (though not an enforceable legal obligation) to bondholders that the bonds would retain their value.

The bonds authorized by the Act were not labelled "moral obligation bonds" by the legislature, and entirely apart from nomenclature the Act does not create such an obligation. The Act requires a statement on the face of the bonds that they are not a debt of the State and are payable only out of the Authorities' funds. Moreover, the Act disavows existence of a moral obligation on the part of the State to appropriate revenues in the future. These disclaimers—particularly when read in light of the constitutional prohibition against State assumption of authority debt (NY Const, art X, § 5)—are sufficient to remove any reasonable expectation on the part of bondholders that the State will guarantee return in the event of default on the part of the Authority or that the bonds place them in privity with the State (*see Matter of Mullane v McKenzie*, 269 NY 369, 376 [1936], *rearg denied* 270 NY 563, *supra* [no moral obligation arises where State acting in accordance with its legal rights]).

Plaintiffs' heavy reliance on *Williamsburgh* (243 NY 231, *supra*) as establishing the possibility that the State could be held liable on a moral obligation is unavailing. First— unlike the Act—the statute at issue in *Williamsburgh* expressly recognized the possibility

---

6. A moral obligation cognizable by the State generally falls into one of two classifications. The first are claims involving benefits conferred by private persons upon the State which the State has continued to enjoy without the return of quid pro quo. The second are claims involving injuries and damages wrongfully inflicted upon individuals by those in state service or others for whose acts the State might justly be regarded as responsible (*Farrington v State of New York*, 248 NY 112, 116 [1928]). Where a moral obligation exists, the legislature may use public money to remedy an injustice in cases even though no legal obligation to do so exists, so long as some higher obligation of honor, fairness or broad public responsibility is recognized (*Matter of Mullane v McKenzie*, 269 NY 369 [1936]). As we recently stated in *Matter of Ruotolo v State of New York*, moral obligation is properly found where legislative failure to act would be a "travesty of justice" (83 NY2d 248, 259 [1994]).

of a moral obligation. Second, article X, § 5 was adopted after *Williamsburgh* precisely to overrule constitutionally the possibility of the State assuming a moral obligation as to debt of a public authority.

Most critically, a moral obligation cannot be judicially imposed upon the State in the absence of its consent to be so bound (*see Williamsburgh*, 243 NY at 247). Even where a moral obligation exists, that circumstance creates no enforceable right on behalf of the aggrieved party. Rather, where circumstances support a determination that the State has a valid moral obligation to honor a private claim, we will permit the State to waive immunity from liability. But that is a unilateral right (*Ruotolo*, 83 NY2d 248, *supra*; *People v Westchester County Natl. Bank*, 231 NY 465, *supra*), and the effect is simply to permit adjudication of a claim.

In short, a moral obligation does not create "debt," since it creates no enforceable right on the part of the one to whom the obligation is owed. Moreover, the Act could not make plainer that the State recognizes no moral obligation on its part to continue appropriations. Plaintiffs' claim that the Act creates a moral obligation to pay which falls within the constitutional definition of "debt" therefore also must fail.

V

Plaintiffs point as well to the State's need to protect our economy as binding future legislatures to continue with annual appropriations to the Funds for the life of the bonds. They claim that, in reality, the bonds are backed by the State's full faith and credit because the consequences of default would be ruinous, assuring that appropriations will be made. Indeed, plaintiffs document instances where State officials appear to have characterized the future appropriations as legal obligations of the State, despite the Act's disclaimers. Thus, in plaintiffs' view, the Act obligates the State to continue appropriations for the life of the bonds—some 30 years—creating long-term state "debt."

We have previously held that a proposal to fund in a subsequent year, subject to legislative appropriation and explicit disclaimer, does not create legally binding debt (*Levy v McClellan*, 196 NY 178, 195–196 [1909]; *see also Public Util. Dist. No. 1 v Washington Pub. Power Supply Sys.*, 104 Wash 2d 353, 370, 705 P2d 1195, 1207 [1985] [WPPS bonds do not constitute legal or equitable pledge upon State]). In *People ex rel. Hopkins v Board of Supervisors* (52 NY 556, 564, *supra*), we observed that while the legislature might endeavor to incur future liabilities, to be appropriated on a year-to-year basis without submitting the spending plan to the people, "[n]o harm or loss has or can come from this practice." Such spending plans are effectual only to the extent subsequent legislatures indeed do "give effect to them by providing the means and directing their payment, but the discretion and responsibility is with them as if no former appropriations had been made. No duty or obligation is devolved upon them by the acts of their predecessors" (*id.* at 565). If uneffected by future legislatures, the laws will simply "remain upon the statute books, but . . . only . . . as monuments of the extravagance, recklessness or folly of those by whom they were enacted," creating no legally binding debt or liability upon the State (*id.* at 565).

Our constitutional limitations, however, have consistently been construed as addressing legally binding debt. As in *Wein I*, where we upheld subsidies for debt service on bonds issued by the Stabilization Reserve Corporation contingent on annual appropriation, indebtedness is precluded by the very terms of chapter 56, as well as the prohibition of article X, § 5 against State assumption of authority debt (36 NY2d at 617). We rejected in *Wein I* the suggestion that a gift of money to a public authority—upheld in *Comereski* (308 NY at 253-254)—violated the letter or spirit of the constitutional limitations on contracting debt (*Wein I*, 36 NY2d at 616).

Next, in *Wein II* (39 NY2d 136, *supra*), we upheld a plan giving aid to New York City and the Municipal Assistance Corporation that would be funded through borrowing pursuant to the short-term debt provision of article VII, § 9 as not violating the constitutional prohibition against giving or lending credit of the State. In *Wein III* (42 NY2d 300, *supra*), a law promising to indemnify state officers from any claims arising from purchase of risky authority bonds was not "borrowing" of any kind, but rather "a contingent cost of doing State business payable routinely out of the general fund" (42 NY2d at 305).

Apart from constituting a line of precedents upon which reliance has been placed in the financial marketplace, these cases established that a contractual obligation on the part of government to make future "gifts" to a special fund created to retire debt of an independent public authority is not offensive to article VII, § 8; article VIII, § 1; or article X, § 5 of the Constitution.

We define "debt" no differently for purposes of article VII, § 11. While the legislature might make the appropriations to the Funds, to be used in turn to service the Authorities' debt, it is not bound to do so. Should it fail to do so, and the Authority default, the State is not liable to the bondholders under the provisions of the Act. Because the State does not become indebted, the financing subject to appropriation does not constitute the lending of credit or assumption of the liability of a public corporation, or indebtedness of the State for purposes of the constitutional limits on such debt (*Wein I*, 36 NY2d at 618). Instead, the funds—if appropriated—constitute a permissible gift of money to a public corporation out of existing revenues, creating no debt (NY Const, art VII, § 8; *Comereski v City of Elmira*, 308 NY 248, *supra*). Laws making annual appropriations from a special fund do not and cannot create debts within the meaning of the referendum requirement (*Rockaway Pac. Corp. v Stotesbury*, 255 F 345, 348 [ND NY 1917]).

Plaintiffs' third argument therefore must fail as well.

VI

In sum, neutral principles of law and consistent precedents of this Court, upon which decades of commercial transactions have been premised, lead us to uphold the validity of the particular legislation before us. If (as plaintiffs urge) modern ingenuity, even gimmickry, have in fact stretched the words of the Constitution beyond the point of prudence, that plea for reform in state borrowing practices and policy is appropriately directed to the public arena, where indeed it is now under serious consideration (*see* NY

Senate Bill S4359, replacing Assembly Bill A7586 [Apr 4, 1993]; Joint Press Release of Governor and Comptroller [Mar 15, 1994]; Op of Atty Gen to Legislature re NY Senate Bill S4359 [May 11, 1993]).

Matter of Jacob,
86 NY2d 651 (1995)

Chief Judge Kaye's opinion in *Matter of Jacob* is a model of legal craftsmanship. The case concerned the rights of unmarried couples, mainly gay and lesbian couples who could not legally marry at the time, and did not have the ability to adopt their nonbiological children. In 1995, Kaye knew an argument about gay rights would not gather the necessary votes, and thus tactfully framed the argument around the best interest of the child. Essentially, children were being born to gay couples whether society liked it or not, and it was clearly in the best interest of the child to have two parents, rather than one. *Matter of Jacob* stands out as a prime example of Kaye's persistent concern for the actual people affected by her judicial decisions, and this is evidenced by her lengthy discussion of the facts in this, and many of her other opinions. Moreover, this case showcases her noteworthy approach to state court statutory interpretation: essentially that state court's common law powers and tradition allow it to choose broader purpose over semantic meaning when the two conflict. Her courageous opinion, yet again, forecasted Justice Kennedy's words in *United States v Windsor* (570 US 744, ___ [2013]), where he explained how the Defense of Marriage Act, "humiliates tens of thousands of children now being raised by same-sex couples. The law in question makes it even more difficult for the children to understand the integrity and closeness of their own family and its concord with other families in their community and in their daily lives."

—Introduction by Roberta A. Kaplan, law clerk 1995–1996

Under the New York adoption statute, a single person can adopt a child (Domestic Relations Law § 110). Equally clear is the right of a single homosexual to adopt (*see* 18 NYCRR 421.16 [h] [2] [qualified adoption agencies "shall not . . . reject( ) (adoption petitions) solely on the basis of homosexuality"]). These appeals call upon us to decide if the unmarried partner of a child's biological mother, whether heterosexual or homosexual, who is raising the child together with the biological parent, can become the child's second parent by means of adoption.

Because the two adoptions sought—one by an unmarried heterosexual couple, the other by the lesbian partner of the child's mother—are fully consistent with the adoption statute, we answer this question in the affirmative. To rule otherwise would mean that the thousands of New York children actually being raised in homes headed by two unmarried persons could have only one legal parent, not the two who want them.

The Adoptions Sought

In *Matter of Jacob*, Roseanne M.A. and Jacob's biological father (from whom she is divorced) separated prior to the child's birth and Roseanne M.A. was awarded sole custody. Jacob was a year old when Stephen T.K. began living with him and his mother in early 1991. At the time of filing the joint petition for adoption three years later, Stephen T.K. was employed as a programmer/analyst with an annual income of $50,000, while Roseanne M.A. was a student at SUNY Health Center. Jacob's biological father consented to the adoption. Though acknowledging that "the granting of an adoption in this matter may be beneficial to Jacob," Family Court dismissed the petition for lack of standing on the ground that Domestic Relations Law § 110 does not authorize adoptions by an unmarried couple. The Appellate Division affirmed, two Justices dissenting (210 AD2d 876 [1994]), and an appeal to this Court was taken as of right.

In *Matter of Dana*, appellants are G.M. and her lesbian partner, P.I., who have lived together in what is described as a long and close relationship for the past 19 years. G.M. works as a special education teacher in the public schools earning $38,000 annually and P.I., employed at an athletic club, has an annual income of $48,000. In 1989, the two women decided that P.I. would have a child they would raise together. P.I. was artificially inseminated by an anonymous donor, and on June 6, 1990, she gave birth to Dana. G.M. and P.I. have shared parenting responsibilities since Dana's birth and have arranged their separate work schedules around her needs. With P.I.'s consent, G.M. filed a petition to adopt Dana in April 1993. In the court-ordered report recommending that G.M. be permitted to adopt (*see* Domestic Relations Law § 116), the disinterested investigator described Dana as an attractive, sturdy and articulate little girl with a "rich family life," which includes frequent visits with G.M.'s three grown children from a previous marriage "who all love Dana and accept her as their baby sister." Noting that G.M. "only has the best interest of Dana in mind," the report concluded that she "provides her with a family structure in which to grow and flourish."

As in *Matter of Jacob*, Family Court, while conceding the favorable results of the home study and "in no way disparaging the ability of [G.M.] to be a good, nurturing and loving parent," denied the petition for lack of standing. In addition, the court held that the adoption was further prohibited by Domestic Relations Law § 117 which it interpreted to require the automatic termination of P.I.'s relationship with Dana upon an adoption by G.M. Despite its conclusion that G.M. had standing to adopt, the Appellate Division nevertheless affirmed on the ground that Domestic Relations Law § 117 prohibits the adoption (209 AD2d 8 [1995]). We granted leave to appeal. . . .

The Context of Our Statutory Analysis

Two basic themes of overarching significance set the context of our statutory analysis.

First and foremost, since adoption in this state is "solely the creature of . . . statute" (*Matter of Eaton*, 305 NY 162, 165 [1953]), the adoption statute must be strictly construed. What is to be construed strictly and applied rigorously in this sensitive area of the law, however, is legislative purpose as well as legislative language. Thus, the adoption statute must be applied in harmony with the humanitarian principle that adoption is a means of securing the best possible home for a child (see *Matter of Malpica-Orsini*, 36 NY2d 568, 571–572 [1975]). . . .

What *Matter of Robert Paul P.* and *Matter of Best* underscore is that in strictly construing the adoption statute, our primary loyalty must be to the statute's legislative purpose—the child's best interest. "The adoptive family arises out of the State's concern for the best interest of the child" (*People ex rel. Sibley v Sheppard*, 54 NY2d 320, 327 [1981]). This profound concern for the child's welfare is reflected in the statutory language itself: when "satisfied that the best interests of the . . . child will be promoted thereby," a court "*shall* make an order approving the adoption" (Domestic Relations Law § 114 [emphasis added]).

This policy would certainly be advanced in situations like those presented here by allowing the two adults who actually function as a child's parents to become the child's legal parents. The advantages which would result from such an adoption include Social Security and life insurance benefits in the event of a parent's death or disability, the right to sue for the wrongful death of a parent, the right to inherit under rules of intestacy (*see In re Tammy*, 416 Mass 205, 619 NE2d 315, 320 [1993]) and eligibility for coverage under both parents' health insurance policies. In addition, granting a second parent adoption further ensures that two adults are legally entitled to make medical decisions for the child in case of emergency and are under a legal obligation for the child's economic support (*see* Domestic Relations Law § 32).

Even more important, however, is the emotional security of knowing that in the event of the biological parent's death or disability, the other parent will have presumptive custody, and the children's relationship with their parents, siblings and other relatives will continue should the coparents separate. Indeed, viewed from the children's perspective, permitting the adoptions allows the children to achieve a measure of permanency with both parent figures and avoids the sort of disruptive visitation battle we faced in *Matter of Alison D. v Virginia M.* (*see* 77 NY2d 651, 656 [1991] ["Petitioner concedes that she is not the child's 'parent' . . . by virtue of an adoption."]).

A second, related point of overriding significance is that the various sections comprising New York's adoption statute today represent a complex and not entirely reconcilable patchwork. Amended innumerable times since its passage in 1873, the adoption statute was last consolidated nearly 60 years ago, in 1938 (L 1938, ch 606). Thus, after decades of piecemeal amendment upon amendment, the statute today contains language from the 1870s alongside language from the 1990s. . . .

That the questions posed by these appeals are not readily answerable by reference to the words of a particular section of the law, but instead require the traditional and often close and difficult task of statutory interpretation is evident even in the length of today's opinions—whichever result is reached. . . .

Domestic Relations Law § 110

Despite ambiguity in other sections, one thing is clear: section 110 allows appellants to become adoptive parents. Domestic Relations Law § 110, entitled "Who May Adopt," provides that an "adult unmarried person or an adult husband and his adult wife together may adopt another person" (Domestic Relations Law § 110). Under this language, both appellant G.M. in *Matter of Dana* and appellant Stephen T.K. in *Matter of Jacob*, as adult unmarried persons, have standing to adopt and appellants are correct that the Court's analysis of section 110 could appropriately end here.

Endowing the word "together" as used in section 110 with the overpowering significance of enforcing a policy in favor of marriage (as the dissent does) would require us to rewrite the statute. The statute uses the word "together" only to describe married persons and thus does not preclude an unmarried person in a relationship with another unmarried person from adopting. Rather, by insisting on the joint consent of the married persons, the statutory term "together" simply insures that one spouse cannot adopt a child without the other spouse's knowledge or over the other's objection (*see* L 1984, ch 218, Mem of State Dept of Social Services, 1984 McKinney's Session Laws of NY at 3184). Since each of the biological mothers here is not only aware of these proceedings, but has expressly consented to the adoptions, section 110 poses no statutory impediment. . . .

A reading of section 110 granting appellants, as unmarried second parents, standing to adopt is therefore consistent with the words of the statute as well as the spirit behind the modern-day amendments: encouraging the adoption of as many children as possible regardless of the sexual orientation or marital status of the individuals seeking to adopt them.

Domestic Relations Law § 117

Appellants having standing to adopt pursuant to Domestic Relations Law § 110, the other statutory obstacle relied upon by the lower courts in denying the petitions is the provision that "[a]fter the making of an order of adoption the natural parents of the adoptive child shall be relieved of all parental duties toward and of all responsibilities for and shall have no rights over such adoptive child or to his property by descent or succession" (Domestic Relations Law § 117 [1] [a]). Literal application of this language would effectively prevent these adoptions since it would require the termination of the biological mothers' rights upon adoption thereby placing appellants in the "Catch-22" of having to choose one of two coparents as the child's only legal parent.

As outlined below, however, neither the language nor policy underlying section 117 dictates that result.

The Language of Section 117. Both the title of section 117 ("Effect of adoption") and its opening phrase ("After the making of an order of adoption") suggest that the section has nothing to do with the standing of an individual to adopt, an issue treated exclusively in section 110 (*see* at 660–662, *supra*). Rather, section 117 addresses the legal effect of an adoption on the parties and their property.

Also plain on the face of section 117 is that it speaks principally of estate law. Words such as "succession," "inheritance," "decedent," "instrument" and "will" permeate the statute. Read contextually, it is clear that the legislature's chief concern in section 117 was the resolution of property disputes upon the death of an adoptive parent or child. . . .

Recent Statutory Amendments. Moving beyond the language and history of section 117 itself, our reading of the statute is further supported by recent amendments to other sections of the adoption law which provide elaborate procedural mechanisms for regulating the relationships between the child, the child's (soon-to-be former) biological parents and the persons who will become the child's parents upon adoption (*see* Social Services Law § 383-c; Domestic Relations Law § 115-b).

In the context of agency adoptions, Social Services Law § 383-c, enacted in 1990 (L 1990, chs 479, 480), provides that biological parents willing to give their child up for adoption must execute a written instrument, known as a "surrender," stating "in conspicuous bold print on the first page" that "the parent is giving up all rights to have custody, visit with, write to or learn about the child, forever" (Social Services Law § 383-c [5] [b] [ii]). . . .

The above-described amendments to Social Services Law § 383-c and Domestic Relations Law § 115-b suggest that the legislature in recent years has devised statutory vehicles other than section 117 to carefully regulate and restrict parental rights during the adoption process, again militating against a rigid application of subdivision (1) (a).

The Ambiguity Should be Resolved in the Children's Favor. Finally, even though the language of section 117 still has the effect of terminating a biological parent's rights in the majority of adoptions between strangers—where there is a need to prevent unwanted intrusion by the child's former biological relatives to promote the stability of the new adoptive family—the cases before us are entirely different. As we recognized in *Matter of Seaman* (78 NY2d 451, 461 [1991]), "complete severance of the natural relationship [is] not necessary when the adopted person remain[s] within the natural family unit as a result of an intrafamily adoption." . . .

Despite their varying factual circumstances, each of the adoptions described above—stepparent adoptions, adoptions by minor fathers and open adoptions—share such an agreement as a common denominator. Because the facts of the cases before us are directly analogous to these three situations, the half-century-old termination language of section 117 should not be read to preclude the adoptions here. Phrased slightly differently, "the desire for consistency in the law should not of itself sever the bonds between the child and the natural relatives" (*People ex rel. Sibley v Sheppard*, 54 NY2d 320, 326, *supra*). . . .

"Where the language of a statute is susceptible of two constructions, the courts will adopt that which avoids injustice, hardship, constitutional doubts or other objectionable results" (*Kauffman & Sons Saddlery Co. v Miller*, 298 NY 38, 44 [1948, Fuld, J.]; *see also* McKinney's Cons Laws of NY, Book 1, Statutes § 150). Given that section 117 is open to two differing interpretations as to whether it automatically terminates parental rights in all cases, a construction of the section that would deny children like Jacob and Dana the opportunity of having their two de facto parents become their legal parents, based solely on their biological mother's sexual orientation or marital status, would not only be unjust under the circumstances, but also might raise constitutional concerns in light of the adoption statute's historically consistent purpose—the best interests of the child. . . .

These concerns are particularly weighty in *Matter of Dana*. Even if the Court were to rule against him on this appeal, the male petitioner in *Matter of Jacob* could still adopt by marrying Jacob's mother. Dana, however, would be irrevocably deprived of the benefits and entitlements of having as her legal parents the two individuals who have already assumed that role in her life, simply as a consequence of her mother's sexual orientation.

Any proffered justification for rejecting these petitions based on a governmental policy disapproving of homosexuality or encouraging marriage would not apply. As noted above, New York has not adopted a policy disfavoring adoption by either single persons or homosexuals. In fact, the most recent legislative document relating to the subject urges courts to construe section 117 in precisely the manner we have as it cautions against discrimination against "nonmarital children" and "unwed parents" (*see* at 664, *supra*). An interpretation of the statute that avoids such discrimination or hardship is all the more appropriate here where a contrary ruling could jeopardize the legal status of the many New York children whose adoptions by second parents have already taken place (*e.g. Matter of Camilla*, 163 Misc 2d 272 [1994]; *Matter of Evan*, 153 Misc 2d 844 [1992]; *Matter of A. J. J.*, 108 Misc 2d 657 [1981]).

Conclusion

To be sure, the legislature that last codified section 117 in 1938 may never have envisioned families that "include[ ] two adult lifetime partners whose relationship is . . . characterized by an emotional and financial commitment and interdependence" (*Braschi v Stahl Assocs. Co.*, 74 NY2d 201, 211 [1989]). Nonetheless, it is clear that section 117, designed as a shield to protect new adoptive families, was never intended as a sword to prohibit otherwise beneficial intrafamily adoptions by second parents.

Accordingly, in each proceeding, the order of the Appellate Division should be reversed, without costs, the adoption petition reinstated and the matter remitted to Family Court for further proceedings consistent with this opinion.

Johnson v. Pataki,
91 NY2d 214 (1997)

From a notorious prosecution following the murder of a New York City police officer arose a conflict between the governor of New York and an independent constitutionally empowered elected district attorney. The Court of Appeals was presented with the issue whether the governor's Executive Order, requiring the attorney general to supersede the district attorney in the potential death penalty murder case, was permissible.

Though the underlying controversy was fraught with tension, the court was bound by principles of justiciability to limit its review to determining whether the state constitution or the legislature had empowered the governor to act. In a 5–2 decision, Chief Judge Kaye calmly guided the court through these turbulent waters, relying on the plain meaning of the state constitution, the statutory language, and clearly defined precedent. The court was careful to leave open the question whether, in any or all circumstances, the exercise of the executive power to supersede an elected district attorney would be beyond judicial review.

—Introduction by Jean M. Joyce, law clerk 2000–2006

By this appeal we are asked to determine whether Governor George E. Pataki had the legal authority to supersede Bronx County District Attorney Robert T. Johnson in a potential death penalty prosecution involving a slain police officer. We hold that the Governor acted lawfully under constitutional and statutory authority, and that even if the rationale for his action were subject to judicial review the superseder order here would be valid.

On March 21, 1996, pursuant to article IV, § 3 of the New York Constitution and Executive Law § 63 (2), Governor Pataki issued Executive Order No. 27 (9 NYCRR 5.27), which required respondent Attorney-General Dennis C. Vacco to replace District Attorney Johnson in all investigations and proceedings arising out of the shooting of Police Officer Kevin Gillespie. As recited in the Executive Order, the District Attorney's statements, correspondence and swift rejection of the death penalty option in prior death-eligible cases indicated that the District Attorney had adopted a "blanket policy" against imposition of the death penalty.

Such a policy, according to the Executive Order, both violated a District Attorney's statutory duty to make death penalty determinations on a case-by-case basis and opened future death sentences to challenge on proportionality grounds. Given his obligation to take care that the death penalty law would be faithfully executed and the possibility that the District Attorney would take action that would irrevocably foreclose the death penalty in the Gillespie matter, the Executive Order continued, the Governor concluded that his immediate intervention through a superseder order was necessary.

Subsequently, the Grand Jury indicted Angel Diaz on two counts of murder in the first degree and related offenses in connection with Officer Gillespie's death. Diaz's alleged accomplices, Jesus Mendez and Ricardo Morales, were indicted for second-degree murder and other lesser crimes. The Attorney-General then filed notice that the People intended to seek the death penalty against Diaz.

Before the Attorney-General's announcement appellants District Attorney Johnson, and Bronx County voters and taxpayers (whose standing is assumed for purposes of this appeal), separately commenced CPLR article 78 proceedings contesting the legality of Executive Order No. 27. Supreme Court dismissed both petitions, holding that the superseder was an executive action pursuant to a valid grant of authority and as such was nonjusticiable. Alternatively, the court found that the District Attorney's pronouncements and practices provided "ample basis" for the Governor's action. During pendency of the appeals, Diaz committed suicide in his jail cell. Mendez and Morales were later tried in Federal court for their involvement in the Gillespie murder. They were found guilty of violating the Racketeer Influenced and Corrupt Organizations statute (18 USC § 1962), and their State indictments were dismissed.

The Appellate Division, concluding the appeals were not moot, unanimously affirmed Supreme Court's dismissal of both petitions (229 AD2d 242 [1997]). Finding that this case fell considerably short of the possible justiciable controversies reserved in *Mulroy v Carey* (43 NY2d 819, 821 [1977]), the court applied the traditional test for determining the validity of a superseder order—whether the Governor had acted within constitutional or statutory authority—and concluded that appellants had not made this requisite showing. Like the trial court, the Appellate Division went on to consider the reasonableness of the order, holding that the Governor's intervention was "fully justified" in light of the possibility that the District Attorney would take steps to preclude the death penalty in the Gillespie matter (229 AD2d at 246). We now affirm. . . .

The Law Regarding Superseder

. . . [W]e begin analysis with a recognition that when the Governor acts by Executive Order pursuant to a valid grant of discretionary authority, his actions are largely beyond judicial review (*see e.g. Matter of Cunningham v Nadjari*, 39 NY2d 314, 317–318 [1976]; *Gaynor v Rockefeller*, 15 NY2d 120, 131 [1965]; *Matter of Nistal v Hausauer*, 308 NY 146, 152–153 [1954], *cert denied* 349 US 962 [1955]).

Judicial review in such cases is generally limited to determining whether the State Constitution or the Legislature has empowered the Governor to act, and does not include the manner in which the Governor chooses to discharge that authority (*see e.g. Mulroy v Carey*, 58 AD2d 207, 214–215 [1977], *affd* 43 NY2d 819 [1977]; *People ex rel. Saranac Land & Timber Co. v Extraordinary Special & Trial Term of Supreme Ct.*, 220 NY 487, 491 [1917]; *People v Kramer*, 33 Misc 209, 219 [1900]). For abuse of lawful discretionary authority, the remedy as a rule lies with the people at the polls, or with a constitutional amendment, or with corrective legislation.

Whether a Governor is empowered to supersede a District Attorney in a particular prosecution is not a novel question. We have long held that article IV, § 3 of the Constitution and Executive Law § 63 (2) together provide the Governor with discretionary authority to supersede the District Attorney in a matter (*see Mulroy v Carey*, 43 NY2d at 821; *see also Matter of Additional Jan. 1979 Grand Jury of Albany Supreme Ct. v Doe*, 50 NY2d 14, 16 [1980]).[1] Article IV, § 3 delegates to the Governor, as head of the executive branch, the duty to "take care that the laws are faithfully executed." Executive Law § 63 (2), the legislative grant of authority, provides:

> The attorney-general shall . . . [w]henever required by the governor, . . . manag[e] and conduc[t] . . . criminal actions or proceedings as shall be specified in such requirement; in which case the attorney-general . . . shall exercise all the powers and perform all the duties in respect of such actions or proceedings, which the district attorney would otherwise be authorized or required to exercise or perform; and in any of such actions or proceedings the district attorney shall only exercise such powers and perform such duties as are required of him by the attorney-general.

The statute neither limits the Governor's authority to supersede nor requires the Governor to explain that choice. Consistent with that authority, Governors have numerous times invoked the superseder power (*see e.g.* Pitler, *Superseding the District Attorneys in New York City—The Constitutionality and Legality of Executive Order No. 55*, 41 Fordham L Rev 517, 522–527 [1973]).

In *Mulroy v Carey* (43 NY2d at 821), this Court reserved the possibility that in some undefined circumstance, the courts could invalidate this executive action. There we upheld the Governor's superseder of the Onondaga County District Attorney, rejecting the argument that the Governor was required to establish "to the satisfaction of the court the necessity of such action" in that case (58 AD2d at 208). We added, however, that "no view is expressed whether in any or all circumstances the exercise of the executive power to supersede an elected District Attorney would be beyond judicial review or correction in a direct or collateral action or proceeding brought or defended by the county or the elected District Attorney involved" (43 NY2d at 821).

---

1. This Court has rejected appellants' argument that Executive Law § 63 (2) should be read narrowly, as merely defining the general duties of the Attorney-General (*see e.g. Matter of Haggerty v Himelein*, 89 NY2d 431, 436 [1997]; *Mulroy v Carey*, 43 NY2d at 821; *Matter of Dondi v Jones*, 40 NY2d 8, 19 [1976]; *People v Rallo*, 39 NY2d 217, 224 [1976]).

Rust v. Reyer,
91 NY2d 355 (1998)

Chief Judge Kaye's decision in this case tackled the societal problem of underage drinking and expanded liability under the Dram Shop Act (General Obligations Law § 11-100). Her decision held that defendant, a high school girl who had made her parents' house available for a "keg party" while they were away, could be liable for furnishing beer to minors even though she herself did not serve or provide beer to anyone. Kaye followed the court's prime directive in interpreting statutes—giving effect to legislative intent—and stayed true to the clear purpose of the statute in deterring this behavior and the collateral harm that could follow.

—Introduction by Jeremy R. Feinberg, law clerk 1996–1998

This appeal centers on the question whether the host of a "keg party" for minors, in the circumstances presented, might be liable as a person who, by "unlawfully furnishing to or unlawfully assisting in procuring alcoholic beverages" for minors, caused the injuries of a third party (General Obligations Law § 11-100). We conclude that there are material factual issues to be resolved and consequently reverse the Appellate Division order summarily dismissing the second cause of action against defendant Heidi Reyer.

Plaintiff Carol Rust, a minor, was injured when she was punched in the face by Stephen Tarantino, also a minor, after a party at Reyer's house on October 7, 1989. Tarantino had been drinking heavily at the party, and in his inebriated state struck plaintiff during a brawl on the street outside Reyer's house in Merrick, New York.

The facts, viewed in a light most favorable to plaintiff, are as follows. When Reyer, then 17, learned that her parents were going to be on vacation over the weekend of October 7, 1989, she planned a party in their absence. Word of the party reached the ears of a high school fraternity of which Tarantino was a member known as the Marquis. Representatives of the fraternity approached Reyer and attempted to convince her to allow them to bring beer. Those attending the party would pay a one-time fee to receive a 16-ounce cup, allowing them unlimited access to the beer. Reyer agreed to have the beer at her party, in exchange for a portion of the proceeds.

On the day of the party, fraternity members arrived with several kegs of beer, which Reyer allowed them to store in the garage. Fraternity members later set up the kegs, where they could be accessed from the Reyers' backyard. As the party started, the fraternity stationed three individuals at the entrance to the backyard, one to collect money, a second to stamp the hands of those who had paid, and a third to hand out cups. Reyer attempted to arrange for her friends to have free beer, and she observed many of the estimated 150 underaged guests consuming alcohol. She did not herself drink or dispense beer at the party, collect money, stamp hands or distribute cups.

Later, responding to neighbors' complaints, the police arrived. Reyer and the police dispersed the party but the guests, including Rust and Tarantino, milled around in the street near Reyer's house. There, a melee erupted and Tarantino impaired by the alcohol he had consumed at the party punched plaintiff once in the face, severely injuring her. After the party the kegs were stored in the Reyers' garage, where they were later retrieved by the fraternity. Reyer never received the promised share of the fees, although she sought payment several times after the party.

Rust ultimately brought suit against Reyer, her parents and Tarantino, alleging negligence and violations of General Obligations Law §§ 11-100 and 11-101. Tarantino settled with plaintiff, and after joinder of issue the remaining defendants moved for summary judgment on all claims. Plaintiff opposed only that portion of the motion dismissing the General Obligations Law § 11-100 claim against Reyer. Supreme Court first dismissed the uncontested claims and then granted the remainder of defendant's motion. Relying on the principle that statutes in derogation of the common law are to be narrowly construed, the court held that while "Heidi Reyer may be said to have 'facilitated' the furnishing of beer to Stephen Tarantino and other party guests, the statute cannot be stretched to impose liability for this type of conduct." The court further concluded that Reyer had not assisted in procuring the alcohol, because fraternity members had purchased the beer, brought it to the party and personally dispensed it.

Plaintiff appealed only that portion of Supreme Court's order dismissing the General Obligations Law § 11-100 claim against Reyer, and the Appellate Division affirmed. That court held that "General Obligations Law § 11-100 is not applicable to a homeowner who has neither supplied alcohol to nor procured alcohol for consumption by an underage person" (235 AD2d 413 [1997]). We granted plaintiff leave to appeal and now reverse.

Analysis

Underage drinking is a significant societal problem that has generated widespread concern (*see e.g.* French, Kaput and Wildman, *Special Project: Social Host Liability for the Negligent Acts of Intoxicated Guests*, 70 Cornell L Rev 1058 [1985]; Comment, *Killer Party: Proposing Civil Liability for Social Hosts who Serve Alcohol to Minors*, 30 J Marshall L Rev 245, 257–258 [1996] [*Killer Party*]). All 50 states have set minimum drinking ages, a measure which has to some extent prevented minors from themselves purchasing alcohol at bars and liquor stores.[1] Those same laws, however, have proven far less effective in stopping minors from obtaining alcohol in a social setting, where it is provided to them by individuals who have little, if any, financial disincentive for doing so (*see e.g. Killer Party, op. cit.* at 260).

---

1. Alcoholic Beverage Control Law § 65 establishes 21 as the minimum drinking age in New York.

States have responded to this circumvention of their minimum age laws in a variety of ways. Some have by statute imposed civil liability, criminal liability or both on gratuitous providers of alcohol. In other states, courts have recognized a common-law duty of the provider (*see generally* Annotation, *Social Host's Liability for Injuries Incurred by Third Parties as a Result of Intoxicated Guest's Negligence*, 62 ALR4th 16). New York has taken the former approach: in addition to making it a crime to furnish alcoholic beverages to a minor in most cases (Penal Law § 260.20 [2]), in 1983 the legislature enacted General Obligations Law § 11-100, which provides:

> Any person who shall be injured in person, property, means of support or otherwise, by reason of the intoxication or impairment of ability of any person under the age of twenty-one years, whether resulting in his death or not, shall have a right of action to recover actual damages against any person who *knowingly causes such intoxication or impairment of ability by unlawfully furnishing to or unlawfully assisting in procuring alcoholic beverages* for such person with knowledge or reasonable cause to believe that such person was under the age of twenty-one years. (General Obligations Law § 11-100 [1] [emphasis supplied]).

Conceding that Reyer herself never actually served alcohol to any party guest, plaintiff nonetheless contends that Reyer's actions constituted "furnishing" under the statute. Neither the relevant statutes (including related enactments General Obligations Law § 11-101 and Alcoholic Beverage Control Law § 65) nor our prior cases define the term "furnishing," which is ordinarily understood to mean "to provide in any way," "to supply" or "to give" (*see e.g.* Black's Law Dictionary 675 [6th ed 1990]; Webster's Deluxe Unabridged Dictionary 743 [2d ed 1983]; *accord Ball v Allstate Ins. Co.*, 81 NY2d 22, 25 [1993]).

Here, Reyer allegedly gave permission for the alcohol at the party she was planning, provided storage for the kegs of beer both before and after the party, negotiated a share of the proceeds from cup sales for herself and at least attempted to arrange for her friends to drink the beer without charge. Her request for a portion of the proceeds from cup sales underscores her complete complicity in the fraternity's plans to furnish beer. As stated in plaintiff's affidavit, Reyer "chose to participate in a scheme to furnish alcohol to underage individuals in return for a payment of money." Moreover, without Reyer's advance permission, the beer could not have been served as it ultimately was. Indeed, many of the 150 minors present may well not have come to the party in the first instance had they not known that alcohol would be available.

We conclude that if proven at trial, these facts could bring Reyer's acts within the meaning of "furnishing" as used in the statute.[2] Reyer's role could well be viewed as part of a deliberate plan to provide, supply or give alcohol to an underage person.

In reaching this conclusion we are mindful that a statute in derogation of the common law must be strictly construed (*see Sherman v Robinson*, 80 NY2d 483, 487

---

2. Given this conclusion, we need not and do not reach plaintiff's alternative contention that defendant "unlawfully assist[ed] in procuring" alcohol for an underage person.

[1992]; *D'Amico v Christie*, 71 NY2d 76, 83 [1987]). We are mindful as well that our prime directive, in matters of statutory interpretation, is to give effect to the intention of the legislature (*see Ferres v City of New Rochelle*, 68 NY2d 446, 451 [1986]; *People v Ryan*, 274 NY 149, 152 [1937]). To interpret "furnishing" as Reyer suggests in effect limiting it to those who hand the alcohol to the minor gives the term an overly narrow reach that undermines the clear legislative goal.

The purpose of General Obligations Law § 11-100 is to employ civil penalties as a deterrent against underage drinking (*Sheehy v Big Flats Community Day*, 73 NY2d 629, 636 [1989]). As the bill's cosponsor noted, "[t]his legislation seeks to protect minors from those persons uncaring enough to provide intoxicating beverages to minors in an indiscriminate manner and by so doing, to endanger the life and safety of the minor as well as of the general public" (Letter of Assembly Member John F. Duane, Bill Jacket, L 1983, ch 641). In the words of Senator William T. Smith, also a cosponsor of the statute:

> Over the years, numerous court cases have dealt extensively with the question of common law liability on the part of those who knowingly furnish alcoholic beverages to under-age persons at graduation parties, church socials, wedding receptions, office parties, and college campuses. Under-age persons consuming excess alcohol at these social events unquestionably have the same propensity to do harm to the traveling public as those who have been served alcohol pursuant to a sale. (1983 NY Legis Ann at 281).

The facts alleged demonstrate that Reyer was more than an unknowing bystander or an innocent dupe whose premises were used by other minors seeking to drink (*cf. Dodge v Victory Mkts.*, 199 AD2d 917 [1993]; *Reickert v Misciagna*, 183 AD2d 151 [1992]). Similarly, she was more than a passive participant who merely knew of the underage drinking and did nothing else to encourage it (*cf. Lane v Barker*, 241 AD2d 739 [1997]; *MacGilvray v Denino*, 149 AD2d 571 [1989]; *see also Pelinsky v Rockensies*, 209 AD2d 392 [1994]). Reyer played an indispensable role in the scheme to make the alcohol available to the underage party guests.

Reading the statute to foreclose responsibility in these circumstances would allow unintended circumvention of the legislation and negate its deterrent purpose (*see* 1983 NY Legis Ann at 281–282 [the "time has come for every individual to accept responsibility for an activity which most people partake in, consumption of alcoholic beverages the responsibility as a consumer, and as a furnisher, as well"]; *see also Killer Party*, op. cit. at 249–250).

Accordingly, the order of the Appellate Division should be reversed, with costs, and the motion for summary judgment dismissing the second cause of action against defendant Heidi Reyer should be denied.

Karlin v. IVF Am.,
93 NY2d 282 (1999)

Writing for the court in *Karlin*, Judge Kaye confirmed an important concept in consumer actions. Plaintiffs, a husband and wife, participated in defendant clinics' in vitro fertilization (IVF) program over a number of years, unsuccessfully. Claiming that defendants had exaggerated success rates and misrepresented health risks, plaintiffs sued defendants pursuant to General Business Law §§ 349–350 for unfair and deceptive trade practices and false advertising.

The court ruled that plaintiffs had satisfactorily stated causes of action; that providers of medical services, such as defendants, were not exempt from those consumer protection statutes, and that plaintiffs were not limited to a suit for lack of informed consent. By allegedly engaging in consumer-related conduct, defendants were subject to the standards of an honest marketplace, setting forth the test for a "deceptive act or practice" as a representation or omission "likely to mislead a reasonable consumer acting reasonably under the circumstances." Aptly rejecting defendants' "floodgates" argument, Kaye wrote that plaintiffs were not precluded from pursuing those claims simply because the alleged misrepresentations related to the provision of medical services.

—Introduction by Hon. Albert M. Rosenblatt

In order to ensure an honest marketplace, the General Business Law prohibits all deceptive practices, including false advertising, "in the conduct of any business, trade or commerce or in the furnishing of any service in this state" (General Business Law § 349 [a]; § 350; . . .). This appeal requires us to determine whether plaintiffs can maintain an action against defendants operating an in vitro fertilization (IVF) program for deceptive practices and false advertising under General Business Law §§ 349 and 350, or are instead limited to a claim for medical malpractice based on lack of informed consent. We hold that plaintiffs have properly stated causes of action under these consumer protection statutes, and are not precluded from pursuing those claims because the alleged misrepresentations relate to the provision of medical services. . . .

In 1987, plaintiffs Jayne and Kenneth R. Karlin sought evaluation and treatment from defendants' IVF program. The IVF procedure involves removal of multiple eggs from a woman's ovaries, fertilization of the eggs outside her body and transfer of the fertilized eggs to her uterus in an attempt to impregnate her. . . . Over the course of 2½ years, Mrs. Karlin completed seven IVF cycles at defendants' clinic but did not become pregnant.

In 1990, the Federal Trade Commission (FTC) charged IVF America and related entities . . . with deceptively advertising and promoting its program, finding the following statements typical of representations in their promotional materials:

1. "LIKELY TREATMENT OUTCOMES . . . Our experience indicates that when a patient at an IVF [America] Program completes four IVF treatment cycles, the chance of giving birth is about 50% . . . If *25* women begin a total of *100* IVF cycles . . . About *13* (or about 50%) of the women give birth to *18* babies (emphasis in original). . . .

2. "[M]ore than 28% of the couples who complete a cycle of treatment are becoming pregnant" . . .

3. "[O]ne out of three couples who complete a cycle of treatment is becoming pregnant."

According to the FTC, these statements were misleading because women who participate in IVF America's treatment program "consisting of four IVF cycles have considerably less than a 50 percent chance of giving birth," and women who participate in IVF America's treatment program "consisting of one IVF cycle have considerably less than a 28 to 33 percent chance of becoming pregnant." By consent decree dated December 31, 1990, IVF America agreed to cease and desist from misrepresenting success rates, and also agreed in the future to disclose the basis used for calculating the percentage of patients who have become pregnant or given birth.

In February 1993, however, the ABC News program "20/20" televised an investigative report on the IVF industry in which IVF America employees were shown informing prospective patients that after four to six cycles, IVF America had pregnancy success rates "between 60 to 80 percent." The report also showed an IVF America representative telling a seminar participant that there are "[a]bsolutely not" any long-term effects of the IVF procedure. This report prompted New York City's Department of Consumer Affairs to charge IVF America with violations of the City's Consumer Protection Law. As part of a settlement reached in April 1993, IVF America agreed to refrain both from marketing its services using unsubstantiated pregnancy success rates and from stating that IVF procedures posed no adverse health risks.

The following year, plaintiffs commenced this action alleging that defendants engaged in fraudulent and misleading conduct by disseminating false success rates and misrepresenting health risks associated with IVF. In particular, plaintiffs claim that defendants "exaggerated success rates, excluding certain subsets of failed treatment procedures, emphasizing numerically false and misleading overall success rates and conceal[ing] and misrepresent[ing] significant health risks, high miscarriage rates and excessive neonatal deaths and abnormalities of infants even if a birth resulted from the treatment rendered by defendants."

Supreme Court dismissed all of plaintiffs' causes of action except those alleging unfair and deceptive trade practices in violation of General Business Law § 349, false advertising in violation of General Business Law § 350 and lack of informed consent in violation of Public Health Law § 2805-d. . . .

We . . . conclude that plaintiffs may pursue their General Business Law §§ 349 and 350 claims. . . .

Pursuant to General Business Law § 349 (a), it is unlawful to perform "[d]eceptive acts or practices in the conduct of *any* business, trade or commerce or in the furnishing of *any* service in this state" (emphasis added). The scope of General Business Law § 350 is equally broad, prohibiting the promulgation of "[f]alse advertising in the conduct of *any* business, trade or commerce or in the furnishing of *any* service in this state" (emphasis added). Advertising is "false" if it "is misleading in a material respect" (General Business Law § 350-a [1]).

These statutes on their face apply to virtually all economic activity, and their application has been correspondingly broad [citing cases]. The reach of these statutes "provide[s] needed authority to cope with the numerous, ever-changing types of false and deceptive business practices which plague consumers in our State" (NY Dept of Law, Mem to Governor, 1963 NY Legis Ann at 105).

When section 349 was enacted in 1970, only the Attorney General was empowered to enforce it (General Business Law § 349 [b]). It soon became clear, however, that the "broad scope of section 349, combined with the limited resources of the Attorney General, [made] it virtually impossible for the Attorney General to provide more than minimal enforcement" (Mem of Assemblyman Strelzin, L 1980, ch 346, § 1, 1980 NY Legis Ann at 146). Accordingly, in 1980 the statute was amended to provide a private right of action (*see* L 1980, ch 346, § 1). Among the remedies available to private plaintiffs are compensatory damages, limited punitive damages and attorneys' fees (General Business Law § 349 [h]).

A blanket exemption for providers of medical services and products is contrary to the plain language of the statutes. Such an exemption is also contrary to legislative history, as supporters of the consumer protection bills recognized that consumers of medical services and products might be particularly vulnerable to unscrupulous business practices. In fact, in a memorandum to the Governor advocating section 350, the only example cited by the Attorney General to underscore the need for such legislation was an Arthritis and Rheumatism Foundation report concluding "that through fraudulent advertising people suffering from such painful diseases as arthritis are being duped out of 250 million dollars annually" (NY Dept of Law, Mem to Governor, 1963 NY Legis Ann at 105–106).

Indeed, while the question before us is a novel one, General Business Law §§ 349 and 350 have long been powerful tools aiding the Attorney General's efforts to combat fraud in the health care and medical services areas. The Attorney General has relied on these provisions to challenge deceptive and fraudulent practices in contexts as diverse as the marketing of AIDS-related products [citing cases].

Not only is the categorical exemption crafted by the Appellate Division at odds with the language and history of sections 349 and 350, but also the apparent simplicity of that excision proves elusive when it is necessary to decide who is a "provider of medical services." IVF America, for example, is a publicly traded company engaged in managing and providing services to clinical facilities and physician practices that specialize in infertility treatments; actual patient medical care, however, is furnished by affiliated medical institutions or groups. Thus, it is unclear whether such an entity could itself even be considered as a "provider of medical services."

Despite the scope of General Business Law §§ 349 and 350 and the historical use of these statutes to combat fraud in the medical context, defendants argue that plaintiffs' claims must be governed exclusively by New York's informed consent statute, Public Health Law § 2805-d. A suit for medical malpractice based on a lack of informed consent is meant to redress a "failure of the person providing the professional treatment or diagnosis to disclose to the patient such alternatives thereto and the reasonably foreseeable risks and benefits involved as a reasonable medical . . . practitioner under similar circumstances would have disclosed, in a manner permitting the patient to make a knowledgeable evaluation" (Public Health Law § 2805-d [1]). In contrast to the latitude afforded plaintiffs suing for deceptive practices and false advertising, there are numerous restrictions on a plaintiff's ability to sue for malpractice based on a lack of informed consent. Such claims, for example, are limited to certain treatments or diagnostic procedures, require a heightened showing of causation, and are subject to several affirmative defenses and an abbreviated Statute of Limitations (*see* Public Health Law § 2805-d; CPLR 214-a). These restrictions were enacted in 1975 as part of a bill intended to ensure the ability of physicians to obtain malpractice insurance coverage at reasonable rates (*see* Governor's Approval Mem, L 1975, ch 109, 1975 McKinney's Session Laws of NY at 1739–1740).

Notwithstanding defendants' procrustean efforts to cast plaintiffs' deceptive acts and false advertising claims as malpractice claims for lack of informed consent, plaintiffs have clearly alleged conduct beyond the purview of Public Health Law § 2805-d. Plaintiffs do not merely charge that "the person providing the professional treatment" failed to disclose certain pertinent information "to the patient" (Public Health Law § 2805-d [1]). Rather, they claim that defendants' "promotional materials, advertisements, slide presentations . . . and so-called 'educational' seminars" contained misrepresentations that had the effect of "deceiving and misleading members of the public." Nor are plaintiffs' claims limited, as defendants urge, to information provided by defendants "during the course of their medical treatment at the Program." On the contrary, plaintiffs assert that before they started any course of treatment, defendants "deceptively lured" plaintiffs and others, including physicians who refer patients to the IVF America programs, by "deceiving and misleading" them.

Defendants' alleged multi-media dissemination of information to the public is precisely the sort of consumer-oriented conduct that is targeted by General Business Law §§ 349 and 350 (*Oswego Laborers' Local 214 Pension Fund v Marine Midland Bank*, 85 NY2d 20, 25 [1995]). By alleging that defendants have injured them with consumer-oriented conduct "that is deceptive or misleading in a material way," plaintiffs have stated claims under General Business Law §§ 349 and 350 even though the subject of the conduct was in vitro fertilization (*id.*; *see also New York Univ v Continental Ins. Co.*, 87 NY2d 308, 320 [1995]).

That a plaintiff has brought General Business Law §§ 349 and 350 claims, of course, does not foreclose additional claims for lack of informed consent. A person who is "deceptively lured into" a course of professional treatment by consumer-oriented misrepresentations may also be harmed by a doctor's failure to disclose information required by Public Health Law § 2805-d. By the same token, the fact that a person may have a claim for lack of informed consent does not preclude a separate claim on the ground that deceptive acts or misleading advertising lured the person to the doctor's office in the first place. . . .

Defendants' concern that allowing plaintiffs to sue doctors for deceptive consumer practices and false advertising may cause a tidal wave of litigation against doctors is misplaced. Because plaintiffs bringing a claim under the consumer protection statutes must demonstrate an impact on consumers at large—something that a physician's treatment of an individual patient typically does not have—these statutes will not supplant traditional medical malpractice actions. Furthermore, as this Court has already observed, the possibility of excessive litigation under the consumer protection statutes is avoided by our "adoption of an objective definition of deceptive acts and practices, whether representations or omissions, limited to those likely to mislead a reasonable consumer acting reasonably under the circumstances" (*Oswego Laborers' Local 214 Pension Fund v Marine Midland Bank, supra*, 85 NY2d at 26).

Finally, the interests at stake in an action under the General Business Law are distinctly different from the interests involved in a suit for professional malpractice. Thus, while physicians providing information to their patients in the course of medical treatment may be afforded the benefits of Public Health Law § 2805-d, when they choose to reach out to the consuming public at large in order to promote business—like clothing retailers, automobile dealers and wedding singers who engage in such conduct—they subject themselves to the standards of an honest marketplace secured by General Business Law §§ 349 and 350.

Plaintiffs' remaining contention is without merit.

Accordingly, the judgment appealed from and the order of the Appellate Division brought up for review should be modified, with costs to plaintiffs, by denying defendants' motion to dismiss the first and second causes of action and, as so modified, affirmed.

Kihl v. Pfeffer,
94 NY2d 118 (1999)

The disclosure process affords litigants an opportunity to gather evidence and prepare for trial. It is often the most time-consuming and most important part of a case. In *Kihl*, writing for the unanimous Court of Appeals, Chief Judge Kaye emphasized that "compliance with a disclosure order requires both a timely response and one that evidences a good-faith effort to address the requests meaningfully." Kaye's message to the bench and bar was unmistakable: if "the credibility of court orders and the integrity of our judicial system are to be maintained, a litigant cannot ignore court orders with impunity." Thus, "when a party fails to comply with a court order and frustrates the disclosure scheme set forth [in New York's rules of procedure], it is well within the Trial Judge's discretion to dismiss the complaint." *Kihl* stands as a strong reminder that to obtain justice through the courts, a party must follow court rules and fulfill its obligations.

—Introduction by Hon. Jennifer G. Schecter, law clerk 1998–2001

At issue is the dismissal of a complaint against defendant Honda Motor Co., Inc. for plaintiff's failure to respond to Honda's interrogatories within court-ordered time frames. We conclude that the trial court did not abuse its discretion in dismissing the complaint, and affirm the Appellate Division order so holding.

On July 26, 1995, plaintiff commenced a damages action for personal injuries arising out of a one-car accident six months earlier. . . . As against Honda she claimed negligence, breach of express and implied warranties, strict products liability and failure to warn in connection with the automobile and its component parts, including the seat belts. Honda responded with a general denial, cross-claims and a host of discovery requests, including demands for expert witness disclosure, collateral source information, no-fault authorizations, medical information and certain records.

On March 18, 1996, the parties convened before the court for a preliminary conference, resulting in an extensive Preliminary Conference Order fixing specific dates for discovery, to be completed within six months. The order was consented to by each party and signed by the Trial Judge. Most pertinently, the order required plaintiff to respond to Honda's interrogatories "within 30 days following receipt of same." That very day Honda served plaintiff with its "First Set of Interrogatories"—34 pages, 92 questions. Having had no response, on September 13, 1996—roughly five months beyond the response date fixed by the Preliminary Conference Order—Honda moved to strike the complaint and dismiss plaintiff's claims against it, or to compel responses within 10 days. Honda alleged that without specificity as to the claimed defect in the automobile it could not adequately prepare its defense. Plaintiff's counsel submitted an affidavit opposing the motion, and that same day—December 10, 1996—served its responses to Honda's interrogatories.

Honda, however, persisted in seeking dismissal of the complaint, portraying plaintiff's responses as "woefully inadequate and totally unresponsive in clear violation of the Court's Order." In particular, Honda claimed that responses 43 through 56 offered no clue as to the claimed defect in the car. . . .

By order dated March 31, 1997, the Trial Judge granted Honda's motion to dismiss the complaint for failure to comply with the Preliminary Conference Order unless plaintiff served further answers to interrogatories 43 through 56 within 20 days after service of a copy of the order on plaintiff's counsel. The court held that plaintiff's answers were "not responsive, lack any reasonable detail and improperly reserve the right to provide answers at a later time."

Honda's Order with Notice of Entry, indicating service by mail on all other parties at their correct addresses, is dated June 6, 1997, and stamped "Filed" by the Nassau County Clerk on June 16, 1997. . . . During the month of June 1997, counsel for Honda twice wrote to plaintiff's counsel referencing the Trial Judge's order, the first letter beginning: "As you are now undoubtedly aware, Judge Kutner has ordered that plaintiff supplement [her] discovery responses." Nevertheless, plaintiff's counsel claimed the March 31, 1997 order was not actually served, as represented, on June 6, 1997. Plaintiff made no further responses to Honda's interrogatories within 20 days after June 6, 1997.

On October 20, 1997, the Trial Judge issued an order reserving decision on Honda's motion to strike the complaint until it received an explanation of when Honda served the court's March 31, 1997 order. Plaintiff's counsel, who was on vacation during the entire month of June, then submitted two affidavits—one from his partner who reviewed his mail during June, the second from his secretary who opened his mail—asserting that they did not see the March 31, 1997 order in the June mail. . . .

On February 9, 1998, the Trial Judge granted Honda's motion to strike the complaint. . . . The Appellate Division affirmed, with two Justices dissenting on the ground that a hearing was required to resolve the question of fact regarding service of the March 31, 1997 order. . . .

Three familiar propositions of law resolve this appeal in Honda's favor. *First*, service of papers on an attorney is complete upon mailing (CPLR 2103 [b] [2]). *Second*, a properly executed affidavit of service raises a presumption that a proper mailing occurred, and a mere denial of receipt is not enough to rebut this presumption. . . . Here, the denials of receipt by persons who reviewed plaintiff's lawyer's June mail were insufficient to create an issue of fact requiring a hearing. *Third*, when a party fails to comply with a court order and frustrates the disclosure scheme set forth in the CPLR, it is well within the Trial Judge's discretion to dismiss the complaint. . . .

Regrettably, it is not only the law but also the scenario that is all too familiar. . . . If the credibility of court orders and the integrity of our judicial system are to be maintained, a litigant cannot ignore court orders with impunity. Indeed, the Legislature, recognizing the need for courts to be able to command compliance with their disclosure directives, has specifically provided that a "court may make such orders . . . as are just," including dismissal of an action (CPLR 3126). Finally, we underscore that compliance with a disclosure order requires both a timely response and one that evinces a good-faith effort to address the requests meaningfully.

Accordingly, the order of the Appellate Division should be affirmed, with costs.

532 Madison Ave. Gourmet Foods, Inc. v. Finlandia Ctr., 96 NY2d 280 (2001)

A tower collapses, sending bricks, mortar, and other material hurtling to the ground in a hectic New York City business district. People are injured, and property destroyed. Only six months before the collapse of the World Trade Center in lower Manhattan, Chief Judge Kaye wrote presciently for a unanimous court that "we have never held . . . that a landowner owes a duty to protect an entire urban neighborhood against purely economic losses" stemming from the owner's fault in an urban disaster.

A great proponent of judge-made law, Kaye believed that "the nature of the common law process [is] constantly to test and retest the rules and principles established by judges of another day, and to retain and build upon what remains sound." In crafting the common law, "always the court's function is the same, that of weighing and balancing the relation of the parties, the nature of the risk and the public interest, and then setting the outer limits of one person's duty of care to another, unquestionably an important element in our social order today" (Kaye, *Human Dimension in Appellate Judging: A Brief Reflection on a Timeless Concern*, 73 Cornell L Rev 1004, 1010–1011 [1988])

—Introduction by Jean M. Joyce, law clerk 2000–2006

The novel issues raised by these appeals—arising from construction-related disasters in midtown Manhattan—concern . . . a landholder's duty in negligence where plaintiffs' sole injury is lost income. . . .

Two of the three appeals involve the same event. On December 7, 1997, a section of the south wall of 540 Madison Avenue, a 39-story office tower, partially collapsed and bricks, mortar and other material fell onto Madison Avenue at 55th Street, a prime commercial location crammed with stores and skyscrapers. The collapse occurred after a construction project, which included putting 94 holes for windows into the building's south wall, aggravated existing structural defects. New York City officials directed the closure of 15 heavily trafficked blocks on Madison Avenue—from 42nd to 57th Street—as well as adjacent side streets between Fifth and Park Avenues. The closure lasted for approximately two weeks, but some businesses nearest to 540 Madison remained closed for a longer period.

In *532 Madison Ave. Gourmet Foods v Finlandia Ctr.*, plaintiff operates a 24-hour delicatessen one-half block south of 540 Madison, and was closed for five weeks. The two named plaintiffs in the companion case, *5th Ave. Chocolatiere v 540 Acquisition Co.*, are retailers at 510 Madison Avenue, two blocks from the building, suing on behalf of themselves and a putative class of "all other business entities [in the vicinity]." Plaintiffs allege that shoppers and others were unable to gain access to their stores during the time Madison Avenue was closed to traffic. Defendants in both cases are Finlandia Center (the building owner), 540 Acquisition Company (the ground lessee) and Manhattan Pacific Management (the managing agent).

On defendants' motions in both cases, Supreme Court dismissed plaintiffs' negligence claims on the ground that they could not establish that defendants owed a duty of care for purely economic loss in the absence of personal injury or property damage. . . . In *5th Ave. Chocolatiere*, plaintiffs' additional claims for gross negligence and negligence per se were dismissed on the ground that plaintiffs could not establish a duty owed by defendants. . . .

Goldberg Weprin & Ustin v Tishman Constr. involves the July 21, 1998 collapse of a 48-story construction elevator tower on West 43rd Street between Sixth and Seventh Avenues—the heart of bustling Times Square. Immediately after the accident, the City prohibited all traffic in a wide area of midtown Manhattan and also evacuated nearby buildings for varying time periods. Three actions were consolidated—one by a law firm, a second by a public relations firm and a third by a clothing manufacturer, all situated within the affected area. Plaintiff law firm sought damages for economic loss on behalf of itself and a proposed class "of all persons in the vicinity of Broadway and 42nd Street, New York, New York, whose businesses were affected and/or caused to be closed" as well as a subclass of area residents who were evacuated from their homes. Plaintiff alleged gross negligence. . . .

Noting the enormity of the liability sought, including recovery by putative plaintiffs as diverse as hot dog vendors, taxi drivers and Broadway productions, Supreme Court concluded that the failure to allege personal injury or property damage barred recovery in negligence. . . .

The Appellate Division affirmed dismissal of the *Goldberg Weprin* complaint, [but] reinstated the negligence . . . claims of plaintiffs 532 Madison and 5th Ave. Chocolatiere, holding that defendants' duty to keep their premises in reasonably safe condition extended to "those businesses in such close proximity that their negligent acts could be reasonably foreseen to cause injury" . . . Two Justices dissented. . . .

Plaintiffs' Negligence Claims

Plaintiffs contend that defendants owe them a duty to keep their premises in reasonably safe condition, and that this duty extends to protection against economic loss even in the absence of personal injury or property damage. Defendants counter that the absence of any personal injury or property damage precludes plaintiffs' claims for economic injury.[1]

---

1. The "economic loss" rule espoused in *Schiavone Constr. Co. v Mayo Corp.* (56 NY2d 667, *revg on dissent* at 81 AD2d 221) and relied on by defendants has no application here. That case stands for the proposition that an end-purchaser of a product is limited to contract remedies and may not seek damages in tort for economic loss against a manufacturer (*see also Bocre Leasing Corp. v General Motors Corp.*, 84 NY2d 685; *Bellevue S. Assocs. v HRH Constr. Corp.*, 78 NY2d 282).

The existence and scope of a tortfeasor's duty is, of course, a legal question for the courts, which "fix the duty point by balancing factors, including the reasonable expectations of parties and society generally, the proliferation of claims, the likelihood of unlimited or insurer-like liability, disproportionate risk and reparation allocation, and public policies affecting the expansion or limitation of new channels of liability" (*Hamilton v Beretta U.S.A. Corp.*, 96 NY2d 222, 232 [quoting *Palka v Servicemaster Mgt. Servs. Corp.*, 83 NY2d 579, 586]). At its foundation, the common law of torts is a means of apportioning risks and allocating the burden of loss. In drawing lines defining actionable duty, courts must therefore always be mindful of the consequential, and precedential, effects of their decisions.

As we have many times noted, foreseeability of harm does not define duty (*see e.g. Pulka v Edelman*, 40 NY2d 781, 785). Absent a duty running directly to the injured person there can be no liability in damages, however careless the conduct or foreseeable the harm. This restriction is necessary to avoid exposing defendants to unlimited liability to an indeterminate class of persons conceivably injured by any negligence in a defendant's act.

A duty may arise from a special relationship that requires the defendant to protect against the risk of harm to plaintiff (*see e.g. Eiseman v State of New York*, 70 NY2d 175, 187–188). Landowners, for example, have a duty to protect tenants, patrons and invitees from foreseeable harm caused by the criminal conduct of others while they are on the premises, because the special relationship puts them in the best position to protect against the risk (*see e.g. Nallan v Helmsley-Spear, Inc.*, 50 NY2d 507, 518–519). That duty, however, does not extend to members of the general public (*see Waters v New York City Hous. Auth.*, 69 NY2d 225, 229). Liability is in this way circumscribed, because the special relationship defines the class of potential plaintiffs to whom the duty is owed.

In *Strauss v Belle Realty Co.* (65 NY2d 399) we considered whether a utility owed a duty to a plaintiff injured in a fall on a darkened staircase during a citywide blackout. While the injuries were logically foreseeable, there was no contractual relationship between the plaintiff and the utility for lighting in the building's common areas. As a matter of policy, we restricted liability for damages in negligence to direct customers of the utility in order to avoid crushing exposure to the suits of millions of electricity consumers in New York City and Westchester.

Even closer to the mark is *Milliken & Co. v Consolidated Edison Co.* (84 NY2d 469), in which an underground water main burst near 38th Street and 7th Avenue in Manhattan. The waters flooded a subbasement where Consolidated Edison maintained an electricity supply substation, and then a fire broke out, causing extensive damage that disrupted the flow of electricity to the Manhattan Garment Center and interrupting the biannual Buyers Week. Approximately 200 Garment Center businesses brought more than 50 lawsuits against Con Edison, including plaintiffs who had no contractual relationship with the utility and who sought damages solely for economic loss. Relying on *Strauss*, we again held that only those persons contracting with the utility could state a cause of action. We circumscribed the ambit of duty to avoid limitless exposure to the potential suits of every tenant in the skyscrapers embodying the urban skyline.

A landowner who engages in activities that may cause injury to persons on adjoining premises surely owes those persons a duty to take reasonable precautions to avoid injuring them (*see e.g. Weitzmann v Barber Asphalt Co.*, 190 NY 452, 457). We have never held, however, that a landowner owes a duty to protect an entire urban neighborhood against purely economic losses. A comparison of *Beck v FMC Corp.* (53 AD2d 118, 121, *affd* 42 NY2d 1027) and *Dunlop Tire & Rubber Corp. v FMC Corp.* (53 AD2d 150, 154–155) is instructive. Those cases arose out of the same incident: an explosion at defendant FMC's chemical manufacturing plant caused physical vibrations, and rained stones and debris onto plaintiff Dunlop Tire's nearby factory. The blast also caused a loss of electrical power—by destroying towers and distribution lines owned by a utility—to both Dunlop Tire and a Chevrolet plant located one and one-half miles away. Both establishments suffered temporary closure after the accident. Plaintiffs in *Beck* were employees of the Chevrolet plant who sought damages for lost wages caused by the plant closure. Plaintiff Dunlop Tire sought recovery for property damage emanating from the blast and the loss of energy, and lost profits sustained during the shutdown.

In *Dunlop Tire*, the Appellate Division observed that, although part of the damage occurred from the loss of electricity and part from direct physical contact, defendant's duty to plaintiffs was undiminished. The court permitted plaintiffs to seek damages for economic loss, subject to the general rule requiring proof of the extent of the damage and the causal relationship between the negligence and the damage. The *Beck* plaintiffs, by contrast, could not state a cause of action, because, to extend a duty to defendant FMC would, "like the rippling of the waters, [go] far beyond the zone of danger of the explosion," to everyone who suffered purely economic loss (*Beck v FMC Corp.*, 53 AD2d at 121). . . .

Policy-driven line-drawing is to an extent arbitrary because, wherever the line is drawn, invariably it cuts off liability to persons who foreseeably might be plaintiffs. The *Goldberg Weprin* class, for example, would include all persons in the vicinity of Times Square whose businesses had to be closed and a subclass of area residents evacuated from their homes; the *5th Ave. Chocolatiere* class would include all business entities between 42nd and 57th Streets and Fifth and Park Avenues. While the Appellate Division attempted to draw a careful boundary at storefront merchant-neighbors who suffered lost income, that line excludes others similarly affected by the closures—such as the law firm, public relations firm, clothing manufacturer and other displaced plaintiffs in *Goldberg Weprin*, the thousands of professional, commercial and residential tenants situated in the towers surrounding the named plaintiffs, and suppliers and service providers unable to reach the densely populated New York City blocks at issue in each case.

As is readily apparent, an indeterminate group in the affected areas thus may have provable financial losses directly traceable to the two construction-related collapses, with no satisfactory way geographically to distinguish among those who have suffered purely economic losses (*see also Matter of Kinsman Tr. Co.*, 388 F2d 821, 825 n 8). In such circumstances, limiting the scope of defendants' duty to those who have, as a result of these events, suffered personal injury or property damage—as historically courts have done—affords a principled basis for reasonably apportioning liability.

We therefore conclude that plaintiffs' negligence claims based on economic loss alone fall beyond the scope of the duty owed them by defendants and should be dismissed.[2] . . .

---

2. Plaintiff Goldberg Weprin & Ustin's bare allegation that the construction project was dangerously handled was insufficient to set forth a cause of action for strict liability based on an abnormally dangerous activity (*see Engel v Eureka Club*, 137 NY 100, 104–105; *Doundoulakis v Town of Hempstead*, 42 NY2d 440, 448). Damage to property—one of the material elements—was not alleged (*see Spano v Perini Corp.*, 25 NY2d 11, 18).

Levin v. Yeshiva Univ., 96 NY2d 484 (2001)

In this 2001 partial concurrence and partial dissent, Judge Kaye demonstrated that she was years ahead of her time in defending the rights of same-sex couples. The plaintiffs, lesbian students at the Albert Einstein College of Medicine (AECOM), sued for the right to live with their life partners in university housing. At the time, state law did not permit same-sex marriage, and university policy prohibited unmarried students from living with their partners in student housing. The majority, citing *Hudson View Props. v Weiss* (59 NY2d 733 [1983]), held that the university's policy did not run afoul of New York state and city laws banning discrimination based on marital status. However, the majority ruled that the university's policy had a disparate impact on gays and lesbians and thus remanded for further proceedings under the City Human Rights Law, which barred housing discrimination based on sexual orientation. Kaye agreed with the majority that the university's policy created a disparate impact under the City Human Rights Law and argued further that the policy constituted impermissible marital status discrimination under city and state law. She explained that the majority rejected the plaintiffs' claims of marital status discrimination by concluding, erroneously, that their same-sex life partners were not members of their immediate "family."

—Introduction by David M. Cohn, law clerk 1999–2001

(Concurring in part and dissenting in part) I concur in the majority's conclusion that plaintiffs have stated a claim that AECOM's housing policy has a disparate impact on gays and lesbians, in violation of the New York City Human Rights Law, and that the disparate impact claim should be remitted to Supreme Court for further proceedings. I further conclude that plaintiffs have stated a claim of marital status discrimination.

Both the State and City Human Rights Laws make it illegal to withhold a housing accommodation from any person because of that person's marital status. . . . Here, plaintiffs allege that they were denied access to partner housing—a type of housing accommodation offered by AECOM—simply because they were not married. AECOM permits married students to live in student housing with their partners; only unmarried students are denied this benefit. When plaintiffs applied for housing for their partners, the sole question asked by AECOM was whether they were married. Since plaintiffs could not present marriage certificates, they were denied access to the housing benefits they sought. For present purposes, these allegations state a claim of discrimination based on marital status.

Our decisions in *Hudson View Props. v Weiss* (59 NY2d 733 [1983]) and *Matter of Manhattan Pizza Hut v New York State Human Rights Appeal Bd.* (51 NY2d 506 [1980]) are not to the contrary. In *Hudson View*, a landlord sought to evict a female tenant for violating a provision in the lease limiting occupancy to the tenant and her "immediate family." The tenant was sharing the apartment with a man who admittedly was not part of her immediate family (59 NY2d at 735). This Court held that the lease provision was enforceable, rejecting the tenant's argument that it constituted marital status discrimination. The Court stated, "the issue arises not because the tenant is unmarried, but because the lease restricts occupancy of her apartment . . . to the tenant and the tenant's immediate family" (*id.*). Thus, the Court concluded, the "applicability of that restriction does not depend on her marital status" (*id.*).

The extent of our holding in *Hudson View* was that a landlord does not engage in marital status discrimination by denying housing to a person who is not part of the tenant's immediate family. Unlike the tenant in *Hudson View*, plaintiffs have never admitted that their life partners are not part of their immediate families. Indeed, the gravamen of plaintiffs' complaint is that they share the same level of commitment with their partners as married persons share with their spouses—that their life partners *are* members of their immediate families. But AECOM's policy does not permit students to live in student housing with all immediate family members; rather, it permits them to live only with *spouses* and children. Thus, AECOM's policy is not "substantially indistinguishable from the policy considered in *Hudson View*" (majority op at 491).

Significantly, in *Braschi v Stahl Assocs. Co.* (74 NY2d 201, 211 [1989]), a plurality of this Court concluded that a tenant's same-sex life partner qualified as "family" under the non-eviction protection provisions of the New York City rent control law, stating that the term "family" includes "two adult lifetime partners whose relationship is long term and characterized by an emotional and financial commitment and interdependence." Indeed, in *Hudson View* the Court noted that it was not called upon to address whether the tenant's boyfriend could become part of her family "by marriage or otherwise" (59 NY2d at 735). Clearly then, this Court has recognized that the concept of "family" can include more than just married couples and their children. . . .

Similarly inapposite is *Matter of Manhattan Pizza Hut v New York State Human Rights Appeal Bd.* In that case, the Court upheld Pizza Hut's anti-nepotism rule forbidding an employee from working under the supervision of a spouse, parent, sibling or offspring. Plaintiff was fired for being married to her supervisor, and she brought suit alleging marital status discrimination under the State Human Rights Law. Recounting the many sound reasons supporting Pizza Hut's anti-nepotism rule, this Court upheld the termination, stating that the Human Rights Law does not prohibit discrimination based on an employee's "relationships" (51 NY2d at 513–514). The Court concluded that plaintiff had not suffered marital status discrimination because she was fired not for being married but "for being married to her supervisor"—a valid anti-nepotism concern (*id.* at 514).

Here, by contrast, plaintiffs were not denied partner housing because of their relationship to any particular person, and certainly not for violating an anti-nepotism or anti-corruption rule. Rather, they were denied partner housing merely because they were unmarried. Indeed, *Pizza Hut* itself states that the Human Rights Law bars decisions from being made on the basis of whether a person is "single, married, divorced, separated or the like" (*id.* at 512). That is exactly what happened here.

As to plaintiffs' disparate impact claim, the City Human Rights Law makes it illegal to deny access to housing accommodations on the basis of sexual orientation (*see* Administrative Code § 8-107 [5] [a] [1]). A prima facie case of discrimination is shown where a facially neutral policy has a disparate impact on a protected group (*see* Administrative Code § 8-107 [17] [a] [1], [2]). If plaintiffs demonstrate a disparate impact and proffer an alternative, less discriminatory policy, the burden then shifts to the defendant to show that a significant business objective is served by its policy (*see* Administrative Code § 8-107 [17] [a] [2]).

Here, AECOM's policy of providing partner housing to married students is facially neutral with respect to sexual orientation. That policy, however, has a disparate impact on homosexual students, because they cannot marry and thus cannot live with their partners in student housing. By contrast, heterosexual students have the option of marrying their life partners.

The Appellate Division erred by holding that the appropriate comparison groups were *unmarried* heterosexual students versus *unmarried* homosexual students. This holding defined plaintiffs' claim out of existence, since the disparate impact is created by AECOM's restriction of partner housing to *married* students. As the United States Supreme Court held in *Griggs v Duke Power* (401 US 424 [1971]), the comparison groups may not be defined in such a way. Further, it is immaterial that State law permits only heterosexual marriage. The City Human Rights Law specifically bans housing discrimination on the basis of sexual orientation. The State marriage law merely defines who can and cannot marry; it was not intended to permit landlords to violate New York City's laws against housing discrimination.

Therefore, since plaintiffs have stated a prima facie case of discrimination based on sexual orientation, the case must be remitted for application of the burden-shifting method mandated by the City Human Rights Law. . . .

Accordingly, I would modify the order of the Appellate Division by . . . reinstating the marital status and sexual orientation claims asserted by plaintiffs Levin and Jones and remitting those claims to Supreme Court for further proceedings.

Matter of Brandon (Nationwide Mut. Ins. Co.), 97 NY2d 491 (2002)

New York law generally holds that when an insurance policy holder submits untimely notice of claim or notice of occurrence to its insurer, the insurer may deny coverage even without demonstrating that it was prejudiced due to the late notice. As discussed in *Brandon*, adherence to the common law "no prejudice" doctrine meant that New York fell out of step with practically every other state, where the doctrine was abandoned either by decision or by statute. In *Brandon*, the Court of Appeals took a new look at the no prejudice doctrine in the specific context of supplementary uninsured motorist coverage—where the issue of whether the rule should apply was open—and concluded that the doctrine should not apply there. The decision included footnote 3, suggesting that the Court might be amenable to reconsidering the "no prejudice" doctrine more generally. Encouraged by footnote 3, policy holders' counsel sought leave to appeal unfavorable notice decisions repeatedly in the years following *Brandon*, and at last the Court took up the issue in *Argo Corp. v Greater N.Y. Mut. Ins. Co.*, 4 NY3d 332 (2005)—a case from which Chief Judge Kaye was recused—and adhered to the "no prejudice" doctrine. Thus, in footnote 3, Kaye and the court opened a door to a possible revision of the law, but in the end, the possibility was not brought to fruition. However, change was in the wind, and a few years later, by statute, the legislature at last laid to rest the no prejudice doctrine, prospectively. Meanwhile, considered simply as an adjudication of the narrow dispute sub judice, *Brandon* was a well-crafted decision and a good result.

—Introduction by Matthew J. Morris, law clerk 2001–2003

Insurance policies providing Supplementary Uninsured Motorists (SUM) coverage typically require the insured not only to submit a notice of claim but also to transmit promptly to the insurer the summons and complaint in any action the insured brings against a tortfeasor. In many contexts, including SUM coverage, an insured's failure to furnish timely notice of claim vitiates the contract, and the insurer may rely on this defense regardless of whether it can demonstrate that the insured's failure operated to its prejudice. Today an insurer asks us, by analogy, to hold that it need not demonstrate prejudice to rely on the defense that the insured forfeited SUM coverage by failing to timely submit the tort action summons and complaint. We decline to take this step, as did the Appellate Division, whose order we now affirm.

On March 1, 1997, a motor vehicle driven by Griselda Cancel [footnote omitted] collided with a parked 1985 Buick in which petitioner was a passenger and which was owned and insured by petitioner's son. Nine days later, petitioner forwarded a sworn "Notice of Intention to Make Claim" to his insurer, respondent Nationwide Mutual Insurance Company. The notice of claim indicated that Cancel negligently struck the Buick, injuring petitioner, and that treating these injuries would cost a sum yet to be determined. The notice also indicated that Cancel drove an "Uninsured Car," and that petitioner was making his claim under his policy's "Uninsured Automobile Endorsement."[1]

Petitioner sent the notice of claim to his local Nationwide agent. An employee of the agency acknowledged receipt, but evidently did not forward it to Nationwide's claims department, and Nationwide did not open a file relating to the accident. During the ensuing months, petitioner underwent a series of medical procedures, including surgery, and sought benefits from his son's insurer, Colonial Penn Insurance Company. After Colonial Penn denied his claim, petitioner submitted a no-fault claim to Nationwide. By December 17, 1997, Nationwide's no-fault file noted petitioner's operation; stated Nationwide's intention to order an injury index to determine whether petitioner had injuries before the accident; and noted "UM/UIM potential . . . due to injuries." The file also reflected Nationwide's belief that petitioner had notified it "over 90 days" after the accident, thus forfeiting coverage. Nationwide made no payment on the no-fault claim and eventually closed the no-fault file.

Meanwhile, on September 19, 1997, petitioner brought a personal injury action against Cancel, but did not forward the summons and complaint to Nationwide. Indeed, it was not until over a year later that Nationwide learned of the personal injury action from petitioner's attorney. Soon afterward, Nationwide sent him a reservation of rights letter, alleging that petitioner was not entitled to SUM coverage both because he had failed to send a timely notice of claim and because he had not promptly forwarded the personal injury summons and complaint. During the following weeks, petitioner finally did forward those papers, and Nationwide, after internal inquiries, recognized that it was mistaken regarding the notice of claim. Accordingly, in a letter dated December 17, 1998, Nationwide denied coverage solely on the basis of failure to forward the personal injury summons and complaint.

The policy language on which Nationwide relied states that if the insured sues any person "legally responsible for the use of a motor vehicle involved in the accident, a copy of the summons and complaint . . . shall be forwarded immediately to us by the insured . . ." Other relevant clauses provide that Nationwide pays on an SUM claim only after the limits of liability under other applicable policies are exhausted; that an insured who receives a settlement offer equal to such limits may release the opposing party after notifying Nationwide unless Nationwide advances the insured a sum equal to the offer; and that the insured may not otherwise settle such a suit without Nationwide's consent. In deference to these latter provisions, petitioner did not immediately accept a January

---

1. In fact, Cancel had $25,000 in liability insurance, but because this sum was less than petitioner's $100,000 in SUM coverage, she remained "uninsured" within the Nationwide policy's definition, which includes underinsured motorists.

1999 offer by Cancel's insurer to settle for her policy limits, but rather notified Nationwide of the offer. That July, after further discussions, Nationwide confirmed that it had denied coverage and that petitioner was "free" to pursue his "best interests" in the matter.

On September 27, 1999, petitioner commenced the instant proceeding, pursuant to CPLR 7503 (a), seeking an order to compel Nationwide to arbitrate his SUM claim. Nationwide moved to stay arbitration permanently, and Supreme Court, assuming that petitioner's failure to provide timely notice of legal action was a sufficient basis for a stay, held a hearing to determine whether Nationwide disclaimed coverage as soon as reasonably possible (*see* Insurance Law § 3420 [d]). Concluding that the interval between when Nationwide ascertained grounds for denial in November 1998 and when it denied coverage the following month was reasonable, Supreme Court dismissed the petition. The Appellate Division reversed, holding, first, that late notice of legal action "will be excused where no prejudice has inured to the insurer," and, second, that Nationwide had in any event failed to disclaim coverage within a reasonable time . . . We granted leave to appeal and now affirm.

Nationwide relies on cases holding that an insured's failure to provide timely notice of claim relieves the insurer of its obligation to perform, whether or not it can show prejudice (*see Security Mut. Ins. Co. v Acker-Fitzsimons Corp.*, 31 NY2d 436, 440 [1972]). This is known as a "no-prejudice" exception.[2] We have, indeed, followed *Security Mutual*, and the "no-prejudice" exception, when the insurers had received late notice of SUM claims. . . . The issue here, however, is whether late notice of legal action should be given the same preclusive effect as late notice of claim. Neither *Mancuso* nor any other decision answers this question, and accordingly we consider whether we should extend the reasoning of *Security Mutual* to this context.

Generally, "one seeking to escape the obligation to perform under a contract must demonstrate a material breach or prejudice" . . . By allowing insurers to avoid their obligations to premium-paying clients without showing prejudice, *Security Mutual* created a limited exception to this general rule. The rationales for this limited exception include the insurer's need to protect itself from fraud by investigating claims soon after the underlying events; to set reserves; and to take an active, early role in settlement discussions. . . . Finding these factors inapposite when a reinsurer asserts a late notice of claim defense against a primary insurer, we declined to extend the *Security Mutual* no-prejudice exception to the reinsurance context. . . .

---

2. New York is one of a minority of states that still maintain a no-prejudice exception (see Ostrager and Newman, Insurance Coverage Disputes § 4.04 [11th ed]). Formerly a majority of states took this approach, but, as the Supreme Court of Tennessee noted when it recently adopted a prejudice requirement in a case involving a late notice of claim for uninsured motorist coverage, "the number of jurisdictions that still follow the traditional view has dwindled dramatically" . . . Indeed, that court noted that in the preceding 20 years, only two states—New York and Colorado—had "considered the issue" and "continued to strictly adhere to the traditional approach" . . . Since then, Colorado adopted the majority rule, requiring insurers to demonstrate prejudice . . .

[S]tates often begin the shift to a prejudice requirement in the uninsured motorist context, where various policy considerations—the adhesive nature of insurance contracts, the public policy objective of compensating tort victims, and the inequity of the insurer receiving a windfall due to a technicality—are clearly implicated. . . . The issue of whether New York should continue to maintain the no-prejudice exception when insurers assert late notice of claim as a defense is not before us.

Here, Nationwide has not shown that the same factors support allowing insurers to evade their obligations, without showing prejudice, when insureds seeking SUM coverage provide late notice of legal action. While immediate notice of legal action may indeed help SUM insurers to protect themselves against fraud, set reserves, and monitor and perhaps settle the tort actions, the notice of claim requirement serves this purpose.[3] More is required to justify extending the *Security Mutual* no-prejudice exception further. Nationwide contends that personal injury claims that result in litigation are especially likely to involve "questionable injuries" or fraud, but it presents no support for this assertion.

The specifics of this case, moreover, do not help Nationwide. There is no allegation that petitioner and Cancel colluded; that Cancel's insurer lacked good reasons when it offered to settle for her policy limits; that petitioner settled without leave from Nationwide; or that Nationwide could have managed a better disposition of the claim if it had known of the tort action sooner. Nationwide also does not explain how it lost track of petitioner's timely notice of claim, or why the information in that notice did not alert it to any need it had to investigate, set reserves and so forth.[4]

At bottom, then, Nationwide's position must be that it needs a no-prejudice exception here too, because it depends on notices of legal action to awaken it in SUM matters where the notices of claim do not at first get its attention. Nationwide articulates something like this point when it asserts, citing *Mancuso*, that "[a] claim for underinsurance benefits . . . has a number of conditions along the way." . . . To Nationwide, the insured's action against the tortfeasor is one of the critical events, the moment when the potential for SUM liability "ripens." But this moment varies widely from case to case. It may come up to three years after the accident (*see* CPLR 214) or possibly years before the tort action is tried or settled. And, as *Mancuso* indicates, the tort action may begin before the insured knows or reasonably should know that the tortfeasor is underinsured and hence before the insured can comply with the policy's notice of claim requirements. . . .

Thus, unlike most notices of claim—which must be submitted promptly after the accident, while an insurer's investigation has the greatest potential to curb fraud—notices of legal action become due at a moment that cannot be fixed relative to any other key event, such as the injury, the discovery of the tortfeasor's insurance limits or the resolution of the underlying tort claim. Contrary to Nationwide's position, then, the timing of the notice

---

3. Nationwide stated at oral argument that notice of claim typically is submitted before notice of legal action, as in this case.

4. When petitioner submitted his no-fault claim, Nationwide was aware of the potential for SUM exposure, and made note of a plan to investigate any injuries petitioner may have had before the accident. The record does not show whether Nationwide followed up on this plan, a procedure designed to limit its exposure to claims based on "questionable injuries" or fraud. The claims file also does not show that Nationwide, aware by late 1997 of the SUM potential and the operation, asked its customer about suit against the tortfeasor.

Nationwide's procedures for handling no-fault and SUM claims doubtless differ, and we do not say that notice of one kind of claim can substitute for the other. Nevertheless, the least that can be said on this record is that neither Nationwide's treatment of the no-fault claim nor its treatment of the SUM claim suggests that Nationwide took any active interest in investigating, settling or setting reserves for petitioner's claim. The emphasis in both cases was solely on determining whether late notice might relieve Nationwide of its coverage obligations.

of legal action requirement does little to make performance of this requirement stand out as an event that informs the insurer of its "ripened" need to investigate, set reserves or take charge of settlement. Possibly another insurer will show that a policyholder's failure to deliver timely notice of action prejudiced it by hindering it from addressing this need. But Nationwide has not established that such prejudice is so inevitable as to justify further extending the no-prejudice exception.

Under these circumstances, and given the protection SUM insurers already enjoy by virtue of the notice of claim requirement and the clauses governing settlement, insurers relying on the late notice of legal action defense should be required to demonstrate prejudice. We place the burden of proving prejudice on the insurer because it has the relevant information about its own claims-handling procedures and because the alternative approach would saddle the policyholder with the task of proving a negative.

In light of this conclusion we need not and do not pass on petitioner's alternative contention that Nationwide's disclaimer was untimely.

Accordingly, the order of the Appellate Division should be affirmed, with costs.

Campaign for Fiscal Equity, Inc. v. State of New York, 100 NY2d 893 (2003)

Few cases came to the Court of Appeals more closely watched, and fraught with deeply felt differences about the role of the courts, than *Campaign for Fiscal Equity*, in which the court was asked to determine whether the state of New York had met its constitutional obligation to provide a sound basic education to schoolchildren in the city of New York. CFE had been wending its way through the courts, including one previous trip to the Court of Appeals, for a decade when, after trial, the court was called on to determine whether the plaintiffs had proved their case. The court tackled this task knowing that holding for the state could mean perpetuating a serious constitutional violation affecting some of the most vulnerable members of society, while holding for the plaintiffs could mean wading into a prolonged confrontation with the political branches of state government, such as had occurred, with debatable results, in other states. Nevertheless, the court had stated a standard, the litigants had produced a massive record, and it was necessary to compare the two and make a decision.

—Introduction by Matthew J. Morris, law clerk 2001–2003

We begin with a unanimous recognition of the importance of education in our democracy. The fundamental value of education is embedded in the Education Article of the New York State Constitution by this simple sentence: "The legislature shall provide for the maintenance and support of a system of free common schools, wherein all the children of this state may be educated" (NY Const, art XI, § 1). Plaintiffs claim that the State has violated this mandate by establishing an education financing system that fails to afford New York City's public schoolchildren the opportunity guaranteed by the Constitution. . . .

This case does not arrive before us on a blank slate. On June 15, 1995—precisely eight years ago—we denied the State's motion to dismiss plaintiffs' claims, thereby resolving three issues of law that now become the starting point for our decision (*Campaign for Fiscal Equity v State of New York*, 86 NY2d 307 [1995] [*CFE*]).

First, echoing *Board of Educ., Levittown Union Free School Dist. v Nyquist* (57 NY2d 27 [1982] [*Levittown*]), in *CFE* we recognized that by mandating a school system "wherein all the children of this state may be educated," the State has obligated itself constitutionally to ensure the availability of a "sound basic education" to all its children. . . . Second, we made clear that this Court is responsible for adjudicating the nature of that duty, and we provided a template, or outline, of what is encompassed within a sound basic education. And third, we concluded from the pleadings that plaintiffs had alleged facts that, if proved, would constitute a violation of the State's constitutional duty as well as the federal regulations. The actual quality of the educational opportunity in New York City, the correlation between the State's funding system and any failure to fulfill the constitutional mandate, and any justification for claimed discriminatory practices involve fact questions. For that reason, we remitted the matter to the trial court for development of the record. . . .

Based on the testimony of 72 witnesses and on 4,300 exhibits, the trial court on January 9, 2001 determined that the State over many years had consistently violated the Education Article of the Constitution. In keeping with our directive, the trial court first fleshed out the template for a sound basic education that we had outlined in our earlier consideration of the issue. To determine whether the State actually satisfied that standard the court then reviewed the various necessary instructional "inputs" we had identified, and concluded that in most of these the New York City schools were deficient. The trial court further held that the "outputs"—test results and graduation rates—likewise reflected systemic failure and that the State's actions were a substantial cause of the constitutional violation. Finally, the court found a violation of title VI, and directed defendants to put in place systemic reforms.

A divided Appellate Division reversed, on the law and facts. The majority rejected the trial court's definition of a sound basic education, as well as the bulk of Supreme Court's findings of fact concerning inputs, outputs and causation. . . . Plaintiffs appealed to us as of right on constitutional grounds.

Plaintiffs' appeal presents various questions of law, but one is paramount: whether the trial court correctly defined a sound basic education. Further—in light of the Appellate Division's express and implicit substitution of its findings of fact for those of the trial court regarding the inputs, outputs and causation—we must determine which court's findings more nearly comport with the weight of the credible evidence (*see* CPLR 5501 [b]). We now modify, affirming for reasons stated by the Appellate Division so much of the decision as dismissed plaintiffs' title VI claim [footnote omitted], and otherwise reversing the Appellate Division's order. . . .

I. Overview

At the time of trial, the New York City public school system comprised nearly 1,200 schools serving 1.1 million children and employing a staff of over 135,000, including 78,000 teachers . . . Some 84% of City schoolchildren were racial minorities; 80% were born outside the United States; and 16% were classified as Limited English Proficient (LEP—persons who speak little or no English)—most of the state's students in each of these categories . . . and 135,000 were enrolled in special education programs.

The New York City public school system was and is supervised by the Board of Education and its Chancellor. . . . The State Education Department (SED) and

Commissioner of Education supervise and manage the State's public schools, promulgating regulations and determining teaching standards and curricula, among other things.

Neither the Regents nor the SED is responsible, however, for the day-to-day operation of the schools or for their funding. Rather, a combination of local, state and federal sources generates school funding. Almost half of the state aid component consists of operating aid, which is allocated using a complex statutory formula that apportions various categories of aid based on a district's combined wealth ratio—which measures its ability to generate revenue—and student attendance. . . .

Every year . . . the Board of Regents and the SED submit a report to the Governor and Legislature on the educational status of the State's schools. The most recent of these "655 Reports" at the time of trial—that of April 1999—provides a comprehensive statistical view of the funding system as of the 1996–1997 school year, the last year for which the record provides such a complete picture. That year, statewide, the State provided 39.9% of all public school funding—$10.4 billion out of a total of $26 billion—while districts provided 56% and the federal government four percent. These figures represented an investment of $9,321 per pupil, $3,714 of it by the State. Per-pupil expenditures in the New York City public schools, at $8,171, were lower than in three quarters of the State's districts, including all the other "large city" districts, as classified by the SED. The State's dollar contribution to this figure was also lower, at $3,562, than its average contribution to other districts; and the City's, at about $4,000, was likewise lower than the average local contribution in other districts.

II. The Standard

In *CFE* we equated a sound basic education with "the basic literacy, calculating, and verbal skills necessary to enable children to eventually function productively as civic participants capable of voting and serving on a jury" . . . We thus indicated that a sound basic education conveys not merely skills, but skills fashioned to meet a practical goal: meaningful civic participation in contemporary society. This purposive orientation for schooling has been at the core of the Education Article since its enactment in 1894. As the Committee on Education reported at the time, the "public problems confronting the rising generation will demand accurate knowledge and the highest development of reasoning power more than ever before" . . .

In keeping with this core constitutional purpose and our direction further to develop the template, the trial court took evidence on what the "rising generation" needs in order to function productively as civic participants, concluding that this preparation should be measured with reference to the demands of modern society and include some preparation for employment. . . . The Appellate Division also recognized that our "term 'function productively' does imply employment" . . . , and we agree with both parties and both lower courts that an employment component was implicit in the standard we outlined in *CFE*. Nevertheless, the parties dispute the nature of the employment—and of civic participation generally—for which a sound basic education should prepare children, as well as the nature of the instruction necessary to achieve such preparation. We address each of these areas of dispute in turn.

First, as to employment, the Appellate Division concluded that the trial court "went too far" in construing the ability to "function productively" as the ability to obtain "competitive employment" or, indeed, as anything more than "the ability to get a job, and support oneself, and thereby not be a charge on the public fisc." . . . More is required. While a sound basic education need only prepare students to compete for jobs that enable them to support themselves, the record establishes that for this purpose a high school level education is now all but indispensable. As plaintiffs' education and economics expert Dr. Henry Levin testified, manufacturing jobs are becoming more scarce in New York and service sector jobs require a higher level of knowledge, skill in communication and the use of information, and the capacity to continue to learn over a lifetime. The record showed that employers who offer entry-level jobs that do not require college increasingly expect applicants to have had instruction that imparts these abilities, if not a specific credential.

Second, as to other aspects of civic participation, the difference between the trial court and the Appellate Division centers on our statement in *CFE* that a sound basic education should leave students "capable of voting and serving on a jury" . . . The State's expert on educational psychology, Dr. Herbert Walberg, testified that pattern jury instructions and newspaper articles typically feature vocabulary and sentence length comparable to those of texts eighth-graders are expected to be able to read. Based on this testimony, the Appellate Division concluded that the skills necessary for civic participation are imparted between eighth and ninth grades. . . .

We agree with the trial court that students require more than an eighth-grade education to function productively as citizens, and that the mandate of the Education Article for a sound basic education should not be pegged to the eighth or ninth grade, or indeed to any particular grade level. . . .

Finally, with these goals in mind, we come to the dispute over the kind and amount of schooling children need in order to be assured of the constitutional minimum of educational opportunity. In *CFE* we refrained from addressing this problem in detail, simply setting forth the "essentials":

> Children are entitled to minimally adequate physical facilities and classrooms which provide enough light, space, heat, and air to permit children to learn. Children should have access to minimally adequate instrumentalities of learning such as desks, chairs, pencils, and reasonably current textbooks. Children are also entitled to minimally adequate teaching of reasonably up-to-date basic curricula such as reading, writing, mathematics, science, and social studies, by sufficient personnel adequately trained to teach those subject areas. . . .

The issue to be resolved by the evidence is whether the State affords New York City schoolchildren the opportunity for a meaningful high school education, one which prepares them to function productively as civic participants. This is essentially the question the trial court addressed, and we conclude that the Appellate Division erred to the extent that it founded a judgment for defendants upon a much lower, grade-specific level of skills children are guaranteed the chance to achieve.

III. The Evaluation

To determine whether New York City schools in fact deliver the opportunity for a sound basic education, the trial court took evidence on the "inputs" children receive—teaching, facilities and instrumentalities of learning—and their resulting "outputs," such as test results and graduation and dropout rates. This organization of the facts follows naturally from our summary of the "essentials" in *CFE* and was not disputed by the Appellate Division. [Footnote omitted.]

A. INPUT

Teaching

The first and surely most important input is teaching. The trial court considered six measures of teacher quality—including certification rates, test results, experience levels and the ratings teachers receive from their principals—and concluded that the quality of New York City schoolteachers is inadequate, despite the commendable, even heroic, efforts of many teachers. The Appellate Division reached a contrary conclusion. . . . In our view, the Appellate Division improperly narrowed the inquiry here. Considering all of the factors, we agree with the trial court's findings and its conclusion that the teaching is inadequate.

The 1999 655 Report noted that schools with the highest percentages of minority children "have the least experienced teachers, the most uncertified teachers, the lowest-salaried teachers, and the highest rates of teacher turnover." The same report showed that well over half of the State's minority children attended New York City schools; that 84% of New York City schoolchildren were minorities; and that most of these children are poor. Taken together, these and other facts and statements in the 655 Report amount to an admission by the state agencies responsible for education that—with respect to teacher experience and retention, certification and pay—New York City schools are inferior to those of the rest of the state.

To be sure, the Education Article guarantees not equality but only a sound basic education . . . But as Judge Levine observed in his concurrence in *CFE*, "the constitutional history of the Education Article shows that the objective was to 'make[ ] it *imperative* on the State to provide *adequate* free common schools for the education of *all* of the children of the State' and that the new provision would have an impact upon 'places in the State of New York where the common schools are not adequate'" . . .

The 655 Report indicates a mismatch between student need in New York City and the quality of the teaching directed to that need, and it is one authoritative source of facts showing the extent of the mismatch. The report, for instance, shows that in 1997 17% of New York City public schoolteachers either were uncertified or taught in areas other than those in which they were certified. The trial court noted this fact and evidence that uncertified and inexperienced teachers tend to be concentrated in the lowest performing schools. . . .

As the trial court's decision shows, the record contains many more facts proving a serious shortfall in teacher quality in New York City schools, proving that this shortfall results from those schools' lack of competitiveness in bidding for and retaining personnel, and proving that better teachers produce better student performance. . . .

In sum, we conclude that the Appellate Division erred in relying solely on principals' evaluations, and we agree with the trial court's holdings that teacher certification, test performance, experience and other factors measure quality of teaching; that quality of teaching correlates with student performance; and that New York City schools provide deficient teaching because of their inability to attract and retain qualified teachers.

School Facilities and Classrooms

As we noted in *CFE*, children are entitled to "classrooms which provide enough light, space, heat, and air to permit children to learn" . . .

Nevertheless, on this record it cannot be said that plaintiffs have proved a measurable correlation between building disrepair and student performance, in general. [Footnote omitted.]

On the other hand, plaintiffs presented measurable proof, credited by the trial court, that New York City schools have excessive class sizes, and that class size affects learning. Even in the earliest years—from kindergarten through third grade—over half of New York City schoolchildren are in classes of 26 or more, and tens of thousands are in classes of over 30. As the trial court noted, federal and state programs seek to promote classes of 20 or fewer. . . .

Although the Appellate Division found "no indication that students cannot learn in classes consisting of more than 20 students" . . . , plaintiffs' burden was not to prove that some specific number is the maximum class size beyond which children "cannot learn." It is difficult to imagine what evidence could ever meet a burden so formulated; nothing in *CFE* required plaintiffs to do so. Rather, . . . plaintiffs had to show that insufficient funding led to inadequate inputs which led to unsatisfactory results. . . .

We conclude that plaintiffs' evidence of the advantages of smaller class sizes supports the inference sufficiently to show a meaningful correlation between the large classes in City schools and the outputs to which we soon turn. In sum, the Appellate Division erred in concluding that there was not "sufficient proof" . . . that large class sizes negatively affect student performance in New York City public schools.

Instrumentalities of Learning

The final input is "instrumentalities of learning," including classroom supplies, textbooks, libraries and computers. The courts below agreed that the textbook supply is presently adequate and the evidence on classroom supplies is inconclusive. . . .

In sum, considering all of the inputs, we conclude that the trial court's findings should be reinstated, as indicated, and that the educational inputs in New York City schools are inadequate. There are certainly City schools where the inadequacy is not "gross and glaring" . . . Some of these schools may even be excellent. But tens of thousands of students are placed in overcrowded classrooms, taught by unqualified teachers, and provided with inadequate facilities and equipment. The number of children in these straits is large enough to represent a systemic failure. A showing of good test results and graduation rates among these students—the "outputs"—might indicate that they somehow still receive the opportunity for a sound basic education. The showing, however, is otherwise.

B. OUTPUTS

School Completion

Concerning the first output, school completion, the proof revealed that of those New York City ninth graders who do not transfer to another school system, only 50% graduate in four years, and 30% do not graduate or receive a general equivalency degree (GED) by the age of 21, when they cease to be eligible for free public education. This rate of school completion compares unfavorably with both state and national figures, and the trial court considered it symptomatic of "system breakdown" . . . The Appellate Division concluded that "there was no evidence quantifying how many drop-outs fail to obtain a sound basic education" . . . That conclusion follows from the Appellate Division's premise that a sound basic education is imparted by eighth or ninth grade. A sound basic education, however, means a meaningful high school education. Under that standard, it may, as a practical matter, be presumed that a dropout has not received a sound basic education. In any event the evidence was unrebutted that dropouts typically are not prepared for productive citizenship, as the trial court concluded. . . .

The State argues nonetheless that it is responsible only to provide the opportunity for a sound basic education and cannot be blamed if some students—perhaps those who enter New York City schools after years of schooling in another country—do not avail themselves of the opportunity it provides. As the trial court correctly observed, this opportunity must still "be placed within reach of all students," including those who "present with socioeconomic deficits" . . .

The evidence on why students drop out suggested mainly that the choice to drop out correlates with poor academic performance and, as noted in the 655 Report for 1999, racial minority status and concentrated poverty. . . .

Test Results

The State's main answer to the proof of graduation and dropout rates in City schools consists of evidence that, in any event, test results are not bad—and this is also where the Appellate Division concentrated its discussion of outputs. . . .
In sum, . . . the trial court's assessment of exam results, like its assessment of completion rates, better comports with the weight of the credible evidence, and supports its conclusion that, whether measured by the outputs or the inputs, New York City schoolchildren are not receiving the constitutionally-mandated opportunity for a sound basic education.

IV. Causation

As we noted in *CFE*, in order to prevail plaintiffs must "establish a correlation between funding and educational opportunity . . . a causal link between the present funding system and any proven failure to provide a sound basic education to New York City school children" . . . The trial court reasoned that the necessary "causal link" between the present funding system and the poor performance of City schools could be established by a showing that increased funding can provide better teachers, facilities and instrumentalities of learning. . . . We agree that this showing, together with evidence that such improved inputs yield better student performance, constituted plaintiffs' prima facie case, which plaintiffs established. . . .

The State nevertheless makes several further arguments concerning the correlation between its funding scheme and the educational results. Most of these points, however, more properly concern the apportionment of responsibility among various government actors than causation. In any event, the trial court interpreted *CFE* correctly when it said that the "law recognizes that there may be many 'causal links' to a single outcome, and there is no reason to think that the Court of Appeals 1995 opinion mandates a search for a single cause of the failure of New York City schools. . . .

Socioeconomic Disadvantage

The State argues that poor student performance is caused by socioeconomic conditions independent of the quality of the schools and better remedied with investment in other resources. The Appellate Division agreed, reasoning that because of "demographic factors, such as poverty, high crime neighborhoods, single parent or dysfunctional homes, homes where English is not spoken, or homes where parents offer little help with homework and motivation . . . more spending on education is not necessarily the answer, and . . . the cure lies in eliminating the socio-economic conditions facing certain students" . . . This is partly an argument about why students fail, which we have rejected in the discussion of outputs. But it is also a distinctly constitutional argument in the sense that choosing between competing beneficial uses of funds is a legislative task.

This is, in fact, the argument that Judge Simons made in his solitary dissent in *CFE*. . . . Had we accepted the argument, we would have saved everyone considerable effort and expense by dismissing the case on the spot. We did not do so. Decisions about spending priorities are indeed the Legislature's province, but we have a duty to determine whether the State is providing students with the opportunity for a sound basic education. While it may be that a dollar spent on improving "dysfunctional homes" would go further than one spent on a decent education, we have no constitutional mandate to weigh these alternatives. And, again, we cannot accept the premise that children come to the New York City schools ineducable, unfit to learn. . . .

City Mismanagement

The State's most sustained arguments on causation, however, are based on evidence that the Board of Education mismanages New York City schools and the City itself fails to devote a sufficient part of its revenues to them. The State reasons that if either proposition is true, then the cause of any shortage of educational inputs in City schools is not the state funding system but City bureaucracy.

Specifically, the State argues first that fraud and corruption in the community school boards and City school construction spending, rather than the funding system, are the cause of any shortage of inputs. The trial court rejected these arguments . . . and the Appellate Division likewise rejected the point about construction spending . . . while saying nothing about the community school boards. We thus have no occasion to review either argument.

The State argues second that, corruption aside, the Board of Education mismanages the schools, particularly by referring too many students to special education and placing too many of these children in costly full-time segregated settings. The trial court credited evidence that better special education practices could save City schools between $105 and $185 million annually, though some of these savings would be offset by the greater cost of instructing children with special education needs in a mainstream environment. . . . The Appellate Division saw the possible savings mounting to "hundreds of millions of dollars, if not $1 billion" . . .

We are thus constrained to accept that some saving on special education is possible, a fact that to some extent undermines plaintiffs' argument that the school funding system is unconstitutional because it leaves New York City schools with insufficient funds to provide a sound basic education. But the magnitude of the savings is in dispute. The Appellate Division appears to have arrived at its "billion" simply by taking the number of full-time special education students, assuming that 80% could be moved to part-time settings, and multiplying the number of students subject to this move by the $10,000 difference between the cost of full-time and part-time placement. No witness for the State sponsored any such calculation, and there was thus no opportunity to test the Appellate Division's assumptions on which it is based. . . .

We need not speculate further on the possible saving from special education placement, however, for the State's argument on Board of Education mismanagement fails for a more basic reason. As the trial court and Appellate Division recognized . . . , both the Board of Education and the City are "creatures or agents of the State," which delegated whatever authority over education they wield. . . . Thus, the State remains responsible when the failures of its agents sabotage the measures by which it secures for its citizens their constitutionally-mandated rights.

As our ensuing discussion of remedy shows, various reforms unrelated to financing— some already in the works—may be part of the package of legislative and administrative measures necessary to ensure a sound basic education to New York City schoolchildren. The requirement stated in *CFE,* however, was for plaintiffs to "establish a causal link between the present funding system and any proven failure" . . . , not to eliminate any possibility that other causes contribute to that failure. . . .

Similar reasoning disposes of the State's argument that the Board of Education's inefficient management of personnel is the supervening cause that, rather than the funding system, accounts for deficiencies in the teaching input. The State points to disturbing evidence that thousands of City schoolteachers do not teach; others teach under contracts that limit their classroom time to under four hours a day; and all are paid according to the same salary schedule, regardless of whether a more flexible system of incentives might be needed, for instance, to induce senior teachers to remain in troubled schools. . . . But as the trial court found, "the allegedly shorter workday of New York City's public school teachers has not provided the City an advantage in the competition for qualified teachers" . . . Such considerations, as well as the simple constitutional principle that the State has ultimate responsibility for the schools, counsel us against the State's rebuttal arguments on causation.

Local Funding

Of the State's rebuttal arguments, one more requires special attention. The State argues that the City actually has a greater capacity to fund education from local revenues than many local governments statewide, yet fails to make anything like the same "tax effort" that other localities make. Indeed, the State marshals evidence that when the State injects funds pursuant to formulas intended to compensate for inequalities in local school funding, the City deducts proportionately from its own contribution, leaving the school budget unimproved. . . .

Here . . . there is next to no dispute. If the State believes that deficient City tax effort is a significant contributing cause to the underfunding of City schools, it is for the State . . . to consider corrective measures. This possibility pertains to the remedy, not to the definition of plaintiffs' burden of proof on causation or—what amounts to the same thing in practice—to the determination of whether plaintiffs' cause of action is viable. . . .

Plaintiffs have established the causation element of their claim.

V. The Remedy

Challenging as the previous issues are, in complexity they pale by comparison to the final question: remedy. Pointing to a long history of State inaction despite its knowledge of the inadequacy of the education finance system, plaintiffs ask us to initiate a legislative/judicial dialogue by issuing guidelines to the Legislature for restructuring the system and directing—with strict timetables—that the necessary resources be provided. The State, by contrast, urges that, should a constitutional violation be found, the Court simply direct the proper parties to eliminate the deficiencies.

Both extremes are problematic. We are, of course, mindful—as was the trial court—of the responsibility, underscored by the State, to defer to the Legislature in matters of policymaking, particularly in a matter so vital as education financing, which has as well a core element of local control. We have neither the authority, nor the ability, nor the will, to micromanage education financing. By the same token, in plaintiffs' favor, it is the province of the judicial branch to define, and safeguard, rights provided by the New York State Constitution, and order redress for violation of them. Surely there is a remedy more promising, and ultimately less entangling for the courts, than simply directing the parties to eliminate deficiencies, as the State would have us do.

The trial court ordered the State first to ascertain the actual cost of providing a sound basic education statewide, and then reform the system to (1) ensure that every school district has the resources necessary to provide a sound basic education; (2) take into account variations in local costs; (3) provide sustained and stable funding in order to promote long-term planning by school districts; (4) provide "as much transparency as possible so that the public may understand how the State distributes school aid"; and (5) ensure a system of accountability to measure the effect of reforms implemented. . . .

The State objects to each of these guidelines on various grounds, but a common theme is that existing reforms already address existing problems. Indeed, ongoing federal, state and City programs—several initiated after the close of trial—likely constitute the most ambitious education reform in recent years. . . .

All of these initiatives promise, but await, demonstrable outcomes. We are, of course, bound to decide this case on the record before us and cannot conjecture about the possible effect of pending reforms, at least when determining whether, on the evidence gathered over four years and presented during the seven-month trial, a constitutional violation exists. To the extent that recent reforms enable more students to receive a sound basic education, the State will have the opportunity on remittal to present evidence of such developments. . . .

Given all of the jurisprudential constraints discussed above, we begin our review of the trial court's directives by rejecting the provision that the remedy be statewide, and that variations in local costs be taken into account. Courts deal with actual cases and controversies, not abstract global issues, and fashion their directives based on the proof before them. Here the case presented to us, and consequently the remedy, is limited to the adequacy of education financing for the New York City public schools, though the State may of course address statewide issues if it chooses.

Second, we recognize that mechanisms in place, including No Child Left Behind and the SURR process, may already to some extent function as a system of accountability. They are not foolproof, and neither is tied to the definition of a sound basic education. Nevertheless, the State should be able to build on existing criteria to identify the schools in greatest need and set measurable goals for their improvement.

Third, we are not prepared to say as a constitutional matter that a new system must ensure the City "sustained and stable funding." The language of this directive may appear unobjectionable, but in the context of the trial court's decision it implies a need for fundamental change in the relationship between New York City schools and their local tax base. The school districts in New York City, Buffalo, Yonkers, Syracuse and Rochester—unlike every other district in the State—are "fiscally dependent": they lack the authority to levy property taxes to support education. [Footnote omitted.] As the trial court observed, City schools are dependent on municipal revenues, largely from other kinds of taxes more susceptible to the vagaries of the business cycle. . . . It may well be that this susceptibility hinders City schools from developing a more stable budgetary plan—and that any plan to improve City schools that required better local tax effort, in particular, would need to address this matter. At the same time, the State has suggested that reforms tending to concentrate responsibility with the Mayor of New York City may prove beneficial, and we do not know that a "sustained and stable funding" requirement addressing fiscal dependency would necessarily fit together with such reforms. Accordingly, while the trial court's directive is understandable, we do not make it mandatory.

Fourth, as the foregoing implies, the trial court properly indicated that reforms may address governance as well as the school funding system. Various factors alleged by the State as causes of deficiencies in the schools—and rejected by us on the ground that the State has ultimate responsibility for the conduct of its agents and the quality of education in New York City public schools—may be addressed legislatively or administratively as part of the remedy. We do not think such measures will obviate the need for changes to the funding system, but they may affect the scope of such changes.

Finally, we know of no practical way to determine whether members of the political branches have complied with an order that the funding process become as transparent as possible, and we therefore decline to incorporate such a directive into our order. No one, however, disputes the trial court's description of the existing education funding scheme as needlessly complex, malleable and not designed to align funding with need. . . .

Thus, the political process allocates to City schools a share of state aid that does not bear a perceptible relation to the needs of City students. While we do not join the trial court in ordering that the process be made as transparent as possible, we do agree that the funding level necessary to provide City students with the opportunity for a sound basic education is an ascertainable starting point. Once the necessary funding level is determined, the question will be whether the inputs and outputs improve to a constitutionally acceptable level. Other questions about the process—such as how open it is and how the burden is distributed between the State and City—are matters for the Legislature desiring to enact good laws.

In view of the alternatives that the parties have presented, we modify the trial court's threshold guideline that the State ascertain "the actual costs of providing a sound basic education in districts around the State" . . . The State need only ascertain the actual cost of providing a sound basic education in New York City [footnote omitted]. Reforms to the current system of financing school funding and managing schools should address the shortcomings of the current system by ensuring, as a part of that process, that every school in New York City would have the resources necessary for providing the opportunity for a sound basic education. Finally, the new scheme should ensure a system of accountability to measure whether the reforms actually provide the opportunity for a sound basic education.

The process of determining the actual cost of providing a sound basic education in New York City and enacting appropriate reforms naturally cannot be completed overnight, and we therefore recognize that defendants should have until July 30, 2004 to implement the necessary measures.

VI. Conclusion

We offer these concluding thoughts, against the backdrop of the dissent.

Courts are, of course, well suited to adjudicate civil and criminal cases and extrapolate legislative intent. . . . They are, however, also well suited to interpret and safeguard constitutional rights and review challenged acts of our co-equal branches of government—not in order to make policy but in order to assure the protection of constitutional rights. That is what we have been called upon to do by litigants seeking to enforce the State Constitution's Education Article. The task began with *Levittown*'s articulation of the constitutional right to a sound basic education—not at all a "catchphrase for an inferred constitutional guarantee" . . . but this Court's careful judgment 21 years ago as to what is meant by our State Constitution's promise in the Education Article. *CFE* built on our definition of the constitutional requirement, adding to the law a determination that the complaint stated a cause of action, and that—if plaintiffs proved their assertions, as they have—they would establish a violation.

Nor is the Court's standard of a sound basic education, articulated both in *Levittown* and *CFE*, "illusory" for failing to fix the moment when a meaningful high school education is achieved. . . . As the dissent itself exemplifies by "of course" rejecting the eighth (or ninth) grade test of the Appellate Division *and offering no other*, a constitutional standard of sound basic education need not pinpoint a date with statutory precision, so long as it defines the contours of the requirement, against which the facts of a case may then be measured. [Footnote omitted.] Indeed, a sound basic education back in 1894, when the Education Article was added, may well have consisted of an eighth or ninth grade education, which we unanimously reject. The definition of a sound basic education must serve the future as well as the case now before us.

Finally, the remedy is hardly extraordinary or unprecedented. . . . It is, rather, an effort to learn from our national experience and fashion an outcome that will address the constitutional violation instead of inviting decades of litigation. A case in point is the experience of our neighbor, the New Jersey Supreme Court, which in its landmark education decision 30 years ago simply specified the constitutional deficiencies, beginning more than a dozen trips to the court . . . , a process that led over time to more focused directives by that court . . . In other jurisdictions, the process has generated considerably less litigation, possibly because courts there initially offered more detailed remedial directions, as we do. . . . We do not share the dissent's belief that in New York any constitutional ruling adverse to the present scheme will inevitably be met with the kind of sustained legislative resistance that may have occurred elsewhere.

Nor is it certain that plaintiffs' success will necessarily inspire a host of imitators throughout the state. . . . Plaintiffs have prevailed here owing to a unique combination of circumstances: New York City schools have the *most* student need in the state and the *highest* local costs yet receive some of the *lowest* per-student funding and have some of the *worst* results. Plaintiffs in other districts who cannot demonstrate a similar combination may find tougher going in the courts.

We trust that fixing a few signposts in the road yet to be traveled by the parties will shorten the already arduous journey and help to achieve the hoped-for remedy.

Accordingly, the order of the Appellate Division should be modified and the case remitted to Supreme Court for further proceedings in accordance with this opinion, and as so modified affirmed, with costs to plaintiffs.

First Financial Ins. Co. v. Jetco Contr. Corp., 1 NY3d 64 (2003)

Judge Kaye here articulated the court's response to two certified questions from the Second Circuit in connection with an injured construction worker's claim of employer negligence. In response to the first, the court determined that insurers cannot delay notification of coverage denial without adequate justification, with the second response declaring an unjustified delay of forty-eight days unreasonable as a matter of law. In essence, this decision strictly interpreted and applied New York Insurance Law § 3420 (d), which remains the dominant method of interpreting this law. In addition to reflecting Kaye's characteristic lucidity and respect for legislative intent, this opinion captures her commonsense approach to creating a fairer system by placing the burden to provide both timely notice and justification for delay squarely on the shoulders of those with the requisite knowledge and power, thereby allowing those in an inferior position to adjust their behavior accordingly in an effort to minimize their losses. In this regard, this decision can be seen as a type of forerunner of *Brill v. City of New York* (2 NY3d 650 [2004]), which required timely motions for summary judgment after interpreting CPLR 3212 (a) in a similarly strict manner.

—Introduction by James D. Fry, law clerk 2003–2004

The United States Court of Appeals for the Second Circuit, by two certified questions, has asked us to clarify whether an insurer's 48-day delay in notifying a policyholder of denial of coverage is unreasonable as a matter of law under Insurance Law § 3420 (d), where the purpose of the delay is to investigate the existence of other, third-party sources of insurance. The central issue is whether such delay is excusable, even though the existence of alternative sources is not a factor in the insurer's decision to deny coverage. We conclude that once the insurer has sufficient knowledge of facts entitling it to disclaim, or knows that it will disclaim coverage, it must notify the policyholder in writing as soon as is reasonably possible. Furthermore, an unexcused 48-day delay is unreasonable as a matter of law.

On July 9, 1998, falling scaffolding hit Gavin Hanna—an employee of Jetco's scaffolding subcontractor—while he was at work restoring the facade of a New York University (NYU) building. On January 6, 1999, Hanna brought suit in Bronx County Supreme Court against Jetco and NYU for negligence under various state statutes. Jetco's president and general manager learned of the accident the very day it occurred but failed to inform its commercial general liability insurer, First Financial Insurance Company, which learned of the accident from NYU on February 23, 1999. By letter dated March 2, 1999, First Financial's authorized agent advised the policyholder that this was "a late notice situation," and reserved its right to deny coverage because Jetco had failed to comply with the policy's provision requiring notice of an occurrence as soon as practicable. On March 30, 1999, First Financial confirmed that Jetco's president had known of the accident since the day it occurred. However, the insurer failed to notify Jetco of its decision to deny coverage until May 17, 1999—48 days after First Financial's agent confirmed the grounds for disclaiming coverage. The insurer claims that this delay was excusable because it resulted from an investigation into other sources of insurance for Jetco.

First Financial sought a declaratory judgment from the United States District Court for the Southern District of New York that the policy did not cover Jetco for Hanna's suit. Whether the 48-day delay was reasonable as a matter of law became material because the insurer's failure to provide notice as soon as is reasonably possible precludes effective disclaimer, even though the policyholder's own notice of the incident to its insurer is untimely (*see Hartford Ins. Co. v County of Nassau*, 46 NY2d 1028, 1029 [1979]).

The District Court concluded that the insurer's 48-day delay was reasonable because its investigation into alternative sources of insurance was clearly for Jetco's benefit, which the court felt should be encouraged even though the insurer would itself have denied coverage regardless of the existence of any other insurance benefitting Jetco.[1] The District Court refused to read Insurance Law § 3420 (d) in a way that would prohibit an insurer from waiting to notify a policyholder of denial of coverage until after the insurer has conducted an alternative source investigation, because insurance companies would be forced to disclaim coverage before seeking additional sources of coverage.[2] In its appeal to the Second Circuit, Jetco challenged the District Court's finding that the insurer's delayed disclaimer was reasonable under Insurance Law § 3420 (d).

Concerned that New York law is unclear as to whether an insurer's investigation into other, third-party sources of insurance is a sufficient excuse for delay, and if not, whether an unexcused delay of 48 days could be unreasonable as a matter of law—both novel policy issues with wider implications—the Second Circuit certified two questions to this Court.

> 1. Under N.Y. Ins. Law § 3420(d), may an insurer who has discovered grounds for denying coverage wait to notify the insured of denial of coverage until after the insurer has conducted an investigation into alternate, third-party

---

1. Three witnesses testified at trial that First Financial's investigation into other sources of insurance did not affect insurer's decision to deny coverage. In the words of one witness: "Whether there is an additional insure[r] really has no bearing on whether it's late. If it's late, it's late and we will deny coverage."

2. The court further noted that Jetco suffered no prejudice from the time it took First Financial to investigate additional sources of coverage—though correctly observing that prejudice is of no legal relevance here (*see Allstate Ins. Co. v Gross*, 27 NY2d 263, 269–270 [1970]).

sources of insurance benefitting the insured, although the existence or non-existence of alternate insurance sources is not a factor in the insurer's decision to deny coverage?

2. If an investigation into alternate sources of insurance is not a proper basis for delayed notification under N.Y. Ins. Law § 3420(d), is an unexcused delay in notification of 48 days unreasonable as a matter of law under § 3420(d)? (322 F3d 750, 752 [2003].)

We now answer the first question in the negative, and the second in the affirmative.

Discussion

New York Insurance Law § 3420 (d) provides:

> If under a liability policy delivered or issued for delivery in this state, an insurer shall disclaim liability or deny coverage for death or bodily injury arising out of a motor vehicle accident or any other type of accident occurring within this state, it shall give written notice as soon as is reasonably possible of such disclaimer of liability or denial of coverage to the insured and the injured person or any other claimant.

While the Legislature specified no particular period of time, its words "as soon as is reasonably possible" leave no doubt that it intended to expedite the disclaimer process, thus enabling a policyholder to pursue other avenues expeditiously. As the Legislature's 1975 Budget Report on the bill that ultimately became section 3420 (d) noted, the purpose "is to assist a consumer or claimant in obtaining an expeditious resolution to liability claims by requiring insurance companies to give prompt notification when a claim is being denied" (30-Day Budget Report on Bills, Bill Jacket, L 1975, ch 775).

That notice of disclaimer must be prompt, however, still leaves unresolved the questions of *when* promptness is to be measured from, and *whether* as a matter of law an insurer may delay notification in order to investigate other sources of insurance potentially available to its policyholder.

As we have made clear, "timeliness of an insurer's disclaimer is measured from the point in time when the insurer first learns of the grounds for disclaimer of liability or denial of coverage" (*Matter of Allcity Ins. Co. [Jimenez]*, 78 NY2d 1054, 1056 [1991], citing *Hartford*, 46 NY2d at 1029). Moreover, an insurer's explanation is insufficient as a matter of law where the basis for denying coverage was or should have been readily apparent before the onset of the delay (*Matter of Firemen's Fund Ins. Co. of Newark v Hopkins*, 88 NY2d 836, 837–838 [1996]). Here, First Financial was aware that Jetco's claim was untimely when the insurer learned of the accident on February 23, 1999 (as noted in its March 2 letter to Jetco), or at the latest on March 30 (when its agent confirmed that Jetco's president had known of the accident since the day it occurred). For present purposes we assume that on March 30, 1999, the clock began to run on First Financial's obligation to give written notice to Jetco disclaiming coverage.

An insurer who delays in giving written notice of disclaimer bears the burden of justifying the delay. While Insurance Law § 3420 (d) speaks only of giving notice "as soon as is reasonably possible," investigation into issues affecting an insurer's decision whether to disclaim coverage obviously may excuse delay in notifying the policyholder of a disclaimer (*see e.g. 2540 Assoc. v Assicurazioni Generali*, 271 AD2d 282, 284 [1st Dept 2000] [delay reasonable because of insurer's need to conduct a "prompt, diligent and good faith investigation of the claim"]; *DeSantis Bros. v Allstate Ins. Co.*, 244 AD2d 183, 184 [1st Dept 1997] [delay reasonable because of need to review 500-page file and conduct legal research]; *Aetna Cas. & Sur. Co. v Brice*, 72 AD2d 927, 928–929 [4th Dept 1979] [delay reasonable due to insurer's difficulty gathering evidence because all those involved in accident had been killed]).

We cannot accept, however, that delay simply to explore other sources of insurance for the policyholder—an excuse unrelated to the insurer's own decision to disclaim—is permissible. While First Financial urges that, as a matter of policy, such inquiries should be encouraged because they are for the benefit of the insured, we note that they may also be in the insurer's interest in reducing its ultimate risk, and further may detrimentally delay the policyholder's own search for alternative coverage. When the insurer promptly disclaims coverage, the policyholder—perhaps with the aid of its own broker or insurance agent—is best motivated by its own interest to explore alternative avenues of protection.

Having concluded that investigation into possible other sources of insurance is not an acceptable reason for delayed disclaimer, we reach the Second Circuit's second question: Is an unexcused delay of 48 days unreasonable as a matter of law?

On the one hand, we appreciate the desire for a fixed yardstick against which to measure the reasonableness, or unreasonableness, of an insurer's delay. In this respect we note that the Appellate Division several times has found fixed periods of less than 48 days unreasonable as a matter of law (citing cases.) On the other hand, the difficulty with imposing a fixed time period—which the Legislature scrupulously avoided—is that most often the question whether a notice of disclaimer has been sent "as soon as is reasonably possible" will be a question of fact, dependent on all of the circumstances of a case that make it reasonable, or unreasonable, for an insurer to investigate coverage (*see Hartford*, 46 NY2d at 1030; *Allstate Ins. Co. v Gross*, 27 NY2d 263, 270 [1970]).

One thing is clear: that it is the responsibility of the insurer to explain its delay. Where, in *Hartford*, the insurer gave absolutely no explanation for its delay, this Court concluded that a delay of 62 days was, as a matter of law, unreasonable. Clearly a delay of 48 days in those circumstances would have been as well. Here, we see no material difference between a delay that is *unexplained* and a delay that is *unexcused*, meaning the explanation is unsatisfactory. The insurer's 48-day delay in giving written notice, on the facts before us, was unreasonable as a matter of law.

Accordingly, certified question No. 1 should be answered in the negative and certified question No. 2 should be answered in the affirmative.

Following certification of questions by the United States Court of Appeals for the Second Circuit and acceptance of the questions by this Court pursuant to section 500.17 of the Rules of the Court of Appeals (22 NYCRR 500.17), and after hearing argument by counsel for the parties and consideration of the briefs and the record submitted, certified question No. 1 answered in the negative and certified question No. 2 answered in the affirmative.

Brill v. City of New York, 2 NY3d 648 (2004)

In this case, the New York Court of Appeals made plain that even the most meritorious motion for summary judgment, which would obviate the need for a trial, cannot be entertained without compliance with New York's civil procedure rules. Chief Judge Kaye began the *Brill* opinion by highlighting a recurring scenario: movants were seeking summary judgment late without showing good cause for their delay, thereby engaging in a practice that ignored statutory law, disrupted trial calendars, and undermined the goals of orderliness and efficiency in state court practice. Writing for a six-judge majority, Judge Kaye explained that a violation of procedure could not be rewarded because doing so would obliterate the ameliorative statute passed by the legislature and encourage sloppy practice. Kaye made clear that to avoid denial of a meritorious summary judgment motion and burdening the courts with "a case that in fact leaves nothing to try, all practitioners had to do was develop a habit of compliance with the statutory deadlines . . . rather than delay until trial looms or show good cause for their failure to do so." It was that simple.

—Introduction by Hon. Jennifer G. Schecter, law clerk 1998–2001

This appeal puts before us a recurring scenario regarding the timing of summary judgment motions that ignores statutory law, disrupts trial calendars, and undermines the goals of orderliness and efficiency in state court practice.

On June 4, 1998, plaintiffs Ona and Maurice Brill brought suit against the City of New York and others for injuries Ona Brill allegedly suffered on February 15, 1998 when she tripped and fell on a public sidewalk in Brooklyn. Following discovery, on June 28, 2001, plaintiffs filed their note of issue and certificate of readiness, and sought a preference due to Ona Brill's age.

On June 18, 2002, close to a year after the trial calendar papers were filed, the City moved for summary judgment. The City gave no explanation for filing the motion after the 120-day limit specified in CPLR 3212 (a), simply arguing that it did not have prior written notice of the alleged defect at the accident site and that plaintiffs could not show an exception to the prior written notice requirement. Supreme Court determined that in the interests of judicial economy, and since Mrs. Brill did not manifest any prejudice from the delay, it would decide the summary judgment motion on the merits. The court granted the City's motion, finding plaintiffs did not prove that the City had notice of a defect at the accident site, and the Appellate Division affirmed.

We now reverse because, on these facts, Supreme Court should not have considered the merits of the City's motion for summary judgment.

Since New York established its summary judgment procedure in 1921, summary judgment has proven a valuable, practical tool for resolving cases that involve only questions of law. Summary judgment permits a party to show, by affidavit or other evidence, that there is no material issue of fact to be tried, and that judgment may be directed as a matter of law, thereby avoiding needless litigation cost and delay. Where appropriate, summary judgment is a great benefit both to the parties and to the overburdened New York State trial courts.

In that a summary judgment motion may resolve the entire case, obviously the timing of the motion is significant. CPLR 3212 (a) . . . originally required only joinder of issue before a summary judgment motion could be made. In practice, however, the absence of an outside time limit for filing such motions became problematic, particularly when they were made on the eve of trial. Eleventh-hour summary judgment motions, sometimes used as a dilatory tactic, left inadequate time for reply or proper court consideration, and prejudiced litigants who had already devoted substantial resources to readying themselves for trial. . . .

At the court system's request, in 1996 the Legislature stepped in to ameliorate the problem by amending CPLR 3212 (a) to provide that "the court may set a date after which no such motion may be made, such date being no earlier than thirty days after the filing of the note of issue. If no such date is set by the court, such motion shall be made no later than one hundred twenty days after the filing of the note of issue, except with leave of court on good cause shown."

By the amendment, the Legislature maintained the courts' considerable discretion to fix a deadline for filing summary judgment motions, after joinder of issue, but mandated that no such deadline could be set earlier than 30 days after filing the note of issue or (unless set by the court) later than 120 days after the filing of the note of issue, except with leave of court on good cause shown. Thus, the Legislature struck a balance, fixing an outside limit on the time for filing summary judgment motions, but allowing courts latitude to set an alternative limit or to consider untimely motions to accommodate genuine need.

Nonetheless, the practice of filing late summary judgment motions persisted, with the statutory "good cause" requirement a new litigation battleground. Some courts concluded that "good cause" required a satisfactory explanation for movant's delay, and refused to entertain the motion if no such showing was made . . . Other courts read "good cause" to permit late filing where the motion had merit and there was no prejudice to the adversary . . .

We conclude that "good cause" in CPLR 3212 (a) requires a showing of good cause for the delay in making the motion—a satisfactory explanation for the untimeliness—rather than simply permitting meritorious, nonprejudicial filings, however tardy. That reading is supported by the language of the statute—only the movant can *show* good cause—as well as by the purpose of the amendment, to end the practice of eleventh-hour summary judgment motions. No excuse at all, or a perfunctory excuse, cannot be "good cause."

Here, it is undisputed that the City did not file its motion within the requisite 120 days specified by the statute, and it did not submit any reason for the delay. Thus, there was no "leave of court on good cause shown," as required by CPLR 3212 (a). The violation is clear. What to do is the more vexing issue.

In *Kihl v Pfeffer* (94 NY2d 118, 123 [1999]), we affirmed the dismissal of a complaint for failure to respond to interrogatories within court-ordered time frames, observing that "[i]f the credibility of court orders and the integrity of our judicial system are to be maintained, a litigant cannot ignore court orders with impunity." The present scenario, another example of sloppy practice threatening the integrity of our judicial system, rests instead on the violation of legislative mandate.

If this practice is tolerated and condoned, the ameliorative statute is, for all intents and purposes, obliterated. If, on the other hand, the statute is applied as written and intended, an anomaly may result, in that a meritorious summary judgment motion may be denied, burdening the litigants and trial calendar with a case that in fact leaves nothing to try. Indeed, the statute should not "provide a safe haven for frivolous or meritless lawsuits" . . . , which is precisely why practitioners should move for summary judgment within the prescribed time period or offer a legitimate reason for the delay.

As Professor David Siegel—who has tracked this "controversial topic"—has promised, "we'd think better of judicial decisions that absolutely refuse to extend the time for meritorious summary judgment motions if they would tell us what is to happen in the case." . . .

What is to happen in this case is that summary judgment will be reversed and the case returned to the trial calendar, where a motion to dismiss after plaintiff rests or a request for a directed verdict may dispose of the case during trial. Hopefully, as a result of the courts' refusal to countenance the statutory violation, there will be fewer, if any, such situations in the future, both because it is now clear that "good cause" means good cause for the delay, and because movants will develop a habit of compliance with the statutory deadlines for summary judgment motions rather than delay until trial looms.

Accordingly, the order of the Appellate Division should be reversed, with costs, and the motion of the City of New York for summary judgment dismissing the complaint against it denied.

Judges Ciparick, Rosenblatt, Graffeo, Read and R.S. Smith concur with Chief Judge Kaye; Judge G.B. Smith dissents and votes to affirm in a separate opinion. Order reversed, etc.

Nicholson v. Scoppetta,
3 NY3d 357 (2004)

Chief Judge Kaye's brilliance is on full display in *Nicholson*, a case concerning battered mothers who had been further victimized by a practice of the Administration for Children's Services (ACS). Their children were summarily removed from their care and custody because they had "engaged in domestic violence" when their intimate partners beat and abused them. *Nicholson* represented an unintended consequence of domestic violence advocacy against awarding custody and visitation to a battering parent. Having established that exposure to domestic violence is harmful to children, advocates now saw their hard-won premise turned against their clients, as their children were removed from loving mothers because of the domestic violence perpetrated against them.

Acutely aware of how devastating removal from the home can be for any child, Kaye ruled in no uncertain terms that removal is to be the last resort, not the first response, of ACS, and that its primary purpose should be to keep children with parents, not separate them. It is an opinion that reflects her great heart and her incisive mind, sparing untold families greater misery at the hands of unthinking municipal policy. The evolution of domestic violence jurisprudence in New York paralleled Chief Judge Kaye's tenure. The Family Protection and Domestic Violence Intervention Act of 1994 placed domestic violence squarely under the auspices of the newly appointed Chief Judge Kaye, and she worked tirelessly to understand the full scope of the issues and find ways for the court system not simply to "hear" cases but to truly resolve them, addressing all of a family's legal needs. Her persistent innovation resulted in creation of the Integrated Domestic Violence courts in 2001. New Because of her leadership, imagination, and courage, New York courts are an international model for providing real, lasting help to domestic violence victims and their families.

—Introduction by Mary Rothwell Davis, law clerk 1993–1995

In this federal class action, the United States Court of Appeals for the Second Circuit has certified three questions centered on New York's statutory scheme for child protective proceedings. The action is brought on behalf of mothers and their children who were separated because the mother had suffered domestic violence, to which the children were exposed, and the children were for that reason deemed neglected by her.

In April 2000, Sharwline Nicholson, on behalf of herself and her two children, brought an action pursuant to 42 USC § 1983 against the New York City Administration for Children's Services (ACS).[1] The action was later consolidated with similar complaints by Sharlene Tillet and Ekaete Udoh—the three named plaintiff mothers. Plaintiffs alleged that ACS, as a matter of policy, removed children from mothers who were victims of domestic violence because, as victims, they "engaged in domestic violence" and that defendants removed and detained children without probable cause and without due process of law. That policy, and its implementation—according to plaintiff mothers—constituted, among other wrongs, an unlawful interference with their liberty interest in the care and custody of their children in violation of the United States Constitution.

In August 2001, the United States District Court for the Eastern District of New York certified two subclasses: battered custodial parents (Subclass A) and their children (Subclass B) (*Nicholson v Williams*, 205 FRD 92, 95, 100 [ED NY 2001]). For each plaintiff, at least one ground for removal was that the custodial mother had been assaulted by an intimate partner and failed to protect the child or children from exposure to that domestic violence.

In January 2002, the District Court granted a preliminary injunction, concluding that the City "may not penalize a mother, not otherwise unfit, who is battered by her partner, by separating her from her children; nor may children be separated from the mother, in effect visiting upon them the sins of their mother's batterer" (*In re Nicholson*, 181 F Supp 2d 182, 188 [ED NY 2002]; *see also Nicholson v Williams*, 203 F Supp 2d 153 [ED NY 2002] [108-page elaboration of grounds for injunction]).

The court found that ACS unnecessarily, routinely charged mothers with neglect and removed their children where the mothers—who had engaged in no violence themselves—had been the victims of domestic violence; that ACS did so without ensuring that the mother had access to the services she needed, without a court order, and without returning these children promptly after being ordered to do so by the court;[2] that ACS caseworkers and case managers lacked adequate training about domestic violence, and their practice was to separate mother and child when less harmful alternatives were available; that the agency's written policies offered contradictory guidance or no guidance at all on these issues; and that none of the reform plans submitted by ACS could reasonably have been expected to resolve the problems within the next year (203 F Supp 2d at 228–229).

The District Court concluded that ACS's practices and policies violated both the substantive due process rights of mothers and children not to be separated by the government unless the parent is unfit to care for the child, and their procedural due process rights (181 F Supp 2d at 185). The injunction, in relevant part, "prohibit[ed] ACS from carrying out *ex parte* removals 'solely because the mother is the victim of domestic

---

1. "ACS" includes all named city defendants, including the City of New York. Apart from defendant John Johnson (Commissioner of the State Office of Children and Family Services, which oversees ACS), state officials are named in the complaint with respect to the assigned counsel portion of the case, which is not before us.

2. The District Court cited the testimony of a child protective manager that it was common practice in domestic violence cases for ACS to wait a few days before going to court after removing a child because "after a few days of the children being in foster care, the mother will usually agree to ACS's conditions for their return without the matter ever going to court" (203 F Supp 2d at 170).

violence,' or from filing an Article Ten petition seeking removal on that basis" (*Nicholson v Scoppetta*, 344 F3d 154, 164 [2d Cir 2003] [internal citations omitted]).[3]

On appeal, the Second Circuit held that the District Court had not abused its discretion in concluding that ACS's practice of effecting removals based on a parent's failure to prevent his or her child from witnessing domestic violence against the parent amounted to a policy or custom of ACS, that in some circumstances the removals may raise serious questions of federal constitutional law, and that the alleged constitutional violations, if any, were at least plausibly attributable to the City (344 F3d at 165–167, 171–176).[4] The court hesitated, however, before reaching the constitutional questions, believing that resolution of uncertain issues of New York statutory law would avoid, or significantly modify, the substantial federal constitutional issues presented (*id.* at 176).

Given the strong preference for avoiding unnecessary constitutional adjudication, the importance of child protection to New York State and the integral part New York courts play in the removal process, the Second Circuit, by three certified questions, chose to put the open state statutory law issues to us for resolution. We accepted certification (1 NY3d 538 [2003]), and now proceed to answer those questions.[5]

Certified Question No. 1: Neglect

Does the definition of a "neglected child" under N.Y. Family Ct. Act § 1012(f), (h) include instances in which the sole allegation of neglect is that the parent or other person legally responsible for the child's care allows the child to witness domestic abuse against the caretaker? (344 F3d at 176.)

We understand this question to ask whether a court reviewing a Family Court Act article 10 petition may find a respondent parent responsible for neglect based on evidence of two facts only: that the parent has been the victim of domestic violence, and that the child has been exposed to that violence. That question must be answered in the negative. Plainly, more is required for a showing of neglect under New York law than the fact that a child was exposed to domestic abuse against the caretaker. Answering the question in the affirmative, moreover, would read an unacceptable presumption into the statute, contrary to its plain language.

---

3. The injunction was stayed for six months to permit ACS to attempt reform on its own, free of the court's involvement, and to allow for an appeal. Thereafter, the City and ACS appealed, challenging the District Court's determination. The Second Circuit denied the City's request for an additional stay pending appeal.

4. Chief Judge Walker dissented, concluding that the injunction should be vacated because the evidence did not support the District Court's findings underpinning the injunction. In his view, the District Court's central factual finding that ACS had a policy of regularly separating battered mothers and children unnecessarily was "simply unsustainable" (*id.* at 177).

5. We are not asked to, nor do we, apply our answers to the trial record, though recognizing that in the inordinately complex human dilemma presented by domestic violence involving children, the law may be easier to state than apply.

Family Court Act § 1012 (f) is explicit in identifying the elements that must be shown to support a finding of neglect. As relevant here, it defines a "neglected child" to mean:

a child less than eighteen years of age

(i) whose physical, mental or emotional condition has been impaired or is in imminent danger of becoming impaired as a result of the failure of his parent or other person legally responsible for his care to exercise a minimum degree of care. . . .

(B) in providing the child with proper supervision or guardianship, by unreasonably inflicting or allowing to be inflicted harm, or a substantial risk thereof, including the infliction of excessive corporal punishment; or by misusing a drug or drugs; or by misusing alcoholic beverages to the extent that he loses self-control of his actions; or by any other acts of a similarly serious nature requiring the aid of the court.

Thus, a party seeking to establish neglect must show, by a preponderance of the evidence (see Family Ct Act § 1046 [b] [i]), first, that a child's physical, mental or emotional condition has been impaired or is in imminent danger of becoming impaired and second, that the actual or threatened harm to the child is a consequence of the failure of the parent or caretaker to exercise a minimum degree of care in providing the child with proper supervision or guardianship. The drafters of article 10 were "deeply concerned" that an imprecise definition of child neglect might result in "unwarranted state intervention into private family life" (Besharov, Practice Commentaries, McKinney's Cons Laws of NY, Book 29A, Family Ct Act § 1012 at 320 [1999 ed.]).

The first statutory element requires proof of actual (or imminent danger of) physical, emotional or mental impairment to the child (see Matter of Nassau County Dept. of Social Servs. [Dante M.] v Denise J., 87 NY2d 73, 78–79 [1995]). This prerequisite to a finding of neglect ensures that the Family Court, in deciding whether to authorize state intervention, will focus on serious harm or potential harm to the child, not just on what might be deemed undesirable parental behavior. "Imminent danger" reflects the Legislature's judgment that a finding of neglect may be appropriate even when a child has not actually been harmed; "imminent danger of impairment to a child is an independent and separate ground on which a neglect finding may be based" (Dante M., 87 NY2d at 79). Imminent danger, however, must be near or impending, not merely possible.

In each case, additionally, there must be a link or causal connection between the basis for the neglect petition and the circumstances that allegedly produce the child's impairment or imminent danger of impairment. In Dante M., for example, we held that the Family Court erred in concluding that a newborn's positive toxicology for a controlled substance alone was sufficient to support a finding of neglect because the report, in and of itself, did not prove that the child was impaired or in imminent danger of becoming impaired (87 NY2d at 79). We reasoned, "[r]elying solely on a positive toxicology result for a neglect determination fails to make the necessary causative connection to all the surrounding circumstances that may or may not produce impairment or imminent risk of impairment in the newborn child" (*id.*). The positive toxicology report, in conjunction with other evidence—such as the mother's history of inability to care for her children because of her drug use, testimony of relatives that she was high on cocaine during her pregnancy and the mother's failure to testify at the neglect hearing—supported a finding of neglect and established a link between the report and physical impairment.

The cases at bar concern, in particular, alleged threats to the child's emotional, or mental, health. The statute specifically defines "[i]mpairment of emotional health" and "impairment of mental or emotional condition" to include "a state of substantially diminished psychological or intellectual functioning in relation to, but not limited to, such factors as failure to thrive, control of aggressive or self-destructive impulses, ability to think and reason, or acting out or misbehavior, including incorrigibility, ungovernability or habitual truancy" (Family Ct Act § 1012 [h]).

Under New York law, "such impairment must be clearly attributable to the unwillingness or inability of the respondent to exercise a minimum degree of care toward the child" (*id.*). Here, the Legislature recognized that the source of emotional or mental impairment—unlike physical injury—may be murky, and that it is unjust to fault a parent too readily. The Legislature therefore specified that such impairment be "clearly attributable" to the parent's failure to exercise the requisite degree of care.

Assuming that actual or imminent danger to the child has been shown, "neglect" also requires proof of the parent's failure to exercise a minimum degree of care. As the Second Circuit observed, "a fundamental interpretive question is what conduct satisfies the broad, tort-like phrase, 'a minimum degree of care.' The Court of Appeals has not yet addressed that question, which would be critical to defining appropriate parental behavior" (344 F3d at 169).

"[M]inimum degree of care" is a "baseline of proper care for children that all parents, regardless of lifestyle or social or economic position, must meet" (Besharov at 326). Notably, the statutory test is *minimum* degree of care"—not maximum, not best, not ideal—and the failure must be actual, not threatened (*see e.g. Matter of Hofbauer*, 47 NY2d 648, 656 [1979] [recognizing, in the context of medical neglect, the court's role is not as surrogate parent and the inquiry is not posed in absolute terms of whether the parent has made the "right" or "wrong" decision]).

Courts must evaluate parental behavior objectively: would a reasonable and prudent parent have so acted, or failed to act, under the circumstances then and there existing (*see Matter of Jessica YY.*, 258 AD2d 743, 744 [3d Dept 1999]). The standard takes into account the special vulnerabilities of the child, even where general physical health is not implicated (*see Matter of Sayeh R.*, 91 NY2d 306, 315, 317 [1997] [mother's decision to demand immediate return of her traumatized children without regard to their need for counseling and related services "could well be found to represent precisely the kind of failure 'to exercise a minimum degree of care' that our neglect statute contemplates"]). Thus, when the inquiry is whether a mother—and domestic violence victim—failed to exercise a minimum degree of care, the focus must be on whether she has met the standard of the reasonable and prudent person in similar circumstances.

As the Subclass A members point out, for a battered mother—and ultimately for a court—what course of action constitutes a parent's exercise of a "minimum degree of care" may include such considerations as: risks attendant to leaving, if the batterer has threatened to kill her if she does; risks attendant to staying and suffering continued abuse; risks attendant to seeking assistance through government channels, potentially increasing the danger to herself and her children; risks attendant to criminal prosecution against the abuser; and risks attendant to relocation.[6] Whether a particular mother in these circumstances has actually failed to exercise a minimum degree of care is necessarily dependent on facts such as the severity and frequency of the violence, and the resources and options available to her (*see Matter of Melissa U.*, 148 AD2d 862 [3d Dept 1989]; *Matter of James MM. v June OO.*, 294 AD2d 630 [3d Dept 2002]).

Only when a petitioner demonstrates, by a preponderance of evidence, that both elements of section 1012 (f) are satisfied may a child be deemed neglected under the statute. When "the sole allegation" is that the mother has been abused and the child has witnessed the abuse, such a showing has not been made. This does not mean, however, that a child can never be "neglected" when living in a household plagued by domestic violence. Conceivably, neglect might be found where a record establishes that, for example, the mother acknowledged that the children knew of repeated domestic violence by her paramour and had reason to be afraid of him, yet nonetheless allowed him several times to return to her home, and lacked awareness of any impact of the violence on the children, as in *Matter of James MM.* (294 AD2d at 632); or where the children were exposed to regular and continuous extremely violent conduct between their parents, several times requiring official intervention, and where caseworkers testified to the fear and distress the children were experiencing as a result of their long exposure to the violence (*Matter of Theresa CC.*, 178 AD2d 687 [3d Dept 1991]).

In such circumstances, the battered mother is charged with neglect not because she is a victim of domestic violence or because her children witnessed the abuse, but rather because a preponderance of the evidence establishes that the children were actually or imminently harmed by reason of her failure to exercise even minimal care in providing them with proper oversight.

Certified Question No. 2: Removals

Next, we are called upon to focus on removals by ACS, in answering the question:

> Can the injury or possible injury, if any, that results to a child who has witnessed domestic abuse against a parent or other caretaker constitute

---

6. The Legislature has recognized this "quandary" that a victim of domestic violence encounters (Senate Mem in Support, 2002 McKinney's Session Laws of NY at 1861). To avoid punitive responses from child protective services agencies, the Legislature attempted to increase awareness of child protective agencies of the dynamics of domestic violence and its impact on child protection by amending the Social Services Law to mandate comprehensive domestic violence training for child protective services workers (*id.*).

"danger" or "risk" to the child's "life or health," as those terms are defined in the N.Y. Family Ct. Act §§ 1022, 1024, 1026–1028? (344 F3d at 176–177)

The cited Family Court Act sections relate to the removal of a child from home. Thus, in essence, we are asked to decide whether emotional injury from witnessing domestic violence can rise to a level that establishes an "imminent danger" or "risk" to a child's life or health, so that removal is appropriate either in an emergency or by court order.

While we do not reach the constitutional questions, it is helpful in framing the statutory issues to note the Second Circuit's outline of the federal constitutional questions relating to removals. Their questions emerge in large measure from the District Court's findings of an "agency-wide practice of removing children from their mother without evidence of a mother's neglect and without seeking prior judicial approval" (203 F Supp 2d at 215), and Family Court review of removals that "often fails to provide mothers and children with an effective avenue for timely relief from ACS mistakes" (id. at 221).

Specifically, as to ex parte removals, the Circuit Court identified procedural due process and Fourth Amendment questions focused on whether danger to a child could encompass emotional trauma from witnessing domestic violence against a parent, warranting emergency removal. Discussing the procedural due process question, the court remarked that:

> there is a strong possibility that if New York law does not authorize *ex parte* removals, our opinion in *Tenenbaum* at least arguably could weigh in favor of finding a procedural due process violation in certain circumstances. If New York law does authorize such removals, *Tenenbaum* likely does not prohibit us from deferring to that judgment. In either case, the underlying New York procedural rules will also be an important component of our balancing. Thus, the state-law question of statutory interpretation will either render unnecessary, or at least substantially modify, the federal constitutional question. (344 F3d at 172)[7]

The court also questioned whether "in the context of the seizure of a child by a state protective agency the Fourth Amendment might impose any additional restrictions above and beyond those that apply to ordinary arrests" (id. at 173).

As to court-ordered removals, the Second Circuit recognized challenges based on substantive due process, procedural due process—the antecedent of Certified Question No. 3—and the Fourth Amendment. The substantive due process question concerned

---

7. In *Tenenbaum v Williams* (193 F3d 581 [2d Cir 1999]), a child's parents brought an action pursuant to 42 USC § 1983 challenging the New York City Child Welfare Administration's removal of their five year old from her kindergarten class—under the emergency removal provision of Family Court Act § 1024—and taking her to the emergency room where a pediatrician and a gynecologist examined her for signs of possible sexual abuse. When they found none, the child was returned to her parents. The Second Circuit reversed the District Court's judgment in pertinent part and held that a jury could have concluded that the emergency removal for the medical examination violated the parents' and child's procedural due process rights, and the child's Fourth Amendment rights.

whether the City had offered a reasonable justification for the removals. The Second Circuit observed that "there is a substantial Fourth Amendment question presented if New York law does not authorize removals in the circumstances alleged" (*id.* at 176).

Finally, in certifying the questions to us, the court explained that:

[t]here is . . . some ambiguity in the statutory language authorizing removals pending a final determination of status. Following an emergency removal, whether *ex parte* or by court order, the Family Court must return a removed child to the parent's custody absent "an imminent risk' or "imminent danger" to "the child's life or health." At the same time, the Family Court must consider the "best interests of the child" in assessing whether continuing removal is necessary to prevent threats to the child's life or health. Additionally, in order to support removal, the Family Court must "find[ ] that removal is necessary to avoid imminent risk." How these provisions should be harmonized seems to us to be the province of the Court of Appeals. (344 F3d at 169 [internal citations omitted])

The Circuit Court summarized the policy challenged by plaintiffs and found by the District Court as "the alleged practice of removals based on a theory that allowing one's child to witness ongoing domestic violence is a form of neglect, either simply because such conduct is presumptively neglectful or because in individual circumstances it is shown to threaten the child's physical or emotional health" (*id.* at 166 n 5).

It is this policy, viewed in light of the District Court's factual findings, that informs our analysis of Certified Question No. 2. In so doing, we acknowledge the Legislature's expressed goal of "placing increased emphasis on preventive services designed to maintain family relationships rather than responding to children and families in trouble only by removing the child from the family" (*see Mark G. v Sabol*, 93 NY2d 710, 719 [1999] [emphasis omitted] [construing Child Welfare Reform Act of 1979 (L 1979, chs 610, 611)]). We further acknowledge the legislative findings, made pursuant to the Family Protection and Domestic Violence Intervention Act of 1994, that

[t]he corrosive effect of domestic violence is far reaching. The batterer's violence injures children both directly and indirectly. Abuse of a parent is detrimental to children whether or not they are physically abused themselves. Children who witness domestic violence are more likely to experience delayed development, feelings of fear, depression and helplessness and are more likely to become batterers themselves. (L 1994, ch 222, § 1; *see also People v Wood*, 95 NY2d 509, 512 [2000] [though involving a batterer, not a victim])

These legislative findings represent two fundamental—sometimes conflicting—principles. New York has long embraced a policy of keeping "biological families together" (*Matter of Marino S.*, 100 NY2d 361, 372 [2003]). Yet "when a child's best interests are endangered, such objectives must yield to the State's paramount concern for the health and safety of the child" (*id.*).

As we concluded in response to Certified Question No. 1, exposing a child to domestic violence is *not* presumptively neglectful. Not every child exposed to domestic violence is at risk of impairment. A fortiori, exposure of a child to violence is not presumptively ground for removal, and in many instances removal may do more harm to the child than good. Part 2 of article 10 of the Family Court Act sets forth four ways in which a child may be removed from the home in response to an allegation of neglect (or abuse) related to domestic violence: (1) temporary removal with consent; (2) preliminary orders after a petition is filed; (3) preliminary orders before a petition is filed; and (4) emergency removal without a court order. The issue before us is whether emotional harm suffered by a child exposed to domestic violence, where shown, can warrant the trauma of removal under any of these provisions.

The Practice Commentaries state, and we agree, that the sections of part 2 of article 10 create a "continuum of consent and urgency and mandate a hierarchy of required review" before a child is removed from home (*see* Besharov, Practice Commentaries, McKinney's Cons Laws of NY, Book 29A, Family Ct Act § 1021 at 5 [1999 ed.]).

CONSENT REMOVAL

First, section 1021 provides that a child may be removed "from the place where he is residing with the written consent of his parent or other person legally responsible for his care, if the child is an abused or neglected child under this article" (Family Court Act § 1021; *see Tenenbaum v Williams*, 193 F3d 581, 590 n 5 [2d Cir 1999]; *Matter of Jonathan P.*, 283 AD2d 675 [3d Dept 2001]). This section is significant because "many parents are willing and able to understand the need to place the child outside the home and because resort to unnecessary legal coercion can be detrimental to later treatment efforts" (Besharov at 6).

POSTPETITION REMOVAL

If parental consent cannot be obtained, section 1027, at issue here, provides for preliminary orders after the filing of a neglect (or abuse) petition. Thus, according to the statutory continuum, where the circumstances are not so exigent, the agency should bring a petition and seek a hearing *prior to* removal of the child. In any case involving abuse—or in any case where the child has already been removed without a court order—the Family Court must hold a hearing as soon as practicable after the filing of a petition, to determine whether the child's interests require protection pending a final order of disposition (Family Ct Act § 1027 [a]). As is relevant here, the section further provides that in any other circumstance (such as a neglect case), after the petition is filed any person originating the proceeding (or the Law Guardian) may apply for—or the court on its own may order—a hearing to determine whether the child's interests require protection, pending a final order of disposition (*id.*).[8]

---

8. Under section 1028, a parent or person legally responsible for the care of a child may petition the court for return of the child after removal, if he or she was not present or given an adequate opportunity to be present at the section 1027 hearing. The factors to be considered when returning a child removed in an emergency mirror those considered in an initial determination under sections 1027 and 1022—best interests, imminent risk, and reasonable efforts to avoid removal.

For example, in *Matter of Adam DD.* (112 AD2d 493 [3d Dept 1985]), after filing a child neglect petition, petitioner Washington County Department of Social Services sought an order under section 1027. At a hearing, evidence demonstrated that respondent mother had told her son on several occasions that she intended to kill herself, and Family Court directed that custody be placed with petitioner on a temporary basis for two months. At the subsequent dispositional hearing, a psychiatrist testified that respondent was suffering from a type of paranoid schizophrenia that endangered the well-being of the child, and recommended the continued placement with petitioner. A second psychiatrist concurred. The Appellate Division concluded that the record afforded a basis for Family Court to find neglect because of possible impairment of the child's emotional health, and continued placement of the child with petitioner.

While not a domestic violence case, *Matter of Adam DD.* is instructive because it concerns steps taken in the circumstance where a child is emotionally harmed by parental behavior. The parent's repeated threats of suicide caused emotional harm that could be akin to the experience of a child who witnesses repeated episodes of domestic violence perpetrated against a parent. In this circumstance, the agency did not immediately remove the child, but proceeded with the filing of a petition and a hearing.

Upon such a hearing, if the court finds that removal is necessary to avoid imminent risk to the child's life or health, it is required to remove or continue the removal and remand the child to a place approved by the agency (Family Ct Act § 1027 [b] [i]). In undertaking this inquiry, the statute also requires the court to consider and determine whether continuation in the child's home would be contrary to the best interests of the child (*id.*).[9]

The Circuit Court has asked us to harmonize the "best interests" test with the calculus concerning "imminent risk" and "imminent danger" to "life or health" (344 F3d at 169). In order to justify a finding of imminent risk to life or health, the agency need not prove that the child has suffered actual injury (*see Matter of Kimberly H.*, 242 AD2d 35, 38 [1st Dept 1998]). Rather, the court engages in a fact-intensive inquiry to determine whether the child's emotional health is at risk. Section 1012 (h), moreover, sets forth specific factors, evidence of which may demonstrate "substantially diminished psychological or intellectual functioning" (*see also Matter of Sayeh R.*, 91 NY2d 306, 314–316 [1997]; *Matter of Nassau County Dept. of Social Servs. [Dante M.] v Denise J.*, 87 NY2d 73, 78–79 [1995]). As noted in our discussion of Certified Question No. 1, section 1012 (h) contains the caveat that impairment of emotional health must be "clearly attributable to the unwillingness or inability of the respondent to exercise a minimum degree of care toward the child" (*see Matter of Theresa CC.*, 178 AD2d 687 [3d Dept 1991]).

Importantly, in 1988, the Legislature added the "best interests" requirement to the statute, as well as the requirement that reasonable efforts be made "to prevent or eliminate the need for removal of the child from the home" (L 1988, ch 478, § 5).[10] These changes were apparently necessary to comport with federal requirements under title IV-E

---

9. The order must state the court's findings which support the necessity of removal, whether the parent was present at the hearing, what notice was given to the parent of the hearing and under what circumstances the removal took place (Family Ct Act § 1027 [b] [i]).

10. The Legislature added these provisions to sections 1022 and 1028 as well.

of the Social Security Act (42 USC §§ 670–679b), which mandated that federal "foster care maintenance payments may be made on behalf of otherwise eligible children who were removed from the home of a specified relative pursuant to a voluntary placement agreement, or as the result of a 'judicial determination to the effect that continuation therein would be contrary to the welfare of the child and . . . that reasonable efforts [to prevent the need for removal] have been made' " (Policy Interpretation Question of US Dept of Health & Human Servs, May 3, 1986, Bill Jacket, L 1988, ch 478 at 32–33). The measures "ensure[d] that children involved in the early stages of child protective proceedings and their families receive appropriate services to prevent the children's removal from their homes whenever possible" (Mem from Cesar A. Perales to Evan A. Davis, Counsel to Governor, July 27, 1988, Bill Jacket, L 1988, ch 478 at 14).

By contrast, the City at the time took the position that

> [t]he mixing of the standards "best interest of the child" and "imminent risk" is confusing. It makes no sense for a court to determine as part of an "imminent risk" decision, what is in the "best interest of the child." If the child is in "imminent risk," his/her "best interest" is removal from the home. A "best interest" determination is more appropriately made after an investigation and a report have been completed and all the facts are available. (Letter from Legis Rep James Brennan, City of New York Off of Mayor, to Governor Mario M. Cuomo, July 27, 1988, Bill Jacket, L 1988, ch 478 at 23)

In this litigation, the City posits that the "best interests" determination is part of the Family Court's conclusion that there is imminent risk warranting removal, and concedes that whether a child will be harmed by the removal is a relevant consideration. The City thus recognizes that the questions facing a Family Court judge in the removal context are extraordinarily complex. As the Circuit Court observed, "it could be argued that the exigencies of the moment that threaten the welfare of a child justify removal. On the other hand, a blanket presumption in favor of removal may not fairly capture the nuances of each family situation" (344 F3d at 174).

The plain language of the section and the legislative history supporting it establish that a blanket presumption favoring removal was never intended. The court *must do more* than identify the existence of a risk of serious harm. Rather, a court must weigh, in the factual setting before it, whether the imminent risk to the child can be mitigated by reasonable efforts to avoid removal. It must balance that risk against the harm removal might bring, and it must determine factually which course is in the child's best interests.

Additionally, the court must specifically consider whether imminent risk to the child might be eliminated by other means, such as issuing a temporary order of protection or providing services to the victim (Family Ct Act § 1027 [b] [iii], [iv]). The Committee Bill Memorandum supporting this legislation explains the intent that "[w]here one parent is abusive but the child may safely reside at home with the other parent, the abuser should be removed. This will spare children the trauma of removal and placement in foster care" (Mem of Children and Families Standing Comm, Bill Jacket, L 1989, ch 727 at 7).

These legislative concerns were met, for example, in *Matter of Naomi R.* (296 AD2d 503 [2d Dept 2002]), where, following a hearing pursuant to section 1027, Family Court issued a temporary order of protection against a father, excluding him from the home, on the ground that he allegedly sexually abused one of his four children. Evidence established that the father's return to the home, even under the mother's supervision, would present an imminent risk to the health and safety of all of the children. Thus, pending a full fact-finding hearing, Family Court took the step of maintaining the integrity of the family unit and instead removed the abuser.

Ex Parte Removal by Court Order

If the agency believes that there is insufficient time to file a petition, the next step on the continuum should not be emergency removal, but ex parte removal by court order (*see e.g. Matter of Nassau County Dept. of Social Servs. [Dante M.] v Denise J.*, 87 NY2d 73 [1995]). Section 1022 of the Family Court Act provides that the court may enter an order directing the temporary removal of a child from home *before* the filing of a petition if three factors are met.

First, the parent must be absent or, if present, must have been asked and refused to consent to temporary removal of the child and must have been informed of an intent to apply for an order. Second, the child must appear to suffer from abuse or neglect of a parent or other person legally responsible for the child's care to the extent that immediate removal is necessary to avoid imminent danger to the child's life or health. Third, there must be insufficient time to file a petition and hold a preliminary hearing.

Just as in a section 1027 inquiry, the court must consider whether continuation in the child's home would be contrary to the best interests of the child; whether reasonable efforts were made prior to the application to prevent or eliminate the need for removal from the home; and whether imminent risk to the child would be eliminated by the issuance of a temporary order of protection directing the removal of the person from the child's residence.[11] Here, the court must engage in a fact-finding inquiry into whether the child is at risk and appears to suffer from neglect.

The Practice Commentaries suggest that section 1022 may be unfamiliar, or seem unnecessary, to those in practice in New York City, "where it is common to take emergency protective action without prior court review" (Besharov, Practice Commentaries, McKinney's Cons Laws of NY, Book 29A, Family Ct Act § 1022 at 10 [1999 ed.]). If, as the District Court's findings suggest, this was done in cases where a court order could be obtained, the practice contravenes the statute. Section 1022 ensures that in most urgent situations, there will be judicial oversight in order to prevent well-meaning but misguided removals that may harm the child more than help. As the comment to the predecessor statute stated, "[t]his section . . . [is] designed to avoid a premature removal of a child from his home by establishing a procedure for an early judicial determination of urgent need" (Committee Comments, McKinney's Cons Laws of NY, Book 29A, Family Ct Act § 322 [1963 ed.]).

Whether analyzing a removal application under section 1027 or section 1022, or an application for a child's return under section 1028, a court must engage in a balancing

---

11. The order must state the court's findings concerning the necessity of removal, whether respondent was present at the hearing and what notice was given.

test of the imminent risk with the best interests of the child and, where appropriate, the reasonable efforts made to avoid removal or continuing removal. The term "safer course" (*see e.g. Matter of Kimberly H.*, 242 AD2d 35 [1st Dept 1998]; *Matter of Tantalyn TT.*, 115 AD2d 799 [3d Dept 1985]) should not be used to mask a dearth of evidence or as a watered-down, impermissible presumption.

EMERGENCY REMOVAL WITHOUT COURT ORDER

Finally, section 1024 provides for emergency removals without a court order. The section permits removal without a court order and without consent of the parent if there is reasonable cause to believe that the child is in such urgent circumstance or condition that continuing in the home or care of the parent presents an imminent danger to the child's life or health, and there is not enough time to apply for an order under section 1022 (Family Ct Act § 1024 [a]; *see generally Matter of Joseph DD.*, 300 AD2d 760, 760 n 1 [3d Dept 2002] [noting that removal under such emergency circumstances requires the filing of an article 10 petition "forthwith" and prompt court review of the nonjudicial decision pursuant to Family Ct Act § 1026 (c) and § 1028]; *see also Matter of Karla V.*, 278 AD2d 159 [1st Dept 2000]). Thus, emergency removal is appropriate where the danger is so immediate, so urgent that the child's life or safety will be at risk before an ex parte order can be obtained. The standard obviously is a stringent one.

Section 1024 establishes an objective test, whether the child is in such circumstance or condition that remaining in the home presents imminent danger to life or health.[12] In construing "imminent danger" under section 1024, it has been held that whether a child is in "imminent danger" is necessarily a fact-intensive determination. "It is not required that the child be injured in the presence of a caseworker nor is it necessary for the alleged abuser to be present at the time the child is taken from the home. It is sufficient if the officials have persuasive evidence of serious ongoing abuse and, based upon the best investigation reasonably possible under the circumstances, have reason to fear imminent recurrence" (*Gottlieb v County of Orange*, 871 F Supp 625, 628–629 [SD NY 1994], citing *Robison v Via*, 821 F2d 913, 922 [2d Cir 1987]). The *Gottlieb* court added that, "[s]ince this evidence is the basis for removal of a child, it should be as reliable and thoroughly examined as possible to avoid unnecessary harm to the family unit" (871 F Supp at 629).

Section 1024 concerns, moreover, only the very grave circumstance of danger to life or health. While we cannot say, for all future time, that the possibility can *never* exist, in the case of emotional injury—or, even more remotely, the risk of emotional injury—caused by witnessing domestic violence, it must be a rare circumstance in which the time would be so fleeting and the danger so great that emergency removal would be warranted.[13]

---

12. Section 1022 also requires that the child be brought immediately to a social services department, that the agency make every reasonable effort to inform the parent where the child is and that the agency give written notice to the parent of the right to apply to Family Court for return of the child.

13. Section 1026 permits the return of a child home, without court order, in a case involving neglect, when an agency determines in its discretion that there is no imminent risk to the child's health in so doing (Family Ct Act § 1026 [a], [b]). If the agency does not return the child for any reason, the agency must file a petition forthwith, or within three days if good cause is shown (Family Ct Act § 1026 [c]).

Certified Question No. 3: Process

Finally, the Second Circuit asks us:

> Does the fact that the child witnessed such abuse suffice to demonstrate that "removal is necessary," N.Y. Family Ct. Act §§ 1022, 1024, 1027, or that "removal was in the child's best interests," N.Y. Family Ct. Act §§ 1028, 1052(b)(i)(A), or must the child protective agency offer additional, particularized evidence to justify removal? (344 F3d at 177)

The Circuit Court has before it the procedural due process question whether, if New York law permits a presumption that removal is appropriate based on the witnessing of domestic violence, that presumption would comport with *Stanley v Illinois* (405 US 645 [1972] [recognizing a father's procedural due process interest in an individualized determination of fitness]). All parties maintain, however, and we concur, that under the Family Court Act, there can be no "blanket presumption" favoring removal when a child witnesses domestic violence, and that each case is fact-specific. As demonstrated in our discussion of Certified Question No. 2, when a court orders removal, particularized evidence must exist to justify that determination, including, where appropriate, evidence of efforts made to prevent or eliminate the need for removal and the impact of removal on the child.

The Circuit Court points to two cases in which removals occurred based on domestic violence without corresponding expert testimony on the appropriateness of removal in the particular circumstance (*Matter of Carlos M.*, 293 AD2d 617 [2d Dept 2002]; *Matter of Lonell J.*, 242 AD2d 58 [1st Dept 1998]). Both cases were reviewed on the issue whether there was sufficient evidence to support a finding of neglect. In *Carlos M.*, the evidence showed a 12-year history of domestic violence between the parents which was not only witnessed by the children but also often actually spurred their intervention. In *Lonell J.*, caseworkers testified at a fact-finding hearing about the domestic violence perpetrated by the children's father against their mother, as well as the unsanitary condition of the home and the children's poor health.

We do not read *Carlos M.* or *Lonell J.* as supportive of a presumption that if a child has witnessed domestic violence, the child has been harmed and removal is appropriate. That presumption would be impermissible. In each case, multiple factors formed the basis for intervention and determinations of neglect. As the First Department concluded in *Lonell J.*, moreover, "nothing in section 1012 itself requires expert testimony, as opposed to other convincing evidence of neglect" (242 AD2d at 61). Indeed, under section 1046 (a)(viii), which sets forth the evidentiary standards for abuse and neglect hearings, competent expert testimony on a child's emotional condition *may* be heard. The *Lonell J.* court expressed concern that while older children can communicate with a psychological expert about the effects of domestic violence on their emotional state, much younger children often cannot (242 AD2d at 62). The court believed that "[t]o require expert testimony of this type in the latter situation would be tantamount to refusing to protect the most vulnerable and impressionable children. While violence between parents adversely affects all children, younger children in particular are most likely to suffer from psychosomatic illnesses and arrested development" (*id.*).

Granted, in some cases, it may be difficult for an agency to show, absent expert testimony, that there is imminent risk to a child's emotional state, and that any impairment of emotional health is "clearly attributable to the unwillingness or inability of the respondent to exercise a minimum degree of care toward the child" (Family Ct Act § 1012 [h]). Yet nothing in the plain language of article 10 requires such testimony. The tragic reality is, as the facts of *Lonell J.* show, that emotional injury may be only one of the harms attributable to the chaos of domestic violence.

Accordingly, the certified questions should be answered in accordance with this opinion.

Judges G.B. Smith, Ciparick, Rosenblatt, Graffeo, Read and R.S. Smith concur.

Following certification of questions by the United States Court of Appeals for the Second Circuit and acceptance of the questions by this Court pursuant to section 500.17 of the Rules of Practice of the Court of Appeals (22 NYCRR 500.17), and after hearing argument by counsel for the parties and consideration of the briefs and the record submitted, certified questions answered in accordance with the opinion herein.

People v. Gonzalez,
1 NY3d 464 (2004)

In reversing defendant's depraved indifference murder conviction, the Court made clear that only a homicide committed in conscious disregard of the risk of death presented to the victim—as opposed to intentionally—can constitute depraved indifference murder. The Court emphasized that depraved indifference murder does not mean an extremely, even heinously intentional killing. Rather, the Court explained, when a defendant's conscious objective is to cause death, the depravity of the circumstances under which the intentional homicide is committed is simply irrelevant. Accordingly, the defendant's aiming of a gun directly at the victim and shooting him 10 times at close range was inconsistent with a reckless, as opposed to an intentional, killing.

—Introduction by Hon. Robert M. Mandelbaum, law clerk 2003–2006

On January 25, 2000, defendant entered a Rochester barber shop and whispered something to another person in the shop. Although both left quickly, defendant soon returned, kicked in the door, stepped inside, pulled a gun from his waistband and shot the victim in the chest from a distance of six to seven feet. As the victim fell to the floor, defendant fired again, shooting him in the head. Defendant then leaned over the prone body and fired eight more shots into the victim's back and head. Defendant waved the gun at the only eyewitness—the barber—warned him not to say anything and walked out the door. Medical testimony established that defendant shot the victim once in the chest, once in the face from 6 to 18 inches away, six times in the back of the head from approximately six inches away, and twice in the back. Any one of the shots could have been fatal.

After his arrest, defendant made a written statement in which he claimed that he had been afraid of the victim, who had repeatedly threatened him because the victim's niece had accused him of raping her. Defendant said that he became tense and panicked when he saw the victim in the barber shop. Defendant further stated that he had been carrying a gun for protection, but had "blanked out" as a result of fear and could not recall the shooting. The next day, he "couldn't believe what had happened." Later, on the way to booking, a police officer asked him, "Well, if you had blacked out, why are you having these nightmares? . . . Could you be having these nightmares because you shot him?" Defendant replied, "Of course I shot him."

Defendant was indicted for both intentional and depraved indifference murder, as well as for criminal possession of a weapon in the second and third degrees. At the conclusion of the People's proof, defendant moved for a trial order of dismissal, arguing that the evidence was legally insufficient to establish his guilt of depraved indifference, as opposed to intentional, murder. Supreme Court denied the motion and submitted both counts to the jury in the alternative. The jury acquitted defendant of intentional murder but convicted him of depraved indifference murder and two counts of criminal possession of a weapon. The Appellate Division, with one Justice dissenting, reversed the murder conviction, concluding that the evidence was legally insufficient to establish depraved indifference, and affirmed the weapon possession convictions, for which defendant is serving 15 years in prison. We now affirm.

Discussion

A defendant is guilty of depraved indifference murder in the second degree when "[u]nder circumstances evincing a depraved indifference to human life, he recklessly engages in conduct which creates a grave risk of death to another person, and thereby causes the death of another person" (Penal Law § 125.25 [2]). "A person acts recklessly with respect to a result or to a circumstance described by a statute defining an offense when he is aware of and consciously disregards a substantial and unjustifiable risk that such result will occur or that such circumstance exists. The risk must be of such nature and degree that disregard thereof constitutes a gross deviation from the standard of conduct that a reasonable person would observe in the situation" (Penal Law § 15.05 [3]).

As the Appellate Division correctly concluded, in this case "defendant was guilty of an intentional shooting or no other" (*People v Wall*, 29 NY2d 863, 864 [1971]). A defendant acts intentionally with respect to a result "when his conscious objective is to cause such result" (Penal Law § 15.05 [1]). The only reasonable view of the evidence here was that defendant intentionally killed the victim by aiming a gun directly at him and shooting him 10 times at close range, even after he had fallen to the ground.

Depraved indifference murder differs from intentional murder in that it results not from a specific, conscious intent to cause death, but from an indifference to or disregard of the risks attending defendant's conduct. Depraved indifference murder is exemplified by a defendant—unconcerned with the consequences—who fires into a crowd (*see e.g. People v Jernatowski*, 238 NY 188 [1924]); drives an automobile down a crowded sidewalk at high speed (*see People v Gomez*, 65 NY2d 9 [1985]); shoots a partially loaded gun at a person's chest during a game of Russian roulette (*see People v Roe*, 74 NY2d 20 [1989]); abandons a helplessly intoxicated person on a snowy highway at night (*see People v Kibbe*, 35 NY2d 407 [1974]); or repeatedly beats a young child over a period of several days (*see People v Poplis*, 30 NY2d 85 [1972]).

When a defendant is in that sense indifferent to whether death will likely result from his or her conduct—including with respect to a single victim—depraved indifference may be manifest. But where, as here, a defendant's conduct is specifically designed to cause the death of the victim, it simply cannot be said that the defendant is indifferent to the consequences of his or her conduct.

The prosecution's speculative argument—that the jury may have concluded that defendant recklessly fired the first shot spontaneously or impulsively and then decided to intentionally shoot nine more times—is unsupported by any reasonable view of the evidence and thus no rational jury could have accepted it. "From this record there exists no valid line of reasoning that could support a jury's conclusion that defendant possessed the mental culpability required for depraved indifference murder" (*People v Hafeez*, 100 NY2d 253, 259 [2003]).

The People also maintain that the evidence was sufficient to support a conclusion that defendant acted recklessly by consciously disregarding the risk that if he came across someone he intended to shoot while carrying a gun, he might intentionally shoot that person, or that if he did, that person would die. But a person cannot act both intentionally and recklessly with respect to the same result. "The act is either intended or not intended; it cannot simultaneously be both" (*People v Gallagher*, 69 NY2d 525, 529 [1987]). Because "guilt of one necessarily negates guilt of the other," intentional and depraved indifference murder are inconsistent counts (*id.*).

Depraved indifference murder does not mean an extremely, even heinously, intentional killing. Rather, it involves a killing in which the defendant does not have a conscious objective to cause death but instead is recklessly indifferent, depravedly so, to whether death occurs. When defendant shot his victim at close range, he was not recklessly creating a grave risk of death, but was creating a virtual certainty of death born of an intent to kill. There is no record evidence that defendant "consciously disregarded" that certainty. Indeed, firing 10 times did not establish extremely reckless homicide under Penal Law § 125.25 (2). Rather, it confirmed the intent to kill. The People's tautology, if accepted, would improperly convert every intentional homicide into a depraved indifference murder.

Our decision in *People v Sanchez* (98 NY2d 373 [2002]) is not to the contrary. In *Sanchez*, depraved indifference murder was established by "the sudden shooting of a victim by a defendant who reached around from behind a door and fired into an area where children were playing, presenting a heightened risk of unintended injury" (*Hafeez*, 100 NY2d at 259). The defendant's conduct in firing from behind a partly closed door established his indifference to the grave risk of death posed by his actions. Here, by contrast, the only conclusion reasonably supported by the evidence was that defendant shot to kill his intended victim.

When a defendant's conscious objective is to cause death, the depravity of the circumstances under which the intentional homicide is committed is simply irrelevant. Nor can the wanton disregard for human life inherent in every intentional homicide convert such a killing into a reckless one. To rise to the level of depraved indifference, the reckless conduct must be " 'so wanton, so deficient in a moral sense of concern, so devoid of regard of the life or lives of others, and so blameworthy as to warrant the same criminal liability as that which the law imposes upon a person who intentionally causes the death of another' " (*People v Russell*, 91 NY2d 280, 287 [1998], quoting *People v Fenner*, 61 NY2d 971, 973 [1984]).

In arguing that the jury might have concluded that defendant acted out of fear and anger, and therefore without intent, the People confuse recklessness with extreme emotional disturbance. A defendant who commits murder because of uncontrollable emotion may be entitled to raise an affirmative defense to murder, but the extreme emotional disturbance defense "does not negate intent. The influence of an extreme emotional disturbance explains the defendant's intentional action, but does not make the action any less intentional" (*People v Patterson*, 39 NY2d 288, 302 [1976], *affd* 432 US 197 [1977]; *accord People v Fardan*, 82 NY2d 638, 644 [1993] [extreme emotional disturbance defense "recognizes that defendant intended to kill his victim but, by legislative prerogative, the accused is viewed as being less blameworthy"]). Indeed, when there is a finding that the defendant acted under extreme emotional disturbance, the offense is reduced from intentional murder in the second degree to intentional—not reckless—manslaughter in the first degree (*see* Penal Law §§ 125.25 [1] [a]; 125.20 [2]).

In short, because the depraved indifference murder count was unsupportable as a matter of law, the trial court erred in allowing the jury to consider it. It may well be that, had the jury not been invited to consider depraved indifference murder, it would have convicted defendant of intentional murder. But the choice to proceed on both theories does not exempt this case from the dictates of the law. Inasmuch as this "was a quintessentially intentional attack directed solely at the victim" (*Hafeez*, 100 NY2d at 258), the trial court erred in denying defendant's motion for a trial order of dismissal as to the depraved indifference count.

Accordingly, the order of the Appellate Division should be affirmed.

Maybee v. State of New York, 4 NY3d 415 (2005)

The New York state constitution provides that no bill may be passed without having been printed and on legislators' desks for three days, unless the governor certifies the facts which in his or her opinion necessitate an immediate vote. In rejecting a challenge to an alleged failure of the governor to certify such facts, the court held that as long as the governor's certificate contains some factual statements, the sufficiency of the message of necessity may not be challenged. Chief Judge Kaye dissented, concluding that the history and text of the constitutional provision required that the facts stated by the governor pertain not merely to the utility of the proposed legislation but to the necessity of its expedited consideration.

—Introduction by Hon. Robert M. Mandelbaum, law clerk 2003–2006

(Concurring in result) I begin, as do my Colleagues, with the clear words of the New York State Constitution. That is the appropriate place to begin, as the Court is obliged to honor the Constitution.

No bill shall be passed or become a law unless it shall have been printed and upon the desks of the members, in its final form, at least three calendar legislative days prior to its final passage, unless the governor, or the acting governor, shall have certified, under his or her hand and the seal of the state, *the facts which in his or her opinion necessitate an immediate vote thereon*, in which case it must nevertheless be upon the desks of the members in final form, not necessarily printed, before its final passage. (NY Const, art III, § 14 [emphasis added])

Today, however, the Court honors neither the words, nor the surprisingly long and substantial history, of this constitutional provision.

In an effort to break with past practice and ensure that both legislators and the public would know the content of bills being voted on by the Legislature, the Constitution of 1894 required—for the first time—that bills be printed and distributed to the members of the Legislature at least three days before final passage (*see* 1894 NY Const, art III, § 15).

The objects of this reform were to prevent hasty and careless legislation, to prohibit last-minute amendments—deemed to be "one of the principal evils in the way of legislation" (1 Revised Rec, 1894 NY Constitutional Convention at 902)—and to secure public comment prior to passage (*see People ex rel. Hatch v Reardon*, 184 NY 431, 439 [1906]; *Matter of Schneider v Rockefeller*, 31 NY2d 420, 434 [1972]). Nevertheless, because of grave doubt expressed as to whether it would be possible to print bills and get them on the desks of the members so quickly, as well as fears that public emergencies might require rapid legislation, an exception was adopted for those instances in which the Governor certified the necessity of immediate passage of the bill.

At both the Constitutional Convention of 1915 and the Constitutional Convention of 1938, the indiscriminate use of gubernatorial messages of necessity was much criticized (*see e.g.* 1 Revised Rec, 1915 NY Constitutional Convention at 767 ["It was intended, beyond a doubt, that these messages should be used only in the case of a real public emergency and it was not intended . . . that they should be used as a dose of strychnine for legislation which was in its last gasps, on the last day or two of the legislative session, and which had not received proper attention earlier in the session . . . I think it may well be doubted whether there ever has been, since 1894, a real emergency where it was actually necessary to pass a bill within three days of its introduction"]; *id.* at 823 ["When this matter was brought before the Convention of 1894 . . . the amendment was proposed for the purpose of preventing hasty and ill-considered legislation . . . It never entered the head of anybody in that Convention that this . . . (message of) necessity . . . should be resorted to for the purpose of defeating the very object which we had in view in incorporating this provision in the Constitution so as to require at least three days for deliberation."]; 2 Revised Rec, 1938 NY Constitutional Convention at 975).

The 1915 Constitution, not adopted by the electorate, proposed to eliminate the exception for such messages altogether (*see e.g.* 1 Revised Rec, 1915 NY Constitutional Convention at 824 ["I do not think among the important things that we have to do, that there is anything more important than the elimination of this so-called emergency message. Nothing can be done which will tend to secure more deliberative legislation in the future than the doing away with this message."]; *id.* ["I have such a strong feeling upon the subject that I believe, if this Convention did nothing more than to take out this emergency message, it would have rendered a very great service to the State."]).

The framers of the 1938 Constitution (our current Constitution) similarly sought to decrease the frequency of these messages—the use of which was especially prevalent in the hectic last few days of each legislative session—by amending the Constitution to its present form, to require that the Governor accompany a message of necessity with a certification of "the facts which in his opinion necessitate an immediate vote thereon" (*see* 1938 NY Const, art III, § 14).

In explaining the intent of this amendment, the sponsor explained:

> It provides first that instead of the Governor certifying as to the necessity for the immediate passage, which is exactly what he does, any Governor does: He has a printed form in which he certifies to the necessity for the immediate passage; under the new proposal the Governor will certify the facts which, in his opinion, necessitate an immediate vote on the bill, not necessarily its

passage, but an immediate consideration of it and an immediate vote upon it. And it is the hope of the members of the committee that if the Governor is required to certify facts which in his opinion constitute an emergency, it will not fall into a pro forma signing of a printed message which reads, in effect, "I hereby certify the necessity for the immediate passage of bill No. so and so." (2 Revised Rec, 1938 NY Constitutional Convention at 1435)

The purpose of the amendment was thus to slow the emergency enactment process, prohibit last-minute amendments, force legislators to bring bills to a vote earlier in the legislative term, and reduce the number of bills requiring an immediate vote at the end of the term (*see* 2 Revised Rec, 1938 NY Constitutional Convention at 975, 980).

In contravention of the clear words and intent of the constitutional framers not only in 1894 and 1915 but also in 1938, the Court today endorses the pro forma issuance of messages of necessity *without limitation*, concluding that by use of the word "hope," the framers recognized that the amendment would in fact have no effect. The common thread woven through 44 years of constitutional history is that messages of necessity were meant to be the exception, not the rule.

I cannot agree that the failure of the Governor to certify facts which in his or her opinion necessitate an immediate vote on the bill when issuing a message of necessity is of no consequence. Rather, when the constitutional command is clear, it may not be waived even with the concurrence of the Legislature.

Here, the facts certified by the Governor stated simply that the bill was "necessary to amend the public health law in relation to the shipment and transportation of cigarettes to any person not licensed as a cigarette tax agent or wholesale dealer. This bill also amends the tax law and the administrative code of the City of New York with respect to imposing and enhancing civil and criminal penalties for unlawfully possessing, selling and transporting cigarettes."

These facts do nothing more than set forth the content of the bill itself and are in no way relevant to the necessity of immediate consideration.[1] To be sure, the facts are relevant to the utility of eventual adoption of the bill—that is, by setting forth the proposed provisions of law, including that penalties would be enhanced for dealing in black-market cigarettes, the message perhaps made the case for *ultimate* passage. But that is not the constitutional test.

In both *Finger Lakes Racing Assn. v New York State Off-Track Pari-Mutuel Betting Commn.* (30 NY2d 207, 219–220 [1972], *appeal dismissed* 409 US 1031 [1972]), and *Matter of Joslin v Regan* (48 NY2d 746 [1979], *affg* 63 AD2d 466, 468–469 [4th Dept 1978]), we rejected challenges to gubernatorial messages of necessity premised on claims that the reasons given by the Governor were not good enough. Of course, as the Constitution makes clear, the facts must justify immediate consideration in the Governor's opinion. That being so, the Court will not analyze whether facts which pertain to a need for expeditiousness are sufficient to justify the asserted need, as long as they are sufficient to

---

1. The message also contained the truism that such a message was needed in order to waive the otherwise constitutionally mandated three-day waiting period.

satisfy the Governor. The Governor, having stated such facts, is the final arbiter of their quality, and the Court will not question that judgment.

Thus, in *Finger Lakes*, we upheld a message setting forth the Governor's opinion that expedited consideration was necessary to permit consideration of the bill before the Legislature's anticipated final adjournment. Similarly, in *Joslin*, we sustained a message—sent on March 31, 1977—providing that "[e]nactment of this bill is necessary in connection with the Budget for the 1977–78 Fiscal Year, which begins April 1" (63 AD2d at 469). But when the Governor states no facts at all that relate to timing, the Constitution has been violated, both "in terms and in spirit" (*Finger Lakes*, 30 NY2d at 219).

The Court relies on *Norwick v Rockefeller* (70 Misc 2d 923, 934 [Sup Ct, NY County 1972]) for the proposition that a message of necessity "may not be challenged" (majority op at 419). There, the messages at issue provided simply that "[b]ecause the bill in its final form has not been on your desks three calendar legislative days the Leaders of your Honorable bodies have requested this message to permit its immediate consideration" (70 Misc 2d at 931). The *Norwick* trial court—in analyzing *Finger Lakes*—expressed the view that our precedent could be read either narrowly (to set forth a rule pertaining only to messages containing facts plainly relating to the need for speed, such as the imminency of a final legislative adjournment) or broadly (to mean that messages of necessity are always beyond judicial review) (70 Misc 2d at 933–934). Stating that to forecast which reading an appellate court would ultimately endorse was "precarious" for a lower court, the trial court assumed the broader interpretation (*id.* at 934). The Appellate Division simply affirmed (40 AD2d 956 [1st Dept 1972]), and this Court affirmed "[n]o opinion" (33 NY2d 537, 538 [1973]), declining an opportunity to affirm on the reasoning of the trial court, as we have done innumerable times when that is our intention. "*[S]tare decisis* does not spring full-grown from a 'precedent' but from precedents which reflect principle and doctrine rationally evolved" (*People v Hobson*, 39 NY2d 479, 488 [1976]).

To sanction the instant message is to read the provision out of the Constitution. This, not the Governor, the Legislature or this Court—nor all three together—is empowered to do.

I concur in the result, however, because—although the very purpose of the amendment at issue here was to avoid pro forma messages of necessity—it has nevertheless become the practice of government that messages like the one before us have been routinely used. To strike or put in doubt legislation enacted on such messages would lead to great unsettlement. Thus, while I conclude that the instant message failed to comply with the constitutional mandate of article III, § 14, I would give this ruling prospective effect only (*see Matter of King v Cuomo*, 81 NY2d 247, 256–257 [1993] [although bicameral recall practice used by Legislature to reacquire bill from Governor's desk found unconstitutional, relief was prospective because of longstanding recall practice and "disorder and confusion" retroactive ruling or ruling with resuscitative effect would produce]; *Matter of Campaign for Fiscal Equity v Marino*, 87 NY2d 235, 239 [1995] [although practice of withholding bills passed by both houses of Legislature from Governor violated State Constitution, retroactive ruling was not warranted]).

Finally, I note that article III, § 14 of the Constitution does not ask much of the Governor when a message of necessity is in order. Any facts which in the Governor's opinion necessitate an immediate vote will satisfy the constitutional test. I therefore hope that, despite the Court's ruling today, the Governor will in the future take the simple step of including in any message of necessity the minimal statement of facts that compliance with the Constitution requires.

People v. Caban,
5 NY3d 143 (2005)

In analyzing various out-of-court statements made by coconspirators, the court explicated the distinction between hearsay and nonhearsay declarations. The court also rejected defendant's claim of ineffective assistance of counsel, explaining that the state constitutional standard of ineffective assistance, which requires meaningful representation, affords greater protection than its federal counterpart. Although this principle may seem self-evident, since a state constitution may establish greater, but not lesser, protections than the Federal Constitution, some federal habeas corpus courts had, prior to *Caban*, misinterpreted New York's absence of a strict prejudice requirement as providing less protection than the federal standard. *Caban* clarified that under New York law, an attorney may be constitutionally ineffective even if the defendant was not federally prejudiced by the inadequacy.

—Introduction by Hon. Robert M. Mandelbaum, law clerk 2003–2006

Defendant was convicted of conspiracy to commit murder, based largely on the testimony of prosecution witness George Castro. By his own admission, Castro was a street-level drug dealer who, along with several others, worked for defendant, selling crack on Fox Street in the Bronx. Castro resided in defendant's stash house, and was there on March 18, 1995, when the charged conspiracy was allegedly hatched. The object of the conspiracy was to kill Angel Ortiz, a rival drug dealer who also sold crack on Fox Street. Castro testified that he was packaging drugs in the stash house on March 18, along with two of defendant's dealers, Pello Torres and Melvin Butler, and defendant's brother, Derrick Garcia, when defendant informed the group that Ortiz "needed . . . to be killed" because his operations were competing with defendant's drug business, and offered to pay $5,000 for the murder. Castro further testified that Garcia responded, "I'll do it," and Torres offered to provide Garcia with a gun.

On June 1, 1995, Ortiz was murdered in a Fox Street playground, in the presence of three of his drug dealers and his girlfriend's four-year-old daughter. According to Castro's account of the killing, he was in front of the stash house when Torres approached him and said, "It's time." Torres then went into the house, whereupon Garcia came out with a friend. Castro testified that he followed Garcia and the friend to the playground and watched from across the street as Garcia approached Ortiz and argued with him over defendant's drug "spot." As Ortiz turned to walk away, Garcia shot him several times, killing him.

On cross-examination, Castro admitted his involvement in a prior, unsuccessful attempt on Ortiz's life, which took place sometime in mid-March 1995. Although the trial testimony did not establish whether this incident occurred before or after the March 18 meeting, on the date in question Castro, Torres and Butler set out to kill Ortiz. Butler was armed with two guns, while Castro acted as a lookout. The plan was aborted, however, when the police appeared.

Defendant was eventually indicted and tried for murder in the second degree, manslaughter in the first degree, conspiracy in the second degree, and criminal possession of a weapon in the second degree. The jury convicted him of conspiracy, but acquitted him of the substantive crimes, and a divided Appellate Division affirmed.

I. Statements of Coconspirators

Defendant's first claim of error relates to the three statements of Garcia and Torres, as testified to by Castro—Garcia's March 18 "I'll do it" and Torres's offer to provide Garcia with a gun, and Torres's June 1 "It's time." Defendant argues that hearsay statements of coconspirators are admissible only when a prima facie case of conspiracy is established independent of the statements, and maintains that the People failed to establish such a case here. We reject that claim.

"A declaration by a coconspirator during the course and in furtherance of the conspiracy is admissible against another coconspirator as an exception to the hearsay rule" (*People v Bac Tran*, 80 NY2d 170, 179 [1992]). The theory underlying the coconspirator's exception is that all participants in a conspiracy are deemed responsible for each of the acts and declarations of the others (*see e.g. People v Rastelli*, 37 NY2d 240, 244 [1975]; Martin, Capra and Rossi, New York Evidence Handbook § 8.3.2.4 at 720 [2d ed]). The exception "is not limited to permitting introduction of a conspirator's declaration to prove that a coconspirator committed the crime of conspiracy, but, rather, may be invoked to support introduction of such declaration to prove a coconspirator's commission of a substantive crime for which the conspiracy was formed" (*People v Salko*, 47 NY2d 230, 237 [1979], *rearg denied* 47 NY2d 1010 [1979]). However, as defendant points out, such declarations may be admitted only when a prima facie case of conspiracy has been established. While the prima facie case of conspiracy "must be made without recourse to the declarations sought to be introduced" (*Salko*, 47 NY2d at 238), "the testimony of other witnesses or participants may establish a prima facie case" (*People v Wolf*, 98 NY2d 105, 118 [2002]).

A. Relevance of the Challenge Statements

At the outset, we note that the same evidence may be admissible under different theories when offered for different purposes. Here, some of the statements at issue were relevant for different purposes with respect to the different charges for which defendant was tried. Specifically, although the March 18 declarations of Garcia and Torres were hearsay when offered to prove the murder and related charges of which defendant was acquitted, they were nonhearsay when offered to prove the only charge now before us—conspiracy.

A conspiracy consists of an agreement to commit an underlying substantive crime (here, murder), coupled with an overt act committed by one of the conspirators in furtherance of the conspiracy (*see* Penal Law §§ 105.15, 105.20). Thus, with respect to the conspiracy charge, Garcia's acceptance of defendant's solicitation to murder Ortiz was relevant not for its truth, but rather as evidence of an agreement to commit the underlying crime—itself an essential element of the crime of conspiracy. In other words, whether or not Garcia in fact killed Ortiz, his acceptance of defendant's invitation to do so was a verbal act which rendered defendant and his coconspirators culpable for the inchoate crime of conspiracy, even if the planned substantive crime never came to fruition. Indeed, even if Garcia had no genuine intent ever to commit the murder, defendant would be guilty of conspiracy if he believed he had entered into such an agreement.

> [T]he "act" of agreeing is concrete and unambiguous as an expression of each actor's intent to violate the law . . . The fact of agreement serves only to unequivocally establish a particular actor's intent to commit the object crime by acting with others.
>
> The identity and degree of participation by the other persons are wholly irrelevant. Also irrelevant are the niceties of contract law concerning when an agreement is consummated (e.g. meeting of the minds). It is the individual who is prosecuted [for conspiracy] and necessarily it is the individual who must have the prescribed *mens rea*. The requisite intent is to join with others to commit a substantive crime. If an individual believes he has so joined, it is sufficient to establish complicity, regardless of the actual fact of agreement . . . This is particularly so . . . where . . . it appears that the individual defendant is the originator of the criminal plan and the one most anxious to see the successful completion of the criminal objective. (*People v Schwimmer*, 66 AD2d 91, 95–96 [2d Dept 1978], *affd for reasons stated in op below* 47 NY2d 1004, 1005 [1979])

Similarly, Torres's statement that he would provide the gun for a later homicide—even if ultimately untrue—was admissible for the fact that it was said, inasmuch as its utterance provided evidence of Torres's unlawful agreement with defendant and Garcia. Thus, because the March 18 statements were nonhearsay with respect to the conspiracy charge, the People had no obligation to establish a prima facie case of conspiracy in order for the statements to be admissible.

The analysis differs respecting the admissibility of these declarations as relevant proof of the substantive crimes. Garcia's inculpatory offer to "do it," if introduced as evidence that he had in fact committed the June 1 homicide, would—although proffered in that event for its truth—nevertheless be admissible at defendant's trial under the coconspirator's exception to the hearsay rule as evidence of defendant's complicity in the murder. In that event, however, a prima facie case would need to be established independent of the hearsay statement. The same rule applies to Torres's offer to provide the gun, if used to establish the conspirators' collective guilt of murder and weapon possession.

Thus, the same declarations—relevant both to conspiracy and to the substantive crimes whose commission formed the basis of the conspiratorial enterprise—were admissible at defendant's trial under different theories and different rules, depending on which crimes they were offered to prove. Since the statements were nonhearsay with respect to the conspiracy charge—the only charge before us—defendant's challenge to their admissibility concerning that charge is without merit. . . .

II. Ineffective Assistance of Counsel

During the charge conference, defense counsel requested an instruction that if the jury found as a fact that Castro was an accomplice, his testimony required corroboration. The court so charged the jury over the prosecutor's objection. Defense counsel did not, however, request the court to charge that Castro was an accomplice as a matter of law. Defendant now contends that his trial counsel was ineffective for failing to request the latter instruction, and for failing to move to dismiss the conspiracy count on the ground that the People failed in their obligation to corroborate the testimony of an accomplice. These contentions lack merit.

To prevail on his claim that he was denied effective assistance of counsel, defendant must demonstrate that his attorney failed to provide meaningful representation (*see People v Benevento*, 91 NY2d 708, 712 [1998]; *People v Baldi*, 54 NY2d 137, 147 [1981]). A single error may qualify as ineffective assistance, but only when the error is sufficiently egregious and prejudicial as to compromise a defendant's right to a fair trial (*see People v Hobot*, 84 NY2d 1021, 1022 [1995]; *People v Flores*, 84 NY2d 184, 188 [1994]). Further, to establish ineffective assistance, a defendant must "demonstrate the absence of strategic or other legitimate explanations" for counsel's allegedly deficient conduct (*People v Rivera*, 71 NY2d 705, 709 [1988]).

There can be no denial of effective assistance of trial counsel arising from counsel's failure to "make a motion or argument that has little or no chance of success" (*People v Stultz*, 2 NY3d 277, 287 [2004]). Because the evidence adduced at trial did not establish that Castro was an accomplice as a matter of law, counsel's failure to request that the jury be charged that he was did not constitute ineffective assistance.

An accomplice is defined as,

> a witness in a criminal action who, according to evidence adduced in such action, may reasonably be considered to have participated in . . .
> [t]he offense charged . . . or . . .
> [a]n offense based upon the same or some of the same facts or conduct which constitute the offense charged. (CPL 60.22 [2])

Where "the undisputed evidence establishes that a witness is an accomplice, the jury must be so instructed but, if different inferences may reasonably be drawn from the proof regarding complicity . . . the question should be left to the jury for its determination" (*People v Basch*, 36 NY2d 154, 157 [1975]). In other words, a "witness is an accomplice as a matter of law only if the jury could reasonably reach no other conclusion but that he participated in the offense charged or an offense based upon the same or some of the same facts or conduct which constitute the offense charged" (*People v Besser*, 96 NY2d 136, 147 [2001]).

While Castro's role in the initial mid-March attempted murder, which may have occurred prior to the March 18 meeting and thus prior to and apart from the conspiracy, coupled with Castro's presence at the March 18 meeting and June murder, may have been sufficient to raise a factual issue as to his accomplice status respecting the charged conspiracy, this testimony was not sufficient to render Castro an accomplice as a matter of law. If the mid-March attempted murder predated the March 18 meeting at which the conspiracy was formed, Castro's participation in it would have been insufficient to render him an accomplice to the conspiracy as a matter of law, even though its intended victim was the same as the subject of the murder conspiracy (*see People v Cobos*, 57 NY2d 798, 801 [1982] [witness's participation in an assault and attempted robbery did not make him an accomplice as a matter of law to murder of the same victim committed a few hours later by accomplices to the earlier crimes]). Further, Castro testified that he did not help Garcia with the June murder. Thus, the jury could have either found, as defense counsel argued, that Castro was indeed an accomplice to the conspiracy because he participated in a prior attempt on Ortiz's life and attended the March 18 meeting, or credited the prosecutor's contrary argument that Castro's presence at the murder did not make him an accomplice inasmuch as the record contained no evidence showing that he was anything more than a benign spectator at the March 18 meeting and the June murder. That being so, the undisputed evidence did not establish Castro's accomplice status, and the issue was therefore left to the jury as a question of fact.

Defendant's further argument that Castro was an accomplice as a matter of law because he was undeniably an accomplice to a separate, uncharged drug conspiracy involving defendant is also without merit. Although it is undisputed that Castro worked for defendant's drug business, the indictment filed in this criminal action did not allege a conspiracy to sell drugs; rather, the sole charges involved a conspiracy to commit (and the substantive commission of) murder. An accomplice is a witness in a criminal action who may reasonably be considered to have participated in either the offense charged or an "offense based upon the same or some of the same facts or conduct which constitute the offense charged" (CPL 60.22 [2] [b]).

Here, the facts and conduct constituting the crimes of murder and conspiracy to commit murder did not involve any sale of drugs in which Castro participated, nor was any sale of drugs alleged in the indictment as an overt act committed in furtherance of the conspiracy. Although the underlying motive for Ortiz's murder reflected a desire to eliminate Ortiz as a competitor of defendant's drug business, motive is not an element of murder or conspiracy. The mere circumstance that the elimination of a competitor may have furthered the ends of the uncharged drug conspiracy is insufficient to confer accomplice-as-a-matter-of-law status on a nonparticipant in the murder (*see e.g. People v McAuliffe*, 36 NY2d 820, 822 [1975] ["To hold, as defendant would have us, that it should suffice to show only that the particular witness was 'in some way implicated' in defendant's criminal activity would be to stretch the statute far beyond the ambit intended by the

Legislature"]; *People v Brooks*, 34 NY2d 475, 477–478 [1974]; *People v Fiore*, 12 NY2d 188, 199–200 [1962] [a conspiracy to conceal a prior conspiracy is an independent crime]).

Defendant has, moreover, failed to demonstrate the absence of strategic or other legitimate explanations for counsel's decision to request only that Castro's accomplice status be submitted to the jury as a question of fact. In order to have been entitled to an accomplice-as-a-matter-of-law charge, defendant would have needed to establish that the initial attempted murder involving Castro postdated the birth of the conspiracy at the March 18 meeting. But had defense counsel endeavored to clarify that sequence of events, he would have risked eliciting testimony that the attempted murder predated the March 18 meeting, thereby potentially depriving him of the opportunity to submit even as a question of fact the issue of Castro's status as an accomplice to the conspiracy to murder Ortiz.

We reject defendant's additional claim that counsel was ineffective for failing to move to dismiss the conspiracy count for lack of corroboration of accomplice testimony. "A defendant may not be convicted of any offense upon the testimony of an accomplice unsupported by corroborative evidence tending to connect the defendant with the commission of such offense" (CPL 60.22 [1]). However, corroborative evidence need not establish all elements of the offense. "New York's accomplice corroboration protection . . . requires only enough nonaccomplice evidence to assure that the accomplices have offered credible probative evidence" that connects "the accomplice evidence to the defendant" (*People v Breland*, 83 NY2d 286, 293 [1994]). Indeed, even "[s]eemingly insignificant matters may harmonize with the accomplice's narrative so as to provide the necessary corroboration" (*People v Steinberg*, 79 NY2d 673, 683 [1992]).

Even if Castro had been found by the jury to be an accomplice, there was sufficient independent evidence of corroboration to satisfy the minimal requirements of CPL 60.22 (1). Castro's testimony regarding defendant's motive for killing Ortiz—to protect his drug-dealing operation—was supported by Ortiz's girlfriend, who testified that defendant and Ortiz were competing drug dealers on Fox Street. In addition, that Garcia—defendant's brother and one of the street-level dealers present at the March 18 meeting—was arrested for Ortiz's murder supported Castro's testimony. Moreover, independent evidence from the police and medical examiner as to the location of Ortiz's body at the scene of the murder and the location of the gunshot wounds corresponded with the details that Castro provided (*see Breland*, 83 NY2d at 293). Thus, there were sufficient "standard confirmatory ties" (*id.* at 294) from which the jury could have concluded that Castro credibly connected defendant to the murder and testified about the events surrounding the June 1 killing. Accordingly, defense counsel was not ineffective for failing to seek dismissal of the conspiracy charge (*see Stultz*, 2 NY3d at 287).

Finally, we note that defendant claims ineffective assistance under both the Federal and State Constitutions (*see* US Const Amend VI; NY Const, art I, § 6). Under the two-pronged test established in *Strickland v Washington* (466 US 668 [1984]), a defendant must, in order to prevail on a federal claim of ineffective assistance, demonstrate both that counsel's performance was deficient and that the deficient performance prejudiced the defendant. Prejudice exists when "there is a reasonable probability that, but for counsel's unprofessional errors, the result of the proceeding would have been different" (466 US at 694). Our state standard of meaningful representation, by contrast, does not require a defendant to "fully satisfy the prejudice test of *Strickland*," although we "continue to regard a defendant's showing of prejudice as a significant but not indispensable element in assessing meaningful representation" (*Stultz*, 2 NY3d at 284), whose prejudice component focuses on the "fairness of the process as a whole rather than its particular impact on the outcome of the case" (*Benevento*, 91 NY2d at 714). Thus, under our State Constitution, even in the absence of a reasonable probability of a different outcome, inadequacy of counsel will still warrant reversal whenever a defendant is deprived of a fair trial. Because our state standard thus offers greater protection than the federal test, we necessarily reject defendant's federal constitutional challenge by determining that he was not denied meaningful representation under the State Constitution.

People v. Catu,
4 NY3d 242 (2005)

This case held that a trial court's failure to declare a defendant's term of postrelease supervision—the period of monitoring following a defendant's release from prison—at the time of his guilty plea constituted a due process violation warranting a reversal of Catu's conviction. Although this tightly worded opinion reflected quintessential Kaye efficiency, its breadth was far reaching, paving the way for hundreds of defendants to challenge their convictions on constitutional grounds.

—Introduction by Jonathan E. Rebold, law clerk 2007–2008

Indicted for robbery in the second degree, feloniously operating a motor vehicle while under the influence of alcohol and related charges, defendant pleaded guilty to attempted robbery in the second degree and operating a motor vehicle while under the influence of alcohol, as a felony, in exchange for an aggregate determinate sentence of three years in state prison and a $1,000 fine. Because defendant was a second felony offender, his sentence included a mandatory period of five years' postrelease supervision, of which he was not advised by the court. We conclude that this failure to advise defendant of a direct consequence of his conviction requires that his plea be vacated.

While a trial court has no obligation to explain to defendants who plead guilty the possibility that collateral consequences may attach to their criminal convictions, the court must advise a defendant of the direct consequences of the plea (*see People v Ford*, 86 NY2d 397 [1995]). Collateral consequences "are peculiar to the individual and generally result from the actions taken by agencies the court does not control" (*id.* at 403). A direct consequence "is one which has a definite, immediate and largely automatic effect on defendant's punishment" (*id.*).

Postrelease supervision is a direct consequence of a criminal conviction. In eliminating parole for all violent felony offenders in 1998, the Legislature enacted a scheme of determinate sentencing to be followed by periods of mandatory postrelease supervision (*see* L 1998, ch 1 [Jenna's Law]), and defined each determinate sentence to "also include[ ], as a part thereof, an additional period of post-release supervision" (Penal Law § 70.45 [1]); *see also* Senate Mem in Support, 1998 McKinney's Session Laws of NY at 1489 [describing postrelease supervision as "a distinct but integral part of the determinate sentence"]). Whereas the term of supervision to be imposed may vary depending on the degree of the crime and the defendant's criminal record (*see* Penal Law § 70.45 [2]), imposition of supervision is mandatory and thus "has a definite, immediate and largely automatic effect on defendant's punishment."

"A trial court has the constitutional duty to ensure that a defendant, before pleading guilty, has a full understanding of what the plea connotes and its consequences" (*Ford*, 86 NY2d at 402–403 [citations omitted]). Although the court is not required to engage in any particular litany when allocuting the defendant, "due process requires that the record must be clear that the plea represents a voluntary and intelligent choice among the alternative courses of action open to the defendant" (*id.* at 403 [citations and internal quotation marks omitted]).

Postrelease supervision is significant. Upon release from the underlying term of imprisonment, a defendant must be furnished with a written statement setting forth the conditions of postrelease supervision in sufficient detail to provide for the defendant's conduct and supervision (*see* Penal Law § 70.45 [3]). In addition to supervision by and reporting to a parole officer, postrelease supervision may require compliance with any conditions to which a parolee may be subject (*see id.*), including, for example, a curfew, restrictions on travel, and substance abuse testing and treatment. Moreover, postrelease supervision may require up to six months of participation in a residential treatment facility immediately following release from the underlying term of imprisonment (*see id.*; Correction Law § 2 [6]). A violation of a condition of postrelease supervision can result in reincarceration for at least six months and up to the balance of the remaining supervision period, not to exceed five years (*see* Penal Law § 70.45 [1]).

Because a defendant pleading guilty to a determinate sentence must be aware of the postrelease supervision component of that sentence in order to knowingly, voluntarily and intelligently choose among alternative courses of action, the failure of a court to advice of postrelease supervision requires reversal of the conviction. The refusal of the trial court and Appellate Division to vacate defendant's plea on the ground that he did not establish that he would have declined to plead guilty had he known of the postrelease supervision was therefore error (*see also People v Coles*, 62 NY2d 908, 910 [1984] ["harmless error rules were designed to review trial verdicts and are difficult to apply to guilty pleas"]).

In light of this result, we do not reach defendant's alternative claim of ineffective assistance of counsel.

Accordingly, the order of the Appellate Division should be reversed and the case remitted to Supreme Court for further proceedings in accordance with this opinion.

People v. Combest,
4 NY3d 341 (2005)

Here, the court revisited, in the context of a criminal case, the scope of the journalist's privilege first recognized in *O'Neill v. Oakgrove Constr.* (71 NY2d 521 [1988]). Writing for the majority, Judge Kaye dealt incisively with the balance of interests implicated where a criminal defendant accused of murder sought nonconfidential material consisting of his own statements to the police, which had been recorded by a private production company for use in a TV program. In holding that defendant had met the statutory three-factor test enunciated in *O'Neill* (enacted as the Shield Law), Kaye avoided an unnecessary constitutional ruling, while taking care to register her concern with a practice that could immunize police from providing defendants with their own statements.

—Introduction by Anne C. Reddy, law clerk 2006–2008

This appeal tests the scope of the journalist's privilege in nonconfidential information in the context of criminal proceedings.

On April 16, 2000, gunfire between two groups of young men erupted across a Brooklyn intersection. When the shots concluded, a bystander, caught in the crossfire, lay dying on the sidewalk. Two days later, detectives from the Brooklyn North Homicide Task Force arrested 17-year-old defendant in his home.

Accompanying these detectives was a film crew from Hybrid Films, Inc., a production company that was in the process of creating a documentary on the Task Force for Court TV. The show, which aired later that year under the title "Brooklyn North Homicide Squad," consisted of five episodes intended to present a behind-the-scenes look at the inner workings of the Task Force. In its press release announcing the series, Court TV advertised the "unprecedented access" it had been given by the Task Force, "which allowed a crew to capture the daily activities of detectives, including their personal lives, over a period of five months." Each episode was to "focus on the discovery, investigation and resolution of a case, interweaving aspects of the detectives' personal interests and family lives."

Among the show's featured detectives was Tony Viggiani, who was assigned to question defendant after his arrest. The police thus permitted Hybrid's crew to film throughout defendant's arrest and subsequent interrogation, during which he gave oral and written statements confessing to his participation in the shootout, but attempting to explain his actions as justified by self-defense. A few hours after the police interrogation, which was filmed only by Hybrid, defendant gave a 14-minute videotaped statement to an assistant district attorney, filmed by the prosecution. According to defendant, he and his friends had been forced to return fire after being shot at by a drug dealer and his associate.

Indicted for murder and related charges, defendant served a subpoena duces tecum upon Hybrid for the production of those portions of the video and audio tapes taken during his arrest and interrogation that had not been broadcast. Although Hybrid voluntarily turned over the arrest videotape that it had taken in defendant's home (that tape is no longer in issue), it moved to quash the subpoena for portions of the tapes depicting defendant's interrogation by detectives, asserting that defendant did not establish his entitlement to these tapes under the three-pronged test set forth in Civil Rights Law § 79-h (c) (the Shield Law), which affords journalists and newscasters a qualified privilege in nonconfidential news.

Without deciding the application, and over Hybrid's objection, Supreme Court ordered Hybrid to produce its tapes, under seal, for in camera review. The court ruled that defendant would, if necessary, have an opportunity during the trial of the criminal action to make the required showing under the Shield Law, and that the tapes would then be reviewed by the court to determine the existence of any relevant material and to redact any irrelevant material. However, the criminal action was subsequently transferred to a different Justice, who directed that the tapes be turned over to the parties, without review and without a showing by defendant that the three-pronged test set forth in Civil Rights Law § 79-h (c) had been satisfied. The tapes were then provided to both defendant and the People.

The following day, Hybrid obtained a stay of Supreme Court's order from the Appellate Division, and the parties were required to return the tapes to the trial court. Shortly thereafter, the Appellate Division reversed the order and remitted the matter to Supreme Court for further proceedings. The Appellate Division held that the trial court's decision had been premature, and directed the court to maintain possession of the tapes until an issue concerning their release arose at trial, at which time defendant would be given an opportunity at a hearing to make the necessary showing under the Shield Law. If defendant satisfied the statutory test, the court was then to review the videotapes in camera and redact any irrelevant material prior to release (*see Matter of Hybrid Films, Inc. v Combest*, 281 AD2d 500, 501 [2001]).

The trial proceeded immediately. After the testimony of Detective Viggiani, a hearing was held on the motion to quash. Concluding that defendant had not met his burden under the Shield Law, the court granted Hybrid's motion. At the trial, defendant's statements were the only evidence connecting him to the crime, as well as supporting his justification defense. The jury, without having seen the subpoenaed tapes, acquitted defendant of murder, but convicted him of manslaughter in the first degree and criminal possession of a weapon in the second degree. The Appellate Division affirmed, holding that the trial court properly granted Hybrid's application to quash the subpoena because defendant failed to satisfy the requirements of Civil Rights Law § 79-h (c). We now reverse and order a new trial.

The Governing Law

We first recognized a journalist's privilege in nonconfidential news in *O'Neill v Oakgrove Constr., Inc.* (71 NY2d 521 [1988]), where we determined that our state constitutional guarantee of freedom of the press requires the protection of a qualified privilege when a party to a civil lawsuit seeks nonconfidential information from a news organization (*see* NY Const, art I, § 8). Explaining that a party's request for a journalist's nonconfidential material calls for a balancing of "competing interests" (71 NY2d at 529), we established a three-pronged test that a litigant must satisfy to obtain such materials. At the same time, however, we noted without deciding that different factors might be involved in criminal cases (*see* 71 NY2d at 528 n 2).

In 1990, the Legislature enacted Civil Rights Law § 79-h (c) to codify our three-pronged test, applying it to both civil and criminal proceedings (*see* L 1990, ch 33, § 2). Under the statute, a news organization may not be required

> to disclose any unpublished news obtained or prepared by a journalist or newscaster in the course of gathering or obtaining news . . . , or the source of any such news, where such news was not obtained or received in confidence, unless the party seeking such news has made a clear and specific showing that the news: (i) is highly material and relevant; (ii) is critical or necessary to the maintenance of a party's claim, defense or proof of an issue material thereto; and (iii) is not obtainable from any alternative source.

Defendant contends that the Shield Law is unconstitutional as applied to criminal cases, arguing that a criminal defendant is entitled to obtain nonconfidential material possessed by a news organization even when he or she cannot meet the three-pronged showing required by the statute. He maintains that his due process rights to a fair trial, presentation of a defense, compulsory process and confrontation entitled him to obtain the nonconfidential videotapes of his own statements that were recorded by Hybrid.

As made clear in *O'Neill*, when faced with a litigant's request for information in the possession of the media, competing interests must be balanced (*see* 71 NY2d at 529). In a criminal case, defendant's interest in nonconfidential material weighs heavy. Of course, in *any* case, the interest in refusing to share nonconfidential information is significantly lower than when confidential material is at issue. When confidential material is at issue, the media may have real reason to fear that their ability to find sources willing to provide information will soon evaporate if their guarantees of confidentiality will not be honored. While we do not question the importance of nonconfidential news gathering, whose significance we recognized in *O'Neill*, defendant argues that this case involves

> no intrusions upon speech or assembly, no prior restraint or restriction on what the press may publish, and no express or implied command that the press publish what it prefers to withhold. No exaction or tax for the privilege of publishing, and no penalty, civil or criminal, related to the content of published material is at issue here. The use of confidential sources by the

press is not forbidden or restricted; reporters remain free to seek news from any source by means within the law. No attempt is made to require the press to publish its sources of information or indiscriminately to disclose them on request. (*Branzburg v Hayes*, 408 US 665, 681–682 [1972])

Thus, he contends, a reporter's privilege in nonconfidential materials does not easily overcome a criminal defendant's fair trial rights.

Because in this case we conclude that defendant met his burden under the Shield Law, we need not decide what standard is constitutionally required in order to overcome a criminal defendant's substantial right to obtain relevant evidence.

Application to This Case

It is beyond dispute that a defendant's own statements to police are highly material and relevant to a criminal prosecution. It is for this reason that such statements are always discoverable, even when the People do not intend to offer them at trial (*see* CPL 240.20 [1]; *cf.* CPL 710.30 [1] [a] [requiring notice of the People's intention to offer a defendant's statement at trial]). Further, the voluntariness of a defendant's statement is highly material and relevant when put in issue by the defense. Indeed, even when a motion to suppress a statement as involuntarily made has been litigated and denied, a defendant is not precluded "from attempting to establish at a trial that evidence introduced by the people of a pre-trial statement made by him should be disregarded by the jury or other trier of the facts on the ground that such statement was involuntarily made" (CPL 710.70). "[T]he defendant may adduce trial evidence" in support of his or her contention, and "the court must submit such issue to the jury under instructions to disregard such evidence upon a finding that the statement was involuntarily made" (*id.*).

Here, defendant expressed to the hearing court his intention to pursue two alternative defenses—that he acted in self-defense, and that his statements were involuntary—and to use the subpoenaed videotapes in support of those defenses. In that there was no dispute that Hybrid's tapes constituted the only depictions of his interrogation by the police, in this case defendant met his burden under Civil Rights Law § 79-h (c) as a matter of law.

Defendant contended that the tapes would support his involuntariness claim in several ways. *First*, he contended that the tapes would show the various ruses undertaken by the interrogating detective in an attempt to induce him to confess. Although the detective admitted that he at times used deception in an effort to elicit a truthful confession, he testified that he could not recall whether in this case he made any of the misleading statements specifically identified by defendant. Defendant, however, maintained that the detective had assured him that if he cooperated, he would be charged only with gun possession, whereas if he did not, he would be prosecuted for murder and subject to the death penalty (which the detective testified he knew to be untrue because of defendant's age). Defendant further asserted that he had been promised, in exchange for his cooperation, that he would get probation. *Second*, defendant contended that the tapes would show the extent to which he would have felt physically intimidated by the detective's close proximity to him. *Third*, defendant argued that the tapes would demonstrate the visibility of the detective's holstered gun, inasmuch as the detective could not recall whether his gun was in view during the interrogation.

Defendant also articulated a number of ways in which the tapes would help to establish his justification defense, as well as to negate the elements of intent and recklessness essential to the intentional and depraved indifference murder counts with which he was charged. *First*, defendant argued that the tapes contained his statement to the police that, when the shooting broke out, his car was not double-parked for a quick getaway, but had instead been parked parallel to the curb, helping to rebut the People's theory that he was the initial aggressor in a premeditated assassination attempt. *Second*, he asserted that the tapes included his statement to the detective that he was unaware that his friend had been armed with a gun until after the shooting began. *Third*, he maintained that the tapes contained his statements that he had warned a woman to get her children off the street before he returned fire, and that he had not seen the deceased until he was hit—evidence offered to rebut depraved indifference.

That defendant was provided with the brief videotaped statement he ultimately gave to the prosecutor does not lessen the importance of the evidence he sought. Defendant was entitled to present evidence, if he could, that he had been coerced into making a statement through a variety of techniques employed during the earlier interrogation period, which occurred behind closed doors and before the People's cameras began to roll. Defendant argues that only after he had been prepared to give a calm and coherent statement was the prosecutor's camera turned on. In that event, any earlier displays of fear, upset, suggestibility, protestation—all relevant to the determination whether the statement ultimately given was voluntary—would not be memorialized, but his eventual, dispassionate (and therefore seemingly truthful and accurate) account would be.

In this case, the trial court erred in considering only the allegedly coercive statements that defendant claimed had been made to him by the police, and in analyzing each such statement in isolation. Because it found that no single alleged threat was by itself sufficient to establish that defendant's statement was involuntary, the court concluded that defendant had failed to make a clear and specific showing that the subpoenaed information was highly material and relevant, and critical or necessary to his defense. But a jury's assessment of the voluntariness of defendant's statements may, as defendant contends, involve more than an analysis of the words spoken to and by him. Here, only the tapes could establish those intangibles that might properly be considered.

Finally, we note our concern with the troubling practice of the police partnering with the media to make a television show depicting custodial interrogations. Defendant argues that by inviting Hybrid into the interrogation room, the police created an agency relationship with the film company, thereby entitling him to copies of his statements. Because we conclude that defendant established his entitlement to the videotapes under the statute, we need not decide whether the indicia of state involvement in this case rise to the level at which private conduct is transformed into state action (*see e.g. People v Ray*, 65 NY2d 282, 286 [1985]).

Nevertheless, the police may not immunize themselves from their obligation to provide defendants with copies of their own taped statements simply by letting a news organization—invited into the room by the police—operate the cameras. Defendant correctly contends that the police here allowed the film company to perform what was in fact a police function—the memorialization of an otherwise private interrogation and admission—by videotaping it, thus possessing the only recording of the event. Had the police made (or had copies of) the videotapes, they would plainly have had to provide them to defendant. Just as plainly, the film company could not have videotaped defendant's interrogation in the absence of an agreement with the police. Of course, much of the difficulty could have been avoided here had the police themselves taped the entire interrogation or conditioned access to the interrogation on Hybrid's agreement to provide the police with a copy of the resulting videotapes.

In light of our determination, we do not address defendant's further contention that the trial court erred in denying his challenge for cause to a prospective juror.

Accordingly, the order of the Appellate Division should be reversed and a new trial ordered.

Deutsche Bank Sec., Inc. v. Montana Bd. of Invs., 7 NY3d 65 (2006)

Writing for the court majority, Chief Judge Kaye interpreted New York's long-arm statute, CPLR 302 (a) (1), to cover purely electronic transactions over the Internet, concluding that it is not the medium at issue but the nature and quality of the contracts. The case arose out of a $15 million bond transaction between plaintiff Deutsche Bank, a Delaware corporation with New York headquarters, and defendant, a Montana state agency. The Montana agency had moved, unsuccessfully, to dismiss for lack of personal jurisdiction. The court went out of its way to point out that the defendant was a sophisticated institutional investor, having entered into several other bond transactions with the plaintiff in New York and knew that the plaintiff was located in New York.

By "initiating" negotiations and entering into a contract with a New York bank via online messaging, the Montana defendant availed itself of the benefits of New York law, thus allowing a New York court to acquire personal jurisdiction over that transaction. The decision recognized that electronic advances enable parties to transact enormous volumes of business within a state without physically entering it.

Purposefully entering into a course of transactions with the New York bank employee was enough for due process purposes to place the defendant's activities within CPLR 302 (a) (1).

The court noted that the situation was distinct from the situation where an out-of-state individual investor makes a phone call to a New York stockbroker, which is not sufficient for jurisdiction.

—Introduction by Hon. Albert M. Rosenblatt

This appeal concerns a March 25, 2002 bond transaction between plaintiff Deutsche Bank Securities, Inc. (DBSI) and defendant Montana Board of Investments (MBOI). DBSI, a Delaware corporation with its headquarters in New York, is (among other things) engaged in trading securities for its own account and for clients. MBOI is a Montana state agency charged with managing an investment program for public funds, the public retirement system and state compensation insurance fund assets. In the 13 months prior to the transaction at issue here, DBSI and MBOI had engaged in approximately eight other bond transactions with a face value totaling over $100 million. These transactions were principally negotiated between Stephen Williams, a director in the Global Markets

Sales Division of DBSI in New York, and Robert Bugni, Senior Investment Officer–Fixed Income with MBOI in Montana.

On the morning of March 25, 2002, from New York City, Williams contacted Bugni to ask if MBOI was interested in swapping its Pennzoil-Quaker State Company 2009 bonds for DBSI's Toys R Us bonds, or selling the Pennzoil bonds to DBSI for a stated price. Williams communicated with Bugni electronically through the Bloomberg Messaging System, an instant messaging service provided to Bloomberg subscribers. Bugni responded that MBOI was not interested in the swap proposal. Williams countered that the Pennzoil bid looked good but Bugni replied that the bonds "will get a lot tighter" (increase in price) and MBOI wanted to hold onto them. Williams ended the exchange with a simple "THX" (thanks).

Approximately 10 minutes later, Bugni, knowing that Williams was in New York, sent him a new instant message asking whether the price originally quoted by Williams applied only to the swap, or if it would be the same for a cash purchase. Bugni indicated that MBOI had $15 million of Pennzoil bonds it might be interested in selling. Williams replied that DBSI would like to purchase $5 million of the bonds outright and could probably "trade the balance with one phone call." Bugni countered with a request that Williams investigate whether all $15 million could be sold at the price he quoted. After a DBSI colleague contacted some of his clients and found that DBSI had a sufficient market for all $15 million, Williams replied to Bugni that DBSI would purchase all $15 million at his quoted price, with a settlement date of March 28, 2002. Bugni agreed, and Williams sent a trade ticket and confirmation of the deal.

Hours after the parties concluded their agreement, on the evening of March 25, 2002, Shell Oil publicly announced that it had agreed to acquire Pennzoil-Quaker State Company, an announcement that would potentially increase the value of the bonds. The following day, MBOI advised DBSI that it was breaking the trade because it believed the buyer had inside information and the trade was "unethical & probably illegal." As a result of MBOI's cancellation, DBSI purchased the Pennzoil bonds elsewhere, paying an additional $1.6 million.

DBSI then commenced this action in Supreme Court, New York County, alleging breach of contract, and MBOI answered. After limited discovery, DBSI sought summary judgment as to liability as well as dismissal of MBOI's affirmative defenses. MBOI cross-moved for dismissal of the action based on its affirmative defenses of lack of personal jurisdiction, sovereign immunity and comity.

MBOI contends that there is insufficient basis for the exercise of long-arm jurisdiction and thus the case must be dismissed for lack of personal jurisdiction. Additionally, MBOI urges that dismissal is mandated by principles of sovereign immunity and comity, and that in any event summary judgment is inappropriate because of triable issues of fact and a need for further discovery. We reject each contention.

Personal Jurisdiction

New York's long-arm statute provides that "a court may exercise personal jurisdiction over any non-domiciliary . . . who in person or through an agent . . . transacts any business within the state or contracts anywhere to supply goods or services in the state" (CPLR 302 [a] [1]). By this "'single act statute' . . . proof of one transaction in New York is sufficient to invoke jurisdiction, even though the defendant never enters New York, so long as the defendant's activities here were purposeful and there is a substantial relationship between the transaction and the claim asserted" (*Kreutter v McFadden Oil Corp.*, 71 NY2d 460, 467 [1988]).

As we noted in *Kreutter*, the growth of national markets for commercial trade, as well as technological advances in communication, enable a party to transact enormous volumes of business within a state without physically entering it. Thus, we held that" [s]o long as a party avails itself of the benefits of the forum, has sufficient minimum contacts with it, and should reasonably expect to defend its actions there, due process is not offended if that party is subjected to jurisdiction even if not 'present' in that State" (*id.* at 466). We have in the past recognized CPLR 302 (a) (1) long-arm jurisdiction over commercial actors and investors using electronic and telephonic means to project themselves into New York to conduct business transactions (*see e.g. Parke-Bernet Galleries v Franklyn*, 26 NY2d 13 [1970]; *Ehrlich-Bober & Co. v University of Houston*, 49 NY2d 574 [1980]), and we do so again here.

MBOI should reasonably have expected to defend its actions in New York. As distinct from an out-of-state individual investor making a telephone call to a stockbroker in New York. . . . MBOI is a sophisticated institutional trader that entered New York to transact business here by knowingly initiating and pursuing a negotiation with a DBSI employee in New York that culminated in the sale of $15 million in bonds. Negotiating substantial transactions such as this one was a major aspect of MBOI's mission. . . . Further, over the preceding 13 months, MBOI had engaged in approximately eight other bond transactions with DBSI's employee in New York, availing itself of the benefits of conducting business here, and thus had sufficient contacts with New York to authorize our courts to exercise jurisdiction over its person. As Professor Siegel has observed, where a defendant "deals directly with the broker's New York office by phone or mail [or e-mail] in a number of transactions instead of dealing with the broker at the broker's local office outside New York, long-arm jurisdiction may be upheld" (Siegel, NY Prac § 86 at 152 [4th ed.]).

In short, when the requirements of due process are met, as they are here, a sophisticated institutional trader knowingly entering our state—whether electronically or otherwise—to negotiate and conclude a substantial transaction is within the embrace of the New York long-arm statute. . . .

Accordingly, the order of the Appellate Division should be affirmed, with costs, and the certified question answered in the affirmative.

Hernandez v. Robles,
7 NY3d 338 (2006)

"I am confident that future generations will look back on today's decision as an unfortunate misstep." In her dissent, Chief Judge Kaye penned these closing words in the historic lawsuit seeking marriage equality for gay couples in New York, in which the majority upheld the state's exclusion of lesbian and gay couples from marriage. Her dissent proved prescient, yet she was uncharacteristically inaccurate in the timing. Rather than taking "generations," a mere seven years later the Supreme Court recognized the fundamental rights of gay and lesbian couples to marry in *United States v Windsor* (570 US 744 [2013]). Nevertheless, Kaye's dissent manages to cover the entire landscape of legal arguments that had and were soon to be presented to courts around the country: the substantive due process fundamental right to marry, gays and lesbians as a suspect class, the recognition of dignity in our equal protection doctrine, the understanding that marriage bans constitute sex discrimination, and finally the utter lack of rational basis surrounding procreation, moral disapproval, tradition, state uniformity, and judicial activism claims from marriage equality opponents. Undoubtedly, Kaye's dissent in *Hernandez* finds its home in the canon of judicial dissents, such as Justice Harlan's in *Plessy v Ferguson* (163 US 537 [1896]), that prophetically recognize the equal dignity of all persons under the law.

—Introduction by Roberta A. Kaplan, law clerk 1995–1996

(Dissenting) Plaintiffs (including petitioners) are 44 same-sex couples who wish to marry. They include a doctor, a police officer, a public school teacher, a nurse, an artist and a state legislator. Ranging in age from under 30 to 68, plaintiffs reflect a diversity of races, religions and ethnicities. They come from upstate and down, from rural, urban and suburban settings. Many have been together in committed relationships for decades, and many are raising children—from toddlers to teenagers. Many are active in their communities, serving on their local school board, for example, or their cooperative apartment building board. In short, plaintiffs represent a cross-section of New Yorkers who want only to live full lives, raise their children, better their communities and be good neighbors.

For most of us, leading a full life includes establishing a family. Indeed, most New Yorkers can look back on, or forward to, their wedding as among the most significant events of their lives. They, like plaintiffs, grew up hoping to find that one person with whom they would share their future, eager to express their mutual lifetime pledge through civil marriage. Solely because of their sexual orientation, however—that is, because of who they love—plaintiffs are denied the rights and responsibilities of civil marriage. This State has a proud tradition of affording equal rights to all New Yorkers. Sadly, the Court today retreats from that proud tradition.

I. Due Process

Under both the state and federal constitutions, the right to due process of law protects certain fundamental liberty interests, including the right to marry. Central to the right to marry is the right to marry the person of one's choice. . . . The deprivation of a fundamental right is subject to strict scrutiny and requires that the infringement be narrowly tailored to achieve a compelling state interest (*see e.g. Carey v Population Services Int'l*, 431 US 678, 686 [1977]).

Fundamental rights are those "which are, objectively, deeply rooted in this Nation's history and tradition . . . and implicit in the concept of ordered liberty, such that neither liberty nor justice would exist if they were sacrificed" . . .

The Court concludes, however, that same-sex marriage is not deeply rooted in tradition, and thus cannot implicate any fundamental liberty. But fundamental rights, once recognized, cannot be denied to particular groups on the ground that these groups have historically been denied those rights . . . Simply put, fundamental rights are fundamental rights. They are not defined in terms of who is entitled to exercise them.

Instead, the Supreme Court has repeatedly held that the fundamental right to marry must be afforded even to those who have previously been excluded from its scope—that is, to those whose *exclusion* from the right was "deeply rooted" . . .

It is no answer that same-sex couples can be excluded from marriage because "marriage," by definition, does not include them. In the end, "an argument that marriage is heterosexual because it 'just is' amounts to circular reasoning" (*Halpern v Attorney Gen. of Can.*, 65 OR3d 161, 172 OAC 276, ¶ 71 [2003]). "To define the institution of marriage by the characteristics of those to whom it always has been accessible, in order to justify the exclusion of those to whom it never has been accessible, is conclusory and bypasses the core question we are asked to decide" (*Goodridge v Department of Pub. Health*, 440 Mass 309, 348, 798 N.E.2d 941, 972–973 [2003] [Greaney, J., concurring]).

The claim that marriage has always had a single and unalterable meaning is a plain distortion of history. In truth, the common understanding of "marriage" has changed dramatically over the centuries (*see* brief of Professors of History and Family Law, as amici curiae in support of plaintiffs). . . .

That restrictions on same-sex marriage are prevalent cannot in itself justify their retention. After all, widespread public opposition to interracial marriage in the years before *Loving* could not sustain the anti-miscegenation laws. "[T]he fact that the governing majority in a State has traditionally viewed a particular practice as immoral is not a sufficient reason for upholding a law prohibiting the practice" (*Lawrence*, 539 US at 577–578 [internal quotation marks and citation omitted]). . . . The long duration of a constitutional wrong cannot justify its perpetuation, no matter how strongly tradition or public sentiment might support it.

II. Equal Protection

By virtue of their being denied entry into civil marriage, plaintiff couples are deprived of a number of statutory benefits and protections extended to married couples under New York law. Unlike married spouses, same-sex partners may be denied hospital visitation of their critically ill life partners. They must spend more of their joint income to obtain equivalent levels of health care coverage. They may, upon the death of their partners, find themselves at risk of losing the family home. The record is replete with examples of the hundreds of ways in which committed same-sex couples and their children are deprived of equal benefits under New York law. Same-sex families are, among other things, denied equal treatment with respect to intestacy, inheritance, tenancy by the entirety, taxes, insurance, health benefits, medical decision-making, workers' compensation, the right to sue for wrongful death and spousal privilege. Each of these statutory inequities, as well as the discriminatory exclusion of same-sex couples from the benefits and protections of civil marriage as a whole, violates their constitutional right to equal protection of the laws.

Correctly framed, the question before us is not whether the marriage statutes properly benefit those they are intended to benefit—any discriminatory classification does that—but whether there exists any legitimate basis for *excluding* those who are not covered by the law . . . On three independent grounds, this discriminatory classification is subject to heightened scrutiny, a test that defendants concede it cannot pass.

A. Heightened Scrutiny

1. Sexual Orientation Discrimination

Homosexuals meet the constitutional definition of a suspect class, that is, a group whose defining characteristic is "so seldom relevant to the achievement of any legitimate state interest that laws grounded in such considerations are deemed to reflect prejudice and antipathy—a view that those in the burdened class are not as worthy or deserving as others" (*Cleburne*, 473 US at 440). Accordingly, any classification discriminating on the basis of sexual orientation must be narrowly tailored to meet a compelling state interest. . . . Although no single factor is dispositive, the Supreme Court has generally looked to three criteria in determining whether a group subject to legislative classification must be considered "suspect." First, the Court has considered whether the group has historically been subjected to purposeful discrimination. Homosexuals plainly have been, as the Legislature expressly found when it recently enacted the Sexual Orientation Non-Discrimination Act (SONDA), barring discrimination against homosexuals in employment, housing, public accommodations, education, credit and the exercise of civil rights. Specifically, the Legislature found "that many residents of this state have encountered prejudice on account of their sexual orientation, and that this prejudice has severely limited or actually prevented access to employment, housing and other basic necessities of life, leading to deprivation and suffering. The legislature further recognizes that this prejudice has fostered a general climate of hostility and distrust, leading in some instances to physical violence against those perceived to be homosexual or bisexual. . . .

Second, the Court has considered whether the trait used to define the class is unrelated to the ability to perform and participate in society. When the State differentiates among its citizens "on the basis of stereotyped characteristics not truly indicative of their abilities" (*Massachusetts Bd. of Retirement v Murgia*, 427 US 307, 313 [1976]), the legislative classification must be closely scrutinized. Obviously, sexual orientation is irrelevant to one's ability to perform or contribute.

Third, the Court has taken into account the group's relative political powerlessness. Defendants contend that classifications based on sexual orientation should not be afforded heightened scrutiny because, they claim, homosexuals are sufficiently able to achieve protection from discrimination through the political process, as evidenced by the Legislature's passage of SONDA in 2002. SONDA, however, was first introduced in 1971. It failed repeatedly for 31 years, until it was finally enacted just four years ago. Further, during the Senate debate on the Hate Crimes Act of 2000, one Senator noted that "[i] t's no secret that for years we could have passed a hate-crimes bill if we were willing to take out gay people, if we were willing to take out sexual orientation" (New York State Senate Debate on Senate Bill S 4691-A, June 7, 2000 at 4609 [statement of Senator Schneiderman]; *accord id.* at 4548–4549 [statement of Senator Connor]). The simple fact is that New York has not enacted anything approaching comprehensive statewide domestic partnership protections for same-sex couples, much less marriage or even civil unions.

In any event, the Supreme Court has never suggested that racial or sexual classifications are not (or are no longer) subject to heightened scrutiny because of the passage of even comprehensive civil rights laws (*see Cleburne*, 473 US at 467 [Marshall, J., concurring in the judgment in part and dissenting in part]). . . .

Nor is plaintiffs' claim legitimately answered by the argument that the licensing statute does not discriminate on the basis of sexual orientation since it permits homosexuals to marry persons of the opposite sex and forbids heterosexuals to marry persons of the same sex. The purported "right" of gays and lesbians to enter into marriages with different-sex partners to whom they have no innate attraction cannot possibly cure the constitutional violation actually at issue here. "The right to marry is the right of individuals, not of . . . groups" (*Perez v Sharp*, 32 Cal 2d 711, 716, 198 P2d 17, 20 [1948]). "Human beings are bereft of worth and dignity by a doctrine that would make them as interchangeable as trains" (32 Cal 2d at 725, 198 P2d at 25). Limiting marriage to opposite-sex couples undeniably restricts gays and lesbians from marrying their chosen same-sex partners whom "to [them] may be irreplaceable" (*id.*)—and thus constitutes discrimination based on sexual orientation.

2. Sex Discrimination

The exclusion of same-sex couples from civil marriage also discriminates on the basis of sex, which provides a further basis for requiring heightened scrutiny. Classifications based on sex must be substantially related to the achievement of important governmental objectives (*see e.g. Craig v Boren*, 429 US 190 [1976]), and must have an "exceedingly persuasive justification" (*Mississippi Univ. for Women v Hogan*, 458 US 718, 724 [1982] [citations omitted]).

Under the Domestic Relations Law, a woman who seeks to marry another woman is prevented from doing so on account of her sex—that is, because she is not a man. If she were, she would be given a marriage license to marry that woman. That the statutory scheme applies equally to both sexes does not alter the conclusion that the classification here is based on sex. The "equal application" approach to equal protection analysis was expressly rejected by the Supreme Court in *Loving*: "[W]e reject the notion that the mere 'equal application' of a statute containing [discriminatory] classifications is enough to remove the classifications from the [constitutional] proscription of all invidious . . . discriminations" (388 US at 8). Instead, the *Loving* court held that "[t]here can be no question but that Virginia's miscegenation statutes rest solely upon distinctions drawn according to race [where the] statutes proscribe generally accepted conduct if engaged in by members of different races" . . .

3. Fundamental Right

"Equality of treatment and the due process right to demand respect for conduct protected by the substantive guarantee of liberty are linked in important respects, and a decision on the latter point advances both interests" (*Lawrence*, 539 US at 575). Because, as already discussed, the legislative classification here infringes on the exercise of the fundamental right to marry, the classification cannot be upheld unless it is necessary to the achievement of a compelling state interest. . . .

B. RATIONAL-BASIS ANALYSIS

Although the classification challenged here should be analyzed using heightened scrutiny, it does not satisfy even rational-basis review, which requires that the classification "rationally further a legitimate state interest" (*Affronti v Crosson*, 95 NY2d 713, 718 [2001], *cert denied sub nom. Affronti v Lippman*, 534 US 826 [2001]). Rational-basis review requires *both* the existence of a legitimate interest *and* that the classification rationally advance that interest. Although a number of interests have been proffered in support of the challenged classification at issue, none is rationally furthered by the exclusion of same-sex couples from marriage. Some fail even to meet the threshold test of legitimacy. . . . In other words, it is not enough that the State have a legitimate interest in recognizing or supporting opposite-sex marriages. The relevant question here is whether there exists a rational basis for *excluding* same-sex couples from marriage, and, in fact, whether the State's interests in recognizing or supporting opposite-sex marriages are rationally *furthered* by the exclusion.

1. Children

Defendants primarily assert an interest in encouraging procreation within marriage. But while encouraging opposite-sex couples to marry before they have children is certainly a legitimate interest of the State, the *exclusion* of gay men and lesbians from marriage in no way furthers this interest. There are enough marriage licenses to go around for everyone.

Nor does this exclusion rationally further the State's legitimate interest in encouraging heterosexual married couples to procreate. Plainly, the ability or desire to procreate is not a prerequisite for marriage. The elderly are permitted to marry, and many same-sex couples do indeed have children. Thus, the statutory classification here—which prohibits only same-sex couples, and no one else, from marrying—is so grossly underinclusive and overinclusive as to make the asserted rationale in promoting procreation "impossible to credit" (*Romer*, 517 US at 635). . . . But no one rationally decides to have children because gays and lesbians are excluded from marriage. . . .

Marriage is about much more than producing children, yet same-sex couples are excluded from the entire spectrum of protections that come with civil marriage— purportedly to encourage other people to procreate. Indeed, the protections that the State gives to couples who do marry—such as the right to own property as a unit or to make medical decisions for each other—are focused largely on the adult relationship, rather than on the couple's possible role as parents. Nor does the plurality even attempt to explain how offering only heterosexuals the right to visit a sick loved one in the hospital, for example, conceivably furthers the State's interest in encouraging opposite-sex couples to have children, or indeed how excluding same-sex couples from each of the specific legal benefits of civil marriage—even apart from the totality of marriage itself—does not independently violate plaintiffs' rights to equal protection of the laws. The breadth of protections that the marriage laws make unavailable to gays and lesbians is "so far removed" from the State's asserted goal of promoting procreation that the justification is, again, "impossible to credit" (*Romer*, 517 US at 635).

The State plainly has a legitimate interest in the welfare of children, but excluding same-sex couples from marriage in no way furthers this interest. In fact, it undermines it. Civil marriage provides tangible legal protections and economic benefits to married couples and their children, and tens of thousands of children are currently being raised by same-sex couples in New York. Depriving these children of the benefits and protections available to the children of opposite-sex couples is antithetical to their welfare, as defendants do not dispute (*see e.g. Baker v State*, 170 Vt 194, 219, 744 A2d 864, 882 [1999] ["(i)f anything, the exclusion of same-sex couples from the legal protections incident to marriage exposes *their* children to the precise risks that the State argues the marriage laws are designed to secure against"]; *cf. Matter of Jacob*, 86 NY2d 651, 656 [1995] ["(t)o rule otherwise would mean that the thousands of New York children actually being raised in homes headed by two unmarried persons could have only one legal parent, not the two who want them"]). The State's interest in a stable society is rationally advanced when families are established and remain intact irrespective of the gender of the spouses. . . .

2. Moral Disapproval

The government cannot legitimately justify discrimination against one group of persons as a mere desire to preference another group (*see Metropolitan Life Ins. Co. v Ward*, 470 US 869, 882 and n 10 [1985]). Further, the Supreme Court has held that classifications "drawn for the purpose of disadvantaging the group burdened by the law" can never be legitimate (*Romer*, 517 US at 633), and that "a bare . . . desire to harm a politically unpopular group cannot constitute a *legitimate* governmental interest" . . .

3. Tradition

That civil marriage has traditionally excluded same-sex couples—i.e., that the "historic and cultural understanding of marriage" has been between a man and a woman—cannot in itself provide a rational basis for the challenged exclusion. To say that discrimination is "traditional" is to say only that the discrimination has existed for a long time. A classification, however, cannot be maintained merely "for its own sake" (*Romer*, 517 US at 635). Instead, the classification (here, the exclusion of gay men and lesbians from civil marriage) must advance a state interest that is separate from the classification itself (*see Romer*, 517 US at 633, 635). Because the "tradition" of excluding gay men and lesbians from civil marriage is no different from the classification itself, the exclusion cannot be justified on the basis of "history." Indeed, the justification of "tradition" does not explain the classification; it merely repeats it. Simply put, a history or tradition of discrimination—no matter how entrenched—does not make the discrimination constitutional. . . .

4. Uniformity

The State asserts an interest in maintaining uniformity with the marriage laws of other states. But our marriage laws *currently* are not uniform with those of other states. For example, New York—unlike most other states in the nation—permits first cousins to marry (*see* Domestic Relations Law § 5). This disparity has caused no trouble, however, because well-settled principles of comity resolve any conflicts. The same well-settled principles of comity would resolve any conflicts arising from any disparity involving the recognition of same-sex marriages. It is, additionally, already impossible to maintain uniformity among all the states, inasmuch as Massachusetts has now legalized same-sex marriage. Indeed, of the seven jurisdictions that border New York State, only Pennsylvania currently affords no legal status to same-sex relationships. Massachusetts, Ontario and Quebec all authorize same-sex marriage. . . . Moreover, insofar as a number of localities within New York offer domestic partnership registration, even the law within the state is not uniform. Finally, and most fundamentally, to justify the exclusion of gay men and lesbians from civil marriage because "others do it too" is no more a justification for the discriminatory classification than the contention that the discrimination is rational because it has existed for a long time. As history has well taught us, separate is inherently unequal.

III. The Legislature

The Court ultimately concludes that the issue of same-sex marriage should be addressed by the Legislature. If the Legislature were to amend the statutory scheme by making it gender neutral, obviously the instant controversy would disappear. But this Court cannot avoid its obligation to remedy constitutional violations in the hope that the Legislature might someday render the question presented academic. After all, by the time the Court decided *Loving* in 1967, many states had already repealed their anti-miscegenation laws. Despite this trend, however, the Supreme Court did not refrain from fulfilling its constitutional obligation. The fact remains that although a number of bills to authorize same-sex marriage have been introduced in the Legislature over the past several years, none has ever made it out of committee. . . . It is uniquely the function of the Judicial Branch to safeguard individual liberties guaranteed by the New York State Constitution, and to order redress for their violation. The Court's duty to protect constitutional rights is an imperative of the separation of powers, not its enemy. I am confident that future generations will look back on today's decision as an unfortunate misstep.

People v. Hill,
9 NY3d 189 (2007)

To knowingly, voluntarily, and intelligently enter a guilty plea, a defendant pleading guilty to a determinate sentence must be aware of the postrelease supervision component of that sentence. A sentencing court's failure to advise the defendant of the period of postrelease supervision to be imposed after incarceration requires vacatur of the guilty plea. In *Hill*, Chief Judge Kaye wrote that harmless error analysis does not apply when addressing these violations.

—Introduction by Hon. Albert M. Rosenblatt

In April 2002, defendant pleaded guilty to rape in the first degree in full satisfaction of the indictment. The court sentenced him to a determinate 15-year imprisonment term. No mention was made, either during the plea or during the sentencing that followed one month later, of an additional five-year term of post-release supervision, which defendant allegedly learned of from a fellow inmate. Defendant now claims that he would not have agreed to the plea had he known of the post-release supervision, and he seeks vacatur of the plea.

As has been well established in our law, when a criminal defendant waives the fundamental right to trial by jury and pleads guilty, due process requires that the waiver be knowing, voluntary and intelligent (. . . *McCarthy v United States*, 394 US 459, 466 [1969] ["if a defendant's guilty plea is not equally voluntary and knowing, it has been obtained in violation of due process and is therefore void"]). Prior to accepting a guilty plea, therefore, a defendant must be informed of the direct consequences of the plea. When a court fails to so advise the defendant, the plea cannot be deemed knowing, voluntary and intelligent, and defendant may withdraw the plea and be returned to his or her uncertain status before the negotiated bargain [citing cases].

Among the direct consequences of pleading guilty is the period of post-release supervision that follows a determinate sentence of incarceration. As we explained in *People v Catu* (4 NY3d 242, 245 [2005]), "[b]ecause a defendant pleading guilty to a determinate sentence must be aware of the post-release supervision component of that sentence in order to knowingly, voluntarily and intelligently choose among alternative courses of action, the failure of a court to advise of post-release supervision requires reversal of the conviction." In that the constitutional defect lies in the plea itself and not in the resulting sentence, vacatur of the plea is the remedy for a *Catu* error since it returns a defendant to his or her status before the constitutional infirmity occurred. [Footnote omitted.]

In *People v Van Deusen* (7 NY3d 744 [2006]), defendant pleaded guilty, and the trial court promised a determinate sentencing range of between 5 to 15 years of incarceration with no mention of the post-release supervision term. On the eve of sentencing, defendant moved to withdraw her guilty plea based on the trial court's failure to inform her of post-release supervision. The court denied her motion and sentenced defendant to a determinate term of eight years of imprisonment with five years of post-release supervision. This Court rejected the Appellate Division's rationale that vacatur of a guilty plea was not required when the sentencing court gave the defendant the benefit of her plea bargain, exposing her to a shorter total period of punishment. We held that "[a]t the time defendant pleaded guilty, she did not possess all the information necessary for an informed choice among different possible courses of action because she was not told that she would be subject to mandatory post-release supervision as a consequence of her guilty plea. Accordingly, defendant's decision to plead guilty cannot be said to have been knowing, voluntary and intelligent" (*id.* at 746).

In effect, the Court rejected harmless error analysis by requiring vacatur of defendant's guilty plea (*see also People v Goss*, 286 AD2d 180 [3d Dept 2001] ["as defendant never knowingly agreed to the five-year post-release period of supervision to follow his 12-year determinate sentence, we reject the People's argument that the error in not disclosing this portion of the sentence to defendant is harmless"]).

Similarly, in *People v Louree* (8 NY3d 541, 545 [2007]), we held it "irrelevant that the prison sentence added to post-release supervision is within the range of prison time promised at the allocution." Harmless error doctrine is inapposite when analyzing remedies for *Catu* errors [citation].

Here, at the time of his plea, defendant was not informed that a period of post-release supervision would follow his term of incarceration. Thus, defendant did not possess the requisite information knowingly to waive his rights and must be permitted to withdraw his plea. That the trial court ultimately resentenced defendant to a total period of incarceration (12½ years) plus post-release supervision (2½ years) equal to his originally promised sentence of incarceration does not change this conclusion.

The dissent incorrectly believes that *Catu* and *Van Deusen* turned on the question whether "the defendant got the full benefit of her plea bargain"; thus, the dissent attempts to undo the prejudice of defendant's involuntary guilty plea. Rather, *Catu*, *Van Deusen* and *Louree* made clear that the courts violated the defendant's due process rights—not the defendant's sentencing expectations. Therefore, we vacated the defendants' involuntary guilty pleas to remedy the constitutional violations. Here, we are constrained to give the same relief, exposing defendant to the full penalty of at least a 25-year prison term.

Accordingly, the order of the Appellate Division should be reversed, defendant's plea vacated and the case remitted to Supreme Court for further proceedings on the indictment.

Ross v. Louise Wise Servs., Inc.,
8 NY3d 478 (2007)

In this sensitive case, Chief Judge Kaye determined that plaintiffs, adoptive parents, presented sufficient facts to proceed to trial on a claim of fraud/wrongful adoption against an adoption agency. Although compensatory damages were a potential proper remedy, punitive damages were not. In 1961, plaintiffs were offered a baby to adopt, and when the child was troubled and violent later, the agency did not disclose in response to inquiries that both biological parents had serious mental illnesses, including schizophrenia. Evidence showed that in the 1960s to mid-1980s, psychiatrists thought the environment was more significant than heredity and believed such disclosure of such history would be detrimental to bonding. The agency's admitted policy to conceal information deprived plaintiffs of the right to make informed parenting decisions and thus plaintiffs raised a cognizable claim of fraud in adoption. However, the conduct, normative at the time, did not evince the high degree of moral turpitude required for punitive damages, and 1980s statutes requiring disclosure obviated the need for deterrence of future similar conduct.

—Introduction by Elaine Unkeless, law clerk 2006–2007

Plaintiffs, adoptive parents Arthur Ross and Barbara Ross, have asserted three causes of action against Louise Wise Services: wrongful adoption/fraud; negligence and breach of fiduciary duty; and intentional infliction of emotional distress. On defendants' motion for summary judgment, we conclude that, while plaintiffs may seek compensatory damages, punitive damages are not available for the first claim in this case, and statutes of limitations bar the second and third claims.

Facts

In 1960 plaintiffs applied to Louise Wise (the Agency) for assistance in adopting an infant.[1] They told the Agency that they preferred a "healthy infant from a healthy family," and

---

1. Founded in 1916, the Agency sought good homes for children placed for adoption. By the late 1990s, it no longer acted as an adoption agency, and instead offered training and support for foster care families and children. Those operations ceased in 2004. . . .

that "it would be nice if the baby's birth family had an artistic background." Mr. Ross was nationally recognized in the advertising field, had won awards and made a good salary, and the couple were engaged in various cultural activities. According to one social worker who had interviewed them, plaintiffs were mature, seemed comfortable about adopting a child and could handle the situation "better than the average couple with whom we place a child."

In the spring of 1961 plaintiffs were offered a boy, born January 11, 1961. In response to plaintiffs' question about the health of the baby and his biological family, the social worker told plaintiffs this was "a demanding baby who likes attention." She described the physical appearance and artistic interests of the birth parents and indicated that they were healthy but the birth father was allergic to penicillin and the maternal grandfather had died of heart disease. The Agency did not, however, disclose that either of the birth parents or members of their families had suffered from emotional disturbance.

According to Agency files, the biological mother never had a "normal" home life. In 1952, her father, the baby's biological grandfather, was hospitalized for 1½ years for schizophrenia when he was in his mid-60s. The report also indicated that the birth mother was worried that her feelings of stress could affect the baby. She and the biological father married only because she was pregnant. She had seen a psychiatrist, who wrote to the Agency that the mother "presented as a girl who was failing in her major adjustments to life: late to school with the result that she failed to maintain matriculation at two colleges; few friends; hostility to most people; and demanding dependency." The biological father, according to the files, saw a psychiatrist, who, after one meeting, stated that the father was "a seriously disturbed young man, classified him as a paranoid, schizophrenic, and felt he had married purely for her [the birth mother's] money." The doctor also noted that, while the birth father could use treatment, "there was no rush."

Plaintiffs accepted the child, and on March 30, 1961, took home the baby they named Anthony. Although he was an active, difficult infant who could not sleep well, Ms. Ross attended to him and he was a happy baby. The adoption was finalized in 1962, and in 1964 plaintiffs adopted a daughter from the Agency. By the time Anthony was four, his troublesome behavior led plaintiffs to seek professional help.

Post-Adoption Events

In 1970, when Anthony was nine years old and the difficulties increased, plaintiffs called the Agency and were directed to Barbara Miller, head of the Post-Adoption Service. Plaintiffs told Miller that Anthony was experiencing "night terrors," cursed at the family, hit his parents and threatened people with objects. Ms. Ross suspected that he was hyperactive and might have brain dysfunction. Plaintiffs asked whether there could have been problems with the birth mother, whether she had taken drugs, whether she attempted to abort the pregnancy or whether there was birth trauma. Miller recommended that plaintiffs see a psychiatrist, Dr. Anne-Marie Weil, associated with the Agency. Miller's letter to Weil noted that Anthony's birth mother and grandfather "had histories of emotional instability"; however, Miller did not give Weil any specifics of the schizophrenia, and neither Miller nor Weil told plaintiffs of any emotional instability. Weil never saw Anthony himself, and her suggestions for behavior modification were to no avail.

While Ms. Ross wished to get treatment for Anthony, Mr. Ross disagreed and hoped that Anthony would grow out of his disruptive behavior. In 1973, after Anthony's school advised plaintiffs that Anthony needed a special school, they called Miller again to ask that she send a summary of Anthony's "birth history, background and foster home experience to Dr. Stella Chess," a well-known child psychiatrist plaintiffs had engaged. Although Miller mentioned in her report to Chess that Anthony was a tense, active baby, she did not tell the doctor of the birth parents' history of schizophrenia. In the same call to Miller, Ms. Ross indicated that she suspected more and more that Anthony's difficulties were organically based and divulged that she was forced to separate herself from her son as much as possible since his violence was getting progressively worse.

When she phoned the Agency in 1981, Ms. Ross told Miller that, fearful of her own and her daughter's physical well-being, she had moved out of her home in 1978 when Anthony had finished a special high school. Plaintiffs divorced in 1979. The daughter then lived with her mother and Anthony with his father. Though Miller stated in her notes that Anthony remained disturbed and undiagnosed, she mentioned nothing to plaintiffs about his biological background.

Anthony continued to live with his father and graduated from college. Over the years, he did see several doctors, none of whom could assist him. He had some odd jobs but could not keep any. Ms. Ross called the Agency in 1994 and told them that she thought Anthony had ADHD. The Agency again did not disclose any information, including that it had received a call in 1984 that Anthony's birth mother had committed suicide in 1973. Anthony's behavior became more erratic, and he started to see a psychiatrist again. In 1995, when Anthony was 34, Mr. Ross woke up to find his son about to hit him with a large flashlight. Anthony was taken to Bellevue, where he was diagnosed as a paranoid schizophrenic.

The Action

The New York Times Magazine on March 14, 1999, published an article, *What the Jumans Didn't Know About Michael*, describing a family who adopted a boy from the Agency and learned years later that the birth family's history included schizophrenia. As a result, plaintiffs sought Anthony's medical records. These were sent in April 1999, and plaintiffs filed suit on June 25, 1999. Plaintiffs testified in their depositions that much as they love Anthony, they would not have adopted him before they saw him if they had been told about the schizophrenia in his biological family, and that psychiatrists might have treated him differently had disclosure been made earlier. Further, they claimed that the stresses in their family resulted in both plaintiffs' clinical depression, the dissolution of their marriage and lost employment.

Agency Policies in the 1960s and 1970s

In the 1960s and 1970s, the belief among the social workers and psychiatrists who worked for the Agency was that, in the development of a child, nurture played a far more significant role than nature. For that reason, the policy of the Agency was not to disclose certain information about a birth family's medical history if the doctors were unsure whether the factors were hereditary. Anita Longo Sorensen, the Agency's expert witness, expressed this opinion in an affidavit and added:

> Moreover, it was the belief and general opinion of social workers and other professionals in the adoption field at those times that mental illness would not be passed on if a child were placed in a loving environment.
>
> It was also the general opinion and belief of social workers and other professionals in the adoption field at those times that the disclosure of certain information to prospective adoptive parents would interfere with the bonding between adoptive parent and child and prove detrimental to the child, the parents and their relationship. Therefore, it was the practice of social workers and other professionals in the adoption field in the 1960s and into the early 1980s not to disclose information that could be viewed as negative and which was not believed to be hereditary for fear that it would influence the family adversely on how they would nurture the adopted child. This practice remained in effect until changes were made in the Social Services Law and the Public Health Law in the early-mid 1980s.

Specifically, psychiatrists were unsure about the hereditary factors of mental illness and therefore would not discuss with adoptive parents mental disturbances of the biological family. Florence Kreech, Executive Director of the Agency during that period, testified that their psychiatrists "felt for many, many years we knew so little about schizophrenia and they felt very strongly about not putting labels on people." Kreech knew that studies were underway, but the Agency's psychiatrists "knew too little about hereditary factors," and had no certain information that a child of a parent or parents who had schizophrenia had a greater risk of developing it. "[T]here were children that may have come from parents—and, again, they wouldn't put labels on them—whose parents were disturbed, but it did not necessarily follow that the children were going to be disturbed."

Miller conceded that she concealed the biological information from all adoptive parents, including plaintiffs, when they called with post-adoptive questions. She followed what the Agency considered normative policy. Generally, the Agency might have told a couple that there was some disturbance in the family background, but more likely the Agency, without divulging aberrant history, would find an adoptive couple who could be accepting of emotional problems. Social workers and psychiatrists were concerned that the child not be stigmatized.

> [I]f there were a history of mental illness which we understood to be noninheritable at that time—and I couldn't find a psychiatrist in New York at the time who would have told you that it was inherited—we would not mention that, simply because our psychiatrist felt that it had no meaning and it would only cause anxiety or might cause anxiety in the parents.

A "healthy baby" at that time meant a physically healthy child.

The Agency has included in the record extracts from literature published in the 1960s through 1980s to underscore the divergent views on the etiology of schizophrenia. For example, Herbert Weiner, M.D., wrote in 1967 that "In psychiatry, the nature-nurture controversy continues to rage" (*Schizophrenia III: Etiology*, in Freedman and Kaplan, Comprehensive Textbook of Psychiatry § 15.3 at 604 [1967]). The author concluded that "The environment may continuously interact with the genotype to elicit certain kinds of general potentialities and more specific dispositions to react to certain categories of environmental stress that lead to the illness" (*id.* at 620).

Plaintiffs too presented the affidavit of an expert, Dr. Dolores Malaspina, whose work concentrates on schizophrenia. She indicated that as far back as 1911 a study showed that schizophrenia "arose from a hereditary taint," and even in the 1920s, studies demonstrated elevated risks for the disease in close relatives. Malaspina affirmed that "[a]lthough a number of American practitioners theorized in the post-World War II era that schizophrenia could arise from a dysfunctional family, the evidence of its genetic familial nature was never questioned." Studies indicated that the likelihood of getting schizophrenia for someone with one affected parent is 12%, and the risk for bi-lineal inheritance is 46%. A doctor's not knowing the family history could make diagnosis "correspondingly difficult."

It was not until 1983 that the legislature enacted Social Services Law § 373-a (L 1983, ch 326, amended by L 1985, chs 103, 142), which provides that medical histories should be disclosed to pre-adoptive parents and adult adoptees. In 1985, the statute was amended to include adoptive parents. The legislature also enacted Public Health Law §§ 4138-b, 4138-c and 4138-d, effective December 6, 1983, establishing an Adoption Information Registry in the Department of Health to allow adult adoptees to obtain nonidentifying medical information.

Decisions of the Lower Courts

In Supreme Court, the Agency moved for an order granting summary judgment dismissing plaintiffs' complaint; granting partial summary judgment dismissing plaintiffs' second and third causes of action as time-barred; dismissing plaintiffs' claim for emotional distress and recovery of business or other losses from that emotional distress, and limiting potential recovery of compensatory damages to extraordinary out-of-pocket expenses of raising plaintiffs' adopted child to age 21; and dismissing plaintiffs' claim for punitive damages. Refusing to grant summary judgment as to the first count (wrongful adoption/ fraud), the court found triable issues of fact as to whether the Agency concealed or misrepresented material facts at the time of the adoption and in subsequent years about the child's biological history. The court dismissed the claims for negligence and intentional infliction of emotional harm on statute of limitations grounds, limited potential recovery of compensatory damages to out-of-pocket expenses before the child reached 21 and allowed the claim for punitive damages to proceed.

The Appellate Division affirmed [and] granted leave [to appeal].

The Agency appeals from the order allowing the issue of punitive damages to proceed; plaintiffs cross-appeal from the order dismissing their second and third causes of action. We agree with the trial court and Appellate Division on the statute of limitations issue, agree with the dissent on the punitive damages issue and accordingly modify the order of the Appellate Division.

Analysis

As a threshold matter, the Agency, in failing to challenge the order leaving in place the action for wrongful adoption, acknowledges that plaintiffs have raised a cognizable claim under common-law fraud principles in the adoption setting (*see Juman v Louise Wise Servs.*, 159 Misc 2d 314, 316–317 [NY County 1994], *affd* 211 AD2d 446 [1st Dept 1995]). . . .

Thus, plaintiffs here will have the opportunity to show that the Agency's admitted policy to withhold information from them concerned material facts on which they relied and as a result of which they sustained monetary losses.

The questions we are called upon to answer are whether plaintiffs may seek punitive damages for wrongful adoption/fraud as alleged, and whether equitable estoppel bars the Agency from asserting the defense of statute of limitations on the second and third causes of action.

Punitive Damages

Compensatory damages are intended to have the wrongdoer make the victim whole—to assure that the victim receive fair and just compensation commensurate with the injury sustained. Punitive damages are not to compensate the injured party but rather to punish the tortfeasor and to deter this wrongdoer and others similarly situated from indulging in the same conduct in the future (*Walker v Sheldon*, 10 NY2d 401, 404 [1961]). Subjecting a wrongdoer to punitive damages serves to deter future reprehensible conduct. Hence the term "exemplary damages" is a synonym for punitive damages.

Punitive damages are permitted when the defendant's wrongdoing is not simply intentional but "evince[s] a high degree of moral turpitude and demonstrate[s] such wanton dishonesty as to imply a criminal indifference to civil obligations" (*Walker*, 10 NY2d at 405; *see Rocanova v Equitable Life Assur. Socy. of the United States*, 83 NY2d 603, 613 [1994]). In *Prozeralik v Capital Cities Communications, Inc.* (82 NY2d 466, 479 [1993]), the Court wrote that punitive damages may be sought when the wrongdoing was deliberate "'and has the character of outrage frequently associated with crime'" (citation omitted). The misconduct must be exceptional, "as when the wrongdoer has acted maliciously, wantonly, or with a recklessness that betokens an improper motive or vindictiveness . . . or has engaged in outrageous or oppressive intentional misconduct or with reckless or wanton disregard of safety or rights" (*Sharapata*, 56 NY2d at 335 [citations and internal quotation marks omitted]. . . .

In this case, the Agency has conceded that it intentionally misrepresented facts about Anthony's background. We are troubled by such concealment, and sympathetic to the suffering plaintiffs have endured. They have presented sufficient triable facts to proceed on their fraud claim for compensatory damages.

In its motion for summary judgment, however, the Agency has shown that, even if its failure to disclose may have been tortious, its conduct in connection with the adoption did not evince the high degree of moral turpitude required for punitive damages. Nor would punitive damages be warranted against the Agency for deterrence.

First, nothing in the record disproves what the Agency's own social workers and its expert stated—in the 1960s and even into the early 1980s the policy was not to disclose certain information about the child's biological background if the professionals were unsure whether the factors were hereditary. Many thought that mental illness could be avoided if a child were placed in a loving environment and that disclosure of birth parents' emotional disturbances would negatively affect the child's bonding with the adoptive parents. While it may be difficult for us in the twenty-first century to envisage not discussing mental or physical illness with prospective parents, and while such normative conduct may be deemed tortious even for that time, we cannot say that the record shows that the Agency's motivation was malicious or vindictive.

Not until 1983 did the legislature enact Social Services Law § 373-a to require disclosure of medical histories to prospective adoptive parents and adult adoptees. Although we address common-law tort and not violation of the statute, that the statute was enacted only in the 1980s is a factor in determining that punitive damages are inappropriate here.

As to deterrence, section 373-a now requires agencies to provide to prospective adoptive parents and, upon request, to adoptive parents "the medical histories of a child legally freed for adoption . . . and of his or her natural parents, with information identifying such natural parents eliminated." Medical histories include "psychological information" (*id.*). Thus, the statute assures that agencies do not conceal relevant history of birth parents. Moreover, defendant Agency no longer acts in placing children for adoption, and its records are now housed at a different agency.

The complaint here includes a single cause of action for wrongful adoption and fraud at the time of the adoption. There are no separate counts of fraud concerning conduct in later years. Thus, even though no justification may exist, for example, for the Agency's failure to disclose information to the doctors plaintiffs consulted for Anthony in the 1970s, the fraud of wrongful adoption must center on the conduct that induced the prospective parents to accept the child. Because we cannot conclude from the record that the initial concealment was motivated by malice so as to warrant punitive damages, or that these damages would deter future reprehensible conduct, we limit plaintiffs' potential recovery to compensatory damages.

Equitable Estoppel

The second and third causes of action—for negligence and infliction of emotional distress— are barred by the statutes of limitations under CPLR 214 (three years) and CPLR 215 (one year) respectively. Plaintiffs do not assert that the discovery rule under CPLR 203 (g) that permits the fraud claim to proceed is applicable to these torts, for plainly it is not. Rather, they argue that the doctrine of equitable estoppel should apply.

Under this doctrine, a defendant is estopped from pleading a statute of limitations defense if the "plaintiff was induced by fraud, misrepresentations or deception to refrain from filing a timely action" (*Simcuski v Saeli*, 44 NY2d 442, 448–449 [1978]). For the doctrine to apply, a plaintiff may not rely on the same act that forms the basis for the claim—the later fraudulent misrepresentation must be for the purpose of concealing the former tort. . . .

Plaintiffs argue that the Agency's fraudulent conduct induced them not to file suit. They cite to *General Stencils Inc. v Chiappa* (18 NY2d 125 [1966]), in which plaintiff company sued its bookkeeper for theft over many years. The Court held that the defendant could not assert a statute of limitations defense because she affirmatively and carefully concealed her crime and "produced the long delay between the accrual of the cause of action and the institution of the legal proceeding" (*id.* at 128). In this case, unlike *General Stencils*, nothing in the record indicates that the Agency attempted after the adoption to conceal medical histories to induce plaintiffs to forbear from filing suit alleging negligence or infliction of emotional distress. Plaintiffs did not get in touch with the Agency until 1970, by which time both torts of negligence and infliction of emotional distress were already time-barred. Therefore, even if the Agency made fraudulent misrepresentations, plaintiffs had not been induced to refrain from filing suit, and equitable estoppel is not warranted in this case.

Accordingly, the order of the Appellate Division should be modified, without costs, by granting defendant's motion to dismiss plaintiffs' demand for punitive damages and, as so modified, affirmed. The certified question should be answered in the negative.

Matter of Piel,
10 NY3d 163 (2008)

Writing for a unanimous court, Judge Kaye concluded that children adopted out of a family by strangers do not presumptively share in a class gift to the biological parent's issue where the grantor's intent is indiscernible. The Court of Appeals first addressed the rights of adopted children to class gifts in *Matter of Best* in 1985. Twenty-three years later, the decision in *Matter of Piel* extended the *Best* rule to irrevocable trusts created prior to 1964 and hinged on three significant policy considerations: the legislative objective of fully assimilating adopted children into their adoptive families, the importance of keeping adoption records confidential, and the finality of judicial decrees.

—Introduction by Ralia E. Polechronis, law clerk 2007–2008

In *Matter of Best* (66 NY2d 151 [1985]), this Court relied on strong policy considerations to conclude that a child adopted out of the family by strangers does not presumptively share in a class gift to the biological parent's issue established in the biological grandmother's 1973 testamentary trust. This appeal presents the same scenario, but with class gifts created by 1926 and 1963 irrevocable trusts. Despite the time difference, we conclude that the policy considerations that were determinative in *Best* equally determine the case before us, and that the adopted-out child does not share in the trust proceeds.

Background

Florence Woodward created two irrevocable trusts, one in 1926 and a second in 1963, for the lifetime benefit of her daughter, Barbara W. Piel, and upon her death the trusts directed the trustee (successor-in-interest Fleet Bank) to distribute the principal to Barbara's descendants. Specifically, the 1926 trust net income was to be paid "to her descendants, if any, in equal shares, *per stirpes*." The 1963 trust principal was to be divided equally for "each then living child of hers." Barbara Piel died in July 2003, and in October 2004 Fleet Bank instituted two proceedings for judicial settlement of the final account for each trust. This appeal concerns the distribution of approximately $9.7 million in trust principal.

Barbara Piel gave birth to three daughters. Her first daughter, intervenor-respondent Elizabeth McNabb, was born out of wedlock on August 15, 1955 in Portland, Oregon.

Within days, Barbara signed a consent to adoption, relinquishing her parental rights and agreeing to Elizabeth's adoption by strangers. An Oregon court finalized the adoption in November 1955 and Elizabeth lived her life in Oregon as a member of the Jones family. There is no indication that Florence Woodward knew of Elizabeth's birth or adoption. Barbara's other two daughters, Stobie Piel, born in 1959, and Lila Piel-Ollman, born in 1961, are the children of her marriage to Michael Piel.

Fleet Bank cited Stobie and Lila in the October 2004 proceedings, but failed to include Elizabeth or her children as interested persons. In November 2004 Elizabeth moved for permission to intervene and file objections to the accounts, later joined by her two children. Elizabeth objected to each account because it failed to provide her with a one-third distribution of the principal and income of each trust. The parties cross-moved for summary judgment.

Surrogate's Court denied Elizabeth's motions for summary judgment and granted petitioner's motions seeking dismissal of Elizabeth's objections. The Surrogate relied on this Court's holding in *Matter of Best* that class gifts to the issue of a beneficiary do not presumptively include adopted-out children. The Appellate Division reversed, finding inapplicable the reasoning and policy considerations in *Best* because the Woodward trusts were executed prior to 1963 and 1966 amendments in the Domestic Relations Law that had been effective in *Best*. We now reverse and reinstate the Surrogate's decrees.

Analysis

We begin with the fundamental premise that a court must first look within the four corners of a trust instrument to determine the grantor's intent [citations omitted]. Only if the terms are ambiguous may a court consider extrinsic evidence. Where, as here, there is no evidence of the grantor's intent to include or exclude a person from the class gift, a court may craft general, yet rebuttable, rules of construction based on statutory interpretation and public policy.

We did just that in *Best*, concluding that a nonmarital child adopted at birth by strangers was not entitled to share in a class gift devised by his biological grandmother to her daughter's issue. The testamentary trust in *Best*, executed in 1973, directed the trustee, upon the biological mother's death, to distribute the trust principal equally among her issue. The mother had two sons—David, born out of wedlock in 1952 and immediately adopted by strangers, and Anthony, born in 1963. The question in *Best*, as here, was whether the adopted-out child was an intended beneficiary of the class gift.

There being no evidence of the grantor's intent, the Court considered the effect of David's status as his biological mother's nonmarital, adopted-out child. Although there was a rebuttable presumption that nonmarital children could share in class gifts to their parent's issue, David's status as a nonmarital child became irrelevant to the class disposition because of his status as an adopted-out child. In holding that adopted-out children should be excluded from general class gifts to the biological parent's issue, the Court held that Domestic Relations Law § 117 did not require inclusion of adopted-out children, and that three "[p]owerful policy considerations" militate against inclusion in the class (*Best*, 66 NY2d at 155). We reach those same conclusions here.

Before addressing the policy considerations relied upon in *Best*, we outline the significant change in the Domestic Relations Law that distinguishes the present facts, but not the result.

From 1896 through 1963, an adopted child's right "of inheritance and succession" from the biological family "remain[ed] unaffected" by the order of adoption (Domestic Relations Law § 64, as codified by L 1896, ch 272). Clearly, between 1896 and 1963, New York law permitted an adopted-out child to inherit in intestacy from biological parents [citations omitted]. Unclear, however, is whether an adopted-out child was presumptively included in a class gift to a biological parent's issue, descendants or children.

In 1963 the Legislature amended Domestic Relations Law § 117 by terminating—for the first time since 1896—an adopted child's rights to inheritance and succession from the biological family (L 1963, ch 406). Effective March 1, 1964, the amendments included a savings clause for wills and irrevocable instruments executed prior to that date.

In 1985, when *Best* was decided, Domestic Relations Law § 117 (1) provided that the "rights of an adoptive child to inheritance and succession from and through his natural parents shall terminate upon the making of the order of adoption" (As amended by L 1970, ch 570, § 10). Subdivision (2) clarified that the termination of rights applied "only to the intestate descent and distribution of real and personal property and *shall not affect the right of any child to distribution of property under the will . . . or under any inter vivos instrument . . .* executed by such natural parent or his or her kindred" (as amended by L 1966, ch 14 [emphasis added]). Significantly, the Court determined that this statutory provision "does not mandate that [an adopted-out] child receive a gift by implication," but only protects an adopted-out child's right to inherit when specifically identified in the instrument (*Best*, 66 NY2d at 156). Thus, section 117 (2) merely preserved rights of inheritance expressly intended by the grantor; it did not create additional rights.

As in *Best*, the Domestic Relations Law in effect at the time Florence Woodward executed the trusts does not create rights for an adopted-out child to share in a class gift by implication. *Best* determined that question, concluding that similar statutory language did not create such a right. Nothing in the pre-1964 legislative history or case law, moreover, indicates that an adopted-out child would share in a class gift to a biological parent's issue, descendants or children.

Having determined that the statutory law effective prior to March 1, 1964 does not require a different result, we turn to the strong policy considerations supporting adherence to *Best*.

In excluding adopted-out children from class gifts to the biological parent's issue, the Court highlighted the legislative objective of fully assimilating the adopted child into the adoptive family and, relatedly, the importance of keeping adoption records confidential. From the very inception of the adoption law the Legislature has sought to promote assimilation of the adopted child by providing the new family with the "legal relation of parent and child" (Domestic Relations Law § 64, as codified by L 1896, ch 272; *see also Matter of Cook*, 187 NY 253, 260–261 [1907]). Additionally, by 1924 the Legislature had explicitly recognized the importance of confidentiality in adoption records, and in 1938 it mandated the sealing of those records (*see Matter of Linda F. M.*, 52 NY2d 236, 238 n 1 [1981]). These policy considerations predate the execution of both Woodward trusts.

The facts of this case also compellingly demonstrate the importance of the third policy concern identified in *Best*. As the Court noted, the finality of judicial decrees would be compromised if adopted-out children were included in such class gifts "because there would always lurk the possibility, no matter how remote, that a secret out-of-wedlock child had been adopted out of the family by a biological parent or ancestor of a class of beneficiaries" (66 NY2d at 156). That lurking possibility materialized here. In this case the adopted-out child intervened and relieved the trustee of the duty to identify and cite her. In other cases, neither the family nor the child may be aware of a birth or adoption, thereby placing on a trustee seeking closure the onerous burden of searching out unknown potential beneficiaries.

This case raises additional policy concerns: here we address classes of beneficiaries created in irrevocable instruments prior to 1964. The chances of unearthing adoption decrees potentially dating back to the late 1800s, or of identifying witnesses to recall the details of an adoption, dwindle as time passes. Permitting adopted-out children to participate in a class created by a pre-1964 instrument would pose greater practical problems to the procedural administration of a gift, and—without any legal basis for doing so—would create two classes of beneficiaries, those receiving a gift in an instrument executed before 1964 and those after. The policy interests of finality in court decrees and stability in property titles weigh heavily in favor of consistency with *Best*.

Therefore, we conclude that the *Best* rule of construction also applies to irrevocable trusts executed prior to March 1, 1964. Where, as here, the grantor's intent is indiscernible and the statutory intent at best ambiguous, we conclude that the policy considerations disfavoring inclusion of adopted-out children in such a class determine this case.

Accordingly, the order of the Appellate Division should be reversed, with costs payable out of the trusts to all parties appearing separately and filing separate briefs, and the decrees of Surrogate's Court reinstated.

ARTICLES AND SPEECHES

INTRODUCTION

Judith Kaye's contributions to the law came not only through judicial opinions but also her massive output of articles and addresses. While a judge of the Court of Appeals, she published more than 200 pieces[1]—on a "kaleidoscopic range of topics"[2]—"confront[ing] as educator, scholar and advocate many of the most important issues facing our country."[3] This astounding outpouring of scholarship and commentary is especially remarkable given the arduous administrative responsibilities she assumed after becoming chief judge in 1993.[4]

Kaye's articles (many of which began as lectures) reveal her love of the law and insatiable curiosity about it. Researching and writing them provided an outlet for expression beyond deciding cases and were a welcome respite from the endless flow of appeals and motions that came before the Court of Appeals. They allowed her to test new ideas and keep abreast of emerging trends in society and law. They also earned her a national reputation as a scholarly "judge's judge."[5]

Reprinted here is a representative sample of Kaye's extrajudicial oeuvre. They include important works on substantive legal doctrine and philosophy. Falling into this category is *Dual Constitutionalism in Practice and Principle*,[6] a lecture delivered in 1987 in which

---

1. For a partial list of Judge Kaye's published articles, see Steven C. Krane, *Judith Smith Kaye*, in The Judges of the New York Court of Appeals: A Biographical History 821–24 (Albert M. Rosenblatt ed., 2007).

2. Susan N. Herman, *Portrait of a Judge: Judith S. Kaye, Dichotomies, and State Constitutional Law*, 75 Alb. L. Rev. 1977, 1983 (2012).

3. Sandra Day O'Connor, *A Distinguished Path in Public Service*, 84 N.Y.U. L. Rev. 662, 663 (2009).

4. Henry M. Greenberg, *The Making of a Judge's Judge: Judith S. Kaye's 1987 Cardozo Lecture*, 81 Brooklyn L. Rev. 1363, 1373 (2017). See also Herman, *Portrait of a Judge*, at 1983 ("When you factor in the amount of time that it consumes to be chief judge of all the courts of New York State as Chief Administrative Judge and to have the full workload of a judge on the Court of Appeals, it is nothing less than astonishing that Judge Kaye managed during that same period of time to publish over two hundred articles").

5. See generally, Greenberg, *The Making of a Judge's Judge*.

6. Judith S. Kaye, *Dual Constitutionalism in Practice and Principal*, 61 St. John's L. Rev. 399 (1987), reprinted from 42 Rec. Ass'n B. City N.Y. 285 (1987).

Kaye planted her flag as a leader of independent state constitutional adjudication—the doctrine that state courts should look to their own constitutions instead of limiting their decisions to analysis under the US Constitution.[7] As Susan N. Herman has aptly noted, this lecture "was one of the first to apply their points to the New York State Constitution and to urge New Yorkers to practice the art of state constitutional law."[8]

In *The Human Dimension in Appellate Judging: A Brief Reflection on a Timeless Concern*,[9] Kaye discussed the appropriate role of an appellate judge and articulated what was the guiding light of her jurisprudence: "The danger is not that judges will bring the full measure of their experience, their moral core, their every human capacity to bear in the difficult process of resolving the cases before bear in the difficult process of resolving the cases before them. It seems to me that a far greater danger exists if they do not."[10] An example of an article in which she experimented with a novel theory is *State Constitutional Common Law: The Common Law as a Full Partner in the Protection of Individual Rights*.[11] She examined the relationship of common law and state constitutional law in protecting individual rights, suggesting a partnership between them. Likewise, in *State Courts at the Dawn of a New Century: Common-Law Courts Reading Statutes and Constitutions*,[12] she broke new ground by arguing that state court judges, when construing statutes, have a responsibility to fill in interstices with policy judgments informed by common law principles. "For state judges, schooled in the common law, to refuse to make the necessary policy choices when properly called upon to do so would result in a rigidity and paralysis that the common-law process was meant to prevent," she wrote.[13]

A trailblazing court administrator, Kaye often used law review articles to promote ideas for improving the administration of justice. Included here are two such articles, describing her initiatives for jury reform[14] and problem-solving courts.[15] Also included are pieces addressing subjects about which Kaye had an abiding interest, such as women

---

7. Greenberg, *The Making of a Judge's Judge*, at 1367; see also Ruth Bader Ginsburg, *In Praise of Judith S. Kaye*, 84 N.Y.U. L. Rev. 653, 653–54 (2009) ("[Judge Kaye] . . . understood that New York's constitution and common law had important roles to play in the protection of fundamental human rights. On her watch, the state's constitution and laws were read to advance due process, freedom of expression, freedom from unreasonable searches and seizures, and genuinely equal opportunity. The U.S. Supreme Court's sometimes constricted reading of parallel provisions of the Federal Constitution did not overwhelm her judgment").

8. Herman, *Portrait of a Judge*, at 1993.

9. Judith S. Kaye, *The Human Dimension in Appellate Judging: A Brief Reflection on a Timeless Concern*, 73 Cornell L. Rev. 1004 (1988).

10. Kaye, *The Human Dimension*, at 1015.

11. Judith S. Kaye, *Foreword: The Common Law and State Constitutional Law as Full Partners in the Protection of Individual Rights*, 23 Rutgers L.J. 727 (1992).

12. Judith S. Kaye, *State Courts at the Dawn of a New Century: Common-Law Courts Reading Statutes and Constitutions*, 70 N.Y.U. L. Rev. 1 (1995).

13. Kaye, *State Courts*, at 34.

14. Judith S. Kaye, *My Life as Chief Judge: The Chapter on Juries*, 78 N.Y.S. B. J. 10 (Oct. 2006).

15. Judith S. Kaye, *Delivering Justice Today: A Problem-Solving Approach*, 22 Yale L. & Policy Rev. 125 (2004).

in the law,[16] the rights of children,[17] the role of academic law review writing in judicial decision making,[18] and her judicial heroes, Benjamin Cardozo[19] and William J. Brennan Jr.[20]

This collection of her writings is rounded out with *The Best Oral Argument I (N)ever Made*,[21] a hilarious piece in which Kaye describes a personal experience as a respondent in a federal appellate court. As she describes it, the judges gave her adversary an especially difficult time:

> As my bowed and bloodied adversary took his seat, I gathered up my papers, and my courage, and moved to the lectern. Justice Clark, however, was busily chatting with his colleagues—first one side, then the other. I had just spoken the words, "May it please the Court" when he interrupted. "Counsel," he said, "it will not be necessary to hear further argument. We have decided to affirm."
>
> Wait a minute! No fair! Can I be heard on this? What about my meticulous preparation? What about my fifteen-minute presentation? What about my hand-picked audience?[22]

---

16. Judith S. Kaye, *Women and the Law: The Law Can Change People*, 66 N.Y.U. L. Rev. 1929 (1991); Judith S. Kaye, *Law Is Pivotal in Advancing Women's Rights*, N.Y. Law Journal, Law Day Supp., 81, col. 3 (May 3, 1993).

17. Judith S. Kaye, *The Changing World of Children: The Responsibility of the Law and the Courts*, 65 N.Y.S. B. J. 7 (Nov. 1993).

18. Judith S. Kaye, *One Judge's View of Academic Law Review Writing*, 39 J. Legal Educ. 313, 319 (1989).

19. Judith S. Kaye, *A Lecture about Judge Benjamin Nathan Cardozo*, presented Dec. 2, 1986, at Congregation Shearith Israel, New York City (published by the Congregation and Sephardic House).

20. Judith S. Kaye, *In Memoriam: William J. Brennan, Jr.*, 111 Harv. L. Rev. 14 (1997).

21. Judith S. Kaye, *The Best Oral Argument I (N)ever Made*, 7 J. App. Prac. & Process 191 (2005).

22. Kaye, *Best Oral Argument*, at 192.

A Lecture about
Judge Benjamin Nathan Cardozo

Preparation for this evening has been a labor of love—*first,* love for this great synagogue, its leaders, and the members of this congregation who have made a spiritual and social home for Stephen, for our children, and for me these past 20 years; and *second,* love for the Court of Appeals, the highest court of this State, to which I had the good fortune to be appointed by Governor Mario Cuomo three and one-half years ago. As I listened in services one day to the prayers so often recited for the government, including the magistrates of this City, it occurred to me that this congregation associates and identifies itself with matters of civic concern. It also occurred to me that these two important influences in my own life came together in the person of Benjamin Nathan Cardozo, a member of this congregation, and that you might enjoy discussing a page of contemporary history tonight.

At the outset I should tell you that Judge Cardozo served on the Court of Appeals for 18 years, from 1914 to 1932, becoming Chief Judge in 1927, and then went on to the Supreme Court of the United States in Washington to succeed Justice Oliver Wendell Holmes. As I sit in our courtroom in Albany hearing cases presented, Judge Cardozo's kind countenance gazes down over my right shoulder. But more than his portrait remains in Albany. A great many things around the courthouse were his, including the magnificent oak desk now belonging to the Chief Judge, Sol Wachtler. When Chief Judge Wachtler was proudly showing his Chambers to his wife he said, "Seventy years ago this desk was Cardozo's desk." She responded, "And seventy years from today, that will still be Cardozo's desk." That indicates the esteem in which Judge Cardozo is held in our Court: whoever may have the privilege of using that desk in the future, the imprint will always be his.

A Timeless List of Judicial Qualifications

Law is, of course, central to Judaism, and disputes of all sorts are central to mankind, so it is no surprise that, even before the Written Law was received, the Bible records that Moses sat tirelessly, from morning to evening, as a judge between man and his fellow man. It became necessary to delegate this power to others and, either on the advice of Jethro (his father-in-law), or on the advice of the people, Moses assigned judicial power to other men, made rulers of the people. But while they determined every small matter, the people continued to bring the most difficult disputes before Moses.

It is an awesome responsibility to judge one's own neighbors, to proclaim that one has violated the laws of society and must be punished, or that one is right and the other wrong. The concern from earliest times to this day has been with the qualifications and conduct of those entrusted with the power to pass judgment on their fellow citizens. The persons designated by Moses were to be able men, God fearing, men of truth, hating unjust gain, and wise men, understanding and full of knowledge. Judges were enjoined to hear the causes between brethren and to judge righteously between a man and his brother and between the stranger that is with him; not to respect persons in judgment but to judge the great and small alike; and not to fear any man, for judgment is God's.

Maimonides identified the following qualifications for judges: they must be wise and sensible; learned in the law and full of knowledge, acquainted with a wide range of subjects (such as astronomy, medicine, astrology) and with the ways of others (such as sorcerers and magicians) so as to know how to judge them; not too old, nor a eunuch nor childless man (meaning, to my mind, a person with the qualities of patience and understanding, like a parent); pure in mind, pure of bodily defects, men of stature and imposing appearance; and conversant in several languages so as not to require interpreters. The seven fundamental qualities of a judge were perceived as wisdom, humility, fear of God, disdain of money, love of truth, love of people and a good reputation. According to the Talmud, a judge must have a good eye, a humble soul, be pleasant in company, speak kindly to people, be strict with himself and conquer lustful impulses, and have a courageous heart. Playing cards for money, or other games of chance and lending money on interest disqualify a person as a judge of others; a judge should not engage in manual work so as to expose himself to popular contempt.

Apart from qualifications of persons designated to serve as judges, the Talmud provides that in the actual conduct or discharge of the judicial function, judges must show patience, humility and respect, hear out both sides, be impartial, proceed with care and deliberation, considering again and again before announcing a decision, yet not unduly delay justice. A judge must conduct himself so that justice is not only done but also seen to be done, and is so understood by the participants.

This same concern for the qualities of judges as people and their qualifications to judge others has endured throughout the centuries. Whether judges are designated by their predecessors, or as in more recent times elected by the voters, or appointed by the mayor, the Governor or the President, always the concern is the same. Judges should ideally be wise and knowledgeable, and people of stature, so that their judgments will be sound and so that they will be accepted, obeyed and respected as the law. But beyond that, judges must be utterly impartial, free of bias, corruption, influence of any sort, so that—right or wrong—the judgments they make are genuine judgments of their own. And particularly in view of the responsibility they bear over the lives of others, judges should have humility and understanding.

Judge Cardozo's Personal Background

Throughout the legal community of this nation, indeed of the world, a name that stands as a magnificent symbol among the great judges of contemporary history is Benjamin

Nathan Cardozo, born into this congregation on May 24, 1870, the seventh child born to Albert Jacob and Rebecca Nathan Cardozo. Cardozo's father was vice president of this congregation, and his relationships with the families of the congregation on his father's side, as well as the Nathans on his mother's side, could easily consume the whole evening. The Judge once wrote to a friend that the name Cardozo was very common in Spain and Portugal and that there was even someone of that name who claimed to be the messiah.

Benjamin Cardozo was named for his uncle, Benjamin Nathan, who at the time of Cardozo's birth was president of Shearith Israel as his own father had been; he was also the brother-in-law of the Rev. Dr. J. J. Lyons, then minister of the congregation. Just weeks after Cardozo's birth, his uncle was mysteriously murdered after returning from services to his home on West 23rd Street, and the family was deeply grieved. In the home of Albert and Rebecca Cardozo, no detail of religious observance was neglected. Indeed, when it became necessary for judges to be in the courthouse on Saturdays, Albert Cardozo—then a State Supreme Court judge—sought counsel from the Beth Din in London. The answer came that required public business took precedence, so every Saturday he left shortly before services were completed and walked to the courthouse.

At the outset, I want to mention particularly two of the judicial qualifications identified by Maimonides: that judges be men of imposing appearance, and that they have great stature, for both Cardozo's physical appearance and his reputation before ascending the bench are the subject of wide comment.

Whether he was tall or not seems to have generated a difference of opinion, and may well lie in the eye of the beholder. In physique, he unquestionably seemed thin and frail. The captivating quality of his physical appearance, however, was his strikingly sensitive, magnetizing face. William Meyerowitz, an artist, wrote, "The extreme delicate and sensitive forms of his face, his penetrating eyes under his heavy eyebrows, gave one an impression never to be forgotten." He was of imposing appearance, whatever his size. Though of great personal charm, sweetness and gentleness in his dealings with others, Judge Cardozo lived a life of intense privacy and intellectual meditation, the life of a scholar. He never married—indeed, only one of his siblings married, and she died childless—and for most of his life, until he very reluctantly left New York to live in Washington, he lived with his older sister, Ellen (Nell), for a time in a house on West 75th Street, going out little in the evenings. Through Edgar Nathan, I have met and spoken with family members who as young children knew the judge, and who remember trailing along on weekend walks the judge was fond of taking in the sun along Central Park West. Above all they recall his quiet gentleness, his desire to know what interested them, and his love of young people. While his voice may not have been powerful, his ideas, his use of language and his manner of delivery were compelling. Thus, in physical appearance, bearing and demeanor, Cardozo embodied the timeless qualities for judges: he had an imposing, unforgettable appearance; he was a man of humility; he was pleasant, kind, and a lover of people.

His reputation when first chosen for the bench similarly was exemplary. He was adored by the leaders of the New York Bar. Cardozo was educated at home by Horatio Alger until, at the age of 15, he entered Columbia College where he graduated with high honors, and thereafter secured a master's degree in Political Science and attended Columbia Law School. He withdrew two years later—one year short of graduation—and entered his brother's commercial law practice, where he remained for the next two decades. In those years he acquired a great reputation as a lawyer's lawyer, a walking encyclopedia of law. His knowledge of the law was astounding; he could prepare a brief, including references to all pertinent cases and materials, simply from memory. He was a great student of literature and philosophy and a lover of the Classics. He truly needed no interpreters of foreign tongues, for he read widely in Greek, German, French, Italian, and other languages. In the year 1913 he was nominated by a fusion group and elected as a judge of the State's Supreme Court—the general entry level trial court of this State. Despite his ardent support from the Bar, political forces made the election close. Cardozo himself attributed his victory to the support of Italian-Americans who, he said, voted for him believing from his name that he was of Italian descent. Cardozo's election to the Supreme Court was particularly meaningful to him, for that is the court from which his father had resigned in 1873 under charges of corruption. Cardozo bore that stain like a personal wound and several times expressed the desire to restore his family's honor.

Cardozo never filled out his term as a trial judge—indeed, he never really began it—because he was immediately designated by Governor Glynn to serve on the Court of Appeals. Years later the Governor said he was prouder of that designation than any other act of his career. Judge Cardozo was a member of that Court, and then Chief Judge, until he was appointed by President Hoover to the Supreme Court of the United States, where he served a brief six years, until his death at the age of 68 in 1938. He was buried alongside his family in Cypress Hills Cemetery. At his funeral, there was no eulogy, and no word of English. While praises of Cardozo were received the world over, at his funeral, as he had requested, only the traditional Sephardic prayers were recited. As Irving Lehman (himself later a distinguished Chief Judge of the Court of Appeals) said of him in a memorial service at the Bar Association:

> There is little of drama in this brief record of Justice Cardozo's life. It was a life of fruitful thought and study, not of manifold activities. Quiet, gentle and reserved, from boyhood till death he walked steadily along the path of reason, seeking the goal of truth; and none could lure him from that path.

An Important Moment in Synagogue History

Before speaking of Judge Cardozo's illustrious career on the bench, I want to refer to a particular affiliation with this synagogue at an important moment in its history. While Cardozo had close ties of family and friendship to Shearith Israel, while we know that he was raised in a religious atmosphere, maintained the dietary laws in his home, and was confirmed by Dr. Mendes, he apparently had little role in the rich history of this synagogue. Whether this related to the death of his mother when he was only nine years old, followed by the death of his father when he was 15, or was somehow connected with his father's earlier difficulties, I do not know. Cardozo, of course, remained an Elector. On June 5, 1895, he appeared at a Special Meeting of Electors, held in the synagogue's vestry rooms on 5th Avenue and 19th Street, to consider particularly the subject of the new synagogue—the building, seating within the building, the introduction of an organ, changes in the form of worship (including more English) and all other pertinent subjects. This was, in the words of Dr. Pool, a "crucial moment for Shearith Israel."

Dr. Gratz Nathan offered a resolution seconded by Harmon Hendricks that in the new synagogue the sexes shall sit together. After several speeches in support of this resolution, the minutes reflect that the Honorable Adolphus S. Solomon, Benjamin Nathan Cardozo and the Rev. Dr. Pereira Mendes spoke against it, "Mr. Cardozo making a long address impressive in ability and eloquence." What a great pity these remarks are unpreserved, for they undoubtedly brought together Cardozo's Jewish learning, his contemporary views, great command of the English language, and his skills as an advocate. He spoke for an hour or more, described by his biographer George Hellman as the most dramatic episode of his undramatic life. The resolution was overwhelmingly defeated (73–7–6). Dr. Pool also mentions in his book that Cardozo, then Chief Judge of the Court of Appeals, presided at a ceremony honoring Dr. Mendes in the year 1927.

I have often wondered why Judge Cardozo appears in the extensive history of this congregation only to make along, impassioned speech against mixed seating, and to honor Dr. Mendes. The second seems readily understandable, since he obviously maintained a close attachment to Dr. Mendes, and close friendships with members of the congregation, so many of whom were his own relatives. And certainly that also explains in part his desire that the bedrock of his family, a unifying factor for hundreds of years, should undergo absolutely no change. But I was also struck by the following passage in a biography of Cardozo that I recently read, for it offers a further insight into his impassioned defense of the traditional ways:

> Cardozo had reverence for the past. He *was,* it must not be forgotten, an aristocrat by descent. Certainty, order, coherence, that make for the "symmetry of the law" meant to him what a sonnet means to a poet. [George S. Hellman, *Benjamin N. Cardozo: American Judge* (Whittlesey House, 1940), 92]

Cardozo's Genius as a Judge

What, then, was Cardozo's genius as a judge? While he may have advocated strict adherence to traditional ways in matters of faith and worship, that assuredly was not his view in matters of secular law. Those who know of Cardozo's contributions to the law know that while he loved form, he detested empty formalism. While he appreciated certainty and stability in the law, his place in history is as a visionary, innovative judge, with an uncommon mastery of the law and of the English language. What made him a *good* judge—to draw again from the list of the ideal judicial qualities—were his humility, his self-effacement, his reputation and stature, his imposing appearance, his love of people. But the remaining qualities from that list are what made him a *great* judge: his wisdom, extraordinary learning of the law and deep knowledge of a wide variety of subjects, great industry and dedication, utter purity of mind and devotion to a just result, and courageous heart. The Talmud says that a judge must conduct himself so that justice is not only done but also seems to be done: in his power to perceive and to extract the principles of the law and express them clearly, strikingly, even poetically, Cardozo left no doubt that justice was done.

Judge Cardozo's genius as a judge lies both in his judicial opinions and his writings about the law.

An Aside about the Court of Appeals

The Court of Appeals is solely an appellate court, not a trial court. The range of problems coming before the Court is equal only to the range of the human imagination. The intention is that, as the court of last resort in this State, the Court of Appeals should settle and declare the law, with decisions in particular cases to have wide application. In this Cardozo excelled.

While we have important constitutional issues to decide, the docket of the Court of Appeals also requires the application of the common law, or judge made law, to everyday problems—breaches of contract, disputes regarding real estate and other property, personal injuries, family controversies, such as matrimonial and child custody matters. Because of the centrality of religion to our everyday lives, every now and again there is even a case touching on religion. For example, a few years ago the Court considered whether as a matter of public policy the agreement of two parties to appear before a Beth Din, which was contained in a Ketubah, might be enforced in our courts by compelling the appearance of defendant-husband before the Beth Din; we held that—just as with any other contract to submit a dispute to a non-judicial forum—it could be. We have been called upon to deal with property disputes within churches. Just now we have pending before us a case where the constitutionality of a criminal statute has been challenged making the disturbance of a religious service more serious than disorderly conduct generally. With the constitutional separation of church and state, a guiding principle in all such disputes is that courts should not resolve controversies in a matter requiring consideration of religious doctrine, but may apply neutral principles of law. Thus, secular judicial involvement is permitted so long as it can be accomplished in purely secular terms.

The business of the Court of Appeals is largely in matters of development and application of the common law, judge-made law. Justice Stone of the United States Supreme Court described the common law as law made by generations of judges, each professing to be a pupil, yet each in fact a builder who has contributed his few bricks and a little mortar, under the illusion that he has added nothing. Applying that definition, it is plain that Judge Cardozo was the master builder: in fact, he built a vast metropolis of durable brick edifices in the law.

Legal systems are built on ultimate values which remain unchanged but are subject to interpretation and re-interpretation as society changes. Judge-made law is the contemporary commentary to the immutable principles, the ultimate values. Today in the law, for example, courts deal with issues involving surrogate mothering, genetic engineering, massive toxic wastes, and AIDS—subjects unheard of decades ago—yet the settled precedents are always the touchstone. The nearly seven decades of Judge Cardozo's life spanned a period of enormous social change—society became more highly industrialized, we had a great war and a great depression—and his genius was in maintaining the order, certainty and regularity of the law while at the same time recognizing that no judge-made rule can or should survive when it has gone out of harmony with the thoughts and customs of the people. He applied existing doctrines to contemporary problems with wisdom and discretion, leaving an indelible mark in the evolutionary process of the law.

Cardozo's Wide Impact on the Law

It is not the purpose of this talk to analyze particular decisions in the law of torts, or the law of contracts, or to recite the opinions written by Judge Cardozo that come quickly to mind and can virtually be quoted by students of the law. Cardozo's impact as felt in every field of the law. Sixty years ago, he perceived, for example, that an automobile was a potentially dangerous instrument and sustained recovery by an injured person on a broader basis than had previously been recognized; others on the Court would have denied recovery, not seeing the potential danger because the same automobile was travelling at a speed of only eight miles per hour, a little faster than the horse and carriage. Elsewhere in the law, Cardozo held the fiduciary to the highest ethical standards; he extended the reaches of liability in some areas of law, and yet limited recovery against public utilities and others on policy grounds where liability otherwise would be crushing. He found implied promises and constructive trusts to achieve the just result in contract cases, and laid sturdy foundations for development of the law away from mechanical application of principles that barred enforcement of promises. And always his opinions were of incomparable beauty, because of his ability and because he believed that judicial writing was also literature and that form of expression had importance.

Apart from his opinions, Cardozo's contribution to society lies in his lectures and other scholarly writings, particularly his writings about the philosophy of law. His fascinating exposition of how judges decide cases remains a classic of legal literature. After first explaining that the result in most cases is foreordained by precedents of the past, Cardozo writes that he has become more and more reconciled to uncertainty: "I have grown to see that the process in its highest reaches is not discovery but creation; and that the doubts and misgivings, the hopes and fears, are part of the travail of mind, the pangs of death and the pangs of birth, in which principles that have served their day expire, and new principles are born." The confession that judges actually *made* law instead of simply, applying existing precedents, was regarded, as one commentator observed, as a legal version of hard-core pornography; a less saintly man, he adds, would have found himself close to impeachment for such expressions [Grant Gilmore, *The Ages of American Law* (New Haven, CT: Yale University Press, 1977), 77]. To this day—more than 60 years later—Cardozo's exposition of the nature of the judicial process and the growth of the law remains new and exciting.

Cardozo also wrote profoundly of the limits of the law: "The law will not hold the crowd to the morality of saints and seers." He recognized that however much one might wish in an ideal society, the law cannot always protect life and limb at the expense of property. If the demands of social utility are sufficiently urgent, and if the operation of an existing rule is sufficiently productive of hardship, utility will triumph. Rules, however well established, must be revised when found after fair trial to be inconsistent with the ends they were meant to serve.

A Choice of Enduring Values

Among Judge Cardozo's writings I particularly enjoy is a commencement address delivered at the Jewish Institute of Religion on his 61st birthday, in 1931. He began with an apology for attempting to address a group of future rabbis on the subject of values, but said he had been assured that anyone would be listened to who had been able to hold fast to certain values transcending the physical and temporal. He spoke that day of choosing values, first telling the parable of Tycho Brahe, born in Denmark and educated in Copenhagen, a student of the stars. For 25 years he had worked devotedly in an observatory built for him by King Frederick, plotting the stars, but when Frederick died his son—Prince Christian—mocked and challenged his labors as worthless because there was little tangible, little to see for so much labor, and the Prince sent him into exile. Is this all you have done? the Prince asked, when shown 700 tables of stars. Tycho responded, Not all, I hope, for I think before I die I shall have worked a thousand such tables, which will bring those after me closer to their goal. "Resounding through the centuries," Cardozo says, "I hear familiar echoes. Never a philosopher has lived, nor a saint nor a scientist nor an artist, but has been summoned to a like proof—to show the value for today—not the value for the unplumbed future, but the value for today." All the study, all the wisdom stored in books, he continues, is wasted except as it strengthens a person to choose among conflicting and competing values. "What does a ministry of religion mean if it does not mean the preaching and living of that truth?" he asks.

> You are going forth today as preachers of the eternal values. You will find mockery and temptation on the highways, and for the values that you hold to be eternal many a tinsel token will be offered in exchange. Sycophants and time-servers and courtiers and all the lovers of the flesh pots will assail you with warnings that you are squandering the happy days under the sun. . . . Then will be the time when you will need to bethink yourselves of the values that were chosen by the prophets and saints of Israel, and by the goodly and noble of every race and clime. You will remember in that hour the choice of Tycho Brahe. When the course is finished, when the task is ended, when the books are closed, may the last appraisal of all values reveal his choice as yours.

There can be no question that, when the books were closed on Judge, Chief Judge, Justice Cardozo, his choice was the lasting human values and not the temptations of the moment. There have been many illustrious members in the long history of this congregation, including judges. Cardozo stands among them both for the recognition he achieved and for his choice of enduring values.

Dual Constitutionalism in Practice and Principle*

In this year of celebration of the federal Constitution's 200th anniversary, we appropriately also focus attention on our state Constitution, adopted ten years earlier. Given that we *have* both a state and federal Constitution, a state and federal Bill of Rights, and state and federal courts that are sworn to uphold them, the relation and accommodation between the two is naturally a subject of interest.

Of particular concern are provisions that are parallel if not identical in both constitutions, including, for example, such significant protections of the Bill of Rights as the right of free speech; the right to counsel, due process and equal protection of the law; and the protection against unreasonable searches and seizures. Should state courts decide such common issues on a state or federal basis? Should they read their own constitutions to provide greater protection than found under the equivalent provisions of the federal charter, or should they simply conform to federal precedents? I would like to explore these questions both as a matter of history and as a matter of theory.

*42 Record of the Association of the Bar of the City of New York 285 (April 1987). Presented February 26, 1987, as the Forty-First Benjamin N. Cardozo Lecture at the House of the Association. Reprinted with the permission of the Association of the Bar of the City of New York. The author is grateful for the assistance of Robert J. Kochenthal and Eric B. Schnurer in the preparation of this article. She also wishes to thank Chief Judge Sol Wachtler, the State Commission on the Bicentennial of the United States Constitution which he chairs, and Larry Hackman, State Archivist, for the presence at the Cardozo Lecture of our four original state Constitutions (see n. 37 *infra*), reinforcing in a most tangible and exciting way that we—the citizens, lawyers and judges of today—are the true keepers and guardians of our Constitutions.

Much has been written on the recent emergence of state constitutional law.[1] The literature indicates that, more often now, state courts are deciding that standards set by the United States Supreme Court under the federal Constitution do not satisfy the more rigorous requirements of similar provisions of state constitutions, as to which state courts are in general the final arbiters.[2] Some describe this as a new judicial federalism; others, more pejoratively, as an unprincipled reaction to particular criminal law decisions and perceived directions of the Supreme Court.

History tells us that, whether in civil or criminal matters, the independent protection of individual rights under state constitutions is not new; nor is it an illegitimate assumption of authority by state courts. Ironically, in this bicentennial year the emergence of state constitutional law is in many respects a return to a philosophy of federalism similar— although admittedly not identical—to that of the framers.

When the framers gathered in Philadelphia, each of the Colonies already had adopted a constitution setting out the fundamental terms by which it was to be governed. In New York, our Constitution, drawn up under the stress of war and revolution, was adopted on April 20, 1777.

The state charters for many years were the sole protection against governmental overreaching. Indeed, when the federal Constitution was first drawn up, a Bill of Rights was viewed as unnecessary, in part because state constitutions already safeguarded the rights of citizens. And when the Bill of Rights was later added, it was taken from and actually mirrored corresponding state enactments.[3] Despite this deliberate duplication, there was no thought that state constitutions were thereby superseded or their Bills of Rights rendered redundant. To the contrary, the contemplation was that the states would remain the principal protectors of individual rights—the "immediate and visible guardian

---

1. *See, e.g.,* Bamberger, *Recent Developments in State Constitutional Law* (P.L.I. 1985) (hereafter *Recent Developments*); Brennan, *State Constitutions and the Protection of Individual Rights,* 90 Harv. L. Rev. 489 (1977) (hereafter *State Constitutions*); Collins, *State Constitutional Law,* Nat'l L. J., Supp., Sept. 29, 1986; Collins and Galie, *Models of Post-Incorporation Judicial Review: 1985 Survey of State Constitutional Individual Rights Decisions,* 55 U. Cinn. L. Rev. 317 (1986); Countryman, *Why a State Bill of Rights?,* 45 Wash. L. Rev. 454 (1970) (hereafter *State Bill*); Developments in State Constitutional Law: The Williamsburg Conference (West 1985) (hereafter *Williamsburg*); *Symposium: The Emergence of State Constitutional Law,* 63 Tex. L. Rev. 959 (1985); Note, *Developments in the Law—The Interpretation of State Constitutional Rights,* 95 Harv. L. Rev. 1324 (1982).

2. State court decisions interpreting the federal Constitution are subject to review by the United States Supreme Court. However, state court decisions—or for that matter, federal court decisions—interpreting state constitutions are subject to Supreme Court review only for federal law violations. *See* Peters, *State Constitutional Law: Federalism in the Common Law Tradition,* 84 Mich. L. Rev. 583, 588 (1986).

3. I B. Schwartz, The Bill of Rights: A Documentary History, 199, 286, 383 (1971), II Schwartz, *id.* at 1204; Oakes, *The Proper Role of the Federal Courts in Enforcing the Bill of Rights,* 54 N.Y.U.L. Rev. 911 (1979). *See also, Project Report: Toward an Activist Role for State Bills of Rights,* 8 Harv. C. R. C. L. L. Rev. 271, 275 (1973) (hereafter *Project Report*); Peters, *Remarks at the Second Circuit Judicial Conference,* _____ F.R. D. _____ (Sept. 5, 1986) (hereafter *Remarks*).

of life and property"[4]—with the powers of the national government principally directed to external objects such as war, peace and foreign commerce.[5]

The framers designed a system of dual federalism—that the federal government and the states constituted separate sovereignties, each supreme within its sphere. For the first century of our history, the federal Bill of Rights was a protection solely in relation to federal authorities; state constitutions protected the People from abuse by state authorities.[6] *Barron v. Baltimore*,[7] decided by the United States Supreme Court in 1833, exemplifies this design. By a series of ordinances, the City of Baltimore had redirected the course of several streams so that they ran into a harbor near a wharf owned by Barron. Barron proved to the satisfaction of the trial court that the soil and debris carried down by the streams made the harbor so shallow that his pier became unusable. After losing before a Maryland court of appeals, Barron appealed to the United States Supreme Court, arguing that the City of Baltimore had taken his property without just compensation in violation of the fifth amendment. In a unanimous decision written by Chief Justice Marshall, himself a great federalist, the Court dismissed the appeal for want of jurisdiction. The fifth amendment—and by analogy, the entire Bill of Rights—in Chief Justice Marshall's words, "is intended solely as a limitation on the exercise of power by the government of the United States, and is not applicable to the legislation of the states."[8] As the Court wrote:

> Each state established a constitution for itself, and, in that constitution, provided such limitations and restrictions on the powers of its particular government as its judgment dictated.

∿

> In their several constitutions, [the states] have imposed such restrictions on their respective governments, as their own wisdom suggested; such as they deemed most proper for themselves. It is a subject on which they judge exclusively.[9]

The state courts, by the same token, understood that they were the arbiters of their own constitutions. In New York, as early as 1856, in *Wynehamer v. People*,[10] the New York

---

4. The Federalist Papers, No. 17 (A. Hamilton).

5. *See, e.g.,* the Federalist Papers, Nos. 45 and 46 (J. Madison). *See also* Mosk, *State Constitutionalism: Both Liberal and Conservative,* 63 Tex. L. Rev. 1081, 1082 (1985) (hereafter *Liberal and Conservative*).

6. *Massachusetts v. Upton,* 466 U.S. 727, 738–39 (1984) (Stevens, J., concurring); Baker, *The Ambiguous Independent and Adequate State Ground in Criminal Cases: Federalism Along a Mobius Strip,* 19 Ga. L. Rev. 799, 824 (1985) (hereafter *State Ground*); Pollock, *Adequate and Independent State Grounds as a Means of Balancing the Relationship between State and Federal Courts,* 63 Tex. L. Rev. 977, 978 (1985) (hereafter *State and Federal Courts*).

7. 32 U.S. (7 Pet.) 243 (1833).

8. *Id.* at 250.

9. *Id.* at 247–48.

10. 13 N.Y. 378 (1856).

State Court of Appeals struck down a statute as violative of the due process clause of the state Constitution. That case involved an 1855 "Act for the prevention of intemperance, pauperism and crime," which made unlawful the possession and sale of "intoxicating liquors." The Court found that the Act constituted a deprivation of property without due process of law, writing that it was:

> not insensible to the delicacy and importance of the duty [it assumed] in overruling an act of the legislature, believed by so many intelligent and good men to afford the best remedy for great and admitted evils in society; but we cannot forget that the highest function entrusted to us is that of maintaining inflexibly the fundamental law. And believing . . . that the prohibitory act transcends the constitutional limits of the legislative power, it must be adjudged to be void.[11]

In the wake of the Civil War and in a spirit of nationalism, the fourteenth amendment was adopted. Although its full reach was not immediately manifest, the fourteenth amendment eventually changed half of the *Barron* formula. After a false start in the *Slaughter-House Cases*,[12] the Supreme Court began repeatedly suggesting that the due process clause of the fourteenth amendment applied to and limited the exercise of power by the states.

As the federal Constitution marked its centennial, the Supreme Court had occasion to consider whether a Kansas statute barring the manufacture and sale of "intoxicating liquors" constituted a denial of due process.[13] Despite counsel's reliance on that leading New York State case—*Wynehamer v. People*, seemingly right on point—the Supreme Court held that it did not. The Court, however, made clear its belief that the fourteenth amendment applied to the states, specifically noting that state legislation would "come within" the amendment if "it is apparent that [the legislation's] real object is not to protect the community, or to promote the general wellbeing, but, under the guise of police regulation, to deprive the owner of his liberty and property, without due process of law."[14]

By the end of the century the Supreme Court's oft-repeated suggestion[15] ripened into a holding. The Court struck down, as violative of the federal due process clause, a Louisiana statute regulating the issuance of marine insurance, ushering in the "*Lochner* era" of substantive due process.[16] Although that era ended dramatically in

---

11. *Id.* at 405–6.

12. In the *Slaughter-House Cases*, 83 U.S. (16 Wall.) 36 (1873), the Supreme Court narrowly construed the fourteenth amendment's "privileges or immunities" clause, which provides that "No State shall make or enforce any law which shall abridge the privileges or immunities of citizens of the United States." The Court held that "the entire domain of the privileges and immunities of citizens of the States . . . lay within the constitutional and legislative power of the States, and without that of the Federal government." *Id.* at 77.

13. *Mugler v. Kansas*, 123 U.S. 623 (1887).

14. *Id.* at 669.

15. *See Railroad commission Cases*, 116 U.S. 307 (1886); *Barbier v. Connolly*, 113 U.S. 27 (1885); *Hurtado v. California*, 110 U.S. 516 (1884); *Munn v. Illinois*, 94 U.S. 113 (1876).

16. *Allgeyer v. Louisiana*, 165 U.S. 578 (1897). The "*Lochner* era" is of course named for *Lochner v. New York*, 198 U.S. 45 (1905), in which the court invalidated a New York law setting maximum working hours for bakers.

1937,[17] two legacies remain viable to this day. *First*, the federal due process clause applies to the states and sets a floor below which state conduct may not fall. And *second*, one of the tasks of the Supreme Court is to establish where that floor should be set. To this extent, the fourteenth amendment modified the vision of two independent sovereigns described by Chief Justice Marshall in *Barron v. Baltimore*. However, for present purposes, it is more important to recognize what the fourteenth amendment did *not* do: it did not alter the other half of the *Barron* formula, that each state by its own constitution may limit and restrict its own powers as its wisdom suggests.

In short, as a historical matter, state constitutions exist and function independently of the federal Constitution. As the New York Court of Appeals concluded in 1911, Supreme Court interpretations of the fourteenth amendment are simply not "controlling of our construction of our own Constitution."[18] Decades after the adoption of the fourteenth amendment, state and federal courts continued to function as a partnership of equals in the protection of constitutional rights.

While dual federalism remained theoretically intact, one of the two partners thereafter began to play a more dominant role. This trend may, for convenience, be dated to 1938—when the Supreme Court suggested in *Carolene Products*[19] that the specific prohibitions of the first ten amendments might be embraced within the fourteenth amendment and apply to the states.[20] The process of incorporation accelerated sharply during the 1960s, until by 1969 all or part of the first,[21] fourth,[22] fifth,[23] sixth[24] and eighth[25] amendments were applied to the states.

---

17. Compare *West Coast Hotel v. Parrish*, 300 U.S. 379 (1937) (upholding minimum wage legislation) with *Morehead v. New York ex rel. Tipaldo*, 298 U.S. 587 (1936) (invalidating similar legislation).

18. *Ives v. South Buffalo Ry. Co.*, 201 N.Y. 271, 317 (1911).

19. *United States v. Carolene Prods. Co.*, 304 U.S. 144, 152 n. 4 (1938).

20. *But see Chicago, B & Q.R. v. Chicago*, 166 U.S. 144, 226 (1897) (due process clause protects right to just compensation); *Fishe v. Kansas*, 274 U.S. 380 (1927) (due process clause protects freedom of speech); *Near v. Minnesota*, 283 U.S. 697 (1931) (same); *DeJonge v. Oregon*, 299 U.S. 353 (1937) (freedom of assembly). Justice Black's well-known view that the fourteenth amendment guaranteed that "no state could deprive its citizens of the privileges and protections of the Bill of Rights," *Adamson v. California*, 332 U.S. 46, 74–75 (1947) (Black, J., dissenting), did not prevail.

21. *See Everson v. Board of Ed.*, 330 U.S. 1 (1947) (non-establishment of religion); *Cantwell v. Connecticut*, 310 U.S. 296 (1940) (free exercise of religion); *Hague v. CIO*, 307 U.S. 496 (1939) (right to petition); *DeJonge v. Oregon*, 299 U.S. 353 (1937) (freedom of assembly); *Near v. Minnesota*, 283 U.S. 697 (1931) (freedom of press); *Fiske v. Kansas*, 274 U.S. 380 (1927) (freedom of speech).

22. *See Mapp v. Ohio*, 367 U.S. 643 (1961) (exclusionary rule); *Wolf v. Colorado*, 338 U.S. 25 (1949) (unreasonable search and seizure).

23. *See Benton v. Maryland*, 395 U.S. 784 (1969) (double jeopardy); *Malloy v. Hogan*, 378 U.S. 1 (1964) (self-incrimination).

24. *See Duncan v. Louisiana*, 391 U.S. 145 (1968) (right to trial by jury in criminal cases); *Washington v. Texas*, 388 U.S. 14 (1967) (right to compulsory process); *Klopfer v. North Carolina*, 386 U.S. 213 (1967) (right to speedy trial); *Pointer v. Texas*, 380 U.S. 400 (1965) (right to confrontation); *Gideon v. Wainright*, 372 U.S. 335 (1963) (right to counsel); *In re Oliver*, 333 U.S. 257 (1948) (right to public trial).

25. *Robinson v. California*, 370 U.S. 660 (1962) (cruel and unusual punishment). Provisions of the first eight amendments that have not been made applicable to the states through incorporation but are found in the New York State Bill of Rights include the fifth amendment right not to be tried except upon indictment by a grand jury, N.Y. Const. art 1, § 6; *see People v. Iannone*, 45 N.Y. 2d 589, 593 n.3 (1978); the seventh amendment right to trial by jury in a civil case, N.Y. Const. art. 1, § 2; and the eighth

At the same time—and expressing dissatisfaction with many state courts' discharge of their "front-line responsibility for the enforcement of constitutional rights"[26]—the Supreme Court began actively widening and raising the federal floor. Individual rights became increasingly federalized. The broadening application of provisions of the federal Bill of Rights to the states "made U.S. Supreme Court law the touchstone for much of the nation's constitutional decision making concerning individual rights."[27] These are the years in which many of us received our professional education and training. As lawyers, we have acquired an easy familiarity with the federal Bill of Rights and have grown accustomed to controlling federal precedents in the adjudication of constitutional rights of the citizens of this State, even though this is in fact a relatively new development in our nation's history.

In our dual system, the Supreme Court's growing dominance necessarily affected constitutional law as applied by state courts. While state courts have at all times been important contributors to the body of constitutional law, they too became involved in the application of federal law. So long as the federal floor, or national minimum, was satisfied, state courts could have imposed ceilings in the form of greater rights applicable within their own borders under their own constitutions, and these judgments would then have been conclusive, beyond Supreme Court review.[28] But as a practical matter, the federal guarantees as then interpreted by the Supreme Court in general not only satisfied but often exceeded their view of the requirements of comparable state provisions.[29]

This same fundamental dualism has more recently sparked the heightened interest in state constitutional law, but now it is the state courts that are expressing dissatisfaction

---

amendment right to nonexcessive bail, N.Y. Const. art. 1, § 5; *see People ex rel. Klein v. Krueger*, 25 N.Y. 2d 497, 499 n. 1 (1969). *See* Countryman, *State Bill, supra* note 1, at 466.

26. *Gideon v. Wainwright*, 372 U.S. at 351 (Harlan, J. concurring); Brennan, *The Bill of Rights and the States*, 36 N.Y.U.L. Rev. 761, 777–78 (1961); *Project Report, supra* note 3, at 274; Countryman, *State Bill, supra* note 1, at 455; "The states had achieved a dismal record of employing their state constitutions. As Professor Paulsen wrote in 1951, '[I]f our liberties are not protected in Des Moines, the only hope is in Washington.'" Mosk, *Liberal and Conservative, supra* note 5, at 1084. *See also* Lukas, Common Ground: A Turbulent Decade in the Lives of Three American Families 222 (Vantage ed. 1986).

27. Collins and Galie, *Judicial Review, supra* note 1, at 322. To give but one example of the expansion, in the 1920s the Supreme Court upheld, as consistent with the first amendment, state statutes prohibiting the advocacy of criminal anarchy. *See Whitney v. California*, 274 U.S. 357 (1927); *Gulow v. New York*, 268 U.S. 652 (1925). Although the progression was not smooth (*see, e.g., Dennis v. United States*, 341 U.S. 494 [1951]), by the late 1950s the Court had moved toward a distinction between advocacy of doctrine and unprotected advocacy of action. *See Yates v. United States*, 354 U.S. 298 (1957). This trend culminated in 1969 in *Brandenburg v. Ohio*, 395 U.S. s444 (1969) (per curiam) overruling *Whitney v. California*, 274 U.S. 357 (1927), in which the Court held that the first amendment barred the states from penalizing advocacy "directed to inciting or producing imminent lawless action" unless it was "likely to incite or produce such action." *Id*. al 447. *See also* Brennan, *State Constitutions, supra* note 1, at 490, 493.

28. *See, e.g., PruneYard Shopping Center v. Robins*, 447 U.S. 74, 81 (1980); *Oregon v. Hass*, 420 U.S. 714, 719 (1978); *Sibron v. New York*, 392 U.S. 40, 60 (1968).

29. *People v. Adams*, 53 N.Y.2d 241, 250 (1981).

with the Supreme Court's role in the enforcement of constitutional rights.[30] While state courts interpreting parallel provisions of their charters may have been satisfied in particular cases that the federal floor also established their own ceiling, reformulation of the floor cannot help but bring the rest of the structure into question. The point to be drawn from history, however, is that in a system of government that is founded upon dual sovereignties, independent state court adjudications based on state constitutions—*two* layers of constitutional protection—are hardly revolutionary or illegitimate.

This heightened interest in state constitutional law has gained impetus from other developments in the United States Supreme Court, not the least of which have been the writings of individual Justices.[31] Of the past few years, to my mind a most significant development in this regard has been the 1983 Supreme Court decision in *Michigan v. Long*.[32]

The question of when a state court judgment is subject to Supreme Court review, and the source of such authority, is not easily answered, except we know that as a matter of policy a state judgment will not be reviewed if it rests on a nonfederal ground which is independent of the federal question in the case and adequate to support the judgment.[33] What is an "adequate and independent" state ground has itself remained elusive, and appears to have been determined by any of several techniques applied on an *ad hoc* and largely unexplained basis. Until *Michigan v. Long*, however, it was safe to assume that any lack of clarity as to the basis of a state court judgment would be resolved in favor of the state court as the final arbiter, and against further review. *Michigan v. Long*, of course, reversed this historical presumption. As a result, more state court judgments extending the rights of its citizens will, for the time being, be brought under Supreme Court scrutiny.

However much one might be discomfited by this shift or by the new methodology, *Michigan v. Long* has sharply focused the issue; it has staked out the state courts' sphere of autonomy; and it has given the state courts the ability to assure that they remain the ultimate arbiters of state law decisions. Where a state court makes clear that its judgment rests on bona fide separate, adequate and independent grounds, the Supreme Court has declared that it will not review that decision. As Justice O'Connor wrote: "We believe that such an approach will provide state judges with a clearer opportunity to develop

---

30. *See, e.g., People v. Disbrow*, 545 P.2d 272 (Cal. 1976), and particularly cases cited in *id.*, at 281; *State v. Ball*, 471 A.2d 347 (N.H. 1983); *State v. Hunt*, 450 A.2d 952 (N.J. 1982); *People v. P.J. Video, Inc.*, 68 N.Y.2d 296 (1986) *cert. denied*, _____U.S._____(1987); *and see* Brennan, *State Constitutions*, *supra* note 1, at 498–502.

31. *See, e.g., Massachusetts v. Upton*, 466 U.S. at 735 (Stevens, J., concurring); *Michigan v. Mosley*, 423 U.S. 96, 120 (1975) (Brennan, J., dissenting); Brennan, *State Constitutions, supra* note 1. "In recent years particularly the Supreme Court has emphasized and encouraged this and related aspects of Federalism by exercising special restraint in prescribing constitutional rules of procedure which would displace or foreclose development of State rules specifically tailored to local problems and experiences." *Adams*, 53 N.Y.2d at 250.

32. 463 U.S. 1032 (1983).

33. The reason for the restraint is that a Supreme Court decision on the federal question would otherwise merely be an advisory opinion. Pollock, *State and Federal Courts, supra* note 6, at 980. *See generally*, Baker, *State Ground, supra* note 6.

state jurisprudence unimpeded by federal interference, and yet will preserve the integrity of federal law."[34]

Justice Stevens has added a further ingredient: that it is not only fundamental that state courts be left free to develop their own jurisprudence but also, from the federal perspective, desirable and important that they do so. Justice Stevens in a recent concurrence took the Massachusetts Supreme Court to task for premising a decision on federal grounds, needlessly inviting Supreme Court review and ultimately a remand for decision on the stale ground, when it might have finally resolved the issue in the first instance under its own Constitution.[35] In charging the Massachusetts court with "a misconception of our constitutional heritage and the respective jurisdiction of state and federal courts,"[36] Justice Stevens echoed a sentiment found in our earliest history, that the states in our federal system are the primary guardian of the liberty of the people. This is a premise of our constitutional system.

As a matter of history, therefore, it is hardly a novel doctrine that underlies contemporary interest in independent state court adjudication of concurrent constitutional provisions.

II

Against this background, I would like to turn to New York State in particular.

As an expression of inviolable principle and fundamental law, the New York Constitution is a curious document—particularly when laid against the United States Constitution. I mean this in two respects.

First, the state Constitution is long and filled with detail, like a volume of miscellaneous statutes, specifying even—as a matter of constitutional dimension—the width of certain ski trails. The article dealing with local finances (article VIII) is alone longer than the entire federal Constitution. Since its enactment 210 years ago, it has swelled in size and scope, particularly in the aftermath of the depression, as part of the amendments of 1938. Provisions relating to barge canals, elimination of railroad grade crossings, social welfare and returning veterans reflect paramount concerns at given moments in the rich history of this State, alongside the abiding concern in our extensive Bill of Rights and throughout the Constitution for fundamental rights and individual liberty.

Second, while the federal Constitution has been amended only 26 times in its entire history, the state Constitution has been amended often, for the most part in isolated fragments initiated by the legislature and thereafter approved by the People at a general

---

34. 463 U.S. at 1041. *But see* Bamberger, *Recent Developments, supra* note 1, at 296, noting that in decisions since *Michigan v. Long* the Supreme Court "has indicated a strong willingness to review state court decisions."

35. *Massachusetts v. Upton*, 466 U.S. at 735 (Stevens, J., concurring); *see also South Dakota v. Neville*, 459 U.S. 553, 566–71 (1983) (Stevens, J., dissenting). As the Vermont Supreme Court wrote in *State v. Badger,* 450 A.2d 336, 347 (Vt. 1982): "Fulfillment of this Court's responsibilities as a member of the federalist system requires us to consider the availability of state grounds before federal appeal."

36. 466 U.S. at 737.

election.[37] The Constitution has also been extensively revised, most recently in 1938, as the consequence of constitutional conventions. The last proposed new constitution of 1967 was resoundingly defeated at the polls, as were the proposed new constitutions of 1869 and 1915. Additionally, as the Constitution itself directs, every 20 years, and whenever the legislature provides, the People are asked at a general election, "Shall there be a convention to revise the Constitution and amend the same?"

The combination of high detail and accessibility of the amendment process gives our Constitution a distinctive New York character; it is a product and expression of this State.

While current interest centers on the common provisions of our two Constitutions, to proceed right to that issue ignores the fact that the People of this State have chosen to "constitutionalize" a great number of other matters in the Bill of Rights and throughout the state Constitution. Fortuitously, the heightened interest in concurrent provisions has drawn attention as well to the many matters uniquely part of the state charter.

I will not linger long on a recitation of the provisions of the state Constitution that have no specific analogue or counterpart in the federal document. No one would question that, though other considerations such as due process or equal protection may also be implicated, these singular provisions must at some point be analyzed as a matter of state law.

Our Constitution provides, for example, the right to a free education,[38] and declares that the aid, care and support of the needy are public concerns.[39] It directs that

---

37. The State has actually had four constitutions: those of 1777, 1821, 1846 (the "People's Constitution") and 1894. The 1894 Constitution, extensively revised and supplemented in 1938, remains in effect today. Since its first amendments in 1801, the Constitution has also undergone steady piecemeal revision, initiated by one legislature, approved by the next, and the approved by the public at a general election. *See* C. Lincoln, The Constitutional History of New York (1905), for a comprehensive early history of the State Constitution, and particularly *id.*, vol. 1 at 613, for a critical assessment of the amendment process as "rather too easy."

While the resolution for a convention to draw a constitution also provided for a bill of rights, the 1777 Constitution contained no bill of rights; indeed, a formal bill of rights was first added to the Constitution in 1846. The 1777 Constitution, however, continued the English bill of rights, and further provided for a right to vote, trial by jury, right to counsel and religious liberty. This Constitution established the three branches of government that persist to this day as the structural framework of our state, as well as national, government. It was at the time regarded as " 'the most excellent of all the American Constitutions.' " *Id.* at 559.

38. Art. XI, § 1; *see Levittown U.F.S.D. v. Nyquist*, 57 N.Y.2d 27, 47–489 (1982), *app. dismissed*, 459 U.S. 1138, 1139 (1983).

39. Art. XVII, § 1. "State aid to the needy was deemed to be a fundamental part of the social contract. . . . it is clear that section 1 of article XVII imposes upon the State an affirmative duty to aid the needy. . . . Although our Constitution provides the Legislature with discretion in determining the means by which this objective is to be effectuated, in determining the amount of aid, and in classifying recipients and defining the term 'needy,' it unequivocally prevents the Legislature from simply refusing to aid those whom it has classified as needy. Such a definite constitutional mandate cannot be ignored or easily evaded in either its letter or its spirit." *Tucker v. Toia*, 43 N.Y.2d 1, 7–8 (1977); *Lee v. Smith*, 43 N.Y.2d 453 (1977). *See also McCain v. Koch*, 117 A.D.2d 198, *lv. granted*, 121 A.D.2d 997 (1st Dep't. 1986); *Wilkins v. Perales*, 119 A.D.2d 1018 (1st Dep't. 1986), *aff'g* 128 Misc.2d 265 (N.Y. Sup. Ct. 1985); *Eldredge v. Koch*, 98 A.D.2d 675 (1st Dep't. 1983); Note, *A Right to Shelter for the Homeless in New York State*, 61 N.Y.U.L. Rev. 272 (186); Note, *Establishing a Right to Shelter for the Homeless*, 50 Brooklyn L. Rev. 939 (1984).

provision be made for the protection and promotion of public health, and it recognizes that the legislature in its discretion may provide for low-rent housing and nursing home accommodations for persons of low income.[40] It specifies that environmental conservation is a policy of this State, and mandates that adequate provision be made for abatement of pollution and noise.[41] As a matter of constitutional directive, certain executive rules and regulations cannot be enforced until they have been publicly filed.[42] The benefits of membership in a state pension or retirement system may not be impaired;[43] and the jurisdiction of the Appellate Division to hear appeals may not be diminished.[44] The Bill of Rights bars the abrogation of a cause of action for wrongful death; it guarantees the right of workers to the prevailing wage, and to organize and bargain collectively; and it provides for workers' compensation.[45]

Given its laborious detail, our Constitution may not in every phrase ring with the majesty of Chief Justice Marshall's declaration: "It is *a constitution* we are expounding."[46] But it *is* a constitution we are expounding, and its commands are therefore entitled to the particular deference that courts are obliged to accord matters of constitutional magnitude. To borrow former Chief Judge Breitel's eloquent words, in overturning the moratorium on enforcement of City obligations as violative of the State constitutional requirement of a pledge of faith and cred it: "But it is a Constitution that is being interpreted and as a Constitution it would serve little of its purpose if all that it promised, like the elegantly phrased constitutions of some totalitarian or dictatorial Nations, was an ideal to be worshipped when not needed and debased when crucial."[47]

One cannot help but wonder, reading our Constitution, why some seemingly everyday matters were elevated to a place in that document of fundamental law and, even beyond, enshrined in its Bill of Rights. Many of these matters were and are the subject of state statutes, some additionally the subject of federal statutes. They were nonetheless purposefully placed in our state Constitution—within an ambit of special deference and protection—in many instances to declare the existence of a right and correlative commitment by the State; to put them beyond repeal by the legislature; and to insure

---

40. Art. XVII, § 3; Art. XVIII, § 1. *See Suffolk Hous. Servs. v. Town of Brookhaven,* 109 A.D.2d 323 (2d. Dep't. 1985), *app. dismissed,* 67 N.Y.2d 917, *lv. granted,* 68 N.Y.2d 603 (1986); *Robert E. Kurzius, Inc. v. Incorporated Vill. Of Upper Brookville,* 51 N.Y.2d 338 (1980), *cert. denied,* 450 U.S. 1042 (1981); *Berenson v. Town of New Castle,* 38 N.Y.2d 102 (1975); *Golden v. Planning Bd. of Ramapo,* 30 N.Y.2d 359, *app. dismissed,* 409 U.S. 1003 (1972). *Compare Southern Burlington Cty. NAACP v. Township of Mount Laurel (Mount Laurel I),* 67 N.J. 151, *app dismissed* and *cert. denied,* 423 U.S. 808 (1975); *Southern Burlington Cty. NAACP v. township of Mount Laurel (Mt. Laurel II),* 92 N.J. 158 (1983).

41. Art. XIV, § 4.

42. Art. IV, § 8. *See Davidson v. Smith,* 69 N.Y.2d 677 (1986); *People ex rel. Roides v. Smith,* 67 N.Y.2d 899 (1986); *Jones v. Smith,* 64 N.Y.2d 1003 (1985); *New York St. Coalition of Pub. Employers v. New York St. Dep't of Labor,* 60 N.Y.2d 789 (1983); *People v. Cull,* 10 N.Y.2d 123 (1961).

43. Art. V, § 7. *See Lippman v. Board of Ed.,* 66 N.Y.2d 313 (1985).

44. Art. VI, § 4(k) provides that the Appellate Division shall have all the jurisdiction possessed by it on the effective date of the article. *See People v. Pollenz,* 67 N.Y.2d 264, 270 (1986).

45. Art. I, § 16 (wrongful death); art. I, § 17 (labor); art. I, § 18 (workers' compensation).

46. *McCulloch v. Maryland,* 17 U.S. (4 Wheat.) 316, 407 (1819).

47. *Flushing Nat'l Bank v. Municipal Assistance Corp.,* 40 N.Y.2d 731, 739 (1976).

that derivative legislation involving the expenditure of state money and credit would not be cast out as unconstitutional by the judiciary. The People have declared to the courts and others that, as part of the Constitution, these matters stand above the miscellaneous statutes as their expression of what they consider to be particularly important and not subject to revision except by them.

This being so as to the provisions that have no federal analogue or counterpart, no less can be said of the provisions of our state Constitution that *do* have a parallel in the federal Constitution. These provisions have obviously also been placed, and retained, in our Constitution as an expression of the significance they have to the People of this State.

III

Where the text of the state Constitution deals with matters not enumerated federally there is obviously basis—indeed necessity—for independent interpretation. Similarly, where there are material textual differences between the state Constitution and a corresponding provision of the federal Constitution, there is little difficulty concluding that something different may have been intended. Does the absence of textual difference in comparable provisions preclude principled independent analysis under the state Constitution?

History itself answers this question. The federal Constitution was, after all, taken from state models; provisions of our state Constitution have been drawn from the federal document; and many of the same individuals—notably John Jay—had their hand in both. Common objectives, common drafters and common models naturally engender common texts. Yet it is most significant that, as a political act, two separate constitutions were adopted, neither expressly superseding the other, and two have endured. As a juridical act, therefore, constitutional analysis by state courts cannot stop with a mechanical matching of texts; significant protections of a state constitution are otherwise relegated to redundancy.[48]

In this State, in fact, there is a long tradition of reading the parallel clauses independently and affording broader protection, where appropriate, under the state Constitution. One commentator, having studied the New York cases between 1960 and 1978, has concluded that the courts of this State have consistently recognized the independent value of their own constitutional traditions, a recognition that "is not a recent phenomenon brought about by the Burger Court's retrenchment in criminal procedure."[49] In this connection, a substantive area that springs to mind is the right of an accused to the assistance of counsel, found in similar words in both Bills of Rights. The right to counsel was first set out in the state Constitution of 1777; from earliest times it

---

48. For an example of a State's choice so to treat a provision of its own constitution, *see* Fla. Const. art. 1, § 12, mandating that the state search and seizure guarantee be construed in conformity with the fourth amendment to the U.S. Constitution as interpreted by the U.S. Supreme Court. *See generally* Wilkes, *First Things Last: Amendomania and State Bills of Rights*, 54 Miss. L.J. 223 (1984).

49. Galie, *State Constitutional Guarantees and Protection of Defendants' Rights: The Case of New York 1960–1978*, 28 Buff. L. Rev. 157, 192 (1979); *see also* Kramer and Riga, *The New York Court of Appeals and the United States Supreme Court*, 1960–76 8 Publius 75 (1978).

has been insisted upon in our case law, and given wider scope than the corresponding federal right. The New York State decisions upholding the right to counsel have been characterized as "the strongest protection of right to counsel anywhere in the country," and cited as "a striking illustration of a constitutional tradition that has developed on its own terms and, thus, was not susceptible to the vagaries of changing Supreme Courts."[50]

The reasons why separate interpretation and broader protection under the state Constitution may be appropriate are perhaps best shown by two additional examples of parallel provisions: the due process clause, and the protection against unreasonable searches and seizures.

Our due process clause, enacted before the fourteenth amendment, concludes: "No person shall be deprived of life, liberty or property without due process of law." The fourteenth amendment to the federal Constitution provides: "nor shall any state deprive any person of life, liberty, or property without due process of law." Does due process under the state Constitution mean whatever the Supreme Court says due process means under the federal Constitution?

Early in its history, in the *Ives* case,[51] our due process clause became the basis for striking down the Workmen's Compensation Act of 1910, a statute requiring employers, irrespective of fault, to contribute to an insurance fund to benefit employees injured in the course of employment. That unanimous opinion of the Court of Appeals was immediately and immensely unpopular. It was publicly declaimed by Theodore Roosevelt, then planning his Progressive political movement; it led to amendment of the state Constitution specifically to include workers' compensation in no less than the Bill of Rights; it was rejected nationally; and it cost the author of the offending opinion the chief judgeship of the Court of Appeals in the next election. That decision has, moreover, earned a permanent place in the study of jurisprudence, as an example of how a court's choice of methodology can dictate the outcome of a case.[52]

But apart from its historical, political and jurisprudential interest, *Ives* is also relevant to the present discussion in that two proffered decisions of the United States Supreme Court which supported the validity of the statute were rejected by the Court of Appeals as "not controlling of our construction of our own Constitution." The Court wrote: "All that it is necessary to affirm in the case before us is that in our view of the Constitution of our state, the liability sought to be imposed upon the employers enumerated in the statute before us is a taking of property without due process of law, and the statute is therefore void."[53] *Ives* thus stands as a declaration of the independence of the state court in construing the due process clause of the state Constitution. A statute possibly valid as a matter of federal due process was nonetheless upset as a matter of state due process.

Since *Ives*, the state courts have drawn on the state's constitutional history as well as its judicial history in having accorded the due process clause wider scope than its federal

---

50. Galie, *The Other Supreme Courts: Judicial Activism among State Supreme Courts*, 33 Syr. L. Rev. 731, 764, 765 (1982). *See also People v. Hobson*, 39 N.Y.2d 479 (1976).

51. 201 N.Y. 271 (1911).

52. *See* F. Bergan, The History of the New York Court of Appeals, 1847–1932, 245–47 (1985); *see also* B. Cardozo, The Growth of the Law 71 (1924); *New York Central R.R. Co. v. White*, 243 U.S. 188 (1916).

53. 201 N.Y. at 317.

counterpart. *Sharrock v. Dell Buick-Cadillac, Inc.*,[54] for example, involved a challenge under the state and federal due process clauses to the statutory lien enabling garage men to foreclose for delinquent repair and storage charges. Two months earlier, the Supreme Court had made clear that a private sale of property subject to a warehouseman's possessory lien did not constitute "state action" for purposes of the fourteenth amendment,[55] a holding which might have been dispositive. The New York Court of Appeals, however, recognized that it could, and should in this instance, give a broader reading to the "state action" requirement because the state due process clause—unlike its federal counterpart—contains no reference to "state." The material factors cited by the Court of Appeals in invalidating the statute were the difference in constitutional text, the history of the clause within the State, the long record of due process protections particularly afforded our citizens, and fundamental principles of federalism.[56]

Thus, the due process example shows that any difference between texts may become significant in particular cases as a point of departure from federal precedents. Moreover, how a concurrent provision arrived in our charter, as well as how it has been interpreted within the State, may signal whether, in certain cases, greater rights should be afforded under the state Constitution.[57]

---

54. 45 N.Y.2d 152 (1978).

55. *Flagg Bros., Inc. v. Brooks*, 436 U.S. 149 (1978).

56. 45 N.Y.2d at 159–61. *See also Svendsen v. Smith's Moving & Trucking Co.*, 54 N.Y.2d 865 (1981), *cert. denied*, 455 U.S. 927 (1982). The dissent in *Sharrock* and the concurrence in *Svendsen* would instead have relied on the *per curiam* opinion in *Central Savings Bank v. City of New York*, 280 N.Y. 9 (1939) (*amending remittitur in* 279 N.Y. 255 (1938)), *cert. denied*, 306 U.S. 661 (1939), in which the Court of Appeals held, on *remittitur*, that the state and federal due process "clauses are formulated in the same words and are intended for the protection of the same fundamental rights of the individual and there is, logically, no room for distinction in definition of the scope of the two clauses." *Id.* at 10. The Court explained that the conclusion in its original opinion that the amendment violated the state due process clause "followed necessarily from our determination that in accordance with a long line of decisions of the Supreme Court of the United States, the statute is repugnant to the Federal Constitution." *Id.*

One is hard pressed, however, to find the "long line" of due process decisions of the Supreme Court purportedly relied upon by the Court of Appeals in *Central Savings Bank*. Moreover, construction of the state and federal due process clauses as identical was wholly unnecessary. As the Court of Appeals noted, "We did not by reference solely to the Constitution of the State intend to indicate that though we cannot give validity to a statute which is repugnant to the due process clause in the Federal Constitution we would give wider scope to the same clause in the State Constitution and hold invalid statutes not repugnant to the Federal Constitution as defined by the Supreme Court. No such question was presented or considered in this court." *Id.*

57. An "interpretive" analysis considers whether the language of a state constitution specifically recognizes rights not enumerated in the federal Constitution; whether language in a state constitution is sufficiently different to support a broader interpretation of the individual right under state law; whether the history of the adoption of the text reveals an intention to make the state provision coextensive with, or broader than, the parallel federal provision; and whether the very structure and purpose of the state constitution serves to affirm certain rights rather than merely restrain the sovereign power of the state. A "noninterpretive" analysis deals with other matters, such as policy and tradition of the state. *P.J. Video*, 68 N.Y.2d at 302–3. *See* Maltz, *The Dark Side of State Court Activism*, 63 Tex. L. Rev. 995 (1985), questioning the value of yet another layer of noninterpretive review.

As a further example, the state protection against unreasonable searches and seizures has neither this textual nor historical distinction from the federal Constitution.[58] Indeed, article 1, § 12, taken word-for-word from the fourth amendment, did not become part of the state Constitution—we were possibly the last state to adopt it—until 1938.

The protection against unreasonable searches and seizures itself generated little dispute at the 1938 convention—that very protection had for a decade already been contained in the Civil Rights Law—but there were heated exchanges regarding the exclusionary rule. The Supreme Court had held that the exclusion of evidence in federal courts was essential to meaningful protection against intrusive searches,[59] but the New York Court of Appeals chose not to accept that holding as a matter of state law. Writing for the New York court, Judge Cardozo observed that state courts were not bound to interpret their own statutes in the same manner as the federal courts had interpreted the federal Constitution, and concluded that the public policy of this State favored rejection of the exclusionary rule.[60] Ultimately, the protection against unreasonable searches and seizures was added to the state Constitution but an explicit exclusionary rule was not, thus leaving open the issue whether the exclusion of evidence was to follow implicitly, as it did under the federal scheme, and the courts have held that it does.[61]

Faced with this history and text, during many years the Court of Appeals in considering state search and seizure arguments chose to follow a policy of uniformity with the federal courts.[62] This meant that the State in general followed fourth amendment precedents, recognizing as a valued consequence that police officers and reviewing courts would thereby have but one bright-line rule to guide them.[63] Two significant factors of course attended that policy. First, as in all things, continuing a policy of conformity necessarily depends upon the continuation of that to which one has chosen to conform. And second, a policy of having a single workable rule can as readily be served by imposing

---

58. The analysis with respect to search and seizure pertains as well to the equal protection clause. Despite an identity of text and history, the Court of Appeals has on occasion concluded that greater rights should be accorded under the equal protection clause of the state Constitution. The equal protection provision approved at the 1938 Constitutional Convention, N.Y. Const. art. 1, § 11, was designed simply to embody "'in our Constitution the provisions of the Federal Constitution which are already binding upon our State and its agencies.'" *Dorsey v. Stuyvesant Town Corp.*, 299 N.Y. 512, 530 (1949), *cert. denied*, 339 U.S. 981 (1950). *See also Under 21 v. City of New York*, 65 N.Y.2d 344, 360 (1985) (applying federal precedents); *Esler v. Walters*, 56 N.Y.2d 306 313–14 (1982) (coverage is same as under federal provision). In *Cooper v. Morin*, 49 N.Y.2d 69 (1979), *cert. denied*, 446 U.S. 984 (1980), however, the Court of Appeals, concluding that the denial of contact visitation privileges to pretrial detainees would not violate the federal Constitution, found this unacceptable as a matter of state law. "We have not hesitated when we concluded that the Federal Constitution as interpreted by the Supreme Court fell short of adequate protection for our citizens to rely upon the principle that the document defines the minimum level of individual rights and leaves the States free to provide greater rights for its citizens through its Constitution statutes or rule-making authority." *Id.* at 79.

59. *Weeks v. United States*, 232 U.S. 383 (1914).

60. *People v. Defore*, 242 N.Y. 13 (1926).

61. For a discussion of the relevant history see *People v. Johnson*, 66 N.Y.2d 398, 408 (1985) (Titone, J., concurring).

62. *See, e.g., People v. Ponder*, 54 N.Y.2d 160, 165 (1981).

63. *Johnson*, 66 N.Y.2d at 406; *People v. Gonzalez*, 62 N.Y.2d 386, 389–90 (1984).

a higher *state* standard as by conforming to the federal standard. As the Court of Appeals recently noted, the interest of uniformity is only "one consideration to be balanced against other considerations that may argue for a different State rule. When weighed against the ability to protect fundamental constitutional rights, the practical need for uniformity can seldom be a decisive factor."[64]

Where the text and history of a provision point to uniformity—and without addressing whether a state court should first consider the federal precedents or its own state law, itself a subject of lively difference[65]—what other factors have nonetheless motivated the conclusion that greater protection should be afforded under state law?

A response to that question lies in the fact that the Supreme Court's role is to establish only the minimal level, the lowest common denominator, of individual rights applicable throughout the nation, while it is the role of state courts, in discharging their additional responsibility to uphold their own constitutions, to safeguard and supplement those rights where necessary.[66] Sound policy considerations have therefore been cited as the basis for different interpretations of common provisions—such considerations as statutes or common law, traditions of the state, and distinctive public attitudes toward the scope, definition and protection of the right in question. An argument for a broader construction under the state Constitution than that established under the federal Constitution requires more than merely urging that some other result is preferred.[67]

It has long been recognized that issues relating to free expression involve community standards and traditions; disputes regarding land use are another example raising policy

---

64. *P.J. Video*, 68 N.Y.2d at 304.

65. Three modes of analysis have been identified: reliance on both state and federal Constitutions; the "primacy" approach—*i.e.*, looking first to the state Constitution; and the "interstitial" or supplemental approach—*i.e.*, consulting the state Constitution if action is first found valid under the federal Constitution. *See* Pollock, *State and Federal Courts, supra* note 6, and Bamberger, *Recent Developments, supra* note 1, at 301. *Compare Sterling v. Cupp*, 290 Ore. 611, 614 (1981), *with Right to Choose v. Byrne*, 91 N.J. 287 (1982). *See also* Baker, *State Ground, supra* note 6, at 833; Linde, *E Pluribus—Constitutional Theory and State Courts*, 18 Ga. L. Rev. 165, 179 (1984); Linde, *First Things First: Rediscovering the State Bills of Rights*, 9 U. Balt. L. Rev. 379 (1980) (hereafter *First Things First*); Hill and Marks, *Foreword: Toward a Federalist System of Rights*, 1984 Ann. Survey Am. L. 1 (1984); Williams, *In the Supreme Court's Shadow: Legitimacy of State Rejection of Supreme Court Reasoning and Result*, 35 S.C.L. Rev. 353 (1984).

66. *See People ex rel. Arcara v. Cloud Books Inc.*, 68 N.Y.2d 553, 557 (1986); *Adams*, 53 N.Y.2d at 250; *see also Cooper*, 49 N.Y.2d 69; Brennan, *The Roles of the State Supreme Court Justice and the United States Supreme Court Justice*, 56 N.Y.S.B.J. 6 (Oct. 1984) (hereafter *Roles of Justice*).

67. *See State v. Hunt*, 91 N.J. 338 (1982), for a list of relevant considerations in this determination. "To make an independent argument under the state clause takes homework—in texts, in history, in alternative approaches to analysis. It is not enough to ask the state court to reject a Supreme Court opinion on the comparable federal clause merely because one prefers the opposite result." Linde, *First Things First, supra* note 65, at 392. *See also* Bamberger, *Recent Developments, supra* note 1, at 306; Howard, *State Courts and Constitutional Rights in the Day of the Burger Court*, 62 Va. L. Rev. 873, 934–44 (1976). And *see State v. Jewett*, 500 A.2d 233 (Vt. 1985), where the Vermont Supreme court declined to address the state constitutional issue raised because the parties had failed to discuss it adequately in their briefs, and directed that supplemental briefs be filed on the issue. In response to the decision, the Vermont attorney general set up a committee to research history and precedents connected with the Vermont Constitution. Collins and Galie, *Judicial Review, supra* note 1, at 335.

concerns peculiar to the state.[68] Considerations of policy have similarly led the Court of Appeals to depart from federal precedents in search and seizure cases.[69] For example, by decisional law developed over the years, clear, definable standards had been established and consistently applied to probable cause determinations within this State. The New York Court in recent cases has continued to apply those standards as a matter of state constitutional law under article 1, § 12. Its departure from fourth amendment precedents has been expressly predicated on policy considerations, particularly the perception that the Supreme Court of late had changed the federal standards, muddying the rules and diluting judicial supervision of the warrant process, thereby heightening "the danger that our citizens' rights against unreasonable police intrusions might be violated."[70]

Thus—despite perceived or even actual identity of texts—there may in particular instances be principled basis for broader protection within this State because of our history in adopting or applying a clause, or for other reasons. While language differences between the two constitutions may determine that there is a need for independent analysis, where our Constitution is at issue the fact that there is no language difference does not spell the end of state judicial review. It invites inquiry into matters of history, tradition, policy and other special State concerns.

IV

I would like to shift the focus from the historical and practical to the theoretical by asking, is independent state court adjudication of parallel protections supported by a cohesive theory, or is this today indeed merely a passing disagreement with particular decisions of the United States Supreme Court?

You are of course familiar with the great debate raging in the law as to how a constitution should be interpreted.[71] Some insist that it must be read by the intent of the framers; others assert that intent of the framers cannot be controlling, and that the document must be interpreted in light of prevailing attitudes and modern values. It

---

68. *See, e.g., PruneYard Shopping Ctr. v. Robins*, 447 U.S. 74 (1980) (speech); *Arcara* 68 N.Y.2d 553 (same); *SHAD Alliance v. Smith Haven Mall*, 66 N.Y.2d 496 (1985) (same); *Bellanca v. State Liq. Auth.*, 54 N.Y.2d 228 (1981) (same); *People v. Barber*, 289 N.Y. 378 (1943) (same); *McMinn v. Town of Oyster Bay*, 66 N.Y.2d 544 (1985) (land use); Pollock, *State Constitutions, Land Use and Public Resources: The Gift Outright*, Williamsburg, *supra* note 1, at 146 (1985).

69. *P.J. Video*, 68 N.Y.2d 296; *People v. Bigelow*, 66 N.Y.2d 417 (1985); *Johnson*, 66 N.Y.2d at 398.

70. *P.J. Video*, 68 N.Y.2d at 305. *State v. Kimbro*, 496 A.2d 498 (Conn. 1985). As Chief Justice Peters recently noted, in choosing as a matter of state constitutional law to adhere to the "well-developed federal test" of *Aguilar-Spinelli* instead of the newer, "less stringent" test of *Illinois v. Gates*, "the Connecticut court was able to profit from a developed history of an established, workable test for warrantless searches, without having to commit itself to changing federal views on the reach of the fourth amendment. We were reinforced in our view of our constitution by a similar decision reached by a Massachusetts court with a similar constitutional history." Peters, *Remarks*, *supra* note 3. Collins and Galie, *Judicial Review*, *supra* note 1, at 318 n.3.

71. *See, e.g.,* Wachtler, *Will America Survive?*, 41 Rec. A.B. City N.Y. 1991 (1986); Powell, *The Original Understanding of Original Intent*, 98 Harv. L. Rev. 885 (1985).

occurs to me that this issue, as well as the one at hand, both propel us to an even more fundamental inquiry. We can answer the question of how to interpret a constitution, whether state or federal, only by first understanding what, in a real sense, a constitution is.

The very word "constitution," in common understanding, means the most basic structure of a thing, how it is constituted. The English regarded themselves as having a constitution long before the Colonials began drawing up constitutions for themselves on paper, and the English constitution has never been written down in a single document. That the English can speak of their unwritten "constitution" helps to underscore exactly what a constitution means. A community's constitution is its basic make-up, the source, delineation and delimitation of rights and powers within that society, the collective assessment of the rules of the game under which the process of decision-making and exercise of power within that community will proceed. As the very basis or a living community, a constitution is necessarily a thing of that community.

The essential difference between British and American constitutionalism is not that American constitutions are written. Rather, it is that the British constitution is founded upon a concept of parliamentary supremacy. Under British theory constitutional sovereignty resides in Parliament. The laws enacted by Parliament, though restrained by traditions and principles, are perforce within the constitution. Our nation, by contrast, is rooted in a concept that sovereignty resides in the People. Thus it is possible that our designated lawmakers can at times enact laws that fall outside the basic law established by the People. Where the People are sovereign, their conception of their constitution exists apart from, and above, ordinary legislative enactments.

The day-to-day function of a constitution, however, goes further. It is a fact of human nature, and of the democratic process, that our actions—both as individuals and as a community—sometimes conflict with our most basic, or overarching, values. Therefore, what we set out to embody in a constitution are those values we do not wish to sacrifice to more transient choices. Our constitutional values can of course be explicitly changed, but amendments are accomplished only through extraordinary political processes—the approval of two successive legislatures followed by a popular referendum in the case of the state Constitution,[72] and the approval of two-thirds of both Houses of Congress and three-fourths of the states in the case of the federal charter.[73] The constitution, in short, is that set of values to which we have bound ourselves, the values that transcend even our currently made choices—or, in the words of James Madison, the values that "counteract the impulses of interest and passion."[74]

This is no abstraction but rather a reflection of the most abiding reality of both our past and present. We talk a great deal about the constitutional shield provided the People against the government, but in a democracy the threats to our values often have popular support. The Constitution throughout history has been called upon to protect long venerated values that are momentarily abandoned or neglected.

---

72. N.Y. Const. art. XIX.

73. U.S. Const. art. V.

74. Letter from J. Madison to T. Jefferson (Oct. 17, 1788), *reprinted in* 5 The Writings of James Madison 273 (G. Hunt ed., 1904).

It is a function of constitutional law, then, to preserve a community's overarching values in the face of its transient choices. And it is a significant function of the courts to ascertain and identify these most basic values, and flag them when they are at risk. As Judge Cardozo aptly wrote in *The Nature of the Judicial Process*:

> The restraining power of the judiciary does not manifest its chief worth in the few cases in which the legislature has gone beyond the lines that mark the limits of discretion. Rather shall we find its chief worth in making vocal and audible the ideals that might otherwise be silenced, in giving them continuity of life and of expression, in guiding and directing choice within the limits where choice ranges. This function should preserve to the courts the power that now belongs to them, if only the power is exercised with insight into social values, and with suppleness of adaptation to changing social need.[75]

What many, most notably Hugo Black, have sought in a jurisprudence of original intent—the protection of civil liberties by fixing us to an *a priori* commitment to them—cannot realistically be achieved in that manner. The right to a fair trial or free speech does not exist today simply because a group of framers two centuries ago intended them to exist. They can and do exist today because we mean them to, even though at times we may do or say otherwise. The overarching values of the past can and surely do inform our inquiry into what values make up our "constitution" today.[76] We are, after all, *interpreting* a text, not *inventing* one. Moreover, we look to the past because our most basic values, when they change, tend to do so very slowly, and then by a process of evolution. But interpreting our Constitution cannot stop with values of the past. It necessarily involves as well the community's present values—identifying the values that this community has declared should limit the ordinary processes of its government.

All of this speaks with particular force, and has special relevance, to the subject of state constitutions.

Where a provision has been adopted into our Constitution from the federal charter, intent-based interpretation would obviously be unusually difficult. When dealing with

---

75. B. Cardozo, The Nature of the Judicial Process, 94 (1921).

76. "We may assume that the framers of the Constitution in adopting that section, did not have specifically in mind the selection and elimination for candidates for Congress by the direct primary any more than they contemplated the application of the commerce clause to interstate telephone, telegraph and wireless communication, which are concededly within it. But in determining whether a provision of the Constitution applies to a new subject matter, it is of little significance that it is one with which the framers were not familiar. For setting up an enduring framework of government they undertook to carry out for the indefinite future and in all the vicissitudes of the changing affairs of men, those fundamental purposes which the instrument itself discloses. Hence we read its words, not as we read legislative codes which are subject to continuous revision with the changing course of events, but as the revelation of the great purposes which were intended to be achieved by the Constitution as a continuing instrument of government." *United States v. Classic*, 313 U.S. 299, 315–16 (1941) (Stone, J.).

intentions of several distinct groups of framers and amenders, are we to look to the intent of the federal framers, or the intent that the state framers believed—perhaps erroneously—the federal framers held? Or did the state framers intend something altogether different? A text-based "contemporary values" approach fares no better. If we read the words of all the constitutions of this nation in terms of what those words mean to us today, it is hard to argue that the same words have any different meaning anywhere. Obviously, if there is any variation across this nation it is not in the meaning of words, it is in the concepts they embody.

It should be immediately apparent that the Constitution established by this community under threat of British invasion in 1777, and painstakingly reviewed and amended throughout the ensuing centuries, reflects its own values, which may or may not be identical to those held elsewhere.

Indeed, the history that has shaped the values of this State is different in many respects from that which has shaped the consensus in other states, not to mention our nation as a whole. Many states today espouse cultural values distinctively their own; Alaska, for instance, is unique in its constitutional guarantee of the right to possess marijuana in one's home.[77] If it is our duty to look at what our "constitution" represents in order to determine what it say, and if what a constitution represents is that community's most basic, overarching values, then it is only right to interpret our state Constitution independently of others, even where concepts are expressed in the same words. An independent interpretation of course does not mean that identical clause will invariably be read differently, or more broadly, than their federal counterparts or those of sister states.[78] The Supreme Court, in reading the federal Constitution, must lay out a minimal rule for a diverse nation, with due concern for principles of federalism. State courts, even when working with the same basic provisions, have a different focus, which is to fashion workable rules for a narrower, more specific range of people and situations. Their solutions thus may at times be identical to the federal solutions, but they are not necessarily so.[79]

Practical considerations support this theory. State courts are generally closer to the public, to the legal institutions and environments within the state, and to the public policy process. This both shapes their strategic judgments, and renders any erroneous assessments they may make more readily redressable by the People. Moreover, building a coherent body of law—one that is not merely reacting to particular Supreme Court decisions, or waiting on the Supreme Court to flesh out the contours of a devel-

---

77. *See Ravin v. State*, 537 P.2dd 494 (Alaska 1975).

78. "Horizontal federalism, a federalism in which states look to each other for guidance, may be the hallmark of the rest of the century." Pollock, *State and Federal Courts, supra* note 6, at 992. Guidance may additionally be taken by state courts from dissenting opinions of the United States Supreme Court.

79. *See* Brennan, *Some Aspects of Federalism*, 39 N.Y.U.L. Rev. 945, 948–49 (1964); Brennan, *Roles of Justice, supra* note 66. *See also* Sager, *Forward: State Courts and the Strategic Space Between the Norms and Rules of Constitutional Law*, 63 Tex. L. Rev. 959 (1985).

oping right—has the advantage of furthering predictability and stability in our state law.[80]

In short, the development of an independent body of state constitutional doctrine not only has deep historical roots but also is theoretically sound.

V

We have so far been concerned with the conditions under which state constitutional rights depend upon the delineation of federal constitutional rights. I think it's only proper to turn the tables and ask, are there conditions under which federal constitutional rights should depend upon the delineation of state constitutional rights?

Development of federal law through experimentation within the states of course has a long tradition. Justice Brandeis in his famous *New State Ice* dissent[81] described as one of the "happy incidents" of the federal system that a state, if its citizens chose, could serve as a laboratory for novel social and economic experiments without risk to the rest of the country.[82] The Supreme Court implicitly recognized this process in *Mapp v. Ohio*,[83] in giving the exclusionary rule national application, noting that since its own prior decision declining to recognize the exclusionary rule as binding nationally, two-thirds of the states had themselves adopted the rule.[84] Only last term the Supreme Court

---

80. *See People v. Hicks*, 68 N.Y.2d 234, 243 (1986); *People v. Elwell*, 50 N.Y.2d 231 (1980); *State v. Williams*, 93 N.J. 39 (1983); *but see Hobson*, 39 N.Y.2d at 488 with respect to *stare decisis* in constitutional law. As the New Jersey Supreme Court recently wrote in *State v. Gilmore*, 103 N.J. 508 (1986), in concluding under the state constitution that defendant's right to an impartial jury had been violated by the prosecutor's use of peremptory challenges:

> That the United States Supreme Court has overruled *Swain* in *Batson* does not mean that the laboratories operated by leading state courts should now close up shop. For one thing, *Batson* rests on federal grounds of equal protection, whereas *Wheeler* and its progeny rest on state constitutional rights to trial by an impartial jury. For another, *Batson* is not the final word in this area—as the majority recognized, and as Justice White emphasized in concurrence, "[m]uch litigation will be required to spell out the contours of the Court's Equal Protection holding" 476 U.S. at _____, 90 *L.Ed.*2d at 90 n. 24 (majority) & 91 (White, J., concurring).
>
> Accordingly, we base our decision on the New Jersey Constitution, which protects fundamental rights independently of the United States Constitution. *Id.* at 522.

81. *New State Ice Co. v. Liebmann*, 285 U.S. 262, 311 (1932) (Brandeis, J., dissenting).

82. A similar process of recognizing constitutional rights—which are then beyond legislative diminution—may occur within state law. In *In re Storar*, 52 N.Y.2d 363 (1981), the Court of Appeals recognized as a matter of common law the right of a competent adult to control the course of his medical treatment, and not to have his life prolonged by medical means; the Court did not reach the question whether this right is also guaranteed by the Constitution. *Id.* at 376–77. The lower court, in *In re Eichner (Fox)*, 73 A.D.2d 431 (2d Dep't. 1980), had held that the right to refuse medical treatment was guaranteed by the constitutional right to privacy. *Id.* at 461. In *Rivers v. Katz*, 67 N.Y.2d 485, 493 (1986), the Court of Appeals concluded that the fundamental common law right to refuse medical treatment "is coextensive with the patent's liberty interest protected by the due process clause of our State Constitution."

83. 367 U.S. 643 (1961).

84. *Id.* at 651.

reversed its prior ruling on the discriminatory use of peremptory challenges.[85] A few years earlier, in denying *certiorari* in a New York case, three Justices explicitly made known their interest in the issue, but said they preferred to allow it to percolate further in the state laboratories, to generate solutions upon which the Supreme Court might rely.[86] The growing trend among the states ultimately led the Court to depart from its holding in *Swain v. Alabama,*[87] and also provided content for the new rule.[88]

This practice comports with the theory outlined earlier.[89] As states may well have different constitutions from the national community; it logically follows that if a value is recognized by enough such communities, then that value has come to be so recognized by—and part of the "constitution" of—the larger community as well. In short, rights that come to be recognized as such by enough of the People acting through the states may become federal rights—values of national, constitutional importance.

Is there a place in our traditional constitutional structure for such a result? I suggest that there is—the ninth amendment, which reads: "The enumeration in the constitution of certain rights shall not be construed to deny or disparage other rights retained by the People."[90]

The ninth amendment is perhaps the one sentence in the federal Constitution that has never been figured out. "In sophisticated legal circles," John Hart Ely tells us, "mentioning the Ninth Amendment is a surefire way to get a laugh. ('What are you planning to rely on to support that argument, Lester, the Ninth Amendment?')."[91] The ninth amendment has been dismissed as stating a mere truism: that all powers not delegated by the Constitution to the federal government remain undelegated as a result of the Bill of Rights. But, as Dean Ely points out, the tenth amendment, added to the Constitution at the same time as the ninth, says this much more clearly. Thus, the ninth

---

85. *Batson v. Kentucky,* 476 U.S. _____, 106 S.Ct. 1712, 90 L. Ed. 2d 69 (1986).

86. *McCray v. New York,* 461 U.S. 961 (1983) (Powell, Blackmun, and Stevens, JJ., concurring).

87. 380 U.S. 202 (1965).

88. After it became apparent that the *Swain* rule had virtually no bite, two state courts—California, *People v. Wheeler,* 22 Cal.3d 258 (1978), and Massachusetts, *Commonwealth v. Soares,* 377 Mass. 461, *cert. denied,* 444 U.S. 881 (1979)—decided on the basis of their *state* constitutions to adopt a stricter rule. Over the course of several years, the mechanics of the rule were fleshed out. *See, e.g., People v. Hall,* 35 cal. 3d 161 (1983); *Commonwealth v. Robinson,* 382 Mass. 189 (1981). Other state courts followed suit. *Riley v. State,* 496 A.2d 997 (Del. 1985); *State v. Neil,* 457 So.2d 481 (Fla. 1984); *see also State v. Crespin,* 94 N.M. 486 (app. 1980). The Supreme Court noted in *Batson v. Kentucky, supra* note 85, that two federal Courts of Appeals had found discriminating peremptory challenges violative of the *federal* Constitution by "[f]ollowing the lead of a number of state courts construing their *state's* Constitution." 106 S.Ct. at 1714 n.1 (emphasis added). The Court's ruling itself basically adopted the California-Massachusetts procedure nationally.

89. *See* text accompanying notes 71–76 *supra.*

90. U.S. Const., amdt. IX.

91. J. Ely, Democracy and Distrust: A Theory of Judicial Review 34 (1980). *See also* B. Patterson, The Forgotten Ninth Amendment (1955); Redlich, *Are There "Certain Rights . . . Retained by the People"?,* 37 N.Y.U.L. Rev. 787 (1962). The Patterson book served as something of a spark for the ninth amendment's brief renaissance. *See Griswold v. Connecticut,* 381 U.S. 479, 484 (1965); *id.* at 487–99 (Goldberg, J., concurring); *cf. id.* at 511–20 (Stewart, J., dissenting). On further approaches to the ninth amendment *see generally* C. Black, Decision According to Law (1981).

amendment becomes not only an unneeded truism but also a redundant unneeded truism. As a commonplace of constitutional interpretation, however, "[i]t cannot be presumed that any clause in the Constitution is intended to be without effect."[92]

In the case of the ninth amendment, then, what might that intended effect be? The amendment's relatively few boosters have been singularly unsuccessful at developing any content for it that would do more than license the federal judiciary to define new rights without providing any standards or mechanisms for so doing. Yet as the text must have been intended to mean something, the task must be to reason our way to some set of standards or mechanisms that make sense of it. Reasoning through what it must mean to say that the enumeration of rights in the original Bill of Rights does not "deny or disparage" other rights retained by the People, one might very well arrive at the point also reached from the opposite direction: approaching state constitutional values as the building blocks of federal constitutional values.[93]

It makes sense that rights protected by the federal Constitution should be expandable by the People acting through the states. Under prevailing political theory when the Constitution was framed—particularly among the recalcitrant ratifiers at whose insistence the Bill of Rights was added—it was fundamental

> that the powers granted under the Constitution, being derived from the people, may be resumed by them whenever perverted to their injury; that every power not therein granted remains in the people at their will; that no right of any denomination can be cancelled, abridged, restrained or modified except in the instances and for the purposes for which power is given; and that among other essentials, liberty of the press and of conscience cannot be abridged.[94]

As Chief Justice Marshall made clear in *Marbury*, "That the people have an original right to establish, for their future government, such principles as, in their opinion, shall most conduce to their own happiness, is the basis on which the whole American fabric has been erected."[95]

---

92. *Marbury v. Madison*, 5 U.S. (1 Cranch) 137, 175 (1803).

93. *See* text accompanying notes 81–87 *supra*.

94. Kelsey, *The Ninth Amendment of the Federal Constitution*, 11 Ind. L.J. 309, 314–15 (1936) (summarizing Virginia's reservations in ratifying Constitution). The theory of the ninth amendment is, essentially, that "nothing has or can be lost by the people because these rights exist independent of the limited powers granted to the federal government." Call, *Federalism and the Ninth Amendment*, 64 Dick. L. Rev. 121, 130 (1960). The problem lies in identifying what these rights might be. One student of the ninth amendment found, upon pursuing its legislative history, that the amendment's purpose was "to guarantee that rights protected under state law would not be construed as supplanted by federal law merely because they were not expressly listed in the Constitution." Caplan, *The History and Meaning of the Ninth Amendment*, 69 Va. L. Rev. 223, 254 (1983). The amendment, as conceived of by its framers, "simply provides that the individual rights contained in state law are to continue in force under the Constitution until modified or eliminated by state enactment, by federal preemption, or by a judicial determination of unconstitutionality." *Id.* at 228. Thus, "[t]he retained rights envisioned by the framers . . . include not only those established by common law and statute as of the Constitution's adoption, but also those to be subsequently established by state legislation." *Id.* at 248.

95. *Marbury v. Madison*, 5 U.S. at 137.

Whatever other rights may have been contemplated by the framers of the ninth amendment, one of these "original" rights was clearly the right to establish, and to alter, the principles of government.

The conception that state-generated constitutional rights could at some point become binding nationally gives the ninth amendment substance without license. First, it allows for growth in the federal Constitution slowly and through cautious experimentation, subject to testing and confirmation, and provides the People the time and opportunity, acting through their state processes, to reject, expand or modify rights declared at the state level before they are taken as part of a national consensus. Second, this conception of the ninth amendment gives the federal judiciary a point of reference as to the overarching values embodied in our Constitution today, insuring that the Constitution grows to fit society, but in a way more accessible to the democratic process and less dependent on any individual judge's divination of "contemporary values." Finally, this view reinforces the role of the states as not only guarantors but also generators of individual rights.

VI

In summary, state constitutional law is significant historically; its independent development is sound today, both practically and theoretically; and it represents an avenue for the future delineation of constitutional rights nationally.

The Human Dimension
in Appellate Judging*

A Brief Reflection on a Timeless Concern

It is impossible to let these historic years pass without commenting on the magnificence of our bicentennial celebration. So many times lately we have gathered on community lawns, in courthouses, in schools—with balloons and bands and the Star Spangled Banner—to pay tribute to our Constitution and to this nation's founders for a document and tradition that have endured as our backbone and conscience through 200 years of societal change. What a great refresher course we are having in American origins.

It is ironic that in 1987—while debate raged over how the Constitution should be interpreted[1]—we were also given a living lesson, a nationwide seminar in United States government, particularly the interaction of its three branches, through the confirmation process of Judge Robert Bork. I have not found anything on television more magnetizing than the Senate Judiciary Committee hearings, and I am delighted that public interest in these lengthy televised sessions was so widespread. Tradespeople in my neighborhood suddenly wanted only to talk about Bork; more than ever I began to dread long red lights and traffic jams while seated in New York City taxicabs; in Albany a woman told me that every night she set up her ironing in front of the television set. (That's a lot of ironing.) The word "Borkian" is probably in serious contention for the next edition of Webster's.

The personalities were fascinating, to be sure, but by the fifth or fifteenth or fiftieth hour it simply had to be the dialogue and not the actors that captivated viewers and held them riveted to their television sets. The public became genuinely absorbed by the issue of "judicial restraint" versus "judicial policy-making": what exactly is the proper role of the flesh and blood human being—the individual judge's own values and philosophy—in Supreme Court adjudication of constitutional questions that are so obviously fundamental to the kind of society we have? The words "judicial policy-making" and "judicial law-

---

*73 Cornell Law Review 1004 (July 1988). This essay is an expanded version of the remarks delivered to the New York County Lawyers' Association, December 10, 1987.

1. *See, e.g.*, Powell, *The Original Understanding of Original Intent*, 98 Harv. L. Rev. 885 (1985); Wachtler, *Our Constitutions—Alive and Well*, 61 St. John's L. Rev. 381 (1987).

making," for some, have become words of terror signifying an arrogation of power, an intrusion into the domain of the legislature, judges gone wild.

If you believe that there can be such a thing as coincidence, then an extraordinary coincidence occurred on September 17, 1987—the day 200 years ago that convention delegates in Philadelphia actually put their signatures to the Constitution. That was Judge Bork's third day of testimony before the Senate Judiciary Committee and, coincidentally, also the day Justice Brennan delivered the Cardozo Lecture at the Association of the Bar of the City of New York—a talk plainly prepared long in advance of Justice Powell's resignation and the Bork nomination. Justice Brennan's lecture was called "Reason, Passion, and 'The Progress of the Law.'"[2] It was the antithesis of the judicial philosophy being expressed that very day in Washington.

Passion, according to Justice Brennan, is "the range of emotional and intuitive responses to a given set of facts or arguments, responses which often speed into our consciousness far ahead of the lumbering syllogisms of reason."[3] I have to admit, I never thought of "passion" quite that way. In eloquent passages intensifying the grace, the sheer poetry of Judge Cardozo's *Nature of the Judicial Process*, Justice Brennan had as his thesis that interpretation of the Constitution—particularly its guarantee of due process—demands the full measure of every human capacity, that we cannot "take refuge in the illusion of rational certainty." The interplay of forces, he said, the "internal dialogue of reason and passion, does not taint the judicial process, but is in fact central to its vitality,"[4] particularly in matters of constitutional interpretation.

I do not intend to discuss the bicentennial or Judge Bork or constitutional decision-making by the United States Supreme Court or by the New York Court of Appeals. But I do wish to share a few related thoughts about one of the many timeless issues rekindled by these most recent chapters in American history—the part played by a judge's own values and sense of justice, or "passion," when sitting in review of *nonconstitutional*

---

2. 42 Rec. Assoc. Bar. City of N.Y. 948 (1987).

3. *Id.* at 958.

4. *Id.* at 951. According to Justice Brennan:

> [The Constitution's] broadly phrased guarantees of our freedoms ensure that the Constitution need never become an anachronism: the Constitution will endure as a vital charter of human liberty as long as there are those with the courage to defend it, the vision to interpret it, and the fidelity to live by it.
>
> Yet the open-ended nature of a written constitution, and the difficulty of reconciling competing principles and passions, places an enormous responsibility on the judge.

Id. at 962. Justice Brennan focused particularly on the Due Process Clause, noting that:

> [it] demands of judges more than proficiency in logical analysis. It requires that we be sensitive to the balance of reason and passion that mark a given age, and the ways in which that balance leaves its mark on the everyday exchanges between government and citizen. In order to do so, we must draw on our own experience as inhabitants of that age, and our own sense of the uneven fabric of social life. We cannot delude ourselves that the Constitution takes the form of a theorem whose axioms need mere logical deduction.

Id. at 966–67.

questions, the statutory issues as well as the everyday problems that are the grist of our common law process. While often less dramatic than the burning constitutional issues, these decisions made day in and day out by appellate courts throughout the nation are obviously also a major force in shaping the kind of society we have, and they touch the lives and affairs of most of us perhaps even more directly.

Long before the issue flared up in connection with the recent Supreme Court nomination, and especially as a judge, I had thought a great deal about the proper balance of person and precedent in deciding the publicly significant issues that come before the courts. By that I do not mean to suggest that any case in our court is unimportant—it is not; but what I wish to focus on are the cases that come to us with lights flashing and bells ringing as issues that likely will have broad social impact.

Every human being—judges included—certainly has a view or philosophy or outlook on life, some notion about what society needs, and all manner of personal feelings, beliefs, and experiences. Yet the Court of Appeals is exclusively a court of law. With few exceptions, we are by constitution, statute, and abundant case law without jurisdiction to decide anything but issues of law.[5] Over the years that it has been my good fortune to serve on the Court of Appeals, I have come to appreciate how as a court of law, deciding only issues of law, within a government of law, we can and do and must, also bring the full measure of every human capacity to bear in resolving the cases before us.

I doubt that anyone today would seriously question the proposition that appellate decision-making is more than a mechanical exercise of locating citations and affixing them to facts found below. The view of the function as entirely formalistic, as a matter of pure reason and scientific search, manifests not judicial restraint but intellectual nonsense. Judge Cardozo himself observed that judges do not stand aloof on the chill and distant heights of pure reason, immune from the tides and currents that engulf the rest of mankind, "and we shall not help the cause of truth by acting and speaking as if they do."[6] He recognized that the judicial process "in its highest reaches is not discovery, but creation."[7] Those sentiments expressed in the year 1920 were apparently widely regarded as a legal version of hard core pornography that no one but a saint like Cardozo could get away with.[8] I suspect that the public view has changed somewhat over the past 68 years—both as to what constitutes hard core pornography and as to the true and proper function of appellate judges.

To my mind, the mere statement of the proposition that human values must be abjured by appellate judges exposes its fallacy: how but by the application of some measure of human understanding and contemporary experience could a judge today resolve the unprecedented legal issues that crowd the court dockets? Even if the law were declared

---

5. See, e.g., N.Y. Const. art. VI, § 3(a); N.Y. Civ. Prac. L. & R. 5501(b) (McKinney, 1983); N.Y. Crim. Proc. Law § 450.90(2)(a) (McKinney, 1983); People v. McRay, 51 N.Y.2d 594, 601, 416 N.E.2d 1015, 1018, 435 N.Y.S.2d 679, 682 (1980).

6. B. Cardozo, The Nature of the Judicial Process 168 (1921).

7. Id. at 166. See also Clark and Trubek, The Creative Role of the Judge: Restraint and Freedom in the Common Law Tradition, 71 Yale L.J. 255 (1961).

8. G. Gilmore, The Ages of American Law 77 (1977). See supra note 2, at 951 for the historical context in which these unorthodox views were expressed.

dead, always to remain static, the problems confronted by the courts are people's problems, and the infinite ingenuity of the human mind seems never to concoct the identical situation twice. Immediately there is judicial hand tailoring to be done, often requiring choices among sound alternatives, simply to fit existing precedents to the very next suit. And even if nothing more were required of appellate courts than the application of codes made by others, the exercise is necessarily more than mechanical. There are inevitably gaps to be filled and anomalies to be treated as statutes are tested in the crucible of live controversies that even the most farseeing legislators could not have contemplated.

With every session of our court in Albany, I am increasingly struck by the changed nature of the business of a common law court in a great commercial state, which is surely reflective of profound changes both in the litigation process and in society generally. Our docket is substantially devoted to criminal appeals, to the interpretation of ever-proliferating statutes as our law has grown increasingly codified, and to review of administrative agency decisions, where the problems of our citizenry seem more and more to be resolved. In the past year, for example, there has likely not been a single session without appeals involving children under the Family Court Act and the penal laws—child abuse and neglect cases, parental rights termination cases, juvenile delinquencies—as the family has taken the law into its midst; and there has likely not been a single session without appeals from prison administrative determinations arising under regulations of the Commissioner of Corrections. In the year 1920, when Judge Cardozo delivered the lectures that became the classic *Nature of the Judicial Process* there were no such cases. The entire law of prisoners' rights probably could have been summarized in one sentence: This page intentionally left blank.

But while the business of the Court of Appeals has changed dramatically as society has evolved, while the number and topics of the cases we hear today are vastly different, when the meaning of a statute is in dispute, there remains at the core the same process of discerning, interpreting, and applying the will of the lawmakers. In applying the laws declared by others—be they statutes, regulations, or orders—there is no question that judges frequently are left to choose among competing policies, thereby narrowing or broadening the reach of the law, and determining its range and direction.

A time-honored principle of statutory construction often may be found to support the position of each party, as is evident in the fact that two courts below ours may already have divided respectably on the meaning of the provision in issue. One principle of construction tells us that courts interpreting statutes must look to the words used by the legislature; explicit statutory provisions should be applied as written. But another principle tells us that if literalness yields absurdity, or if it fails to give effect to the underlying legislative purpose, courts are not to apply the statutory provisions as written but are to seek some other meaning. McKinney's Book on Statutes is filled with such bedeviling points and counterpoints.[9]

I am reminded by several recent volumes of Court of Appeals opinions that, just within the past few years, the court has determined, under one rubric of statutory construction or another, many socially significant issues within the state statutory law. The

---

9. *See generally* Breitel, *The Lawmakers*, 65 Colum. L. Rev. 749, 767–69 (1965), and particularly, K. Llewellyn, The Common Law Tradition 521–35 (1960).

court has determined, for example, that a medical license acquired by one spouse during marriage may be "marital property" as that term is used in the Domestic Relations Law,[10] and that increases in the value of separate property of one spouse may also fall within that statutory term;[11] that there is no private right of action for securities fraud under the General Business Law;[12] that the term "environment" as used in environmental conservation laws may include short-term and long-term effects of secondary displacement of local residents and businesses;[13] that only communications made confidentially to journalists come within the Shield Law;[14] that letters of credit are not attachable "property" as that word is used in the Civil Practice Law and Rules.[15] The court in a recent celebrated criminal case defined the statutory defense of "justification,"[16] and it defined the word "death" for purposes of homicide prosecutions under the Penal Law.[17]

The legislature has established the requirement of corroboration for certain crimes, but it remains for the court as a matter of statutory construction to give substance to the word "corroboration,"[18] and the phrase "mistake of law,"[19] and the term "actually present"[20] as used in the penal statutes. These words can rarely be defined by simply consulting a good dictionary. The cases would hardly reach us if there were not genuine ground for difference. Yet when the court interpreting a statute concludes that an indictment must be dismissed or a conviction affirmed or a damages award modified, that determination not only affects the litigants but also influences future decisions of others as to what crimes will be prosecuted and what lawsuits brought—in short, what conduct will be tolerated by society generally.

If this is so as to statutory law, where the role of the court is circumscribed by the words and intent of the legislature—if human value judgments can play any part in a judge's choice between one reading of key statutory provisions and another—then it

---

10. *O'Brien v. O'Brien*, 66 N.Y.2d 576, 489 N.E.2d 712, 498 N.Y.S.2d 743 (1985).

11. *Price v. Price*, 69 N.Y.2d 8, 503 N.E.2d 684, 511 N.Y.S.2d 219 (1986).

12. *CPC Int'l, Inc. v. McKesson Corp.*, 70 N.Y.2d 268, 514 N.E.2d 116, 519 N.Y.S.2d 804 (1987). *See also All Seasons Resorts, Inc. v. Abrams*, 68 N.Y.2d 81, 497 N.E.2d 33, 506 N.Y.S.2d 10 (1986) (defining "securities" under, Section 352-e of New York General Business Law).

13. *Chinese Staff and Workers Ass'n v. City of New York*, 68 N.Y.2d 359, 502 N.E.2d 176, 509 N.Y.S.2d 499 (1986). *See also Jackson v. New York Urban Dev. Corp.*, 67 N.Y.2d 400, 494 N.E.2d 429, 503 N.Y.S.2d 298 (1986).

14. *In re Knight-Ridder Broadcasting v. Greenberg*, 70 N.Y.2d 151, 511 N.E.2d 1116, 518 N.Y.S.2d 595 (1987).

15. *In re Supreme Merchandise Co. v. Chemical Bank*, 70 N.Y.2d 344, 514 N.E.2d 1358, 520 N.Y.S.2d 734 (1987).

16. *People v. Goetz*, 68 N.Y.2d 96, 497 N.E.2d 41, 506 N.Y.S.2d 18 (1986). *See also People v. Magliato*, 68 N.Y.2d 24, 496 N.E.2d 856, 505 N.Y.S.2d 836 (1986) and *People v. McManus*, 67 N.Y.2d 541, 496 N.E.2d 202, 505 N.Y.S.2d 43 (1986).

17. *People v. Eulo*, 63 N.Y.2d 341, 472 N.E.2d 286, 482 N.Y.S.2d 436 (1984).

18. *People v. Groff*, 71 N.Y.2d 101, 518 N.E.2d 908, 524 N.Y.S.2d 13 (1987); *People v. Moses*, 63 N.Y.2d 299, 472 N.E.2d 4, 482 N.Y.S.2d 228 (1984). *See also In re Nicole V.*, 71 N.Y.2d 112, 518 N.E.2d 914, 524 N.Y.S.2d 19 (1987) (defining "corroboration" in child protective proceedings).

19. *People v. Marrero*, 69 N.Y.2d 382, 507 N.E.2d 1068, 515 N.Y.S.2d 212 (1987).

20. *People v. Hedgman*, 70 N.Y.2d 533, 517 N.E.2d 858, 523 N.Y.S.2d 46 (1987).

must be all the more so as to the common law. Common law, after all, is law that is out-and-out made by judges.

The value judgments of appellate judges can hardly be alien to the development of the common law; they are essential to it. Choices among the precedents of another day—which to bring forward, which to leave behind, which to extend to meet some new condition, which to limit or overrule—mark the progress of the law. This process breathes life into our law; it gives relevance and rationality in the year 1988 to rules fashioned for another day, so that they command acceptance as principles by which we live.

Reflecting on the subject of this article, I have read the Court of Appeals decisions of the year 1928—which will no doubt lend a wonderful freshness and vitality to my own opinions in 1988. I have a new wealth of knowledge on the law relating to barge canals and the common law of insurance. I picked 1928 because it yielded an even number, and because it fell within the tenure of Chief Judge Cardozo, before he left our court for the United States Supreme Court. That was the year of *Moch v. Rensselaer*,[21] *Meinhard v. Salmon*,[22] and *Palsgraf v. The Long Island Railroad*,[23] to name a few. In one sense I found it disheartening; so few of the hundreds of decisions of that year are familiar to me today, and so many utterly unknown. That is a sobering thought for the future as I prepare for the argument of new cases, which seem to me, as always, to raise momentous issues that will live forever in the law. But it is in another sense elevating that, even given the small relative number, so many of the 1928 decisions remain central to the law today, which perhaps best illustrates the nature of the common law process—constantly to test and retest the rules and principles established by judges of another day, and to retain and build upon what remains sound.

Mrs. Palsgraf, as every student of the law knows, was waiting for the Rockaway Beach train when a Long Island Railroad employee dislodged a wrapped package of fireworks carried by another passenger. The impact of the package falling to the ground caused an explosion that toppled scales at the other end of the platform, injuring her. Four judges voted to dismiss her case against the railroad. Three of the seven thought she should have won. Ample authority was collected by both sides; the opinions made a plausible, reasoned argument for both conclusions. Yet in thousands of guises, that bare majority decision—which of course became the law of the state—has lived through the decades as a root principle of the law of negligence. To this day we cite *Palsgraf*. The facts are modern—should a landlord be liable when a 16-year-old is forced into his unlocked building and attacked;[24] should the state be liable to a murdered student's family when a prison physician, completing a college medical form for an inmate about to be released to attend the college, fails to disclose the inmate's extensive psychiatric history;[25] should the Transit Authority be liable when a young student waiting for a subway train is beaten

21. *H.R. Moch Co. v. Rensselaer Water Co.*, 247 N.Y. 160, 159 N.E. 896 (1928).

22. 249 N.Y. 458, 164 N.E. 545 (1928).

23. 248 N.Y. 339, 162 N.E. 99, *reargument denied*, 249 N.Y.511, 164 N.E. 564 (1928).

24. *Waters v. New York City Hous. Auth.*, 69 N.Y.2d 225, 505 N.E.2d 922, 513 N.Y.S.2d 356 (1987).

25. *Eiseman v. State of New York*, 70 N.Y.2d 175, 511 N.E.2d 1128, 518 N.Y.S.2d 608 (1987).

to death, while a toll collector stands in the booth?[26] What standard of care is owed to baseball spectators,[27] to baseball players,[28] to jockeys,[29] to trespassers,[30] to fetuses?[31] Should damages be allowed for purely psychic injury, and if so how far should responsibility for such injury be extended?[32] The times are different, the facts are different, the answers vary. But always the court's function is the same, that of weighing and balancing the relation of the parties, the nature of the risk and the public interest, and then setting the outer limits of one person's duty of care to another, unquestionably an important element in our social order today.

By the same token, only four judges of the Court of Appeals several decades ago joined in another famous opinion, *MacPherson v. Buick*,[33] upholding the liability of an automobile manufacturer for a defective wheel on a car purchased by the injured plaintiff. The dissenting opinion—again replete with creditable authorities—rejected the imposition of liability on the automobile manufacturer because it was the wheel that was defective, the wheel was made by someone else, and the plaintiff was not the customer of the wheel manufacturer. There was no "privity of contract" between the injured plaintiff and the automobile manufacturer, and the dissent concluded that under existing law there could be no liability. But the court's majority chose a different route. Although the dissent saw the automobile as an innocuous object moving at the speed of eight miles an hour, the majority saw that same object as a potentially dangerous instrument that could travel 50 miles an hour and had space for passengers. The majority therefore chose an entirely separate line of authority that bypassed the notion of privity and instead treated the automobile as a dangerous instrument for which the manufacturer should be held liable, likening an automobile with a bad wheel to a deadly poison falsely labeled.[34] And from that choice, an entire body of product liability law has emerged and flowered.

---

26. *Crosland v. New York City Transit Auth.*, 68 N.Y.2d 165, 498 N.E.2d 143, 506 N.Y.S.2d 670 (1986).

27. *Davidoff v. Metro. Baseball Club, Inc.*, 61 N.Y.2d 996, 463 N.E.2d 1219, 475 N.Y. 367 (1984); *Akins v. Glens Falls City School Dist.*, 53 N.Y.2d 325, 424 N.E.2d 531, 441 N.Y.S.2d 644 (1981).

28. *Maddox v. City of New York*, 66 N.Y.2d 270, 487 N.E.2d 553, 496 N.Y.S.2d 726 (1985).

29. *Turcotte v. Fell*, 68 N.Y.2d 432, 502 N.E.2d 964, 510 N.Y.S.2d 49 (1986).

30. *Basso v. Miller*, 40 N.Y.2d 233, 352 N.E.2d 868, 386 N.Y.S.2d 564 (1976).

31. *See, e.g., Tebbutt v. Virostek*, 65 N.Y.2d 931, 483 N.E.2d 1142, 493 N.Y.S.2d 1010 (1985); *Martinez v. Long Island Jewish-Hillside Medical Center*, 70 N.Y.2d 697, 512 N.E.2d 538, 518 N.Y.S.2d 955 (1987). *See also Woods v. Lancet*, 303 N.Y. 349, 102 N.E.2d 691 (1951) (recognizing the right of an infant to recover against a doctor for injuries in utero). The Court wrote: "We act in the finest common-law tradition when we adapt and alter decisional law to produce common-sense justice." *Id.* at 355, 102 N.E.2d at 694.

32. *Bovsun v. Sanperi*, 61 N.Y.2d 219, 461 N.E.2d 843, 473 N.Y.S.2d 357 (1984).

33. 217 N.Y. 382, 111 N.E. 1050 (1916). Judges Hiscock, Chase, and Cuddeback joined in the opinion of Judge Cardozo; Judge Hogan concurred in result only; Chief Judge Bartlett dissented; and Judge Pound did not participate in the case at all.

34. For an analysis of *MacPherson*, see K. Llewellyn, *supra* note 9, at 430–37. "[P]rinciple, in terms of 'the needs of life,' must be recurred to constantly, so as to correct and to readjust precedent—that is vital. But so far as it suggests that principles themselves do not change, the suggestion is legal convention and not legal fact. Principles are born in travail, and some of them die, and sometimes, like the one here, they take new shape in mid-career." *Id.* 436–37.

MacPherson too has lived countless additional lives as appellate courts throughout the country, responding to changing social needs and social conditions, have inch by inch, case by case, moved the law beyond privity of contract and beyond liability to the ultimate purchaser, beyond the manufacturer,[35] beyond actual negligence,[36] and some courts, even beyond strict liability to enterprise or "market share" liability,[37] openly using policy-based justifications such as the superior ability of manufacturers and sellers both to recognize and cure defects, and to minimize and spread the risk among all consumers. In our sophisticated, materialistic society, can anyone today doubt the profound influence of judge-made product liability law on our social development?

In *Moch v. Rensselaer*,[38] a waterworks company furnishing the water for city fire hydrants was sued by a warehouse owner when his property burned to the ground because there was no water in the hydrants to put out the fire. This time, however, the court denied recovery because there was no "privity of contract" between the warehouse owner and the waterworks company. The only contract was with the city. The court perceived that to allow recovery, to enlarge the company's duty beyond its contract, would have been to extend potential liability indefinitely. Today that same principle also lives in many forms, most recently as the basis for decisions favoring Consolidated Edison in suits for personal injuries suffered by New York City residents during the last blackout. It was the court's perception in 1985, just like *Moch* in 1928, that it would impose a crushing burden on the utility if every person in the City of New York who suffered injury during the blackout were allowed to recover against Consolidated Edison. As a matter of public policy the complaints were dismissed.[39] That same concept of "privity of contract" as limiting the ambit of tort responsibility was again critical in the famous case of *Ultramares Corp. v. Touche*,[40] defining an accountant's liability in negligence. More than 50 years later in *Credit Alliance*,[41] the Court of Appeals chose to adhere to the "wisdom and policy"[42] of *Ultramares*; state supreme courts elsewhere, for policy reasons, have chosen otherwise.

---

35. The cases, of course, are legion in this burgeoning area of law. For an interesting development at ten-year intervals, see *Voss v. Black & Decker Mfg. Co.*, 59 N.Y.2d 102, 450 N.E.2d 204, 463 N.Y.S.2d 398 (1983); *Codling v. Paglia*, 32 N.Y.2d 330, 298 N.E.2d 022, 345 N.Y.S.2d 461 (1973); and *Goldberg v. Kollsman Instrument Corp.*, 12 N.Y.2d 432, 191 N.E.2d 81, 240 N.Y.S.2d 592 (1963).

36. *See, e.g., Micallef v. Miehle Co.*, 39 N.Y.2d 376, 348 N.E.2d 571, 384 N.Y.S.2d 115 (1976); *Sage v. Fairchild-Swearingen Corp.*, 70 N.Y.2d 579, 517 N.E.2d 1304, 523 N.Y.S.2d 418 (1987).

37. *See Sindell v. Abbott Laboratories*, 26 Cal. 3d 588, 607 P.2d 924, 163 Cal. Rptr. 132, *cert. denied*, 449 U.S. 912 (l 980); *Martin v. Abbott Laboratories*, 102 Wash. 2d 581, 689 P.2d 368 (1984).

38. 247 N.Y. 160, 159 N.E. 896 (1928).

39. *Strauss v. Belle Realty*, 65 N.Y.2d 399, 482 N.E.2d 34, 492 N.Y.S.2d 555 (1985). The judge-made law of municipal immunity comes quickly to mind as another *Moch* derivative. *See, e.g., Cuffy v. City of New York*, 69 N.Y.2d 255, 505 N.E.2d 937, 513 N.Y.S.2d 372 (1987).

40. 255 N.Y. 170, 174 N.E. 441 (1931).

41. *Credit Alliance Corp. v. Arthur Andersen & Co.*, 65 N.Y.2d 536, 483 N.E.2d 110, 493 N.Y.S.2d 435 (1985).

42. *Id.* at 551, 483 N.E.2d at 118, 493 N.Y.S.2d at 443.

I believe I could multiply these examples in every area of the law—substantive and procedural.[43] There is no question that appellate courts and appellate judges throughout the nation traditionally and necessarily do shape the law and sometimes even make the law, and that this is not a subject for sheepishness or apology.[44] Judges exercising their policy-making function are not exhibiting a lack of judicial restraint, and it strikes me as a false issue to equate the two. Moreover, this accepted judicial function so permeates our social order that, even if in principle subject to legislative correction, as a practical matter its effects cannot readily be undone by legislative action.

The concern—and I believe a valid one—is that there must be limits. Judicial policy-making cannot be a freewheeling exercise. If appellate adjudication is not a cold, scientific process of affixing precedents to facts found below, neither is it a free-form exercise in imposing a judge's personal beliefs about what would be a nice result in a particular case.

---

43. Indeed, there are so many examples that I find it hard to stop reciting them. *See, e.g., Bing v. Thunig*, 2 N.Y.2d 656, 143 N.E.2d 3, 163 N.Y.S.2d 3 (1957) abrogating the judge-made charitable immunity doctrine, in which the court wrote:

> To the suggestion that *stare decisis* compels us to perpetuate it until the legislature acts, a ready answer is at hand. It was intended, not to effect a "petrifying rigidity," but to assure the justice that flows from certainty and stability. If, instead, adherence to precedent offers not justice but unfairness, not certainty but doubt and confusion, it loses its right to survive, and no principle constrains us to follow it.

Id. at 667, 143 N.E.2d at 9, 163 N.Y.S.2d at 11. *See also Buckley v. City of New York*, 56 N.Y.2d 300, 305, 437 N.E.2d 1088, 1090, 452 N.Y.S.2d 331, 333 (1982) (abolishing the fellow servant rule in New York) and *McGee v. Adams Paper & Twine Co.*, 20 N.Y.2d 921, 233 N.E.2d 289, 286 N.Y.S.2d 274 (1967), *aff'g* 26 A.D.2d 186, 271 N.Y.S.2d 698 (1966) (adopting the fireman's rule).

44. While Judges Cardozo and Holmes more than a half-century ago described judicial lawmaking as interstitial and molecular—even that recognition of a limited policymaking role was at the time regarded as radical—I think it has long been true that the traditional judicial activity is broader:

> It is now a commonplace that courts, not only of common-law jurisdictions but also those which have codified statutory law as their base, participate in the lawmaking process. The commonplace, for which the Holmeses and the Cardozos had to blaze a trail in the judicial realm, assumes the rightness of courts in making interstitial law, filling gaps in the statutory and decisional rules, and at a snail-like pace giving some forward movement to the developing law. . . . The simplest observation of the vast, direct and profound overriding of old rules and principles and the substitution of new ones in both the state and federal courts establishes the contrary, namely, that the courts do not confine their lawmaking activity to the interstitial.

Breitel, *supra* note 9, at 765.

> It is evident that the massive changes in the field of public law are greater because of the need to interpret broadly-worded constitutional provisions and the difficulty of constitutional amendment. But the capacity, and the habit perhaps, of significant law creation under the pressure of constitutional interpretation has extended to private law, and here without the public and political controversy engendered by issues involved in public law.

Id. at 766. In his article, former Chief Judge Breitel offers an excellent analysis of the reasons for and the limitations of judicial lawmaking.

Our government is after all a government of law, and our court is a court of law. Though it must move, the law also must have stability, certainty, and predictability so that people will know how to conduct themselves in order to come within the law, and will know what rights they may reasonably expect will be protected or enforced. An appellate court decision resolves a dispute between litigants, but it also establishes the rule for the future. Stability is essential for fairness and evenhandedness: if certain conduct produces a result in one case, then blind justice should produce the same result for other people in other cases like it. Courts simply cannot decide one way one day and another way the next.[45]

The point, however, is that they do not. There must be limits, and there are limits. There is first and foremost respect for the separate functions of the legislative and executive branches of government. I have found no better lesson in the significance of the distribution of powers than the profound and enduring Cardozo Lecture delivered by former Chief Judge Breitel, which concludes with the observation that "self-restraint by the courts in lawmaking must be their greatest contribution to the democratic society."[46] Statutes are limits; the court's focus is to implement the will of the legislature, not its own will. Cases are limits; courts do not render advisory opinions, they resolve live disputes on the facts before them. Then too, appellate decisions are not written on blank sheets of paper. They are the product of a system that values stability and faithful adherence to precedent. They are the product of a process of extracting the principles of the past and assiduously following their path through history and logic. They are the product of consensus among independent judges who are restrained additionally by the traditions of the institution, not the least of which is the tradition of making public a reasoned explanation for the results they reach.

My concluding thought from all of this is that the danger is not that judges will bring the full measure of their experience, their moral core, their every human capacity to bear in the difficult process of resolving the cases before them. It seems to me that a far greater danger exists if they do not.

---

45. *[S]tare decisis* does not spring full-grown from a "precedent" but from precedents which reflect principle and doctrine rationally evolved. Of course, it would be foolhardy not to recognize that there is potential for jurisprudential scandal in a court which decides one way one day and another way the next; but it is just as scandalous to treat every errant footprint barely hardened overnight as an inescapable mold for future travel.

People v. Hobson, 39 N.Y.2d 479, 488, 348 N.E.2d 894, 901, 384 N.Y.S.2d 419, 425 (1976). *See also Bing v. Thunig*, 2 N.Y.2d 656, 143 N.E.2d 3, 163 N.Y.S.2d 3 (1957).

46. Breitel, *supra* note 9, at 777.

One Judge's View of
Academic Law Review Writing*

Last year I was invited to join in a full-day conference on contract theory at New York University Law School, principally with contract law teachers from around the country. My friend Stewart Pollock, a distinguished member of the New Jersey Supreme Court, was the only other judge participating. I remember how startled I was to receive the invitation—it was so different from the more usual bar invitations I receive. In the midst of a docket crammed with pressing civil and criminal cases, I was offered the opportunity to carve out a whole Saturday to consider a body of developing legal theory, with people I generally encounter only in graduation processions and card catalogs. The invitation was irresistible.

Although it was a thoroughly successful conference,[1] there was a persistent undercurrent that frankly surprised me. Concern was several times voiced that academic writing was having little influence on the development of the law, that the professors seemed to be writing for each other. One of the conference papers measured the impact of law and economics theory by compiling the number of times law review articles on the subject had been cited in opinions, and then grading the degree of actual reliance placed on each cited article.[2] Finally, during a question period, a professor addressed the following remarks to me:

---

*39 Journal of Legal Education 313 (September 1989). This article is an outgrowth of remarks delivered at a conference on contracts sponsored by the Association of American Law Schools, at Cornell Law School, June 3–8, 1989. The author is grateful for the enthusiastic research assistance of her law clerk Henry Greenberg.

1. The day's proceedings are printed in 1988 Ann. Surv. Am. L. 1, 1–272.

2. Jeffrey L. Harrison, *Trends and Traces: A Preliminary Evaluation of Economic Analysis in Contract Law*, 1988 Ann. Surv. Am. L., supra note 1, at 73 & app. Many cited articles were found to be of no actual importance to the decision, which says something about opinions that cite a lot of law review articles. Although the idea of measuring impact by counting citations struck me as odd—I read a great many more law review articles than I cite in my opinions—I have since learned that this is an established method for determining the impact of articles, known as "citation analysis." Fred R. Shapiro, *The Most Cited Law Review Articles*, 73 Calif. L. Rev. 1540 (1985).

Several of the speakers today have pointed to the distressingly low impact that they perceive of legal academic writing on what practicing lawyers do or what judges do. I was wondering if there was some way we might improve the effect of our output into which so much effort goes.[3]

It is an excellent question for academics to put to judges, and to practitioners, who represent not only their empirical data but also a substantial portion of their readership. I did not know anyone was interested in my views on the subject; I considered the situation analogous to that of my friend's father, who well into his nineties steadfastly kept his hardware store open daily between 6 a.m. and 10 a.m., when there were few customers in the area, because it suited him.

I would now like to offer a more thoughtful response, centering on the law reviews.

One Sure-Fire Solution

My initial surprise about the concern expressed at the conference was in fact a realization that as academics search through opinions for references to their articles, judges search through articles for references to their opinions. When I find none, I have mixed emotions—gratitude and relief. It is like stage performers and the morning notices, and the reviews can be blistering; such is the character of the critic. When a scholar who has devoted years of study to an area comments on the opinion of a generalist judge constrained by a record, a full calendar, and a need to decide cases with some dispatch, there is usually little for the majority author to write home about. Dissents are something else. With rare exception, it is only dead majority writers who fare well in the literature, and then only really dead ones.

But I do have a suggestion for increasing citations to academic articles in opinions: write only flattering things about judges' opinions. As Chief Justice Taft cautioned a group of law review editors of a bygone era: "Remember, if you will, we are the only courts you have."[4]

If an opinion reaches the wrong result, instead of immortalizing it as myopic or blundering, why not describe it as thought-provoking or interesting? If the result is right but the rationale wrong, forget the rationale. It is the result that counts, and who

---

3. *Supra* note 1, at 270 (Hilary Josephs was the questioner).

4. *Quoted in* Stanley H. Fuld, *A Judge Looks at the Law Review*, 28 N.Y.U. L. Rev. 915, 921 (1953). Judge Fuld observes:

> [I]t is difficult to describe the judge's bliss when he discovers a law review affirming an opinion that he wrote for the court. And nothing can be more cheering than the note that agrees with his lone dissent. That, he says to himself, that bespeaks an intelligent farseeing student of the law-a veritable Solomon come to judgment. And so he rests content, until once more the review "reverses" another of his opinions.

Id. at 916.

remembers rationales anyway? If the opinion is turgid or incomprehensible, why not stay focused on the result or the rationale? And if the writing is an unprincipled break from *stare decisis*, a misstep in the mighty path of the law, is it not adequately put down as bold or novel? Common sense tells us that if being cited more often in opinions is an objective of academic writers, articles of unabashed praise and downright reverence for the judiciary would stand a far better chance of success than the devastating criticism that traditionally motivates scholarly comment on court decisions.

What also surprises me is that I now discover that scholarly law review articles going back more than half a century have been devoted to measuring the impact of scholarly law review articles,[5] and the subject is once again being studied.[6] The concern is particularly surprising today because it seems that most modern appellate opinions cite a treatise, law review article, book, or other academic writing. Substantial opinions today are likely to cite everything.

The phenomenon may in part be attributable to a marked ambivalence of *our* consuming public about what constitutes a creditable opinion. On the one hand, there is avowed hostility to overlong, overblown, overfootnoted opinions.[7] On the other hand, there is an expectation that Significant Opinions will be long, elaborate, splintered, and laced with references to all manner of arcane sources. Opinions that are shorn of adornments—the crisp, plain statements of an earlier day—do not seem "scholarly" or "reasoned" when written today. The principle appears to be that if an opinion is short, unanimous, and readable, it is unsophisticated or unimportant; if not, it is positively brilliant. Because judges generally would rather be perceived as scholarly than simple, academic law review writing for courts would seem to be a growth industry.

---

5. *See, e.g.*, Douglas B. Maggs, *Concerning the Extent to Which the Law Review Contributes to the Development of the Law*, 3 S. Cal. L. Rev. 181 (1929–30); Comment, *Legal Periodicals: Their Use in Kansas*, 7 U. Kan. L. Rev. 490 (1959); William M. Landes and Richard A. Posner, *Legal Precedent: A Theoretical and Empirical Analysis*, 19 J. L. & Econ. 249 (1976); Olavi Maru, *Measuring the Impact of Legal Periodicals*, 1976 Am. B. Found. Res. J. 227; John Merryman, *Toward a Theory of Citations: An Empirical Study of the Citation Practice of the California Supreme Court in 1950, 1960 and 1970*, 50 S. Cal. L. Rev. 381 (1976–77); Ira Mark Ellman, *A Comparison of Law Faculty Production in Leading Law Reviews*, 33 J. Legal Educ. 681 (1983); Fred R. Shapiro, *supra* note 2; [Mary Anne Bobinski], *Citation Sources and the New York Court of Appeals*, 34 Buff. L. Rev. 965 (1985); Louis J. Sirico, Jr. and Jeffrey B. Margulies, *The Citing of Law Reviews by the Supreme Court: An Empirical Study*, 34 UCLA L. Rev. 131 (1986).

6. In January 1989, Professor Michael Saks of the University of Iowa presented a preliminary, partial draft of his study, *Law Journals: Their Shapes and Contents, 1960 and 1985*, as part of a symposium on legal scholarship sponsored by the Executive Committee of the Association of American Law Schools.

7. Abner J. Mikva, *Goodbye to Footnotes*, 56 U. Colo. L. Rev. 647 (1984–85); Milton Handler, *The Supreme Court's Footnote Addiction*, 58 N.Y. St. B.J. 18 (Dec. 1986). I concur in Handler's view that it is not a court's function to produce a new edition of Corpus Juris in its opinions. Judicial opinions are not encyclopedias or law review articles and need not round out the law—or display the writer's erudition, or the clerk's industry—by including every possible citation to the cases and literature. For an analysis of changes in opinion-writing style, see Lawrence M. Friedman, Robert A. Kagan, Bliss Cartwright, and Stanton Wheeler, *State Supreme Courts: A Century of Style and Citation*, 33 Stan. L. Rev. 773 (1981).

Historical Perspective

It was not always that way. Judicial opinions have been around longer than legal periodicals, which officially began in the United States with *The American Law Journal and Miscellaneous Repertory* in 1808. The *Harvard Law Review*, founded in 1887, is generally credited with being the first of the student-edited law reviews.[8] Apart from references to the likes of Blackstone, Coke, and Littleton, a judge before the turn of the century was belittling the office if anything other than an opinion was cited.[9] When a lawyer in the early 1900s had the temerity to refer to law review writings during a Supreme Court argument, Justice Holmes admonished that they were merely the "work of boys."[10] Chief Judge Cardozo described the early distrust of law reviews—which quickly emerged as the perfect outlet for shorter faculty writings—as a "vague terror of the nihilistic and explosive power of thinking and of theory. . . . Teachers being notoriously given to thinking, one can never know what they may do in unsettling the foundations of the established legal order."[11]

There was a glaring exception—the pioneering article written by two practicing lawyers, Louis Brandeis and Samuel Warren, "The Right to Privacy," published in the *Harvard Law Review* a century ago.[12] The article envisioned a common-law right to privacy, and a tort for its invasion, before it had been formally recognized by the courts of England or America. The trial and intermediate appellate courts in New York wisely accepted the notion of such a right, but the Court of Appeals in *Roberson v. Rochester Folding-Box Co.*[13] had the misfortune to reject it. *Roberson* is notable for yet another reason: in his four-judge majority opinion Chief Judge Alton Parker discussed a law review article. He observed that the theory espoused by Brandeis and Warren "was presented with attractiveness and no inconsiderable ability."[14] Not bad.

Brandeis and Warren actually fared a lot better than Parker. His opinion was unanimously overruled both in the court of public opinion and in the legislature, and two years after the decision he resigned the bench to run for president of the United States—against Theodore Roosevelt. Indeed, the strong public reaction even drove one of the majority judges to an unprecedented counterattack: he wrote a law review article

---

8. Both Harvard and the University of Pennsylvania claim the distinction of being the oldest continuously published American university law review. Pennsylvania dates itself from the founding of the *American Law Register* in 1852. See William O. Douglas, *Law Reviews and Full Disclosure*, 40 Wash. L. Rev. 227, 228 n.3 (1965). For law review histories, see Roger C. Cramton, *"The Most Remarkable Institution": The American Law Review*, 36 J. Legal Educ. 1 (1986); Michael I. Swygert and Jon W. Bruce, *The Historical Origins, Founding, and Early Development of Student-Edited Law Reviews*, 36 Hastings L.J. 739 (1985); Lawrence Meir Friedman, A History of American Law 630, 2d ed. (New York, 1985).

9. Benjamin N. Cardozo, *Introduction*, Selected Readings in the Law of Contracts at viii, ix (New York, 1931).

10. *Quoted in* Charles E. Hughes, *Foreword*, 50 Yale L.J. 737 (1941).

11. Cardozo, *supra* note 9, at viii.

12. Samuel D. Warren and Louis D. Brandeis, *The Right to Privacy*, 4 Harv. L. Rev, 193 (1890–91).

13. 171 N.Y. 538, 64 N.E. 442 (1902).

14. *Id.* at 544, 64 N.E. at 443.

defending the decision.[15] Of course both the privacy right and the Brandeis-Warren article have won wide recognition. To this day, the article stands as perhaps "the outstanding example of the influence of legal periodicals upon the American law."[16]

In time the judiciary's prejudice against citing law review articles gave way. More precisely, it collapsed and vanished without a trace. Writing in 1931, Chief Judge Cardozo noted that the old prejudice had disappeared within the last ten or fifteen years:

> Judges and advocates may not relish the admission, but the sobering truth is that leadership in the march of legal thought has been passing in our day from the benches of the courts to the chairs of universities. . . . [T]he outstanding fact is here that academic scholarship is charting the line of development and progress in the untrodden regions of the law.[17]

In a similar vein, Judge Learned Hand, addressing a meeting of the Association of American Law Schools in 1925, predicted that law teachers would "be recognized in another generation . . . as the only body which can be relied upon to state a doctrine, with a complete knowledge of its origin, its authority and its meaning. Judges shall in very shame, if we have sense enough, acknowledge that preeminence which your position and your opportunities secure."[18]

It was inevitable that Judge Hand's prediction would come true. We are beyond embarrassment about it. The explosion of codes and calendars makes it impossible for judges to maintain expertise in every corner of the law. As Judge Hand observed, judges are "predetermined sciolists, compelled to maintain some working acquaintance with the whole field, and consequently incapable of thorough knowledge in any part."[19] Increasingly the judiciary has turned to academia. From the day Justice Brandeis first began tucking law review citations into Supreme Court opinions—ostensibly not as authorities but only as collections of cases[20]—we have reached a time in which reliance on academic writing is so pervasive that anything less requires a specific disclaimer.[21]

There can be no question that academic writing has established its impact on the law. The "Corbinizing" of contract law[22] and influence of scholars such as Williston,

---

15. Denis O'Brien, *The Right of Privacy*, 2 Colum. L. Rev. 437 (1902).

16. William L. Prosser, *Privacy*, 48 Cal. L. Rev. 383 (1960).

17. Cardozo, *supra* note 9, at ix.

18. Learned Hand, *Have the Bench and Bar Anything to Contribute to the Teaching of Law?*, 24 Mich. L. Rev. 466, 468 (1926).

19. *Id.* at 466.

20. *See* Philippa Strum, Louis D. Brandeis: Justice for the People 363–64 (Cambridge, Mass., 1984).

21. *See Montana v. United States*, 440 U.S. 147, 164 (1978) (Rehnquist, J., concurring) ("I join the Court's opinion on the customary understanding that its references to law review articles and drafts or finally adopted versions of the Restatement of Judgments are not intended to bind the Court to the views expressed therein on issues not presented by the facts of this case").

22. Peter Linzer, A Contracts Anthology 154 (Cincinnati, 1989)—an excellent collection of materials, itself demonstrating the impact of academic writing on the development of contract law.

Llewellyn, and Prosser come immediately to mind. Strict product-liability law—indeed much of the law of torts today—can be traced to academic writings. Lon Fuller and William Perdue's "Reliance Interest in Contract Damages"[23] has "become the standard exposition of what might be considered the 'modern' approach to contract remedies."[24] These few examples can be multiplied throughout history. I have no doubt that law professors today are highly influential in shaping and formulating the law—whether through their own work with public and private clients, or through their teachings, their students, and their writings.[25]

The influence of academics does not, however, extinguish the concern evidenced at the N.Y.U. Conference. Law reviews have more than quadrupled over the past twenty-five years, now totaling well over 300 publications that appear several times a year and consume over 150,000 printed pages annually.[26] No wonder some of that enormous, expensive output influences the development of the law. With such a proliferation of material, it could hardly be otherwise. The concern nonetheless remains a valid and important one: how can academics *improve* the impact of their writings on the work of judges? I recognize that although my subject is limited to articles by academics, these perceptions are relevant to law reviews generally.[27]

Modern Times

Law reviews have changed in the century since the *Harvard Law Review* was launched with law school news, lecture notes, case summaries, book reviews, student comments on common law topics, and a few lead articles by faculty members on subjects such as the law of electric poles and tickets, elevated road litigation, disseisin of chattels and privity of contract. Many law schools now have four or more separate journals, all student edited—itself an unusual tradition among professional journals.[28] As Dean Havighurst notes,

---

23. L. L. Fuller and William R. Perdue, Jr., *The Reliance Interest in Contract Damages* (pts. 1 & 2), 46 Yale L.J. 52, 373 (1936–37).

24. Charles L. Knapp and Nathan M. Crystal, Problems in Contract Law: Cases and Materials 768, 874–76 (Boston, 1987).

25. On the influence of American Jaw professors, particularly as contrasted with their English counterparts, see P. S. Atiyah and Robert S. Summers, Form and Substance in Anglo-American Law: A Comparative Study in Legal Reasoning, Legal Theory and Legal Institutions 398–403 (New York, 1987).

26. Cramton, *supra* note 8, at 2. According to Saks's preliminary data, law reviews not only have multiplied in number but also have grown fatter, and individual articles have grown longer. Saks, *supra* note 6.

27. Law review form and style are beyond the purview of this piece. Much could be said on both scores—and has been said, masterfully. See Fred Rodell, *Goodbye to Law Reviews*, 23 Va. L. Rev. 38 (1936); Fred Rodell, *Goodbye to Law Reviews—Revisited*, 48 Va. L. Rev. 279 (1962); Richard A. Posner, *Goodbye to the Bluebook*, 53 U. Chi. L. Rev. 1343 (1986). See also David Margolick, *At the Bar*, N.Y. Times, June 9, 1989, at B5, col. 2.

28. See Cramton, *supra* note 8, observing that the student-run law reviews "now have rivals and their future is in doubt." *Id.* at 10.

law reviews are unique among publications in that they do not exist because of any large demand on the part of a reading public. Whereas most periodicals are published primarily in order that they may be read, the law reviews are published primarily in order that they may be written. This, I imagine, was not the view of that small group of students, including young Wigmore and the young Beale, when they first started the *Harvard Law Review*.[29]

Nor is this my view of law reviews, or the view of academics concerned that their articles should have greater impact on the law. Law review articles should be of value to their readers as well as their writers.

Most significant is a perceptible change in law review content, supporting Dean Havighurst's observation that the reviews are published primarily to serve their writers, not their readers. Prominent law reviews are increasingly dedicated to abstract, theoretical subjects, to federal constitutional law, and to federal law generally, and less and less to practice and professional issues, and to the grist of state court dockets.

In chambers, I regularly receive a half-dozen or more law reviews as well as the indices of scores more. Some days, just reading titles is sufficient mental exercise. Consider, for example, "Epistemological Foundations and Meta-Hermeneutic Methods: The Search for a Theoretical Justification of the Coercive Force of Legal Interpretation." I read law review articles generally, for background and for currents in legal thought; the feminist jurisprudence emerging in the literature is an example.[30] But most of the time I read law reviews particularly, as an aid to resolving the cases before us. It is hard to think of *completing* an opinion without venturing into the literature, and ideally I like *starting* an opinion with good briefs and articles. I do not seek out law review articles for case compilations—we have a variety of manual and computerized research tools for such information. I look to law review articles for something much different—for the newest thinking on the subject, for a sense of the direction of the law and how the case before us fits within it, for a more global yet profound perspective on the law and its social context than any individual case presents.

Although it is the function of a state's highest court to develop, fashion, pronounce, settle, and declare broadly applicable principles in particular cases that will not only resolve litigants' disputes but also serve society generally, courts are formally guided only by the parties. Parties do not necessarily have in mind the sensible, incremental development of generally applicable principles of law; they often do not have that in mind at all. Academic writers therefore become genuine partners in the courts' search for wisdom—for determining when and where to move the law to meet the needs of our rapidly changing society. When, for example, should a court first recognize that an automobile moving

---

29. Harold C. Havighurst, *Law Reviews and Legal Education*, 51 NW. U. L. Rev. 22, 24 (1956). Indeed, the Harvard editors in their inaugural issue expressed the hope that their law review would be of service to the profession at large. 1 Harv. L. Rev. 35 (1887).

30. See Eleanor M. Fox, *Being a Woman, Being a Lawyer and Being a Human Being—Women and Change*, 57 Fordham L. Rev. 955 (1989); *Symposium, Women in Legal Education-Pedagogy, Law, Theory, and Practice*, 38 J. Legal Educ. 1, 1–193 (1988).

at the speed of only eight miles an hour is a dangerous instrumentality;[31] when should it first recognize a right to privacy?[32] Such dilemmas—which faced my predecessors on the Court of Appeals when they split four-three in decisions that today are so plainly right, and so plainly wrong—are endlessly repeated on modern state court dockets, in tort and commercial cases, administrative appeals, criminal matters, individual rights cases, even to some extent in cases involving statutes. Such cases are overwhelmingly nonconstitutional, but they are nonetheless significant both to the state's citizens and to the development of the law.

Despite a challenging, important array of issues, despite themes of material the law reviews generate, and despite diligent searching, I am disappointed not to find more in the law reviews that is of value and pertinence to our cases. Invariably the treatises are better source material, though they have neither the purpose nor the potential of law review articles.

Another noticeable change in law reviews is that fewer contributions today are made by judges and practitioners. Most articles are written by full-time academics.[33] There are any number of possible explanations, among them litigation pressures and academic pressures; the tastes and predilections of student editors (getting published can be a bruising experience); and the reluctance of practicing lawyers and judges to commit themselves publicly on issues they may yet confront.

Although there is no necessary correlation to the increasingly abstract law review menus, the decrease in judges and practitioners writing for law reviews may evidence a growing distance between academia and the rest of us. Roger Cramton recently observed:

> In the last twenty-five years, law faculties, especially at the best schools, have become much more academic and scholarly in their orientation. . . . Practitioners, of course, are particularistic problem solvers. They are always dealing with problems that are embedded in a rich institutional and social context. Writing that will meet their needs has to reflect the context in which lawyers do their problem solving. Much that is currently fashionable in legal scholarship seems like pushing smoke into bottles, interminably and at great length.[34]

It is of some comfort—small comfort—that several dedicated educators have concluded that academic writing is now distinctly directed toward the theoretician/scholar and not

---

31. *MacPherson v. Buick Motor Co.*, 217 N.Y. 382, 111 N.E. 1050 (1916).

32. *Roberson v. Rochester Folding Box Co.*, 171 N.Y. 538, 64 N.E. 443 (1902). For more modern examples of similar dilemmas, see my article, *The Human Dimension in Appellate Judging: A Brief Reflection on a Timeless Concern*, 73 Cornell L. Rev. 1004 (1988) [reprinted in this volume].

33. Saks found that in 1960 almost as many articles were authored by judges or practicing lawyers as by law professors. In 1985, for every article authored by a judge or practicing lawyer, there were more than three authored by law professors. Saks, *supra* note 6. Nowak finds that all to the good. The all-too-infrequent contributions of judges and lawyers, he says, "are commonly the subject of faculty room sneers and pejorative comments. Law reviews are the property of professors." John E. Nowak, *Woe Unto You, Law Reviews!*, 27 Ariz. L. Rev. 317 (1985).

34. Roger C. Cramton, *The Next Century: The Challenge: A Panel Discussion*, 73 Cornell L. Rev. 1275, 1276–77 (1988). See also Cramton, *supra* note 8.

the problem-solver/practitioner and judge.[35] The concern that academics are writing for each other is indeed well founded.

After considerable reflection, I would answer the question put to me with more questions. In a legal environment in which the glittering issues revolve around the Supreme Court, the federal Constitution, and federal law, how much do you follow and write about our work? Do you stay current with what state courts are doing? State cases far outnumber federal cases, reaching into every corner of our lives. Are you students of the common-law process? Do you appreciate the traditions and institutional principles that constrain these courts?[36] Are you interested in how state courts operate, how they handle their dockets, how they decide cases? It is nothing short of exciting to come upon a law review article that evidences both scholarship and comprehension of our process, including the remarkable growth and change in the common law. I can only conclude that enhanced interest in what the "other" courts are doing necessarily would improve the impact of academic law review writing on large numbers of lawyers and judges.

My own day at New York University Law School, which blossomed into a second at Cornell Law School, persuades me that there is much to be gained from strengthening the bridges that connect the various islands of the legal profession. Students of course forge a connection when as practicing lawyers they bring fresh ideas from the academy to the law offices and courts; writings forge a connection; so do conferences. As Judge Hand observed, judges "furnish the momentum, [academics] the direction; but each is necessary to the other, each must understand, respect and regard the other, or both will fail."[37] When Judge Hand uttered those words, law reviews were in their infancy, still viewed with skepticism by the bench. Although law reviews have matured into significant contributors to the judicial process, it is no less true today that judges and academics must "understand, respect and regard" each other in order for both to succeed. I sense that, in the rising mountain of law review output, some of that essential quality has been lost.

---

35. Cramton, *supra* note 8; Nowak, *supra* note 33; Sirico and Margolies, *supra* note 5; Havighurst, *supra* note 29; Rodell, *supra* note 7.

36. See Jon O. Newman, *Between Legal Realism and Neutral Principles: The Legitimacy of Institutional Values*, 72 Calif. L. Rev. 200, 216 (1984); Hugh R. Jones, *Cogitations on Appellate Decision-Making*, 34 Rec. Assoc. Bar City of N.Y. 543 (1979).

37. Hand, *supra* note 18, at 480.

Women in Law*

The Law Can Change People

Graduations, for all their pomp and public display, are quintessentially private affairs. A personal rite of passage, graduations tend to be a time of deep distraction and intense introspection for the graduates as well as those who surround them. This is so of a law school graduation especially, for it is the culmination of decades of formal schooling, with its attendant effort and expense, and the gateway to dreams and ambitions that have been nurtured for a good long time. So I understand if during my speech you occupy yourselves fully with your own private thoughts about this auspicious occasion. As a matter of fact, I intend to do exactly the same.

This convocation happens to be a milestone for me as well as for you. I mean this in several ways, most of all as a mother. Like the other parents, grandparents, spouses, siblings, and friends who are here today, I am filled with love and pride to see my daughter, Luisa, a member of this extraordinary class. That gives me the opportunity, if not the right, to say to every graduate that we applaud and admire your achievement and fervently wish for your happiness and success in whatever you may choose to do.

Then too, this law school is my alma mater, the source of my learning and license for a professional life that has been rich beyond imagination. I feel a bit about my law school as I do about my daughter: in both instances what I have received from them far exceeds any contribution I may have made to their lives.

Your graduation is my personal celebration in yet another way. I cannot look upon this class without noting that about half are women. I recall that we were only eleven women back in 1962, my graduation year—a mere four percent of the class. And one hundred years ago this school, indeed this state, had yet to graduate a single female law

*66 New York University Law Review 1929 (1991). This essay formed the basis for remarks delivered as a Commencement Address for the New York University School of Law on May 17, 1991, at Carnegie Hall.

student.[1] For me, therefore, this convocation also is a celebration of change, of society's slow but perceptible movement toward recognizing human beings for who and not what they are, and of the role played by the law in that process. Several examples come to mind—of course, one in particular on this day of days, the thirty-seventh anniversary of the Supreme Court's historic decision in *Brown v. Board of Education.*[2] But the examples that seem most opportune in this hundredth anniversary year of women in the Law School are those of women, of changing attitudes toward women, and especially of the part the law has played in stimulating that change.

It is on this subject that my thoughts center today, after nearly thirty years as a lawyer and judge and considerably more years as a woman in American society. And while I have been reflecting privately on the changes that have taken place since my own graduation, this centennial highlights the even greater distances women have traveled since we were allowed into the Law School.

A century ago, in May 1891, I imagine that New York University's first women law students were doing some celebrating of their own, kicking up their heels for having survived the rigors of the first year of law school. Remember that feeling? They may well have come to this very place, marking their triumph of survival by listening to the works of Beethoven, Mendelssohn, Mozart, Wagner, and Tchaikovsky—the doors of this magnificent Music Hall[3] having opened precisely one hundred years ago this month.

If the music those students heard in this Hall one hundred years ago retains its great beauty today, many other sounds they were hearing—especially those emanating from the Halls of Justice—distinctly do not. The ink barely had dried on the thirteenth, fourteenth, and fifteenth amendments, with their promise of equal rights, when those women heard the Supreme Court of the United States uphold a state's denial of a woman's right to become a member of the Bar. In *Bradwell v. Illinois,*[4] the Court reasoned that bar membership was not one of the "privileges" of a citizen protected by the Constitution.[5] In a separate opinion, Justice Bradley, joined by two colleagues, elaborated on the different

---

1. New York's first woman lawyer, Albany teacher and suffragist Kate Stoneman, was admitted to practice five years earlier—in May 1886—but she qualified for the Bar by law office study, not by law school attendance. *See Centennial Celebration for First Woman Admitted to the Bar*, St. B. News, April 1986, at 11. Prior to New York University's acceptance of women law students, New York women had to leave the state in order to attend law school. K. Morello, The Invisible Bar: The Woman Lawyer in America, 1638 to the Present 76 (1986); *see also* Tokarz, *A Tribute to the Nation's First Women Law Students*, 68 Wash. U. L.Q. 89 (1990) (commemorating first two female law graduates of University of Washington); Weisberg, *Barred from the Bar: Women and Legal Education in the United States, 1870–1890*, in 2 Women and the Law: The Social Historical Perspective 231 (D. Weisberg, ed., 1982) (discussing reasons behind exclusion of women from Bar).

2. 347 U.S. 483 (1954).

3. What is now known as "Carnegie Hall" opened in May 1891 as the "Music Hall," that name prominently etched on the building's facade where it remains to this day. See Keller, *The House That Carnegie Built*, Seaport Mag., Winter–Spring 1991, at 24, 26.

4. 83 U.S. (16 Wall.) 130 (1872).

5. *See id.* at 139; see also *Minor v. Happersett*, 88 U.S. (21 Wall.) 162, 178 (1875) (holding right to vote not necessary privilege of United States citizen and, therefore, that women do not have right to vote if their state prohibits them from doing so).

"spheres and destinies" of men and women under the Law of the Creator—a law those Justices were of no mind to modify.[6] Women needed the protection of men, and society needed healthy mothers; women therefore were inherently unfit for careers in the law.[7] Soon after, New York University's first female law students heard the same themes echoed by the Supreme Court of Wisconsin, which observed, "It would be revolting to all female sense of innocence and sanctity of sex, shocking to man's reverence for womanhood and faith in woman . . . that women should be permitted to mix professionally in all the nastiness of the world which finds its way into courts of justice."[8]

So I have been wondering, what could those first female law students have thought lay ahead when they overthrew tradition and entered law school? Could they possibly have foreseen that they would inspire a centennial? Could they have envisioned a full year of celebration, an unbroken hundred years of women graduates following after them, a class in which women number just under fifty percent,[9] or a time when women would comprise nearly forty percent of all lawyers, as they will by this decade's end?[10] Given the attitudes toward women in 1891, it is hard to imagine that anyone could have had such prescience.

Of course those women were somewhat more fortunate to be living in this enlightened state, where one hundred years ago a woman could be admitted to the practice of law,[11] retain control of her property upon marriage,[12] enter into contracts, collect rents, and

---

6. See *Bradwell*, 83 U.S. (16 Wall.) at 141 (Bradley, J., concurring).

7. *See id.* (Bradley, J., concurring).

8. *In re Goodell*, 39 Wis. 232, 245–46 (1875). *Bradwell* rejected a challenge that would have had nation-wide impact, making it necessary to litigate the issue under each state's constitution. See K. Morello, *supra* note 1, at 22; see also Rhode, *Perspectives on Professional Women*, 40 Stan. L. Rev. 1163, 1164–77 (1988) (providing additional examples of early stereotypes); Weisberg, *supra* note 1, at 231–32 (discussing similar litigation in other states).

9. Women comprise forty-six percent of the graduating J.D. class of 1991. Telephone interview with Karen Stember, Executive Assistant to the Dean, New York University School of Law (Jan. 27, 1992).

10. *See* note 34 *infra*.

11. In 1885, Kate Stoneman was denied admission to the Bar on the ground that "her sex was against her." *In re Leonard*, 53 Am. Rep. 323, 325 (1885). At the time, New York prescribed rules for the admission of "a male citizen of the State of full age," N.Y. Civ. Prac. L. & R. § 56 (1871), and in Stoneman's case the state trial court concluded that the legislature would not have used the word "male" if it had intended to extend eligibility to women. *See Leonard*, 53 Am. Rep. at 325. Stoneman spearheaded efforts to amend the statute, and the legislature complied in 1886, declaring that race and sex would "constitute no cause for refusing such person admission to practice in the courts of record of this State as an attorney and counselor." 1886 N.Y. Laws 425. Stoneman then renewed her application for admission to the Bar which the committee granted. *See Decisions in Cases Not Reported*, 40 Hun. 638 (N.Y. 1886).

From a study of the names of admitted attorneys, it appears that the New York Bar admitted only one other woman besides Stoneman between 1886 and 1890, the year New York University first accepted female law students. See Official Register of Attorneys and Counsellors-at-Law of the State of New York 1–167 (1899).

12. See 1848 N.Y. Laws 200 (declaring that "real and personal property of any female who may hereafter marry, and the rents and profits thereof shall not be subject to the disposal of her husband"). Until 1848, the legal presumption was that husband and wife were "one flesh"—that of the husband. The common law perpetuated this presumption which dates back at least to the Norman Conquest. A married woman

invoke the power of the courts.[13] By no means did women throughout the nation have these same rights.[14]

But even in this enlightened state, in 1891 womanhood remained a "protected occupation."[15] New York laws shielded women from such "burdens" as voting[16] and serving on juries.[17] And, not surprisingly, the laws were particularly protective of women in their anticipated destiny: marriage and childbearing.[18] Well into the present century, the

could not sue or be sued in her own name, nor could she execute a will or enter into contract. Any wages she earned belonged to her husband, who upon marriage acquired the right to control and manage her property. *Sec* N. Basch, In the Eyes of the Law: Women, Marriage, and Property in Nineteenth-Century New York 17 (1982) (discussing development of marital unity doctrine); Speth, *The Married Women's Property Acts 1839–1865: Reform, Reaction, or Revolution?*, in 2 Women and the Law: The Social Histori-cal Perspective 69–70 (D. Weisberg, ed., 1982) (summarizing married women's property rights prior to enactment of married women's property legislation).

13. The New York Earnings Act, 1860 N.Y. Laws 90, allowed a woman to hold property, collect rents, bargain, sell, and transfer her separate property, and sue or be sued. A series of statutes enacted in New York between 1848 and 1884 radically altered the "one flesh" presumption of the common law. *See gen-erally* N. Basch, *supra* note 12, at 113–200 (discussing effect of New York statutes and their relationship to women's suffrage). Describing these statutes which allowed married women a measure of personal identity, Professor Basch notes, "In the context of the nineteenth century, the right of wives to own property entailed their right not to be property." *Id.* at 38; *see also* L. Friedman, A History of American Law 184–86 (1985) (discussing common-law rules regarding property ownership by married women and mid-nineteenth-century changes in those rules).

14. For example, as Justice Sandra Day O'Connor has pointed out, as late as the 1970s, Arizona stat-utes gave exclusive control of community property to the husband and set maximum working hours for women but not for men. S. O'Connor, *Women in Power*, 1990 Sixteenth Annual Olin Conference, Washington University 4 (Nov. 14, 1990) (on file at New York University Law Review).

15. V. Woolf, A Room of One's Own 41 (1957); see also Law, *The Founders on Families*, 39 U. Fla. L. Rev. 583, 586–93 (1987) (despite promise of fourteenth amendment, dominant assumptions of nineteenth century portrayed women as centerpiece of home and "denied women the right or capacity to participate in most forms of economic and political life").

16. While Congress did not ratify the nineteenth amendment until 1920, New York women gained the right to vote on January 1, 1918 when the amended Article II, § 1 of the New York Constitution, conferring equal suffrage on women, took effect.

17. New York state did not deem women eligible for jury service until March 1938, when the state leg-islature amended Civil Rights Law § 13. *See* 1938 N.Y. Laws 163 ("No citizen of the state possessing all other qualifications which are or may be required or prescribed by law, shall be disqualified to serve as a grand or petit juror in any court of the state on account of race, creed, color or sex"); *see also People v. Irizarry*, 142 Misc. 2d 793, 800–803, 536 N.Y.S.2d. 630, 633–35 (Sup. Ct. 1988) (discussing history of 1938 law that enabled women to serve as jurors), *rev'd on other grounds*, 165 A.D.2d 715, 560 N.Y.S.2d 279 (1990); Bamberger, *Democratizing the Supreme Court: 300 Years of the Jury*, 63 N.Y. St. B.J., May/June 1991, at 30, 32 (same).

18. A brief foray into the New York Court of Appeals cases of 1891 makes clear the prevailing expectation that a woman's career involved marriage and dependency on her husband. *See, e.g., Chellis v. Chapman*, 125 N.Y. 214, 219, 221 (1891) (holding trial court did not err in admitting evidence of defendant's wealth in action for breach of marriage contract since "ability of the man to support [a woman] in comfort and the station in life, which marriage with him holds forth, are matters which may be weighed, in connec-tion with an agreement to marry"); *Zimmer v. Settle*, 124 N.Y. 37, 42 (1891) (noting that "primary duty to take care of and support a wife is with the husband"); *Duval v. Wellman*, 124 N.Y. 156, 160 (1891) (ruling in favor of woman who sued publisher of matrimonial journal for failing to find her suitable

courts and others served periodic public reminders that women by nature and structure were timid and weak and that they were at all times in need of care and dependent on the superior strengths of men, especially when the "burdens of motherhood were upon them."[19] Even when the distinguished graduates from the decade of the 1920s who are here with us today persisted in their quest for a legal education, revered individuals and institutions continued to hold and unabashedly to give voice to these widely accepted beliefs.[20]

Whatever drew those first women to this Law School one hundred years ago, we know for certain that they—and the pioneers who followed them—paid a high price for admission to the legal profession. Decades after courts no longer openly spoke of the "sphere and destiny" of women as limited to marriage and childbearing,[21] those deep-seated views continued to flourish. As I myself can attest, even as late as the 1960s, jobs for women lawyers—surely among the most educated and privileged of all women in society—were hard to find; quotas were commonplace; compensation lower; partnerships all but impossible. Women were excluded from bar associations, lawyers' luncheon and athletic clubs, and even firm outings. Humiliation and degradation at the hands of judges, fellow lawyers, and support personnel were the order of the day.[22] The law tolerated this behavior long into the twentieth century, and quite frankly, so did many of us. Getting in was what mattered.

But while the stereotypes and inequities are by no means yet eradicated, efforts that began more than a century ago at last have borne fruit. Public attitudes about women have indeed begun to change. And the law and the courts have had a substantial role in facilitating that change.

In the nineteenth and early twentieth centuries anyone who saw an injustice in prejudice toward women—and most people did not—hardly would have turned to the law for redress. The law, after all, legitimated, perpetuated, and institutionalized society's belief that women were unequal, subordinate. Indeed, even where there were legislative

---

husband, court reasoned that marriage brokerage contracts bring about fraudulent marriages and "destroy the hopes and fortunes of the weaker party, especially of women").

19. *Muller v. Oregon*, 208 U.S. 412, 422 (1907) (holding that statutes regulating woman's work hours fall within states' police powers because "woman's physical well-being and her ability to discharge her maternal functions are objects of public interest").

20. *See, e.g.*, W. Chafe, The American Woman: Her Changing Social, Economic, and Political Roles, 1920–1970, at 25–111 (1972) (discussing prejudices against women during 1920s); Rhode, *supra* note 8, at 1166 (citing 1920 editorial in prominent legal periodical which stated that female practitioners were sure to "treat the law much the way they treat changing fashion: One season all wills will be cut short, [in] another all wills will be drawn long").

21. *See* note 18 *supra*.

22. The abundance of evidence of pervasive discrimination makes choosing sources for this footnote nearly impossible. Nevertheless, *see generally The Report of the New York Task Force on Women in the Courts*, 15 Fordham Urb. L.J. 7, 126–60 (1986–87) (summarizing status of women attorneys and other female employees in New York courts); The American Bar Association Commission on Women in the Profession, *Report to the House of Delegates*, reprinted in N.Y.L.J., Aug. 19, 1988, at 1–3 (discussing current barriers to advancement of women in legal profession).

reforms, such as married women's property acts, in many instances the courts, through cramped statutory interpretation, negated their beneficial effect.[23]

Until I sat down with a dozen dusty volumes from the last century, I quite frankly had forgotten how sharp the contrast is between courts then and now. Above all, the courts of 1891 were forums for resolving private disputes through scientific discovery and application of the correct rule of law.[24] Property taxes, mortgages, and foreclosures; inheritances; steamer, railway, and barge contracts; insurance of every variety; bondholders and interest coupons—these were the burning subjects that consumed the New York Reports as business burgeoned throughout the state and nation.[25] Similarly, the Federal Reports were thick with controversies about bridges and seas, collisions and customs duties, and page upon page about patents.[26]

By 1891, New York had adopted four successive constitutions replete with the lofty language of freedom, liberty, and the rights of citizens.[27] And we had as a nation adopted and already amended the federal Constitution and Bill of Rights. Yet there was no hint of a relationship between those words—equal rights, equal justice, equal opportunity—and many of the inequities that abounded in society.[28] In fact, there was precious little by way of individual rights litigation or administrative proceedings to compel the government to honor its explicit promises to its citizens. A review of the cases litigated a century ago plainly reflects that the community did not regard its courts as a forum for adjusting social imbalances.

Since the middle of this century, however, society has come to view its courts quite differently. I can hardly recall a Court of Appeals session, for example, that has not included several statutory and constitutional challenges against the government for breaching its responsibilities, whether by deprivation of public entitlements, inattention

---

23. See N. Basch, *supra* note 12, at 200–223 (discussing ways in which New York courts limited effectiveness of married women's property acts).

24. See Brennan, *Reason, Passion and "The Progress of the Law,"* 42d Benjamin N. Cardozo Lecture Before the Association of the Bar of the City of New York (Sept. 17, 1987), reprinted in 42 Record of the Ass'n of the Bar of the City of New York 948, 958 (1987) ("[T]he focus on reason had become so tight that all else was excluded from view, and the legal community became convinced that a broader focus would gravely threaten the legitimacy and authority of the judicial branch").

25. See, e.g., volumes 122 to 127 of the New York Reports (1891).

26. See, e.g., volumes 46 to 48 of the Federal Reports (1891).

27. New York adopted its first constitution—among the first in the nation—in 1777; by 1891, the State had replaced the 1777 constitution with the constitutions of 1821, 1846, and 1867. *See generally* P. Galle, The New York State Constitution: A Reference Guide (1991) (providing historical overview of New York Constitution).

28. See G. Boutwell, The Constitution of the United States at the End of the First Century (1895) (devoting 180 pages to case summaries involving Articles of Constitution and 48 pages to Bill of Rights). Imagine such a book today. The concept of "rights" was "consistent with moral and social stratification and clear recognition that the country 'belonged' to the dominant group, white Protestant men. The modern concept is more plural." Friedman, *State Constitutions and Criminal Justice in the Late Nineteenth Century*, 53 Albany L. Rev. 265, 270–71 (1989).

to the environment, or denial of individual rights.[29] Such disputes were virtually unheard of a century ago. And I believe it is no exaggeration to say that the expansion of the judiciary's role in private disputes has been as great as it has been in the public law.[30]

Certainly by the middle of this century, it became clear that the law could be "a vital engine . . . of civilizing change";[31] that courts indeed have a role to play in advancing the enlightenment and progress of this country, in bringing day-to-day reality closer to this nation's stated ideals. It became clear that the law is more than a sheaf of rules, the right rule simply to be discovered and applied mechanically. Rather, there is a necessary and desirable human dimension in the judicial process. There is a recognition that courts and judges shape and at times even make policy, that their insights born of a greater understanding of this changing world can and do contribute to a thoroughly principled yet contemporary, compassionate Rule of Law.[32] And whether by rightful inheritance, the

---

29. For recent examples from the New York Court of Appeals, *see, e.g., Jiggetts v. Grinker*, 75 N.Y.2d 411, 553 N.E.2d 570, 554 N.Y.S.2d 92 (1989) (suit against Social Services Commissioner to require reasonable shelter allowances for families receiving public assistance); *McCain v. Koch*, 70 N.Y.2d 109, 511 N.E.2d 62, 517 N.Y.S.2d 918 (1987) (suit to require New York City agencies to provide housing for homeless families); *Chinese Staff & Workers Ass'n v. City of New York*, 68 N.Y.2d 359, 502 N.E.2d 176, 509 N.Y.S.2d 499 (1986) (suit to require city, in its environmental review, to consider secondary effects on residents of proposed special zoning district). About one-third of our docket today is concerned with individual rights in criminal cases and prison disciplinary proceedings, which have no parallel in the reports of 1891. *See* text accompanying note 25 *supra*.

30. Whole new fields of private law have arisen within the past century including, for example, the law of products liability, where courts openly make policy-based decisions about the proper allocation of risk for safety hazards associated with certain products. *See, e.g., Hymowitz v. Eli Lilly & Co.*, 73 N.Y.2d 487, 539 N.E.2d 1069, 541 N.Y.S.2d 941 (1989) (adopting form of enterprise liability); *Micallef v. Miehle Co.*, 39 N.Y.2d 376, 348 N.E.2d 571, 384 N.Y.S.2d 115 (1976) (determining that manufacturer has duty to avoid unreasonable harm in intended and foreseeable uses, and plaintiff has duty of reasonable care when danger is open and obvious). Other traditional private law fields, such as family law, have enlarged enormously, as the courts now are drawn into all manner of intrafamily disputes. *See, e.g., Alison D. v. Virginia M.*, 77 N.Y.2d 651, 572 N.E.2d 27, 569 N.Y.S.2d 586 (1991) (upholding denial of visitation rights to lesbian woman who had agreed to raise child with estranged lover who was birth mother); *In re Raquel Marie*, 76 N.Y.2d 387, 559 N.E.2d 418, 559 N.Y.S.2d 855 (1990) (declaring unconstitutional portion of statute requiring mother's consent before newborn surrendered for adoption, but requiring father's consent only when he has openly lived with mother for six months immediately preceding surrender). It is Lawrence Friedman's thesis that "legal culture and legal character have been moving in a single direction, toward . . . total justice. Total justice is a social norm; it is also, more and more, a working principle transforming legal and social institutions." *See* L. Friedman, Total Justice 147 (1985).

31. Brennan, *Space Law in the Next Century*, 63 N.Y. St. B.J., May/June 1991, at 42, 44.

32. *See* Tribe, *Revisiting the Rule of Law*, 64 N.Y.U. L. Rev. 726, 731 (1989) (calling for decency and compassion to shape idea of law and for legal community to play special role in furthering nation by advancing law); *see also* K. Karst, Belonging to America: Equal Citizenship and the Constitution 42 (1989) ("In our society one of the most prominent bridges between ideology and behavior is the law. In particular, constitutional litigation is a process in which ideology can be brought to life in the behavior of litigants and of law professionals, including judges. *Brown v. Board of Education* was just such an occasion"); Wald, *"One Nation Indivisible, with Liberty and Justice for All": Lessons from the American Experience for New Democracies*, 59 Fordham L. Rev. 283, 296 (1990) (noting that principles of nation's best judges "have emerged from an intuition of justice, a way of understanding a total situation not just analytically but in context, an empathy with the plight of the parties before them").

defaults of others, or natural forces—that societal perception, indeed public demand and now tradition, of the courts in recent decades has gained an unstoppable momentum.[33]

The law as it relates to women is an example of a recent "civilizing change" that has not merely followed but also shaped and advanced society's perceptions. To be sure, people have changed the law, but the more interesting and significant point is that the law also has succeeded in changing people, and particularly some—though by no means enough—of their invidious stereotypes about women's roles and capacities.

While many forces have helped to change societal attitudes toward women—women's own perseverance[34] and economic necessity[35] chief among them[36]—indisputably the law

---

33. I do not ignore the concern about the appropriate limits of judicial authority—the raging debate on original intent in matters of constitutional interpretation comes immediately to mind. *See, e.g.,* Meese, *The Law of the Constitution,* 61 Tul. L. Rev. 979,985 (1987) (arguing constitutional law derived only from "the original document of 1787 plus its amendments," and not from judges' interpretations of Constitution); Powell, *The Original Understanding of Original Intent,* 98 Harv. L. Rev. 885, 887–88 (1985) (arguing that Framers themselves did not believe Constitution should be interpreted according to "Framers' intent"). For example, is the definition of the constitutional "liberty" interest today to be found in the views of a father of the fourteenth amendment in the society of 1868 or a biological father seeking visitation in a vastly different society more than one hundred years later? *See Michael H. v. Gerald D.,* 491 U.S. 110 (1989) (denying visitation to biological father of child born out of wedlock). The underlying point, I believe, is an incontrovertible one, as evidenced even by recent decisions of the United States Supreme Court. *See* Stevens, *A Bill of Rights: A Century of Progress,* The University of Chicago Centennial Celebration & Bicentennial of the Bill of Rights 7–10 (Oct. 25, 1991) (on file at New York University Law Review) (citing 1991 criminal procedure cases as examples of how "an extraordinarily aggressive Supreme Court has reached out to announce a host of new rules narrowing the Federal Constitution's protection of individual liberties"); Greenhouse, *Conservatively Speaking, It's an Activist Supreme Court,* N.Y. Times, May 26, 1991, § 4, at 1 (pointing to *Rust v. Sullivan,* 111 S. Ct. 1759 [1991], *McCleskey v. Zant,* 111 S. Ct. 1454 [1991], and *Arizona v. Fulminante,* 111 S. Ct. 1246 [1991], as examples of current Court's activism).

34. Unquestionably, the presence of women in the legal profession has helped to bring about change much in the same way as their exclusion helped to perpetuate laws and traditions that discriminated against women. As Professor Basch observed, in the nineteenth century,

> The law, the most effective instrument of social control in a modern society, was in all of its manifestations male. It was created, shaped, disseminated, altered, and adjudicated by men. Men fashioned disabilities for women, subsequently devised ways of remedying them for women, and ultimately determined how far concessions to women should go. Few social institutions offer a clearer view of the way men delineated the boundaries of women's lives than the law.

See N. Basch, *supra* note 12, at 225. It is somewhat startling to consider that one hundred years ago there were approximately 135 female lawyers and law students in the United States. *See* Weisberg, *supra* note 1, at 240. Today, more female lawyers and law students assembled in Carnegie Hall for the Law School Convocation. There are approximately 157,000 female lawyers (about twenty-one percent of all lawyers) and 54,000 female law students (about forty-three percent of total enrollments). My source for these statistics is the American Bar Association Commission on Women in the Profession, of which I am pleased to be a member. See ABA Comm'n on Women in the Profession, Fact Sheet (1991).

35. The evidence overwhelmingly suggests that throughout history economic forces have affected the status of women. *See generally* W. Chafe, *supra* note 20, at 48–65 (discussing how economic experience of women after 1920 became measure of female freedom); Speth, *supra* note 12, at 69 (arguing that economics was one factor that led to adoption of married women's property legislation).

36. Without doubt, the scholarly literature on gender-related issues, which reaches and influences a wide audience of students, practicing lawyers, judges, and legislators, has contributed as well to effecting change

also has had a key role in stimulating the process of reform. Within recent decades, new statutes have been accompanied by court decisions assuring that their words and spirits would be honored scrupulously.[37] Court decisions have helped the public at last to comprehend that the constitutional guarantees include women.[38] Indeed, it is hard to imagine a judicial interpretation of the Bill of Rights today that would allow a state to deny women the right to practice law or to limit their right to work. Litigation has been a powerful tool in eroding discriminatory barriers in the workplace, including barriers to club memberships,[39] even to partnerships,[40] and it has awakened public awareness to the disparate treatment of women in divorce, child support, employment, and other private and public aspects of life.[41] Where courts were once a forum for legitimating and institutionalizing barriers to equal justice for women, in our own lifetimes we have seen them become a forum for challenging stereotypes, for opening paths, and for punishing and deterring harassment and discrimination.

Thus far, I have spoken mostly of courts and judges in describing the civilizing, humanizing process that can advance the law beyond ugly stereotypes and prejudices and thereby bring this nation closer to its constitutional ideals. But it also should be apparent that, while a vital engine of civilizing change, the law and the courts are not self-directed or self-driven engines. Courts and judges—necessarily somewhat removed and isolated from everyday affairs, necessarily somewhat passive and reactive to issues put before

---

in perceptions about women. *See* Fox, *Being a Woman, Being a Lawyer and Being a Human Being—Woman and Change*, 57 Fordham L. Rev. 955, 959 (1989) ("Feminist legal scholars provide a new window for law formation, and may fill a void in the understanding of law and the possibilities for its development").

37. *See, e.g., International Union v. Johnson Controls, Inc.*, 111 S. Ct. 1196, 1210 (1991) (stating that Pregnancy Discrimination Act "means what it says").

38. *See, e.g., Davis v. Passman*, 442 U.S. 228, 234–35 (1979) (holding that equal protection component of due process clause prohibits gender classifications unless they are substantially related to an important government objective); *Califano v. Goldfarb*, 430 U.S. 199, 217 (1977) (holding that equal protection clause prevents gender-based discrimination in distribution of employment-related benefits); *Taylor v. Louisiana*, 419 U.S. 522, 537 (1975) (holding that state cannot exclude women as class from serving on juries since sixth amendment requires that juries be drawn from fair cross section of the community); *Frontiero v. Richardson*, 411 U.S. 677, 690–91 (1973) (holding statute that classified spouses of male members of armed forces as dependents without doing same for spouses of female members violates due process clause of fifth amendment).

39. *See New York State Club Ass'n, Inc. v. City of New York*, 69 N.Y.2d 211, 505 N.E.2d 915, 513 N.Y.S.2d 349 (1987) (upholding New York City law which prohibited discrimination in private clubs because "denial of access to club facilities constitutes a significant barrier to the professional advancement of women and minorities"), *aff'd*, 487 U.S. 1 (1988).

40. *See Hopkins v. Price Waterhouse*, 490 U.S. 228 (1989) (suit by woman claiming she was denied partnership in major accounting firm because of gender discrimination); *Hishon v. King & Spaulding*, 467 U.S. 69, 73–79 (1984) (holding that Title VII of the Civil Rights Act of 1964, which forbids unlawful discrimination as to "terms, conditions, or privileges of employment," would bind law firm to consider woman for partnership if promise of partnership was term, condition, or privilege of employment); *see also* K. Morello, *supra* note 1, at 211–18 (describing suits brought by women against several New York City law firms).

41. *See* Symposium, Developments in the Law Affecting Women, Presented to the Judges and Staff of the New York State Court of Appeals by the Court's Central Legal Research Staff on Law Day 1988 (on file at New York University Law Review) (discussing current issues facing women in workplace and courts).

them by litigants—look to and depend upon the sensitivity, creativity, and dedication of lawyers to enlighten them with new insights into old principles. As the world changes and values evolve, courts look to the Bar to deepen their understanding of the context and ramifications of legal issues, to help keep the law attuned to the needs of modern society, and to lead in the progress of the law. As is evident in the example of women during the hundred years since 1891, the law can perpetuate ideas in need of reform, but the vigilance of lawyers who perceive wrongdoing and press for relief can assure that the law also is an instrument of justice.

So you see, in the end it all comes back to law graduates today. They have a unique responsibility as superbly motivated and educated lawyers to question unfair practices and attitudes, however entrenched, so that our justice system can remain one. The American Bar long ago established itself as a guardian of human rights, and it has always maintained that role.

I would be less than candid if I did not, in closing, tell you what a deep down, abiding pleasure it is to see my daughter among the graduates, along with other sons and daughters and loved ones, not only because they are now rewarded for their hard work, but also because I know from my own life how much it means to be a lawyer. I have yet to discover any calling that offers such opportunity for intellectual stimulation; for helping people who entrust their lives and fortunes to us, whether by drawing a will, or defending against potentially ruinous charges, or seeking redress for injury, or executing worldwide commercial transactions. Lawyers can influence others through writing, teaching, and legislating; and they can continue to advance this nation toward its dream of equality for women and the multitudes for whom that promise also remains unfulfilled.

I hope that today's graduates never will forget the aspirations that led them to the law and to this joyous day in their lives. Now they have the tools to make their dreams, and ours, a reality. May they have the courage and commitment always to pursue the ideal of justice.

State Constitutional Common Law*

The Common Law as a Full Partner in the Protection of Individual Rights

The inaugural Rutgers Law Journal Annual Issue on State Constitutional Law opened with the declaration that the 1980s "might well be designated as the decade of revival of state constitutional law."[1] That spirited statement was followed a year later with the forecast that the 1990s will be "a decade in which state constitutional law should finally be recognized as 'real' constitutional law."[2] Clearly, this publication does not shrink from bold pronouncements.

It would be easy to quarrel with the second assertion—that state constitutional law is at last fully emerged from the shadows and recognized as real constitutional law. Fifty-two percent of those responding to a poll conducted by the Advisory Committee on Intergovernmental Relations did not even know their state had a constitution.[3] In New York City, after a lecture I delivered on the subject, a lawyer thanked me effusively because he had been unaware that New York had a constitution. He said, "I feel like I'm swimming in a whole new sea of culture." Regrettably, already one-fourth of the way through this new decade, state constitutions are still too often sniffed at or ignored by lawyers and educators.

*23 Rutgers Law Journal 727 (1992), originally published as "Foreword: The Common Law and State Constitutional Law as Full Partners in the Protection of Individual Rights." The author is grateful to Henry M. Greenberg, Michael J. Garcia, and Joseph Lee Matalon for their assistance in preparing this article.

1. Robert F. Williams and Earl M. Maltz, *Introduction*, 20 Rutgers L.J. 877, 877 (1989).

2. Robert F. Williams, *Introduction*, 21 Rutgers L.J. 793, 793 (1990).

3. John Kincaid, *State Court Protections of Individual Rights Under State Constitutions: The New Judicial Federalism*, 61 J. St. Gov't 163, 169 (1988). *See also* Robert F. Williams, *State Constitutional Law: Teaching and Scholarship*, 41 J. Legal Educ. 243 (1991). One state constitutional law scholar, Peter Galie, recently opined that "the movement has slacked off nationally [with the three most activist judges of California's Supreme Court losing a recall election and Florida judges facing similar voter difficulty]. Most courts do not take it seriously and most lawyers do not brief state constitutional questions." Gary Spencer, *Judicial Federalism Remains Viable But Judges Are Deeply Divided over How and When to Apply Doctrine*, 206 N.Y. L.J. Oct. 15, 1991, at S31 (Special Supplement).

But I would not dispute the idea that state constitutional law has steadily gained acceptance, and certainly I would not do so here, the home of pre-eminent scholars, influential literature, even an annual review of developments in the field. Where there are annual developments there must be a field. Anyway, I would rather take issue with the first pronouncement—that what we have been witnessing these past ten or so years is a *revival* of state constitutional law. Frankly, if that is meant to suggest a revival of the sort of state court activity we are witnessing today, I have difficulty locating the "vival."[4]

As two knowledgeable commentators recently observed, "most of the literature, like many of the state cases themselves, offers more in terms of approval and encouragement than of analytical insight and innovation."[5] Taking that criticism to heart, I have decided that instead of proliferating the congratulations, I would venture what I hope might be considered an analytical insight, even if not an out-and-out innovation. And I know no better place to turn for new perceptions than back into history.

It is the search for the "vival" that inspires and informs these observations. Plainly, state constitutional decision-making as we know it today, particularly the open rejection by state courts of United States Supreme Court interpretations of analogous if not identical constitutional texts, has no parallel in American history. In state courts, the grand tradition has been not of constitutional but of common law decision-making, a tradition peculiar to state courts, and one that has been diminished over this century by rampant codification and constitutionalization of the law. Indeed, the Supreme Court's constitutionalization of individual rights in recent history has fostered a federal fascination that all but obscured state constitutions, let alone protections offered by the independent body of law within each state known as common law.[6]

I believe that what we are experiencing is in fact not a revival of state constitutional decision-making at all, but a new chapter in American federalism, that unique balance struck between state and federal sovereignties.[7] The emergence of state constitutional case law necessarily changes the balance as state courts, by plain statements indicating adequate and independent state law grounds for their determinations, establish themselves as the final arbiters of fundamental questions affecting society, insulating those questions from review by the United States Supreme Court.[8] It is the shift in the balance as we approach the end of the century that invites attention to a subject that dominated state court decision-making at its inception: the common law.

---

4. History does reflect waves of state constitutional revision, *see* Williams, *supra* note 3, at 244–45, and some state constitutional decision-making, but nothing compared to the current judicial activity. *See also* James A. Henretta, *Foreword: Rethinking the State Constitutional Tradition*, 22 Rutgers L.J. 819 (1991).

5. Ronald K.L. Collins and David M. Skover, *The Future of Liberal Legal Scholarship*, 87 Mich. L. Rev. 189, 217 (1988).

6. *See generally* Kevin Cole, *Federal and State "State Action": The Undercritical Embrace of a Hypercriticized Doctrine*, 24 Ga. L. Rev. 327 (1990).

7. The basic question of federalism is how power should be allocated between the federal and state governments. Every time common law is replaced by federal constitutional rules, power has shifted away from state law; but, conversely, each refusal to apply constitutional standards to the common law is a reaffirmation of state authority. Erwin Chemerinsky, *The Constitution and the Common Law*, 73 Judicature 149, 149 (1989).

8. *See Michigan v. Long*, 463 U.S. 1032 (1983) (state court decision not reviewable by Supreme Court where plain statement reflects bona fide separate, adequate and independent state law grounds).

In the ensuing sections, I will revisit the common law, beginning with our nation's beginnings and ultimately considering the relationship of the common law and state constitutional law in the protection of individual rights today. So as not to raise (or lower) expectations unduly, I should tell you at the outset that I do not plan to restate the history of the law from the start of time, but only to set forth a sufficient picture of the past for an appreciation of how changed the legal landscape is, and to suggest that the real revival may be not in state constitutional law but in state common law.

To refine the framework of this discussion even further, I should make clear that I am not urging that common law supplant constitutional law for the protection of fundamental values. That would be an abdication of courts' responsibility, to say the least. I do, however, suggest that as new demands now turn to state courts, the enormous capacity of the common law for fairness and justice not be overlooked. In short, there is more to be celebrated in state law than our constitutions.

I. The Common Law in Historical Perspective

In trying to state the history of the common law succinctly, I feel a bit like Father Guido Sarducci. "Saturday Night Live" fans will understand my reference to his five-minute university, which taught everything you would remember ten years after graduation, and even included a one-minute spring break in Fort Lauderdale. What you need to remember is that the common law is old; a lot has been written about it, much of it unread;[9] and it is familiar yet enigmatic.

The common law is of course lawmaking and policymaking by judges.[10] It is law derived not from authoritative texts such as constitutions, statutes and regulations, but from human wisdom collected case by case over countless generations to form a stable body of rules. While at its core durable, certain and predictable, the common law is not static. It proceeds and grows incrementally, in principled fashion, to fit a changing society. In our justice system the state courts, not the federal courts, are largely responsible for developing the common law.[11]

A. The Colonial Era

The precise source of the common law, worldly or otherworldly, could be debated interminably (and is). It is clear, however, that the common law in England was viewed as a principal safeguard against infringements of individual rights. It was pictured "invested with a halo of dignity," the "highest expression of human reason and of the

---

9. *See* Grant Gilmore, The Ages of American Law 76 (1977).

10. *See* Benjamin N. Cardozo, The Nature of the Judicial Process 10–11 (1921); Charles D. Breitel, *The Lawmakers*, 65 Colum. L. Rev. 749, 765–76 (1965). *See generally* Melvin A. Eisenberg, The Nature of the Common Law (1988); Cyril J. Radcliff, The Law and Its Compass (1960).

11. Burt Neuborne, *Foreword: State Constitutions and the Evolution of Positive Rights*, 20 Rutgers L.J. 881, 896–97 (1989). Federal common law does exist; however, it is specialized and limited. *See* Thomas S. Schrock and Robert C. Welsh, *Reconsidering the Constitutional Common Law*, 91 Harv. L. Rev. 1117 (1978).

law of nature implanted by God in the heart of man."[12] As natural reason developed, expounded and tested over time, common law was preferred over acts of Parliament and royal ordinances, which could be repealed at any moment. It was described as "the most perfect, and most excellent [of all law], and without comparison the best, to make and preserve a Common-wealth."[13] Though a far cry from "rights" and "justice" as we know them today, English common law embraced such concepts as the right to trial by jury, "that finest Barrier of English liberty,"[14] and the writ of habeas corpus to prevent undue detention of a suspect before trial.[15]

The colonists carried this law and attitude with them across the Atlantic Ocean.[16] When asked by the home government in 1773, "What is the constitution of the government?," the Governor of New York replied, the "Common Law of England is considered as the Fundamental law of the Province."[17] But obviously conditions in the colonies were markedly different from life in England and, with necessity always the "supreme lawmaker,"[18] so was our common law. If English precedents rested on what were considered mistaken, inconvenient or repugnant principles, our courts changed them. "In such cases," an early commentator explained, the courts "do not determine the prior decisions to be bad law; but that they are not law. Thus in the very nature of the institution, is a principle established which corrects all errors and rectifies all mistakes."[19] The common law—that "golden and sacred rule of reason"[20]—was accepted

---

12. J. Neville Figgis, The Theory of the Divine Right of Kings 226–27 (1896).

13. Sir John Davies, Irish Reports, Dublin: 1674, Preface, *quoted in* Charles M. Haar and Daniel W. Fessler, The Wrong Side of the Tracks: A Revolutionary Rediscovery of the Common Law Tradition of Fairness in the Struggle against Inequality 227 (1986).

14. Arthur M. Schlesinger, The Birth of the Nation 15 (1968). "The tradition of peremptory challenges for both the prosecution and the accused was already venerable at the time of Blackstone." *Holland v. Illinois*, 493 U.S. 474, 481 (1990).

15. *See* Herbert Pope, *The English Common Law in the United States*, 24 Harv. L. Rev. 6 (1910); Robert F. Williams, *The State Constitutions of the Founding Decade: Pennsylvania's Radical 1771 Constitution and its Influence on American Constitutionalism*, 62 Temp. L.Q. 541 (1989). No one today would urge a return to the common law rights of Elizabethan England. *See* J.A.C. Grant, *Our Common Law Constitution*, 11 B.U. L. Rev. 1, 1 (1960).

16. Cornelia Geer LeBoutillier, American Democracy and Natural Law 139 (1950); *see generally* Lawrence M. Friedman, A History of American Law 33–93 (1973). Blackstone was widely read here, and the custom early established of studying law in England. Roscoe Pound, The Spirit of the Common Law 116 (1921).

17. 1 Charles Z. Lincoln, Constitutional History of New York 39 (1906); Albert M. Rosenblatt, *The Foundations of the New York State Supreme Court (1691–1991): A Study in Sources*, 63 N.Y. St. B.J. 10 (1991) (in New York the English common law co-existed with Dutch law and the Bible codes).

18. Friedman, *supra* note 16, at 37.

19. 1 Zephaniah Swift, A System of the Laws of the State of Connecticut 41 (Arno Press, 1972). For example, in England, the right to counsel was hardly a "right" at all. For persons accused of capital offenses, which included most serious offenses, counsel would be appointed only to argue matters of law, leaving defendants to handle the examination of witnesses. Significantly greater protection was afforded in several of the colonies. *See* Grant, *supra* note 15, at 9. *See also* 2 Zephaniah Swift, A System of the Laws of the State of Connecticut 392, 399 (Arno Press, 1972) (discussing eighteenth-century common law).

20. Charles F. Mullett, Fundamental Law and the American Revolution, 1760–1776 48 (1966); Charles G. Haines, The American Doctrine of Judicial Supremacy 63 (1959).

as superior even to positive law. A statute that contravened the common law "was no law at all."[21]

Perhaps most significant in the colonial era are the events that closed it: the creation of written constitutions, a distinctively non-British, American tradition. Before the eighteenth century ended, sixteen states had adopted thirty-one constitutions,[22] and the federal Constitution and Bill of Rights were in place. The first New York Constitution, adopted in 1777, was a brief but masterful document setting out the structure of the new government.[23] In 1777, state governance, and not the protection of individual rights against governmental interference, topped the constitutional agenda. To safeguard citizens' liberties against governmental interference we also had the common law, which we in New York were careful to declare and incorporate in our first charter, as did many other states.[24] Our national government drew on these constitutions and the common law for the Bill of Rights.[25] As Professor Leonard Levy has observed,

> The mere fact that a common-law right, such as the liberty of the press, received constitutional status in America did not argue that its meaning had changed. . . . In the national Bill of Rights, for example, the guarantees of the right against self-incrimination, indictment by grand jury, and trial by jury in civil and criminal cases simply declared the common law, as indeed was the case concerning numerous provisions of the Bill of Rights.[26]

---

21. Mullett, *supra* note 20, at 48. *See* Pound, *supra* note 16, at 75–76. Thomas C. Grey, *Origins of the Unwritten Constitution: Fundamental Law in American Revolutionary Thought*, 30 Stan. L. Rev. 843, 868 (1978); Theodore F.T. Plucknett, *Bonham's Case and Judicial Review*, 40 Harv. L. Rev. 30 (1926).

22. Stephen E. Gottlieb, *Foreword: Symposium on State Constitutional History: In Search of a Usable Past*, 53 Alb. L. Rev. 255, 256 (1989).

23. 1 Lincoln, *supra* note 17, at 55.

24. The 1777 New York Constitution, in article 35, explicitly continued the English common law and statute law, and the legislation of the colony, so long as they were applicable under the new form of government. *See also* Suzanna Sherry, *The Founders' Unwritten Constitution*, 54 U. Chi. L. Rev. 1127, 1131–34 (1987).

25. *See Boddie v. Connecticut*, 401 U.S. 371, 375 (1971) (noting that American society "bottoms its systematic definition of individual rights and duties, as well as its machinery for dispute settlement, not on custom or the will of strategically placed individuals, but on the common-law model"); *Murray's Lessee v. Hoboken Land and Improvement Co.*, 59 U.S. (18 How.) 272, 276 (1855) ("The words, 'due process of law,' were undoubtedly intended to convey the same meaning as the words, 'by the law of the land,' in *Magna Charta*").

26. Leonard W. Levy, Emergence of a Free Press 324–25 (1985). *See also* Vincent M. Bonventre, *A Classical Constitution: Ancient Roots of Our National Charter*, 59 N.Y. B.J. 10, 17 (1987) (the Bill of Rights represents the embodiment of certain principles and liberties which preceded the government); Chemerinsky, *supra* note 7, at 150; Paul K. Conkin, Self-Evident Truths 133 (1974); Mullett, *supra* note 20, at 25–26, 58; Edward S. Corwin, *The "Higher" Law Background of American Constitutional Law*, 42 Harv. L. Rev. 149, 170 (1928) (Bill of Rights meant to ensure that government could not violate natural law rights).

As was immediately apparent, the mere fact that a common law right received constitutional recognition did not signify that it was thereby extinguished as a common law right.[27]

B. The Early Life of the Republic

Despite a brief backlash against all things British,[28] English common law held its place within the American legal system even after the Revolution.[29] In time, however, our courts turned their energies to the development of our own case law, and tailored the common law to the social and economic needs of this young republic.[30]

American lawyers believed that the "doctrines of the common law [were] part of the universal jural order."[31] The common law "was taken to exist in order to secure individual interests, not merely against aggression by other individuals, but even more against arbitrary invasion by state or society."[32] Since bills of rights were expressions of the common law, it thus "became usual to think not of the text of the bills of rights, but of these supposed fundamental principles of which they were but declaratory."[33] As a consequence, despite the making and remaking of constitutions during this period, state courts often resolved cases involving transcendent issues without a passing reference to the text of a constitution. The common law was a source no less fundamental.[34]

Connecticut Supreme Court Chief Justice Ellen Peters has concluded from a study of three decades of Connecticut's earliest reports that "rights now denominated as constitutional had well-recognized common law antecedents,"[35] typically found in tort actions for misuse of process, false imprisonment, or trespass. On common law grounds, the courts set aside overbroad and defective warrants, and routinely safeguarded rights

---

27. Sherry, *supra* note 24, at 1155–77; Grant, *supra* note 15. The Ninth Amendment made plain that the "enumeration in the Constitution, of certain rights, shall not be construed to deny or disparage others retained by the people." U.S. Const. amend. IX. *See generally* Sol Wachtler, *Judging the Ninth Amendment*, 59 Fordham L. Rev. 597 (1991).

28. New Jersey, Pennsylvania and Kentucky took the drastic step of legislating against citations to English cases. Pound, *supra* note 16, at 117.

29. In the post-Revolutionary period, English law was the only law American lawyers knew. Gilmore, *supra* note 9, at 19. *See also* Pope, *supra* note 15.

30. Pound, *supra* note 16, at 120.

31. Roscoe Pound, *Liberty of Contract*, 18 Yale L.J. 454, 466 (1909); Morton J. Horwitz, The Transformation of American Law, 1780–1860, at 4 (1977).

32. Pound, *supra* note 16, at 101. "Bills of rights [in eighteenth-century America] especially were viewed as providing a statement of broad principles rather than a set of legally enforceable rights." Donald S. Lutz, *Political Participation in Eighteenth-Century America*, 53 Alb. L. Rev. 327, 331 (1989).

33. Pound, *supra* note 16, at 76.

34. *See generally*, Suzanna Sherry, *The Early Virginia Tradition of Extra-Textual Interpretation*, 53 Alb. L. Rev. 297 (1989); Sherry, *supra* note 24, at 1134–46. *See also Fletcher v. Peck*, 10 U.S. (Cranch 6) 87, 136 (1810) (state restrained by constitutional provisions and "general principles which are common to our free institutions").

35. Ellen A. Peters, *Common Law Antecedents of Constitutional Law in Connecticut*, 53 Alb. L. Rev. 259, 261 (1989).

today located within the ambit of constitutional "due process."[36] The common law offered security against self-incrimination and double jeopardy; it protected freedom of speech and religion; and it disfavored retroactive laws which could operate to impair contracts. Though the culture of the times did not look to the courts for "rights" as we know them today, there are many parallels to the Connecticut experience in the law of other states, in criminal as well as civil cases.[37]

During this period, the common law courts were "our preferred problem-solvers."[38] Common law judges "creatively manipulated and changed common law rules in reaction to changing circumstances to a degree that the subsequent period of formalism and judicial modesty has made us almost forget."[39] Their innovative spirit "openly and legitimately"[40] kept the common law up to date, and remained the basic reference point for construing the Constitution.[41] Thus, whether attributable to the perceived merit of the common law, or to the relatively limited expectation of the legal culture for justice,[42] or to the view that constitutions were declaring rights already in existence, the common law and the common law courts enjoyed a "happy primacy"[43] during the early life of the republic.

C. The Twentieth Century

That was not long to continue. The twentieth century saw the exponential growth of statutory and constitutional grounds for vindicating individual rights, an explosion of "rights" litigation, and a concomitant decline in resort to the common law for this purpose.[44] While the common law continued to flourish—modern product liability and property law are

---

36. *Id.* at 263–64.

37. *See, e.g., State v. Zdanowicz,* 69 N.J.L. 619, 55 A.743 (1903) (common law privilege against self-incrimination); *Hamilton v. Eno,* 81 N.Y. I 16, 126 (1880) (official acts of public officers may be freely criticized absent actual malice); *People v. McMahon,* 15 N.Y. 384 (1857) (involuntary statements inadmissible); *Henry v. Salinas Bank,* 1 N.Y. 83 (1847) (witness cannot be compelled to testify when forfeiture or penalty may result). A noteworthy example from the common law of contracts and property is the common law "duty to serve," an ancient principle that required parties engaged in public callings to serve the public on a non-arbitrary, non-discriminatory basis. *See* Note, *The Antidiscrimination Principle in the Common Law,* 102 Harv. L. Rev. 1993 (1989).

38. Gilmore, *supra* note 9, at 35–36.

39. Guido Calabresi, A Common Law for the Age of Statutes 183–84 (1982). *See also* Friedman, *supra* note 16, at 17, 99–100; Horwitz, *supra* note 31, at 1–4; William E. Nelson, The Americanization of the Common Law: The Impact of Legal Change on Massachusetts Society, 1760–1830, at 171–72 (1975).

40. Calabresi, *supra* note 39, at 184.

41. Grant, *supra* note 15, at 19–56; Sherry, *supra* note 34, at 299–300.

42. Lawrence M. Friedman, *State Constitutions and Criminal Justice in the Late Nineteenth Century,* 53 Alb. L. Rev. 265 (1989). Professor Friedman notes the differences in the legal cultures of the nineteenth and early twentieth centuries. State courts were constitutionally active on issues of taxing power and labor legislation, but not criminal justice legislation. *Id.* at 267. In addition, courts gave greater deference to zones of immunity, such as teachers, the state, prison wardens and husbands. *Id.* at 270–71.

43. Ellen A. Peters, *Common Law Judging in a Statutory World: An Address,* 43 U. Pitt. L. Rev. 995, 996 (1982).

44. *See generally,* Calabresi, *supra* note 39; Ruggero J. Aldisert, *The Nature of the Judicial Process: Revisited,* 49 U. Cin. L. Rev. 1 (1980).

conspicuous examples of its vitality—in this century the common law has been eclipsed as a source of human rights.[45]

It is no longer widely believed that rights are derived from natural law.[46] Today it is more commonly thought that rights are found in positive enactments.[47] The shift from a jurisprudence based in large part on natural law to one founded primarily on positivism has limited the interest in recognizing and protecting new rights on a common law basis. In addition, a dichotomy has emerged between public and private law—a clear separation between constitutional, criminal and regulatory law on the one hand, and torts, contracts, property and commercial law on the other.[48]

Of course, the legal soil of the nineteenth century was not fertile for the growth of individual rights litigation. The Supreme Court's pronouncement that the liberties protected by the Bill of Rights did not apply to the states left state law the sole protection against state encroachment on personal freedoms.[49] This was not a concern, however, because "the states were perceived as protectors of, rather than threats to, the civil and political rights of individuals."[50] But in the aftermath of the Civil War, it became apparent that the states could no longer be trusted to safeguard the liberty of *all* citizens. Thus, the ratification of the Fourteenth Amendment in 1868 mandated, as a constitutional imperative, that no state may "deprive any person of life, liberty, or property, without due process of law."[51]

In the ensuing years, the courts struggled to define the broad promises of the Fourteenth Amendment. The notion that the amendment imported, in wholesale fashion, the entire Bill of Rights against the states was rejected early in this century.[52] The constitutional guarantees of life, liberty and property came to be recognized, to be sure. But in accordance with the mindset of the day, it was the property rights of business interests, rather than individual liberties, that were first emphasized.[53] As one judge observed, "of the three fundamental principles which underlie government, and for which government exists, the protection of life, liberty and property, the chief of these is property."[54]

This limited recognition of due process rights continued until 1938 and the remarkable footnote in an otherwise unremarkable case involving a federal statute prohibiting the

---

45. State constitutional law also suffered "terminal decline." *See* Friedman, *supra* note 42, at 265.

46. *See, e.g.,* John H. Ely, Democracy and Distrust 52 (1980) ("The concept [of natural law] has consequently all but disappeared in American discourse").

47. *See, e.g., Southern Pac. Co. v. Jensen*, 244 U.S. 205, 222 (1917) (Holmes, J., dissenting) ("The common law is not a brooding omnipresence in the sky but the articulate voice of some sovereign or quasi-sovereign that can be identified"); Ely, *supra* note 46, at 54.

48. Morton J. Horwitz, *The History of the Public/Private Distinction*, 130 U. Pa. L. Rev. 1423, 1424 (1982).

49. *See, e.g., Barron v. Baltimore*, 32 U.S. (7 Pet.) 242, 247 (1833) (Fifth Amendment prohibition against takings without just compensation inapplicable to state legislation).

50. William J. Brennan, Jr., *The Bill of Rights: State Constitution as Guardians of Individual Rights*, 59 N.Y. St. B.J. 10, 11 (l 987).

51. U.S. Const. Amend. XIV.

52. *Twining v. New Jersey*, 211 U.S. 78, 99 (1908).

53. *See, e.g., Lochner v. New York*, 198 U.S. 45, 57–64 (1905) (Constitution protects an employer's freedom of contract).

54. *Children's Hosp. of D.C. v. Adkins*, 284 F. 613,622 (D.C. Cir. 1922) (Van Orsdel, J.).

shipment of imitation milk in interstate commerce.[55] Justice Stone there suggested that heightened judicial scrutiny "under the general prohibitions of the Fourteenth Amendment" may be appropriate for legislation impinging on personal freedoms,[56] and that view ultimately garnered the Court.[57]

The process of applying the Bill of Rights to the states through the Fourteenth Amendment escalated sharply during the 1960s. By the end of the decade, the search for rights that are at the "very essence of a scheme of ordered liberty"[58] led the Supreme Court to conclude that virtually the entire Bill of Rights applied to the states. The Court then proceeded to forge a national human rights law and new legal framework for society, with the federal Constitution and the Supreme Court at its center.[59]

The rising federal constitutional floor, together with technological, biomedical and social revolutions, awakened an awareness of the role courts—especially *federal* courts—might play in ameliorating social inequities. Profound new questions arrived in court: reapportionment; contraception; abortion; affirmative action; unequal education; exclusionary zoning; racial and gender discrimination.

Legislative activity also erupted during this century. In the New Deal years, a series of national and international forces, including the frustrating slowness of the courts in accepting change, made codes and statutes seem the appropriate solution, and the "statutorification"[60] of American law was underway. From dockets dominated by common law controversies early in the century, as the decades passed state courts increasingly confronted the meaning and legality of statutes.[61] Whole fields once determined under the common law were overtaken by codes.

This "orgy of statute making"[62] included laws to protect citizens from public and private infringements of their liberty and security. For example, New York in 1903 enacted a "Right to Privacy" statute, which prohibited the use of a person's name or

---

55. *United States v. Carolene Prods. Co.*, 304 U.S. 144, 152 n.4 (1938).

56. *Id.*

57. *See* Judith S. Kaye, *Dual Constitutionalism in Practice and Principle*, 61 St. John's L. Rev. 399, 404 (1987).

58. *Palko v. Connecticut*, 302 U.S. 319, 325 (1937) (Cardozo, J.). Justice Brennan has characterized the decisions that were handed down between 1961 and 1969, binding the states to virtually all of the restraints of the Bill of Rights, as the most important decisions of the Warren Court era. Brennan, *supra* note 50, at 16.

59. The Supreme Court in this era constitutionalized even causes of action that had been relegated to common law tort remedies. For example, in *Bivens v. Six Unknown Named Agents of Federal Bureau of Narcotics*, 403 U.S. 388 (1971), the Court held that an individual aggrieved by a federal officer's unlawful search or seizure could recover damages directly under the Fourth Amendment. *Bivens* exemplifies the move away from the common law and toward the Constitution. *See* Elaine W. Shoben, *Uncommon Law and the Bill of Rights: The Woes of Constitutionalizing State Common-Law Torts*, 1992 U. Ill. L. Rev. (difficulties created when Supreme Court unnecessarily constitutionalizes state tort claims).

60. Calabresi, *supra* note 39, at 1, 44.

61. Peters, *supra* note 43, at 996, 998. Roger J. Traynor, *Statutes Revolving in Common-Law Orbits*, 17 Cath. U. L. Rev. 401, 402 (1968).

62. Gilmore, *supra* note 9, at 95. Significant codification of the common law is often simply a means of making and updating uniform rules first elaborated by the courts. The Uniform Commercial Code is a leading example of this process. *See* Charles D. Breitel, *The Lawmakers*, 65 Colum. L. Rev. 749, 765 (1965).

picture for advertising or business purposes without consent.[63] New York also passed a law prohibiting discrimination in public accommodations on the basis of race, religion or national origin.[64] Decades later, Congress followed suit with the landmark Civil Rights Act of 1964[65] and other statutes which prohibit discrimination in public accommodations, employment and education. The recent Americans with Disabilities Act[66] is a legislative response to intolerable discrimination against the disabled. Thus, human rights claims that might once have been adjudicated under the common law, in this century have become matters of statutory interpretation or, more likely, constitutional challenge.

Whether or not it is undergoing a revival, state constitutional law today is plainly developing on a legal landscape that has been remade since our nation's beginnings.

II. A Common Law Infused with Constitutional Values

It is always interesting to ponder causes: causes for the march toward codification of the law; causes for increased resort to the courts to adjust social imbalances; causes for the constitutionalization of individual rights over the past decades;[67] causes for the recent rise in state constitutional decision-making. With interest so high, it is no surprise that a wide range of causes has been suggested, from politics and expediency, to surrender of the Supreme Court's central role in defining and expanding the rights of minorities,[68] to implementation of the founders' design for our system of government.

Rather than enter the debate on causes, however, I would like to consider effects, particularly the effect of the rise in state constitutional decision-making on the common law, once revered but significantly devalued as a fount of individual rights. For the protection of human liberty, it is the federal courts and federal charter, not state courts and certainly not the common law, that electrify law teachers, practicing lawyers and judges. Free speech is intuitively First Amendment, search and seizure Fourth, due process Fifth, right to counsel Sixth, and on and on. These are matters of *public* law, by definition of supervening importance.

Yet as we are challenged to think beyond the intuitive federal constitutional responses, and turn to state constitutions and state courts for justice, new questions emerge. There is, for example, the issue of methodology.[69] Should state constitutions be considered first, or only in the event the right propounded is not found federally? What attention should be

---

63. L. 1903, c. 132 § 1, codified at N.Y. Civ. Rights Law § 50 (McKinney 1992).

64. N.Y. Exec. Law § 296(2)(a) (McKinney 1992).

65. 42 U.S.C.A. § 2000a (West 1992) (public accommodations); 42 U.S.C.A. § 2000c (West 1992) (public education); 42 U.S.C.A. § 2000e (West 1992) (employment).

66. 42 U.S.C.A. § 6000 *et seq.* (West 1992).

67. *See* Calabresi, *supra* note 39, at 8 (suggesting as a reason the need for a mechanism to invalidate anachronistic statutes).

68. Frederick A.O. Schwarz, *The Constitution Outside the Courts*, 47 Record of Ass'n of the Bar of the City of N.Y. 9 (January/February 1992).

69. *See, e.g.,* now-Senior Judge Hans A. Linde's newest article on the subject, *Are State Constitutions Common Law?*, 34 Ariz. L. Rev. 215 (Summer 1992).

given decisions of the United States Supreme Court construing analogous if not identical texts? What if the parties do not raise, or adequately brief, state constitutional issues? What if sources for interpreting state texts are wholly unenlightening or, worse yet, nonexistent? After all, the process, if not new, has been decidedly dormant during the Federal Age.

Interesting, difficult questions like these have generated extensive commentary, as the scholarly literature continues to fuel a movement toward constitutional decision-making. They have also generated deep divisions on state high courts, as turf is defined and theory evolved. On the New York Court of Appeals, for example, where consensus ordinarily prevails, the state constitutional law cases often divide us; one case provoked four opinions, all seven judges agreeing on result, differing only as to methodology.[70]

Curiously, one of the effects of the perceived ongoing movement toward the outermost extreme of state constitutional decision-making for recognizing new rights has been to draw attention to the other extreme of state court decision-making, the common law. Whatever the historical causes for the devaluation of common law as a guarantor of human liberty, there is every good reason for renewed interest in the subject today. Three examples illustrate the point: shopping mall cases, medical treatment cases, and fundamental fairness cases.

A. SHOPPING MALL CASES

Of the recent state constitutional law decisions, the shopping mall cases likely have generated the most print.[71]

The central legal question is whether individuals have a right of access to privately-owned shopping malls to gather petitions or engage in other expressive activity. Pitting individuals seeking access against property owners is surely not new. What is new is that the conflict is staged in mammoth, sprawling malls, sometimes a million or more square feet of space beckoning the public to enter, linger, relax, enjoy—in some communities supplanting whole downtown areas. Gargantuan malls are decidedly something new in the way of private property.

The United States Supreme Court declined to recognize a First Amendment right of expression on someone else's private property,[72] and in *PruneYard v. Robins*[73] handed

---

70. *Immuno A.G. v. Moor-Jankowski*, 567 N.E.2d 1270 (N.Y. 1991).

71. *See, e.g.*, William Barnett, *A Private Mall Becomes a Public Hall*, 26 Loy. L. Rev. 739 (1980); Elizabeth Hardy, Note, *Post-PruneYard Access to Michigan Shopping Centers; The "Malling" of Constitutional Rights*, 30 Wayne L. Rev. 93 (1983); Cordelia S. Munroe, Note, *Granting Access to Private Shopping Center Property for Free Speech Purposes on the Basis of a State Constitutional Provision Does Not Violate the Shopping Center Owner's Federal Constitutional Property Rights or First Amendment Free Speech Rights*, 64 Marq. L. Rev. 507 (1981); Note, *Private Abridgment of Speech and the State Constitutions*, 90 Yale L.J. 165 (1980); Todd F. Simon, *Independent But Inadequate: State Constitutions and Protection of Freedom of Expression*, 33 U. Kan. L. Rev. 305 (1985); Robert F. Utter, *The Right to Speak, Write and Publish Freely: State Constitutional Protection Against Private Abridgment*, 8 U. Puget Sound L. Rev. 157 (1985); Stuart E. Wachs, *Access to Private Fora and State Constitutions: A Proposed Speech and Property Analysis*, 46 Alb. L. Rev. 1501 (1982).

72. *See Hudgens v. NLRB*, 424 U.S. 507, 519–21 (1976).

73. *PruneYard Shopping Ctr. v. Robins*, 441 U.S. 74, 81 (1980).

the baton to the states to decide whether, under their own constitutions, they would offer more expansive rights than had been found under the federal Constitution. In the dozen or so years since, state courts throughout the nation, joining issue on the constitutional battleground defined by Chief Justice Rehnquist in *PruneYard*, have reached divergent results, some favoring the petitioners,[74] others the property owners.[75] The decisions reflect impassioned differences about declaring constitutional rights of access to private property, especially the necessity for "state action." For the New York Court of Appeals, which held against the petitioners as a matter of state constitutional law (the only ground the petitioners put before us), this was a rare venture into the murky "state action" waters under state law.[76]

As demonstrated by the scorecard heavily favoring property owners over petitioners, a constitutional right to petition on private property is problematical. The right has been denied federally, and likewise denied overwhelmingly by state courts under state constitutions.

In 1989, however, the Oregon Supreme Court, in *Lloyd Corp. Ltd. v. Whiffen*,[77] declared that, despite the parties' importunings, it simply would not join the nationwide constitutional debate without first examining the parties' rights on a *subconstitutional* level.[78] "If there is no duty to decide the constitutionality of a law, there is a duty not to decide it. This rule prevents premature foreclosure of opportunities for legislators who are better equipped to consider and choose among different policies."[79] Then applying basic principles of equity and property law, the court balanced the owner's interest against the petitioners' interest as defined in the state Constitution, and concluded that the balance tipped decidedly in petitioners' favor, so long as they observed reasonable time, place and manner restrictions.

> The signature-gathering process for political petitions is a form of political speech and no one contests that free speech is one of our society's most precious rights. As Justice Brandeis said in his concurring opinion in *Whitney v. California*, "[t]hose who won our independence believed that . . . the greatest menace to freedom is an inert people; that public discussion is a political duty; and that this should be a fundamental principle of the American government." We might add that this is a fundamental principle of the Oregon government as well. No doubt defendants' activity involves a very important public interest.

---

74. *Robins v. PruneYard Shopping Ctr.*, 592 P.2d 341 (Cal. 1989), *aff'd sub. nom. PruneYard Shopping Ctr. v. Robins*, 447 U.S. 74 (1980); *Batchelder v. Allied Stores Int'l, Inc.*, 445 N.E.2d 590 (Mass. 1983); *Alderwood Assocs. v. Washington Envtl. Council*, 635 P.2d 108 (Wash. 1981).

75. *Cologne v. Westfarms Assocs.*, 469 A.2d 1201 (Conn. 1984); *Woodland v. Michigan Citizens Lobby*, 378 N.W.2d 337 (Mich. 1985); *Shad Alliance v. Smith Haven Mall*, 488 N.E.2d 1211 (N.Y. 1985); *State v. Felmet*, 273 S.E.2d 708 (N.C. 1981); *Western Pennsylvania Socialist Workers 1982 Campaign v. Connecticut Gen. Life Ins. Co.*, 515 A.2d 1331 (Pa. 1986); *Jacobs v. Major*, 407 N.W.2d 832 (Wis. 1987).

76. *Shad Alliance v. Smith Haven Mall*, 488 N.E.2d 1211 (N.Y. 1985).

77. 773 P.2d 1294 (Or. 1989).

78. *Id.* at 1297.

79. *Id.* at 1297 n.4

But is that public interest seriously injured if defendants' activity is completely blocked at the Center? We believe that it is.[80]

Thus, without constitutionalizing the result, the court injected state constitutional values—here, Oregon's constitutional provisions regarding the process of filing petitions and obtaining signatures—into a traditional balancing test, finding in favor of petitioners yet leaving open the possibility of legislative action or some other result when materially different interests are at stake.[81]

A decade earlier, the New Jersey Supreme Court in *State v. Shack*,[82] also on nonconstitutional grounds, held that the ownership of real property did not include the right to bar access to governmental service available to migrant workers housed on the premises.[83] As in *Whiffen*, the New Jersey court saw no need to decide the constitutional claims pressed by the workers, concluding that the

> policy considerations which underlie that conclusion may be much the same as those which would be weighed with respect to one or more of the constitutional challenges, but a decision in nonconstitutional terms is more satisfactory, because the interests of migrant workers are more expansively served in that way than they would be if they had no more freedom than these constitutional concepts could be found to mandate if indeed they apply at all.[84]

---

80. *Id.* at 1299–1300 (citation omitted). *See* Christine M. Durham, *Obligation or Power? The New Judicial Federalism and the Policy-Making Role of State Supreme Courts*, 2 Emerging Issues St. Const. L. 219, 229–30 (1989) (discussing *Whiffen*).

81. The Pennsylvania Superior Court employed a similar methodology in *Coatesville Development Co. v. United Food and Commercial Workers*, 542 A.2d 1380 (Pa. Super. 1988), to deny a preliminary injunction to a supermarket owner against picketing on its property. For further discussion of this case, see Suzanne Cooperstein, Note, *Developments in State Constitutional Law: 1988*, 20 Rutgers L.J. 903, 936–37 (1989). The Pennsylvania Supreme Court had earlier upheld state constitutional free speech rights on private university property in *Commonwealth v. Tate*, 432 A.2d 1382 (Pa. 1981), but rejected similar rights on private shopping center property in *Western Pennsylvania Socialist Workers 1982 Campaign v. Connecticut General Life Insurance Co.*, 515 A.2d 1331 (Pa. 1986). In rejecting the state constitutional grounds asserted, the court stated: "We should be wary of insulating that development against legislative, judicial or private change by enshrining a particular position in the text of the constitution. Social and economic developments require a flexible legal framework which can adapt to them." *Socialist Workers*, 515 A.2d at 1335.

82. 58 N.J. 297, 277 A.2d 369 (1971).

83. *Id.* The holding in *Shack* was later extended by a lower New Jersey court in *Freedman v. New Jersey State Police*, 135 N.J. Super. 297, 343 A.2d 148 (Law Div. 1975), which concluded that Shack's access right to agricultural labor camps extended to members of the press. The lower courts in New Jersey have decided other free expression cases on subconstitutional grounds. *See, e.g., Streeter v. Brogan*, 113 N.J. Super. 486, 274 A.2d 312 (Ch. Div. 1971) (display of peace symbol); *Zelenka v. Benevolent & Protective Order of Elks of the United States*, 129 N.J. Super. 379, 324 A.2d 35 (App. Div.), *cert. denied*, 66 N.J. 317, 331 A.2d 17 (1974) (newspaper advertisement).

84. *Shack*, 277 A.2d at 372. *See also Shad Alliance v. Smith Haven Mall*, 488 N.E.2d 1211, 1218 (N.Y. 1985) (Jasen, J., concurring) (suggesting that when a landowner "open[s] the doors to the public to participate in the exchange of noncommercial ideas . . . the common-law right of the owner to exclude any expressionist from his private property must be limited to nondiscriminatory and nonarbitrary grounds" as a matter of public policy).

Whatever the disappointments,[85] decisions like these must give pause even to "[c]ontemporary lawyers, law professors, and jurists, weaned from the common-law tradition."[86] After all, petitioners did succeed against the property owner where they might otherwise have failed—not a banner headline perhaps, but a victory nonetheless. I have more in mind, however, than a result.

Unlike federal litigation, state litigation routinely proceeds under the common law, particularly in disputes between private parties, where according greater rights to one person means taking rights from the other. To be sure, state courts, like federal courts, deal with statutory, regulatory and constitutional questions, but state court traditions— let alone their authority and jurisdiction—may be quite different. Those accustomed to litigating in federal forums may in some respects find less on the state side, but they also may find appreciably more.[87]

It is of course fundamental that constitutional issues are reached only when necessary. In *Whiffen*, the Oregon court revealed one disadvantage of unnecessary constitutionalization: the premature foreclosure of action by other branches of government. In *Shack*, the New Jersey court spoke of another disadvantage: limitation of the judiciary's own flexibility in later dealing with the subject.

Cases like these remind us of principles learned early in law school, not only about legal method but also about the exquisite capacity of the common law for growth. There is perhaps no better example of common law growth to accommodate our progressing sense of social justice than the road traversed by property law, from ancient England to modern America, a road which "grudgingly, but steadily, [has broadened] the recognized scope

---

85. *See, e.g.*, Note, *Private Abridgment of Speech and the State Constitutions*, 90 Yale L.J. 165, 178 (1980):

> An important feature of an effective system of freedom of expression is its reliance on independent judicial institutions, rather than elective political ones, such as legislatures, to supervise the functioning, as opposed to the outcomes, of democratic process. Courts, rather than legislatures, are relied upon to safeguard democratic process from governmental abridgment of speech. Similarly, courts should be relied upon to protect the democratic process from private abridgment. Unlike reliance on statutory or common law, use of state constitutional law would ensure effective judicial protection of access to privately held public forums and residential communities.

Id. (footnotes omitted). The author continues, "[a]lthough the common law approach initially achieves judicial protection of speech, it leaves the legislature the option to nullify the judicial initiative with new statutory law." *Id.* at 178 n.63 (citation omitted).

86. Curtis J. Berger, *PruneYard Revisited: Political Activity on Private Lands*, 66 N.Y.U. L. Rev. 633, 661 (1991) (proposing a common law rationale and statutory scheme to protect free speech on private property).

87. *See* Phylis Skloot Bamberger, *Beware the Dark Side of Constitutional Law*, 19 Hum. Rts. 22 (1992); Hans A. Linde, *First Things First: Rediscovering the States' Bills of Rights*, 9 U. Balt. L. Rev. 379, 390 (1980); Robert F. Williams, *State Constitutional Law Processes*, 24 Wm. & Mary L. Rev. 169, 190 (1983); *see also* Lawrence G. Sager, *Fair Measure: The Legal Status of Underenforced Constitutional Norms*, 91 Harv. L. Rev. 1212, 1255–56 (1978) (state courts are not burdened as the federal courts are concerning the effects of setting a nationwide rule).

of social interest in the utilization of things."[88] Cases like these remind us that a rush to state constitutions as the ground for a new right may overlook the common law, which is not burdened by considerations of "state action" or the constraints of a constitutional holding that can be changed only by amending a charter or overturning a precedent.

The real significance of cases such as *Whiffen* and *Shack*, however, may well lie in their explicit reminder that, as the common law once nourished the constitutions, constitutional values—especially the values so meticulously set out in our lengthy state charters—also can enrich the common law. Indeed, that may be a particularly timely message as society continues to deposit brand new issues of unimagined societal impact at the doorstep of the courts. My next example is just such a situation.

B. Medical Treatment Cases

Historically, no common law principle was more carefully guarded than the right of competent individuals to control their person, free of restraint and interference by others except by clear authority of law.[89] Drawing on that principle, two young lawyers, Louis Brandeis and Samuel Warren, in 1890 envisioned a right to privacy and tort for its invasion, which they cogently advocated in their famous article *The Right to Privacy*.[90] In the years that followed, their vision became reality as common law judges found causes of action, several since made statutory, for such wrongdoing as misappropriating an individual's name or likeness; public disclosure of private facts; and publicity that paints its subject in a false light.[91]

The right to privacy has also figured prominently outside the tort context, particularly in cases involving medical treatment. In New York, the courts have consistently recognized the common law right of every competent adult to refuse treatment, even treatment necessary to preserve life.[92] Whether addressed as a right to privacy, or a matter of

---

88. 5A Powell on Real Property § 746, at 494.

> These adjustments have been guided by a generally prevailing desire to preserve the rights of individuals as far as they prove to be consistent with the welfare of the group; by the necessities of distributing the natural resources as effectively as is possible among multiple claimants; and by the underlying effort to promote the social and economic policies finding current acceptance.

Id. at 496. *See also* Richard R.B. Powell, *The Relationship between Property Rights and Civil Rights*, 15 Hastings L.J. 135 (1963); Berger, *supra* note 86, at 663.

89. *Union Pac. Ry. Co. v. Botsford*, 141 U.S. 250, 251 (1891). *See, e.g., Schloendorff v. Society of N.Y. Hosp.*, 105 N.E. 92 (N.Y. 1914).

90. Louis D. Brandeis and Samuel D. Warren, *The Right to Privacy*, 4 Harv. L. Rev. 193 (1890). As Justice Brandeis later wrote: "The makers of our Constitution . . . conferred, as against the Government, the right to be let alone—the most comprehensive of rights and the right most valued by civilized men." *Olmstead v. United States*, 277 U.S. 438, 478 (1928) (Brandeis, J., dissenting).

91. *See* W. Page Keeton, et al., Prosser and Keeton on the Law of Torts 849–69 (5th ed. 1984).

92. *E.g., Fosmirev. Nicoleau*, 551 N.E.2d 77 (N.Y. 1990); *In re Westchester County Medical Ctr.*, 531 N.E.2d 607 (N.Y. 1988); *In re Storar*, 420 N.E.2d 64 (N.Y.), *cert. denied*, 454 U.S. 858 (1981).

informed consent, individual self-determination or bodily autonomy, state courts have embedded in law an individual's right to disagree with the medical assessments, even as to life-sustaining measures.

1. Right to Die Cases

Biomedical technology has, however, added awesome new dimension to that principle. Scientific advances extending life, sometimes simply prolonging the process of dying, have engendered new ethical and moral questions implicating interests that are critical not only to the individual but also to all of society as available resources dwindle and an aging population grows. As the courts are drawn to the bedside of terminally ill, even irreversibly comatose patients, they have struggled to find modern moorings for what seems like an individual's right to bodily autonomy, but is in fact without historical precedent. With the right to privacy found in the "penumbras" of the federal Constitution[93] and implicitly, sometimes even explicitly, in state constitutions, many ports beckon.

Several courts recognizing a right to privacy in the dying-patient context, have located that right in the common law rather than a constitution; others have not. Lacking clear expression from the Supreme Court, which has hinted at the dying patient's constitutional liberty interest, the Illinois Supreme Court, for example, rejected an invitation to address "whether Federal privacy guarantees the right to refuse life-sustaining medical treatment."[94] By the same token, lacking clear expression from the drafters of the State Constitution, the Illinois court abstained from expanding the state constitutional privacy provision to embrace that right, grounding its decision instead in the state's common law.[95]

The New Jersey Supreme Court, surely a national leader in this area, may well exemplify the persisting search for moorings. In the landmark case *In re Quinlan*,[96] the court premised its decision squarely on the federal Constitution. Shortly thereafter, the same court in *In re Conroy*[97] shifted ground first to New Jersey common law as well as

---

93. *Griswold v. Connecticut*, 381 U.S. 479, 483 (1965).

94. *In re Estate of Longeway*, 549 N.E.2d 292, 297 (Ill. 1989).

95. *Id. See also Bartling v. Superior Court*, 163 Cal. App. 3d 186 (1984); *In re Colyer*, 660 P.2d 738 (Wash. 1983) (en banc); *Severns v. Wilmington Medical Ctr., Inc.*, 421 A.2d 1334 (Del. 1980); *Satz v. Perlmutter*, 362 So. 2d 160 (Fla. Dist. Ct. App. 1978), *aff'd* 379 So. 2d 359 (Fla. 1980); *In re Storar*, 420 N.E.2d 64 (N.Y. 1981).

96. *In re Quinlan*, 70 N.J. 10, 355 A.2d 647, *cert. denied sub nom., Garger v. New Jersey*, 429 U.S. 922 (1976).

97. Finally, in *Quinlan* . . .

> we indicated that the right of privacy enunciated by the Supreme Court "is broad enough to encompass a patient's decision to decline medical treatment under certain circumstances," even if that decision might lead to the patient's death. . . . While this right of privacy might apply in a case such as this, we need not decide that issue since the right to decline medical treatment is, in any event, embraced within the common-law right to self-determination.

In re Conroy, 98 N.J. 321, 346–48, 486 A.2d 1209, 1222–23 (1985) (citations omitted).

constitutional law, and then in *In re Farrell*[98] "primarily" to the common law. While a shift from constitutional to common law grounds is obviously significant, it was accomplished without fanfare, indeed without explanation.

Reasons are obvious. By common law solutions, illuminated by "privacy" and "liberty interest" precedents, courts leave it open for legislatures to fix comprehensive standards for addressing these broad scale questions of social policy. But legislatures may be slow to act in this delicate area, their ultimate enactments may not address the innumerable human variations that characterize individual cases, and statutes would in any event be subject to judicial interpretation and review. Thus it is clear that these issues, including most particularly when they are of constitutional magnitude and when not, will continue to occupy the courts and challenge them to explicate their decisional groundings.[99]

2. Rights of Mental Patients

A related area where scientific advances have radically remade the legal questions, and courts have shifted ground between common law and constitutional solutions, is the treatment of institutionalized mental patients with mind-altering drugs. Again, the individual's right to refuse treatment, to disagree with the doctors, has sparked controversy over the correct basis for deciding cases.[100] As in the case of life-and-death decision-making, where the long-awaited Supreme Court decision[101] suggested federal due process protections but left a wide swath for the states, the Court's most recent holdings concerning the treatment of mental patients[102] have left commentators predicting that "state law is to be the vehicle for any extension of due process."[103] This surely would include state common law, which has over the years relaxed its barriers to challenges by the institutionalized mentally ill.[104]

---

98. *In re Farrell*, 108 N.J. 335, 347–48, 529 A.2d 404, 410 (1987). *See* Nancy J. Moore, *"Two Steps Forward, One Step Back": An Analysis of New Jersey's Latest "Right to Die" Decisions*, 19 Rutgers L.J. 955 (1988); Stewart G. Pollock, *Life and Death Decisions: Who Makes Them and by What Standards?*, 41 Rutgers L. Rev. 505 (1989).

99. In *In re Jobes*, 108 N.J. 394, 529 A.2d 434 (1987), concurring Justice Handler noted that the court may well have erred in *Quinlan* in its constitutional grounding. *Id.* at 432 n.3, 529 A.2d at 454 n.3 (Handler, J., concurring). *See also* the concurrence of Justice Mountain in *Southern Burlington County NAACP v. Township of Mount Laurel*, 67 N.J. 151,193,336 A.2d 713, 735 (1975) (urging statutory rather than constitutional basis for decision).

100. Jonathan P. Bach, Note, *Requiring Due Care in the Process of Patient Deinstitutionalization: Toward a Common Law Approach to Mental Health Care Reform*, 98 Yale L.J. 1153 (1989); Jessica Litman, Note, *A Common Law Remedy for Forcible Medication of the Institutionalized Mentally Ill*, 82 Colum. L. Rev. 1720 (1982); Steven G. Mintz, Note, *The Nightmare of Forcible Medication: The New York Court of Appeals Protects the Rights of the Mentally Ill Under the State Constitution*, 53 Brook. L. Rev. 885 (1987).

101. *Cruzan v. Director of Missouri Dep't of Health*, 497 U.S. 261 (1990).

102. *Washington v. Harper*, 494 U.S. 210 (1990); *Youngberg v. Romeo*, 457 U.S. 307 (1982).

103. Jeannette Brian, *The Right to Refuse Antipsychotic Drug Treatment and the Supreme Court: Washington v. Harper*, 40 Buff. L. Rev. 251, 282 (1992). *See also* Phyllis P. Dietz, Note, *The Constitutional Right to Treatment in Light of Youngberg v. Romeo*, 72 Geo. L.J. 1785 (1984) (summarizing Department of Justice's narrow interpretation of *Youngberg* and suggesting a broader approach).

104. Litman, *supra* note 100 (suggesting common law theories).

In New York, these issues have fluctuated between common law and constitutional solutions. Our most recent decision, coming after years of common law cases with no significant legislative response, identified a mental patient's right of autonomy or self-determination as "coextensive with the patient's liberty interest protected by the due process clause of our State Constitution."[105] In other states, the same qualified right to refuse medication in nonemergency situations has been premised on state common law, state statutes, state constitutions, the federal Constitution, or some combination of them.[106]

As I watch new miracles of modern science arrive on court dockets, it occurs to me that the "incremental pragmatism and seasoned skepticism"[107] of the common law process may be uniquely suited to these unparalleled cases. In fixing the permissible outer limits of medical interference, a social policy issue of enormous importance, courts may indeed "best serve the interests of justice if [they] build upon [their] common law strengths and make haste slowly."[108]

C. Fundamental Fairness Cases

The final example of common law decision-making infused with constitutional values concerns what might loosely be described as "common law due process," an example of the flexibility and adaptability of the common law in fullest flower. While the principle can take many forms—most notably, New Jersey's extraordinary "fairness and rightness" doctrine[109]—the example I have chosen is the public service doctrine, or duty to serve.

---

105. *Rivers v. Katz*, 495 N.E.2d 337, 341 (N.Y. 1986). In *In re Storar*, 420 N.E.2d 64 *cert. denied*, 454 U.S. 858 (1981), the New York Court of Appeals recognized as a matter of *common law* the right of a competent adult to control the course of medical treatment; the intermediate appellate court had reached that same result as a matter of *constitutional* law (426 N.Y.S.2d 517) (1980). *See* William M. Brooks, *A Comparison of a Mentally Ill Individual's Right to Refuse Medication Under the United States and the New York State Constitutions*, 8 Touro L. Rev. 1 (1991).

106. *See, e.g., Large v. Superior Court*, 714 P.2d 399, 406 (Ariz. 1986) (en banc) (state constitution); *People v. Woodall*, 257 Cal. Rptr. 601, 607 (1989) (state statute); *Riese v. St. Mary's Hosp. & Medical Ctr.*, 243 Cal. Rptr. 241, 246 (1988) (state statute); *People v. Medina*, 705 P.2d 961, 967 (Colo. 1985) (en banc) (state statute and common law); *In re Orr*, 531 N.E.2d 64, 71 (Ill. App. Ct. 1988) (state statute); *In re Mental Commitment of M.P.*, 510 N.E.2d 645 (Ind. 1987) (state statute); *In re Guardianship of Linda*, 519 N.E.2d 1296, 1299 (Mass. 1988) (state and federal constitutional rights to privacy and bodily integrity); *Jarvis v. Levine*, 418 N.W.2d 139, 148 (Minn. 1988) (state constitution); *State rel Jones v. Gerhardstein*, 416 N.W.2d 883, 892–93 (Wis. 1987) (federal and state constitutions).

107. Ellen A. Peters, *State Constitutional Law: Federalism in the Common Law Tradition*, 84 Mich. L. Rev. 583, 592 (1986).

108. *Id. See also* Cole, *supra* note 6, at 396; Norman L. Cantor, *Conroy, Best Interests, and the Handling of Dying Patients*, 37 Rutgers L. Rev. 543 (1985).

109. New Jersey's "fairness and rightness" doctrine is an "elusive concept" with "undefinable" boundaries that enables the court to reach a just result. *State v. Yoskowitz*, 116 N.J. 679, 704–5, 563 A.2d 1, 13 (1989) (quoting Bruce D. Greenberg, *New Jersey's "Fairness and Rightness" Doctrine*, 15 Rutgers L.J. 927, 928 [1984]); *State v. Ramseur*, 106 N.J. 123, 379, 524 A.2d 188, 318–19 (1987) (Handler, J., dissenting). Openly based on public policy, the doctrine has been invoked in civil and criminal matters, against private and public actors. The doctrine has facilitated providing indigent municipal court defendants with counsel, *Rodriquez v. Rosenblatt*, 58 N.J. 281, 294, 277A.2d 216 (1971), non-tenured teachers with reasons for dismissal, prisoners with reasons for the denial of their parole, and the guilty with access

Traditionally, private persons engaged in public callings—for example, innkeepers, victuallers, warehouse operators, common carriers—were required to serve the public on a nondiscriminatory basis.[110] That venerable principle was as familiar to old England as it is to every first-year law student today. Whether based on a rationale that such persons had monopoly power, or had affirmatively undertaken to serve the general public, or some other rationale, it was *status* that limited both the property owners' freedom of contract and their absolute right to exclude others. Those serving the public had an affirmative obligation to provide adequate and nondiscriminatory access, and members of the public had a correlative right to reasonable treatment.

The common law duty to serve has extensive modern application in the area of private associations, such as cooperative boards, professional societies and labor unions. In contrast to the social and fraternal orders of the past, many private organizations today have virtual monopolistic control over their members' economic interests. Common law due process recognizes that such associations, although not governmental, by reason of their status often exercise powers that affect the public interest—for example, the cooperative board imposing rules, the union acting as sole bargaining agent, and the local medical society controlling physicians' hospital affiliations.[111] As with any authority to govern, those powers hold potential for arbitrary and malicious decision-making, favoritism and discrimination. Because of the potential public impact, courts have compelled them as a matter of common law to exercise their powers fairly, not to exclude individuals unreasonably. Like the constitutional doctrine, how much process is due varies with the circumstances, but may include a full range of procedural protections. These common law limits on self-government by private actors mirror constitutional due process both because they share the core requirements of notice and an opportunity to be heard, and because they are triggered by a deprivation of property rights or pecuniary benefits.[112]

---

to their presentence reports. *See State v. Kunz*, 55 N.J. 128, 259 A.2d 895 (1969). The doctrine has also been employed to enhance double jeopardy principles. *See State v. Godfrey*, 139 N.J. Super. 135,353 A.2d 101 (App. Div.), *cert. denied*, 73 N.J. 40, 372 A.2d 306 (1976).

Two recent New York decisions illustrate the common law fairness doctrine. *See Beer Garden, Inc. v. New York State Liquor Auth.*, 590 N.E.2d 1193 (N.Y. 1992) (*common law* fairness violated in license suspension proceeding); *contrast 1616 Second Ave. Restaurant, Inc. v. New York State Liquor Auth.*, 550 N.E.2d 910 (N.Y. 1990) (federal constitutional due process violated in license suspension proceeding).

110. *See* C.M. Haar and D.W. Fessler, The Wrong Side of the Tracks: A Revolutionary Rediscovery of the Common Law Tradition of Fairness in the Struggle against Inequality (1986); Note, *The Antidiscrimination Principle in the Common Law*, 102 Harv. L. Rev. 1993 (1989); Matthew O. Tobriner and Joseph R. Grodin, *The Individual and Public Service Enterprise in the New Industrial State*, 55 Cal. L. Rev. 1247 (1967).

111. *See, e.g., Levandusky v. One Fifth Avenue Apt.*, 553 N.E.2d 1317, 1320 (N.Y. 1990) (describing condominium association as a "quasi-government"); *Collins v. International Alliance of Theatrical Stage Employees*, 119 N.J. Eq. 230, 240–42, 182 A. 37, 43–44 (Ch. 1935) (motion picture union control over its members is dictatorial); *Falcone v. Middlesex County Medical Soc'y*, 34 N.J. 582, 170 A.2d 791 (1961) (County Medical Society's actions stricken when they run counter to public policy).

112. *See, e.g., Blende v. Maricopa County Medical Soc'y*, 393 P.2d 926, 930 (Ariz. 1964) (judicial inquiry limited to reasonableness standard in reviewing denial of physicians' application for membership in medical society, must comport with the legitimate goals of the society and the rights of the individual and the public); *Pinsker v. Pacific Coast Soc'y of Orthodontists*, 460 P.2d 495, 499 (Cal. 1969) (dentist seeking admission to professional society had judicially enforceable right to have his application considered in

As a doctrine of fairness and equality, the common law principle also has been invoked, despite a web of statutes and constitutional protections, to prevent unfair exclusion from public places such as restaurants, hospitals, even blackjack tables.[113] "Property owners have no legitimate interest in unreasonably excluding particular members of the public when they open their premises for public use."[114] The doctrine is seriously advocated, as well, as a basis for challenging inequities in municipal services.[115] Others have urged that courts adopt a broader, more realistic definition of "public service companies," to account for the public importance of goods and services furnished by private entities.[116] The full potential for adding common law grounds to the arsenal for addressing racial and other invidious discrimination remains to be explored.[117]

III. Conclusion: An Invitation to Dialogue

I am confident that I could multiply, many times over, examples of existing common law protections of individual rights, in civil as well as criminal cases, in statutory as well as constitutional areas, and we could together speculate endlessly on potential future applications.[118] Surely in the great reaches of the common law an ancestor can be found for every claimed right.

---

a manner comporting with the fundamentals of due process); *International Union of Operating Eng'rs v. Pierce*, 321 S.W.2d 914,918 (Tex. Civ. App. 1959) (constitutional bylaws of trade unions will be upheld if applied and administered in good faith and upon probable cause); *Mixed Local of Hotel & Restaurant Employees v. Hotel and Restaurant Employees Int'l Alliance*, 4 N.W.2d 771, 775 (Minn. 1942) (in the matter of expulsion and suspension of members, a trade association is bound by the rules of fair play, or as it is sometimes called, due process); *Johnson v. Prince Hall Grand Lodge*, 325 P.2d 45, 49 (Kan. 1958) (in determining whether fraternal organization fairly exercised its disciplinary powers, close adherence to the form of legal procedure is not required; rather it is sufficient if the accused is accorded those essentials which make for justice); *Washington Local Lodge No. 104 v. International Bhd. of Boilermakers*, 203 P.2d 1019, 1061 (Wash. 1949) (it is within the powers of the courts to protect the property rights of the members of labor unions and other voluntary organizations where they are threatened or endangered without specific charges and an opportunity to be heard); *see also*, James C. Harrington, *The Texas Bill of Rights and Civil Liberties*, 17 Tex. Tech. L. Rev. 1487, 1528–29 (1986).

113. *Uston v. Resorts Int'l Hotel, Inc.*, 89 N.J. 163, 445 A.2d 370 (1982).

114. *Id.* at 173, 445 A.2d at 375.

115. *See generally* Haar and Fessler, *supra* note 110.

116. *See generally* Tobriner and Grodin, *supra* note 110.

117. Note, *The Antidiscrimination Principle in the Common Law*, 102 Harv. L. Rev. 1993 (1989).

118. I have not touched on criminal law, which itself offers many examples. The New York Court of Appeals recently invoked the common law to define requisite levels of suspicion for official inquiry of passengers in bus and train terminals, *People v. Hollman*, 581 N.Y.S.2d 619 (1992), levels which surpass the federal floor established in *Terry v. Ohio*, 392 U.S. 1 (1968). We also continue to explore the limits of a discovery principle which the Court of Appeals added to the criminal law as a matter of common law fairness. *People v. Rosario*, 173 N.E.2d 881 (N. Y. 1961). Free press protections are another example of the continued operation of the common law alongside statutes and constitutional guarantees. *See, e.g., In re John Doe Grand Jury Investigation*, 574 N.E.2d 373 (Mass. 1991) (grand jury subpoenas of reporters quashed as a matter of common law; constitutional value of disseminating information considered in balance). *See also* Joseph W. Singer, *The Reliance Interest in Property*, 40 Stan. L. Rev. 611, 746–48 (1988)

Instead of multiplication or prognostication, however, I would like to venture what might be called a conclusion but is more accurately an invitation to further dialogue. Having spent considerable time researching and reflecting on the subject, I must admit that I am left with questions. Not doubts, questions.

I have no question, however, as to the legitimacy and good sense of suggesting that the movement of individual rights cases toward the state courts should awaken greater attention to the common law as a source of new rights.[119] A cast-in-stone constitutional decision ties the hands of the judiciary and other institutions of government, perhaps precluding the development of flexible solutions to complex new policy choices generated by a changing society with an expectation of "total justice."[120] Positing only constitutional arguments and ignoring common law arguments may in some instances be appropriate, but in other instances unnecessarily close a door.

The common law, lifeblood of state courts from their inception, "enables courts to intervene resolutely and persistently without completely overthrowing legislative discretion and priorities."[121] Nourished by our bedrock constitutional values and updated by our evolving sense of justice, the common law can embolden state courts confronting new demands and encourage the sort of experimentation that has long been a strength of the American justice system.[122] Indeed, one might well ask, why should it *not* be the common law that is determinative of demands for new rights?

The answer is not simple. Clearly, there are matters that must stand as constitutional, beyond ready revision. Constitutional issues cannot be avoided, or constitutional principles diluted, or the law manipulated, or responsibility shirked or deflected to other institutions by resort to the common law for core policies of that nature. But which are the core

---

(urging development of common law doctrines to solve problems of plant closing); F. Eric Fryar, Note, *Common Law Due Process Rights in the Law of Contracts*, 66 Tex. L. Rev. 1021, 1048 (1988) (common law due process in contract law); Jonathan P. Graham, Note, *Privacy, Computers, and the Commercial Dissemination of Personal Information*, 65 Tex. L. Rev. 1395, 1425–26 (1987) (proposing formulation for new common law doctrines to address invasions of privacy resulting from computer databases).

119. The dignity of the individual "affords the true basis for a doctrine of public interest to be applied by the courts as a substantive part of the law." Cyril J. Radcliff, The Law and Its Compass 57 (1960). "Every system of jurisprudence needs, I think, a constant preoccupation with the task of relating its rules and principles to the fundamental moral assumptions of the society to which it belongs." *Id.* at 63. *See* Henry P. Monaghan, *Foreword: Constitutional Common Law*, 89 Harv. L. Rev. 1 (1975) (suggesting a *federal* constitutional common law). *See also* Thomas Schrock and Robert Welsh, *Reconsidering the Constitutional Common Law*, 91 Harv. L. Rev. 1117 (1978); Thomas W. Merrill, *The Common Law Powers of Federal Courts*, 52 U. Chi. L. Rev. 1 (1985).

120. Lawrence M. Friedman, Total Justice (1985).

121. Bach, *supra* note 100, at 1159. *See* Calabresi, *supra* note 39, at 11; Tobriner and Grodin, *supra* note 110, at 1283. I do not propose resort to the common law to invalidate statutes, but merely that the common law should be fully investigated before courts confronting new demands turn to constitutions.

122. *New State Ice Co. v. Liebmann*, 285 U.S. 262, 311 (1932) (Brandeis, J., dissenting). See also the thoughtful concurrence of Justice Stewart G. Pollock in *Hennessey v. Coastal Eagle Point Oil Co.*, 129 N.J. 81, 108, 609 A.2d 1 l, 24 (1992), urging a common law rather than constitutional grounding for the court's decision, referring to the state court's "common-law birthright."

policies of that nature? Where there is no clear discontinuity between common law and constitutional law, the difficult question is one of definition.[123]

When is a matter properly one of common law and when does it cross the threshold of constitutional law? A court's stated desire to preserve flexibility and options by common law solutions is as much a consequence as a cause for choosing one ground over the other. The shifts and vacillation among courts, even *within* courts, between constitutional and nonconstitutional premises suggests that a rationale has yet to emerge.

I would contribute two thoughts to the dialogue. First, I think of the attention now focused on state constitutional law methodology, as courts and commentators enrich even our vocabulary with talk of "primacy interstitial-lockstep," and "interpretive-noninterpretive" approaches. As the "new" judicial federalism approaches majority, we are increasingly challenged to formulate a constitutional theory that recognizes the distinctive origins and character of state charters.[124] With the common law a necessary and desirable step in the response of state courts confronting demands for new rights, fixing the line that divides common law from constitutional law is yet another facet of the challenge to formulate state constitutional theory. Drawing the distinction is, moreover, a matter in which state court judges have genuine expertise, not only because of their long experience with the subject but also because it is the very essence of the common law process of incremental growth to make such choices. That is, after all, the process by which our constitutional rights have evolved.

Second, there is something very positive in all of this. A full two *centuries* after the federal charter, courts and commentators are still actively engaged in theorizing about correct models of federal constitutional interpretation. Now barely two *decades* into a state constitutional law "vival," does this same sort of discussion not itself establish overwhelmingly that state constitutional law is "real" constitutional law? I surely think so. The partnership of real common law and real constitutional law holds great promise for the future.

---

123. Professor Monaghan suggests that the question is only a difference in degree, citing the example of defamation as an interpretive constitutional rule, and the law governing reasonable warrantless searches of automobiles as not. Monaghan, *supra* note 119, at 33. I would surely agree that defamation is an example of an interpretive *constitutional* rule, but even on the Court of Appeals, that view is not unanimous. *See Immuno A.G. v. Moor-Jankowski*, 567 N.E.2d 1286 (Titone, J., concurring on state common law grounds).

124. *See* G. Allan Tarr, *Constitutional Theory and State Constitutional Interpretation*, 22 Rutgers L.J. 841 (1991).

Law Is Pivotal in Advancing Women's Rights*

Law Day '93: Justice for All

Law Day began in 1958 as a Cold War counterpoint to the Soviet Union's May Day celebration. With the end of the Cold War, many countries in the former Soviet Union and Eastern Bloc are now taking their first steps toward democracy—a difficult journey, we are daily reminded, whose outcome is far from certain.

Law Day is no less important in America today. It is a time to reflect on the privileges of American citizenship and the principles and institutions that have secured our liberty for more than 200 years—principles and institutions which many other nations are now studying and emulating.

The genius of our bedrock American principles is that they are sturdy enough to form the foundation of the longest-lasting constitutional democracy in the world today and supple enough to permit necessary refinement in a constantly evolving, hopefully progressing society. The principles have lasted because the law has continually developed to provide fuller measures of justice to more Americans. Law Day permits us to renew our commitment to the critical struggle for a more just society.

For me, the theme of this year's Law Day celebration, Justice for All—All for Justice, has taken on special, personal significance since my swearing in as Chief Judge exactly six weeks ago.

Constraints on Women

I cannot help but think that, during much of our nation's early history, the law played a central role in constraining women's dreams and ambitions. The law denied them even the right to practice law. The ink barely had dried on the Thirteenth, Fourteenth and Fifteenth Amendments, with their promise of equal protection, when the U.S. Supreme Court upheld a state's denial of a woman's right to become a member of the Bar. Several

---

*New York Law Journal, Law Day Supplement, S1, col. 3 (May 3, 1993), special pullout section.

of the justices joined in elaborating on the different spheres and destinies of men and women under the Law of the Creator—a law they were of no mind to modify.

Shortly thereafter, the Supreme Court of Wisconsin held that a similar prohibition did not violate that State's Constitution, observing: ["]It would be revolting to all female sense of innocence and sanctity of sex, shocking to man's reverence for womanhood and faith in woman that women should be permitted to mix professionally in all the nastiness of the world which finds its way into courts of justice.["] Almost half a century later, women still were denied rights as basic as the right to vote and the right to serve on juries.

Even when I entered the profession in the early 1960s, women lawyers found it hard to secure employment; quotas were the rule; compensation lower; and law firm partnerships all but impossible. Women were openly excluded from bar associations and lawyers' clubs, and the subject of pejorative remarks even in the courtroom. In more recent years, women have gained recognized status under our constitutions; sexual harassment has become a firmly rooted cause of action; and the law generally has become more responsive to crimes and other wrongdoing against women.

Civilizing Force

As in this nation's early history, the law—again—has played a central role in shaping society's attitudes toward women. Now, however, it has become clear that the law can be a vital engine of civilizing change (to quote Justice Brennan) for women and other historically marginalized groups, and that lawyers and courts have an important role to play in advancing the progress of this country by bringing day-to-day reality closer to the nation's stated ideals.

It has become clear that the law is more than a sheaf of rules to be mechanically applied to each controversy brought to court. Rather, there is a necessary and desirable human dimension in the judicial process. There is a recognition that lawyers who bring and frame cases, and courts and judges who rule on them, shape and at times even make policy, that their insights born of a greater understanding of this changing world can and do contribute to a thoroughly principled yet contemporary, compassionate Rule of Law. And whether by rightful inheritance, the defaults of others or natural forces, that societal perception, indeed public demand and now tradition, of the courts in recent decades has gained an unstoppable momentum.

Litigation has been a powerful tool in eroding discriminatory barriers in the workplace, including barriers to club memberships, even to partnerships, and it has awakened public awareness to the disparate treatment of women in divorce, child support, employment and other private and public aspects of life. Where courts were once a forum for legitimating and institutionalizing barriers to equal justice for women, in our own lifetimes we have seen them also serve as a forum for challenging stereotypes, for opening paths, and for punishing and deterring harassment and discrimination.

The law as it relates to women is but one example of a civilizing change that has not merely followed but also shaped and advanced society's perceptions. People have changed the law to be sure, but the more interesting and significant point is that the law has also succeeded in changing people, and particularly some—though by no means enough—of their invidious stereotypes about the roles and capacities of traditionally excluded social groups.

This may be the most significant contribution the law has made to the broader culture in this century. As the recent fall of the Eastern Bloc reminds us, the hearts and minds of free-thinking citizens cannot be changed by governmental fiat or military might. But the American experience shows that the organic development of the law, coupled with the independence of the judiciary and a tradition of respect for the Rule of Law, can change attitudes. Recent decades have witnessed a progressive dialectic between legal doctrine and the views of many Americans, a process which has led to greater justice for all.

In spite of these hopeful developments, there is of course a great deal yet to be done. Discrimination is perhaps even more invidious today for its greater subtlety, even within the justice system. Injustices persist although women are more than half our populace. For other groups, the barriers to full social inclusion and self-determination have been even slower to fall. And the barriers remain formidable.

Profession's Role

The Bar must continue its active role in breaking down these barriers. Courts and judges depend upon the sensitivity, creativity and dedication of lawyers for new insights into old principles. As the world changes and values evolve, courts look to the Bar to deepen their understanding of the context and ramifications of legal issues, to help keep the law attuned to the needs of modern society, and to lead in the progress of the law.

The emerging democracies of Eastern Europe now look to the United States for leadership in such areas as the independence of the judiciary, the Rule of Law, and the role of the courts in unifying a diverse nation with inclusive, evolving principles of justice. As we celebrate Law Day and reflect on the unifying, elevating power of the law, it is crucial for all lawyers to reaffirm their commitment to refining our traditions and principles for today's world and bringing us closer to the ideal of Justice for All.

The Changing World of Children*

The Responsibility of the Law and the Courts

After ten years as a Judge, thirty years as a lawyer, and considerably more as a member of society, I knew that our knottiest problems somehow inevitably landed on the doorstep of the courts. But even as a lifetime New Yorker I could not have imagined the sort of questions that technological progress and social enlightenment are every day adding to court dockets. Courts today are asked whether frozen embryos are marital property subject to distribution on divorce. Should a sperm donor have visitation rights? Should "families of choice"—linked by love and commitment but not a traditional marriage ceremony—be awarded child custody?

So often I have marveled at Judge Cardozo's deft analogy to a poison labeling case, to find liability against a car manufacturer when the wooden spokes of a wheel crumbled and the car collapsed. What analogy, I wonder, would Judge Cardozo have found in our precedents to determine the right of a gay life partner to succeed to a New York City rent-controlled apartment?

Of course, not all the change has been so intriguing, so fascinating. Much of it has been unwelcome and downright distressing—especially the change in the lives of children. A tragic combination of forces—largely sociological and economic—combine to rob millions of children of what we envision when we think of childhood: playing in the park; smiling faces; loving, nurturing homes; well-functioning public schools; safe neighborhoods. Instead, many children live with poverty, violence, drugs, crime, homelessness, hopelessness. Tens of thousands are crack-addicted at birth.

The Plight of Today's Children

Caring citizens—looking around, reading the newspapers—could only be deeply moved, horrified by the plight of children today. There is no respite in the media from tales of torture, cruelty, death inflicted on children, sometimes by children.

---

*Reprinted with permission from New York State Bar Association Journal, November 1993, vol. 65, no. 7, published by the New York State Bar Association, One Elk Street, Albany, NY 12207.

But lawyers and judges have an even more intimate, personal connection because troubled children are not just in the newspapers, they are increasingly in the courts. The courts, especially the state courts, have in a sense become societal reception centers, often the very first of a lifetime of escalating encounters with the State. Children may be in court as victims of sexual abuse or neglect, or because of foster care failures. They may be in court because of crimes they have committed, sometimes violent crimes; or they may be the object of contests for visitation, custody or support in adoption or matrimonial litigation. All litigation has exploded, but in each of these categories—abuse, foster care placements, juvenile delinquency, matrimonial actions—the percentage growth in the numbers of new cases is positively staggering.

So for lawyers and judges, and particularly for state trial and appellate courts, the heartbreaking plight of children and families is not just the concern of a caring citizenry: it's today's docket, and tomorrow's too, growing wildly, both in volume of cases and in gravity of offenses. What might begin with a neglected young child snatching a purse, too soon can become burglary, drug dealing, robbery, rape, murder. Only yesterday I read of the alarming nationwide rise in teenage sex crimes, children not only themselves lost lives but also major menaces to all of society.

Family Cases Are Different

It doesn't take a family law expert to know immediately that, in so many ways, these cases are different from the controversies typically found on court dockets and in law reviews. Disputes typically are adjudicated through the adversary process, and finite. Someone wins, someone loses—eventually. In family cases, by contrast, both sides may be asserting the identical interest—the child's interest—and continuing court intervention may be mandatory.

Where abuse or neglect is found, for example, a child may be removed from the home, with periodic hearings concerning efforts to reunify the family, inquiries involving social service theory and practice, and other disciplines. That is true also of foster care placements: indeed, the laws are by definition not adversarial; they are child protective and seek only the "best interest of the child." In delinquency cases as well, the goals may be therapeutic as much as punitive, to help children become responsible adults, again requiring courts and agencies to work cooperatively. Court delays and congestion, undesirable in any litigation, become utterly intolerable when measured by children's time—long delays in resolving custody, with rotating placements, can have deadly lifetime impact on a child.

In many ways, therefore, the burgeoning numbers of cases involving children are different. With so many lives in the balance, determining what in the child's best interest is truly God's work—too often denigrated within the justice system, too often ignored and debased by others, particularly by branches of government whose financial support is so vital.

The Significance of Family Law

While litigation involving children and families is unquestionably different in many ways—most especially its human toll—it is at the same time true that family law cases are fundamentally like other adjudicated disputes. That too is a point often ignored. Courts deciding family law controversies are courts of law, not social service agencies. They require not just big hearts and good intentions but jurisdiction to proceed, competent proof, sound legal principles to guide their determinations, and uniformity of result to assure equal justice.

From the perspective of new developments in the law, moreover, few are more significant than in family law, today a frontier in defining individual rights, rights to form families, rights to conduct family life. The family would seem to be the ultimate private preserve, immune from State intervention, yet at the same time children in danger are a public responsibility. Family law today exemplifies the tension in the law between traditional notions of privacy and autonomy on the one hand and the state's need to protect its most vulnerable citizens on the other.

Perhaps most interesting of all is how pervasively modern family law infuses and influences the law generally. Even in corporate and business matters, the marital property cases guide the law in valuing closely-held businesses, in pension rights, even in bankruptcy.

Whether essentially different or essentially the same—and I believe it is both—family law today is clearly essential in our struggle toward a better society. It is a struggle we seem to be losing, as the lives of more and more children—America's future—are wasted and devastated. As a nation, we need nothing short of a Marshall Plan to turn around the lives and life chances of children. While we continue to search for that global solution, however, we can as concerned individuals at least lend support to programs we know are working—programs that get children off to a decent start in life, as well as programs that can help keep families together by providing assistance during times of crisis. As individuals, we can lend support to strengthening the public schools—once the key to the American dream.

What Lawyers and Judges Can Do

But lawyers and judges can do more. However daunting the root problems that cause families increasingly to resort to the courts, it is a simple, sad truth that they are today a major presence in the justice system. And while we may not be able to resolve the global problem, we certainly can address our own discrete, tangible piece of it.

We can spearhead and inspire task forces and other groups dedicated to improvements in the law relating to children and families. We can offer advocacy in the political arena to upgrade the resources available for courts dealing with children. We can take steps to assure that courthouse facilities accommodate the special needs of children and families, and that the necessary services will be available to minimize the prospect of their perpetual return visits. We can facilitate procedural reform so that matters involving children are more expeditiously and painlessly resolved. We can offer advocacy in the courts for children who need representation. Whether in the law schools, the organized bar, or in daily practice, we can recognize and thereby elevate scholarship in the area of family law. The American Law Institute's ongoing family law project, like the Restatements generally, will surely advance that objective.

Above all, we must visibly, openly, in every way possible, demonstrate respect and value for the enormous contributions to the law and to society made by family courts and family law.

As Chief Judge, I now receive complaints from every imaginable source about every imaginable subject—in fact, complaint letters are the fastest growing file in Chambers. A recent complaint letter ended with this endearing phrase: "*You judges have a really tough job.*" And of course we do. It is perhaps nowhere more difficult than in the area of family law, where on both the abstract and the human levels the impact is incomparable. The other side of it all is that we also have enormous satisfaction because we can, every now and then, make things a little better, for one person or many. We can, and must, seize that opportunity for children.

State Courts at the Dawn of a New Century*

Common-Law Courts Reading Statutes and Constitutions

Introduction: Justice Brennan's Marvelous Contribution

To begin with what is uppermost in my mind, I have to tell you how pleased I am to be a participant, with all of you, in this wonderful tribute to Justice Brennan. As the first of what I am confident will be an illustrious tradition of convocations centering on the comparatively neglected subject of our nation's state courts, these proceedings also honor my alma mater, the New York University School of Law, and its Dean, John Sexton.

At the outset, I would like to touch on Justice Brennan's marvelous contribution, beginning with what I believe to be his most profound teaching—that as judges we can and must bring the full measure of our human capacities to bear in resolving the cases before us. That has proven a beacon to me in my own years on the bench, as I know it has to so many of my colleagues.[1]

As he underscored most recently when writing of his friend Justice Harry Black-mun, Justice Brennan has always believed that humanity and dignity are no strangers to reason.[2] In his view, passion, which he defines—as only a lawyer could—as "the range of emotional and intuitive responses to a given set of facts or arguments, responses which often speed into our consciousness far ahead of the lumbering syllogism of reason," does not taint the judicial process but is instead central to its vitality.[3] Thus, Justice Brennan has

---

*70 New York University Law Review 1 (1995). The author is grateful to her law clerk Roberta A. Kaplan for her unflagging enthusiasm, which, in addition to her innumerable other contributions to this lecture, made the project so pleasurable.

1. *See generally* Judith S. Kaye, *The Human Dimension in Appellate Judging: A Brief Reflection on a Timeless Concern*, 73 Cornell L. Rev. 1004 (1988).

2. William J. Brennan, Jr., *A Tribute to Justice Harry A. Blackmun*, 108 Harv. L. Rev. 1, 1 (1994).

3. William J. Brennan, Jr., *Reason, Passion, and "The Progress of the Law,"* 42 The Rec. of the Ass'n of the Bar of the City of N.Y. 948, 958 (1987) (42nd annual Benjamin N. Cardozo Lecture).

been a tenacious opponent of those who would have us believe in the concept of "rational certainty"[4]—that there is "no room for compassion in the cold calculus of judging."[5]

This process of deciding each case with its own parties, facts, and issues, according to Justice Brennan, involves a Jeffersonian dialogue between head and heart, a dialogue legitimated by the inarguable fact that judges "are flesh-and-blood human beings, not demi-gods to whom objective truth has been revealed."[6]

In his thirty-four terms on the Supreme Court, Justice Brennan left us with a precious inheritance of deep humanity and principled decision-making—a true dialogue of heart and head—that will live long beyond us. Given the volumes that have been written about his federal constitutional jurisprudence, as well as the fact that we are here today to celebrate our state court heritage, I will linger not on his landmark Supreme Court opinions, but on his equally significant contribution to the way we have come to think about our state courts.

I. The "Topography"[7] of State Courts Today

Justice Brennan is of course most often associated with his distinguished tenure on the Supreme Court of the United States, but prior to that appointment he served seven years as a state court judge, the last four as a member of the New Jersey Supreme Court. Remarkably, at the time of his confirmation, he was only the third state judge appointed to the Supreme Court this century. And what a magnificent trio it was: Holmes, Cardozo, and Brennan!

A decade into his tenure on the Supreme Court, Justice Brennan delivered a lecture at the University of Florida in which he reflected on how both the kinds of cases and the manner in which he decided them had changed fundamentally, noting that this change was the inevitable result of the very different roles of the federal and state courts in our justice system.[8] As he wrote:

> Our states are not mere provinces of an all powerful central government. They are political units with hard-core constitutional status and with plenary governmental responsibility for much that goes on within their borders. . . . [T]he composite work of the courts of the fifty states probably has greater significance in measuring how well America attains the ideal of equal

---

4. *Id.* at 974.

5. Brennan, *supra* note 2, at 1.

6. Brennan, *supra* note 3, at 953.

7. Abner Mikva, *The Shifting Sands of Legal Topography*, 96 Harv. L. Rev. 534, 540 (1982) (reviewing Guido Calabresi, A Common Law for the Age of Statutes [1982]).

8. *See generally* William J. Brennan, Jr., *State Supreme Court Judge versus United States Supreme Court Justice: A Change In Function and Perspective*, 19 Univ. Fla. L. Rev. 225, 225–37 (1966) (explaining different roles of federal and state courts in constitutional interpretive theory and practice).

justice for all. . . . We should remind ourselves that it is state court decisions which finally determine the overwhelming aggregate of all legal controversies in this nation.[9]

Justice Brennan's description of the influence and importance of state courts rings even truer today.[10] Overwhelmingly, our nation's legal disputes are centered in the state courts, which handle more than ninety-seven percent of the litigation—tens of millions of new filings each year compared to some 250,000 in the federal courts.[11] Given these numbers, it is no surprise that the top courtroom dramas to flicker across the nation's television screens—the trials of Joel Steinberg, William Kennedy Smith, the Menéndez brothers, Lorena Bobbitt, O.J. Simpson—have unfolded in state courts.

Not only the number but also the nature of state court cases has changed dramatically. As society has evolved in ways our grandparents could hardly have dreamed, so have our cases, which present an inexhaustible array of novel issues. Today's state court dockets comprise the battlefields of first resort in social revolutions of a distinctly modern vintage: whether frozen embryos are marital property to be distributed equitably upon divorce;[12] whether it is a crime to assist a terminally ill patient in committing suicide;[13] whether DNA evidence should be admitted to establish a defendant's guilt.[14]

In addition, whole categories of cases affecting the day-to-day circumstances, indeed survival, of our citizens are largely if not exclusively adjudicated in the state courts. As societal reception centers, we confront daily the very crises—AIDS, homelessness, drugs,

---

9. *Id.* at 227, 236.

10. For example, in 1976, a decade after Justice Brennan's lecture, there were approximately twenty-three million civil and criminal cases filed in the state courts. National Center for State Courts, State Court Caseload Statistics: Annual Report 1981, at 157–58 (1985). In 1992, the number exceeded thirty-three million. National Center for State Courts, State Court Caseload Statistics: Annual Report 1992, at 3 (1994) (hereafter 1992 State Court Caseload Statistics Report).

11. While the total United States population increased approximately eight percent during the seven years from 1985 to 1992, the number of federal filings increased approximately twenty-three percent, and the number of cases initiated in the state courts increased approximately thirty percent. 1992 State Court Caseload Statistics Report, *supra* note 10, at xii, 43–45.

12. *See, e.g., Davis v. Davis*, 842 S.W.2d 588 (Tenn. 1992); *see also Hecht v. Superior Court*, 20 Cal. Rptr. 2d 275 (2d Dist. 1993) (holding that no public policy forbade posthumous artificial insemination with cryogenically preserved sperm).

13. *People v. Kevorkian*, 527 N.W.2d 714 (Mich. 1994); *see also Kane v. Kulongoski*, 871 P.2d 993 (Or. 1994) (considering constitutionality of assisted suicide ballot provision).

14. *See, e.g., People v. Wesley*, 633 N.E.2d 451 (N.Y. 1994); *see also Ex parte Perry*, 586 So. 2d 242 (Ala. 1991) (putting forth three-pronged test for analyzing admissibility of DNA matching or population frequency statistical evidence); *State v. Bible*, 858 P.2d 1152 (Ariz. 1993) (applying *Frye* test for admissibility of DNA evidence), *cert. denied*, 114 S. Ct. 1578 (1994); *Prater v. State*, 820 S.W.2d 429 (Ark. 1991) (using "relevancy approach" to determine admissibility of DNA evidence); *State v. Brown*, 470 N.W.2d 30 (Iowa 1991) (holding that DNA evidence must be both established as reliable and meet general test of expert testimony admissibility); *State v. Carter*, 524 N.W.2d 763 (Neb. 1994) (considering different approaches to testing admissibility of DNA evidence); *State v. Cauthron*, 846 P.2d 502 (Wash. 1993) (applying *Frye* test to determine admissibility of different types of DNA evidence).

juvenile violence—that continue to frustrate so many others in and out of government.[15] In Chief Justice Ellen Peters's words, state "courts are not ivory towers, sheltered from the vicissitudes of everyday life and controversy. Working in an adversarial context, facing a tide of new cases, [state court] judges . . . devote their learning and their energies and their compassion to the search for just solutions."[16]

As the courts both literally and figuratively closest to the people, it is beyond question that state courts continue to play a vital role in shaping the lives of our citizenry. Plainly Justice Brennan had much more in mind than mere statistics when he equated the work of state courts with how well this nation attains its ideal of equal justice. I think he had in mind as well the common law, that "golden and sacred rule of reason"[17] and the process by which state courts fundamentally address their dockets.

II. The Common Law as the Core Element

The common law is, of course, law-making and policy-making by judges.[18] It is law derived not from authoritative texts such as constitutions and statutes, but from human wisdom collected case by case over countless generations to form a stable body of rules that not only determine immediate controversies but also guide future conduct.[19] While it is durable, certain, and predictable at its core, the common law is not static. It proceeds and grows incrementally, in restrained[20] and principled fashion, to fit into a changing society.

Policy-making under the common law is not however, a freewheeling exercise. Cases are themselves limits; courts do not render advisory opinions but instead resolve

---

15. Between 1989 and 1992, for example, the number of domestic relations and juvenile filings in the state courts rose thirty-eight percent and thirty-three percent, respectively. 1992 State Court Caseload Statistics Report, *supra* note 10, at 26, 30. Not only has there been an alarming growth in this area, "but these cases often remain in the courts for long periods of time and require ongoing court supervision." *Id.* at 24. Similarly, although criminal cases increased twenty-two percent in the federal courts from 1985 to 1992, they increased by nearly twice that amount in the state courts during the same period. *Id.* at 44.

16. The Hon. Ellen Ash Peters, Remarks at the State of the Judiciary, State of Connecticut (March 8, 1995) (transcript on file with author).

17. See Charles F. Mullett, Fundamental Law and the American Revolution, 1760–1776, at 48 (1966) (describing intellectual origins of the common law).

18. *See generally* Benjamin N. Cardozo, The Nature of the Judicial Process 10 (1921); Oliver W. Holmes, Jr., The Common Law 35 (1881); Roscoe Pound, The Spirit of the Common Law 116 (1921).

19. See Janet Reno, *Address Delivered at the Celebration of the Seventy-Fifth Anniversary of Women at Fordham Law School*, 63 Fordham L. Rev. 5, 7 (1994) ("There is on the wall of the east side of the building that houses the Justice Department in Washington, D.C., a statement that reads, 'The Common Law is the Will of Mankind Issuing From the Life of the People Framed Through Mutual Confidence Sanctioned by the Light of Reason' ").

20. See *People v. Hobson*, 348 N.E.2d 896, 900 (N.Y. 1976) ("[S]tare decisis does not spring full-grown from a 'precedent' but from precedents which reflect principle and doctrine rationally evolved. . . . [I]t . . . would be foolhardy not to recognize that there is potential for jurisprudential scandal in a court which decides one way one day and another way the next").

live disputes on the facts and law before them. Appellate decisions, moreover, are the product of a system that requires the agreement of several judges, values stability and faithful adherence to precedent, and safeguards those values by the requirement of written opinions publicly explaining the results reached.

That state courts—not federal courts—are the keepers of the common law has long been American orthodoxy.[21] Even in today's legal landscape, dominated by statutes, the common-law process remains the core element in state court decision-making.

Every day, for example, state courts delineate the limits of tort liability, thereby defining socially acceptable conduct: which members of the general public can recover against a utility for damages incurred during a New York City black-out;[22] whether a victim of rape in an urban apartment building can recover against the landlord;[23] whether the State is liable to a murdered student's family for failure to disclose a former inmate's extensive psychiatric history to the school;[24] whether the Transit Authority is responsible when a young student waiting for a subway train is beaten to death.[25] Not unlike other state tribunals, my court has set the standard of care owed to baseball spectators,[26] baseball players,[27] jockeys,[28] firefighters,[29] swimmers and divers,[30] trespassers,[31] and

---

21. See generally Charles Z. Lincoln, Constitutional History of New York 37 (1906); Thomas C. Grey, *Origins of the Unwritten Constitution: Fundamental Law in American Revolutionary Thought*, 30 Stan. L. Rev. 843, 849; Burt Neubome, *Foreword: State Constitutions and the Evolution of Positive Rights*, 20 Rutgers L.J. 881, 896–97 (1989).

22. See, e.g., *Milliken & Co. v. Consol. Edison Co.*, 644 N.E.2d 268 (N.Y. 1994); *Strauss v. Belle Realty Co.*, 482 N.E.2d 34 (N.Y. 1985); *Koch v. Consol. Edison Co.*, 468 N.E.2d 1 (N.Y. 1984); *Food Pageant v. Consol. Edison Co.*, 429 N.E.2d 738 (N.Y. 1981).

23. See *Jacqueline S. v. City of New York*, 614 N.E.2d 723 (N.Y. 1993); *Waters v. New York City Housing Auth.*, 505 N.E.2d 922 (N.Y. 1987).

24. See *Eiseman v. State*, 511 N.E.2d 1128 (N.Y. 1987).

25. See *Crosland v. New York City Transit Auth.*, 498 N.E.2d 143 (N.Y. 1986).

26. See *Davidoff v. Metro. Baseball Club, Inc.*, 463 N.E.2d 1219, 1220 (N.Y. 1984) (requiring that only seating area behind home plate be screened); *Akins v. Glens Falls City School Dist.*, 424 N.E.2d 531, 533–34 (N.Y. 1981) (same).

27. See *Maddox v. City of New York*, 487 N.E.2d 553, 555 (N.Y. 1985) (holding "assumption of risk to be implied from plaintiff's continued participation in the game with the knowledge and appreciation of the risk").

28. See *Turcotte v. Fell*, 502 N.E.2d 964, 967 (N.Y. 1986) (holding that duty of care owed to plaintiff by defendant "was no more than a duty to avoid reckless or intentionally harmful conduct").

29. See, e.g., *Kenavan v. City of New York*, 517 N.E.2d 872, 875 (N.Y. 1987) (holding that duty of care to firefighters "engaged in extinguishing a fire" only extends insofar as "the owner or other person in control [of the premises] negligently failed to comply with . . . [some] rule respecting the maintenance and safety of such premises").

30. See *Heard v. City of New York*, 623 N.E.2d 541, 544 (N.Y. 1993) (holding that municipality's duty to plaintiff was satisfied once lifeguard "made clear that diving from the jetty was to cease"); *Amatulli v. Delhi Constr. Corp.*, 571 N.E.2d 645, 649–50 (N.Y. 1991) (holding as matter of law that manufacturer is not liable for "injuries resulting from substantial alterations . . . of the product . . . which render [it] . . . unsafe," but liability of retailer and pool installer is question of fact for jury).

31. See *Sega v. State*, 456 N.E.2d 1174, 1175 (N.Y. 1983) (finding landowners of property that is open to the public "are not liable for injuries unless caused by [owners'] willful or malicious acts or omissions"); *Basso v. Miller*, 352 N.E.2d 868, 872 (N.Y. 1976) (holding landowners to a "single standard of reasonable care [for invitees, licensees, and trespassers] whereby foreseeability shall be a measure of liability").

fetuses.[32] Though the facts of each case are different and the answers vary, the court's function is always the same—to weigh and balance the relation of the parties, the nature of the risk, and of course the public interest.

Time and again, state courts have openly and explicitly balanced considerations of social welfare and have fashioned new causes of action where common-sense justice required, most recently in the area of "cancerphobia"[33] and emotional distress suffered by persons exposed to the HIV virus.[34] Conversely, state courts have refused to enlarge the boundaries of the common law by declining to recognize new torts. Only this year, our court refused to allow a cause of action for a third-party's intentional interference with the attorney-client relationship, noting that while the creation of new tort liability is unquestionably a part of our common-law responsibility, we "exercise that responsibility with care, mindful that a new cause of action will have foreseeable and unforeseeable consequences, most especially the potential for vast, uncircumscribed liability."[35]

Whole categories of what can best be described as "gateway" issues like standing,[36] choice of law,[37] and admissibility of evidence[38] are decided every day by state courts as a matter of pure policy. Applying the common law, the New York Court of Appeals even decided the 1988 America's Cup match between New Zealand and San Diego.[39]

---

32. *See Martinez v. Long Island Jewish Hillside Medical Ctr.*, 512 N.E.2d 538, 539 (N.Y. 1987) (finding that doctor owes patient a duty not to give "erroneous advice" concerning the need for an abortion); *Tebbutt v. Virostek*, 483 N.E.2d 1142, 1144 (N.Y. 1985) ("den[ying] damages for emotional distress to parents of children . . . injured [in utero] but born alive"); *see also Woods v. Lancet*, 102 N.E.2d 691, 694 (N.Y. 1951) (recognizing right of infant to recover against doctor for injuries sustained in utero and stating "[w]e act in the finest common-law tradition when we adapt and alter decisional law to produce common-sense justice").

33. *See Criscuola v. Power Auth.*, 621 N.E.2d 1195, 1196–97 (N.Y. 1993) (discussing level of proof required of landowners claiming "cancerphobia"-related damages due to power lines).

34. *See Tischler v. Dimenna*, 609 N.Y.S.2d 1002, 1009 (Sup. Ct. 1994) (allowing claim of "emotional distress for the fear of contracting AIDS" made by plaintiff against boyfriend's estate); *Castro v. New York Life Ins. Co.*, 588 N.Y.S.2d 695, 696 (Sup. Ct. 1991) (holding that "fear of developing AIDS in the future" is a legitimate cause of action). But *see Kaufman v. Physical Measurements, Inc.*, 207 A.D.2d 595, 596 (N.Y. App. Div. 1994) (holding that emotional distress claim was too remote and too speculative to permit recovery, absent proof of likelihood of contracting AIDS); *Hare v. State*, 570 N.Y.S.2d 125, 127 (App. Div. 1991) (denying damages for emotional distress resulting from a fear of contracting AIDS); *Petri v. Bank of New York Co.*, 582 N.Y.S.2d 608, 610 (Sup. Ct. 1992) (denying claim of intentional infliction of emotional distress where employer is alleged to have undertaken "a campaign to terminate plaintiff before he developed AIDS in order to save money").

35. *Madden v. Creative Servs., Inc.*, 84 N.Y.2d 738, 746 (1995) (citations omitted).

36. *See In re Schulz*, 615 N.E.2d 953, 955–56 (N.Y. 1993) (discussing standing to sue); *Society of Plastics Indus. v. County of Suffolk*, 573 N.E.2d 1034, 1040–42 (N.Y. 1991) (discussing development of state standing law in public interest cases); *People v. Wesley*, 538 N.E.2d 76, 77–84 (N.Y. 1989) (discussing standing in criminal law constructive possession cases).

37. *See In re Allstate Ins. Co.*, 613 N.E.2d 936, 938–40 (N.Y. 1993) (discussing choice of law issue); *Cooney v. Osgood Mach., Inc.*, 612 N.E.2d 277, 279–85 (N.Y. 1993) (same).

38. In New York, unlike in the federal system, rules for the admissibility of evidence are developed by the courts largely as a matter of common law. The New York legislature has for many years considered proposals for a comprehensive evidence code analogous to the Federal Rules of Evidence but has to date failed to enact such legislation. See Barbara C. Salken, *To Codify or Not to Codify—That Is the Question: A Study of New York's Efforts to Enact an Evidence Code*, 58 Brook. L. Rev. 641, 641 (1992).

39. *Mercury Bay Boating Club, Inc. v. San Diego Yacht Club*, 577 N.E.2d 87 (N.Y. 1990).

Yet despite the continued vitality of the common law, it is clear that "common law judging" now takes place in a "world of statutes."[40] In my court, like other state courts, the ratio of strictly common-law cases unquestionably has declined, and even in traditional common-law fields like torts, contracts, and property we often confront statutes that affect our decision-making.[41] This ubiquitous web of statutes, combined with more political concerns about "judicial activism,"[42] may in fact have caused state judges to feel that our role as common-law judges, cautiously and creatively developing the law in ways appropriate to a changing society, has been circumscribed.[43]

Increasingly, judicial opinions reflect the notion that, in the absence of a statute, courts should not make law.[44] In 1889, the New York Court of Appeals held, as a matter of common law, that a defendant who poisoned his grandfather could not inherit under the grandfather's will, and the court did so even though no such exception existed in the probate statute.[45] One hundred years later, we would more likely say—as we in fact did

---

40. Ellen A. Peters, *Common Law Judging in a Statutory World: An Address*, 43 U. Pitt. L. Rev. 995, 995–96 (1982).

41. *Farnham v. Kittinger*, 634 N.E.2d 162 (N.Y. 1994) (applying recreational use statute, N.Y. Gen. Oblig. Law § 9-103(1)(a) (Consol. 1977 & Supp. 1993) (granting special immunity to landowners from liability in negligence in connection with injuries sustained by individuals who enter or use property in pursuit of certain recreational activities); *Iannotti v. Consolidated Rail Corp.*, 542 N.E.2d 621 (N.Y. 1989) (same).

42. *See, e.g.,* Abner J. Mikva, *Statutory Interpretation: Getting the Law to Be Less Common*, 50 Ohio St. L.J. 979, 979 (1990); *see also* Cass R. Sunstein, After the Rights Revolution 157–59 (1990).

43. *See* Allan C. Hutchinson and Derek Morgan, *Calabresian Sunset: Statute in the Shade*, 82 Colum. L. Rev. 1752, 1753 (1982) (reviewing Guido Calabresi, A Common Law for the Age of Statutes [1982]) ("The distinguishing feature of twentieth-century legal history has been the shift from the common law to statutes as the major source of law"); Peters, *supra* note 40, at 997 ("Even in cases to which no statute presently applies, the fact that the legislature is always, or virtually always, in session casts a considerable shadow on innovation in common law growth and development").

44. *See Donaca v. Curry County*, 734 P.2d 1339, 1342 (Or. 1987) (stating that the court has not "embraced freewheeling judicial 'policy declarations'"); Kenneth J. O'Connell, *Oregon's Common Law Tradition: An Endangered Species*, 27 Willamette L. Rev. 197, 197 (1991) ("In the course of the last decade, the Oregon Supreme Court has formulated a methodology of appellate adjudication which seriously limits the scope of the judicial decisionmaking process. The limits are set by the court's pronouncement that, in the absence of statutory sources of public policy, courts do not have the authority to articulate and justify rules of law"); Patricia K. Fenske, Note, *Oregon's Hostility to Policy Arguments*, 68 Or. L. Rev. 197, 206–7 (1989) (discussing *Donaca*).

45. *Riggs v. Palmer*, 22 N.E. 188, 190 (N.Y. 1889) ("[A]ll laws . . . may be controlled in their operation and effect by general, fundamental maxims of the common law. . . . These maxims are dictated by public policy, have their foundation in universal law administered in all civilized countries, and have nowhere been superseded by statutes"); *see also Barker v. Kallash*, 468 N.E.2d 39, 41, 43 (N.Y. 1984) (applying principle established by *Riggs* that one may not profit from his own wrong); Reed Dickerson, *Statutory Interpretation: Dipping into Legislative History*, 11 Hofstra L. Rev. 1125, 1153–56 (1983) (discussing *Riggs*). Although we continue to construe statutes in derogation of the common law strictly, *see, e.g., Morris v. Snappy Car Rental, Inc.*, 84 N.Y.2d 21, 28 (1994) (stating that "legislative enactments . . . are deemed to abrogate the common law only to the extent required by the clear import of the statutory language" [citations omitted]), would any among us today be willing to suggest that a statute be modified or ignored because it is in derogation of the common law? I doubt that law students even hear of the now obsolete doctrine of "the equity of the statute," which once permitted common law judges to write exceptions into statutes based on concepts of fundamental fairness. *See, e.g.,* Roger J. Traynor, *Statutes Revolving in Common-Law Orbits*, 17 Cath. U. L. Rev. 401, 403–4 (1968) (discussing history of the doctrine); Peters,

in refusing to recognize a tort of wrongful discharge[46] and in refusing to expand "dram shop" liability[47]—that "such a significant change in our law is best left to the Legislature."[48]

In spite of the anxiety surrounding the legitimacy of judicial law-making, I believe that the inherent, yet principled flexibility of the common law remains the defining feature of the state court judicial process today.[49] As our former Chief Judge Benjamin Cardozo observed more than seventy years ago, though the "fissures in the common law are wider than the fissures in a statute," the resulting "gaps" must still "be filled, whether their size be great or small."[50]

In keeping with that sentiment, former Chief Judge Mikva more recently defined "judicial activism" as "the decisional process by which judges fill in the gaps that they perceive in a statute or the ambiguities that they find in a constitutional phrase."[51] Given the inevitability of this process, he continued, "*all* judges are activists."[52] Thus, "[t]he 'judicial activism' . . . so criticized by today's conservatives (and yesterday's liberals) is really judicial 'naturalism'—judges doing what comes naturally—what most of them were taught to do."[53]

Today, as in the past, in applying the law declared by others (whether a constitution or a statute) there is little doubt that state judges are frequently left to choose among competing policies—to fill the gaps—thereby narrowing or broadening the reach of the law. The choices state judges make are based on a consideration of the "social welfare" which Cardozo described as "public policy, the good of the collective body"[54] which may mean "expediency or prudence"[55] or "the standards of right conduct, which find expression in the *mores* of the community."[56]

---

supra note 40, at 1005 (observing that "the equity of the statute" doctrine has "fallen into disrepute"). For a discussion of the canons of statutory interpretation and their relationship to the common law, *see* David L. Shapiro, *Continuity and Change in Statutory Interpretation*, 67 N.Y.U. L. Rev. 921, 936–40 (1992).

46. *Murphy v. American Home Prods. Corp.*, 448 N.E.2d 86, 89–90 (N.Y. 1983); *see also Sabetay v. Sterling Drug, Inc.*, 506 N.E.2d 919, 923 (N.Y. 1987) (following *Murphy* and reiterating that "significant alteration of employment relationships . . . is best left to the Legislature"). But *see Wieder v. Skala*, 609 N.E.2d 105, 107–10 (N.Y. 1992) (distinguishing *Murphy* and *Sabetay* and allowing claim for wrongful discharge by attorney who reported ethical wrongdoing by law firm).

47. *Sherman v. Robinson*, 606 N.E.2d 1365, 1368 (N.Y. 1992); *D'Amico v. Christie*, 518 N.E.2d 896, 899 (N.Y. 1987); see N.Y. Gen. Oblig. Law §§ 11-100 to 11-101 (Consol. 1977 & Supp. 1993) ("Dram Shop Act").

48. *Murphy*, 448 N.E.2d at 89. For an early example of this type of deference to the legislature, *see Agar v. Orda*, 190 N.E. 479, 480 (N.Y. 1934), where the court reasoned that by passing a statute, the legislature had "shattered or destroyed general common-law rules inconsistent with the statutory code."

49. *See* Mikva, *supra* note 42, at 979 ("Our judicial system, indeed our entire legal system, was forged in the age of the common law. Most judges still function in the mold of their common law predecessors").

50. Cardozo, *supra* note 18, at 71.

51. Mikva, *supra* note 42, at 979.

52. *Id.*

53. *Id.* at 979.

54. Cardozo, *supra* note 18, at 72.

55. *Id.*

56. *Id.*

No one disputes our role—indeed our responsibility—to draw and redraw the bounds of socially tolerable conduct by explicitly adapting established principles to changing circumstances, not by simply picking a result out of a hat but by reference to our precedents and our perceptions of the common good.[57] Few would complain that state court decisions defining the scope of foreseeability, for example, were an arrogation of power. One might disagree with particular policy choices we make,[58] but no one questions our authority to make them. Yet when it comes to constitutional and statutory adjudication—where we engage in a similar process—some are loath to admit that there is *any* "freedom of choice" at all.

My task today is thus both descriptive and normative. It is descriptive in the sense that I believe state courts effectively "make law," and do so by reference to social policy, not only when deciding traditionally common-law cases but also when faced with cases that involve difficult questions of constitutional and statutory interpretation. My ambition is normative in the sense that I believe that this function is necessary both to fill the "gaps" inevitably arising from the complex interplay between human facts and abstract laws, and to fill the far deeper void that would result if state courts were to abrogate their traditional role as interstitial lawmakers.

Let me illustrate what I mean by examining the social policy choices state courts necessarily make (whether we admit it or not). First, I will address the role state judges have in interpreting state constitutions, and then I will focus on state judges interpreting state statutes.

III. Common Law Courts Construing State Constitutions

No doubt in part attributable to his experience as a state court judge, nearly twenty years ago Justice Brennan issued his now famous wake-up call for state courts to "step into the breach" and resuscitate our state constitutions as the living documents they are.[59] I

---

57. *See, e.g.,* O'Connell, *supra* note 44, at 225 (stating that "judges . . . mak[ing] policy decisions" is a "function which most members of the legal community have assumed was an inherent feature of the common-law system").

58. *See, e.g.,* the debate engendered by a recent Court of Appeals conflict of laws decision—*Symposium, Reflections on Cooney v. Osgood Machinery Inc.,* 59 Brook. L Rev. 1323 (1994) (discussing *Cooney,* 612 N.E.2d 277 [N.Y. 1993])—as well as the debate among the judges on the court itself over the municipal liability question presented in a case where the police department failed to react to reports of an abduction (and eventual rape) in progress, *Kircher v. City of Jamestown,* 74 N.Y.2d 251, 260–70 (1989) (Hancock & Bellacosa, JJ., dissenting in separate opinions); *see also* Stewart F. Hancock, Jr., *Municipal Liability Through a Judge's Eyes,* 44 Syracuse L. Rev. 925, 926–31 (1993) (discussing judicial debate over policy behind exceptions to New York's statutory waiver of immunity); Horace B. Robertson, *Municipal Tort Liability: Special Duty Issues of Police, Fire and Safety,* 44 Syracuse L. Rev. 943, 946–55 (1993) (discussing principles underlying municipal liability relating to police protection, fire protection, and safety inspections).

59. William J. Brennan, Jr., *State Constitutions and the Protection of Individual Rights,* 90 Harv. L. Rev. 489, 503 (1977) (hereafter Brennan, *State Constitutions*); *see also* William J. Brennan, Jr., *The Bill of Rights and the States: The Revival of State Constitutions as Guardians of Individual Rights,* 61 N.Y.U. L. Rev. 535, 549 (1986) ("[T]he state courts have responded with marvelous enthusiasm to many not-so-subtle invitations to fill the constitutional gaps left by the decisions of the Supreme Court majority").

still remember the excitement those stirring words generated. Many of us had grown so federalized, so accustomed to the Supreme Court of the United States as the fount of constitutional wisdom, that we barely remembered that our state even had a constitution.

No serious idea is without its critics, and the movement toward active state constitutional interpretation has certainly attracted its share.[60] But it is now clear that the promise inherent in Justice Brennan's challenge has made giant steps toward fulfillment.[61] Perhaps the most accurate assessment of state constitutionalism today is that it has emerged from the cauldrons of our nation's law reviews[62] into the crucible of our state courts, regrettably (I trust not fatally) missing most of our nation's law schools.[63] In the words of the author of a new treatise on the subject: "The past ten years will be known as the era in which state appellate courts issued a Declaration of Independence."[64] Examples

---

60. *See, e.g.,* James A. Gardner, *The Failed Discourse of State Constitutionalism,* 90 Mich. L. Rev. 761, 764 (1992) (arguing that "failure of state constitutional discourse" results from inherent and theoretical weaknesses in very idea of state constitution); Paul W. Kahn, *Interpretation and Authority in State Constitutionalism,* 106 Harv. L. Rev. 1147, 1163 (1993) (arguing that state courts should participate in "common interpretive enterprise" in "American constitutionalism," rather than interpreting their own state constitutions as distinctive documents reflecting their own state's political identity and tradition). But *see* Daniel Gordon, *Superconstitutions Saving the Shunned: The State Constitutions Masquerading as Weaklings,* 67 Temp. L. Rev. 965, 968–70 (1994) (responding to Gardner's article); Burt Neuborne, *A Brief Response to Failed Discourse,* 24 Rutgers L.J. 971 (1993) (same); David Schuman, *A Failed Critique of State Constitutionalism,* 91 Mich. L. Rev. 274 (1992) (same).

61. *See* Brennan, *State Constitutions, supra* note 59, at 502 ("I suggest to the bar that, although in the past it might have been safe for counsel to raise only federal constitutional issues in state courts, plainly it would be most unwise these days not also to raise the state constitutional questions").

62. For an early example of scholarly attention to state constitutional law, *see Developments in the Law— The Interpretation of State Constitutions,* 95 Harv. L. Rev. 1324 (1982) (reviewing development and current status of state constitutional jurisprudence), For more recent examples of such scholarship, see authorities cited in Tim J. Watts, State Constitutional Law Development: A Bibliography (1991); Earl M. Maltz, *Selected Bibliography on State Constitutional Law, 1980–1989,* 20 Rutgers L.J. 1093–113 (1989); *see also* Judith S. Kaye, *Contributions of State Constitutional Law to the Third Century of American Federalism,* 13 Vt. L. Rev. 49, 49 (1988) ("In the fascinating area of state constitutional law, the trickle of deep scholarly interest evident during the 1970's has grown thunderously" [citations omitted]); Robert F. Williams, *State Constitutional Law: Teaching and Scholarship,* 41 J. Legal Educ. 243, 247–49 (1991) (discussing expansion of scholarly interest in state constitutional law).

63. I believe it is largely the failure of our nation's law schools to teach state constitutional law that has resulted in the poor grade earned by the vast majority of counsel who fail to develop state constitutional issues in their court filings. *See, e.g., Davenport v. Garcia,* 834 S.W.2d 4, 20–21 (Tex. 1992) ("Our consideration of state constitutional issues is encumbered when they are not fully developed by counsel. Many of our sister states, when confronted with similar difficulties, have . . . ordered additional briefing of the state issue. We will follow this procedure as necessary and appropriate, when asserted state grounds have not been adequately briefed" [citation omitted]); *see also State v. Jewett,* 500 A.2d 233, 235 (Vt. 1985) (noting that "[d]espite the burgeoning developments in state constitutional law, only about a dozen law schools have courses in state constitutional jurisprudence"); Daniel R. Gordon, *The Demise of American Constitutionalism: Death by Legal Education,* 16 S. Ill. U. L.J. 39 (1991) (arguing that unwillingness and/ or inability of attorneys to employ, and law schools to teach, state constitutional law has paved way for evisceration of constitutional jurisprudence). With rare exceptions, our court will not consider an argument unless it has been preserved by counsel in the trial court.

64. Jennifer Friesen, *Adventures in Federalism: Some Observations on the Overlapping Spheres of State and Federal Constitutional Law,* 3 Widener J. Pub. L. 25, 25 (1993); *see generally* Jennifer Friesen, State Constitutional Law: Litigating Individual Rights, Claims & Defenses (1992) (providing a practitioner's

---

of recent cases where state courts have concluded that their own constitutions afford greater protection than the minimum floor provided by the federal Constitution include decisions from Louisiana, Kentucky, and Michigan holding that it is unconstitutional to medicate a condemned prisoner forcibly so that the prisoner can be executed,[65] that a criminal statute prohibiting "deviate sexual intercourse with another person of the same sex" violates privacy and equal protection guarantees,[66] and that a sentence of life without the possibility of parole for possession of cocaine is improper.[67] In the area of free speech and assembly, the Texas Supreme Court recently held that its constitution was violated by a civil gag order,[68] and the New Jersey Supreme Court, in a decision released just before Christmas, joined at least four other states[69] in concluding that its state constitution guarantees the right of free speech in large, privately owned shopping malls.[70]

Every one of these cases is distinguished by close, heated divisions unusual in the jurisprudence of those courts.[71] Like the debate in the scholarly literature, these divisions reflect important differences about methodology—about when and how a state court should rely on its own constitution.[72] They also reflect deep differences about the role of state constitutions in our judicial system.

These debates are not limited to the pages of law reports or law reviews but have extended to media campaigns and political action committees, one judicial candidate

---

guide to state constitutional law); Robert F. Williams, State Constitutional Law: Cases and Materials (2d ed. 1993) (same).

65. *State v. Perry*, 610 So. 2d 746, 755–56, 762 (La. 1992).

66. *Commonwealth v. Wasson*, 842 S.W.2d 487, 492–99 (Ky. 1992).

67. *People v. Bullock*, 485 N.W.2d 866, 870–72 (Mich. 1992).

68. *Davenport v. Garcia*, 834 S.W.2d 4, 10–11 (Tex. 1992).

69. See *Robins v. Pruneyard Shopping Ctr.*, 592 P.2d 341, 346–48 (Cal. 1979); *Bock v. Westminster Mall Co.*, 819 P.2d 55, 56 (Colo. 1991); *Batchelder v. Allied Stores Int'l Inc.*, 445 N.E.2d 590, 593–96 (Mass. 1983); *Lloyd Corp. v. Whiffen*, 849 P.2d 446, 447 (Or. 1993).

70. *New Jersey Coalition Against War in the Middle East v. J.M.B. Realty Corp.*, 650 A.2d 757, 760–62 (N.J. 1994).

71. *See, e.g., Bullock*, 485 N.W.2d at 883–84 (Riley, J., concurring in part and dissenting in part) ("In its analysis of the role this Court plays in state constitutional adjudication, the majority . . . contends that the Michigan Constitution is an independent source of rights, different in scope from the federal counterpart, and that the federal court decisions interpreting the parallel constitutional provisions are not presumptively correct. I cannot subscribe to the majority's argument because it is evidence of its decision to eschew the historical foundations which the Michigan constitutional provision shares with the federal counterpart. Furthermore, I view it as nothing more than an attempt to substitute a judicial policy choice for the policy choice already made by our Legislature" [citations omitted]).

72. *See, e.g.,* the description in *West v. Thomson Newspapers*, 872 P.2d 999, 1005–7 (Utah 1994) where the Utah Supreme Court outlined "four models for determining when and under what circumstances courts should base decisions on their own constitutions where there are related or similar federal constitutional provisions": the court embraced the "primacy" model, thus committing itself to reaching state constitutional concerns before federal ones. The other three models discussed by the court were: (1) the "interstitial" model (presumption that federal law is controlling; state issues reached only when case cannot be resolved under federal law); (2) the "dual sovereignty" model (both federal and state grounds analyzed even if case can be resolved solely on federal grounds); and (3) the "lockstep" model (independent analysis of state constitution considered improper); *see also Immuno A.G. v. Moor-Jankowski*, 567 N.E.2d 1270, 1282 n.6 (N.Y. 1991) (discussing the grounds on which the four concurrences diverge in their approaches to interpreting the interaction between state and federal constitutional law).

even calling for term limits for judges.[73] Because so many elected state court judges do not have the shield of life tenure—another contrast with the federal system—they have been swept into the whirlwind of new age politics.[74] The intensity of these campaigns has had its effects, with some perceiving the vibrancy of state constitutions as linked to more overtly political debates about specific results, for example, how expansively a court will interpret its citizens' state constitutional right to be free from unreasonable searches and seizures.[75] It is well to remember that even the principle that the Supreme Court has the power to authoritatively interpret the Federal Constitution was forged against a backdrop of fierce political partisanship.[76]

---

73. A candidate was elected to the Texas Court of Criminal Appeals during this past election season based in part on his campaign promises to be "tough" on criminals and advocating a two-term limit for all judges. See *Q&A with Stephen Mansfield: "The Greatest Challenge of My Life,"* Texas Lawyer, Nov. 21, 1994, at 8, 8, available in LEXIS, Legnew Library, Txlawr File.

74. For example, in 1986, for the first time since California's judicial retention process was set in place in 1934, the voters refused to retain three members of the California Supreme Court (Chief Justice Rose Bird, Justice Joseph Grodin, and Justice Cruz Reynoso), a refusal based largely on their rulings in the area of criminal law and criminal procedure and specifically on their unwillingness to impose the death penalty. *See, e.g.,* Judith S. Kaye, *Book Review,* 64 Tul. L. Rev. 985, 986–87 (1990) (reviewing Joseph R. Grodin, In Pursuit of Justice: Reflections of a State Supreme Court Justice [1989]); Robert S. Thompson, *Judicial Retention Elections and Judicial Method: A Retrospective on the California Retention Election of 1986,* 61 S. Cal. L. Rev. 2007 (1988).

More recently, Wyoming Justice Walter Urbrigkit was defeated in a 1992 election after he was attacked for his positions in criminal cases, while Chief Judge Rosemary Barkett of the Florida Supreme Court retained her position despite a retention election in which she was attacked for her votes in cases involving criminal procedure and abortion rights. Andrew Blum, *Jurists, Initiatives on Ballot,* Nat'l L. J., Nov. 16, 1992, at 1, 1; *see also Harris v. Alabama,* 130 L.Ed.2d 1004, 1018, 1020 (1995) (Stevens, J., dissenting) ("Voting for a political candidate who vows to be 'tough on crime' differs vastly from voting . . . to condemn a specific individual to death. . . . Not surprisingly, given the political pressures they face, judges are far more likely than juries to impose the death penalty"); Hans A. Linde, *The Judge as Political Candidate,* 40 Clev. St. L. Rev. 1, 1–4 (1992).

75. *See* Fla. Stat. Ann. § 933.19(2) (West 1985) (providing that "[t]he same rules as to admissibility of evidence [with respect to] unreasonable searches and seizures as were laid down . . . by the Supreme Court of the United States shall apply to and govern the rights, duties and liabilities of . . . citizens in the state under the like provisions of the Florida Constitution relating to searches and seizures."); *cf. Grisson v. Gleason,* 418 S.E.2d 1:1, 29 (Ga. 1992) (Georgia Supreme Court "disapprove[s]" of its previous decision in *Denton v. Con-Way Southern Express,* 402 S.E.2d 269 [Ga.1991], to interpret equal protection clause of Georgia Constitution more expansively than that of federal Constitution).

Though some critics of state constitutionalism have charged it with the bare desire to achieve a political agenda, *see* Earl M. Maltz, *The Political Dynamic of the "New Judicial Federalism,"* 2 Emerging Issues in St. Const. L. 233, 235–38 (1989) (arguing state constitutionalism is a device to advance "liberal politics"), even one of its foremost critics has acknowledged "that an overwhelming consensus has developed . . . that 'reactive' state constitutional jurisprudence-state rulings that reject federal constitutional decisions merely because the state court disagrees with the result-is generally inappropriate." Gardner, *supra* note 60, at 772.

76. *See* Brennan, *supra* note 3, at 956 ("The Judicial branch was . . . born not on the lofty peaks of pure reason, but in the trenches of partisan politics"); *see also Marbury v. Madison,* 5 U.S. (1 Cranch) 137 (1803); 3 Albert J. Beveridge, The Life of John Marshall 101–56 (1919) (delineating conflict between Federalist and Republican parties preceding *Marbury*); Richard E. Ellis, The Jeffersonian Crisis: Courts and Politics in the Young Republic 43–45, 58, 64–68 (1971) (discussing role of partisan politics in development of federal judiciary).

Apart from extraordinary divisiveness, what distinguishes these state constitutional decisions from federal constitutional decisions is that, while federal constitutional law is cabined by the text of the Constitution,[77] state courts move seamlessly between the common law and state constitutional law, the shifting ground at times barely perceptible.

Indeed, the common law and state constitutional law often stand as alternative grounds for individual rights,[78] as one of my colleagues wrote recently of New York libel law.[79] In New Jersey, common-law principles of privacy and "fundamental fairness," as distinguished from the analogous constitutional guarantees of equal protection and due process, have been invoked in situations as factually diverse as endorsing a dying patient's right to refuse medical treatment[80] and preventing unfair exclusion of members of the public from blackjack tables.[81] A decade after the California Supreme Court decision in *Bakke v. Regents of the University of California*,[82] the author of that opinion, Justice Mosk, noted that, given another opportunity, instead of equal protection he would have seriously considered relying on the duty to serve (a common law doctrine that requires persons providing goods or services to the public to do so on a nondiscriminatory basis).[83]

There is of course a "critical difference" between when courts make constitutional law and when they make common law.[84] Outside the area of constitutional adjudication, state court decisions "are subject to overrule or alteration by ordinary statute. The court is standing in for the legislature, and if it has done so in a way the legislature does

---

77. *See* Ellen A. Peters, *Common Law Antecedents of Constitutional Law in Connecticut*, 53 Alb. L. Rev. 259, 261 (1989) (suggesting common law as interpretive source in reading state constitutions); Suzanna Sherry, *The Founders Unwritten Constitution*, 54 U. Chi. L. Rev. 1127, 1155–77 (1987) (arguing that debate surrounding drafting and ratification of Constitution suggests framers' intent for Constitution to be read in context of fundamental law, a project the Supreme Court long ago abandoned).

78. *See* Judith S. Kaye, *The Common Law and State Constitutional Law as Full Partners in the Protection of Individual Rights*, 23 Rutgers L.J. 727, 745–46 (1992) (presenting historical analysis of state common law and constitutions as pertains to individual rights).

79. *Immuno AG. v. Moor-Jankowski*, 567 N.E.2d 1270, 1286–90 (N.Y. 1991) (Titone, J., concurring) (opting to ground speech rights in state common and constitutional doctrine rather than on narrower federal constitutional grounds).

80. *In re Farrell*, 529 A.2d 404, 414 (N.J. 1987); *see also Bartling v. Superior Court*, 163 Cal. App. 3d 186, 193–95 (Cal. Ct. App. 1984); *Severns v. Wilmington Medical Ctr., Inc.*, 421 A.2d 1334, 1341–44 (Del. 1980); *In re Estate of Longeway*, 549 N.E.2d 292, 297–98 (Ill. 1989); *In re Storar*, 420 N.E.2d 64, 70 (N.Y.), *cert. denied*, 454 U.S. 858 (1981).

81. *See Uston v. Resorts Int'l Hotel, Inc.*, 445 A.2d 370, 375–76 (N.J. 1982).

82. 553 P.2d 1152, 1162–64 (Cal. 1976) (holding in part that discrimination based on race, even if favoring majority, is still subject to Fourteenth Amendment scrutiny), *aff'd in part and rev'd in part*, 438 U.S. 265 (1978).

83. Stanley Mosk, *The Common Law and the Judicial Decision-Making Process*, 11 Harv. J.L. & Pub. Pol'y 35, 37 (1988). For a description of the duty to serve, *see* Charles M. Haar and Daniel W. Fessler, The Wrong Side of the Tracks: A Revolutionary Rediscovery of the Common Law Tradition of Fairness in the Struggle against Inequality (1986) (exploring potential, and urging use of, common law duty to serve in fighting discrimination); Note, *The Antidiscrimination Principle in the Common Law*, 102 Harv. L. Rev. 1993 (1989) (reviewing history and analyzing power of common-law duty to serve on non-discriminatory basis).

84. John H. Ely, Democracy and Distrust 4 (1980).

not approve, it can soon be corrected."[85] But when a case is decided on constitutional grounds, the court solidifies the law in ways that may not be as susceptible to subsequent modification either by courts or by legislatures. Because of this crucial difference, use of the common law to define rights at times has been preferable in that it has allowed both courts and legislatures room to adapt principles to changed circumstances,[86] for example in areas like the "right to die"[87] and forcible medication of mental patients.[88] Of course, that same flexibility is not an option for the federal courts which must decide either that a constitutional right has been violated or that it has not—a distinction perhaps not fully appreciated by those accustomed to litigating "rights" issues in federal court.

In the area of "rights" adjudication, state courts plainly have a distinct advantage in that the common law allows them to shape evolving legal standards more cautiously. It is therefore important that they be explicit about whether and why they are deciding cases on common-law or constitutional grounds.[89] The New Jersey Supreme Court did exactly that in its recent shopping mall case involving the right of free speech on private property.[90] The court had earlier been reluctant to rest that right on constitutional grounds and had decided instead on what it called the "more satisfactory" common-law free speech grounds.[91] Given the more than two decades of "experimentation"[92] that elapsed since the court first addressed the scope of those rights,[93] it transplanted what had previously been a common-law right to firmer constitutional ground.

Despite the controversy that has surrounded the movement toward active state constitutionalism, and given the inherent role of state courts under the common law and the clear similarities between deciding a common-law case and what is currently required,

---

85. *Id.*

86. Kaye, *supra* note 78, at 745.

87. *See, e.g., In re Conroy*, 486 A.2d 1209, 1222–25 (N.J. 1985), and *In re Farrell*, 529 A.2d 404, 408 (N.J. 1985), in which the New Jersey Supreme Court abandoned its previous reliance on the federal Constitution and *In re Quinlan*, 355 A.2d 647, 671–72 (N.J. 1976), where it held that the right to remove life-sustaining medical support from a comatose patient was grounded in New Jersey common law.

88. *See, e.g., In re Storar*, 420 N.E.2d 64, 73–74 (N.Y.) (holding based, in absence of specific legislative or constitutional provisions, on common law), *cert. denied*, 454 U.S. 858 (1981); *Rivers v. Katz*, 495 N.E.2d 337, 342–45 (N.Y. 1986) (holding that right of mental patient to refuse treatment was based on state constitution).

89. Kaye, *supra* note 78, at 745–46.

90. *New Jersey Coalition Against War in the Middle East v. J.M.B. Realty Corp.*, 650 A.2d 757, 770–84 (N.J. 1994) (holding on state constitutional grounds that speech is protected in shopping centers).

91. *See State v. Shack*, 277 A.2d 369, 372 (N.J. 1971) ("[The] policy considerations which underlie that conclusion may be much the same as those which would be weighed with respect to one or more of the constitutional challenges, but a decision in nonconstitutional terms is more satisfactory, because the interests of migrant workers are more expansively served in that way than they would be if they had no more freedom than these constitutional concepts could be found to mandate if indeed they apply at all").

92. *See, e.g., New State Ice Co. v. Liebmann*, 285 U.S. 262, 311 (1932) (Brandeis, J., dissenting) ("It is one of the happy incidents of the federal system that a single courageous state may, if its citizens choose, serve as a laboratory; and try novel social and economic experiments without risk to the rest of the country").

93. *See Shack*, 277 A.2d at 372–74 (basing migrant workers' right to receive visitors on common-law limitations on property rights of employers).

for example, by the constitutional guarantee of "due process,"[94] I think it beyond doubt that we are well embarked on what has been called a "larger interpretive enterprise of American constitutionalism."[95] I am confident that courts will continue to consult their own constitutions to vindicate the rights of their citizens.

My primary concern, however, in this age of political "sound bites" and "spin control" is that state courts continue to do so without reluctance or apology.[96] As Justice Brennan wrote: "Each age must seek its own way to the unstable balance of those qualities that make us human, and must contend anew with the questions of power and accountability with which the Constitution is concerned."[97] Those words are as true of the state constitutions as they are of the federal Constitution, which lawyers and judges are sworn to uphold.

IV. Common Law Courts Construing State Statutes

Vital though the common law still may be, I think it inarguable that it has been surpassed as the preeminent source of law it once was.[98] Why?

The primary reason, of course, is the "orgy of statute making"[99] engaged in by legislatures not only at the federal but also at the state level.[100] In the years since the Depression and the Second World War, "statutorification"[101] of the law has continued unabated so that today, after a half-century of the "relentless annual . . . grinding of more than fifty legislative machines,"[102] statutory interpretation is likely the principal task engaged in by state courts.[103] The current set of New York statutes, like the full set of the United States Code, takes up an entire wall of shelving in my Chambers.

---

94. *See, e.g.*, Brennan, *supra* note 3, at 963 ("Perhaps more than any other provision of the Constitution, the Due Process Clause requires reliance on both reason and passion for its interpretation").

95. Kahn, *supra* note 60, at 1159.

96. *See, e.g.*, Kaye, *supra* note 62, at 50 ("What has to my mind been decisively established . . . if ever it was in doubt—is the legitimacy of state constitutional decision-making by state courts. We do, after all, have state constitutions, a fact that is central to American Government" [emphasis omitted]).

97. Brennan, *supra* note 3, at 974; *see also* Mosk, *supra* note 83, at 41 ("Judges must be fearless and independent, unafraid of applying the Constitution and laws to the least among us").

98. *See* Guido Calabresi, A Common Law for the Age of Statutes 1, 1 (1982) ("In [the last 50 to 80 years] we have gone from a legal system dominated by the common law . . . to one in which statutes . . . have become the primary source of law"); Ruggero J. Aldisert, *The Nature of the Judicial Process: Revisited*, 49 U. Cin. L. Rev. 1, 48 (1980) ("The common law is no longer the major source of legal precepts").

99. Grant Gilmore, The Ages of American Law 95 (1977) (discussing difficulties created by recasting, in statutory form, substantive law once left to judges "for decision in light of common law principles").

100. Thomas G. Alexander and David R. Hall, *State Legislatures in the Twentieth Century*, in Encyclopedia of the American Legislative System 215, 225 (Joel H. Silbey ed., 1994) ("[T]he New Deal changed the idea of 'states' rights' from a negative to a positive concept. While the role of the federal government expanded dramatically during the era, so too did that of state governments").

101. Calabresi, *supra* note 98, at 1.

102. Max Radin, *Statutory Interpretation*, 43 Harv. L. Rev. 863, 863 (1930).

103. Peters, *supra* note 40, at 998 (stating that "statutes are central to the law in courts, and judicial lawmaking must take statutes into account virtually all of the time").

Perhaps in reaction to the proliferation of statutes, perhaps inspired by Judge (then Professor) Guido Calabresi's thought-provoking work *A Common Law for the Age of Statutes*,[104] or perhaps nudged along by the lively and ongoing debate at the Supreme Court,[105] in the last decade the subject of statutory interpretation has seized center-stage in scholarly journals.[106] In the words of a foremost proponent, statutory interpretation, once Cinderella, "now dances in the ballroom."[107] And as tends to happen in scholarly places, Cinderella speaks a whole new language of elusive polysyllabic labels: "new textualists," "dynamic statutory interpreters," "metademocrats."[108]

Despite the outpouring of scholarly ink, analysis has focused almost entirely on how *federal* courts read *federal* statutes. Few, if any, of the recent commentators have considered whether the subject of statutory interpretation presents a different set of issues for state judges reading state statutes.[109]

I submit that it does. And of the many reasons that come to mind, perhaps most important, as is evident in the area of state constitutional law, is the fact that state courts

---

104. Calabresi, *supra* note 98.

105. *See, e.g., United States v. X-Citement Video, Inc.*, 115 S. Ct. 464, 473–76 (1994) (Scalia, J., dissenting) (arguing that majority's reading of statutory scienter requirement is unsupported by precedent or statute's language); *Dewsnup v. Timm*, 502 U.S. 410, 420–36 (1992) (Scalia, J., dissenting) (arguing that the majority's "misinterpretation" of § 506(d) of the Bankruptcy Code destroys predictability by "disregarding well-established and off-repeated principles of statutory construction"); *Chisom v. Roemer*, 501 U.S. 380, 417 (1991) (Scalia, J., dissenting) ("When we adopt a method that psychoanalyzes Congress rather than reads its laws, when we employ a tinkerer's toolbox, we do great harm").

106. William N. Eskridge, Jr. and Philip P. Frickey, *Statutory Interpretation as Practical Reasoning*, 42 Stan. L. Rev. 321, 321 (1990) ("In the last decade, statutory interpretation has reemerged as an important topic of academic theory and discussion"); Daniel A. Farber, *Statutory Interpretation and Legislative Supremacy*, 78 Geo. L.J. 281, 281 (1989) ("In the [past] six years . . . , there has been . . . a renaissance of scholarship about statutory interpretation").

This renewed interest has no doubt also been influenced by current theories of literary criticism that question the concept of a text having an intelligible and stable meaning, *see, e.g.*, William N. Eskridge, Jr., *Dynamic Statutory Interpretation*, 135 U. Pa. L Rev. 1479, 1482–83 (1987) (describing "recent developments in the philosophy of interpretation"), as well as new theories about the behavior of legislatures in democratic governments, *see, e.g.*, Daniel A. Farber and Philip P. Frickey, *In the Shadow of the Legislature: The Common Law in the Age of the New Public Law*, 89 Mich. L. Rev. 875, 875 (1991) (discussing "how modern common law judges should view their role vis-à-vis the legislature").

For examples of this new scholarship, see Shirley S. Abrahamson and Robert L. Hughes, *Shall We Dance? Steps for Legislators and Judges in Statutory Interpretation*,75 Minn. L. Rev. 1045, 1051 n.16 (1991) (compiling recent scholarship).

107. William N. Eskridge, Jr., Dynamic Statutory Interpretation 1 (1994).

108. Examples of scholarship using this type of terminology include William N. Eskridge, Jr., *The New Textualism*, 37 UCLA L. Rev. 621 (1990); Eskridge, *supra* note 106, at 1479; Jane S. Schacter, *Metademocracy: The Changing Structure of Legitimacy in Statutory Interpretation*, 108 Harv. L. Rev. 593 (1995).

109. *See* Larry Kramer, *The Lawmaking Power of the Federal Courts*, 12 Pace L. Rev. 263, 279 n.55 (1992) ("Contemporary scholars speak in general terms and offer general solutions while in fact dealing only with a narrow set of issues associated with the federal government. . . . State courts and state legislatures are ignored"); Larry Kramer, *More Notes on Methods and Objectives in the Conflict of Laws*, 24 Cornell Int'l. L.J. 245, 260 n.50 (1991) ("Most recent scholarship on interpretation," dealing only with the federal context, is incomplete because "[m]any issues that seem easy from a federal perspective are less so from the states' point of view. Conversely, issues . . . controversial in the federal context may become relatively straightforward from the perspective of the states").

regularly, openly, and legitimately speak the language of the common law whereas federal courts do not.[110] The federal courts, after all, may have jurisdiction over a dispute only because a federal statute exists.[111]

Accepting the reality of today's statutory world and its concomitant obligations, however, does not oust state courts from their traditional role. Even in a world dominated by statutes, there remain clear, direct links with: the common law. In the words of one recent commentator, we now live in a "world where common and statutory law are woven together in a complex fabric defining a wide range of rights and duties."[112]

As one rather obvious sample of this modern-day fabric, state legislatures frequently endorse court decisions by codifying causes of action created and carefully crafted by state courts as a matter of common law.[113] A prominent instance in the law of New York is the legislature's endorsement of the ground-breaking court decision some twenty years ago discarding as unfair the concept of contributory negligence and embracing instead

---

110. *See, e.g., City of Milwaukee v. Illinois,* 451 U.S. 304, 312 (1981) ("Federal courts, unlike state courts, are not general common-law courts and do not possess a general power to develop and apply their own rules of decision."); *see also Texas Indus., Inc. v. Radcliff Materials, Inc.,* 451 U.S. 630, 640–42 (1981) ("(A)bsent some congressional authorization to formulate substantive rules of decision, federal common law exists only in such narrow areas as those concerned with the rights and obligations of the United States, interstate and international disputes implicating the conflicting rights of States or our relations with foreign nations, and admiralty cases"). *But see Bob Jones Univ. v. United States,* 461 U.S. 574 (1983) (using common-law concept of "charitable" as starting point for Court's analysis).

111. *See* 28 U.S.C. § 1331 (1988) ("The district courts shall have original jurisdiction of all civil actions arising under the Constitution, laws, or treaties of the United States"); *see also United States v. Standard Oil Co.,* 332 U.S. 301, 313 (1947) ("We would not deny . . . the law's capacity for growth, or that it must include the creative work of judges. . . . But in the federal scheme our part in that work, and the part of the other federal courts, outside the constitutional area is more modest than that of state courts, particularly in the freedom to create new common-law liabilities"); Martha A. Field, *Sources of Law: The Scope of Federal Common Law,* 99 Harv. L. Rev. 881, 899 (1986) ("[S]tate courts . . . can fill in any gap, as long as no directive to the contrary exists. Federal judges by contrast . . . can fill in a gap only if some enactment permits them to do so").

112. Shapiro, *supra* note 45, at 937. Of course, this same fabric is woven by courts and legislatures in the realm of constitutional law, for example, when legislatures employ court originated phrases such as "fighting words" in statutes intended to prohibit certain forms of "hate speech." *See* Ira C. Lupu, *Statutes Revolving in Constitutional Law Orbits,* 79 Va. L. Rev. 1, 3–4 (1992) (noting, as one focus, statutes that utilize "the language of judicial gloss on the Constitution").

113. For a detailed description of the relationship of state courts and state legislatures, *see generally* Abrahamson and Hughes, supra note 106; *see also* Peters, *supra* note 40, at 1007 ("The state court house is, if anything, too close to the state legislative house."); *cf. People v. Rosario,* 173 N.E.2d 881, 883–84 (N.Y. 1961) (holding that fairness entitles the defense to examine witness's prior statement) (this requirement was later enacted by the legislature in N.Y. Crim. Proc. Law § 240.45 [McKinney 1993] [requiring that people produce written statements of prosecution witnesses prior to testimony]); *Caceci v. Di Canio Constr. Corp.,* 526 N.E.2d 266 (N.Y. 1988) (holding that implied warranty of habitability and workmanlike construction applies to purchase of newly-constructed home) (this, too, was ultimately codified by the legislature in N.Y. Gen. Bus. Law §§ 777–a to 777–b [McKinney Supp. 1995] [initially effective March 1, 1989]); Note, *New York's Implied Merchant Warranty for the Sale of New Homes: A Reasonable Extension to Reach Initial Owners?,* 1990 Colum. Bus. L. Rev. 373 (examining history of debate over the extension of implied warranty to reach initial owners).

the principle of comparative fault.[114] The Tennessee Supreme Court, in a more recent decision adopting comparative fault, stated as follows: "We recognize that this action could be taken by our General Assembly. However, legislative inaction has never prevented judicial abolition of obsolete common law doctrines, especially those . . . conceived in the judicial womb."[115] By the same token, legislatures at times express their disagreement by "repealing" or "vetoing" other common-law doctrines.[116]

Legislatures have this same "veto" power over judicial interpretations of statutes.[117] Although some scholars have concluded that the incidence of legislative "overruling" of court interpretations is exaggerated,[118] I find this sort of "re-interpretation" not an altogether infrequent occurrence.[119] In her State of the Judiciary Address earlier this month, Chief

114. *Dole v. Dow Chem. Co.*, 282 N.E.2d 288, 294–95 (N.Y. 1972); *see* N.Y. Civ. Prac. L & R 1411 (McKinney 1976) ("In any action to recover damages for personal injury, injury to property, or wrongful death, the culpable conduct attributable to claimant . . . , including contributory negligence or assumption of risk, shall not bar recovery, but the amount of damages otherwise recoverable shall be diminished in the proportion which the culpable conduct attributable to the claimant . . . bears to culpable conduct which caused the damages").

115. *McIntyre v. Balentine*, 833 S.W.2d 52, 56 (Tenn. 1992); *see also Alvis v. Ribar*, 421 N.E.2d 886, 896 (Ill. 1981) (describing "a mutual state of inaction in which the court awaits action by the legislature and the legislature awaits guidance from the court").

116. *See* N.Y. Gen. Mun. Law § 205-a (McKinney 1995) (creating a cause of action in negligence for firefighters in connection with injuries where the defendant had failed to comply with an applicable statute or ordinance, thus "repealing" in part New York's common law "firefighter's rule" ("Santangelo" rule) which precludes firefighters and police officers from recovering damages when the injuries sustained are related to the particular duties and dangers police officers and firefighters are expected to assume); *see, e.g., Santangelo v. State*, 521 N.E.2d 770 (N.Y. 1988) (police officers injured while apprehending escaped mental patient could not recover damages against state for negligence); *see also Zanghi v. Niagara Frontier Transp. Comm'n*, 85 N.Y.2d 423 (1995) (applying firefighter's rule, disallowing recovery by policemen and firefighter); *Cooper v. City of New York*, 619 N.E.2d 369 (N.Y. 1993) (holding suit barred by "Santangelo" rule).

117. *See, e.g.*, N.Y. Elec. Law § 6–134(15) (McKinney 1995) (overruling courts' longstanding practice of strictly construing technical requirements of New York election law in providing that "[t]he provisions of . . . this section shall be liberally construed, not inconsistent with substantial compliance thereto"); *cf. Staber v. Fidler*, 482 N.E.2d 1204, 1206 (N.Y. 1985) (holding that incorrect statement of number of signatures was sufficient reason to invalidate petitions); *Hargett v. Jefferson*, 468 N.E.2d 1114, 1114 (N.Y. 1984) (validating petitions where misstatement of number of signatories was insignificant); see generally Note, *A Call for Reform of New York State's Ballot Access Laws*, 64 N.Y.U. L. Rev. 182 (1989) (examining constitutional test applied by judiciary in cases about New York's designating petition rules).

118. Otto J. Hetzel, *Instilling Legislative Interpretation Skills in the Classroom and the Courtroom*, 48 U. Pitt. L. Rev. 663, 678–79 (1987) (questioning ease with which "[J]udges often imply that judicial decisions can be overruled by the legislature"); *see also* Abrahamson and Hughes, *supra* note 106, at 1054–55 ("[P]rompt legislative reaction to judicial [statutory] interpretation is probably the exception, . . . not the rule"); Schacter, *supra* note 108, at 605 ("The frequency of strategic avoidance and legislative gamesmanship suggest that legislators will generally be tempted to hide behind, rather than to contest, judicial interpretations of statutory law. . . . [L]egislators have a strong incentive to avoid taking up a question that has been provisionally settled by a court and have little incentive to spend precious political capital vindicating the claimed 'real' intention of the prior legislature that enacted the law").

119. *See, e.g.*, Abrahamson and Hughes, *supra* note 106, at 1054–55 (describing examples of such "overruling" by legislatures in Wisconsin, California, and Colorado); William N. Eskridge, Jr., *Overriding*

Justice Peters described precisely such a situation—where the Connecticut legislature passed a statute effectively overruling the "common law gloss"[120] courts had placed on a divorce statute when they limited judicial authority to modify child support orders.[121] Based on the legislative policy choice to permit such modifications, the Connecticut Supreme Court then proceeded to extend the new principle—"as a matter of common law adjudication"—to alimony payments as well.[122]

No one can question the legislature's authority to correct or redirect a state court's interpretation of a statute.[123] Indeed, on our court we especially strive for consensus in statutory interpretation cases as a matter of policy, knowing that the legislature always can, and will, step in if it feels we have gotten it wrong.

In addition, the state legislative/judicial relationship often takes the form of an open dialogue.[124] Some years ago, for example, the New York Court of Appeals felt constrained by the language of the New York private placement adoption statute[125] to uphold an "irrevocable consent" to adoption by a newborn infant's biological parents, though they

Supreme Court Statutory Interpretation Decisions, 101 Yale L.J. 331, 332–34 (1991) (examining only Supreme Court decisions but finding that rate at which Congress overrides statutory interpretations of the Supreme Court may be higher than previously thought).

120. *See Fahy v. Fahy*, 630 A.2d 1328, 1333 (Conn. 1993).

121. *See* Peters, *supra* note 16; *see also* Conn. Gen. Stat. Ann. § 46b-86 (West 1994) "overruling" *Darak v. Darak*, 556 A2d 145 (Conn. 1989) (statute permitting modification of financial orders entered in dissolution agreement without regard to prior contemplation of financial changes had to be applied prospectively); *Turner v. Turner*, 595 A.2d 297, 304 (Conn. 1991) (recognizing that legislature's enactment of current version of § 46b-86 was intended "to reverse the effect of our judgment in Darak v. Darak").

122. *See Fahy*, 630 A.2d at 1334 (concluding that "as a matter of common law adjudication, it is appropriate to extend elimination of the noncontemplation of the circumstances requirement to orders of alimony"); *see also Schuster v. City of New York*, 154 N.E.2d 534, 540 (N.Y. 1958) (stating that "[s]tatutes have played their part in the formation of the common law, and, like court decisions that are not strictly analogous, sometimes point the way into other territory when the animating principle is used as a guide").

123. *See In re Randy K.*, 570 N.E.2d 210, 214 (N.Y. 1991) (holding that bench warrant issued after juvenile's failure to appear at first scheduled fact-finding hearing did not relieve presentment agency and Family Court of statutory obligations), subsequently "overruled" by N.Y. Fam. Ct. Act § 340.1(7) (McKinney 1995). For other examples of such legislative "overruling," *see Sullivan v. Brevard Assocs.*, 488 N.E.2d 1208 (N.Y. 1985) (holding that New York City's Rent Stabilization Law did not obligate landlord to offer renewal lease to tenant's sister); *Festa v. Leshen*, 537 N.Y.S.2d 147 (App. Div. 1989) (upholding amendments to Rent Stabilization Law that provide that relatives who reside with a named tenant may succeed to the tenant's lease rights); *see also People v. Sturgis*, 345 N.E.2d 331 (N.Y. 1976) (holding that where adjusted period between commencement of action and time prosecution was ready for trial exceeded six months, defendant was entitled to dismissal on ground of denial of speedy trial) as "overruled" by N.Y. Crim. Proc. Law § 30.30(4) (c) (McKinney 1992). Indeed, a bill was recently signed by the governor effectively overruling a court of appeals decision holding that in prosecutions for possession of a controlled substance the people must prove that the defendant had knowledge as to the weight of the controlled substance at issue. *See* Assembly Bill No. 210, 218th Gen. Assembly, 1st Sess., 1995 N.Y. A.B. 210 § 1 ("The legislature hereby finds that a recent decision of the Court of Appeals, *People v. Ryan* [82 N.Y.2d 497], . . . will greatly diminish the ability of the district attorney's office across the state to prosecute narcotics offenses").

124. *See* William N. Eskridge, Jr. and Philip P. Frickey, *Legislation Scholarship and Pedagogy in the Post-Legal Process Era*, 48 U. Pitt. L. Rev. 691, 724 (1987) (describing "new legal process" school of statutory interpretation as assuming that "[l]aw is conversation rather than coercion").

125. N.Y. Dom. Rel. Law § 115–b (McKinney 1988 & Supp. 1995).

argued that they had not been given fair notice of the legal consequences.[126] Courts having previously expressed difficulty applying that statute,[127] we ended that opinion by suggesting to our legislative colleagues—who sit directly across the street from us in Albany—that they reexamine the statute "in light of 13 years' experience, for it appears that the well-founded concerns that engendered the law are not yet dispelled."[128] And indeed, the statute was amended the following year.[129]

A similar dialogue took place concerning the statute of limitations for injuries caused by harmful substances, like asbestos, that are discoverable only years after initial exposure.[130] After the court's repeated expressions of frustration over the unfairness of commencing the statute of limitations with exposure to the harmful substance,[131] the legislature passed a law providing that the limitations period might accrue, instead, upon discovery of the injury.[132]

Sometimes, of course, the outcome is not quite so felicitous. I think, for example, of the "right to die" cases, where state courts around the country have struggled with these complex social policy issues, sometimes as a matter of constitutional law, sometimes as a matter of common law.[133] In 1985, then Governor Mario Cuomo appointed a Task Force on Life and the Law which actually did draft legislation.[134] To date, however, the New York legislature has enacted only a statute permitting individuals to designate a "proxy" to make their health care decisions if they are unable to do so.[135]

---

126. *In re Sarah K.*, 487 N.E.2d 241, 249 (N.Y. 1985), *cert denied*, 475 U.S. 1108 (1986). Before *In re Sarah K.*, § 115-b was read to provide that where the consent is not executed or acknowledged before a judge or surrogate, the consent is irrevocable thirty days after the commencement of the adoption proceeding. After *In re Sarah K.*, where there is an extrajudicial consent, the consent is irrevocable forty-five days after its execution.

127. *See In re Daniel C.*, 472 N.Y.S.2d 666, 692 (App. Div.) (Gibbons, J., dissenting) (arguing that adoption of consent form signed by natural mother was invalid as a matter of statutory and constitutional law), *aff'd sub nom. In re Adoption of Daniel C.*, 473 N.E.2d 31 (N.Y. 1984) (Jasen, J., dissenting); *In re Anonymous*, 390 N.Y.S.2d 433, 436 (App. Div. 1977) (Suozzi, J., dissenting).

128. *In re Sarah K.*, 487 N.E.2d at 251.

129. *See* 1986 N.Y. Laws 817, Memorandum in Support of State of New York Unified Court System, Office of Court Administration ("This measure is being introduced at the request of the Court of Appeals").

130. *See Steinhardt v. Johns-Manville Corp.*, 430 N.E.2d 1297, 1299 (N.Y. 1981) (holding that statute of limitations begins to run at time of injury); *Thornton v. Roosevelt Hosp.*, 391 N.E.2d 1002, 1003 (N.Y. 1979) (same); *Victorson v. Bock Laundry Mach. Inc. Co.*, 335 N.E.2d 275, 278 (N.Y. 1975) (same).

131. *See, e.g., Thornton*, 391 N.E.2d at 1005–6 (Fuchsberg, J., dissenting).

132. N.Y. Civ. Prac. L. & R. § 214-c (McKinney 1990 & Supp. 1995) (initially enacted in 1986 in response to *Steinhardt*).

133. *See, e.g., Fosmire v. Nicoleau*, 551 N.E.2d 77, 84 (N.Y. 1990) (holding on common law grounds that patient had right to refuse medically necessary blood transfusion); *In re Westchester County Medical Ctr. ex rel. O'Connor*, 531 N.E.2d 607, 614–15 (N.Y. 1988) (holding on common-law grounds that hospital could insert feeding tube in critically ill patient); *see also Schloendorff v. Society of New York Hosp.*, 105 N.E. 92, 93 (N.Y. 1914) (Cardozo, J.) ("Every individual of adult years and sound mind has a right to determine what shall be done with his own body").

134. See New York State Task Force on Life and the Law, When Others Must Choose: Deciding For Patients without Capacity, app. A at 247–68 (1992) (listing proposed legislation for surrogate decisions).

135. N.Y. Pub. Health Law §§ 2980–2994 (McKinney 1993 & Supp. 1995); *see generally* Judith S. Kaye, *Surrogate Decisionmaking: Staking Out the Law*, 58 Mount Sinai J.M. 369 (1991) (discussing the New York common-law treatment of right to die cases).

Surely, it would be better for a legislature with its greater fact-finding powers and direct accountability to address such questions. Yet I doubt that anyone would seriously contend that a court should decline to decide the next case in this area, stating that it could not resolve the dispute because the legislature had not acted. Indeed, in a recent decision, my court indicated that as a matter of common law we would recognize the concept of a "living will," which the legislature has yet to sanction formally.[136] The Supreme Judicial Court of Massachusetts manifested a similar willingness to fill a gap, when, in light of advances in medical technology, it overruled its common-law rule that a homicide could not be prosecuted if the victim had died more than a year and a day after the criminal act.[137] In so doing, the Court acknowledged that though it would have been better for the legislature to enact a statute "reflect[ing] modern enhanced scientific capabilities, . . . [s]uch a task . . . if not undertaken by that branch, may fall to the courts."[138]

Even when interpreting statutes that have been passed, ascertaining the legislative intent is often no less difficult than drawing common-law or constitutional distinctions, requiring "a choice between uncertainties,"[139] surely an "ungainly judicial function."[140] When the meaning of a statute is in dispute, there remains at the core the same common-law process of discerning and applying the purpose of the law. As one commentator noted, "courts have not only a *law-finding* function . . . but [also] . . . a *law-making* function that engrafts on the statute meaning appropriate to resolving the controversy."[141] Indeed, "there is no sharp break of method in passing from 'common law,' old style, to the combinations of decisional and statutory law now familiar. Statutes, after all, need to be interpreted, filled in, related to the rest of the corpus."[142]

I certainly do not mean to suggest that as judges we are not always mindful of the "legislature's authority, within constitutional limits, to formulate whatever law it chooses."[143] Unless a statute in some way contravenes the state or federal constitution, we

---

136. *In re Westchester County Medical Ctr.*, 531 N.E.2d at 613.

137. *Commonwealth v. Lewis*, 409 N.E.2d 771, 773 (Mass. 1980), *cert. denied*, 450 U.S. 929 (1981).

138. *Id.* at 775; *see also* N.Y. Crim. Proc. Law § 40.20(2)(d) (McKinney 1992) ("delayed death" exception from statutory double jeopardy protection); *People v. Latham*, 631 N.E.2d 83, 85 (N.Y. 1994) ("Particularly in an era where medical advances can prolong the life of a critically injured victim, a prosecution must proceed on the basis of the victim's present condition. Where death follows, however, it is also in society's interest that a homicide be redressed" [citations omitted]); *People v. Brengard*, 191 N.E. 850 (N.Y. 1934) (abandoning New York's common-law "year-and-a-day" rule).

139. *Burnet v. Guggenheim*, 288 U.S. 280, 288 (1933).

140. Abner J. Mikva, *Reading and Writing Statutes*, 48 U. Pitt. L. Rev. 627, 627 (1987) ("The interpretation of statutes—as opposed to the administration of the common law—is a very ungainly judicial function").

141. Dickerson, *supra* note 45, at 1127–28.

142. Benjamin Kaplan, *Encounters with O.W. Holmes, Jr.*, 96 Harv. L. Rev. 1828, 1845 (1983).

143. O'Connell, *supra* note 44, at 231; *see also* Felix Frankfurter, *Some Reflections on the Reading of Statutes*, 47 Colum. L. Rev. 527, 533 (1947) ("(N)o one will gainsay that the function in construing a statute is to ascertain the meaning of words used by the legislature. To go beyond is to usurp a power which our democracy has lodged in its elected legislature"); William D. Popkin, *Law-Making Responsibility and Statutory Interpretation*, 68 Ind. LJ. 865, 867 (1993) ("A court's relationship to statutes is not the same as a common-law court's relationship to the common Jaw. Statutes are not as malleable as common-law precedents").

are obliged to follow it—and of course we do.[144] In many instances the "plain meaning" of the statutory language dictates a clear result.[145] But that is not always invariably so. Statutory interpretation is not a mechanical exercise.

At times the common-law method compels courts even to read a statute in a way that appears contrary to its "plain meaning." Only recently, for example, my court construed the words "currently dangerous" in a criminal statute governing whether a paranoid schizophrenic, found not responsible for attempted murder by reason of mental disease or defect, should remain confined in a secure mental hospital.[146] Surely the word "currently" is clear enough: it means right now, at this moment. But, as the court wrote, to apply those words strictly "would lead to the absurd conclusion that a defendant in a straightjacket, surrounded by armed guards, is not currently dangerous under the statute."[147] Instead, we applied concepts of "common-sense and substantial justice" to give the term "currently" what must have been its intended meaning: dangerous not at the moment of confinement and treatment, but foreseeably dangerous if confinement and treatment were not continued into the future.[148] Indeed, had our courts interpreted the word "currently" in its most literal sense, we would have been less than faithful to the underlying legislative purpose—to protect society from potentially dangerous insanity acquitees.

The very fact that a controversy over statutory interpretation has found its way to a state's high court—quite possibly after several other trial and appellate judges have divided on the question—signals that discerning the statutory meaning may not be quite so simple.[149] As our late Chief Judge Charles Breitel noted, "[t]he words men use are never absolutely certain in meaning; the limitations of finite man and the even greater limitations of his language see to that."[150] Modern linguists speak of language's innate "structural ambiguity," its "opaque context," "categorical indeterminacy," and "shared

---

144. *See, e.g., Doctor's Council v. New York City Employees' Retirement Sys.*, 525 N.E.2d 454, 457 (N.Y. 1988) ("'Where the statute is clear and unambiguous on its face, the legislation must be interpreted as it exists'" [citation omitted]).

145. Justice Cardozo, of course, believed that in some ninety percent of the cases, the law was clear and in only a portion of these was the application of the law to the facts doubtful. Benjamin N. Cardozo, The Growth of the Law 60 (1924). While I might argue with the percentage, I would agree that many of our statutory cases are not "difficult" in the sense of discerning the meaning of the statutory language. *See* Shirley S. Abrahamson, *Judging in the Quiet of the Storm*, 24 St. Mary's L.J. 965, 972 n.27 (1993) (discussing more recent judicial commentary on Cardozo's "tripartite topology of appellate cases"). Yet even in such cases, the process of statutory interpretation has an analog to the common law: finding that a statute's meaning is sufficiently "plain" to end the question is not all that different from finding, as a matter of law, that the language in a contract is unambiguous and thus that extrinsic evidence of its purported ambiguity should not be consulted. *See, e.g., W.W.W. Assocs. v. Giancontieri*, 566 N.E.2d 639, 642 (N.Y. 1990).

146. *In re George L.*, 648 N.E.2d 475, 478–80 (N.Y. 1995).

147. *Id.* at 479.

148. *Id.* at 481.

149. *See* Clark D. Cunningham et al., *Plain Meaning and Hard Cases*, 103 Yale L.J. 1561, 1561 (1994) (reviewing Lawrence M. Solan, The Language of Judges [1993]) ("If the language of a statute is plain, how can interpreting that statute create a hard case? And if a case is hard, how can recourse to the statutory language help resolve the case?").

150. *Bankers Ass'n v. Albright*, 343 N.E.2d 735, 738 (N.Y. 1975).

understandings."[151] And everyone is by now familiar with Karl Llewellyn's demonstration, almost a half-century ago, that two equally time-honored maxims of statutory construction often support the contrary positions of each party to a litigation.[152]

In preparation for this lecture, I have revisited the recent decisions of my court where, in deciding cases based on statutory language, we stated that we were following the "will of the Legislature"—and indeed we were. Although in several of those cases the plain language dictated an obvious result,[153] it was an interesting, even an eye-opening experience to realize that a good many of the cases were among the most difficult we have encountered in recent years, many with impassioned dissents, despite our extra efforts to achieve consensus in matters of statutory interpretation.[154]

I do not think one has to be a "metademocrat," a "public law theorist," or even (heaven forfend) a "dynamic statutory interpreter"[155] to acknowledge that the "will of the legislature" is not always easy (or even possible) to discern when it comes to specific facts before a court.[156] I would venture the guess that in nearly every statutory case that reaches a state's highest court, there exist at least two plausible interpretations, each in some way supported by the text.

My own firsthand experience, study, and good sense convince me that state judges construing statutes are more than pharmacists filling prescriptions written by the legislature: often they are involved as well in treating the ailment. And that task becomes considerably more difficult when the legislature's handwriting is hard to decipher.

---

151. *See, e.g.*, Cunningham et al., *supra* note 149 (discussing how Solan's methodology can provide useful information as to whether text of statute is ambiguous).

152. Karl N. Llewellyn, *Remarks on the Theory of Appellate Decision and the Rules or Canons about How Statutes Are to Be Construed*, 3 Vand. L. Rev. 395, 395–96 (1950). For more recent discussions of the use of the canons of statutory construction, *see generally* Shapiro, *supra* note 45; John C. Yoo, Note, *Marshall's Plan: The Early Supreme Court and Statutory Interpretation*, 101 Yale L.J. 1607 (1992) (examining Marshall Court's approach to statutory interpretation).

153. See *Longway v. Jefferson County Bd. of Supervisors*, 628 N.E.2d. 1316 (N.Y. 1993) (holding that local statute's definition of population did not necessarily exclude transients); *Sutka v. Conners*, 538 N.E.2d 1012 (N.Y. 1989) (giving plain meaning interpretation of firefighters' benefits statute).

154. *See People v. Luperon*, 647 N.E.2d 1243, 1250–56 (N.Y. 1995) (Bellacosa, J., dissenting) (disagreeing with court's decision to dismiss an indictment on statutory interpretation grounds); *People v. Thompson*, 633 N.E.2d 1074, 1081–88 (N.Y. 1994) (Bellacosa, J., dissenting) (dissenting from majority's application of a mandatory sentencing law); *People v. Ryan*, 626 N.E.2d 51, 58 (N.Y. 1993) (Bellacosa, J., dissenting) (objecting to holding that knowledge requirement in criminal statute applies to knowledge of weight of controlled substance); *Jensen v. General Elec. Co.*, 623 N.E.2d 547, 554–59 (N.Y. 1993) (Smith and Hancock, JJ., dissenting in separate opinions) (dissenting from holding that statute of limitations on personal injury actions runs from time of the injury without exception); *People v. Smith*, 591 N.E.2d 1132, 1135–36 (N.Y. 1992) (Titone, J., dissenting) (objecting to holding that defendant had requisite mental state for robbery conviction).

155. *See generally* Calabresi, *supra* note 98.

156. In articulating the concept of the "will of the legislature" we necessarily create a fiction of the legislature—comprised, after all, of many individuals—as a single being "because we want to imagine that there is a contemporary speaker behind the text [of a statute] whose meaning [we judges are] trying to determine." William D. Popkin, *An "Internal" Critique of Justice Scalia's Theory of Statutory Interpretation*, 76 Minn. L. Rev. 1133, 1186 (1992); *see also* Radin, *supra* note 102, at 870–71 (discussing the difficulty of discussing the true "intention" of a legislature).

At times, of course, the delegation of lawmaking authority from the legislature to the courts is explicit. New York's "poison pill" statute, for example, specifies that decisions by a corporation's board of directors "shall be subject to judicial review in an appropriate proceeding in which courts formulate or apply appropriate standards."[157]

But most often the delegation is implicit. I think, for instance, of cases where our court has had to define statutory terms such as "extraordinary circumstances,"[158] "due diligence,"[159] "best interests of the child,"[160] and "prejudice."[161] The court had to decide whether equitable "circumstances" or "conditions"—words I am quoting directly from a New York statute—existed to grant standing where a child's grandparents were seeking visitation over the parents' objection.[162]

Let's be frank: issues like these that reach a state appeals court cannot be resolved simply by consulting a good dictionary or communing with the statutory text.[163] Yet. as with common-law cases, no one could doubt our authority-indeed our responsibility-to define these terms, and to fit each case within the body of the law, thereby necessarily fixing the range and direction of the statute and the course of future litigation. A recent law review article concluded that:

> if a state court can legitimately make public policy when the legislature has said nothing at all about a subject, the same court should also be able to make policy when the legislature has spoken, but spoken so unclearly that the court cannot confidently decipher its directions. In such a case, the fact that the legislature has spoken makes it clear that the legislature intends for something to be done about the particular issue. . . . [T]he line between common law policymaking and statutory construction is just not as sharp as it might seem.[164]

---

157. N.Y. Bus. Corp. Law § 505(a)(2)(ii) (McKinney 1995); *see also* N.Y. Fam. Ct. Act § 303.1(2) (McKinney 1995) ("A court may . . . consider judicial interpretations of . . . the criminal procedure law to the extent that such interpretations may assist the court in interpreting similar provisions of this article").

158. *See, e.g., Yalango v. Popp*, 644 N.E.2d 1318, 1323 (N.Y. 1994).

159. *See, e.g., People v. Luperon*, 647 N.E.2d 1243, 1247 (N.Y. 1995); *People v. Bolden*, 613 N.E.2d 145, 149–50 (N.Y. 1993).

160. *See, e.g., In re Michael B.*, 604 N.E.2d 122, 130–32 (N.Y. 1992).

161. *See, e.g., People v. Sayavong*, 635 N.E.2d 1213, 1217–18 (N.Y. 1994); *People v. Jackson*, 585 N.E.2d 795, 797 (N.Y. 1991).

162. *See Emanuel S. v. Joseph E.*, 577 N.E.2d 27, 28 (N.Y. 1991) (interpreting N.Y. Dom. Rel. Law § 72 as amended in 1975).

163. *See* James Oakes, *Personal Reflections on Learned Hand and the Second Circuit*, 47 Stan. L. Rev. 387, 390–91 (1995) ("[O]ne principle area of [Learned) Hand's work . . . remains relevant today and bears mention—the field of statutory interpretation. . . . Hand firmly believed that a good judge must not fear the unknown or the ambiguous. Rather, he insisted that 'it is one of the surest indexes of a mature and developed jurisprudence not to make a fortress out of the dictionary; but to remember that statutes always have some purpose or object to accomplish, whose sympathetic and imaginative discovery is the surest guide to their meaning'" [quoting *Cabell v. Markham*, 148 F.2d 737, 739 (2d Cir. 1945)]).

164. Farber, *supra* note 106, at 286; *see also* Schacter, *supra* note 108, at 604 ("There is growing recognition that legislators often deliberately employ vague, symbolic, and sometimes meaningless statutory language . . . in order to placate warring interests and achieve compromise, to please as many and

Yet another crucial distinction between state courts and federal courts interpreting statutes is the quantity of the legislative history that is available. Five years ago, in arguing against the "new textualists" (who would preclude all reference to legislative history),[165] Abner Mikva wrote that "seeking legislative intent is [not] a fool's errand. [Though] the quest is difficult and will never provide the holy grail . . . , an informed, careful use of legislative history can limit the number of interstices that judges plug."[166]

Viewed from a state court perspective, I am not at all sure that Mikva's solution is a workable one. In the federal system, legislative history abounds. Debates are routinely printed in the *Congressional Record*, while more authoritative sources such as joint or conference committee reports of both Houses of Congress are customary.[167] But in New York and likely other states as well, legislative history is relatively sparse with legislative intent evidenced primarily by the language of the statute itself. Rarely is a committee report available.[168] Just last month, to give one example of the problem, the Court of Appeals was required to give practical application to a broadly worded statute forbidding "[d]eceptive acts and practices in the conduct of any business, trade or commerce or in the furnishing of any service," with no further indication as to the nature of the prohibited conduct.[169] Having as guidance only the words of the statute and minimal background indicating that the statute was designed for consumers, we held, much as any common-law court, that for a cause of action to be stated, the alleged deceptive acts or practices need not be a course of conduct—a single act will suffice; that the conduct must be judged objectively, meaning is it "likely to mislead a reasonable consumer acting reasonably under the circumstances"; and that the conduct must be "consumer-oriented in the sense that [it] potentially affect[s] similarly situated consumers."[170]

---

alienate as few constituencies as possible, or to avoid difficult policy choices by postponing decision or transferring responsibility to an agency through a broad delegation").

165. *See, e.g.*, Eskridge, *supra* note 108; W. David Slawson, *Legislative History and the Need to Bring Statutory Interpretation Under the Rule of Law*, 44 Stan. L Rev. 383 (1992). For a discussion of new textualism, *see* Nicholas S. Zeppos, *Justice Scalia's Textualism: The "New" New Legal Process*, 12 Cardozo L. Rev. 1597 (1991).

166. Mikva, *supra* note 42, at 981.

167. *See, e.g.*, William N. Eskridge, Jr. and Philip P. Frickey, Cases and Materials on Legislation: Statutes and the Creation of Public Policy 709 (2d ed., 1994) ("Most scholars and judges agree that committee reports should be considered as authoritative legislative history and should be given great weight [i.e., a statement in a committee report will usually count more than a statement by a single legislator.]").

168. *Id.* at 710 ("In state legislatures, committee reports can take a variety of forms, not all of which are published or are readily available to the public"). This situation is confirmed by Frances Murray, the Court of Appeals' (absolutely extraordinary) law librarian, who reports that the New York Legislature ceased publishing joint legislative committee reports in the mid 1970s. *See also City of Lafayette v. Louisiana Power & Light Co.*, 435 U.S. 389, 437 (1978) (Brennan, J., dissenting) ("[S]tate statutes often are enacted with little recorded legislative history, and the bare words of a statute will often be unilluminating in interpreting legislative intent"); Eric Lane, *Legislative Process and Its Judicial Renderings: A Study in Contrast*, 48 U. Pitt. L. Rev. 639, 651 (1987) ("More simply stated, legislative history is generally ignored because [state] legislators see no need for it").

169. *Oswego Laborers' Local 214 Pension Fund v. Marine Midland Bank*, 647 N.E.2d 741, 744 (N.Y. 1995).

170. *Id.* at 745.

Acknowledging the dilemma and drawing on the traditions of the common law, Calabresi has suggested that a solution is for courts simply and openly to "update" obsolete statutes to ensure that the law remains responsive to changes in society.[171] Although there is a great deal of value in Calabresi's ideas, I am not sure that such a radical step is necessary in that the incidence of obsolete statutes seems relatively infrequent.[172]

Rather, I think the more serious dilemma judges face occurs in circumstances where, though the balance of a statute remains relevant, a litigant raises a novel theory of a statute's applicability to a category of cases unforeseen, perhaps even unforeseeable, by the legislature. In other words, courts are often faced with requests to extend a legislatively-created right or duty to facts not previously considered. And that such situations arise with some regularity is not difficult to understand given that no legislature could possibly envision the infinite variety of fact patterns that the human mind, assisted by counsel, can devise. I would submit that once again such analysis is not altogether different from reasoning under the common law.

Thirty years ago, former Chief Judge Traynor stated the proposition as follows:

> Suppose, for example, a statute . . . specifying that it shall apply to A and B and clearly unconcerned with anyone else. Why not an equivalent rule for C, the judge might ask himself, when there is a perplexing C before the court who appears to be a little cousin, if not the sibling of A and B. Before the fortuitous appearance of the statute, the judge might have deemed it prudent to abandon C to his legislative fate. Now he might deem it proper to compose a judgment as to C that would be in keeping with the newly declared legislative policy, even though the legislative authors bad ended their text with B. He would thus make law to govern C by virtue of the analogy he would draw from the statute governing A and B. Whatever he chose to call his method, he would be creating law with a capital C.[173]

---

171. Calabresi, *supra* note 98, at 81–145; *see also* Jack Davies, *A Response to Statutory Obsolescence: Toe Nonprimacy of Statutes Act*, 4 Vt. L. Rev. 203, 204 (1979) (suggesting that legislature, in exercise of its law making authority, create an age of "semi-retirement" for its enactments).

172. Indeed, the only example that comes to mind is a recent case involving a 1933 New York law which on its face prevents an applicant, owned directly or indirectly in any proportion by a foreign company that manufactures alcohol, from obtaining a license to serve liquor to the public. Though we acknowledged that the Act, passed at the close of Prohibition to prevent monopolies in the alcoholic beverages industry, may no longer be relevant in today's economy of global conglomerates, we nevertheless felt constrained to apply the statute as written. *See Rihga Intl. U.S.A., Inc. v. New York State Liquor Auth.*, 644 N.E.2d 1340, 1341 (N.Y. 1994) (referring to N.Y. Alco. Bev. Cont Law § 101(l)(a), originally enacted in 1933).

173. Traynor, *supra* note 45, at 405. For a more modern formulation of this metaphor, see Farber and Frickey, *supra* note 106, at 892 ("Public choice [theory] teaches that a statute reflects not only the preferences of the legislature, but also the procedural obstacle course of enactment The fact that a statute explicitly regulates situations A and B, but not C, should not necessarily be interpreted as a decision to immunize C from regulation. It may only indicate that, for whatever reason, the legislative process failed to produce a bill covering C. Thus, the meandering boundaries of a statute may reflect only the exigencies of the legislative process rather than any majority view about the treatment of excluded cases."); *see also* discussion of *Fahy v. Fahy*, 630 A.2d 1328 (Conn. 1993), *supra* at text accompanying notes 120–22.

Some years ago our court issued a much-discussed[174] decision reading the term "marital property" in New York's equitable distribution statute to include a spouse's professional license.[175] We accepted our responsibility, making clear in the court's writing that "[h]aving classified the 'property' subject to distribution, the legislature did not attempt to go further and define it but left it to the courts to determine what interests come within the terms of [the statute]."[176] And in rejecting the argument that the statutory provision referred not to a professional license but only to an already established practice, the court stated, in the best common-law tradition, that

> [t]here is no reason in law or logic to restrict the plain language of the statute to existing [medical] practices, [which] merely represent[]the exercise of the privileges conferred upon the professional spouse by the license. . . . That being so, it would be unfair not to consider [a medical] license a marital asset.[177]

In perhaps the most commented-on statutory decision handed down by the New York Court of Appeals in recent years,[178] a plurality interpreted the term "family member" in the non-eviction provisions of the New York City rent control statute—a statute originally passed in 1946 to alleviate the perceived housing crisis at the end of World War II—to include the deceased tenant's homosexual partner.[179] In so doing, the plurality reasoned

---

174. *See, e.g.*, Kenneth R. Davis, *The Doctrine of O'Brien v. O'Brien: A Critical Analysis*, 13 Pace L. Rev. 863 (1994); Herma H. Kay, *Toward a Theory of Fair Distribution*, 57 Brook. L. Rev. 755, 761 (1991) (noting that the New York Court of Appeals believed it was following the legislature in *O'Brien*); Scott E. Willoughby, Note, *Professional Licenses as Marital Property: Responses to Some of O'Brien's Unanswered Questions*, 73 Cornell L. Rev. 133 (1987) (approving of result in *O'Brien*).

175. *O'Brien v. O'Brien*, 489 N.E.2d 712 (N.Y. 1985) (holding that husband's newly acquired license to practice medicine was marital property).

176. *Id.* at 715.

177. *Id.* at 717.

178. *See, e.g.*, Paris R. Baldacci, *Pushing the Law to Encompass the Reality of Our Families: Protecting Lesbian and Gay Families from Eviction from Their Homes—Braschi's Functional Definition of "Family" and Beyond*, 21 Fordham Urb. L.J. 973 (1994) (discussing *Braschi v. Stahl Assocs.*, 543 N.E.2d 49 (N.Y. 1989), and its inclusive interpretation of "family" and its potential impact on gay and lesbian equality); Schacter, *supra* note 108; Hubert J. Barnhardt III, Comment, *Let the Legislatures Define the Family: Why Default Statutes Should Be Used to Eliminate Potential Confusion*, 40 Emory L.J. 571 (1991) (arguing *Braschi* invites courts to discard concrete definition of "family" for determination on case by case basis, with great potential for confusion); Note, *Braschi v. Stahl Associates Co.: Much Ado About Nothing?*, 35 Vill. L. Rev. 361 (1990) (discussing *Braschi* decision and limited effect it will have outside of context of protection against eviction); Note, *Looking for a Family Resemblance: The Limits of the Functional Approach to the Legal Definition of Family*, 104 Harv. L. Rev. 1640 (1991) (citing the *Braschi* decision as example of the courts using functional approach to defining "family"); Heidi A. Sorenson, Note, *A New Gay Rights Agenda? Dynamic Statutory Interpretation and Sexual Orientation Discrimination*, 81 Geo. L.J. 2105 (1993) (citing *Braschi* as classic case of dynamic statutory interpretation in protecting gay partner of deceased tenant from eviction).

179. *Braschi v. Stahl Assocs.*, 543 N.E.2d 49, 54–55 (N.Y. 1989). *But see In re Alison D.*, 572 N.E.2d 27 (N.Y. 1991) where, in the context of a child visitation determination, the court declined to construe the term "parent" in New York domestic relations law to encompass the former lesbian lover of the child's biological mother who helped to raise the child. Dissenting in *Alison D.*, I noted that the statutory provision at issue "does not define the term 'parent' at all. That remains for the courts to do, as often happens when statutory terms are undefined." *Id.* at 31.

that though the record was devoid of a specific legislative will with respect to the question at issue, the overall policy expressed in the statute "of protecting a . . . class of occupants from the sudden loss of their homes," required the result reached.[180] Significantly, only months after that decision, regulations were enacted enlarging the definition of family member to include "[a]ny other person residing with a tenant . . . who can prove emotional and financial commitment and interdependence [with] the tenant."[181]

Given the enormous volume of state court litigation, the unending array of novel fact patterns pushing the law to progress, and the inability of legislatures to react immediately to the many changes in society,[182] I think it clear that common-law courts interpreting statutes and filling the gaps have no choice but to "make law" in circumstances where neither the statutory text nor the "legislative will" provides a single clear answer.[183] Indeed, it is my perception that state legislatures not only accept such judicial decision-making as entirely legitimate, but also expect that within defined boundaries courts will make such choices, which can of course then be embraced, enlarged, or entombed.[184]

---

180. *Braschi,* 543 N.E.2d at 53; *see also id.* at 52 ("The present dispute arises because the term 'family' is not defined in the rent-control code and the legislative history is devoid of any specific reference to the noneviction provision. All that is known is the legislative purpose underlying the enactment of the rent-control laws as a whole"); *East Tenth St. Assocs. v. Estate of Goldstein,* 552 N.Y.S.2d 257, 25S.59 (App. Div. 1990) (extending *Braschi* to rent stabilization regulations).

181. *See Rent Stabilization Ass'n v. Higgins,* 630 N.E.2d 626, 629 (N.Y. 1993) (upholding new regulations); *see also People v. Capolongo,* 647 N.E.2d 1286, 1287 (N.Y. 1995) (holding that pretrial notice provisions of New York wiretap statute applied to foreign wiretap evidence, and noting that "[t]he central question we confront is . . . not expressly answered by our comprehensive statutory scheme for electronic eavesdropping").

182. Some public law theorists have suggested that current legislative processes lead to arbitrary or incoherent outcomes. For a brief overview of this theory, *see* Eskridge and Frickey, *supra* note 167, at 52–61; Eskridge and Frickey, *supra* note 124, at 701–10; Farber and Frickey, *supra* note 106, at 877–82; *see also* John Ferejohn and Barry Weingast, *Limitations of Statutes: Strategic Statutory Interpretation,* 80 Geo. L.J. 565, 565–66 (1992) ("It is no longer possible to assume that Congress is simply a deliberative institution devoted wholly to determining the best course of public action and putting it into statutory commands"). My former colleague on the New York Court of Appeals, Bernard S. Meyer, expressed similar thoughts (though I doubt he had public choice theory in mind) when he wrote that "[t]he deference courts give to legislative action or inaction is predicated upon assumptions many of which are little more than fiction: that legislatures act in the interest of the majority, that most legislators who vote upon a given bill . . . are knowledgeable concerning its provisions." Bernard S. Meyer, *Justice, Bureaucracy, Structure and Simplification,* 42 Md. L. Rev. 659, 677–78 (1983).

183. *See* Bernard S. Meyer, *Some Thoughts on Statutory Interpretation with Special Emphasis on Jurisdiction,* 15 Hofstra L. Rev. 167, 167–68 (1987) ("Unlike his civil law counterpart, who . . . was expected to refer problems of statutory interpretation in a given case to the legislature for solution, a common law judge is faced at various times with arguments that he construe an unclear statutory provision, or that he interpolate interstitially what can be found to be within the purpose though not the wording of a statute [or even] with applying a statute the terms of which have remained constant to circumstances which have changed sufficiently since a prior interpretation to require a different interpretation in the case presently before him").

184. An illustration of this legislative acceptance of judicial lawmaking, which is essentially superimposed upon a relatively simple statutory enactment, is in the area of sovereign immunity. Although a statute was passed more than a half-century ago, pursuant to which "[t]he state hereby waives its immunity from liability and action and hereby assumes liability . . . ," *see* N.Y. Court of Claims Act § 8 (McKinney 1995) (no substantive changes have been made to statute since its enactment in 1929), the courts in applying

However much we might prefer in this age of anxiety about "legislating from the bench" and "judicial activism" for only our elected representatives to make all the sensitive decisions, so long as human language remains imprecise and the human capacity to predict the future limited, the cascade of cases that call upon judges to fill the gaps—and to do so by reference to social justice—will unquestionably continue.[185] For state judges, schooled in the common law, to refuse to make the necessary policy choices when properly called upon to do so would result in a rigidity and paralysis that the common-law process was meant to prevent.[186]

Conclusion

I have two concluding thoughts. The first is that I would be delighted if my comments about the unique tradition, competence, and role of the state courts stimulated others to focus attention on state courts and state lawmaking. Those are serious subjects too often overlooked in many of our nation's law schools. I am willing even to run the risk that some future commentator will conclude that I have overstated both the differences between state and federal court decision-making and the capacity of the common law to explain those differences.

Second, I would like to end where I began, with the inspiring words of Justice Brennan, which for me genuinely capture the sense of my remarks:

> The struggle for certainty, for confidence in one's interpretive efforts, is real and persistent. Although we may never achieve certainty, we must continue in the struggle, for it is only as each generation brings to bear its experience and understanding, its passion and reason, that there is hope for progress in the law.[187]

---

the principle that statutes in derogation of sovereign immunity must be strictly construed, *see Smith v. State*, 125 N.E. 841, 842 (N.Y. 1920), have engrafted upon that statute various mechanisms designed to limit its far-reaching ramifications. For example, a municipality cannot be held liable for injuries resulting from a failure to provide police protection absent a "special relationship" between the municipality and the inured party. *See, e.g., Sorichetti v. New York*, 482 N.E.2d 70, 74 (N.Y. 1985); *see also Survey of New York Practice: Court of Claims Act § 8*, 58 St. John's L. Rev. 199 (1983) (discussing court of appeals decisions interpreting the Act).

185. *See, e.g.,* Eskridge, *supra* note 106, at 1554 (describing judges interpreting statutes as analogous to "diplomats . . . [who] must often apply ambiguous or outdated communiques to unforeseen situations, which they do in a creative way, not strictly constrained by their orders. But they are, at bottom, agents in a common enterprise, and their freedom of interpretation is bounded by the mandates of their orders, which are not necessarily consistent or coherent over time, or even at any one time").

186. *United States v. Standard Oil Co.*, 332 U.S. 301, 313 (1947) (describing advantage of common law process as preventing law from becoming "antiquated straight jacket and then dead letter").

187. Brennan, *supra* note 3, at 962.

In Memoriam*

William J. Brennan, Jr.

A pal. "Yankee Doodle Dandy dressed up in judicial robes."[1] "The leprechaun of the Supreme Court."[2] Hardly the words one would expect when speaking of a towering figure in the law, a Justice of the United States Supreme Court for thirty-four years, and author of opinions that have helped to shape America. Yet they *are* apt words to describe Justice William J. Brennan, Jr., a jurist who happily—perhaps uniquely—conjoined a passion for human rights with a love of human beings.

Justice Souter, in his eulogy,[3] described the Brennan touch when he recalled how the Justice would tell him:

> [S]ome pedestrian opinion . . . was not just a very good opinion but a truly great one. Then, a minute later, he'd go on and tell me it wasn't just great but a genuine classic of the judge's art. And I'd sit there and listen to him, and after a while, I'd start to think that maybe he was right. Maybe it *was* pretty good. And when, inevitably, I'd realize again that it wasn't, I'd still feel great myself. I always felt great when I'd been with Bill.[4]

I know the phenomenon. I came to consider Justice Brennan a pal about a decade ago, after I sent him a copy of my Cardozo Lecture,[5] on a subject dear to his heart,

---

*111 Harvard Law Review 14 (1997).

1. Nina Totenberg, *A Tribute to Justice William J. Brennan, Jr.*, 104 Harv. L. Rev. 33, 34 (1990).

2. *Id.* at 39.

3. *See* David H. Souter, *Remarks at the Funeral Mass for Justice Brennan* (July 29, 1997), 111 Harv. L. Rev. 1 (1997).

4. *Id.* at 2.

5. The Benjamin N. Cardozo Memorial Lecture was established in 1940 at the Association of the Bar of the City of New York to celebrate the life and works of New York State Court of Appeals Chief Judge, later Supreme Court Associate Justice, Benjamin N. Cardozo. My lecture—*Dual Constitutionalism in Practice and Principle*—was delivered at the House of the Association on February 26, 1987. Justice Brennan's Cardozo Lecture—*Reason, Passion, and "The Progress of the Law"*—followed on September 17, 1987. *See* William J. Brennan, Jr., *Reason, Passion, and "The Progress of the Law*," 10 Cardozo L. Rev. 3 (1988), reprinted in 3 The Benjamin N. Cardozo Memorial Lectures 1941–1995, at 1435 (1995) [hereafter

state constitutional law. His response knocked my socks off: "That is one of the very best lectures it has been my pleasure to read in many, many years. . . . May I keep the typed copy you sent me?"[6]

Over the years other notes followed: "I thought your article, as usual, was right on the mark. . . . My wife and I look forward eagerly to seeing you."[7] "It's been much too long since our paths last crossed."[8] Finally, after the inaugural Brennan Lecture at New York University School of Law,[9] he thanked me for my tribute to him and added: "I miss terribly being with you."

At first, quite frankly, I was skeptical. He couldn't *possibly* mean all that, could he? But as I turned his words over in my mind, I was able to persuade myself that he was (to use his words) "right on the mark." Even after coming back to Earth from those flights of fancy, messages from Justice Brennan always left me feeling great. The details were irrelevant.

Countless others undoubtedly have had that same experience.[10] Justice Brennan's list of pals was a long one, and he made each of us feel great. I believe he had that effect because, even after we put aside the lovely puffery, we knew his interest in us—his interest in people generally—was wholehearted, genuine. Every aspect of his life validated his sincere interest in people. Too often people of power or achievement are oblivious to the efforts of others, indifferent to their achievements. That was never true of Justice Brennan.

Of course, not all the messages from Justice Brennan came in the form of letters. Some were Supreme Court opinions, some speeches and articles. Just as his pats on the back were uplifting, his more formal messages were also elevating, particularly to those of us who labor in the state courts. Given his tremendous contribution to the national justice system, his considerable influence on the state courts tends to be overlooked.

Cardozo Lectures]; Judith S. Kaye, *Dual Constitutionalism in Practice and Principle*, 61 St. John's L. Rev. 399 (1987), *reprinted in* 3 Cardozo Lectures, *supra*, at 1397.

6. Letter from Justice William J. Brennan, Jr., to the author 1 (Mar. 17, 1987) (on file at the Harvard Law School Library).

7. Letter from Justice William J. Brennan, Jr., to the author 1 (Jan. 19, 1990) (on file at the Harvard Law School Library).

8. Letter from Justice William J. Brennan, Jr., to the author 1 (Dec. 5, 1989) (on file at the Harvard Law School Library).

9. The Justice William J. Brennan, Jr., Lecture Series on State Courts and Social Justice was established in 1995 by New York University School of Law in cooperation with the Institute of Judicial Administration. My lecture, *State Courts at the Dawn of a New Century: Common Law Courts Reading Statutes and Constitutions*, appears at 70 N.Y.U. L. Rev. 1 (1995).

10. David Halberstam writes that, several years ago, he took a brand new lawyer for a thirty-minute visit with the Justice at a summer cottage in Nantucket. The meeting, instead, lasted two hours, as "[t]he Justice peppered him with questions, about Newark, about lawyers and judges they both knew, about what my young friend wanted to do with his life. It was a marvelous morning." David Halberstam, *The Common Man as Uncommon Man*, in Reason and Passion: Justice Brennan's Enduring Influence 22, 25 (E. Joshua Rosenkranz and Bernard Schwartz, eds., 1997). There, again, Justice Brennan's interest left both of them feeling great.

As only the third state supreme court judge in this century named to the United States Supreme Court,[11] Justice Brennan's was one of the few national voices that highlighted the importance of state courts. As he put it:

> [T]he composite work of the courts of the fifty states probably has greater significance in measuring how well America attains the ideal of equal justice for all. The state courts of all levels must annually hand down literally millions of decisions which determine vital issues of life, liberty, and property of human beings of this nation. . . . We should remind ourselves that it is these state court decisions which finally determine the overwhelming aggregate of all legal controversies in this nation.[12]

And it was not merely the volume of cases, staggering though it may be, that made the state courts so significant. He saw us as full partners in shaping the legal landscape of the nation. In Justice Brennan's view, one of the most provocative developments in contemporary constitutional jurisprudence was the emergence of state constitutional law.

Exactly two decades ago, in these very pages, he sounded a call for state courts, no less than federal, to take up their role as guardians of individual liberties:

> [S]tate courts cannot rest when they have afforded their citizens the full protections of the federal Constitution. State constitutions, too, are a font of individual liberties, their protections often extending beyond those required by the Supreme Court's interpretation of federal law. The legal revolution which has brought federal law to the fore must not be allowed to inhibit the independent protective force of state law—for without it, the full realization of our liberties cannot be guaranteed.[13]

He reminded us that "one of the strengths of our federal system is that it provides a double source of protection for the rights of our citizens,"[14] that our nation's infrastructure includes both a federal constitutional floor and a state constitutional ceiling. "Federalism need not be a mean-spirited doctrine that serves only to limit the scope of human liberty. Rather, it must necessarily be furthered significantly when state courts thrust themselves into . . . the struggle to protect the people of our nation from governmental intrusions on their freedoms."[15]

---

11. And what a glittering trio it was: Holmes, Cardozo, and Brennan. *See* William J. Brennan, Jr., *State Supreme Court Judge versus United States Supreme Court Justice: A Change in Function and Perspective,* 19 U. Fla. L. Rev. 225, 237 n.24 (1966).

12. *Id.* at 236.

13. William J. Brennan, Jr., *State Constitutions and the Protection of Individual Rights,* 90 Harv. L. Rev. 489, 491 (1977).

14. *Id.* at 503.

15. *Id.*

And what a response that call evoked—thousands of decisions, articles, state constitutional law journals, texts, treatises, bibliographies, and even the surest mark of an important movement: serious critics.[16] Hardly the passive bystander, Justice Brennan in 1986 observed with obvious delight that "the state courts have responded with marvelous enthusiasm to many not-so-subtle invitations to fill the constitutional gaps left by the decisions of the Supreme Court majority."[17] Regrettably, the subject of state constitutional law has yet to assume an established position in our nation's law school curricula. But I have no doubt that, having been awakened to the issue, state judges will continue to look to the state constitutions that they all have sworn to support, and consequently those who litigate before them will as well.

I have left for last what for me has been Justice Brennan's most profound teaching: that as judges we can and must bring the full measure of our human capacities to bear in applying the law to resolve current problems and present needs. Justice Brennan delivered that message in living color on Bicentennial Day here in New York City, before the largest, most rapt audience I have seen gathered at the Association of the Bar of the City of New York. The speech was entitled *Reason, Passion, and "The Progress of the Law,"*[18] and it centered on due process.

It was in more ways than one a New York event, with *Lochner v. New York*[19] exemplifying "reason" (which he defined to mean cold and sterile rationality, formal rules, static solutions) and *Goldberg v. Kelly*[20]—another New York case—representing the polar opposite, "passion" (meaning not thoughtless emotion, but rather awareness of and sensitivity to human realities). The lecture drew heavily on the insights of Benjamin Cardozo, who nearly seventy years earlier, when he was an Associate Judge of the Court of Appeals of the State of New York, stepped forth and openly acknowledged that judges are not oracles of pure reason, demigods to whom objective truth has been revealed. They are flesh-and-blood human beings necessarily bringing their experience, emotion, and passion to the judicial process.

The proper relationship between the judicial head and heart remains controversial to this day. But no one was surprised to hear Justice Brennan come out on the side of "passion." While his choice of the labels "reason" and "passion" added drama to the discussion, his scholarship, his eloquence, and his sincerity made it hard to argue with his conclusion: "it is only as each generation brings to bear its experience and understanding, its passion and reason, that there is hope for progress in the law."[21]

Justice Brennan brought a full measure of humanity to all his endeavors, whether private correspondence or published writings. He truly personified justice. And I mean

---

16. *See, e.g.,* James A. Gardner, *The Failed Discourse of State Constitutionalism,* 90 Mich. L. Rev. 761, 812–32 (1992).

17. William J. Brennan, Jr., *The Bill of Rights and the States: The Revival of State Constitutions as Guardians of Individual Rights,* 61 N.Y.U. L. Rev. 535, 549 (1986).

18. William J. Brennan, Jr., *Reason, Passion, and "The Progress of the Law,"* 10 Cardozo L. Rev. 3 (1988), *reprinted in* 3 Cardozo Lectures, *supra* note 5, at 1435.

19. 198 U.S. 45 (1905).

20. 397 U.S. 254 (1970).

21. Brennan, *supra* note 5, at 12, *reprinted in* Cardozo Lectures, *supra* note 5, at 1453.

this in two ways. As a person, his own life reflected the values of integrity, decency, and respect for the dignity of others. As a judge, his working definition of justice recognized the positive effect that law could have on the lives of people. The pal, the "Yankee Doodle Dandy dressed up in judicial robes,"[22] "the leprechaun of the Supreme Court"[23]—his passion touched the lives of all Americans and contributed mightily to the progress of the law.

---

22. Totenberg, *supra* note 1, at 34.

23. *Id.* at 39.

Delivering Justice Today*

A Problem-Solving Approach

When New York Chief Judge Benjamin Nathan Cardozo delivered the Storrs Lectures at Yale Law School, he spoke of the inevitability of change in the common law in words that give me comfort in my adjudicative capacity as presiding officer of the state's high court and my executive capacity as head of the state's court system.[1] As he observed:

> The work of a judge is in one sense enduring and in another sense ephemeral. What is good in it endures. What is erroneous is pretty sure to perish. The good remains the foundation on which new structures will be built. The bad will be rejected and cast off in the laboratory of the years. Little by little the old doctrine is undermined. Often the encroachments are so gradual that their significance is at first obscured. Finally we discover that the contour of the landscape has been changed, that the old maps must be cast aside, and the ground charted anew. . . .
>
> Ever in the making, as law develops through the centuries, is this new faith which silently and steadily effaces our mistakes and eccentricities. I sometimes think that we worry ourselves overmuch about the enduring consequences of our errors. They may work a little confusion for a time. In the end, they will be modified or corrected or their teachings ignored. The future takes care of such things. In the endless process of testing and retesting, there is a constant rejection of the dross, and a constant retention of whatever is pure and sound and fine.[2]

---

*22 Yale Law & Policy Review 125 (2004). This article is based on the Robert P. Anderson Memorial Lecture presented at Yale Law School on April 15, 2003. The author expresses gratitude to her Counsel, Mary C. Mone, and to Greg Berman, Director of the Center for Court Innovation, for their collaboration both in the preparation of this article and in the problem-solving initiatives it describes.

1. The Storrs Lectures were published as The Nature of the Judicial Process (1921).

2. *Id.* at 178–79.

Seated at Cardozo's desk in Albany, using his books, I cannot help every now and then thinking back on that extraordinary jurist. It occurs to me that he might even have penned the quoted words while seated at that desk, using those books, wondering at the time whether he was creating dross, or something pure and sound and fine. We all have those moments.

The landscape clearly was far different for New York's Chief Judge, say seventy-five years ago, the very year Cardozo erected at least three mansions of the common law: *Moch v. Rensselaer Water Co.*,[3] *Palsgraf v. Long Island Railroad Co.*,[4] and *Meinhard v. Salmon*.[5] Page after page of the official New York Reports back then are consumed with cases concerning carriers, canals and shipping; contracts, corporations and fiduciary duties; mortgages; personal injury; and property damage. Commercial subjects in the Court's index of opinions far outstripped criminal law, which today is easily a third of our docket.[6] Then too, twenty-first-century society and science have brought our courts so many frontier issues, like the meaning of family and the very definition of life.[7] Additionally, much of today's case law deals with the interpretation of statutes, as our law has grown increasingly codified.[8]

Those changes, however, are not the ones that most worry me as Chief Judge, challenging as the issues are. The changes that I confront as Chief Judge of the State of New York, my executive and administrative role, worry me more. Since 1977, the New York courts have been unified under the authority of the Chief Judge: roughly four thousand state and local judges with close to four million new cases every year,[9] plus a budget

---

3. 159 N.E. 896, 899 (N.Y. 1928) (limiting a water company's duty to a property owner for failure to supply sufficient water pressure to the city's hydrants because "liability would be unduly and indeed indefinitely extended by this enlargement of the zone of duty").

4. 162 N.E. 99 (N.Y. 1928) (limiting a defendant's duty for personal injury to the reasonably foreseeable consequences of its negligence).

5. 164 N.E. 545, 546 (N.Y. 1928) (setting the standard for fiduciaries as "[n]ot honesty alone, but the punctilio of an honor the most sensitive").

6. *See, e.g.,* Stuart M. Cohen, Annual Report of the Clerk of the Court to the Judges of the Court of Appeals of the State of New York 7 (2003).

7. *E.g., Kass v. Kass,* 696 N.E. 2d 174 (N.Y. 1998) (disposition of a divorcing couple's frozen embryos); *In re Jacob,* 660 N.E. 2d 397 (N.Y. 1995) (adoptions by unmarried couples); *People v. Eulo,* 472 N.E. 2d 286, 295 (N.Y. 1984) (defining termination of life in homicide case).

8. *See, e.g.,* Guido Calabresi, A Common Law for the Age of Statutes 1 (1982) (noting that the primary source of American law, previously dominated by the common law, is now statutory); Shirley S. Abrahamson and Robert L. Hughes, *Shall We Dance? Steps for Legislators and Judges in Statutory Interpretation,* 75 Minn. L. Rev. 1045, 1046 (1991) ("[R]esolution of many, if not most, cases today involves statutes").

9. *E.g.,* Twenty-Fourth Annual Report of the Chief Administrator of the Courts 3, 8, 36 (2002) (indicating 1,199 authorized state-paid judgeships and 4,014,962 new cases in 2001). New York also has 2,300 Town and Village Justice Courts. *Id.* at 3. The jurisdiction of these locally financed courts includes minor civil matters, small claims proceedings, traffic and parking violations, minor criminal matters, local ordinances and the processing of arrests and criminal warrants. They may also handle preliminary proceedings in felony cases, including domestic violence and death penalty cases. N.Y. Uniform Justice Ct. Act §§ 201–204, 2001–2005 (McKinney 1989 & Supp. 2003). The Unified Court System does not have caseload statistics for Justice Courts, but we have estimated that they have well more than two million new filings a year.

of more than one billion dollars to match the judiciary's breathtaking responsibilities.[10] That is the role that causes the most headaches, or put more positively, it is the one that allows for—indeed demands—new thinking about the effective delivery of justice today.

Like any committed executive, I would like to leave the New York courts in good shape, to improve operations, from the management of cases and selection of juries, to the enforcement of orders and sentencing of offenders. Perhaps most importantly, I would like to help restore public confidence in the courts, which has frayed in recent years. Indeed, if our justice system is to remain vital and strong, all of us need to think seriously not only about the exquisite nuances of the substantive law but also about the hard reality of how our courts—state as well as federal—are responding to the needs of contemporary society.

I am pleased to report that since 1993 many new ideas have taken root in New York. These new initiatives include "community courts" that address pervasive quality-of-life offenses that can erode the vitality of neighborhoods.[11] They include "drug courts" that attempt to stop the cycle of drugs, crime, jail for addicted offenders. They include "domestic violence courts" that shine a spotlight on a group of cases—violence between intimates—that have historically gotten short shrift from the justice system.

What these courts have in common is an idea we call problem-solving justice. The underlying premise is that courts should do more than just process cases—really people— who we know from experience will be back before us again and again with the very same problem, like drug offenders. Adjudicating these cases is not the same thing as resolving them. In the end, the business of courts is not only getting through a day's calendar, but also dispensing effective justice. That is what problem-solving courts are about.

In this essay, I want to tell the story of problem-solving courts in New York, starting with an explanation of how we reached this point. I also want to address two basic areas of concern about these courts. The first is: Do they work? Do they actually make a dent in the complicated social, human and legal problems they set out to address? The second is: Are they fair? Do they tip the balance in one direction or the other? Do they compromise our responsibility to protect both individual rights and public safety? As Chief Judge, I wanted these questions answered before going forward.

I. Snapshot of New York State Court Dockets

An understanding of why a problem-solving approach has captured our interest starts with an honest look at what happens in the trenches of our nation's state courts today.

---

10. *See* John Caher, *Judiciary Emerges a Winner in Albany Game of Numbers: OCA Budget Showed Restraint in Time of Fiscal Crisis*, N.Y. L. J., May 16, 2003, at 1 (estimating Judiciary budget between $1.2 billion or $1.8 billion, depending on "how you do the math").

11. "Quality-of-life offenses" generally refers to "low-level offenses, like prostitution, street level drug possession, and vandalism." David Rottman et al., A Leadership Guide to Statewide Court and Community Collaboration 101 (2002). *See, e.g.,* Michael D. Schrunk and Judith N. Phelan, *Problem Solving Courts: Impact at the Local Level,* Judges J., Winter 2002, at 17, 17–18 (discussing low-level offenses like disorderly conduct, trespass, shoplifting and prostitution as quality-of-life crimes that "erode communal order, lead to neighborhood deterioration, and create an environment where more serious crime can thrive").

While we certainly have more than our share of mind-bending constitutional, statutory, and common-law questions, the bulk of our caseload is not made up of complex conspiracies and corporate collapses. State court dockets tend overwhelmingly to be the stuff of everyday life: defendants who return to court again and again on a variety of minor criminal charges, landlords and tenants with disagreements over rent and repairs, families who turn to us when their relationships sour—bringing heart-wrenching issues like domestic violence, child abuse, and juvenile delinquency. These categories alone account for roughly two million new cases a year in the New York State courts, about half our total annual filings.[12]

If you think about it for a moment, this docket is not at all surprising. Courts are, after all, a mirror of society, and even in these years of declining violent crime,[13] we have seen an explosion in misdemeanor arrests, an erosion of community support systems, and a rise in family dysfunction.[14] Much of this is drug-driven, and much of it quite naturally lands in the state courts.

Despite the open floodgates and high tides, our judges have done a fine job of delivering justice and providing due process. In the face of staggering caseloads, the wheels of justice continue to turn. That is good, and we are proud of what we accomplish every day in the New York courts. But another perspective looks at case outcomes. Here, the statistics tell us that we are recycling many of the same people again and again, as their lives spiral downward. Like the child who grows up in the courts, graduating from neglect, to delinquency, to serious crime—from Family Court to Criminal Court. Like the abusive spouse who appears on an assault charge one day and a homicide soon after. Like the drug addict who after each court encounter returns to the same street corner and the same criminal conduct—for example, prostitution and shoplifting—to support a habit.

Conventional case processing may dispose of the legal issues in these cases, but it does little to address the underlying problems that return these people to court again and again. It does little to promote victim or community safety. In too many cases, our courts miss an opportunity to aid victims and change the behavior of offenders. So we started to ask ourselves whether the courts' interventions in these cases could be more constructive—whether it was possible to use our time and resources to help break the cycle, to stop the downward spiral.

---

12. *See, e.g.,* Twenty-Fourth Annual Report of the Chief Administrator of the Courts, *supra* note 9, at 8–21.

13. *See* Brian J. Ostrom et al., National Ctr. for State Courts, Examining the Work of State Courts, 2002: A National Perspective from the Court Statistics Project 82 (2003) ("[C]rime rates for some of the most serious criminal offenses are at the lowest levels in a generation."); New York State Division of Criminal Justice Services, New York Crime Trends: Index Crime in New York State: 1994–2001 (graphing declines in murder, forcible rape, robbery and aggravated assault).

14. Rottman et al., *supra* note 11, at 3–4. *See also* Sol Wachtler, The State of the Judiciary 3 (1989) (citing failures of society seen in New York Courts, including "endless streams of crack addicts; drug-addicted parents; women battered and bruised; young boys in handcuffs; exhausted police officers; dispirited social workers; and grim-faced judges and court personnel"). An Administrator of the New York City Family Court wrote: "In many of the case brought to the Family Court today, a lack of viable community institutions and resources created the extreme situation which requires judicial intervention. Unfortunately, this same lack of community resources often limits the court's ability to devise an effective solution." Kathryn McDonald, *Changes in Children's Issues through the Eyes of Family Court*, N.Y. St. B.J., May–June 1992, at 42.

After several closely watched experiments, we have concluded that a problem-solving approach holds promise for the future. While problem-solving courts can, and do, vary greatly from place to place, the good ones all share some key elements. First is careful planning involving the usual courtroom participants, like prosecutors and defenders, as well as a broad spectrum of social service agencies and community groups we refer to as "stakeholders." Second, and equally important, is having an assigned judge to ensure both continuity in the courtroom and expertise in the issue at hand, be it addiction, domestic violence or neighborhood crime. Third, in one way or another, problem-solving courts all employ close judicial monitoring—a luxury that most of our teeming urban courts simply do not have. Requiring regular court appearances by the parties involved in a case reinforces a message of accountability to defendants and to "the system." Just as important, regular appearances provide comprehensive, up-to-date information so the judge can make better decisions in individual cases.

Before elaborating on my themes of effectiveness and fairness, I want to give you a closer look at three specific examples of the problem-solving approach in action—community court, drug court, and domestic violence court.

Along the way, I will try to separate misconception from reality. Recently, I have seen articles that suggest that community courts abdicate sentencing authority to neighborhood vigilantes.[15] This is not true—at least not in the New York State experience. I have had people ask whether drug court judges have become social workers in robes. Again, this is not true. Some even seem to think that these new courts have dispensed with defense attorneys altogether.[16] Again, this is simply not true.

Problem-solving courts are courts. They strive to ensure due process, to engage in neutral fact-finding, and to dispense fair and impartial justice. What is different is that these courts have developed a new architecture—including new technology, new staffing, and new linkages—to improve the effectiveness of court sanctions, particularly intermediate sanctions like drug treatment and community restitution.[17]

II. The First Step: Community Courts

In New York City in the early 1960s, we abandoned a system of neighborhood-based courts and centralized our criminal courts, establishing one in each of the five boroughs. This was done to promote efficiency and achieve economies of scale.

---

15. *See, e.g.,* Morris B. Hoffman, *Therapeutic Jurisprudence, Neo-Rehabilitationism, and Judicial Collectivism: The Least Dangerous Branch Becomes Most Dangerous,* 29 Fordham Urb. L.J. 2063, 2091–92 and n.120 (2002).

16. *Id.* at 2092–93.

17. People often ask how the court system can create these courts on its own. These are, technically, not new courts, but actually court parts set up and staffed pursuant to the court system's administrative authority. Except for community courts, which by definition in New York are located in facilities within the community being served, problem-solving courts are typically located alongside traditional court parts, and they exercise existing statutory authority. Where additional statutory authority will facilitate drug court operations, the court system has proposed, and the Legislature has enacted, new provisions—such as authorization for transfer of cases from the court where initiated to drug courts. *See* N.Y. Crim. Proc. Law § 170.15 (McKinney Supp. 2003) (allowing removal to drug court of an action based on an information or a misdemeanor complaint).

Twenty years later, crack cocaine hit the streets. Drug arrests went through the roof.[18] Dockets mushroomed.[19] We did not know it at the time, but that was just the start of the flood. Then came the 1990s. On the theory that taking minor offenses more seriously would help drive violent crime down—what came to be known as a "broken windows" theory[20]—police increased their enforcement of quality-of-life crimes, like low-level drug possession, fare-beating, and illegal vending.

The courts were not given much warning—or extra resources—to deal with this explosion of cases. With limited time and manpower, our energies had to be directed to serious offenses, often at the expense of these more minor cases. The cases were duly "processed"—legally disposed of—but without any real attention to the cumulative real-world impact of all the processing. As a result, many defendants ended up leaving court with sentences of time served, conditional discharge, or adjournments in contemplation of dismissal.[21] Fewer than one percent of the cases actually went to trial.[22] Very few defendants received jail time.[23] Those given alternative sentences—like community service or a drug treatment program—all too often did not serve out their sentences because the court simply lacked the resources to monitor compliance rigorously. The process became the punishment, as others before me have observed.[24]

The other branches of government—to say nothing of the public—clearly expected better. They knew that quality-of-life cases were not the stuff of CourtTV or law reviews, but they also knew that these crimes profoundly affect how secure people feel at home, how safe tourists feel on the street, and how confident employers feel about opening new businesses.

The court system began planning a community court in midtown Manhattan, a neighborhood renowned for many things, including pervasive quality-of-life

---

18. *See* N.Y. State Comm'n on Drugs & the Courts, Confronting the Cycle of Addiction and Recidivism: A Report to Chief Judge Judith S. Kaye 10, 129 (2000); Wachtler, *supra* note 14, at 3–5.

19. N.Y. State Comm'n on Drugs & the Courts, *supra* note 18, at 1 ("In the last two decades, New York State's criminal justice system has been confronted with a staggering number of drug cases, the volume of which has risen by over four hundred percent in twenty years"); *see also id.* at 10 (estimating the courts' increased drug caseload since 1980 at 430 percent). Nationwide, arrest rates for drug abuse violations increased 168 percent between 1980 and 1998. Nat'l Ctr. for State Courts, Caseload Highlights: Examining the Work of State Courts 2 (2000) (noting that arrests went from 580,900 in 1989 to 1,559,100 in 1998). The crack epidemic also had a dramatic effect on families and children, and impacted our Family Court dockets. *See* Lenore Gittis and Carol Sherman, *Crack/Cocaine, Children and New York City's Family Court,* N.Y. St. B.J., May/June, 1992, at 22 (noting that the docket of Family Court neglect/abuse cases reflected the epidemic on the streets).

20. *See* James Q. Wilson and George L. Kelling, *Broken Windows: The Police and Neighborhood Safety,* Atlantic Monthly, Mar. 1982, at 29.

21. *See, e.g.,* Linda M. Ricci, *Hawking Neighborhood Justice: Unlicensed Vending in the Midtown Community Court,* 12 Yale L. & Pol'y Rev. 231, 232–33 (1994) (stating that "turnstile justice . . . abounds in New York City Criminal Court"); N.Y. State Comm'n on Drugs & the Courts, *supra* note 18, at 86 (finding defendants often "processed and released without any significant supervision or sanction").

22. N.Y. State Comm'n on Drugs & the Courts, *supra* note 18, at 86.

23. *Id.*

24. *E.g.,* John Feinblatt et al., U.S. Dep't of Justice, Neighborhood Justice: Lessons from the Midtown Community Court 2 NJ, 10 (1998) (citing Malcolm M. Feeley, The Process Is the Punishment: Handling Cases in a Lower Criminal Court [1979]).

offenses.[25] This became our first attempt at problem-solving justice. In addition to the Bar, we collaborated with the City of New York, the surrounding business and residential neighborhoods, corporations and foundations, and two dozen social service agencies and civic organizations. After two years of study and planning, in October 1993 the midtown Community Court opened its doors.[26]

Located a few blocks from Times Square, the goal of the Midtown Court is to ensure that justice in misdemeanor cases is prompt, restorative, and rehabilitative, and that the community views this local tribunal as a fair and effective dispenser of justice. Strictly speaking, this is a branch of the New York City Criminal Court. Indeed, it is not a new courthouse at all, but a refurbished version of one of the local courts before consolidation. The words "XI Judicial Dist. Court" are prominently etched into the facade of the building.

Some of the community court's procedures are naturally quite similar to those in the centralized courts. Before seeing the judge, defendants receive a detailed pretrial assessment—just as they do in other criminal courts—although with additional questions about housing, employment, financial status, health, and substance abuse.[27] What is completely new in Midtown is a state-of-the-art computer application, for use by the judge in making individual decisions about defendants.[28] Also new in the courtroom is a Resource Coordinator, a court employee who serves as a link between the judge and the interested social service agencies.[29]

The Midtown Community Court is one of the busiest arraignment parts in the state.[30] As is true in the centralized criminal courts, most cases at the Midtown Community Court are disposed of at the first appearance.[31] Wherever appropriate, the judge in imposing

---

25. The origin and development of the concept of a community court in Midtown Manhattan is described in David C. Anderson, U.S. Dep't of Justice, In New York City, a "Community Court" and a New Legal Culture 3–4 (1996); Rottman et al., *supra* note 11, at 30–33, 101–3; and Ricci, *supra* note 21, at 250–63.

26. For a brief description of the initial project, *see* Michele Sviridoff et al., U.S. Dep't of Justice, Dispensing Justice Locally: The Implementation and Effects of the Midtown Community Court 1 (1997) [hereafter Dispensing Justice Locally].

27. Eric Lee and Jimena Martinez, U.S. Dep't of Justice, How It Works: A Summary of Case Flow and Interventions at the Midtown Community Court 1–2 (1998).

28. The computer application allows the judge, while on the bench, immediately to access all relevant information about the defendant, such as pretrial assessment, the district attorney's complaint, the defendant's criminal record, prior appearances at the Midtown Community Court, and compliance with past sentences. *See* Lee and Martinez, *supra* note 27, at 1–3. Sample screen images can be found in Anderson, *supra* note 25, at 5–6.

29. Lee and Martinez, *supra* note 27, at 3.

30. Anderson reports:

> [T]he Midtown Community Court arraigned 11,959 cases from the time it first opened in October 1993 through the end of 1994. Most were commonplace misdemeanors. Theft-of service (turnstile-jumping) cases accounted for 38 percent of the total; unlicensed vending, 17 percent; petty larceny (shoplifting in the area's big department stores), 16 percent; and prostitution, 10 percent. A mix of assaults, minor drug possession cases, and other offenses made up the remaining 19 percent.

Anderson, *supra* note 25, at 3.

31. For an outline of procedures at the Midtown Community Court, see Lee and Martinez, *supra* note 27.

a sentence seeks to combine punishment and help, sentencing offenders to perform community service and receive social services like drug treatment and job training. In the process, the midtown Court has significantly reduced the number of people who walk out of court with no sanction whatsoever. It has also significantly reduced the use of short-term jail sentences as a response to low-level crime.[32]

Community service takes place in the neighborhood where the crime was committed. The punishment, in effect, restores the community that has suffered injury. Most of the projects are designed to be visible, whether it is removing graffiti, cleaning subway stations, or planting trees. This sends a message not only to defendants, who learn that even minor offenses do harm that must be repaired, but also to the community, which sees its justice system at work. Justice is neither remote nor abstract.

In addition to emphasizing alternative sanctions, the Midtown Court has tested a variety of new methods to engage the local community in the Court's goals, including advisory boards, neighborhood newsletters, community mediation programs, and victim-offender impact panels.[33]

The Midtown Court has received several recognitions for these efforts[34] and was a key reason why the Center for Court Innovation—a full-time research and development arm of the New York courts[35]—received an Innovations in American Government Award from the Ford Foundation and the John F. Kennedy School of Government in 1998.[36] Nice as they are, the public accolades are less important than the recognition we have received from other state court systems.[37] Building on the Midtown model, more than thirty community courts are operating or in the planning stage across the country.[38]

---

32. Michele Sviridoff et al., Executive Summary, Dispensing Justice Locally: The Impact, Costs and Benefits of the Midtown Community Court 3 (2000) [hereafter Executive Summary]; Dispensing Justice Locally, *supra* note 26, at 6.

33. *See* Dispensing Justice Locally, *supra* note 26, at 2–4 (discussing advisory boards, newsletters, and mediation); Feinblatt et al., *supra* note 24, at 11 (discussing the operation of advisory boards and related issues); Robin Campbell, U.S. Dep't of Justice, "There Are No Victimless Crimes": Community Impact Panels at the Midtown Community Court (2000) (detailing the origins and operation of panels in Midtown). For a brief report on a discussion between offenders and citizens at a community impact panel, *see Offenders Face Community Residents at NYC's Midtown Community Court,* N.Y. State Jury Pool News, Winter 2002, at 4.

34. The court's awards are listed at the Center for Court Innovation web site at http://www.courtinnovation. org/center_3honors.html (last visited Aug. 12, 2003).

35. For a description of the Center, see http://www.courtinnovation.org (last visited Aug. 12, 2003), and Rottman et al., *supra* note 11, at 40, 44, 48, 99–101.

36. John F. Kennedy School of Government, The Taubman Center Report 28 (1999) (listing the 1998 award winners). The reasons for the center's selection can be found through the "Awards Recipients" link at the "Innovations Award" page at http://innovations.harvard.edu.

37. *See* Bureau of Justice Assistance, U.S. Dep't of Justice, Community Courts: An Evolving Model iii (Community Justice Series No. 2, 2000) ("The community court movement has come a long way since the first opened in midtown Manhattan in 1993. The concepts pioneered by that court have taken root across the country.").

38. Nat'l Ctr. for State Courts, Court and Community Initiatives: Executive Summary (listing twenty operating courts in Atlanta, Ga.; Austin, Tex.; Denver, Colo.; Midtown Manhattan, Red Hook, Harlem, Hempstead, and Syracuse, N.Y.; Hartford and Waterbury, Conn.; Indianapolis, Ind.; Los Angeles (Van Nuys) and San Diego, Cal.; Memphis, Tenn.; Minneapolis, Minn.; Philadelphia, Pa.; Portland, Or.; South

We now have other community courts in operation in New York State, with several more being planned.[39] In the spring of 2003, Great Britain's Home Secretary and Lord Chancellor announced that they had engaged the Center for Court Innovation to help develop community justice centers in England and Wales.[40]

III. Drug Courts

Statistics about the relationship between drugs and crime are grim. Approximately seventy-five percent of arrests in New York City, for example, are linked to drug or alcohol abuse.[41] Clearly, the scourge of substance abuse drives much of our criminal caseloads. All too many people commit crimes to feed an addiction. Given this reality, the idea of testing a problem-solving approach to addiction—as had been done in Miami since 1989[42]—made sense.

New York's first drug court opened in the upstate community of Rochester in 1995.[43] As with most things in life, it is thoughtful, dedicated people who get new ideas going. In this case, it was a Rochester judge, frustrated by the daily flow of drug addicts before him, who was determined that the court system do better. The immediate public reaction—I well remember—was cool to downright hostile: "soft on crime" was the

Tucson, Ariz.; West Palm Beach, Fla.; and Washington, D.C.); Quintin Johnstone, *The Hartford Community Court: An Experiment That Has Succeeded*, 34 Conn. L. Rev. 123, 124 n.3 (2001) (listing other locations planning community courts); Bureau of Justice Assistance, *supra* note 37, at iii (stating that concepts pioneered by the Midtown Community Court have "taken root" across the country).

39. Some commentators have expressed concern that "[c]ommunity courts are rarely focused on the interests of low-income communities." Anthony C. Thompson, *Courting Disorder: Some Thoughts on Community Courts*, 10 Wash. U.J. L. & Pol'y 63, 89 (2002); *see also* David Anderson, *supra* note 25, at 10 (stating that the Midtown Community Court raised "concerns about elitism"). However, in 2000, the first multi-jurisdictional community court opened in Red Hook, a poor neighborhood in Brooklyn, to hear criminal, delinquency, housing, and family offense matters. *See* Greg Berman, Red Hook Diary: Planning a Community Court (1998) (describing the early planning stages for the Red Hook community court); Alex Calabrese, *"Team Red Hook" Addresses Wide Range of Community Needs*, 42 N.Y. St. B.J. 14 (June 2000). In 2001, the Harlem Community Justice Center in Manhattan officially opened as a multijurisdictional court, focusing on Family Court and housing matters. *See* Rolando Acosta, *The Birth of a Problem-Solving Court*, 29 Fordham Urb. L.J. 1758, 1759–62 (2002). (Acosta is the presiding judge of the Harlem Community Justice Center.) Planning is underway for community courts in the city of Buffalo, as well as in Queens and Staten Island within New York City. In 1999, a community court opened in suburban Long Island to address low-level crime in the Village of Hempstead and four neighboring communities. *See* Bureau of Justice Assistance, *supra* note 37, at 13–14 (describing the Hempstead court).

40. Press Release, Home Office, Support Package for the Development of Community Centres Agreed (Apr. 2, 2003). The Home Secretary later announced that the first "American-style community justice centre" would be established in Liverpool to "act as [a] focal point for the community's fight against the selfish minority whose loutish and criminal behaviour is impairing their quality of life. It will combine punishment and help by providing services such as drug treatment, family and parenting support and education and training." Press Release, Home Office, Liverpool to Pioneer One-Stop Crime Busting Centre (Sept. 11, 2003).

41. N.Y. State Comm'n on Drugs & the Courts, *supra* note 18, at 15.

42. *See id.* at 17.

43. *Id.* at 41.

criticism.[44] Today, eight years later, there are ninety-six drug courts spread across New York State and about a thousand nationwide.[45]

Like the community courts, each of our drug courts was preceded by rigorous planning with a wide spectrum of stakeholders. In most of our drug courts, defendants plead guilty at the outset with the understanding that, if they complete court-mandated treatment, the court will vacate the plea and dismiss the charges or reduce the sentence. In a few, prosecution is deferred pending the outcome of treatment.[46]

Several features are common among New York's drug courts. One is that the judge, prosecution, and defense must all agree that a defendant meets the eligibility criteria—typically a nonviolent charge and history of addiction. Another is that participants must agree to a formal plan stipulating the length and type of treatment, and the consequences for failure to comply with court orders. In addition, to help insure successful transition from addiction to sobriety—and from crime to law-abiding behavior—drug courts link defendants to services like job training, health care, education, and housing.

Once defendants are in treatment, they are closely monitored, reporting to the court at regular intervals and submitting to frequent drug testing. Like community courts, drug courts have Resource Coordinators charged with the responsibility of assuring that the judge has comprehensive, up-to-date information at each court appearance.

Drug courts tend to look a lot like conventional courts pre-adjudication. But after a plea has been entered, judge, prosecutor, and defense counsel, together with treatment providers, social service agencies, and case managers, all focus on the defendant's future, rather than the merits of the original charges.[47] So when a drug treatment court defendant tests positive for drugs, a prosecutor may acknowledge that relapse is part of the recovery process and urge that a lesser sanction than jail is appropriate. A defense attorney may agree with the prosecutor that a move from out-patient to in-patient treatment is appropriate. The judge may speak directly to the defendant and not only impose sanctions but also reward success in treatment with applause or a graduation ceremony in the courtroom.[48]

---

44. Gary Craig, *Verdict Still Out on City Experiment,* Democrat & Chronicle (Rochester), Oct. 8, 1995, at 1A (citing County Executive describing drug court as having a "soft-on-crime approach"); *see* Janet H. Cho, *Judge Defends Drug Court: Aim Is to Stop Addiction, Not Legalize Drugs, He Says,* Democrat & Chronicle (Rochester), Jan. 22, 1995, at 1 (charging that drug court will mean legalization of drugs); Trif Alatzas, *Conservatives Rip Creation of "Drug Court,"* Times-Union (Rochester), Jan. 19, 1995, at 1A (claiming that drug courts are "unfair, illogical and anti-democratic").

45. The drug courts in operation are listed on the Unified Court System's web site. At this writing, eighty-nine additional drug courts were in the planning stages. *Id.* National data reported in September 2003 indicates that 1,078 drug courts were in operation and 418 in the planning process, and that more than 300,000 adults and 12,500 juveniles had been enrolled. National Drug Court Institute, Drug Courts Today.

46. *See* N.Y. State Comm'n on Drugs & the Courts, *supra* note 18, at 35–36; Michael Rempel et al., The New York State Adult Drug Court Evaluation: Policies, Participants and Impacts 13–27 (2003) (reviewing the policies of eleven drug courts under study).

47. *See generally* Office of Justice Programs, Drug Court Program Office, Defining Drug Courts: The Key Components (1997) (describing benchmarks developed by court practitioners and experts to describe the best practices, designs and operations of drug courts).

48. *See* N.Y. State Comm'n on Drugs & The Courts, *supra* note 18, at 33–40 (reviewing the workings of a drug treatment court); Jo Ann Ferdinand, *The Judicial Perspective,* 29 Fordham Urb. L.J. 2011–14 (2002) (discussing the effect on proceedings of the judge, prosecution and defense sharing the goal of successful

The program is voluntary, and some defendants reject the opportunity to participate, preferring jail time to the rigors of court-monitored treatment.[49] Those who do elect to participate can have a life-changing experience, moving from the streets to a home, a job, and a family.[50]

I think it worth noting at this point that drug courts are not the only effort in the state criminal justice system to provide treatment alternatives for addicted defendants. Several prosecutors in our state and others also offer diversion programs for non-violent drug offenders facing mandatory prison sentences. I have seen debates about who is the preferable gatekeeper and monitor for such programs—courts or prosecutors—and which programs are fairer and more successful, with defenders opting for the courts.[51] At least in New York, both programs have operated side-by-side with seeming success.[52]

---

treatment); *see also* Judicial Div., American Bar Ass'n, *Standard 2.77: Procedures in Drug Treatment Courts*, in Standards Relating to Trial Courts (Aug. 7, 2001) (noting that drug treatment courts "have become one of the fastest growing innovations in the American Judicial system," and establishing procedures to ensure that "treatment is ordered and implemented on the basis of adequate information, in accordance with applicable law, and with due regard for the rights of the individual and of the public").

49. Currently, in the New York court system, data on defendants who are offered, but decline, the opportunity to enter a drug court program is not available for each and every drug court. However, available data shows that fifteen percent of eligible defendants refused to enter drug court in Suffolk County, Rempel et al., *supra* note 46, at 199; thirteen percent in Queens, *id.* at 180; eleven percent in Brooklyn, *id.* at 159; and eight percent in the Bronx, *id.* at 140. See also Jeff Storey, *Rockland Drug Court Leads the Way*, N.Y. L.J., Dec. 26, 2000 (noting that many defendants considered drug court too difficult, as evidenced by an estimate by the Rockland District Attorney's office that forty-five of ninety-three eligible defendants enrolled in drug court, and one defense attorney's estimate that only one half of her clients volunteered for drug court participation). One researcher has noted several studies showing that "25 to 35 percent of offenders offered some the [*sic*] type of correctional treatment program refused the program with a preference for jail time" and "prefer incarceration to participation in a treatment program because the jail time is 'easier time' than being held accountable for their behavior." Faye S. Taxman, Reducing Recidivism through a Seamless System of Care: Components of Effective Treatment, Supervision, and Transition Services in the Community 7 (1998).

50. Perhaps the best evidence of the effect on those who complete drug court are their own words, which have been quoted in many publications. *See, e.g.,* N.Y. State Comm'n on Drugs & the Courts, *supra* note 18, at 143–48; Larry Fisher-Hertz, *Drug Court Enjoys First Success: Man Stays Sober for 1 Year,* Poughkeepsie J., July 23, 2003, at B1; John Caher, *Albany Family Treatment Program Holds First Graduation Ceremony,* N.Y. L.J., June 6, 2003, at 1; Christiana Sciaudone, *Choosing Treatment over Time,* Newsday (N.Y.), Feb. 23, 2003, at G6; Steve Lieberman, *Drug Court Turns Lives Around,* Journal News, Dec. 7, 2001; Elizabeth Stull, *Brooklyn Treatment Court Dismisses 30 Cases,* Brook. Daily Bulletin, Dec. 6, 2001, at 9; Barbara Ross, *Cleaned-Up Moms Get Final Applause,* Daily News (N.Y.), June 10, 1999, Suburban Section, at 3.

51. One such debate was an exchange of letters to the editor of New York's daily legal newspaper. Compare Daniel L. Greenberg, Letter to the Editor, *Prosecutors Are the Wrong Gatekeepers,* N.Y. L.J., Mar. 17, 2003, at 2 (president and attorney-in-chief of the Legal Aid Society, arguing that "greater promise of fairness and success lies with returning discretion to judges" than in leaving the roles of gatekeeper and monitor to district attorneys), with Charles J. Hynes, Letter to the Editor, *Prosecutors Should Run Drug Diversion Program,* N.Y. L.J., Mar. 18, 2003, at 2 (District Attorney for Kings County, arguing that the success of prosecutors' Drug Treatment Alternative to Prison [DTAP] programs show that "prosecutors are the right gatekeepers").

52. *See* Nat'l Ctr. on Addiction and Substance Abuse at Columbia Univ., Crossing the Bridge: An Evaluation of the Drug Treatment Alternative-to-Prison (DTAP) Program 12–13 (2003); Anne Swem, *The Birth of a Problem-Solving Court,* 29 Fordham Urb. L.J. 1755, 1763–66 (2002) (commenting on the co-existence of prosecutor's program with drug court program).

Indeed, the success of criminal drug treatment courts has encouraged us to adapt the model to serve other litigants. Since the opening of the first drug court in 1995, we have created mental health courts to link mentally ill offenders to community-based treatment instead of incarceration. We have created juvenile drug courts to give young people arrested for drug-related crimes the structure and support they need to get on the right track. And we have created family treatment courts to help substance-abusing parents charged with neglect in Family Court.

I next turn briefly to the subject of family treatment courts. The goal of family treatment court is to assure that children do not languish in foster-care limbo for what, to a child, can seem an eternity. By providing parents with a meaningful, immediate opportunity to get clean and sober, the court seeks to expedite the permanency planning process, reuniting children with their biological parents or, where that is not possible, placing them in a permanent adoptive home.[53]

To participate in a family treatment court, parents must admit to neglect due to drug or alcohol abuse—parents charged with sexual or physical abuse are ineligible. The family's social service needs—like housing, job training, parenting skills—are assessed at the beginning of the case, and compliance with treatment is closely monitored. Here too, the problem-solving judge, instead of being a remote adjudicator, asks what needs to be done to get the parent off drugs, and takes a leadership role in seeing that everyone works together—from Medicaid eligibility specialists, to private foster care agencies, to drug treatment providers, to child welfare agency caseworkers.

Respondents progressing well through the early phases of treatment may be given enhanced visitation rights and greater responsibility for the child while in foster care. Parents who are drug-free for a time may have the child provisionally released to their care while court monitoring continues. To graduate from a family treatment court program and receive full custody, participants usually must be drug-free for at least a year and working or attending school.

As a veteran of drug court graduations—whether adult or family treatment court—I can tell you that these are very moving events. Typically, a lifelong drug addict who never before could complete treatment tearfully thanks everyone, including the judge, for giving her a chance to start her life again. Frequently I hear, "I wasn't just arrested, I was saved." Grown men report that for the first time in their lives they are able to have an apartment, a credit card. I heard a graduate in New York City say: "My head was bowed when I was brought before you in handcuffs, Judge, but today my head is high. I'm looking you right in the eye."

A Rochester graduate said:

I don't know if I'd be around today if not for the court, which motivated me to stay clean and take responsibility for my life. I had a healthy baby,

---

53. *See* generally Robert Victor Wolf, *Fixing Families: The Story of the Manhattan Family Treatment Court,* 2 J. Ctr. for Fam., Child. & Cts 5 (2000). The children of substance-abusing parents have been described as "the most vulnerable and endangered individuals in America." Nat'l Ctr. on Addiction and Substance Abuse at Columbia Univ., No Safe Haven: Children of Substance-Abusing Parents (1999).

obtained joint custody of the middle son, resumed my relationship with my eldest child and became reacquainted with my mom.[54]

At family treatment court graduations, I have heard parents express gratitude for the opportunity to regain their dignity and self-esteem, re-establish connections with family members, and raise their own children. I have seen a child stand up in a crowded audience and proclaim, "Mom, I'm proud of you."

For me, the only thing better than hearing statements like these is hearing from the judges themselves—hardly revolutionaries—many of whom for years have presided over a docket of recycling addicted offenders. Their message: "This is what I became a judge to do."[55] One drug court judge initially resisted accepting that assignment, but after two years he declined the opportunity for reassignment to another court part.[56] Quite frankly, for me as Chief Judge, these firsthand evaluations from people I respect are compelling evidence from the front lines of the value and effectiveness of these courts.

The success stories from our drug courts are only the anecdotal evidence. In 2000, I appointed a blue-ribbon Commission on Drugs and the Courts headed by former United States Attorney for the Southern District of New York Robert Fiske, that spent the better part of a year studying drug courts. At the conclusion of its study, the Commission issued an exhaustive report recommending that judicially monitored treatment be extended throughout New York State.[57] Acting on that recommendation, we expect by the close of 2003 to have more than 6,000 active participants in our drug courts.[58]

---

54. *Court Adopts New Strategy to Fight Addiction and Crime,* N.Y. State Jury Pool News, Winter 1999, at 1, 2.

55. I heard these precise words spoken at a graduation ceremony by a New York City Family Court Judge, but many judges have expressed the same sentiment to me. By coincidence, only months ago, while I was on vacation in upstate New York, the local paper carried an article about a retiring judge who disclosed that he was initially pessimistic about family treatment court, but was subsequently sold on the program after seeing the progress of its participants. In his words: "That was one of the highlights of my life experience, that treatment court." Don Lehman, *Judge Reflects on Decades of Service: Austin Cites Family Court, Drug Court, as Career Highlights,* Post-Star (Glens Falls, N.Y.), Aug. 18, 2003, at B5; *see also* Emer Scott, *Judge Jo, the Queen of Care,* Manchester Evening News, Sept. 25, 2000, at 19 ("The drug court is the most satisfying thing I have ever done as a judge"); *see generally Judicial Roundtable: Reflections of Problem-Court Justices,* 72 N.Y. St. B.J. 9, 12–14 (2000) (containing comments of several judges who have presided at problem-solving courts).

56. This was State Supreme Court Justice Joseph D. Valentino of Rochester. In addition, Deputy Chief Administrative Judge Joseph J. Traficanti, who has headed our Office of Drug Treatment Programs since the fall of 2000, describes himself as initially "one of the doubters." Jim O'Hara, *Judge Praises Court, Grads,* Post-Standard (Syracuse, N.Y.), Feb. 1, 2001, at B3; *see* Terry Corcoran, *7 Graduate from Putnam Drug Court,* Journal News (N.Y.), June 26, 2003 (containing a former drug court judge's explanation that he originally worked against the idea of drug courts but became a drug court judge himself after attending Rockland County's first graduation).

57. N.Y. State Comm'n on Drugs & the Courts, *supra* note 41.

58. In January, the Office of Drug Treatment Programs estimated that there would be 5541 by September 2003. Joseph J. Traficanti, Office of Court Drug Treatment Programs, The Second Year: Report to Chief Judge Judith S. Kaye 13 (2003). Internal estimates bring that number to more than 6000 active participants by the end of 2003.

III. Domestic Violence Courts

My third example of problem-solving in New York concerns domestic violence, another modern-day scourge. Just to give you some sense of the dimension of this problem, between 1984 and 1995, domestic violence case filings increased ninety-nine percent nationally.[59] In addition, in October 1995, New York began a Statewide Domestic Violence Registry, an automated data bank that allows judges and law enforcement to know immediately a person's prior domestic violence orders of protection and warrants.[60] Our Registry now exceeds one million entries. That is more than one million orders of protection reported to the Registry by the New York State courts in the past seven years.

I will start with my own education on the subject of domestic violence. Shortly before I became Chief Judge ten years ago, tragedy struck in an affluent community in Westchester County, north of New York City. Sadly, it often takes a tragedy to galvanize attention. A woman was bludgeoned to death by her husband of four years, who then jumped to his death from a nearby bridge. The wife, an educated, articulate woman, had appeared in Family Court weeks earlier. With no lawyer or victim advocate to assist her, she stood before the judge, asked for an order of protection, and received precisely what she requested: an order that allowed the husband to remain in the house but prohibited him from harassing her or removing their child. Her death was headline news, and the media heaped blame on the judge for permitting the husband to stay in the home.[61] I wondered what more might have been done.

Not long after that, in Brooklyn, a Russian immigrant was murdered by her ex-boyfriend. While the ex-boyfriend was awaiting trial on prior charges of assaulting her and violating prior orders of protection, a judge modified the bail terms into terms the ex-boyfriend was able to satisfy. Shortly after his release, he went to the car dealership where she worked, shot her in the head, and then fatally shot himself. Again, press coverage was unrelenting, with blame heaped on the courts.[62] Again I asked myself, what more could be done to prevent tragedies like these?

Sad to say, tragedies like these proliferate all across the nation, and they have many familiar elements, like murder-suicide and young children left behind. They also remind us

---

59. Nat'l Ctr. for State Courts, Report on Trends in the State Courts 34 (1997). From the opening of New York City's first drug court in 1995, through December 2002, more than 16,000 have participated in our adult drug court programs. *See* Rempel et al., *supra* note 46, at 6, 7 tbl. 1.1.

60. *See* N.Y. Exec. Law § 221-a (McKinney 2003) (requiring the Superintendent of the State Police, the Division of Criminal Justice Services, the Office of Court Administration, the Division of Probation and Correctional Alternatives, and the Division for Women to establish and maintain a statewide computerized registry of specified orders of protection issued in New York State and by courts of competent jurisdiction in other states).

61. *See, e.g.,* Jonathan Bandier, *Westchester Family Court Judge Announces Retirement,* Journal News (N.Y.), Nov. 27, 1999, at 38 (stating the judge "came under fire in 1994 following the death of . . . the newspaper heiress"); Michael Moss, *Heiress' Mom: Judge Let Abusive Hubby Stay,* Newsday (N.Y.), Jan. 8, 1994, at 2 (stating that the mother of deceased "blasted the judge who allowed her daughter's husband—now suspected in her beating death—to stay in the couple's home").

62. *See, e.g.,* Press Release, New York City Mayor's Office, Mayor Giuliani Honors the Memory of Domestic Violence Victim Galina Komar (Feb. 19, 1997); Max Boot, *What Does It Take to Fire a Judge?,* Wall St. J., Sept. 17, 1997, at A23 ("New York tabloids went into a frenzy").

that family violence knows no boundaries. It can affect the most and the least privileged among us. In both of the cases I have described, there was an alleged history of violence but—again, not atypically—the women remained with, or returned to, their abusers. And perhaps most critically from my perspective, prior to each death the parties had been in court. Indeed, we know that recidivism rates are high and that many domestic violence victims die with judicial orders of protection in their pockets.

At some point during my first months as Chief Judge, I happened to see a video of a police officer in a patrol car, on his way to answering a woman's call that her husband was assaulting her. The woman's voice over the car radio begged the officer not to come to the house: "It was all my fault." "I overreacted." "Please don't come." But he persisted. Finally, he said, "Ma'am, if everything really is OK, please say a number between one and five." A pause. Then her chilling response: "Six."[63]

The message was powerful. Clearly, domestic violence cases demand special skills and special training. The surface response, the ready answer, may not reflect the grim reality.[64] Recognizing this, our first step was to establish a Family Violence Task Force, which for the past several years has presented first-rate training sessions throughout the state for judges and court staff.[65] The idea is to raise awareness about the nature of domestic violence and encourage the sort of probing questions that need to be asked.[66]

---

63. The video was entitled *Agents of Change*, produced by Victims Services Agency (now Safe Horizon). I viewed the video during one of the training sessions conducted by our Family Violence Task Force. Although that particular video is no longer in distribution, videos have become an important tool for education of the public as well as training of judges, police officers and others. *See, e.g.*, National Resource Center on Domestic Violence, at http://www.nrcdv.org (containing a video list on its "Resources" page with the titles of more than 200 videos on the subject of domestic violence). Among the videos we have used in New York is the Academy Award–winning documentary *Defending Our Lives* (regarding battered women imprisoned for killing their abusers). *See, e.g.*, Elizabeth Stull, *Court's Domestic Violence Series Continues with "Defending Our Lives": Documentary Film Features Former D.A.*, Brook. Daily Eagle & Bull., Oct. 17, 2000, at 8 (describing the film's showing during Domestic Violence Awareness Month).

64. In the view of one of the leading advocates for battered women:

> Domestic violence must be understood as a planned pattern of coercive control that may involve physical, sexual, or psychological abuse rising to the level of torture as understood in human rights discourse. An understanding of domestic violence and human rights paradigms shifts battered women's call for justice away from victim-blaming pathologies toward a more accurate view of the systemic oppression of women evidenced in individual relationships.

Sarah M. Buel, *Effective Assistance of Counsel for Battered Women Defendants: A Normative Construct*, 26 Harv. Women's L.J. 217, 218–19 (2003) (footnotes omitted).

65. For a brief description of the Task Force and its programs, see Judith S. Kaye, The State of the Judiciary 1999, at 14. *See generally* Michael Dowd, *Dispelling the Myths about the "Battered Women's Defense": Towards a New Understanding*, 19 Fordham Urb. L.J. 567 (1992) (explaining how lack of knowledge about domestic violence in the legal system diminishes the battered woman's access to a fair trial, and describing Dowd's own lack of knowledge on the topic until he represented a woman who had killed her abusive husband).

66. Though still inadequate, public sensitivity to domestic violence was aroused beginning in the early 1990s. Significantly, in February 1995, the American Bar Association launched a multidisciplinary Commission on Domestic Violence, of which it was my privilege to be a member. *See* Roberta Cooper Ramo,

We also began an experiment with the problem-solving approach, starting in Brooklyn, at first for the most serious of these cases, domestic violence felonies. With the help of many others—prosecutors and defense, criminal justice agencies, social service agencies, victims' advocates, community groups—we put our resources to work in a new and different way, beginning with an assigned courtroom and an assigned judge to work on these cases exclusively, from arraignment through plea, trial, and post-sentence monitoring.

Our focus, of course, is always on fairly judging the merits of each case, but in domestic violence cases we also want to take special care to ensure victim safety and defendant accountability. To reduce victim safety risks, a Resource Coordinator ensures that the court has all information available for decision-making.[67] To promote defendant accountability, the court monitors defendants closely, requiring frequent returns to court so that the judge can ensure there is no violation of bail conditions, orders of protection, or conditions of probation. Defendants know that they will be held accountable for any errant behavior.[68]

Here too we have seen signs of success.[69] Signs of success in getting complainants to place greater trust in the justice system. Signs of success in reducing probation violation rates.[70] Success—and I say this always with fingers crossed, and prayer—in that there have been no fatalities in the cases before domestic violence courts.

As important as they are, the criminal domestic violence courts in New York are handling just a fraction of the cases involving family violence.[71] The sad truth is that families with domestic violence issues in New York can find themselves whipsawed among a variety of different courtrooms at the same time, including Family Court, a Supreme

---

Ending the Violence: With Cooperation and Commitment, We Can Banish Domestic Abuse, A.B.A. J., Feb. 1996, at 6; Steven Keeva, *Striking Out at Domestic Abuse: New ABA Commission Plans Interdisciplinary Programs to Aid Victims,* A.B.A. J., April 1995, at 115; Robert A. Stein, *Changing Attitudes about Abuse: Awareness, Education Are Linchpins of Domestic Violence Prevention Effort,* A.B.A. J., Oct. 1996, at 106.

67. A special computer application assists the court in monitoring the case. *See* Pamela Young, An Informed Response: An Overview of the Domestic Violence Court Technology Application and Resource Links (2001).

68. For a profile of the first presiding judge in the Brooklyn Felony Domestic Violence Court, Supreme Court Justice John Leventhal, see Lynda Richardson, *His Specialty and His Burden: Domestic Violence,* N.Y. Times, Apr. 25, 2001, at 82.

69. *See* Robyn Mazur and Liberty Aldrich, *What Makes a Domestic Violence Court Work? Lessons from New York,* Judges J., Spring 2003, at 5, 41–42 (describing the difficulty of defining and measuring success in domestic violence courts, but concluding that they play an important role in helping to eliminate family violence).

70. Probation Department statistics for the year 2000 suggested a decline in probation violation rates in Brooklyn's Felony Domestic Violence Court, although researchers found equivocal results in studying early cases for the year 1997. *See* Lisa Newmark et al., Specialized Felony Domestic Violence Courts: Lessons on Implementation and Impacts from the Kings County Experience 69, 76 (2001).

71. Domestic violence cases can also be litigated civilly, and at times even concurrently with criminal matters. New York's Family Courts have jurisdiction over "family offense" petitions in specified situations. In 2001, Family Courts had close to 60,000 family offense filings. Twenty-Fourth Annual Report of the Chief Administrator, *supra* note 9, at 21. In addition, domestic violence matters can arise in divorce cases pending in New York Supreme Court.

Court matrimonial part, and a criminal court. It is difficult to imagine, but as currently constructed, our fractured court system makes these families appear in separate locations in front of separate decision makers even though the underlying problem in each case is the same. The potential for inefficiency and redundancy is obvious. What may be less obvious is the potential for conflicting court orders and judicial decisions based on only a partial picture of the legal problems of the families before them.

In an effort to address this problem, we have created a series of Integrated Domestic Violence (or "IDV") courts to hear all cases involving a family with domestic violence issues—for this class of cases, in effect, a unified family court. We began with a few pilots, and in January 2003 announced a comprehensive three-year plan to replicate these courts statewide.[72]

These courts, we believe, will better protect and assist victims, and better promote defendant accountability. IDV judges will know, for example, when an abuser sent to a court-mandated drug treatment program shows up intoxicated at supervised visitation with his children. There will be less opportunity for a defendant to slip through the cracks. More opportunity for the judge to monitor the abusers, to see that child support is paid and visitation and treatment orders are satisfied. Better linkages to social services and other resources to address family needs like housing, employment, and child care. Maybe, above all, more information that leads to better judicial decisions in individual cases, which, in a nutshell, is the goal of our integrated domestic violence courts.

IV. Effectiveness

Having described the origins and operations of problem-solving courts, I want to return to the questions posed at the outset of this essay: Do they work, and are they fair?

A generation ago, in 1974, Robert Martinson wrote an article for *The Public Interest* that examined prison-based rehabilitation programs and concluded that they had no significant effect on recidivism.[73] Although subsequent researchers successfully challenged his conclusions on methodological grounds,[74] his bleak assessment that nothing

---

72. Judith S. Kaye, The State of the Judiciary 2003 6–7 (2003). *See* New York State Unified Court System, Integrated Domestic Violence Courts (providing information about the plan and courts that are already in operation).

73. Robert Martinson, *What Works? Questions and Answers about Prison Reform,* The Public Interest, Spring 1974, at 22–54.

74. One of the researchers whose work was summarized in Martinson's article recently wrote:

> [F]ew people who espoused the view that nothing works questioned the validity of the research on which it was based or understood the problems inherent in the design of most treatment programs and in the methodologies used to evaluate them. They also did not recognize the difference between the pessimistic viewpoint of the summary article [by Martinson] and the more guarded conclusion, arrived at by my colleagues and me, which left open the possibility that rehabilitation could work.

works in many respects "cast a pall" over the criminal justice community that lingers to this day.[75]

Looking back on three decades of debate about criminal justice reform, I think we have learned two important lessons. The first is the need to be realistic about our expectations—about what we can achieve as we take on complicated and deeply entrenched social problems like addiction, domestic violence, mental illness, and child neglect. We need to acknowledge that, despite our best efforts, problem-solving courts are not going to change every offender's life. Some people will fail. Some people belong in prison. The innovations discussed here—enhanced treatment, special staffing, and judicial monitoring—can accomplish only so much in an individual's life. They are not going to make up for problems like chronic poverty, substandard education, shoddy housing, and inferior health care.

Hand in hand with the need for realistic expectations is the need for solid research. Almost all of the experiments launched in New York State have rigorous evaluation plans.[76] We want to know not just whether they work, but why and for which populations.

It is still too early to offer definitive conclusions about the problem-solving approach. Some of our projects, like the IDV and mental health courts, are just months old. It takes years to track recidivism. It takes years to weigh program costs and benefits. It takes years to compare new practices to traditional ones.

Yet our experience has taught us quite a bit about the impact of problem-solving courts, and most of what we know is positive and encouraging. I want to highlight findings in five principal areas, beginning with recidivism.

A. Recidivism

In a recent review of drug court evaluations from across the country, researchers found that thirty-five of the forty-one studies showed reductions in recidivism among drug court participants compared to control groups.[77] In October 2003, the Center for Court

---

Douglas S. Lipton, U.S. Dep't of Justice, The Effectiveness of Treatment for Drug Abusers under Criminal Justice Supervision (1995). Lipton also notes that Martinson himself later acknowledged that "some treatment programs do have an appreciable effect on recidivism." *Id.*

75. Greg Berman and Anne Gulick, *Just the (Unwieldy, Hard to Gather but Nonetheless Essential) Facts, Ma'am: What We Know and Don't Know about Problem-Solving Courts,* 30 Fordham Urb. L.J. 1027, 1027–28 (2003); *see* John S. Goldkamp, *The Drug Court Response: Issues and Implications for Justice Change,* 63 Alb. L. Rev. 923, 926 & n. 17, 960–61 (2000); Rick Sarre, Beyond "What Works?": A 25 Years Jubilee Retrospective of Robert Martinson 5 (Dec. 1999); Jerome Miller, *Criminology: Is Rehabilitation a Waste of Time?,* Wash. Post, Apr. 23, 1989, at C3.

76. *See* Berman and Gulick, *supra* note 75, at 1035, 1038–40, 1041–48 (discussing studies of the New York family treatment courts, Midtown Community Court, and domestic violence courts); N.Y. State Comm'n on Drugs & the Courts, *supra* note 18 (studying drug court pilot programs).

77. *See* Rempel et al., *supra* note 46, at 118 (citing David B. Wilson et al., A Systematic Review of Drug Court Effects on Recidivism, Paper Presented at the Annual Meeting of the American Society of Criminology, at 11 & 23, March 2002).

Innovation released its evaluation of New York's drug courts in a report that I believe will be important not just to New York, but also to the field of criminal justice research.[78] It is the first multisite study that evaluates the impact of drug courts on recidivism by participants both while they are in a drug court program and after they leave. It also details the backgrounds of drug court participants, retention rates (how long participants stay in treatment), and predictors of successful treatment. Examining data from half a dozen drug courts, the Center found an average decline in recidivism of thirty-two percent in the year following program completion.[79] The impact of a reduction of this size is far-reaching—both for the future of the drug court participants and their families, and for the safety of communities and the functioning of our criminal justice system. It also has the potential for saving substantial amounts of money for the state.[80]

B. Street Conditions

Independent evaluators from the National Center for State Courts spent three years investigating the midtown Community Court and its effect on the streets of Manhattan.[81] Street prostitution arrests dropped by fifty-six percent. Illegal vending dropped by twenty-four percent.[82] Just as important, supervised work crews from the Court each year contribute tens of thousands of dollars worth of labor to the local community, repairing conditions of disorder like graffiti-marred buildings and trash-strewn parks.

C. Improved Accountability

One of the hallmarks of the problem-solving approach is accountability ensuring, to the extent we can, that court orders are followed. Researchers tell us that compliance rates for community service at New York's community courts are consistently fifty percent

---

78. The report, Rempel et al., *supra* note 46, is among the first large-scale evaluations of whether drug courts have a long-lasting impact on criminal behavior. *Id.* at ix. Only Ohio has done a statewide study, and only a handful of studies addressed long-term impacts of drug courts beyond the first one or two years after entry into program participation. *Id.* at 13. Previous studies had been criticized "for failing to establish the long-term impacts of drug court participation—especially over a *post-program* period when participants are no longer under court supervision." *Id.* at 9. *See also id.* at 117–24 (reviewing prior recidivism studies).

79. *Id.* at x. Among the study's conclusions are that drug courts "reduce recidivism when compared with conventional prosecution," *id.* at 288, that their "impacts extend beyond the period of program participation," *id.*, and that "[t]he exact magnitude of [their] impact varies across different sites," *id.* at 289. The study also suggests that "while statewide institutionalization efforts will presumably want to promote statewide accountability and training, as well as some uniformity of key policy principles, it appears sound to promote a measure of local innovation, diversity, and adaptation to the available community-based resources." *Id.* at 290. Questions about "best practices," however, will persist, since "we do not adequately understand *how* and *why* drug courts work, and which approaches are most cost-effective." *Id.*

80. *See* N.Y. State Comm'n on Drugs & the Courts, *supra* note 18, at 25–30 (outlining the financial benefits of treatment instead of jail).

81. See Dispensing Justice Locally, *supra* note 26.

82. *Id.* at 7.

higher than in traditional courts.[83] Meanwhile, the study of several New York drug courts shows that drug courts in the Bronx, Queens, Manhattan, and Tonawanda County have one-year retention rates exceeding seventy percent.[84] By way of contrast, addict stays in voluntary treatment programs over three-month periods range only from thirty to sixty percent.[85] These statistics support what common sense suggests: that judicial monitoring keeps addicts in treatment.

D. Stronger Families

The data shows that New York's family treatment courts are having a profound impact on the permanency planning process. Prior to the creation of these courts, children languished in the city's child welfare system for an average of more than four years while their parents' cases wended their way through the courts. By giving parents an immediate and realistic chance to get clean and sober, family treatment courts have reduced the average foster-care stay for these children to about a year.[86]

E. Public Confidence

Last, increasing evidence suggests that problem-solving courts can help counter the erosion of public trust and confidence in justice that we have experienced in recent generations. In Red Hook, Brooklyn, for example, a poor, predominantly minority neighborhood with high levels of crime, seventy-two percent of local residents surveyed were aware of the Red Hook Community Justice Center and seventy-one percent of them viewed it favorably.[87] This contrasts sharply with a survey conducted before the community court opened, in which only twelve percent approved of the job that courts were doing in Brooklyn.[88]

We have learned a lot from the first generation of research into problem-solving courts and undoubtedly we will learn more in the days ahead. Among the questions that researchers are currently studying in New York are these: Which is a more effective response to misdemeanor domestic violence judicial monitoring or batterers' intervention programs? Are rewards more important than sanctions in motivating behavioral change among drug court participants?

There is one answer, however, that I do know: while the challenges of a contemporary urban criminal court or family court docket may be fierce, we can unquestionably find ways to meet them and do better. I am simply unwilling to adopt a despairing and

---

83. *Id.* at 7 (initial results showed fifty percent better compliance than traditional Manhattan courts); Executive Summary, *supra* note 32, at 2, 4 (compliance rate essentially sustained over three years).

84. Rempel et al., *supra* note 46, 85–86 & tbl. 8.1 (reporting retention rates, respectively, of seventy-two, eighty-one, seventy-three and eighty-two percent).

85. *Id.* at 85 ("Since attrition always increases over time, one-year retention rates across these same programs, if they were available, would presumably drop much lower than the 30–60% three-month range").

86. N.Y. State Comm'n on Drugs & the Courts, *supra* note 18, at 67.

87. Greg Berman and Aubrey Fox, Justice in Red Hook: An Experiment in Government-Community Collaboration 2 (2003) (unpublished manuscript, on file with the author).

88. *Id.*

defeatist attitude that "nothing works," or put another way—"everything stinks, but don't change a thing."

V. Fairness

Measuring the effectiveness of problem-solving courts is no easy matter, but at least we have recourse to studies, statistics, and surveys. Gauging the fairness of problem-solving courts is a far more challenging task. Does this new approach tilt the scales of justice? Does it shake the foundation of the adversarial system or compromise courts' ability to make fair and impartial decisions?

Any serious effort to address these questions must take place not in the world of abstraction but in the real world. It is crucial to remember the context out of which problem-solving courts emerged.

I wish I could tell you that our misdemeanor and family courthouses resemble the pristine temples of law you find in books. If you come to these courthouses looking for meaty motions and trials, you will be gravely disappointed. On a typical day in a New York City arraignment part, there are eighty or more cases before the court, which means that the judge and attorneys can devote just minutes to each.[89] Most of the cases, as I have discussed, involve quality-of-life offenses or minor drug possession. The vast majority are disposed of at arraignment, many by plea to reduced charges and community service. Very few will ultimately go to trial. The rest will be settled in plea negotiations between the prosecution and defense.[90] The picture is no different in Family Court: scores of new cases on the calendar each day; little time for more than brief appearances before a judge; difficulty in finding counsel to appoint; frequent delays and adjournments; bargains often negotiated in hallway conferences.[91]

Lest you think this is a New York phenomenon, I offer this quotation from Chief Justice Kathleen Blatz, speaking about Minnesota's busy trial courts. In her words:

> [J]udges are very frustrated. . . . I think the innovation that we're seeing now
> is a result of judges processing cases like a vegetable factory. Instead of cans

---

89. This simple arithmetic assumes a judge can spend the entire day on the daily calendar of appearances, which does not even account for other activities, like studying written submissions, researching and writing opinions, conducting trials, performing ordinary administrative tasks, etc. In 1989. my predecessor Chief Judge pointed out that the typical court calendar in New York City Criminal Court consisted of 250 cases a day, leaving judges "at most two to three minutes to take meaningful action in each case." Wachtler, *supra* note 14, at 5.

90. *See* Twenty-Fourth Annual Report of the Chief Administrator of the Courts, *supra* note 9, at 17 (stating that in 2001, forty-two percent of arrest cases in New York City Criminal Court were concluded by plea, thirty percent by dismissal, twenty-two percent by "other means"). Only two tenths of one percent of the cases were resolved by verdict. *Id.*

91. *See* Charlie LeDuff, *Handling Sinners and Victims of Domestic Hell: Sad Hallways and Broken Lives in an Overburdened Family Court System,* N.Y. Times, May 28, 2000, at B1; Stephen J. Bogacz, *Family Court Faces Funding Crisis,* Newsday (N.Y.), Mar. 14, 2001, at A24; Laura Mansnerus, *For Lawyers in Family Court, Preparing for Cases Is Luxury,* N.Y. Times, Mar. 10, 2001, at 83.

of peas, you've got cases. You just move 'em, move 'em, move 'em. One of my colleagues on the bench said: "You know, I feel like I work for McJustice: we sure aren't good for you, but we are fast."[92]

Clearly, compared to McJustice, carefully planned, well-operated problem-solving courts offer a far better opportunity for both prosecutors and defendants. That, I presume, is why District Attorneys, the Legal Aid Society, and other respected public defenders work cooperatively with us in these new initiatives.[93] That is why defendants choose to participate in, rather than challenge, these courts. What is the alternative is a question that needs to be answered by critics of a problem-solving approach.[94]

But "compared to what?" and "what's the alternative?" are not the end of my answer. Indeed, I think it is worth lingering for a moment on the roles of the judge and defender in a problem-solving court.

Drug courts, for example, until the treatment phase, can look very much like conventional courts before a plea is entered. Lawyers argue about eligibility criteria, the length of treatment mandates, and appropriate treatment methods, like whether a defendant merits residential or out-patient treatment. Judge, prosecutor, and defender perform their roles much as they do in any court.

In the next phase, however, when the focus is on defendant's success in treatment, there is an understandable concern about ethical obligations and a need for heightened sensitivity both in the design of these courts and in daily practice. Serious questions may arise, such as sanctions for relapses and possibly even failure. It should be clear that a judge's engagement with drug court defendants in no way diminishes or obscures the

---

92. Greg Berman, *What Is a Traditional Judge Anyway? Problem Solving in the State Courts*, 84 Judicature 78, 80 (2000).

93. A variety of perspectives on problem-solving courts (from judges, prosecutors, defense attorneys, academicians, and researchers) were expressed at the Eleventh Annual Symposium in Contemporary Legal Challenges at Fordham Law School on February 28, 2002. The proceedings of this Symposium were published in the Fordham Urban Law Journal. *See* Symposium, *Problem Solving Courts: From Adversarial Litigation to Innovative Jurisprudence*, 29 Fordham Urb. L.J. 1751 (2002).

94. For a more detailed critique of problem-solving courts, *see, for example*, James L. Nolan, Jr., Reinventing Justice: The American Drug Court Movement (2001); Hoffman, *supra* note 15; Morris B. Hoffman, *The Drug Court Scandal*, 78 N.C.L. Rev. 1437 (2000); Anthony C. Thompson, *Courting Disorder: Some Thoughts on Community Courts*, 10 Wash. U. J.L. & Pol'y 63 (2002). It is worth noting that the first article by Judge Hoffman cited above relies on data on "Drug Court Recidivism" in New York City in 1993, Hoffman, *supra* note 15, at 2070 n.29. However, in 1993, New York's first drug treatment court had not even begun operations, *see supra* note 43 and accompanying text. Hoffman's source, *see* Hoffman, *supra* note 15, at 2070 n.29, was Steven Belenko and Tamara Dumanovsky, Program Brief: Special Drug Courts (1993) (reporting that "53.5 percent of the 'N Part' cases and 50.9 percent of those processed through other parts were rearrested"). In 1993, New York City operated Narcotics Parts ("N Parts"), which were not treatment courts. Those parts were intended to facilitate prosecution of felony narcotics cases so as "to remove more narcotics peddlers from our streets, deter professional drug traffickers and stem the flow of drugs into our communities." Memorandum from Nelson A. Rockefeller, Governor, New York State (June 17, 1971), *in* 1971 N.Y. Laws 2614. *See also* N.Y. Jud. Ct. Acts Law §§ 177-a to 177-e (McKinney 1983 & 2003 Supp.) (establishing and governing Narcotics Parts); Belenko and Dumanovsky, *supra* (noting that the Narcotics Parts were intended solely to reduce disposition time). As for the recidivism impact of New York's drug courts, see Rempel et al., *supra* note 46, at 274–81.

court's responsibility at all times to retain the role of impartial, independent decision maker and guardian of legal rights. Nor do defense counsel cease being their clients' advocates. In the words of one problem-solving judge, counsel always have "to take care that cooperation does not turn into capitulation."[95]

While I cannot deny that there may be bad practice in some problem-solving courts,[96] just as there may be bad practice anywhere, these courts have been planned to avoid unfairness by assiduously including both prosecutor and defense among the planners and implementers, and by closely overseeing these courts in daily practice. That there may be issues, moreover, is not a condemnation of the problem-solving idea, but rather a signal, or reminder, of the need for care in the planning and operation of these courts.[97] Attempting to stop the cycle of drug addiction and domestic violence as cases come before us not only is no perversion of our roles as lawyers and judges but indeed represents an effort to fulfill the highest values of our profession.

VI. Conclusion

I conclude with the observation that New York has made a significant commitment to problem-solving, but we are not alone in our enthusiasm for this new approach. In 2000, the Conference of Chief Justices and the Conference of State Court Administrators passed a joint resolution endorsing the concept of problem-solving courts. The resolution encouraged the broad integration of the principles and methods used in those courts into the administration of justice, in order "to improve court processes and outcomes while preserving the rule of law, enhancing judicial effectiveness, and meeting the needs and expectations of litigants, victims and community."[98] The American Bar Association adopted a similar resolution the following year.[99]

---

95. Judy H. Kluger, *The Impact of Problem Solving on the Lawyer's Role and Ethics,* 29 Fordham Urb. L.J. 1892, 1894 (2002). Kluger was a former presiding judge of the Midtown Community Court, and is currently responsible for overseeing the expansion of New York's Integrated Domestic Violence Courts.

96. Compare Morris B. Hoffman, *The Denver Drug Court and Its Unintended Consequences,* in Drug Courts in Theory and Practice 67, 87 (James J. Nolan, Jr. ed., 2002) (judge who participated in the decision to open the Denver Drug Court describing its many failures), with N.Y. State Comm'n on Drugs & the Courts, *supra* note 18, at 105 (blue-ribbon commission recommending statewide expansion of New York's drug court program). *See also* Rempel et al., *supra* note 46, at 274–81 (finding, inter alia, that drug court participants had lower recidivism than comparable defendants not entering drug court); Steven Belenko, *What the Data Shows,* 29 Fordham Urb. L.J. 1827, 1839 (2002) (noting that although the majority of drug courts achieved a reduction in recidivism, Denver is one of a few that did not).

97. For example, Professor Eric Lane reviewed three case studies—of the Stanford Drug Treatment Court, the Brownsberg Community Court, and the West Jackson Domestic Violence Court—to examine "whether problem-solving courts can be effectively maintained without damage to the individual protections afforded defendants under the due process mantle" of federal and state constitutions. Eric Lane, *Due Process and Problem-Solving Courts,* 30 Fordham Urb. L.J. 955–57 (2003). He concluded that "with certain cautions, problem-solving judging and lawyering, as described by the case studies and other available material, need not be in conflict with due process standards." *Id.* at 958.

98. Conference of Chief Justices, Resolution 22, and Conference of State Court Administrators, Resolution 4, In Support of Problem-Solving Courts (2000).

99. A.B.A. House of Delegates Rep. No. 117, cited in Daily Journal, 2001 Annual Meeting, A.B.A. House of Delegates, Aug. 6–7, 2001, at 13, 25.

I think the next step is to take up the challenge presented by these resolutions, to explore incorporating the strategies and technologies we have tested in problem-solving courts into the broader administration of justice.

This means asking some hard questions. How do we make the current problem-solving courts better? Should we consider additional problem-solving parts, or should we—can we—systemize these efforts and encourage every courtroom to adopt the underlying principles? How do we help lawyers and judges think about more effective outcomes? How do we incorporate these principles into legal education?

These are just a few of the challenges that confront us in the days ahead. They are not insignificant, but given the current size and state of our dockets, as well as the tangible evidence of success with our innovations, I believe this approach is well worth pursuing.

I close by returning full circle to Chief Judge Cardozo. To be sure, the subject of this essay is a far cry from the novel common law issues that captivated Chief Judge Cardozo. But the spirit that motivates us is much the same: using our best skills and best judgment, we try to fit the law to the new challenges an evolving society leaves at our courthouse doors—whether a newfangled Buick automobile with a defective wooden wheel,[100] or a recycling docket of drug-driven behavior. The process of testing and retesting new ideas, retaining and refining what is good and rejecting what is not, keeps the law relevant and responsive to a changing world. It is a great privilege for me, as Chief Judge, to be part of that process.

---

100. *MacPherson v. Buick Motor Co.*, 111 N.E. 1050 (1916).

The Best Oral Argument I (N)ever Made*

Back in my days as a litigator, I often faced the same preargument dilemma: Do I invite my family or not? Plainly I would want them all there at the conclusion of a flawless performance, but what if things didn't go so well? What if I was trapped by a question from the Court, or shown up by the adversary? Embarrassing enough in a roomful of strangers. But why heighten the risk, and pressure, by bringing family?

Baldt v. Tabet was an exception. Though we had lost on summary judgment, the trial had gone well before United States District Judge Charles Tenney,[1] and I felt sufficiently confident about our client's prospects on appeal to spread the word as the date for oral argument in the Second Circuit neared. The client, my husband, my in-laws, and countless others accompanied me on that sunny and beautiful June 26, 1975, as I made my way down to Foley Square in lower Manhattan.

I cannot honestly say today—a full three decades later—that I was surprised to find retired United States Supreme Court Justice Tom Clark presiding. Surely I must have known in advance that he would be on my panel. But most definitely I did not know that he would be so lively, so engaging, so entertaining. As he tore into my adversary, dismembering his arguments, I had fifteen minutes of exquisite pleasure/pain—pleasure witnessing the skillful demolition of my adversary's case, pain at the prospect that the panel was merely warming up for the next round: me. Definitely a mistake to have issued all those invitations.

As my bowed and bloodied adversary took his seat, I gathered up my papers, and my courage, and moved to the lectern. Justice Clark, however, was busily chatting with his colleagues—first one side, then the other. I had just spoken the words, "May it please the Court" when he interrupted. "Counsel," he said, "it will not be necessary to hear further argument. We have decided to affirm."[2]

---

*7 Journal of Appellate Practice and Process 191 (Fall 2005).

1. *Baldt Corp. v. Tabet Mfg. Co., Inc.*, 412 F. Supp. 249 (S.D.N.Y. 1974), *aff'd*, 517 F.2d 1395 (2d Cir. 1975) (table).

2. I'm pleased to learn that the Second Circuit long ago discontinued the practice of announcing a decision at argument. Memo. from Karen Greve Milton, Cir. Exec., U.S. Ct. of App. for the 2d Cir., to Judith S. Kaye, Chief Judge, St. of N.Y., *History Inquiry about the Second Circuit* (July 21, 2005) (noting that the practice stopped "in the early 1980's" and referring to Wilfred Feinberg, *Unique Customs and Practices of the Second Circuit*, 14 Hofstra L. Rev. 297, 317 [1986]) (copy on file with Journal of Appellate Practice and Process). It's hard on "sore winners" to be sure, but far worse for the other side.

Wait a minute! No fair! Can I be heard on this? What about my meticulous preparation? What about my fifteen-minute presentation? What about my hand-picked audience?

In the end, I have come to believe that this was my best oral argument ever, brief and to the point: "May it please the Court. Thank you, Your Honor."

My client and family thought I was great.

My Life as Chief Judge*

The Chapter on Juries

A recent speaking engagement prompted me to reflect on my years as Chief Judge. Ultimately, these ruminations took shape, and I share my thoughts with readers of the *Journal*.

As Chief Judge I hold two positions, each genuinely a full-time job. As Chief Judge of the Court of Appeals, I am one of seven equals, hearing appeals on a range of issues that defies human imagination. On any one day at Court of Appeals Hall we could be hearing argument on budget-making authority, or education funding, under the State Constitution; a slip-and-fall on a patch of ice; a construction site injury under Labor Law § 240; a multiple murder case; and a teacher's claim that his right to tenure under the Education Law has been violated.

Honest, we have days like that. The very idea of a court such as ours—a second level of appeal—is that we will, through a relatively few cases raising novel issues of statewide significance, settle and declare law that has widespread application. I am proud of our Court, which is sound and efficient in its work, and true to its awesome responsibility. I think of my judicial role, as a Judge of the Court of Appeals, as Lawyer Heaven. That is as true today as it was on September 12, 1983, over twenty-three years ago, when I first took my seat on the Court of Appeals.

But the second box of stationery, which I acquired more than thirteen years ago, Chief Judge of the State of New York, a chief executive officer role, is right up there too. When I saw *Pride of the Yankees* recently on television, for the 100th time, I thought I could adopt Lou Gehrig's closing line as my own. Genuinely, I feel that I am the luckiest person on the face of the Earth.

Two Basic Questions

As I stepped back and thought hard about what I do, particularly as head of the Third Branch of government, it occurred to me that most often I was returning to two overlapping

*Reprinted with permission from New York State Bar Association Journal, October 2006, vol. 78, no. 8, published by the New York State Bar Association, One Elk Street, Albany, NY 12207.

questions. First, how do we assure the delivery of justice in this modern, fast-paced, rapidly changing society? And second, how do we maintain the trust and confidence of the public so that our work and our decrees are respected? I could think of no better context for a discussion of both questions than the subject of juries.

The jury system is central to the delivery of justice in the New York State courts, where we have close to 10,000 jury trials a year. Jury service, moreover, is the courts' direct link, often our *only* direct link, with the millions of citizens called to serve as jurors—more than 650,000 a year in New York State alone. Surely, 650,000 positive jury experiences would be a great means of fostering public confidence in the justice system. How do we best assure public trust and confidence when jurors come into our courts? Jury issues run the gamut of my responsibilities; I've even been summoned several times to serve as a juror. Believe me, I know the pain of people being rejected during *voir dire*.

The jury, of course, is the subject of innumerable Court of Appeals decisions, on issues such as discrimination in selection, juror misconduct, even how jurors are seated in a courtroom for *voir dire*. But instead of Court of Appeals jurisprudence, I will focus on my executive and administrative Chief Judge role. Both of the fundamental questions I've posed are pertinent to the subject of juries.

The Roots of Our Jury System

The jury system came to our shores with our earliest settlers. Throughout the colonies, the jury was seen as a fundamental right and a way for the public to restrain government power. As you might imagine, the colonists were none too pleased when the Crown dispensed with jury trials for anyone accused of violating the despised Stamp and Navigation Acts. That added to the many grievances against King George III listed in the Declaration of Independence. So it's no surprise that Article III of the United States Constitution provided for a right to trial by jury for all crimes except impeachment; the omission of that right in civil cases ultimately led to inclusion of the Seventh Amendment in the Bill of Rights, guaranteeing jury trials in certain civil cases. Every state constitution separately secured those rights.

The jury in many ways reflects the progress of America. The right to have, and to serve on, juries has been part of our nation's struggle from its beginnings. Just think: critical as the jury was to the founders of a free nation, they limited service to white male landowners. Although the requirement of property ownership did not last long, it was not until 1880 that the Supreme Court held that jury service could not be restricted by race; not until 1975 that the Court prohibited the systematic exclusion of women from jury service; and not until 1986 that it banned the discriminatory use of peremptory challenges.

New York's public policy echoes our proud history. In the words of Judiciary Law § 500, litigants entitled to a jury "shall have the right to grand and petit juries selected at random from a fair cross section of the community[,] . . . all eligible citizens shall have the opportunity to serve . . . and shall have an obligation to serve when summoned for that purpose, unless excused."

Reality vs. Rhetoric

Regrettably, the reality of jury service has not always matched the rhetoric. By the early 1990s in New York, we were calling the same people every two years like clockwork, and they served on average two full weeks, even if not selected for a trial. One reason for this was that our statutes allowed dozens of automatic exemptions and disqualifications from jury service, ranging from judges, doctors, lawyers, police officers, firefighters, and elected officials to embalmers, podiatrists, people who wore prosthetic devices and people who made them, to individuals with principal child-care responsibilities. Seemingly every group that could lobby Albany for an automatic exemption successfully did, and that sorely depleted our jury pools. To makes things worse, the court system did little follow-up on the rooms filled with summonses returned as undeliverable.

Given the huge demand for jurors, and the short supply, New York State used what were called Permanent Qualified Lists. Once qualified for jury service, a person remained qualified. Not a choice list to be on, especially given the condition of our juror facilities, which often were shabby and neglected.

How was the reality measuring up to the rhetoric? I knew for sure that we weren't earning points with the public. So in 1993, months after I became Chief Judge, we convened a commission of lawyers, judges and public members to review jury service in New York, with the goal of making the New York State jury system one that would be valued and appreciated by jurors, judges, attorneys and litigants alike. In six months, with a dynamic trial lawyer—Colleen McMahon, now a United States District Judge—as chair, The Jury Project handed us a blueprint for comprehensive reform, which we have been implementing ever since.

In fact, this experience was so encouraging that again and again we have convened task forces and commissions to help us address other vexing issues. Over the years, superb commissions of lawyers, judges and others have paved the way on virtually every one of our successful reforms: business courts, fiduciary appointments, drug courts, judicial selection, matrimonial litigation, the legal profession and more.

A Reform Agenda

Without doubt, the centerpiece of New York jury reform was legislation adopting The Jury Project's top recommendation—end automatic exemptions. How shocking, especially for groups that lost their exemption! Fortunately, the Legislature resisted pressure to restore exemptions, and about one million potential new jurors were added to the court lists. Then, the Legislature adopted the recommended expansion of juror source lists to include unemployment and public assistance rosters, adding yet another 500,000 potential jurors.

These reforms sent a strong message: no person, no group is more privileged, or less important, when it comes to jury service, and no one gets excused automatically from this fundamental right, and obligation, of citizenship. We underscored that message with assiduous follow-up of all summonses returned as undeliverable. Besides gaining a more diverse jury pool, we could now spread the burdens and benefits of jury duty more widely, ending the Permanent Qualified Lists, the customary two-week service and the every-two-years-like-clockwork callbacks. The Legislature also increased juror pay and ended automatic sequestration in criminal cases.

These successes were also a powerful lesson for a new Chief Judge. We treasure the independence of the Judiciary, and rightly so. It's essential to our democracy, to our system of checks and balances, that the Judiciary be wholly independent in its core decision-making function. But in so many other ways—most notably systemic reform— we are vitally connected to our partners in government. The jury program—still, by the way, a work in progress—is one of the best examples of profound system-wide reform within the Third Branch.

Which brings me to my next subject: how best to manage the bounty—or, in other words, be careful what you wish for. Not all of the potential new jurors were as pleased as the Chief Judge. Thus, the court system faced a huge new challenge, but always the vision has been clear: to deliver justice for the litigants while affording a positive experience for jurors. This means efficient use of jurors' time in their summoning, selection and service; and it means courteous, respectful treatment. A lawyer friend—the general counsel of a major media corporation—told me that her recent jury service ranked among the great experiences of her life. We need to multiply that. Invariably the most satisfied jurors are those who have actually served to verdict on a well-run trial—they are more likely to have a favorable impression of service and feel that they have made a contribution.

Implementing the Agenda

The easier part of the challenge, without question, has been the internal administrative part—like employee training in dealing with jurors; an online system for submitting juror qualification questionnaires; more efficient summoning procedures, like allowing jurors to call in by telephone to see if they really need to show up on the summons date; obtaining one automatic postponement by telephone or on the Web; orientation of jurors through handbooks, as well as live and video presentations (which are also available at www.nyjuror. gov); decent facilities and quiet work space, including wireless Internet access and even laptop work stations in juror waiting rooms; clean restrooms with locks on bathroom doors, paper towels and liquid (instead of bar) soap (the Chief Judge checks out that sort of stuff—ladies' *and* men's rooms); and assuring prompt payment of juror fees. We have excellent court staff, who are always finding new ways to improve the jury experience.

Yes, definitely the easy part, though still—and I would think forever—a work in progress. The really hard part—changes that would give jurors tools to help improve the way they do their job—would involve cultural change.

The entrenched culture I have in mind includes age-old practices of experienced lawyers and judges, such as settling cases only after (instead of before) the jury is selected; endless, unsupervised *voir dire* in civil cases; and proceedings conducted in a foreign language—legalese—before passive jurors, who are assumed to be taking in information uncritically, recalling it accurately and not thinking about it until they are told, at the end of the trial, what the rules will be for evaluating all the information they've absorbed.

Two decades of solid research and experience in other states have shown that change is both possible and desirable.

Earlier, I mentioned statutory reforms that radically changed the face of our juries, best described as top-down reform. New rules and statutes imposed requirements, and court administration made the appropriate adjustments. But changing how trials are conducted by experienced lawyers and judges cannot be accomplished by order of a chief executive officer, particularly a CEO without power to hire, fire or promote; particularly for wonderful people at the pinnacle of their careers, mindful of affording due process and avoiding reversible error, and thus understandably more comfortable staying with ways that are tried-and-true. The sort of change I am advocating here can be accomplished only by the judges and lawyers themselves, from the ground up.

To stimulate the process of reform inside the courtroom, we convened a group of judges from around the state willing to try out some of the well-researched and best-known modern aids to juror comprehension, and we very carefully documented their experience by surveying lawyers and jurors who participated in using these aids. Perhaps the most telling finding was that, where jurors reported that the trials were "very complex," judges and lawyers reported that those same trials were not "complex." Doesn't that speak volumes? What lawyers and judges understand easily does not necessarily get through clearly to the jurors.

At the conclusion of its study, the group issued an overwhelmingly positive report, endorsing such "innovations" as opening statements that give jurors some idea of the nature of the case before *voir dire*; allowing juror notetaking to facilitate better recall of the evidence; permitting jurors to submit written questions to the judge, who would then determine whether they should be asked of witnesses; and providing jurors with a copy of the judge's final instructions to take into deliberations. This was followed by publication of a "Practical Guide" describing these practices, which we have distributed to all judges.

Will this succeed in changing the picture? Only time will tell.

Public Trust and Confidence

I turn next, and finally, to what may be the most difficult issue of all, how to assure the trust and confidence of the public—jurors and nonjurors—in the work of the courts, particularly given an abysmal lack of civic education and a flood of negative news. A major part of the answer to my question, perhaps a complete answer, is what I have just been describing: improving in every possible way the jury experience for those called to serve, and generally doing a first-rate job. Still, we need to do more. The public *should* know more about us, and *should* think well of us.

In the words of the great French statesman and observer of American life, Alexis de Tocqueville, "The jury may be regarded as a . . . public school ever open, in which every juror learns his [or her] rights." I have no doubt that de Tocqueville's observation remains true today, and that serving on a case to verdict is not only an educational experience but also a satisfying one for a juror.

Sadly, only eighteen percent of those summoned to jury service will actually get selected for a trial. For the other eighty-two percent, we depend on courtesy, efficiency and outreach efforts, such as our orientation video, the availability in every juror assembly room of copies of informational periodicals, and Juror Appreciation Week events in courthouses throughout the state. We have also just completed a booklet about juries for teachers and students, *Democracy in Action*, designed to be shared with family, neighbors and friends.

But how do we address the fact that New Yorkers for the most part are unaware of the role of the courts in their daily lives? That is a challenge I put to the Bar: help us build a citizenry that is better informed about all three branches of government, but especially about the courts, which of necessity—and, I must admit, habit—remain somewhat remote and detached. One of our newest initiatives, announced in the 2006 State of the Judiciary, will be a Center for the Courts and the Community, a nonprofit public-private partnership now in formation, to focus on fortifying educational alliances with schoolchildren and adults, and on establishing programs to inform and facilitate the work of the media in reporting on the courts. I'd appreciate your ideas, in whatever form you see fit, for furthering the success of this new effort.

Conclusion

And there, in brief capsule, is the jury chapter in my life as Chief Judge of the State of New York. A dozen other chapters—such as children in the courts, domestic violence, drug courts, matrimonial issues, fiduciary appointments, commercial courts—have the same questions at their core: are we meeting today's needs, and how are we perceived by the public? Sometimes the answers lie in legislation, sometimes in court rules, sometimes in task forces and commissions, sometimes in small groups seeding reform, always in vital partnerships with our great Judiciary and court staff, with the Bar and with others. When the mountain moves, even a millimeter—as it clearly has in the New York State jury system—it's absolutely exhilarating.

That's one of the reasons why, as Chief Judge, I believe I am the luckiest person on the face of the Earth.

ACKNOWLEDGMENTS

The editors and the Historical Society of the New York Courts (the Society) convey their special appreciation to William J. Hooks, former state reporter, Law Reporting Bureau, New York State Court of Appeals, and his staff for their stellar technical contributions by way of case citations and the table of contents.

The editors and the Society are grateful to Susan N. Herman, Centennial Professor of Law, Brooklyn Law School, and president, American Civil Liberties Union, for her biographical introduction to the memoir. She has provided important insights into Judge Kaye's record as chief judge from the perspective of her writings and initiatives and, in so doing, enriches our understanding of the memoir. We thank Hon. Jonathan Lippman, former NYS chief judge, who was the chief administrative judge of the courts during Judge Kaye's tenure as chief judge, for his review of and additions to the Milestones, and his general advice on administrative proceedings during Judge Kaye's tenure as chief judge.

We would also like to acknowledge the many others who helped research, write, and publish this book. They include the following Society trustees: Hon. Carmen Beauchamp Ciparick, of counsel and co-chair, National Appellate Practice Group, Greenberg Traurig LLP; Frances Murray, former chief legal reference attorney to the New York State Court of Appeals and charter trustee of the Society; and Barry Garfinkel, of counsel, international litigation and arbitration at Skadden, Arps, Slate, Meagher & Flom LLP. Special thanks to John Q. Barrett, professor of law, St. John's University, School of Law, for his important advice and assistance in the planning of the book. We also wish to note the helpful administrative assistance of Allison Morey and Daniel O. Sierra, staff of the Society.

We are grateful to Jennifer L. Smith and Grace M. Haidar, who worked with Judge Kaye for a number of years at Skadden, Arps, Slate, Meagher & Flom LLP as attorney and legal assistant, respectively, for their assistance in organizing and delivering Judge Kaye's articles and speeches to us.

Thanks to Marjorie McCoy, former deputy clerk of the New York State Court of Appeals, and Mary C. Mone, counsel to Judge Kaye from 2000 to 2008, attorneys who worked with Judge Kaye during her tenure on the Court of Appeals and continued to assist her in preparing her memoir.

Finally, we thank the following former law clerks of Judge Kaye who contributed opening comments on the decisions selected for this book. They participated in the decision-making and know the process from an insider's perspective:

David M. Cohn, senior supervising appellate counsel, New York County
    District Attorney's Office

Mary Rothwell Davis, volunteer counsel, Immigration Justice Campaign

Jeremy R. Feinberg, statewide special counsel for ethics and the commercial
    division, Office of Court Administration

James D. Fry, associate professor of law, University of Hong Kong, Faculty
    of Law

Jean M. Joyce, senior assistant district attorney, Kings County District Attor-
    ney's Office

Roberta A. Kaplan, partner, Kaplan Hecker & Fink LLP

Hon. Robert M. Mandelbaum, acting justice, New York State Supreme Court,
    New York County

Matthew J. Morris, special litigation counsel, Proskauer Rose LLP

Ralia E. Polechronis, counsel, Wilkinson Walsh + Eskovitz

Jonathan E. Rebold, assistant United States attorney for the Southern District
    of New York

Anne C. Reddy, of counsel, Greenberg Traurig LLP

Hon. Jennifer G. Schecter, justice, New York State Supreme Court, Commercial
    Division, New York County

Jennifer L. Smith, special assistant to the superintendent, New York State
    Department of Financial Services*

Elaine Unkeless, retired professor of law, City University of New York School
    of Law

We thank James Peltz, co-director of SUNY Press, and Dana Foote, production editor,
James for his wise guidance as we developed the format and content for the book and
Dana for her meticulous review of the edited transcript.

---

*Jennifer was an associate at Skadden, Arps, Slate, Meagher & Flom LLP dedicated to working with
Judge Kaye.

APPENDIX

Law Clerks of Judith S. Kaye

Gary Hoppe (1983–1984)
Darren O'Connor (1983–1985)
Steven C. Krane (1984–1985)
Robert Kochenthal (1985–1986)
Grace M. Healy (1986–1987)
David P. Friedman (1986–1988)
Siobhan Shanks (1987–1988)
Laura R. Johnson (1988–1990)
Henry M. Greenberg (1988–1990)
Michael J. Garcia (1990–1992)
Deirdre Roney (1990–1992)
Joseph L. Matalon (1991–1993)
Wendy H. Schwartz (1992–1993)
Elise A. Yablonski (1993–1994)
Mary Rothwell Davis (1993–1995)
Alesia D. Selby Flemming (1994–1995)
Roberta A. Kaplan (1995–1996)
Audra Zuckerman (1995–1997)
James A. Shifren (1996)
Stephen Kong (1996–1998)
Jeremy R. Feinberg (1996–1998)
Christina B. Dugger (1997–1999)
Kenneth Ian Weissman (1998–2000)
Jennifer G. Schecter (1998–2001)
David M. Cohn (1999–2001)
Jean M. Joyce (2000–2006)
Matthew J. Morris (2001–2003)
Lisa M. Schweitzer (2001–2003)
Gregory A. Call (2001–2003)

James D. Fry (2003–2004)
Anne Marie Bowler (2003–2005)
Robert M. Mandelbaum (2003–2006)
Megan Wolfe Benett (2004–2006)
Devin Jai Burstein (2005–2007)
Elaine Unkeless (2006–2007)
Anne C. Reddy (2006–2008)
Harold E. Bahr III (2006–2008)
Jonathan E. Rebold (2007–2008)
Ralia E. Polechronis (2007–2008)

ABOUT THE EDITORS

HENRY M. GREENBERG is president of the New York State Bar Association and a shareholder at Greenberg Traurig, LLP, in Albany, New York. He served as a law clerk to Judge Kaye from 1988 to 1990.

LUISA M. KAYE is Judge Kaye's daughter. After practicing law as a commercial litigator in New York for over twenty years, she started a new career, making pastry and baking bread, with plans to open a bakery in Denver, Colorado.

MARILYN MARCUS is an attorney and the executive director of the Historical Society of the New York Courts since 2004. As executive director, she developed a treasured working and personal relationship with Judge Kaye, who founded the organization in 2002 and remained closely involved with it for the rest of her life. The mission of the Society is to preserve, protect, and promote New York legal history.

ALBERT M. ROSENBLATT served with Judge Kaye on the New York State Court of Appeals from 1999 through 2006. His previous books include *Opening Statements: Law, Jurisprudence, and the Legacy of Dutch New York* (coedited with Julia C. Rosenblatt), also published by SUNY Press.

INDEX OF CASES

People v. Wheeler, 335n88
People v. Wolf, 262
Perez v. Sharp, 282
Petri v. Bank of New York Co., 401n34
Pinsker v. Pacific Coast Soc'y of Orthodontists, 385n112
Pollitz v. Wabash R. R. Co., 133
Prater v. State, 169n9
Price v. Price, 342n11
Prozeralik v. Capital Cities Communications, Inc., 294
PruneYard v. Robins, 377–378, 380n86

Regan v. Taxation with Representation of Wash., 160
Rent Stabilization Ass'n v. Higgins, 423n181
Riggs v. Palmer, 402n45
Rihga Intl. U.S.A., Inc. v. New York State Liquor Auth., 421n172
Rivera v. State, 169n9
Rivers v. Katz, 334n82, 384n105, 409n88
Roberson v. Rochester Folding-Box Co., 351, 355n32
Robins v. PruneYard Shopping Ctr., 378n74
Robinson v. California, 319n25
Rockaway Pac. Corp. v. Stotesbury, 181
Rodriquez v. Rosenblatt, 384n109
Ross v. Louise Wise Servs., Inc., xiv, 289–296
Rust v. Reyer, 192–195

Sabetay v. Sterling Drug Inc., 403n46
Santagelo v. State, 413n116
Schiavone Constr. Co. v. Mayo Corp., 205n1
Schloendroff v. Society of New York Hosp., 415n133
Schulz v. State of New York, xiv, 171–182
Schuster v. City of New York, 414n122
Scott v. News-Herald, 149
Security Mut. Ins. Co. v. Acker-Fitzsimons Corp., 213–214
Sega v. State, 400n31
Sega v. State of New York, 24
Shad Alliance v. Smith Haven Mall, 378n75, 379n84
Sharrock v. Dell Buick-Cadillac, Inc., 327
Sheehy v. Big Flats Community Day, 195
Sherbert v. Verner, 160n7
Sherman v. Robinson, 403n47

Silver v. Pataki, 48
Silverman v. Benmor Coats, 30–31
Simcuski v. Saeli, 296
Slaughter-House Cases, 318
Southern Pac. Co. v. Jensen, 374n47
Spells v. Spells, 144
Staber v. Fidler, 413n117
Stanley v. Illinois, 250
State v. Anderson, 169n9
State v. Badger, 322n35
State v. Bible, 169n9
State v. Felmet, 378n75
State v. Gilmore, 334n80
State v. Houser, 169n9
State v. Jewett, 329n67, 405n63
State v. Kimbro, 330n70
State v. Pennell, 169n9
State v. Perry, 406n65
State v. Schwartz, 169n9
State v. Shack, 379–381, 409n91, 409n93
State v. Vandebogart, 169n9
State v. Yoskowitz, 384n109
State v. Zdanowicz, 373n37
Steinhardt v. Johns-Manville Corp., 415n130
Steinhilber v Alphonse, 152–154
Sterling Vil. Condominium v. Breitenbach, 133
Strauss v. Belle Realty Co., 206, 345n39
Strickland v. Washington, 266–267
Sullivan v. Brevard Assocs., 414n123
Sutka v. Conners, 418n153
Svendsen v. Smith's Moving & Trucking Co., 327n56
Swain v. Alabama, 334n80, 335
Symphony Space v. Pergola Properties, 23

Taylor v. Louisiana, 365n38
Tebbutt v. Virostek, xiv, 127, 401n32
Tenenbaum v. Williams, 243
Texas Indus., Inc. v. Radcliff Materials, Inc., 412n110
Texas v. Brown, 124
Tischler v. Dimenna, 401n34
Tucker v. Toia, 323N39
Turcotte v. Fell, 344n29, 400n28
Turner v. Turner, 414n121
Twining v. New Jersey, 374n52

Ultramares Corp. v. Touche, 345

GENERAL INDEX

Photographs are numbered consecutively and indexed with an italic *P*.
Photographs 1 to 20 are found after page 76; 21 to 31 are found after page 90.

Burger, Warren E., 74, 325
Burstein, Devin Jai, 466
Business Judgment Rule, xiv, 130
Butler, Melvin, 261–262

Calabresi, Guido, 402n43, 410n98, 411, 421
Call, Gregory A., 465
Cancel, Griselda, 212
Cannon, John, 98
capital punishment, xx, 36–40, 189, 407n74
Cardozo, Benjamin Nathan, 27, 28, 305,
    307–314, 392; on common law, 403, 453; on
    exclusionary rule, 328; Holmes and, 346n44,
    397; on judicial process, 332, 339, 340; on
    law reviews, 351, 352; on legal language,
    417n145; Storrs Lectures of, 430
Carter, Robert, 101
Castro, George, 261–266
Center for Court Innovation, xxvii, 64,
    437–438
Chess, Stella, 291
chief executive officer of State of New York,
    57–58, 72
Chihuly, Dale, 90
Christopher, Warren, 54–55
Ciparick, Carmen Beauchamp, *P5–P7*, *P18*,
    P28, 51, 107
citation analysis, 348n2
Civil Practice Law and Rules, 342
Clark, Thomas, 454
Clinton, Bill, xxii, 54–56
Cobb, Henry N., 13
Cohen, Stuart, 12
Cohn, David M., 465
Cohn, Roy, 100
Colman, Neville, 165
Colonial Penn Insurance Company, 212
Commercial Division of the Supreme Court,
    xxiii, 57, 59, 61–62
Committee on the Profession and the Courts,
    xxvi
common interest communities (CICs), 130
common law, 27–31, 50, 61, 76, 341, 356;
    Brennan on, 399–404; Cardozo on, 403;
    duty to serve in, 363n37, 384–385, 408;
    euthanasia and, 382–383; fundamental
    fairness and, 384–386, 408; history of,
    369–376; medical treatment and, 196,

199–200, 381–386; mental patients and,
    383–384; New York State Constitution and,
    304, 367–388; policy-making and, 399–400,
    403–404, 415; shopping mall cases and,
    377–381; state constitutions and, 404–410;
    state statutes and, 402, 410–424; Stone on,
    312
community courts, 57, 64–65, 432, 434–438
compensatory damages, 289, 293–295, 313,
    353
Conference of Chief Justices, 40–41, 74–76
Connors, Patrick, 105
consumer protection statutes, 196
contract law, 29–30, 137–140, 211–215, 348,
    352–353
Cooke, Lawrence H., *P1*, xx, 24–26, 40
Cooper, Michael, 98
Court Children's Center, *P13*
Court of Appeals Hall, 11–13
Craco, Lou, 60
Cramton, Roger, 355
Cravath, Swaine & Moore, 97, 99
Criminal Procedure Law, 33
Crosson, Matt, 58
Cuomo, Andrew, 49–51, 85
Cuomo, Mario M.: on death penalty, 36;
    on Highway Fund, 171–172; judgeship
    appointments of, *P8*, *P11*, xix, xxii, 19, 37,
    53, 56–57; on right to die, 415

Dautel, Susan, 104
Davis, Mary Rothwell, 162, 171, 237, 465
death penalty. *See* capital punishment
DeCapriles, Miguel, 99
DeCataldo, Kathleen, 88
Delivering Justice Today (Kaye), 430–453
Delphi method, 67
Denman, Dolores, 59
"depraved indifference murder," 31–32, 34,
    252–255, 274
Desmond, Charles, 15
Diaz, Angel, 190
Dicker, Sheryl, 67
Dickinson, Emily, 6
DiFiore, Janet, xi–xii, 3
Dinkins, David, 64
disclosure orders, 201–203
divorce cases, 58–59, 98, 414, 422, 445n71

DNA evidence, 162–170, 398
Domestic Relations Law, 36, 298–299, 342;
  Alison D. v. Virginia M. and, 50, 142–144;
  Matter of Jacob and, 22, 183–188
domestic violence, xiv, 18, 65–66, 432, 433,
  443–446
Donovan, Dan, 87
Down syndrome, 35–36
Dreiser, Theodore, xxiii
drug courts, 57, 59, 64–65, 432, 438–442,
  451–453
drug use, 333, 392, 399, 433, 435
dual constitutionalism, xxi, 40–46, 303–304,
  315–337, 425n5
Duane, John F., 195
Dugger, Christina B., 465
duty of care, 27
duty to serve, 363n37, 384–385, 408

Edelman, Marian Wright, 81
education, right to, 49, 216–228, 323
Ellerin, Betty Weinberg, xx
Ely, John Hart, 335–336
Emigh, Brian, 12
emotional distress damages, 28–29, 50,
  295–296
Eskridge, William N., Jr., 413n119, 414n124,
  420n167, 424n185
euthanasia, 382–383, 398, 415
evidence, 401n38; disclosure order for,
  201–203; DNA, 162–170, 398; exclusion of,
  328; hearsay, 261–264

Fabe, Dana, 87
Fagan-Solis, Elijah, *P17*
"fairness and rightness" doctrine, 384n109
family issues, 49–52, 58–60, 64–68, 109;
  court responsibilities in, 392–395; domestic
  violence and, xiv, 18, 65–66, 432; education
  and, 223; gender equality and, 100; parental
  rights and, xiv, 50, 141–145, 341–342,
  364n33. *See also* adoption
family treatment courts, 441–442, 449
Farber, Daniel A., 411n106, 421n173
Farr, Bartow, 98
Fearon, George, 177–178
Feinberg, Jeremy R., 192, 465
Ferejohn, John, 423n182

Field, Martha A., 412n111
Fishman, Charlotte, 101–102
Flemming, Alesia D. Selby, 465
Folkman, Joseph, 107
Frankfurter, Felix, 416n143
Frickey, Philip P., 411n106, 414n124, 420n167,
  421n173, 424n185
Friedman, David P., 465
Friedman, Lawrence M., 373n42
Friendly, Henry, 109
Friesen, Jennifer, 405n64
Fry, James D., 229, 466
Fuchsberg, Jack, 25
Fuld, Stanley H., 349n4
Fuller, Lon, 353
fundamental fairness, 377, 384–386, 402n45,
  408

Galie, Peter, 367n3
Garcia, Derrick, 261–266
Garcia, Michael J., 465
Garfinkel, Barry, 84
Garibaldi, Marie, 21
gender equality, xviii–xix, 18–19, 99–100,
  104–111, 311; feminist jurisprudence and,
  354; inclusive language and, xviii–xix;
  Law Day speech on, 73, 365n41, 389–391;
  property rights and, 359nn12–13; women
  lawyers and, 97, 100, 101, 357–366; women's
  suffrage and, 358n5, 360n16
Gillespie, Kevin, 189–190
Gilmore, Grant, 313, 410n99
Ginsburg, Ruth Bader, xxii, 60, 86, 110, 304n7
Glass, Elliot, 130
Goldstein, Marcia, 101
Goodhue, Mary, 67
Goodman, Norman, 62–63
Gordon, Daniel R., 405n63
Graffeo, Victoria A., *P7*, *P18*, *P28*, 107
Grand, Paul, 98
Greenberg, Henry "Hank," xv, 3, 45, 54, 55,
  303–305, 465
Griesa, Tom, 62

Haig, Robert, 62
Halberstam, David, 426n10
Hancock, Steward F., Jr., *P2–P4*, 46, 128
Hand, Learned, 352, 356, 419n163

Handler, Milton, 350n7

Hanna, Gavin, 229–230

Harvard Law Review, 351, 353–354

Hate Crimes Act, 281–282

hate speech, 412n112

Havinghurst, Harold C., 353–354

Healy, Grace M., 465

hearsay, 261–264

Hellman, George, 311

Herman, Susan N., xvii–xxiv, 3, 105, 304

Highway Fund, 171–172

Historical Society of the New York Courts, P30, 3

Hoffman, Morris B., 451n94, 452n96

Holmes, Oliver Wendell, Jr., 29, 307, 346n44, 351, 374n47, 397

Holtzman, Elizabeth, 20

homosexuality. *See* LGBTQ rights

Honda Motor Co., 201–202

Hope, Jane, 158–161

Hoppe, Gary, 15, 20, 24, 465

Hughes, Kyle, 73

Human Dimension in Appellate Judging (Kaye), 204, 304, 338–347

In Memoriam: William J. Brennan, Jr. (Kaye), 425–429

in vitro fertilization (IVF), 141, 196–200, 392

International Dispute Resolution Center, 88

Jasen, Matthew J., *P1*, xx, 25, 32

Jeffreys, Alec, 165n5

Jenna's Law, 268

Jobs, Steve, 83

Johnson, Laura R., 465

Johnson, Lyndon B., 59

Johnson, Robert T., 189–190

Jones, Hugh R., *P1*, xx, 25, 28–29, 50

Jones, Theodore T., Jr., *P7*

Joyce, Jean M., 189, 204, 465

judicial activism, 279, 346, 368n4, 402–403, 424

judicial compensation, 70–71

jury service, *P14*, xxiii, 57, 61–63, 360, 457–461

Justice for Children Commission, xxvi, 57, 58, 66–68, 88

juvenile delinquency, 86–88, 341, 393, 399, 441

Kaplan, Roberta A., 62, 183, 279, 465

Karst, K., 363n32

Katzmann, Robert, 74

Kaye, Judith S., 97–103; biographies of, 303nn1–4; as chief executive officer of State of New York, 57–58; Cuomo's appointment of, *P8, P11*, xix, xxii, 19, 37, 53; family of, *P21–P27*, xviii–xix, 14, 19, 80, 93–96, 99, 103; at law school, 95–96; marriage of, 79–80; milestones of, xxv–xxvii; photographs of, *P1–P20, P23–P31*; retirement of, *P28*, xvii

Kaye, Luisa M., xvii, 3–4, 6, 14n2, 19, 80, 130, 357

Kaye, Stephen Rackow, *P25*, 19, 53–56, 79–80, 98, 102–103, 109

Kearse, Amalya, 54, 102

Kennedy, Anthony, 41, 86

Kidd, Kenneth, 164

Klein, Andrew, 104

Koch, Ed, 37

Kochenthal, Robert, 465

Kong, Stephen, 465

Kramer, Larry, 411n109

Krane, Steven C., 303n1, 465

Kreech, Florence, 292

Kunstler, William, 38

Lack, James, 62

Lagarde, Christine, 106

Lane, Eric, 420n168, 452n96

Lang, Toni, 88

Lauren, Ralph, 94

Law Day speech, 73, 365n41, 389–391

Legal Aid Society, 102

Lehman, Irving, 310

Lelyveld, Joe, 74

Levin, Henry, 219

Levine, Howard A., *P4–P6*, 220

Levy, Leonard, 371

Lewis, Anthony, 46, 95

LGBTQ rights, xiii, xxi, 41, 50, 281–282, 422–423; adoption laws and, 183–188; university housing and, 208–210; visitation rights and, xiv, 50, 141–145. *See also* marriage equality

Liman, Arthur, 20

Linde, Hans A., 329n67

Lippman, Jonathan, *P29*, *P31*, 46, 104; as chief operating officer, 57, 72; on jury reform, 62; Justice for Children Commission and, 68; on privacy protections, 47; sentencing reform project of, 59; Task Force on Commercial Litigation in the 21st Century and, 68

Lipton, Douglas S., 446n74

Llewellyn, Karl, 418

Loomis, Arphaxed, 171, 175

Louise Wise Services, 289–296

MacCrate, Robert, 98

MacMahon, Colleen, 62

Madison, James, 331

Maimonides, Moses, 308, 309

Malaspina, Dolores, 293

Maltz, Earl M., 407n75

Mandelbaum, Robert M., 156, 252, 256, 261, 466

Marcus, Marilyn, 3

Margolick, David, 60

marriage, interracial, 51, 280, 283, 285–286

marriage equality, 34, 49–52, 86, 279–286

Marshall, John, 317–319, 324, 336

Martinson, Robert, 446–447

Matalon, Joseph L., 55, 465

McCaffrey, Barry, 65

McCaghey, Charlie, 100

McCoy, Marge, 3, 86

McGreal, Shirley, 147–154

McMahon, Colleen, 458

McNabb, Elizabeth, 297–300

Medicaid, 156–157, 160

medical treatment cases, 196, 199–200, 381–386

Mendez, Jesus, 190

mens rea, 31, 32, 263

Mental Health Courts, 64–66

mental illness, 35–36, 289–293, 383–384, 417, 441

Metropolitan Transportation Authority (MTA), 172–174, 178–179

Meyer, Bernard S., *P1*, xx, 15, 24, 25, 423nn182–183

Meyerowitz, William, 309

Midtown Community Court, xxvi

Mikva, Abner J., 403, 416n140, 420

Miller, Barbara, 290

Milonas, E. Leo, 57, 58, 62

Moe, Jane, 158–161

Monaghan, Henry P., 388n123

Moor-Jankowski, Jan, 45–46, 147

"moral obligation bond," 171

Morales, Ricardo, 190

Morgenthau, Robert, 65

Morpurgo, Michael, 6

Morris, Matthew J., 216, 465

Mosk, Stanley, 408, 410n97

My Life as Chief Judge (Kaye), 456–461

National Center for State Courts, 40–41, 74–76

Nationwide Mutual Insurance Company, 211–215

New Deal policies, 375, 410n100

New York State Constitution, 40–49, 128–129, 175, 257–260; common law and, 304, 367–388, 404–410; Education Article of, 49, 216–218, 228; governor's discretionary authority and, 190–191; Kaye's articles on, xv, xxi, xxv–xxvi, 304; revisions to, 42, 256–258, 323, 326, 362n27; US Constitution and, xiv, 40–46, 303–304, 315–337

New York State Judicial Institute, xxvii

New York Women's Bar Association, xx–xxi

Newton, Juanita, 105

Nierzwicki-Bauer, Sandra, 164

Niles, Russell, xix, 99

No Child Left Behind policy, 226

no prejudice doctrine, 211, 213

no-fault insurance, 212, 214n4

Nowak, John E., 355n33

Nussbaum, Bernie, 57, 71

Oakes, James, 419n163

Obama, Barack, 82

O'Connell, Kenneth J., 402n44, 404n57

O'Connor, Darren, 20, 465

O'Connor, John, 62–63

O'Connor, Sandra Day, 43, 44, 46, 74, 97, 105; on state law decisions, 321–322

O'Donnell, Jack, 99, 100
Olwine, Connelly, Chase, O'Donnell & Weyhar, xix, xxv, 99–102
One Judge's View of Academic Law Review Writing (Kaye), 348–356
Ortiz, Angel, 261–266

Pace University Law School, xxvii
Parker, Alton, 351–352
"parol evidence," 30, 139
parole from prison, 86, 268–269, 287–288, 384n109, 406
Pataki, George, 48–49, 73; on death penalty, 36, 38, 189; discretionary authority of, 189–191; on judicial compensation, 70–71
Paterson, David, xxiii, 71
Perdue, William, 303–304
Permanent Judicial Commission on Justice for Children, xxii
Peters, Ellen A., 399; on state constitutions, 330n70, 372, 408n77; on state statutes, 402n43, 410n103, 413–414
Pfau, Ann, 57, 87
Phelan, Judith N., 432n11
Piel, Barbara W., 297–300
Piel, William, 98
Pigott, Eugene F., Jr., *P7*, 32
Pinker, Steven, 106–107
Poindexter, Alma, 158
Polechronis, Ralia E., 297, 466
Pollock, Stewart, 333n78, 348, 387n122
Popkin, William D., 416n143, 418n156
Prenatal Care Assistance Program (PCAP), 156–161
Prince, Alfred, 151
prison reform, 88, 341, 440, 446–448
privacy rights, 43, 44–47, 351–352, 375–376, 381–383, 408
punitive damages, 289, 293–296
Purnick, Joyce, 74

Ravitch, Richard, 48–49
Read, Susan Phillips, *P7, P18, P28*, 32, 105, 107
Rebold, Jonathan E., 268, 466
recidivism, 447–448

Reddy, Anne C., 270, 466
religion, freedom of, 160n7
Reno, Janet, xxii, 56, 399n19
Reyer, Heidi, 192–195
Ricci, Linda M., 435n21
Richardson, H. H., 11–12
Rifkind, Simon, 84
Rivera, Jenny, 85
Roberts, John G., Jr., *P29*
Roberts, Richard, 164
Robinson, Laurie, 64–65
Rometty, Ginni, 106
Roney, Deirdre, 465
Roosevelt, Theodore, 326, 351
Rosenblatt, Albert M., *P6, P31*, xiii–xv, 3, 38, 121; on "depraved indifference murder," 32; on *Deutsche Bank Sec., Inc. v. Montana Bd. of Invs.*, 276; on *Immuno AG v. Moor-Jankowski*, 146; on *Karlin v. IVF Am.*, 196; on *Matter of Levandusky v. One Fifth Ave. Apt. Corp.*, 130; on *People v. Hill*, 287; on *Tebbutt v. Virostek*, 127
rule against perpetuities, 23, 280, 346n43, 359n12, 364n34
rule of law, 362–364, 390–391, 452
Rust, Carol, 192–195

Saks, Michael, 350n6, 353n26, 355n33
Sandberg, Sheryl, 110
Scalia, Antonin, 43, 47
Schacter, Jane S., 413n118, 419n164
Schall, Ellen, 67, 81–82
Schecter, Jennifer, 69, 137, 201, 234, 465
schizophrenia, 289–293, 417
Schrunk, Michael D., 432n11
Schulz, Robert L., 171–181
Schumer, Charles, 20
Schwartz, John, 65
Schwartz, Wendy H., 465
Schweitzer, Lisa M., 465
search and seizure, 42–43, 46–47, 123–126, 326, 328, 330
sentencing reform project, 59
September 11 attacks (2001), 63, 69–70
Shanks, Siobhan, 465
Shepard, Randy, 75
Sherry, Suzanna, 408n77

Shield Law, 270–272, 342
Shifren, James A., 465
shopping mall cases, 377–381
Siedman, Betsy, 101
Siegel, David, 236
Silver, Sheldon, 71
Simons, Richard D., *P1–P5*, 15, 25, 56; on
  death penalty, 37; on "depraved indifference
  murder," 31–35; on protected speech, 46
Skadden, Arps, Slate, Meagher & Flom, xxiii,
  59, 81–90, 123, 141
Slaughter, Anne-Marie, 110–111
Smith, Allen, *P23, P27*, xviii
Smith, Benjamin, *P21, P22*, xviii, 93–94, 96
Smith, George Bundy, *P3–P6*
Smith, Jennifer L., 141
Smith, Judith Ann. *See* Kaye, Judith S.
Smith, Lena Cohen, *P23*, xviii, 93–94, 96
Smith, Robert S., *P7*, 51, 101
Smith, William T., 195
Sorensen, Anita Longo, 292
Sotomayor, Sonia, 47, 86
Souter, David, 39–40, 425
Spar, Debora, 110
speech, freedom of, 45, 146, 148–155,
  329–330, 371. *See also* Bill of Rights
Spitzer, Eliot, 71, 81
State Constitutional Common Law (Kaye), 304,
  367–388
State Courts at the Dawn of a New Century
  (Kaye), 304, 396–424
Stevens, John Paul, 44, 46, 322
Stewart, Potter, 38
Stone, Harlan Fiske, 312, 332n76, 375
Stoneman, Kate, 97, 358n1, 359n11
Sullivan & Cromwell, xix, 19, 79, 82, 98
Supplementary Uninsured Motorists (SUM),
  211–215
Supreme Court Historical Society, xxiii, 86

Taft, William Howard, 349
Task Force on Commercial Litigation in the
  21st Century, 68
Tenney, Charles, 454
Thruway Authority, 171–174, 178–179
Titone, Vito J., *P2–P5*, 25, 33, 46
Tocqueville, Alexis de, 460

Tolan, James, 100
Torres, Pello, 261–262
Traficanti, Joseph J., 442n56
Traynor, Roger J., 421
Tyler, Harold, 84

uninsured motorists, 211–215
Unkeless, Elaine, 289, 466
US Constitution, 37, 317, 404–410; first
  amendment to, 45, 146, 148–155, 329–330,
  371; ninth amendment to, 335–337,
  372n27; fourteenth amendment to, 360n15,
  374; nineteenth amendment to, 360n16;
  New York State Constitution and, 40–46,
  303–304, 315–337

Vacco, Dennis C., 189
Valentino, Joseph D., 442n56
Viggiani, Tony, 270–271
Vobis family, *P12*

Wachtler, Sol, *P1, P2*, 24, 25; arrest of, 53–54;
  Cardozo and, 307; commercials courts
  and, 61; Committee to Examine Lawyer
  Conduct in Matrimonial Actions of, 58–60;
  on Criminal Procedure Law, 33; Justice for
  Children Commission and, 67; resignation
  of, xxii, 54
Walberg, Herbert, 219
Wald, Patricia, 54, 56, 363n32
Warren, Samuel, 351–352, 381
Weil, Anne-Marie, 290
Weiner, Herbert, 293
Weinfeld, Edward, 102
Weingast, Barry, 423n182
Weissman, Kenneth Ian, 465
Wesley, Richard C., *P6*, 12, 72
White, Byron, 56
Williams, Stephen, 276–277
Women in Law (Kaye), 357–388
Women's Bar Association, 37
Woodward, Florence, 297
Woolf, Virginia, 360n15
workers' compensation, 324, 326

Yablonski, Elise A., 465
Yerawadeker, Prakash, 20n1

Yeshiva University, 208–210
youth courts, 86–88, 393

Zambello, Francesca, xxiii

Zander, Richard, 18
Zenger, Jack, 107
"zone of danger" rule, 28, 29
Zuckerman, Audra, 465